Cognitive Technologies

T0190249

Pierre M. Nugues

An Introduction to Language Processing with Perl and Prolog

An Outline of Theories, Implementation, and Application
with Special Consideration of English, French, and German

With 153 Figures and 192 Tables

 Springer

Author:

Pierre M. Nugues
Institutionen för Datavetenskap
Lunds Tekniska Högskola
E-huset
Ole Römers väg 3
223 63 Lund, Sweden
Pierre.Nugues@cs.lth.se

Managing Editors:

Prof. Dov M. Gabbay
Augustus De Morgan Professor of Logic
Department of Computer Science, King's College London
Strand, London WC2R 2LS, UK

Prof. Dr. Jörg Siekmann
Forschungsbereich Deduktions- und Multiagentensysteme, DFKI
Stuhlsatzenweg 3, Geb. 43, 66123 Saarbrücken, Germany

ACM Computing Classification (1998): D.1.6, F.3, H.3, H.5.2, I.2.4, I.2.7, I.7, J.5

ISSN 1611-2482

ISBN-13 978-3-642-06405-0   e-ISBN-13 978-3-540-34336-3

Springer is a part of Springer Science+Business Media
springer.com

© Springer-Verlag Berlin Heidelberg 2006
Softcover reprint of the hardcover 1st edition 2006

Cover Design: KünkelLopka, Heidelberg

À mes parents,
À Madeleine

Preface

In the past 15 years, natural language processing and computational linguistics have considerably matured. The move has mainly been driven by the massive increase of textual and spoken data and the need to process them automatically. This dramatic growth of available data spurred the design of new concepts and methods, or their improvement, so that they could scale up from a few laboratory prototypes to proven applications used by millions of people. Concurrently, speed and capacity of machines became an order of magnitude larger enabling us to process gigabytes of data and billions of words in a reasonable time, to train, test, retrain, and retest algorithms like never before. Although systems entirely dedicated to language processing remain scarce, there are now scores of applications that, to some extent, embed language processing techniques.

The industry trend, as well as the user's wishes, towards information systems able to process textual data has made language processing a new requirement for many computer science students. This has shifted the focus of textbooks from readers being mostly researchers or graduate students to a larger public, from readings by specialists to pragmatism and applied programming. Natural language processing techniques are not completely stable, however. They consist of a mix that ranges from well mastered and routine to rapidly changing. This makes the existence of a new book an opportunity as well as a challenge.

This book tries to take on this challenge and find the right balance. It adopts a hands-on approach. It is a basic observation that many students have difficulties to go from an algorithm exposed using pseudo-code to a runnable program. I did my best to bridge the gap and provide the students with programs and ready-made solutions. The book contains real code the reader can study, run, modify, and run again. I chose to write examples in two languages to make the algorithms easy to understand and encode: Perl and Prolog.

One of the major driving forces behind the recent improvements in natural language processing is the increase of text resources and annotated data. The huge amount of texts made available by Internet and the never-ending digitization led many of the practitioners to evolve from theory-oriented, armchair linguists to frantic empiricists. This books attempts as well as it can to pay attention to this trend and stresses the importance of corpora, annotation, and annotated corpora. It also tries to go beyond English-only and expose examples in two other languages, namely French and German.

The book was designed and written for a quarter or semester course. At Lund, I used it when it was still under the form of lecture notes in the EDA171 course. It comes with a companion web site where slides, programs, corrections, an additional chapter, and Internet pointers are available: www.cs.lth.se/~pierre/ilppp/. All the computer programs should run with Perl available from www.perl.com or Prolog. Although I only tested the programs with SWI Prolog available from www.swi-prolog.org, any Prolog compatible with the ISO reference should apply.

Many people helped me during the last 10 years when this book took shape, step-by-step. I am deeply indebted to my colleagues and to my students in classes at Caen, Nottingham, Stafford, Constance, and now in Lund. Without them, it could never have existed. I would like most specifically to thank the PhD students I supervised, in chronological order, Pierre-Olivier El Guedj, Christophe Godéreaux, Dominique Dutoit, and Richard Johansson.

Finally, my acknowledgments would not be complete without the names of the people I most cherish and who give meaning to my life, my wife, Charlotte, and my children, Andreas and Louise.

Lund,   Pierre Nugues
January 2006

Contents

1

An Overview of Language Processing

1.1 Linguistics and Language Processing

Linguistics is the study and the description of human languages. Linguistic theories on grammar and meaning have been developed since ancient times and the Middle Ages. However, modern linguistics originated at the end of the nineteenth century and the beginning of the twentieth century. Its founder and most prominent figure was probably Ferdinand de Saussure (1916). Over time, modern linguistics has produced an impressive set of descriptions and theories.

Computational linguistics is a subset of both linguistics and computer science. Its goal is to design mathematical models of language structures enabling the automation of language processing by a computer. From a linguist's viewpoint, we can consider computational linguistics as the formalization of linguistic theories and models or their implementation in a machine. We can also view it as a means to develop new linguistic theories with the aid of a computer.

From an applied and industrial viewpoint, language and speech processing, which is sometimes referred to as natural language processing (NLP) or natural language understanding (NLU), is the mechanization of human language faculties. People use language every day in conversations by listening and talking, or by reading and writing. It is probably our preferred mode of communication and interaction. Ideally, automated language processing would enable a computer to understand texts or speech and to interact accordingly with human beings.

Understanding or translating texts automatically and talking to an artificial conversational assistant are major challenges for the computer industry. Although this final goal has not been reached yet, in spite of constant research, it is being approached every day, step-by-step. Even if we have missed Stanley Kubrick's prediction of talking electronic creatures in the year 2001, language processing and understanding techniques have already achieved results ranging from very promising to near perfect. The description of these techniques is the subject of this book.

1.2 Applications of Language Processing

At first, language processing is probably easier understood by the description of a result to be attained rather than by the analytical definition of techniques. Ideally, language processing would enable a computer to analyze huge amounts of text and to understand them; to communicate with us in a written or a spoken way; to capture our words whatever the entry mode: through a keyboard or through a speech recognition device; to parse our sentences; to understand our utterances, to answer our questions, and possibly to have a discussion with us – the human beings.

Language processing has a history nearly as old as that of computers and comprises a large body of work. However, many early attempts remained in the stage of laboratory demonstrations or simply failed. Significant applications have been slow to come, and they are still relatively scarce compared with the universal deployment of some other technologies such as operating systems, databases, and networks. Nevertheless, the number of commercial applications or significant laboratory prototypes embedding language processing techniques is increasing. Examples include:

- Spelling and grammar checkers. These programs are now ubiquitous in text processors, and hundred of millions of people use them every day. Spelling checkers are based on computerized dictionaries and remove most misspellings that occur in documents. Grammar checkers, although not perfect, have improved to a point that many users could not write a single e-mail without them. Grammar checkers use rules to detect common grammar and style errors (Jensen et al. 1993).
- Text indexing and information retrieval from the Internet. These programs are among the most popular of the Web. They are based on spiders that visit Internet sites and that download texts they contain. Spiders track the links occurring on the pages and thus explore the Web. Many of these systems carry out a full text indexing of the pages. Users ask questions and text retrieval systems return the Internet addresses of documents containing words of the question. Using statistics on words or popularity measures, text retrieval systems are able to rank the documents (Salton 1988, Brin and Page 1998).
- Speech dictation of letters or reports. These systems are based on speech recognition. Instead of typing using a keyboard, speech dictation systems allow a user to dictate reports and transcribe them automatically into a written text. Systems like IBM's ViaVoice have a high performance and recognize English, French, German, Spanish, Italian, Japanese, Chinese, etc. Some systems transcribe radio and TV broadcast news with a word-error rate lower than 10% (Nguyen et al. 2004).
- Voice control of domestic devices such as videocassette recorders or disc changers (Ball et al. 1997). These systems aim at being embedded in objects to provide them with a friendlier interface. Many people find electronic devices complicated and are unable to use them satisfactorily. How many of us are tape recorder illiterates? A spoken interface would certainly be an easier means to control them. Although there are many prototypes, few systems are commercially available yet. One challenge they still have to overcome is to operate in noisy environments that impair speech recognition.

- Interactive voice response applications. These systems deliver information over the telephone using speech synthesis or prerecorded messages. In more traditional systems, users interact with the application using touch-tone telephones. More advanced servers have a speech recognition module that enables them to understand spoken questions or commands from users. Early examples of speech servers include travel information and reservation services (Mast et al. 1994, Sorin et al. 1995). Although most servers are just interfaces to existing databases and have limited reasoning capabilities, they have spurred significant research on dialogue, speech recognition and synthesis.
- Machine translation. Research on machine translation is one of the oldest domains of language processing. One of its outcomes is the venerable SYSTRAN program that started with translations between English and Russian. Since then, SYSTRAN has been extended to many other languages. Another pioneer example is the *Spoken Language Translator* that translated spoken English into spoken Swedish in a restricted domain in real time (Agnäs et al. 1994, Rayner et al. 2000).
- Conversational agents. Conversational agents are elaborate dialogue systems that have understanding faculties. An example is TRAINS that helps a user plan a route and the assembling trains: boxcars and engines to ship oranges from a warehouse to an orange juice factory (Allen et al. 1995). Ulysse is another example that uses speech to navigate into virtual worlds (Godéreaux et al. 1996, Godéreaux et al. 1998).

Some of these applications are widespread, like spelling and grammar checkers. Others are not yet ready for an industrial exploitation or are still too expensive for popular use. They generally have a much lower distribution. Unlike other computer programs, results of language processing techniques rarely hit a 100% success rate. Speech recognition systems are a typical example. Their accuracy is assessed in statistical terms. Language processing techniques become mature and usable when they operate above a certain precision and at an acceptable cost. However, common to these techniques is that they are continuously improving and they are rapidly changing our way of interacting with machines.

1.3 The Different Domains of Language Processing

Historically linguistics has been divided into disciplines or levels, which go from sounds to meaning. Computational processing of each level involves different techniques such as signal and speech processing, statistics, pattern recognition, parsing, first-order logic, and automated reasoning.

A first discipline of linguistics is **phonetics**. It concerns the production and perception of acoustic sounds that form the speech signal. In each language, sounds can be classified into a finite set of **phonemes**. Traditionally, they include **vowels**: *a, e, i, o*; and **consonants**: *p, f, r, m*. Phonemes are assembled into **syllables**: *pa, pi, po*, to build up the words.

A second level concerns the **words**. The word set of a language is called a **lexicon**. Words can appear under several forms, for instance, the singular and the plural forms. **Morphology** is the study of the structure and the forms of a word. Usually a lexicon consists of root words. Morphological rules can modify or transform the root words to produce the whole vocabulary.

Syntax is a third discipline in which the order of words in a sentence and their relationships is studied. Syntax defines word categories and functions. Subject, verb, object is a sequence of functions that corresponds to a common order in many European languages including English and French. However, this order may vary, and the verb is often located at the end of the sentence in German. **Parsing** determines the structure of a sentence and assigns functions to words or groups of words.

Semantics is a fourth domain of linguistics. It considers the meaning of words and sentences. The concept of "meaning" or "signification" can be controversial. Semantics is differently understood by researchers and is sometimes difficult to describe and process. In a general context, semantics could be envisioned as a medium of our thought. In applications, semantics often corresponds to the determination of the sense of a word or the representation of a sentence in a logical format.

Pragmatics is a fifth discipline. While semantics is related to universal definitions and understandings, pragmatics restricts it – or complements it – by adding a contextual interpretation. Pragmatics is the meaning of words and sentences in specific situations.

The production of language consists of a stream of sentences that are linked together to form a **discourse**. This discourse is usually aimed at other people who can answer – it is to be hoped – through a **dialogue**. A dialogue is a set of linguistic interactions that enables the exchange of information and sometimes eliminates misunderstandings or ambiguities.

1.4 Phonetics

Sounds are produced through vibrations of the vocal cords. Several cavities and organs modify vibrations: the vocal tract, the nose, the mouth, the tongue, and the teeth. Sounds can be captured using a microphone. They result in signals such as that in Fig. 1.1.

Fig. 1.1. A speech signal corresponding to *This is* [ðɪs ɪz].

A speech signal can be sampled and digitized by an analog-to-digital converter. It can then be processed and transformed by a Fourier analysis (FFT) in a moving window, resulting in spectrograms (Figs. 1.2 and 1.3). Spectrograms represent the distribution of speech power within a frequency domain ranging from 0 to 10,000 Hz over time. This frequency domain corresponds roughly to the sound production possibilities of human beings.

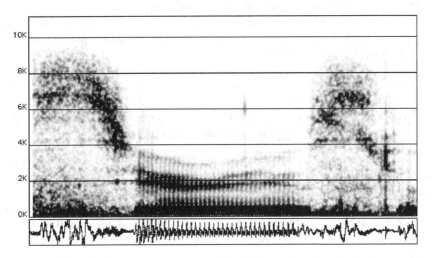

Fig. 1.2. A spectrogram corresponding to the word *serious* [sɪərɪəs].

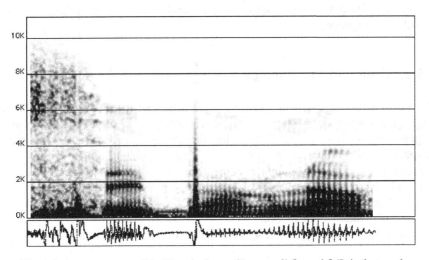

Fig. 1.3. A spectrogram of the French phrase *C'est par là* [separla] 'It is that way'.

Phoneticians can "read" spectrograms, that is, split them into a sequence of relatively regular – stationary – patterns. They can then annotate the corresponding segments with phonemes by recognizing their typical patterns.

A descriptive classification of phonemes includes:

- Simple vowels such as /ɪ/, /a/, and /ε/, and nasal vowels in French such as /ã/ and /ɔ̃/, which appear on the spectrogram as a horizontal bar – the fundamental frequency – and several superimposed horizontal bars – the harmonics.
- Plosives such as /p/ and /b/ that correspond to a stop in the airflow and then a very short and brisk emission of air from the mouth. The air release appears as a vertical bar from 0 to 5,000 Hz.
- Fricatives such as /s/ and /f/ that appear as white noise on the spectrogram, that is, as a uniform gray distribution. Fricatives sounds a bit like a loudspeaker with an unplugged signal cable.
- Nasals and approximants such as /m/, /l/, and /r/ are more difficult to spot and and are subject to modifications according to their left and right neighbors.

Phonemes are assembled to compose words. Pronunciation is basically carried out though **syllables** or diphonemes in European languages. These are more or less stressed or emphasized, and are influenced by neighboring syllables.

The general rhythm of the sentence is the **prosody**. Prosody is quite different from English to French and German and is an open subject of research. It is related to the length and structure of sentences, to questions, and to the meaning of the words.

Speech synthesis uses signal processing techniques, phoneme models, and letter-to-phoneme rules to convert a text into speech and to read it in a loud voice. **Speech recognition** does the reverse and transcribes speech into a computer-readable text. It also uses signal processing and statistical techniques including Hidden Markov models and language models.

1.5 Lexicon and Morphology

The set of available words in a given context makes up a lexicon. It varies from language to language and within a language according to the context: jargon, slang, or gobbledygook. Every word can be classified through a lexical category or **part of speech** such as article, noun, verb, adjective, adverb, conjunction, preposition, or pronoun. Most of the lexical entities come from four categories: noun, verb, adjective, and adverb. Other categories such as articles, pronouns, or conjunctions have a limited and stable number of elements. Words in a sentence can be annotated – tagged – with their part of speech.

For instance, the simple sentences in English, French, and German:

The big cat ate the gray mouse
Le gros chat mange la souris grise
Die große Katze ißt die graue Maus

are annotated as:

> *The*/article *big*/adjective *cat*/noun *ate*/verb *the*/article *gray*/adjective *mouse*/noun
>
> *Le*/article *gros*/adjectif *chat*/nom *mange*/verbe *la*/article *souris*/nom *grise*/adjectif
>
> *Die*/Artikel *große*/Adjektiv *Katze*/Substantiv *ißt*/Verb *die*/Artikel *graue*/Adjektiv *Maus*/Substantiv

Morphology is the study of how root words and affixes – the **morphemes** – are composed to form words. Morphology can be divided into **inflection** and **derivation**:

- Inflection is the form variation of a word under certain grammatical conditions. In European languages, these conditions consist notably of the number, gender, conjugation, or tense (Table 1.1).
- Derivation combines affixes to an existing root or stem to form a new word. Derivation is more irregular and complex than inflection. It often results in a change in the part of speech for the derived word (Table 1.2).

Most of the inflectional morphology of words can be described through morphological rules, possibly with a set of exceptions. According to the rules, a morphological parser splits each word as it occurs in a text into morphemes – the root word and the affixes. When affixes have a grammatical content, morphological parsers generally deliver this content instead of the raw affixes (Table 1.3).

Morphological parsing operates on single words and does not consider the surrounding words. Sometimes, the form of a word is ambiguous. For instance, *worked* can be found in *he worked* (*to work* and preterit) or *he has worked* (*to work* and past

Table 1.1. Grammatical features that modify the form of a word.

Features	Values	English	French	German
Number	singular	*a car*	*une voiture*	*ein Auto*
	plural	*two cars*	*deux voitures*	*zwei Autos*
Gender	masculine	*he*	*il*	*er*
	feminine	*she*	*elle*	*sie*
	neuter	*it*		*es*
Conjugation	infinitive	*to work*	*travailler*	*arbeiten*
and	finite	*he works*	*il travaille*	*er arbeitet*
tense	gerund	*working*	*travaillant*	*arbeitend*

Table 1.2. Examples of word derivations.

	Words	Derived words
English	*real*/adjective	*really*/adverb
French	*courage*/noun	*courageux*/adjective
German	*Der Mut*/noun	*mutig*/adjective

Table 1.3. Decomposition of inflected words into a root and affixes.

	Words	**Roots and affixes**	**Lemmas and grammatical interpretations**
English	*worked*	*work + ed*	*work* + verb + preterit
French	*travaillé*	*travaill + é*	*travailler* + verb + past participle
German	*gearbeitet*	*ge + arbeit + et*	*arbeiten* + verb + past participle

participle). Another processing stage is necessary to remove the ambiguity and to assign (to annotate) each word with a single part-of-speech tag.

A lexicon may simply be a list of all the **inflected** word forms – a wordlist – as they occur in running texts. However, keeping all the forms, for instance, *work*, *works*, *worked*, generates a useless duplication. For this reason, many lexicons retain only a list of canonical words: the **lemmas**. Lemmas correspond to the entries of most ordinary dictionaries. Lexicons generally contain other features, such as the phonetic transcription, part of speech, morphological type, and definition, to facilitate additional processing. Lexicon building involves collecting most of the words of a language or of a domain. It is probably impossible to build an exhaustive dictionary since new words are appearing every day.

Morphological rules enable us to generate all the word forms from a lexicon. Morphological parsers do the reverse operation and retrieve the word root and its affixes from its inflected or derived form in a text. Morphological parsers use finite-state automaton techniques. Part-of-speech taggers disambiguate the possible multiple readings of a word. They also use finite-state automata or statistical techniques.

1.6 Syntax

Syntax governs the formation of a sentence from words. Syntax is sometimes combined with morphology under the term morphosyntax. Syntax has been a central point of interest of linguistics since the Middle Ages, but it probably reached an apex in the 1970s, when it captured an overwhelming attention in the linguistics community.

1.6.1 Syntax as Defined by Noam Chomsky

Chomsky (1957) had a determining influence in the study of language, and his views have fashioned the way syntactic formalisms are taught and used today. Chomsky's theory postulates that syntax is independent from semantics and can be expressed in terms of logic grammars. These grammars consist of a set of rules that describe the sentence structure of a language. In addition, grammar rules can generate the whole sentence set – possibly infinite – of a definite language.

Generative grammars consist of syntactic rules that fractionate a phrase into subphrases and hence describe a sentence composition in terms of phrase structure. Such rules are called **phrase-structure rules**. An English sentence typically comprises two main phrases: a first one built around a noun called the noun phrase, and a second one around the main verb called the verb phrase. Noun and verb phrases are rewritten into other phrases using other rules and by a set of terminal symbols representing the words.

Formally, a grammar describing a very restricted subset of English, French, or German phrases could be the following rule set:

- A **sentence** consists of a **noun phrase** and a **verb phrase**.
- A **noun phrase** consists of an **article** and a **noun**.
- A **verb phrase** consists of a **verb** and a **noun phrase**.

A very limited lexicon of the English, French, or German words could be made of:

- articles such as *the, le, la, der, den*
- nouns such as *boy, garçon, Knabe*
- verbs such as *hit, frappe, trifft*

This grammar generates sentences such as:

The boy hit the ball
Le garçon frappe la balle
Der Knabe trifft den Ball

but also incorrect or implausible sequences such as:

The ball hit the ball
*Le balle frappe la garçon
*Das Ball trifft den Knabe

Linguists use an asterisk (*) to indicate an ill-formed grammatical construction or a nonexistent word. In the French and German sentences, the articles must agree with their nouns in gender, number, and case (for German). The correct sentences are:

La balle frappe le garçon
Der Ball trifft den Knaben

Trees can represent the syntactic structure of sentences (Fig. 1.4–1.6) and reflect the rules involved in sentence generation.

Moreover, Chomsky's formalism enables some transformations: rules can be set to carry out the building of an interrogative sentence from a declaration, or the building of a passive form from an active one.

Parsing is the reverse of generation. A grammar, a set of phrase-structure rules, accepts syntactically correct sentences and determines their structure. Parsing requires a mechanism to search the rules that describe the sentence's structure. This mechanism can be applied from the sentence's words up to a rule describing the sentence's structure. This is **bottom-up parsing**. Rules can also be searched from a sentence structure rule down to the sentence's words. This corresponds to **top-down parsing**.

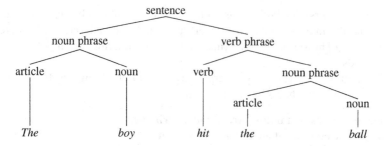

Fig. 1.4. Tree structure of *The boy hit the ball*.

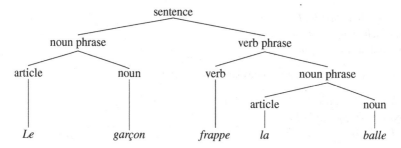

Fig. 1.5. Tree structure of *Le garçon frappe la balle*.

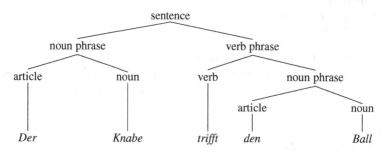

Fig. 1.6. Tree structure of *Der Knabe trifft den Ball*.

1.6.2 Syntax as Relations and Dependencies

Before Chomsky, pupils and students learned syntax (and still do so) mainly in terms of functions and relations between the words. A sentence's classical parsing consists in annotating words using parts of speech and in identifying the main verb. The main verb is the pivot of the sentence, and the principal grammatical functions are determined relative to it. Parsing consists then in grouping words to form the subject and the object, which are the two most significant functions in addition to the verb.

In the sentence *The boy hit the ball*, the main verb is *hit*, the subject of *hit* is *the boy*, and its object is *the ball* (Fig. 1.7).

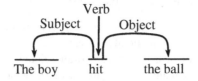

Fig. 1.7. Grammatical relations in the sentence *The boy hit the ball.*

Other grammatical functions (or relations) involve notably articles, adjectives, and adjuncts. We see this in the sentence

The big boy from Liverpool hit the ball with furor.

where the adjective *big* is related to the noun *boy*, and the adjuncts *from Liverpool* and *with furor* are related respectively to *boy* and *hit*.

We can picture these relations as a dependency net, where each word is said to modify exactly another word up to the main verb (Fig. 1.8). The main verb is the head of the sentence and modifies no other word. Tesnière (1966) and Mel'cuk (1988) have extensively described dependency theory.

The big boy from Liverpool hit the ball with furor

Fig. 1.8. Dependency relations in the sentence *The big boy from Liverpool hit the ball with furor.*

Although they are less popular than phrase-structure grammars, **dependency grammars** often prove more efficient to parse texts. They provide a theoretical framework to many present parsing techniques and have numerous applications.

1.7 Semantics

The semantic level is more difficult to capture and there are numerous viewpoints on how to define and to process it. A possible viewpoint is to oppose it to syntax: there are sentences that are syntactically correct but that cannot make sense. Such a description of semantics would encompass sentences that make sense. Classical examples by Chomsky (1957) – sentences 1 and 2 – and Tesnière (1966) – sentence 3 – include:

1. *Colorless green ideas sleep furiously.*
2. **Furiously sleep ideas green colorless.*
3. *Le silence vertébral indispose la voile licite.*
   'The vertebral silence embarrasses the licit sail.'

Sentences 1 and 3 and are syntactically correct but have no meaning, while sentence 2 is neither syntactically nor semantically correct.

In computational linguistics, semantics is often related to logic and to predicate calculus. Determining the semantic representation of a sentence then involves turning it into a predicate-argument structure, where the predicate is the main verb and the arguments correspond to phrases accompanying the verb such as the subject and the object. This type of logical representation is called a **logical form**. Table 1.4 shows examples of sentences together with their logical forms.

Table 1.4. Correspondence between sentences and logical forms.

Sentences	Logical forms (predicates)
Pierre wrote notes	`wrote(pierre, notes).`
Pierre a écrit des notes	`a_écrit(pierre, notes).`
Pierre schrieb Notizen	`schrieb(pierre, notizen).`

Representation is only one facet of semantics. Once sentence representations have been built, they can be interpreted to check what they mean. *Notes* in the sentence *Pierre wrote notes* can be linked to a dictionary **definition**. If we look up in the *Cambridge International Dictionary of English* (Procter 1995), there are as many as five possible senses for *notes* (abridged from p. 963):

1. **note** [WRITING], *noun*, a short piece of writing;
2. **note** [SOUND], *noun*, a single sound at a particular level;
3. **note** [MONEY], *noun*, a piece of paper money;
4. **note** [NOTICE], *verb*, to take notice of;
5. **note** [IMPORTANCE], *noun*, of note: of importance.

So linking a word meaning to a definition is not straightforward because of possible ambiguities. Among these definitions, the intended sense of *notes* is a specialization of the first entry:

notes, *plural noun*, notes are written information.

Finally, *notes* can be interpreted as what they refer to concretely, that is, a specific object: a set of bound paper sheets with written text on them or a file on a computer disk that keeps track of a set of magnetic blocks. Linking a word to an object of the real world, here a file on a computer, is a part of semantics called **reference resolution**.

The **referent** of the word *notes*, that is, the designated object, could be the path `/users/pierre/language_processing.html` in Unix parlance. As for the definition of a word, the referent can be ambiguous. Let us suppose that a database contains the locations of the lecture notes Pierre wrote. In Prolog, listing its content could yield:

```
notes('/users/pierre/operating_systems.html').
notes('/users/pierre/language_processing.html').
notes('/users/pierre/prolog_programming.html').
```

Here this would mean that finding the referent of *notes* consists in choosing a document among three possible ones (Fig. 1.9).

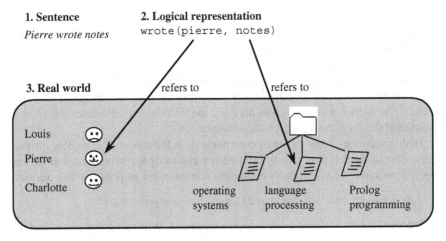

Fig. 1.9. Resolving references of *Pierre wrote notes*.

Obtaining the semantic structure of a sentence has been discussed abundantly in the literature. This is not surprising, given the uncertain nature of semantics. Building a logical form often calls on the **composition** of the semantic representation of the phrases that constitute a sentence. To carry it out, we must assume that sentences and phrases have an internal representation that can be expressed in terms of a logical formula.

Once a representation has been built, a reasoning process is applied to resolve references and to determine whether a sentence is true or not. It generally involves rules of deduction, or **inferences**.

Pragmatics is semantics restricted to a specific context and relies on facts that are external to the sentence. These facts contribute to the inference of a sentence's meaning or prove its truth or falsity. For instance, pragmatics of

Methuselah lived to be 969 years old. (Genesis 5:27)

can make sense in the Bible but not elsewhere, given the current possibilities of medicine.

1.8 Discourse and Dialogue

An interactive conversational agent cannot be envisioned without considering the whole **discourse** of (human) users – or parts of it – and apart from a **dialogue** between a user and the agent. Discourse refers to a sequence of sentences, to a sentence context in relation with other sentences or with some background situation. It is often linked with pragmatics.

Discourse study also enables us to resolve references that are not self-explainable in single sentences. Pronouns are good examples of such missing information. In the sentence

John took it

the pronoun *it* can probably be related to an entity mentioned in a previous sentence, or is obvious given the context where this sentence was said. These references are given the name of **anaphors**.

Dialogue provides a means of communication. It is the result of two intermingled – and, we hope, interacting – discourses: one from the user and the other from the machine. It enables a conversation between the two entities, the assertion of new results, and the cooperative search for solutions.

Dialogue is also a tool to repair communication failures or to complete interactively missing data. It may clarify information and mitigate misunderstandings that impair communication. Through a dialogue a computer can respond and ask the user:

I didn't understood what you said! Can you repeat (rephrase)?

Dialogue easily replaces some hazardous guesses. When an agent has to find the potential reference of a pronoun or to solve reference ambiguities, the best option is simply to ask the user clarify what s/he means:

Tracy? Do you mean James' brother or your mother?

Discourse processing splits texts and sentences into segments. It then sets links between segments to chain them rationally and to map them onto a sort of structure of the text. Discourse studies often make use of **rhetoric** as a background model of this structure.

Dialogue processing classifies the segments into what are called **speech acts**. At a first level, speech acts comprise dialogue turns: the user turn and the system turn. Then turns are split into sentences, and sentences into questions, declarations, requests, answers, etc. Speech acts can be modeled using finite-state automata or more elaborate schemes using **intention** and **planning** theories.

1.9 Why Speech and Language Processing Are Difficult

For all the linguistic levels mentioned in the previous sections, we outlined models and techniques to process speech and language. They often enable us to obtain excellent results compared to the performance of human beings. However, for most levels, language processing rarely hits the ideal score of 100%. Among the hurdles that often prevent the machine from reaching this figure, two recur at any level: ambiguity and the absence of a perfect model.

1.9.1 Ambiguity

Ambiguity is a major obstacle in language processing, and it may be the most significant. Although as human beings we are not aware of it most of the time, ambiguity is ubiquitous in language and plagues any stage of automated analysis. We saw examples of ambiguous morphological analysis and part-of-speech annotation, word senses, and references. Ambiguity also occurs in speech recognition, parsing, anaphora solving, and dialogue.

McMahon and Smith (1996) illustrate strikingly ambiguity in speech recognition with the sentence

The boys eat the sandwiches.

Speech recognition comprises generally two stages: first, a phoneme recognition, and then a concatenation of phoneme substrings into words. Using the International Phonetic Association (IPA) symbols, a perfect phonemic transcription of this utterance would yield the transcription:

[ˈðəbˈɔɪzˈiːtˈðəsˈændwɪdʒɪz],

which shows eight other alternative readings at the word decoding stage:

*The boy seat the sandwiches.
*The boy seat this and which is.
*The boys eat this and which is.
The buoys eat the sandwiches.
*The buoys eat this and which is.
The boys eat the sand which is.
*The buoys seat this and which is.

This includes the strange sentence

The buoys eat the sand which is.

For syntactic and semantic layers, a broad classification occurs between lexical and structural ambiguity. Lexical ambiguity refers to multiple senses of words, while structural ambiguity describes a parsing alternative, as with the frequently quoted sentence

I saw the boy with a telescope,

which can mean either that I used a telescope to see the boy or that I saw the boy who had a telescope.

A way to resolve ambiguity is to use a conjunction of language processing components and techniques. In the example given by McMahon and Smith, five out of eight possible interpretations are not grammatical. These are flagged with an asterisk. A further syntactic analysis could discard them.

Probabilistic models of word sequences can also address disambiguation. Statistics on word occurrences drawn from large quantities of texts – corpora – can capture grammatical as well as semantic patterns. Improbable alternatives <boys eat sand> and <buoys eat sand> are also highly unlikely in corpora and will not be retained (McMahon and Smith 1996). In the same vein, probabilistic parsing is a very powerful tool to rank alternative parse trees, that is, to retain the most probable and reject the others.

In some applications, logical rules model the context, reflect common sense, and discard impossible configurations. Knowing the physical context may help disambiguate some structures, as in the boy and the telescope, where both interpretations of the isolated sentence are correct and reasonable. Finally, when a machine interacts with a user, it can ask her/him to clarify an ambiguous utterance or situation.

1.9.2 Models and Their Implementation

Processing a linguistic phenomenon or layer starts with the choice or the development of a formal model and its algorithmic implementation. In any scientific discipline, good models are difficult to design. This is specifically the case with language. Language is closely tied to human thought and understanding, and in some instances models in computational linguistics also involve the study of the human mind. This gives a measure of the complexity of the description and the representation of language.

As noted in the introduction, linguists have produced many theories and models. Unfortunately, few of them have been elaborate enough to encompass and describe language effectively. Some models have also been misleading. This explains somewhat the failures of early attempts in language processing. In addition, many of the potential theories require massive computing power. Processors and storage able to support the implementation of complex models with substantial dictionaries, corpora, and parsers were not widely available until recently.

However, in the last decade models have matured, and computing power has become inexpensive. Although models and implementations are rarely (never?) perfect, they now enable us to obtain exploitable results. Most use a limited set of techniques that we will consider throughout this book, namely finite-state automata, logic grammars, and first-order logic. These tools are easily implemented in Prolog. Another set of tools pertains to the theory of probability and statistics. The combination of logic and statistical techniques now enables us to parse running-text sentences with a success rate of nearly 90%, a figure that would have been unimaginable ten years ago.

1.10 An Example of Language Technology in Action: the Persona Project

1.10.1 Overview of Persona

The Persona prototype from Microsoft Research (Ball et al. 1997) illustrates a user interface that is based on a variety of language processing techniques. Persona is a conversational agent that helps a user select songs and music tracks from a record database. Peedy, an animated cartoonlike parrot, embodies the agent that interacts with the user. It contains speech recognition, parsing, and semantic analysis modules to listen and to respond to the user and to play the songs. Table 1.5 shows an example of a dialogue with Peedy.

Table 1.5. An excerpt of a Persona dialogue. After Ball et al. (1997).

Turns	Utterances
	[Peedy is asleep on his perch]
User:	Good morning, Peedy.
	[Peedy rouses]
Peedy:	**Good morning.**
User:	Let's do a demo.
	[Peedy stands up, smiles]
Peedy:	**Your wish is my command, what would you like to hear?**
User:	What have you got by Bonnie Raitt?
	[Peedy waves in a stream of notes, and grabs one as they rush by.]
Peedy:	**I have "The Bonnie Raitt Collection" from 1990.**
User:	Pick something from that.
Peedy:	**How about "Angel from Montgomery"?**
User:	Sounds good.
	[Peedy drops note on pile]
Peedy:	**OK.**
User:	Play some rock after that.
	[Peedy scans the notes again, selects one]
Peedy:	**How about "Fools in Love"?**
User:	Who wrote that?
	[Peedy cups one wing to his 'ear']
Peedy:	**Huh?**
User:	Who wrote that?
	[Peedy looks up, scrunches his brow]
Peedy:	**Joe Jackson**
User:	Fine.
	[Drops note on pile]
Peedy:	**OK.**

Certain interactive talking assistants consider a limited set of the linguistic levels we have presented before. Simple systems bypass syntax, for example, and have only a speech recognition device to detect a couple of key words. In contrast, Persona has components to process more layers. They are organized in modules carrying out speech recognition, speech synthesis, parsing, semantics analysis, and dialogue. In addition, Persona has components specific to the application such as a name substitution module to find proper names like *Madonna* or *Debussy* and an animation module to play the Peedy character.

Persona's architecture organizes its modules into a pipeline processing flow (Fig. 1.10). Many other instances of dialogue systems adopt a similar architecture.

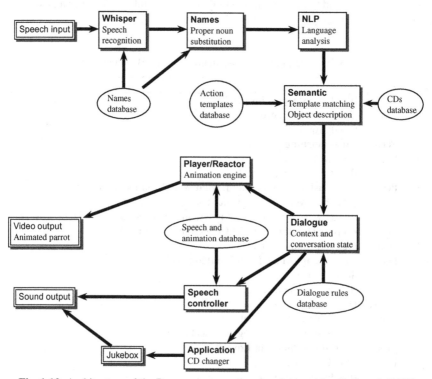

Fig. 1.10. Architecture of the Persona conversational assistant. After Ball et al. (1997).

1.10.2 The Persona's Modules

Persona's first component is the Whisper speech recognition module (Huang et al. 1995). Whisper uses signal processing techniques to compare phoneme models to the acoustic waves, and it assembles the recognized phonemes into words. It also uses a grammar to constrain the recognition possibilities. Whisper transcribes continuous speech into a stream of words in real time. It is a speaker-independent system. This means that it operates with any speaker without training.

The user's orders to select music often contain names: artists, titles of songs, or titles of albums. The Names module extracts them from the text before they are passed on to further analysis. Names uses a pattern matcher that attempts to substitute all the names and titles contained in the input sentence with placeholders. The utterance *Play before you accuse me by Clapton* is transformed into *Play track1 by artist1*.

The NLP module parses the input in which names have been substituted. It uses a grammar with rules similar to that of Sect. 1.6.1 and produces a tree structure. It creates a logical form whose predicate is the verb and the arguments the subject and the object: `verb(subject, object)`. The sentence *I would like to hear something* is transformed into the form `like(i, hear(i, something))`.

The logical forms are converted into a task graph representing the utterance in terms of actions the agent can do and objects of the task domain. It uses an application-dependent notation to map English words to symbols. It also reverses the viewpoint from the user to the agent. The logical form of *I would like to hear something* is transformed into the task graph: `verbPlay(you, objectTrack)` – *You play (`verbPlay`) a track (`objectTrack`)*.

Each possible request Peedy understands has possible variations – paraphrases. The mapping of logical forms to task graphs uses transformation rules to reduce them to a limited set of 17 canonical requests. The transformation rules deal with synonyms, syntactic variation, and colloquialisms. The forms corresponding to

> *I'd like to hear some Madonna.*
> *I want to hear some Madonna.*
> *It would be nice to hear some Madonna.*

are transformed into a form equivalent to

> *Let me hear some Madonna.*

The resulting graph is matched against actions templates the jukebox can carry out.

The dialogue module controls Peedy's answers and reactions. It consists of a state machine that models a sequence of interactions. Depending on the state of the conversation and an input event – what the user says – Peedy will react: trigger an animation, utter a spoken sentence or play music, and move to another conversational state.

1.11 Further Reading

Introductory textbooks to linguistics include *An Introduction to Language* (Fromkin et al. 2003) and *Linguistics: An Introduction to Linguistics Theory* (Fromkin 2000). *Linguistics: The Cambridge Survey* (Newmeyer et al. 1988) is an older reference in four volumes. The *Nouveau dictionnaire encyclopédique des sciences du langage* (Ducrot and Schaeffer 1995) is an encyclopedic presentation of linguistics in French, and *Studienbuch Linguistik* (Linke et al. 2004) is an introduction in German. *Fundamenti di linguistica* (Simone 1998) is an outstandingly clear and concise work in Italian that describes most fundamental concepts of linguistics.

Concepts and theories in linguistics evolved continuously from their origins to the present time. Historical perspectives are useful to understand the development of central issues. *A Short History of Linguistics* (Robins 1997) is a very readable introduction to linguistics history. *Histoire de la linguistique de Sumer à Saussure* (Malmberg 1991) and *Analyse du langage au XXe siècle* (Malmberg 1983) are comprehensive and accessible books that review linguistic theories from the ancient Near East to the end of the 20th century. *Landmarks in Linguistic Thought, The Western Tradition from Socrates to Saussure* (Harris and Taylor 1997) are extracts of founding classical texts followed by a commentary.

The journal of best repute in the domain of computational linguistics is *Computational Linguistics*, published by the Association for Computational Linguistics (ACL). Some interesting articles can also be found in the ACL conference proceedings and in more general journals such as *IEEE Transactions on Pattern Analysis and Machine Intelligence*, other IEEE journals, *Artificial Intelligence*, and the Association for Computing Machinery (ACM) journals. The French journal *Traitement automatique des langues* is also a source of interesting papers. It is published by the Association de traitement automatique des langues (http://www.atala.org).

Available books on natural language processing include (in English): *Natural Language Processing in Prolog* (Gazdar and Mellish 1989), *Prolog for Natural Language Analysis* (Gal et al. 1991), *Natural Language Processing for Prolog Programmers* (Covington 1994), *Natural Language Understanding* (Allen 1994), *Foundations of Statistical Natural Language Processing* (Manning and Schütze 1999), *Speech and Language Processing: An Introduction to Natural Language Processing, Computational Linguistics, and Speech Recognition* (Jurafsky and Martin 2000), *Foundations of Computational Linguistics: Human-Computer Communication in Natural Language* (Hausser 2001). Avalaible books in French include: *Prolog pour l'analyse du langage naturel* (Gal et al. 1989), *L'intelligence artificielle et le langage* (Sabah 1990), and in German *Grundlagen der Computerlinguistik. Mensch-Maschine-Kommunikation in natürlicher Sprache* (Hausser 2000).

There are plenty of interesting resources on the Internet. Web sites include digital libraries, general references, corpus and lexical resources, together with software registries. A starting point is the official home page of the ACL, which provides many links (http://www.aclweb.org). An extremely valuable anthology of papers published under the auspices of the ACL is available from this site (http://www.aclweb.org/anthology). Wikipedia (http://www.wikipedia.org) is a free encyclopedia that contains definitions and general articles on concepts and theories used in computational linguistics and natural language processing.

Many source programs are available on the Internet, either free or under a license. They include speech synthesis and recognition, morphological analysis, parsing, and so on. The German Institute for Artificial Intelligence Research maintains a list of them at the Natural Language Software Registry (http://registry.dfki.de).

Lexical and corpus resources are now available in many languages. Valuable sites include the Oxford Text Archive (http://ota.ox.ac.uk/), the Linguistic Data Consortium of the University of Pennsylvania (http://www.ldc.upenn.edu/), and the European Language Resources Association (http://www.elra.info).

There are nice interactive online demonstrations covering speech synthesis, parsing, translation and so on. Since sites are sometimes transient, we don't list them here. A good way to find them is to use directories like Yahoo, or search engines like Google.

Finally, some companies and laboratories have a very active research in language processing. They include major software powerhouses like Microsoft, IBM, and Xerox. The paper describing the Peedy animated character can be found at the Microsoft Research Web site (http://www.research.microsoft.com).

Exercises

1.1. List some computer applications that are relevant to the domain of language processing.

1.2. Tag the following sentences using parts of speech you know:
The cat caught the mouse.
Le chat attrape la souris.
Die Katze fängt die Maus.

1.3. Give the morpheme list of: *sings, sung, chante, chantiez, singt, sang.* List all the possible ambiguities.

1.4. Give the morpheme list of: *unpleasant, déplaisant, unangenehm.*

1.5. Draw the tree structure of the sentences:
The cat caught the mouse.
Le chat attrape la souris.
Die Katze fängt die Maus.

1.6. Identify the main functions of these sentences and draw the corresponding dependency net linking the words:
The cat caught the mouse.
Le chat attrape la souris.
Die Katze fängt die Maus.

1.7. Draw the dependency net of the sentences:
The mean cat caught the gray mouse on the table.
Le chat méchant a attrapé la souris grise sur la table.
Die böse Katze hat die graue Maus auf dem Tisch gefangen.

1.8. Give examples of sentences that are:
• Syntactically incorrect
• Syntactically correct
• Syntactically and semantically correct

1.9. Give the logical form of these sentences:
The cat catches the mouse.
Le chat attrape la souris.
Die Katze fängt die Maus.

1.10. Find possible phonetic interpretations of the French phrase *quant-à-soi*.

1.11. List the components you think necessary to build a spoken dialogue system.

2

Corpus Processing Tools

2.1 Corpora

A corpus, plural corpora, is a collection of texts or speech stored in an electronic machine-readable format. A few years ago, large electronic corpora of more than a million of words were rare, expensive, or simply not available. At present, huge quantities of texts are accessible in many languages of the world. They can easily be collected from a variety of sources, most notably the Web, where corpora of hundreds of millions of words are within the reach of most computational linguists.

2.1.1 Types of Corpora

Some corpora focus on specific genres, law, science, novels, news broadcasts, transcriptions of telephone calls, or conversations. Others try to gather a wider variety of running texts. Texts collected from a unique source, say from scientific magazines, will probably be slanted toward some specific words that do not appear in everyday life. Table 2.1 compares the most frequent words in the book of Genesis and in a collection of contemporary running texts. It gives an example of such a discrepancy. The choice of documents to include in a corpus must then be varied to survey comprehensively and accurately a language usage. This process is referred to as balancing a corpus.

Balancing a corpus is a difficult and costly task. It requires collecting data from a wide range of sources: fiction, newspapers, technical, and popular literature. Balanced corpora extend to spoken data. The Linguistic Data Consortium from the University of Pennsylvania and The European Language Resources Association (ELRA), among other organizations, distribute written and spoken corpus collections. They feature samples of magazines, laws, parallel texts in English, French, German, Spanish, Chinese, telephone calls, radio broadcasts, etc.

In addition to raw texts, some corpora are annotated. Each of their words is labeled with a linguistic tag such as a part of speech or a semantic category. The annotation is done either manually or semiautomatically. Spoken corpora contain the

Table 2.1. List of the most frequent words in present texts and in the book of Genesis. After Crystal (1997).

	English	French	German
Most frequent words in a collection	*the*	*de*	*der*
of contemporary running texts	*of*	*le* (article)	*die*
	to	*la* (article)	*und*
	in	*et*	*in*
	and	*les*	*des*
Most frequent words in Genesis	*and*	*et*	*und*
	the	*de*	*die*
	of	*la*	*der*
	his	*à*	*da*
	he	*il*	*er*

transcription of spoken conversations. This transcription may be aligned with the speech signal and sometimes includes prosodic annotation: pause, stress, etc. Annotation tags, paragraph and sentence boundaries, parts of speech, syntactic or semantic categories follow a variety of standards, which are called markup languages.

Among annotated corpora, treebanks deserve a specific mention. They are collections of parse trees or more generally syntactic structures of sentences. The production of a treebank generally requires a team of linguists to parenthesize the constituents of a corpus or to arrange them in a structure. Annotated corpora require a fair amount of handwork and are therefore more expensive than raw texts. Treebanks involve even more clerical work and are relatively rare. The Penn Treebank (Marcus et al. 1993) from the University of Pennsylvania is a widely cited example for English.

A last word on annotated corpora: in tests, we will benchmark automatic methods against manual annotation, which is often called the Gold Standard. We will assume the hand annotation perfect, although this is not true in practice. Some errors slip into hand-annotated corpora, even in those of the best quality, and the annotators may not agree between them. The scope of agreement varies depending on the annotation task. The inter-annotator agreement is high for parts of speech. It is lower when annotating the sense of a word.

2.1.2 Corpora and Lexicon Building

Lexicons and dictionaries are intended to give word lists, to provide a reader with word senses and meanings, and to outline their usage. Dictionaries' main purpose is related to lexical semantics. Lexicography is the science of building lexicons and writing dictionaries. It uses electronic corpora extensively.

The basic data of a dictionary is a word list. Such lists can be drawn manually or automatically from corpora. Then, lexicographers write the word definitions and choose citations illustrating the words. Since most of the time current meanings are

obvious to the reader, meticulous lexicographers tended to collect examples – citations – reflecting a rare usage. Computerized corpora can help lexicographers avoid
this pitfall by extracting all the citations that exemplify a word. An experienced lexi-
cographer will then select the most representative examples that reflect the language
with more relevance. S/he will prefer and describe more frequent usage and possibly
set aside others.

Finding a citation involves sampling a fragment of text surrounding a given word.
In addition, the context of a word can be more precisely measured by finding recurrent pairs of words, or most frequent neighbors. The first process results in concordance tables, and the second one in collocations.

Concordance tables were first produced for antiquity and religious studies.
Hugues de Saint Cher is known to have compiled the first Bible concordance in the
thirteenth century. Concordances consist of text excerpts centered on a specific word
and surrounded by a limited number of words before and after it (Table 2.2). Other
more elaborate concordances take word morphology into account or group words
together into semantic themes. Sœur Jeanne d'Arc (1970) produced an example of
such a concordance for Bible studies.

Table 2.2. Concordance of *miracle* in the Gospel of John.

Language	Concordances
English	s beginning of miracles did Je
	n they saw the miracles which
	n can do these miracles that t
	ain the second miracle that Je
	e they saw his miracles which
French	le premier des miracles que fi
	i dirent: Quel miracle nous mo
	om, voyant les miracles qu'il
	peut faire ces miracles que tu
	s ne voyez des miracles et des
German	ist das erste Zeichen, das Je
	du uns für ein Zeichen, daß du
	en, da sie die Zeichen sahen,
	emand kann die Zeichen tun, di
	Wenn ihr nicht Zeichen und Wun

Concordancing is a powerful tool to study usage patterns and to write definitions.
It also provides evidences on certain preferences between verbs and prepositions, adjectives and nouns, recurring expressions, or common syntactic forms. These couples
are referred to as **collocations**. Church and Mercer (1993) cite a striking example of
idiosyncratic collocations of *strong* and *powerful*. While *strong* and *powerful* have
similar definitions, they occur in different contexts, as shown in Table 2.3.

Table 2.4 shows additional collocations of *strong* and *powerful*. These word preferences cannot be explained using rational definitions, but can be observed in cor-

Table 2.3. Comparing *strong* and *powerful*.

	English	**French**	**German**
You say	*Strong tea*	*Thé fort*	*Kräftiger Tee*
	Powerful computer	*Ordinateur puissant*	*Starker Computer*
You don't say	*Strong computer*	*Thé puissant*	*Starker Tee*
	Powerful tea	*Ordinateur fort*	*Kräftiger Computer*

pora. A variety of statistical tests can measure the strength of pairs, and we can extract them automatically from a corpus.

Table 2.4. Word preferences of *strong* and *powerful* collected from the Associated Press corpus. Numbers in columns indicate the number of collocation occurrences with word w. After Church and Mercer (1993).

Preference for *strong* over *powerful*			Preference for *powerful* over *strong*		
strong w	*powerful w*	*w*	*strong w*	*powerful w*	*w*
161	0	*showing*	1	32	*than*
175	2	*support*	1	32	*figure*
106	0	*defense*	3	31	*minority*
...					

2.1.3 Corpora as Knowledge Sources for the Linguist

In the beginning of the 1990s, computer-based corpus analysis completely renewed empirical methods in linguistics. It helped design and implement many of the techniques presented in this book. As we saw with dictionaries, corpus analysis helps lexicographers acquire lexical knowledge and describe language usage. More generally, corpora enable us to experiment with tools and to confront theories on real data. For most language analysis programs, collecting relevant corpora of texts has then become a necessary step to define specifications and measure performances. Let us take the examples of part-of-speech taggers, parsers, and dialogue systems.

Annotated corpora are essential tools to develop part-of-speech taggers or parsers. A first purpose is to measure the tagging or parsing performance. The tagger or parser is run on texts and their result is compared to hand annotation, which serves as a reference. A linguist or an engineer can then determine the accuracy, the robustness of an algorithm or a parsing model and see how well it scales up by applying it to a variety of texts.

A second purpose of annotated corpora is to be a knowledge source to refine tagging techniques and improve grammars. While developing a grammar, a linguist can see if changing a rule improves or deteriorates results. The tool tuning is then done manually. Using statistical techniques, annotated corpora also enable researchers to

acquire grammar rules or language models automatically or semiautomatically to tag
or parse a text. We will see this in Chap. 7.

A dialogue corpus between a user and a machine is also critical to develop an
interactive spoken system. The corpus is usually collected through fake dialogues
between a real user and a person simulating the machine answers. Repeating such
experiments with a reasonable number of users enables us to acquire a text set covering what the machine can expect from potential users. It is then easier to determine
the vocabulary of an application, to have a precise idea of word frequencies, and
to know the average length of sentences. In addition, the dialogue corpus enables
the analyst to understand what the user expects from the machine, that is, how s/he
interacts with it.

2.2 Finite-State Automata

2.2.1 A Description

The most frequent operation we do with corpora consists in searching words or
phrases. To be convenient, search must extend beyond fixed strings. We may want
to search a word or its plural form, uppercase or lowercase letters, expressions containing numbers, etc. This is made possible using finite-state automata (FSA) that we
introduce now. FSA are flexible tools to process texts and one of the most adequate
to search strings.

FSA theory was designed in the beginning of computer science as a model of
abstract computing machines. It forms a well-defined formalism that has been tested
and used by generations of programmers. FSA stem from a simple idea. These are
devices that accept – recognize – or reject an input stream of characters. FSA are very
efficient in terms of speed and memory occupation and are easy to implement in Prolog. In addition to text searching, they have many other applications: morphological
parsing, part-of-speech annotation, and speech processing.

Figure 2.1 shows a three-state automaton numbered from 0 to 2, where state
q_0 is called the start state and q_2 the final state. An automaton has a single start
state and any number of final states, indicated by double circles. Arcs between states
designate the possible transitions. Each arc is annotated by a label, which means that
the transition accepts or generates the corresponding character.

An automaton accepts an input string in the following way: it starts in the initial state, follows a transition where the arc character matches the first character of
the string, consumes the corresponding string character, and reaches the destination
state. It makes then a second transition with the second string character and continues in this way until it ends up in one of the final states and there is no character left.
The automaton in Fig. 2.1 accepts or generates strings such as: *ac, abc, abbc, abbbc,
abbbbbbbbbbbbc*, etc. If the automaton fails to reach a final state, either because it has
no more characters in the input string or because it is trapped in a nonfinal state, it
rejects the string.

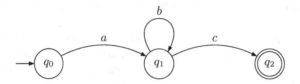

Fig. 2.1. A finite-state automaton.

As an example, let us see how the automaton accepts string *abbc* and rejects *abbcb*. The input *abbc* is presented to the start state q_0. The first character of the string matches that of the outgoing arc. The automaton consumes character *a* and moves to state q_1. The remaining string is *bbc*. Then, the automaton loops twice on state q_1 and consumes *bb*. The resulting string is character *c*. Finally, the automaton consumes *c* and reaches state q_2, which is the final state. On the contrary, the automaton does not accept string *abbcb*. It moves to states q_0, q_1, and q_2, and consumes *abbc*. The remaining string is letter *b*. Since there is no outgoing arc with a matching symbol, the automaton is stuck in state q_2 and rejects the string.

Automata may contain ε-transitions from one state to another. In this case, the automaton makes a transition without consuming any character of the input string. The automaton in Fig. 2.2 accepts strings *a*, *ab*, *abb*, etc. as well as *ac*, *abc*, *abbc*, etc.

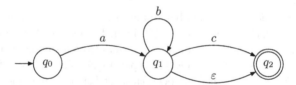

Fig. 2.2. A finite-state automaton with an ε-transition.

2.2.2 Mathematical Definition of Finite-State Automata

FSA have a formal definition. An FSA consists of five components $(Q, \Sigma, q_0, F, \delta)$, where:

1. Q is a finite set of states.
2. Σ is a finite set of symbols or characters: the input alphabet.
3. q_0 is the start state, $q_0 \in Q$.
4. F is the set of final states, $F \subseteq Q$.
5. δ is the transition function $Q \times \Sigma \rightarrow Q$, where $\delta(q, i)$ returns the state where the automaton moves when it is in state q and consumes the input symbol i.

The quintuple defining the automaton in Fig. 2.1 is $Q = \{q_0, q_1, q_2\}$, $\Sigma = \{a, b, c\}$, $F = \{q_2\}$, and $\delta = \{\delta(q_0, a) = q_1, \delta(q_1, b) = q_1, \delta(q_1, c) = q_2\}$. The state-transition table in Table 2.5 is an alternate representation of the δ function.

Table 2.5. A state-transition table where $\emptyset$ denotes nonexisting or impossible transitions.

State\Input	a	b	c
q_0	q_1	$\emptyset$	$\emptyset$
q_1	$\emptyset$	q_1	q_2
q_2	$\emptyset$	$\emptyset$	$\emptyset$

2.2.3 Finite-State Automata in Prolog

A finite-state automaton has a straightforward implementation in Prolog. It is merely the transcription of the quintuplet definition. The following code describes the transitions, the start, and the final states of the automaton in Fig. 2.1:

```
% The start state
start(q0).

% The final states
final(q2).

% The transitions
% transition(SourceState, Symbol, DestinationState)
transition(q0, a, q1).
transition(q1, b, q1).
transition(q1, c, q2).
```

The predicate `accept/1` selects the start state and runs the automaton using `accept/2`. The predicate `accept/2` is recursive. It succeeds when it reaches a final state, or consumes a symbol of the input string and makes a transition otherwise.

```
accept(Symbols) :-
   start(StartState),
   accept(Symbols, StartState).

% accept(+Symbols, +State)
accept([], State) :-
   final(State).
accept([Symbol | Symbols], State) :-
   transition(State, Symbol, NextState),
   accept(Symbols, NextState).
```

`accept/1` either accepts an input symbol string or fails:

```
?- accept([a, b, b, c]).
Yes

?- accept([a, b, b, c, b]).
No
```

The automaton in Fig. 2.2 contains ε-transitions. They are introduced in the database as facts:

```
epsilon(q1, q2).
```

To take them into account, the `accept/2` predicate should be modified so that there are two possible sorts of transitions. A first rule consumes a character and a second one, corresponding to an ε-transition, passes the string unchanged to the next state:

```
accept([], State) :-
   final(State).
accept([Symbol | Symbols], State) :-
   transition(State, Symbol, NextState),
   accept(Symbols, NextState).
accept(Symbols, State) :-
   epsilon(State, NextState),
   accept(Symbols, NextState).
```

2.2.4 Deterministic and Nondeterministic Automata

The automaton in Fig. 2.1 is said to be deterministic (DFSA) because given a state and an input, there is one single possible destination state. On the contrary, a nondeterministic automaton (NFSA) has states where it has a choice: the path is not determined in advance.

Figure 2.3 shows an example of an NFSA that accepts the strings ab, abb, $abbb$, $abbbb$, etc. Taking abb as input, the automaton reaches the state q_1 consuming the letter a. Then, it has a choice between two states. The automaton can either move to state q_2 or stay in state q_1. If it first moves to state q_2, there will be one character left and the automaton will fail. The right path is to loop onto q_1 and then to move to q_2. ε-transitions also cause automata to be nondeterministic as in Fig. 2.2 where any string that has reached state q_1 can also reach state q_2.

A possible strategy to deal with nondeterminism is to use backtracking. When an automaton has the choice between two or more states, it selects one of them and remembers the state where it made the decision: the choice point. If it subsequently fails, the automaton backtracks to the choice point and selects another state to go to. In our example in Fig. 2.3, if the automaton moves first to state q_2 with the string bb, it will end up in a state without outgoing transition. It will have to backtrack and select state q_1. Backtracking is precisely the strategy that Prolog uses automatically.

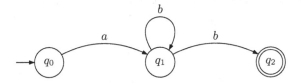

Fig. 2.3. A nondeterministic automaton.

2.2.5 Building a Deterministic Automata from a Nondeterministic One

Although surprising, any nondeterministic automaton can be converted into an equivalent deterministic automaton. We outline here an informal description of the determinization algorithm. See Hopcroft et al. (2001) for a complete description of this algorithm.

The algorithm starts from an NFSA $(Q_N, \Sigma, q_0, F_N, \delta_N)$ and builds an equivalent DFSA $(Q_D, \Sigma, \{q_0\}, F_D, \delta_D)$, where:

- Q_D is the set of all the possible state subsets of Q_N. It is called the power set. The set of states of the automaton in Fig. 2.3 is $Q_N = \{q_0, q_1, q_2\}$. The corresponding set of sets is $Q_D = \{\emptyset, \{q_0\}, \{q_1\}, \{q_2\}, \{q_0, q_1\}, \{q_0, q_2\}, \{q_1, q_2\}, \{q_0, q_1, q_2\}\}$. If Q_N has n states, Q_D will have 2^n states. In general, many of these states will be inaccessible and will be discarded.
- F_D is the set of sets that include at least one final state of F_N. In our example, $Q_D = \{\{q_2\}, \{q_0, q_2\}, \{q_1, q_2\}, \{q_0, q_1, q_2\}\}$.
- For each set $S \subset Q_N$ and for each input symbol a, $\delta_D(S, a) = \bigcup_{s \in S} \delta_N(s, a)$. The state-transition table in Table 2.6 represents the automaton in Fig. 2.3. Table 2.7 represents the determinized version of it.

Table 2.6. The state-transition table of the nondeterministic automaton shown in Fig. 2.3.

State\Input	a	b
q_0	q_1	$\emptyset$
q_1	$\emptyset$	q_1, q_2
q_2	$\emptyset$	$\emptyset$

2.2.6 Searching a String with a Finite-State Automaton

Searching the occurrences of a string in a text corresponds to recognizing them with an automaton, where the string characters label the sequence of transitions. However, the automaton must skip chunks in the beginning, between the occurrences, and at

Table 2.7. The state-transition table of the determinized automaton in Fig. 2.3.

State\Input	a	b
$\emptyset$	$\emptyset$	$\emptyset$
$\{q_0\}$	$\{q_1\}$	$\emptyset$
$\{q_1\}$	$\emptyset$	$\{q_1, q_2\}$
$\{q_2\}$	$\emptyset$	$\emptyset$
$\{q_0, q_1\}$	$\{q_1\}$	$\{q_1, q_2\}$
$\{q_0, q_2\}$	$\{q_1\}$	$\emptyset$
$\{q_1, q_2\}$	$\emptyset$	$\{q_1, q_2\}$
$\{q_0, q_1, q_2\}$	$\{q_1\}$	$\{q_1, q_2\}$

the end of the text. The automaton consists then of a core accepting the searched
string and of loops to process the remaining pieces. Consider again the automaton in
Fig. 2.1 and modify it to search strings ac, abc, $abbc$, $abbbc$, etc., in a text. We add
two loops: one in the beginning and the other to come back and start the search again
(Fig. 2.4).

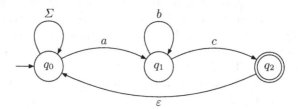

Fig. 2.4. Searching strings ac, abc, $abbc$, $abbbc$, etc.

In doing this, we have built an NFSA that it is preferable to convert into a DFSA.
Hopcroft et al. (2001) describe the mathematical properties of such automata and an
algorithm to automatically build an automaton for a given set of patterns to search.
They notably report that resulting DFSA have exactly the same number of states as
the corresponding NFSA. We present an informal solution to determine the transitions of the automaton in Fig. 2.4.

If the input text does not begin with an a, the automaton must consume the beginning characters and loop on the start state until it finds one. Figure 2.5 expresses
this with an outgoing transition from state 0 to state 1 labeled with an a and a loop
for the rest of the characters. $\Sigma - a$ denotes the finite set of symbols except a. From
state 1, the automaton proceeds if the text continues with either a b or a c. If it is
an a, the preceding a is not the beginning of the string, but there is still a chance
because it can start again. It corresponds to the second loop on state 1. Otherwise, if
the next character falls in the set $\Sigma - \{a, b, c\}$, the automaton goes back to state 0.
The automaton successfully recognizes the string if it reaches state 2. Then it goes

back to state 0 and starts the search again, except if the next character is an a, for which it can go directly to state 1.

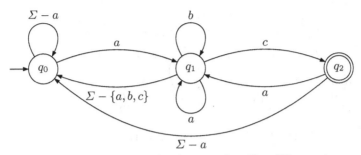

Fig. 2.5. An automaton to search strings ac, abc, $abbc$, $abbbc$, etc., in a text.

2.2.7 Operations on Finite-State Automata

FSA can be combined using a set of operations. The most useful are the union, the concatenation, and the closure.

The union or sum of two automata A and B accepts or generates all the strings of A and all the strings of B. It is denoted $A \cup B$. We obtain it by adding a new initial state that we link to the initial states of A and B (Fig. 2.6) using ε-transitions (Fig. 2.7).

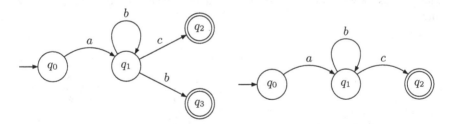

Fig. 2.6. Automata A (left) and B (right).

The concatenation or product of A and B accepts all the strings that are concatenations of two strings, the first one being accepted by A and the second one by B. It is denoted $A.B$. We obtain the resulting automaton by connecting all the final states of A to the initial state of B using ε-transitions (Fig. 2.8).

The iteration or Kleene closure of an automaton A accepts the concatenations of any number of its strings and the empty string. It is denoted A^*, where $A^* = \{\varepsilon\} \cup A \cup A.A \cup A.A.A \cup A.A.A.A \cup \ldots$. We obtain the resulting automaton by linking the final states of A to its initial state using ε-transitions and adding a new

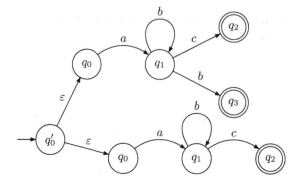

Fig. 2.7. The union of two automata: $A \cup B$.

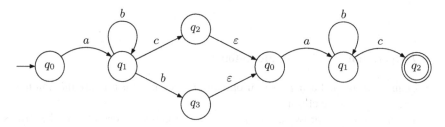

Fig. 2.8. The concatenation of two automata: $A.B$.

initial state, as shown in Fig. 2.9. The new initial state enables us to obtain the empty string.

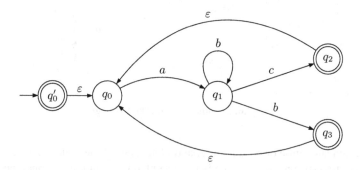

Fig. 2.9. The closure of A.

The notation Σ^* designates the infinite set of all possible strings generated from the alphabet Σ. Other significant operations are:

- The intersection of two automata $A \cap B$ that accepts all the strings accepted both by A and by B. If $A = (\Sigma, Q_1, q_1, F_1, \delta_1)$ and $B = (\Sigma, Q_2, q_2, F_2, \delta_2)$, the resulting automaton is obtained from the Cartesian product of states $(\Sigma, Q_1 \times Q_2, \langle q_1, q_2 \rangle, F_1 \times F_2, \delta_3)$ with the transition function $\delta_3(\langle s_1, s_2 \rangle, i) = \{\langle t_1, t_2 \rangle \mid t_1 \in \delta_1(s_1, i) \wedge t_2 \in \delta_2(s_2, i)\}$.
- The difference of two automata $A - B$ that accepts all the strings accepted by A but not by B.
- The complementation of the automaton A in Σ^* that accepts all the strings that are not accepted by A. It is denoted $\bar{A}$, where $\bar{A} = \Sigma^* - A$.
- The reversal of the automaton A that accepts all the reversed strings accepted by A.

Two automata are said to be equivalent when they accept or generate exactly the same set of strings. Useful equivalence transformations optimize computation speed or memory requirements. They include:

- ε-removal, which transforms an initial automaton into an equivalent one without ε-transitions
- determinization, which transforms a nondeterministic automaton into a deterministic one
- minimization, which determines among equivalent automata the one that has the smallest number of states

Optimization algorithms are out of the scope of this book. Hopcroft et al. (2001) as well as Roche and Schabes (1997) describe them in detail.

2.3 Regular Expressions

The automaton in Fig. 2.1 generates or accepts strings composed of one a, zero or more b's, and one c. We can represent this set of strings using a compact notation: ab*c, where the star symbol means any number of the preceding character. Such a notation is called a regular expression or regex. Regular expressions are very powerful devices to describe patterns to search in a text. Although their notation is different, regular expressions can always be implemented under the form of automata, and vice versa. However, regular expressions are generally easier to use.

Regular expressions are composed of literal characters, that is, ordinary text characters like abc, and of metacharacters like * that have a special meaning. The simplest form of regular expressions is a sequence of literal characters: letters, numbers, spaces, or punctuation signs. Regexes regular or Prolog match strings *regular* or *Prolog* contained in a text. Table 2.8 shows examples of pattern matching with literal characters. Regular expressions are case-sensitive and match the first instance of the string or all its instances in a text, depending on the regex language that is used.

There are currently a dozen major regular expression languages freely available. Their common ancestor is grep, which stands for global/regular expression/print.

Table 2.8. Examples of simple patterns and matching results.

Pattern	String
regular	"A section on regular expressions"
Prolog	"The Prolog language"
the	"The book of the life"

grep is a standard Unix tool that prints out all the lines of a file that contain a given pattern. The grep user interface conforms to the Unix command-line style. It consists of the command name, here grep, options, and the arguments. The first argument is the regular expression delimited by single straight quotes. The next arguments are the files where to search the pattern:

    grep 'regular expression' file1 file2 ... filen

The Unix command:

    grep 'abc' myFile

prints all the lines of file myFile containing the string *abc* and

    grep 'ab*c' myFile1 myFile2

prints all the lines of file myFile1 and myFile2 containing the strings *ac*, *abc*, *abbc*, *abbbc*, etc.

grep had a considerable influence on its followers. Most of them adhere to a comparable syntax. Among the most popular languages featuring regexes now are Perl and Python, Java, and C#. In the following sections, the description of the syntactic features refers to egrep, which is a modern version of grep available for most operating systems.

2.3.1 Repetition Metacharacters

We saw that the metacharacter * expressed a repetition of zero or more characters, as in ab*c. Other characters that describe repetitions are the question mark, ?, the plus, +, and the dot, . (Table 2.9). The star symbol is also called the closure operator or the Kleene star.

If the pattern to search contains a character that is also a metacharacter, for instance, "?", we need to indicate it to the regex engine using a backslash \ before it. We saw that abc? matches *ab* and *abc*. The expression abc\? matches the string *abc?*. In the same vein, abc\. matches the string *abc.*, and a*bc matches *a*bc*. The backslash is also called the escape character. It transforms a metacharacter into a literal symbol. In most regex languages, we must quote characters ., ?, (,), [,], {, }, *, +, |, ^, $, and \ to search them literally.

Table 2.9. Repetition metacharacters.

Metachars	Descriptions	Examples
`*`	Matches any number of occurrences of the previous character – zero or more	`ac*e` matches strings ae, ace, acce, accce, etc. as in "The <u>ae</u>rial ac<u>ce</u>leration alerted the <u>ace</u> pilot"
`?`	Matches at most one occurrence of the previous characters – zero or one	`ac?e` matches ae and ace as in "The <u>ae</u>rial acceleration alerted the <u>ace</u> pilot"
`+`	Matches one or more occurrences of the previous characters	`ac+e` matches ace, acce, accce, etc. as in as in "The aerial ac<u>ce</u>leration alerted the <u>ace</u> pilot"
`{n}`	Matches exactly n occurrences of the previous characters	`ac{2}e` matches acce as in "The aerial ac<u>ce</u>leration alerted the ace pilot"
`{n, }`	Matches n or more occurrences of the previous characters	`ac{2,}e` matches acce, accce, etc.
`{n,m}`	Matches from n to m occurrences of the previous characters	`ac{2,4}e` matches acce, accce, and acccce.
`.`	Matches one occurrence of any characters of the alphabet except the new line character	`a.e` matches aae, aAe, abe, aBe, ale, etc. as in "The aerial accelera-tion al<u>erte</u>d the <u>ace</u> pilot"
`.*`	Matches any string of characters and until it encounters a new line character	

2.3.2 The Longest Match

The description of repetition metacharacters in Table 2.9 sometimes makes string matching ambiguous, as with the string aabbc and the regex a+b*, which has six possible matches: *a*, *aa*, *ab*, *aab*, *abb*, and *aabb*. In fact, matching algorithms use two rules that are common to all the regex languages:

1. They match as early as they can in a string.
2. They match as many characters as they can.

Hence, a+b* matches *aabb*, which is the longest possible match. The matching strategy of repetition metacharacters is said to be greedy.

In some cases, the greedy strategy is not appropriate. To display the sentence

*They match **as early** and **as many** characters as they can.*

in a Web page with two phrases set in bold, we need specific tags that we will insert in the source file. Using HTML, the language of the Web, the sentence will probably be annotated as

```
They match <b>as early</b> and <b>as many</b>
characters as they can.
```

where `<b>` and `</b>` mark respectively the beginning and the end of a phrase set in bold. (We will see annotation frameworks in more detail in Chap. 3.)

A regular expression to search and extract phrases in bold could be:

```
<b>.*</b>
```

Unfortunately, applying this regex to the sentence will match one single string:

```
<b>as early</b> and <b>as many</b>
```

which is not what we wanted. In fact, this is not a surprise. As we saw, the regex engine matches as early as it can, i.e., from the first `<b>` and as many characters as it can up to the second `</b>`.

A possible solution is to modify the behavior of repetition metacharacters and make them "lazy." They will then consume as few characters as possible. We create the lazy variant of a repetition metacharacter by appending a question mark to it (Table 2.10). The regex

```
<b>.*?</b>
```

will then match the two intended strings,

```
<b>as early</b> and <b>as many</b>.
```

Table 2.10. Lazy metacharacters.

Metachars	Descriptions
*?	Matches any number of occurrences of the previous character – zero or more
??	Matches at most one occurrence of the previous characters – zero or one
+?	Matches one or more occurrences of the previous characters
{n}?	Matches exactly n occurrences of the previous characters
{n,}?	Matches n or more occurrences of the previous characters
{n,m}?	Matches from n to m occurrences of the previous characters

2.3.3 Character Classes

We saw that the dot, ., represents any character of the alphabet. It is possible to define smaller subsets or **classes**. A list of characters between square brackets [. . .] matches any character contained in the list. [abc] means one occurrence of either a, b, or c. [ABCDEFGHIJKLMNOPQRSTUVWXYZ] means one uppercase unaccented letter, and [0123456789] means one digit. We can concatenate character classes, literal characters, and metacharacters, as in the expressions [0123456789]+ and

`[0123456789]+\.[0123456789]+`, that match respectively integers and decimal numbers.

Character classes are useful to search patterns with spelling differences, such as `[Cc]omputer [Ss]cience`, which matches four different strings:

Computer Science
Computer science
computer Science
computer science

We can define the complement of a character class, that is, the characters of the alphabet that are not member of the class, using the caret symbol, ^, as the first symbol inside the angle brackets. `[^a]` means any character that is not an *a*. `[^0123456789]` means any character that is not a digit. The expression `[^ABCD]*` means any string that does not contain *A*, *B*, *C*, or *D*. The caret must be the first character after the brackets. The expression `[a^b]` matches either *a*, ^, or *b*.

Inside angle brackets, we can also specify ranges using the dash character -. The expression `[1-4]` means any of the digits *1*, *2*, *3*, or *4*, and a `[1-4]b` matches *a1b*, *a2b*, *a3c*, or *a4b*. The expression `[a-zàâäæçéèêëîïôöœßùûüÿ]` matches any lowercase accented or unaccented letter of French and German. If we want to search the dash character itself, we need to quote it as `\-`. The expression `[1\-4]` means any of the characters *1*, -, or *4*.

Most regex languages have also predefined classes. Table 2.11 lists some useful ones. Some classes may be specific to one regex language. In case of doubt, refer to the corresponding manual.

2.3.4 Nonprintable Symbols or Positions

Some metacharacters match positions and nonprintable symbols. Positions or **anchors** enable one to search a pattern with a specific location in a text. They encode the start and end of a line, using respectively the caret, ^, and the dollar, $.

The expression `^Chapter` matches lines beginning with *Chapter* and `[0-9]+$` matches lines ending with a number. We can combine both in `^Chapter [0-9]+$` that matches lines consisting only of the *Chapter* word and a number as *Chapter 3*, for example.

The command line

```
egrep '^[aeiou]+$' myFile
```

matches lines of `myFile` containing only vowels.

Similarly, metacharacters `\<` and `\>` match the start and end of a word. The expression `\<ace` matches *aces* and *acetylene* but not *place*. Conversely, `ace\>` matches *place* but neither *aces* nor *acetylene*. The expression `\<act\>` matches exactly the word *act* and not *react* or *acted*. Table 2.12 summarizes anchors and some nonprintable characters.

In Perl, word boundaries are indicated by `\b` instead of `\<` and `\>`, as in `\bact\b`.

Table 2.11. Predefined character classes.

Expressions	Descriptions	Examples
\d	Any digit. Equivalent to [0-9]	A\dC matches A0C, A1C, A2C, A3C etc.
\D	Any nondigit. Equivalent to [^0-9]	
\w	Any word character: letter, digit, or underscore. Equivalent to [a-zA-Z0-9_]	1\w2 matches 1a2, 1A2, 1b2, 1B2, etc
\W	Any nonword character. Equivalent to [^\w]	
\s	Any white space character: space, tabulation, new line, form feed, carriage return, or backspace.	
\S	Any nonwhite space character. Equivalent to [^\s]	
[:alpha:]	Any alphabetic character. It includes accented characters	1[:alpha:]2 matches 1a2, 1A2, 1b2, 1B2, etc.
[:digit:]	Any digit	A[:digit:]C matches A0C, A1C, A2C, A3C etc.
[:upper:]	Any uppercase character. It includes accented characters	A[:upper:]C matches AAC, ABC, ACC, ADC etc.
[:lower:]	Any lowercase character. It includes accented characters	A[:lower:]C matches AaC, AbC, AcC, AdC etc.

Table 2.12. Some metacharacters matching nonprintable characters.

Metachars	Descriptions	Examples
^	Matches the start of a line	^ab*c matches ac, abc, abbc, abbbc, etc. when they are located at the beginning of a new line
$	Matches the end of a line	ab?c$ matches ac and abc when they are located at the end of a line
\<	Matches the start of a word	\<abc matches abcd but not dabc
\>	Matches the end of a word	bcd\> matches abcd but not abcde
\n	Matches a new line	a\nb matches a b
\t	Matches a tabulation	–
\r	Matches the carriage return character	–
\f	Matches the form feed character	–
\e	Matches the escape character	–
\a	Matches the bell character	–

2.3.5 Union and Boolean Operators

We reviewed the basic constructs to write regular expressions. A powerful feature is that we can also combine expressions with operators, as with automata. Using a mathematical term, we say that they define an algebra. Using a simpler analogy, this means that we can arrange regular expressions just like arithmetic expressions. This greatly eases the design of complex expressions and makes them very versatile.

Regex languages use three main operators. Two of them are already familiar to us. The first one is the Kleene star or closure, denoted `*`. The second one is the concatenation, which is usually not represented. It is implicit in strings like abc, which is the concatenation of characters *a*, *b*, and *c*. To concatenate the word *computer*, a space symbol, and *science*, we just write them in a row: `computer science`.

The third operation is the union and is denoted "`|`". The expression a|b means either *a* or *b*. We saw that the regular expression `[Cc]omputer [Ss]cience` could match four strings. We can rewrite an equivalent expression using the union operator: `Computer Science|Computer science|computer Science| computer science`. A union is also called an alternation because the corresponding expression can match any of the alternatives, here four.

2.3.6 Operator Combination and Precedence

Regular expressions and operators are grouped using parentheses. If we omit them, expressions are governed by rules of precedence and associativity. The expression a|bc matches the strings *a* and *bc* because the concatenation operator takes precedence over the union. In other words, the concatenation binds the characters stronger than the union. If we want an expression that matches the strings *ac* and *bc*, we need parentheses `(a|b)c`.

Let us examine another example of precedence. We rewrote the expression `[Cc]omputer [Ss]cience` using a union of four strings. Since the difference between expressions lies in the first letters only, we can try to revise this union into something more compact. The character class `[Cc]` is equivalent to the alternation C|c, which matches either *C* or *c*. A tentative expression could then be `C|computer S|science`. But it would not match the desired strings; it would find occurrences of either *C*, *computer S*, or *science* because of the operator precedence. We need parentheses to group the alternations `(C|c)omputer (S|s)cience` and thus match the four intended strings.

The order of precedence of the three main operators union, concatenation, and closure is as follows:

1. closure and other repetition operator (highest)
2. concatenation, line and word boundaries
3. union (lowest)

This entails that abc`*` describes the set *ab*, *abc*, *abcc*, *abccc*, etc. To repeat the pattern *abc*, we need parentheses. And the expression `(abc)*` corresponds to *abc*, *abcabc*, *abcabcabc*, etc.

2.4 Programming with Regular Expressions

2.4.1 Perl

grep and egrep are tools to search patterns in texts. If we want to use them for more elaborate text processing such as translating characters, substituting words, counting them, we need a full-fledged programming language, for example, Perl, Python, AWK, and Java with its java.util.regex package. They enable the design of powerful regular expressions and at the same time, they are complete programming languages. This section intends to give you a glimpse of Perl programming. We discuss features of Perl in this chapter and the next one. Further references include Wall et al. (2000) and Schwartz and Phoenix (2001).

2.4.2 Matching

Perl has constructs similar to those of the C language. It has analogous control flow statements, and the assignment operator is denoted =. However, variables begin with a dollar sign and are not typed. Comments start with the # symbol. The short program

```
# A first program
$integer = 30;
$pattern = "My string";
print $integer, " ", $pattern, "\n";
```

prints the line

```
30 My string
```

We run it with the command:

```
perl -w program.pl
```

where the option -w asks Perl to check syntax errors.

The next program reads the input line and searches the expression ab*c. If it finds the expression, it prints the line:

```
while ($line = <>) {
  if ($line =~ m/ab*c/) {
    print $line;
  }
}
```

The program uses repeat and conditional statements. The symbol <> designates the standard input, and the instruction $line = <> assigns the current line from the input to the $line variable. The while instruction reads all the lines until it encounters an end of file. The m/.../ instruction delimits the regular expression to match, and the =~ operator instructs Perl to search it in the $line variable. If the expression matches a string in $line, the =~ operator returns true, or false otherwise. The if instruction tells the program to print the input when it contains the pattern. We run the program to search the file file_name with the command:

```
perl -w program.pl file_name
```

The match operator supports a set of options also called modifiers. Their syntax is m/regex/modifiers. Useful modifiers are

- Case insensitive: i. The instruction m/regex/i searches regex in the target string regardless of its case.
- Multiple lines: m. By default, the anchors ^ and $ match the start and the end of the input string. The instruction m/regex/m considers the input string as multiple lines separated by new line characters, where the anchors ^ and $ match the start and the end of any line in the string.
- Single line: s. Normally, a dot symbol "." does not match new line characters. The /s modifier makes a dot in the instruction m/regex/s match any character including new lines.

Modifiers can be grouped in any order as in m/regex/im, for instance, or m/regex/sm, where a dot in regex matches any character and the anchors ^ and $ match just after and before new line characters.

2.4.3 Substitutions

One of the powerful features of Perl is pattern substitution. It uses a construct similar to the match instruction: s/regex/replacement/. The instruction

```
$line =~ s/regex/replacement/
```

matches the first occurrence of regex and replaces it by replacement in the $line variable. If we want to replace all the occurrences of a pattern, we use the g modifier, where g stands for globally:

```
$line =~ s/regex/replacement/g
```

We shall write a program to replace the occurrences of ab*c by ABC in a file and print them. We read all the lines of the input. We use the instruction m/ab*c/ to check whether they match the regular expression ab*c. We then print the old line and we substitute the matched pattern using the construct s/ab*c/ABC/:

```
while ($line = <>) {
  if ($line =~ m/ab*c/) {
    print "Old: ", $line;
    $line =~ s/ab*c/ABC/g;
    print "New: ", $line;
  }
}
```

2.4.4 Translating Characters

The instruction `tr/search_list/replacement_list/` replaces all the occurrences of the characters in `search_list` by the corresponding character in `replacement_list`. The instruction `tr/ABC/abc/` replaces the occurrences of *A*, *B*, and *C* by *a*, *b*, and *c*, respectively. The string

```
AbCdEfGhIjKlMnOpQrStUvWxYzÉö
```

results in

```
abcdEfGhIjKlMnOpQrStUvWxYzÉö
```

The hyphen specifies a character range, as in the instruction

```
$line =~ tr/A-Z/a-z/;
```

which converts the uppercase characters to their lowercase equivalents. The instruction `tr` has useful modifiers:

- `d` deletes any characters of the search list that are not found in the replacement list.
- `c` translates characters that belong to the complement of the search list.
- `s` reduces – squeezes, squashes – sequences of characters translated to an identical character to a single instance.

The instruction

```
$line =~ tr/AEIOUaeiou//d;
```

deletes all the vowels in `$line` and

```
$line =~ tr/AEIOUaeiou/\$/cs;
```

replaces all nonvowel characters by a $ sign. The contiguous sequences of translated dollar signs are reduced to a single sign.

2.4.5 String Operators

Perl operators are similar to those of the C and Java languages. They are summarized in Table 2.13. The string operators are notable differences. They enable us to concatenate and compare strings.

The Boolean operators `eq` (equal) and `ne` (not equal) compare two strings. The dot is the concatenation operator:

```
$string1 = "abc";
$string 2 = "def";
$string3 = $string1 . $string2;
print $string3;
#prints abcdef
```

As with the C and Java operators, the shorthand notation `$var1 .= $var2` is equivalent to `$var1 = $var1 . $var2`. The following program reads the content of the input line by line, concatenates it in the `$text` variable, and prints it:

```
while ($line = <>) {
   $text .= $line;
}
print $text;
```

Table 2.13. Summary of the main Perl operators.

Unary operators	!	Logical not
	+ and -	Arithmetic plus sign and negation
Binding operators	=~	Returns true in case of match success
	!~	Returns false in case of match success
Arithmetic operators	* and /	Multiplication and division
	+ and -	Addition and subtraction
String operator	.	String concatenation
Arithmetic comparison operators	> and <	Greater than and less than
	>= and <=	Greater than or equal and less than or equal
	== and !=	Equal and not equal
String comparison operators	ge and le	Greater than and less than
	gt and lt	Greater than or equal and less than or equal
	eq and ne	Equal and not equal
Logical operators	&&	Logical and
	||	Logical or

2.4.6 Back References

It is sometimes useful to keep a reference to matched patterns or parts of them. Let us imagine that we want to find a sequence of three identical characters, which corresponds to matching a character and checking if the next two characters are identical to the first character. To do this, we first tell Perl to remember the matched pattern and we put parentheses around it. It creates a buffer to hold the pattern and we refer back to it by the sequence `\1`. The instruction `s/(.)\1\1/\*\*\*/g` replaces these sequences by three stars.

Perl can create as many buffers as we need. It allocates a new one when it encounters a left parenthesis and refers it back by references \1, \2, \3, etc. The first pair of parentheses corresponds to \1, the second pair to \2, the third to \3, etc. Outside the match expression the \<digit> reference is denoted by $<digit>: $1, $2, $3, etc. As an example, the next program captures occurrences of money amounts in dollars. It prints the dollars and cents:

```
while ($line = <>) {
  while ($line =~ m/\$ *([0-9]+)\.?([0-9]*)/g) {
    print "Dollars: ", $1, " Cents: ", $2, "\n";
  }
}
```

2.5 Finding Concordances

2.5.1 Concordances in Prolog

Concordances of a word, an expression, or more generally any string in a corpus are easy to obtain with Prolog. Let us suppose that the corpus is represented as one single big string: a list of characters. Concordancing simply consists in matching the pattern we are searching as a substring of the whole list. There is no need to consider the corpus structure, that is, whether it is made of blanks, words, sentences, or paragraphs.

We implement the search with two auxiliary predicates: prefix(+List, +Span, -Prefix) that extracts the prefix of a list with up to Span characters, and prepend(+List, +Span, -PrependedList) that adds Span variables onto the beginning of a list.

Now let us write the concordance/4 predicate. It finds Pattern in List and returns the first Line where it occurs. Span is the window size, for example, 15 characters to the left and to the right, within which Pattern will be displayed. We first prepend Pattern with Span variables before it to match the pattern and its right context. We find it with a combination of two append/3 calls; then we use prefix/3 to extract up to Span characters after it.

```
% concordance(+Pattern, +List, +Span, -Line)
% finds Pattern in List and displays the Line
% where it appears within Span characters
% surrounding it.

concordance(Pattern, List, Span, Line) :-
  name(Pattern, LPattern),
  prepend(LPattern, Span, LeftPattern),
  append(_, Rest, List),
  append(LeftPattern, End, Rest),
  prefix(End, Span, Suffix),
```

```
  append(LeftPattern, Suffix, LLine),
  name(Line, LLine).
```

```
% prefix(+List, +Span, -Prefix) extracts the prefix
% of List with up to Span characters.
% The second rule is to check the case where there
% are less than Span character in List.
```

```
prefix(List, Span, Prefix) :-
  append(Prefix, _, List),
  length(Prefix, Span),
  !.
prefix(Prefix, Span, Prefix) :-
  length(Prefix, L),
  L < Span.
```

```
% prepend(+List. +Span, -Prefix) adds Span variables
% to the beginning of List.
```

```
prepend(Pattern, Span, List) :-
  prepend(Pattern, Span, Pattern, List).
```

```
prepend(_, 0, List, List) :- !.
prepend(Pattern, Span, List, FList) :-
  Span1 is Span - 1,
  prepend(Pattern, Span1, [X | List], FList).
```

Let us apply this program to retrieve the concordances of *Helen* in the *Iliad*. We make concordance/4 backtrack until all the occurrences have been found:

```
?- read_file('iliad.txt', L), concordance('Helen', L,
20, C), write(C),nl, fail.
```

```
ry of still keeping Helen, for whose sake so
ry of still keeping Helen, for whose sake so
red for the sake of Helen. Nevertheless, if a
red for the sake of Helen. The men of Pylos
 in their midst for Helen and all her wealth.
he midst of you for Helen and all her wealth.
nwhile Iris went to Helen in the form of her
ke the goddess, and Helen's heart yearned aft
wood. When they saw Helen coming towards the
"   "Sir," answered Helen, "father of my husb
...
No
```

Because the pattern is prepended with exactly Span variables, the concordance program will not examine the first Span characters of the file. This means that it will not find a possible pattern in this sublist. In our example above, the program finds all the occurrences of *Helen* except the ones that could occur in the first 15 characters of the text. This is easily corrected in the program and is left as an exercise.

2.5.2 Concordances in Perl

Arrays in Perl. Writing a basic concordance program is also easy in Perl. However, to be convenient, the program must be able to read parameters from the command line – the file name, the pattern to search, and the span size of the concordance – as in

```
perl -w concordance.pl corpus.txt my_word 15
```

These arguments are passed to Perl by the operating system under the form of an array. Before writing the program, we introduce this feature now.

Arrays in Perl are data structures that can hold any number of elements of any type. Their name begins with an at sign, @, for example, @array. Each element has a position where the programmer can store and read data using the position index.

An array grows or shrinks automatically when elements are appended, inserted, or deleted. Perl manages the memory without any intervention from the programmer. Here are some examples of arrays:

```
@array1 = ();          # The empty array
@array2 = (1, 2, 3); # Array containing 1, 2, and 3

$var1 = 3.14;
$var2 = "my string";
@array3 = (1, $var1, "Prolog", $var2);
# Array containing four elements of different type

@array4 = (@array2,@array3);
#Same as (1, 2, 3, 1, 3.14, "Prolog", "my string")
```

Reading or assigning a value to a position of the array is done using its index between square brackets starting from 0:

```
print $array2[1];  # prints 2
```

If an element is assigned to a position that did not exist before, Perl grows the array to store it. The positions in-between are not initialized. They hold the value undef:

```
$array4[10] = 10;
print $array4[10]; # prints 10
print $array4[9];
# prints a message telling it is undefined
```

The existence of a variable can be tested using the `defined` Boolean function as in:

```
if (defined($array4[9])) {
  print "yes", "\n";
} else {
  print "no", "\n";
}
```

If an `undef` value is used as a number, it is considered to be a zero. The next two lines print 1.

```
$array4[9]++;
print $array4[9];
```

The variable `$#array` is the index of the last element of the array. It can be assigned to grow or shrink the array:

```
$length4 = $#array4;
print $length4;    # prints 10
print $#array2;    # prints 2
$#array4 = 5;      # shrinks the array to 6 elements.
                   # Other elements are lost.
print $array4[10];
# prints a message telling it is undefined
$#array2 = 10;     # extends the array to 11 elements.
                   # Indices 3..10 are undefined.
```

You can also assign a complete array to an array and an array to a list of variables as in:

```
@array5 = @array2;
($v1, $v2, $v3) = @array2;
```

where `@array5` contains a copy of `@array2`, and `$v1`, `$v2`, `$v3` contain respectively 1, 2, and 3.

Printing Concordances in Perl. Now let us write a concordance program modified from Cooper (1999). First, we read the command line arguments: the file name, the pattern to search, and the span size. They are stored in the reserved variable `@ARGV`. We open the file using the `open` function, which assigns the stream to the `FILE` identifier. If `open` fails, the program exits using `die` and prints a message to inform us that it could not open the file.

The notation `<FILE>` designates the input stream, which is assigned to the `$line` variable. We read all the text and we assign it to the `$text` variable. To allow matching across spaces, tabulations, and new lines, we replace spaces in the regular expression `$pattern` representing the pattern to search by the space metacharacter `\s`. We also replace the new lines in the text by a space.

Finally, we use a `while` loop to match the pattern with `$width` characters to the left and to the right. The `/g` modifier enables the `m/.../` instruction to match a pattern and to start a new search from its current position – where the previous match ended. When `m/.../g` fails to match, the start position is reset to the beginning of the string. We create a back reference by setting parentheses around the regular expression to remember the matched pattern and we print it.

```
($file_name, $pattern, $width) = @ARGV;
open(FILE, "$file_name") ||
      die "Could not open file $file_name.";
while ($line = <FILE>) {
  $text .= $line;
}
$pattern =~ s/ /\\s/g;
      # spaces match tabs and new lines
$text =~ s/\n/ /g;
      # new lines are replaced by spaces
while ($text =~ m/(.{0,$width}$pattern.{0,$width})/g){
      # matches the pattern with 0..width
      #to the right and left
  print "$1\n"; #$1 contains the match
}
```

Now let us run the command:

```
perl -w concordance.pl odyssey.txt Penelope 20
```

```
itors of his mother Penelope, who persist in eat
ying out yet, while Penelope has such a fine son
 upon the Achaeans. Penelope, daughter of Icariu
d of Ulysses and of Penelope in your veins I see
long-suffering wife Penelope, and his son Telema
It was not long ere Penelope came to know what t
reshold of her room Penelope said: "Medon, what
```

2.6 Approximate String Matching

So far, we have used regular expressions to match exact patterns. However, in many applications, such as in spell checkers, we need to extend the match span to search a set of related patterns or strings. In this section, we review techniques to carry out approximate or inexact string matching.

2.6.1 Edit Operations

A common method to create a set of related strings is to apply a sequence of edit operations that transforms a source string s into a target string t. The operations are

carried out from left to right using two pointers that mark the position of the next
character to edit in both strings:

- The copy operation is the simplest. It copies the current character of the source
  string to the target string. Evidently, the repetition of copy operations produces
  equal source and target strings.
- Substitution replaces one character from the source string by a new character
  in the target string. The pointers are incremented by one in both the source and
  target strings.
- Insertion inserts a new character in the target string. The pointer in the target
  string is incremented by one, but the pointer in the source string is not.
- Deletion deletes the current character in the target string, i.e., the current character is not copied in the target string. The pointer in the source string is incremented by one, but the pointer in the target string is not.
- Reversal (or transposition) copies two adjacent characters of the source string
  and transposes them in the target string. The pointers are incremented by two
  characters.

Kernighan et al. (1990) illustrate these operations with the misspelled word
acress and its possible corrections (Table 2.14).

Table 2.14. Typographical errors (typos) and corrections. Strings differ by one operation. The
correction is the source and the typo is the target. Unless specified, other operations are just
copies. After Kernighan et al. (1990).

Typo	Correction	Source	Target	Position	Operation
acress	actress	–	t	2	Deletion
acress	cress	a	–	0	Insertion
acress	caress	ac	ca	0	Transposition
acress	access	r	c	2	Substitution
acress	across	e	o	3	Substitution
acress	acres	s	–	4	Insertion
acress	acres	s	–	5	Insertion

If we allow only one edit operation on a source string of length n, and if we consider an alphabet of 26 unaccented letters, the deletion will generate n new strings;
the insertion, $(n + 1) \times 26$ strings; the substitution, $n \times 25$; and the transposition,
$n - 1$ new strings.

2.6.2 Minimum Edit Distance

Complementary to edit operations, edit distances measure the similarity between
strings. They assign a cost to each edit operation, usually 0 to copies and 1 to deletions and insertions. Substitutions and transpositions correspond both to an insertion
and a deletion. We can derive from this that they each have a cost of 2. Edit distances

tell how far a source string is from a target string: the lower the distance, the closer the strings.

Given a set of edit operations, the minimum edit distance is the operation sequence that has the minimal cost needed to transform the source string into the target string. If we restrict the operations to copy/substitute, insert, and delete, we can represent the edit operations using a table, where the distance at a certain position in the table is derived from distances in adjacent positions already computed. This is expressed by the formula:

$$edit\_distance(i, j) = \min \begin{pmatrix} edit\_distance(i-1, j) + del\_cost \\ edit\_distance(i-1, j-1) + subst\_cost \\ edit\_distance(i, j-1) + ins\_cost \end{pmatrix}.$$

The boundary conditions for the first row and the first column correspond to a sequence of deletions and of insertions. They are defined as $edit\_distance(i, 0) = i$ and $edit\_distance(0, j) = j$.

We compute the cell values as a walk through the table from the beginning of the strings at the bottom left corner, and we proceed upward and rightward to fill adjacent cells from those where the value is already known. Arrows in Fig. 2.10 represent the three edit operations, and Table 2.15 shows the distances to transform *language* into *lineage*. The value of the minimum edit distance is 5 and is shown at the upper right corner of the table.

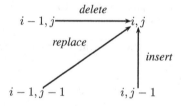

Fig. 2.10. Edit operations.

Table 2.15. Distances between *language* and *lineage*.

e	7	6	5	6	5	6	7	6	5
g	6	5	4	5	4	5	6	5	6
a	5	4	3	4	5	6	5	6	7
e	4	3	4	3	4	5	6	7	6
n	3	2	3	2	3	4	5	6	7
i	2	1	2	3	4	5	6	7	8
l	1	0	1	2	3	4	5	6	7
Start	0	1	2	3	4	5	6	7	8
–	**Start**	**l**	**a**	**n**	**g**	**u**	**a**	**g**	**e**

The minimum edit distance algorithm is part of the **dynamic programming** techniques. Their principles are relatively simple. They use a table to represent data, and they solve a problem at a certain point by combining solutions to subproblems. Dynamic programming is a generic term that covers a set of widely used methods in optimization.

We implement the minimum edit distance in Perl. We introduce the `length` function to compute the length of the source and target, and we use `split(//,` `$string)` to convert a string into an array of characters. The instruction

```
@array = split(regex, $string)
```

breaks up the `$string` variable as many times as `regex` matches in `$string`. The `regex` expression acts as a separator, and the string pieces are assigned sequentially to `@array`. In the program, `regex` is reduced to nothing and assigns all the characters `$string` as elements of `@array`.

```perl
($source, $target) = @ARGV;
$length_s = length($source);
$length_t = length($target);
# Initialize first row and column
for ($i = 0; $i <= $length_s; $i++) {
  $table[$i][0] = $i;
}
for ($j = 0; $j <= $length_t; $j++) {
  $table[0][$j] = $j;
}
# Get the characters. Start index is 0
@source = split(//, $source);
@target = split(//, $target);
# Fills the table.
# Start index of rows and columns is 1
for ($i = 1; $i <= $length_s; $i++) {
  for ($j = 1; $j <= $length_t; $j++) {
    # Is it a copy or a substitution?
    $cost = ($source[$i-1] eq $target[$j-1]) ? 0: 2;
    # Computes the minimum
    $min = $table[$i-1][$j-1] + $cost;
    if ($min > $table[$i][$j-1] + 1) {
      $min = $table[$i][$j-1] + 1;
    }
    if ($min > $table[$i-1][$j] + 1) {
      $min = $table[$i-1][$j] + 1;
    }
    $table[$i][$j] = $min;
  }
}
```

```
print "Minimum distance: ",
$table[$length_s][$length_t], "\n";
```

2.6.3 Searching Edits in Prolog

Once we have filled the table, we can search the operation sequences that correspond to the minimum edit distance. Such a sequence is also called an **alignment**.

The depth-first strategy is an economical way to traverse a search space. It is easy to implement in Prolog and has low memory requirements. The problem with it is that it blindly selects the paths to follow and can explore very deep nodes while ignoring shallow ones. To avoid this, we apply a variation of the depth-first search where we fix the depth in advance to the minimum edit distance. We assign it in the call parameter Cost of edit_distance/4.

The code of the depth-limited search is similar to the depth-first program (see Appendix A). We add a counter in the recursive case that represents the current search depth and we increment it until we have reached the depth limit. We compute each individual edit operation and its cost with the edit_operation/6 predicate.

```
% edit_distance(+Source, +Target, -Edits, +Cost).
edit_distance(Source, Target, Edits, Cost) :-
   edit_distance(Source, Target, Edits, 0, Cost).

edit_distance([], [], [], Cost, Cost).
edit_distance(Source, Target, [EditOp | Edits], Cost,
      FinalCost) :-
   edit_operation(Source, Target, NewSource,
       NewTarget, EditOp, CostOp),
   Cost1 is Cost + CostOp,
   edit_distance(NewSource, NewTarget, Edits, Cost1,
       FinalCost).

% edit_operation carries out one edit operation
% between a source string and a target string.
edit_operation([Char | Source], [Char | Target],
      Source, Target, ident, 0).
edit_operation([SChar | Source], [TChar | Target],
      Source, Target, sub(SChar,TChar), 2) :-
   SChar \= TChar.
edit_operation([SChar | Source], Target, Source,
      Target, del(SChar), 1).
edit_operation(Source, [TChar | Target], Source,
      Target, ins(TChar), 1).
```

Using backtracking, Prolog finds all the alignments. We obtain with the minimum distance of 5:

```
?- edit_distance([l,a,n,g,u,a,g,e], [l,i,n,e,a,g,e],
   E, 5).

E = [ident, sub(a, i), ident, sub(g, e), del(u),
     ident, ident, ident] ;

E = [ident, sub(a, i), ident, del(g), sub(u, e),
     ident, ident, ident] ;

E = [ident, sub(a, i), ident, del(g), del(u), ins(e),
     ident, ident, ident]
...
```

with 15 possible alignments in total. Figure 2.6.3 shows the first and third ones.

	First alignment	**Third alignment**
Without epsilon symbols	l a n g u a g e / l i n e a g e	l a n g u a g e / l i n e a g e
With epsilon symbols	l a n g u a g e / l i n e ε a g e	l a n g u ε a g e / l i n ε ε e a g e

Fig. 2.11. Alignments of *lineage* and *language*. The figure contains two possible representations of them. In the upper row, the deletions in the source string are in italics, as are the insertions in the target string. The lower row shows a synchronized alignment, where deletions in the source string as well as the insertions in the target string are aligned with epsilon symbols (null symbols).

We can apply this Prolog search program alone to find the edit distance. We avoid going an infinite path with an iterative deepening. We start with an edit distance of 0 (the Cost parameter) and we increment it – 1, 2, 3, 4 – until we find the minimum edit distance. The first searches will fail, and the first one that succeeds corresponds to the minimum distance.

2.7 Further Reading

Corpora are now easy to obtain. Organizations such as the Linguistic Data Consortium and ELRA collect and distribute texts in many languages. Although not widely cited, the first fiction corpus with more than 100 million words was probably FranText, which helped write the *Trésor de la langue française* (Imbs 1971–1994). Other early corpora include the Bank of English, which contributed to the *Collins COBUILD Dictionary* (Sinclair 1987).

Text and corpus analysis are an active focus of research in computational linguistics. They include the description of word distributions that were theorized at the beginning of the 20th century by Bloomfield and followers such as Harris (1962). Paradoxically, natural language processing conducted by computer scientists largely ignored corpora until the 1990s, when it rediscovered techniques routinely used in humanities. For a short history, see Zampolli (2003).

Roche and Schabes (1997, Chap. 1) is a concise and clear introduction to automata theory. It makes an extensive use of mathematical notations, however. Hopcroft et al. (2001) is a standard and comprehensive textbook on automata and regular expressions. Friedl (2002) is a thorough presentation of regular expressions oriented toward applications and programming techniques.

Although the idea of automata underlies some mathematical theories of the 19th century such as those of Markov, Gödel, or Turing, Kleene (1956) was first to give a formal definition. He also proved the equivalence between regular expressions and FSA. Thompson (1968) was the first to implement a widely used editor embedding a regular expression tool: Global/Regular Expression/Print, better known as `grep`.

There are several FSA toolkits available from the Internet. The FSA utilities (van Noord and Gerdemann 2001) is a Prolog package to manipulate regular expressions, automata, and transducers (odur.let.rug.nl/˜vannoord/Fsa/). The FSM library (Mohri et al. 1998) is another set of tools (www.research.att.com/sw/tools/fsm/). Both include rational operations – union, concatenation, closure, reversal – and equivalence transformation – ε-elimination, determinization, and minimization.

Exercises

2.1. Implement the automaton in Fig. 2.5.

2.2. Implement a Prolog program to automatically construct an automaton to search a given input string.

2.3. Write a regular expression that finds occurrences of *honour* and *honor* in a text.

2.4. Write a regular expression that finds lines containing all the vowels *a, e, i, o, u,* in that order.

2.5. Write a regular expression that finds lines consisting only of letters *a, b,* or *c.*

2.6. List the strings generated by the expressions:

```
(ab)*c
(a.)*c
(a|b)*
a|b*|(a|b)*a
a|bc*d
```

2.7. Complement the Prolog concordance program to sort the lines according to words appearing on the right of the string to search.

2.8. Write the iterative deepening search in Prolog to find the minimum edit distance.

3

Encoding, Entropy, and Annotation Schemes

3.1 Encoding Texts

At the most basic level, computers only understand binary digits and numbers. Corpora as well as any computerized text have to be converted into a digital format to be read by machines. From their American early history, computers inherited encoding formats designed for the English language. The most famous one is the American Standard Code for Information Interchange (ASCII). Although well established for English, the adaptation of ASCII to other languages led to clunky evolutions and many variants. It ended (temporarily?) with Unicode, a universal scheme compatible with ASCII and intended to cover all the scripts of the world.

We saw in Chap. 2 that some corpora include linguistic information to complement raw texts. This information is conveyed through annotations that describe quantities of structures. They range from text organization, such as titles, paragraphs, and sentences, to semantic information including grammatical data, part-of-speech labels, or syntactic structures, etc. In contrast to character encoding, no annotation scheme has yet reached a level where it can claim to be a standard. However, the Extensible Markup Language (XML), a language to define annotations, is well underway to unify them under a shared markup syntax. XML in itself is not an annotation language. It is a scheme that enables users to define annotations within a specific framework.

In this chapter, we will introduce the most useful character encoding schemes and review the basics of XML. We will examine related topics of standardized presentation of time and date, and how to sort words in different languages. Finally, we will introduce two significant theoretical concepts behind codes – entropy and perplexity – how they can help design efficient codes, and how we can use them in a machine-learning algorithm.

3.2 Character Sets

3.2.1 Representing Characters

Words, at least in European languages, consists of characters. Prior to any further digital processing, it is necessary to build an encoding scheme that maps the character or symbol repertoire of a language to numeric values – integers. The Baudot code is one of the oldest electric codes. It uses five bits and hence has the capacity to represent $2^5 = 32$ characters: the Latin alphabet and some control commands like the carriage return, the bell. The ASCII code uses seven bits. It can represent $2^7 = 128$ symbols with positive integer values ranging from 0 to 127. The characters use the contiguous positions from 32 to 126. The values in the interval [0, 31] and 127 correspond to controls used, for instance, in data transmission (Table 3.1).

Table 3.1. The ASCII character set.

Code	Char	Code	Char	Code	Char	Code	Char
32		33	!	34	"	35	#
36	$	37	%	38	&	39	'
40	(	41	)	42	*	43	+
44	,	45	-	46	.	47	/
48	0	49	1	50	2	51	3
52	4	53	5	54	6	55	7
56	8	57	9	58	:	59	;
60	<	61	=	62	>	63	?
64	@	65	A	66	B	67	C
68	D	69	E	70	F	71	G
72	H	73	I	74	J	75	K
76	L	77	M	78	N	79	O
80	P	81	Q	82	R	83	S
84	T	85	U	86	V	87	W
88	X	89	Y	90	Z	91	[
92	\	93	]	94	^	95	_
96	`	97	a	98	b	99	c
100	d	101	e	102	f	103	g
104	h	105	i	106	j	107	k
108	l	109	m	110	n	111	o
112	p	113	q	114	r	115	s
116	t	117	u	118	v	119	w
120	x	121	y	122	z	123	{
124			125	}	126	~	127	

ASCII was created originally for English. It cannot handle other European languages that have accented letters, such as *é, à*, or other diacritics like *ø* and *ä*, not to mention languages that do not use the Latin alphabet. Table 3.2 shows characters used in French and German that are ignored by ASCII. Most computers used to represent characters on octets – words of eight bits – and ASCII was extended with the eighth unoccupied bit to the values [128, 255] ($2^8 = 256$). Unfortunately, these extensions were not standardized and depended on the operating system. The same character, for instance, $\hat{e}$, could have a different encoding in the Windows, Macintosh, and Unix operating systems.

Table 3.2. Characters specific to French and German.

	French	German
Lowercase	à â æ ç é è ê ë î ï ô œ ù û ü ÿ	ä ö ü ß
Uppercase	À Â Æ Ç É È Ê Ë Î Ï Ô Œ Ù Û Ü Ÿ	Ä Ö Ü

The ISO Latin 1 character set (ISO-8859-1) is a standard that tried to reconcile Western European character encodings (Table 3.3). Unfortunately, Latin 1 was ill-designed and forgot characters such as the French Œ, œ, the German quote „ or the Dutch ij, IJ. Operating systems such as Windows and Mac OS used a variation of it that they had to complement with the missing characters. They used positions in the interval ranging from 128 to 159 (Table 3.4). Later, ISO Latin 9 (ISO-8859-15) updated Latin 1. It restored forgotten French and Finnish characters and added the euro currency sign, €.

3.2.2 Unicode

While ASCII has been very popular, its 128 positions could not support the characters of many languages in the world. Therefore a group of companies formed a consortium to create a new, universal coding scheme: Unicode. Unicode is quickly replacing older encoding schemes, and Windows, Mac OS, and Java platforms now adopt it while sometimes ensuring backward compatibility.

The initial goal of Unicode was to define a superset of all other character sets, ASCII, Latin 1, and others, to represent all the languages of the world. The Unicode consortium has produced character tables of most alphabets and scripts of European, Asian, African, and Near Eastern languages, and assigned numeric values to the characters. Unicode started with a 16-bit code that could represent up to 65,000 characters. It has subsequently been extended to 32 bits.

The Universal Character Set (UCS) is the standardized name of the Unicode character representation. The 2-octet code (UCS-2) is called the Basic Multilingual Plane (BMP). All common characters fit on 16 bits, with the exception of some Chinese ideograms. The 4-octet code (UCS-4) can represent more than a million characters. They cover all the UCS-2 characters and rare characters: historic scripts, some mathematical symbols, private characters, etc.

Unicode groups characters or symbols by script – Latin, Greek, Cyrillic, Hebrew, Arabic, Indic, Japanese, Chinese – and identifies each character by a single hexadecimal number, called the code point, and a name as

Table 3.3. The ISO Latin 1 character set (ISO-8859-1).

Code	Char	SGML	Code	Char	SGML	Code	Char	SGML
160			161	¡	¡	162	¢	¢
163	£	£	164	¤	¤	165	¥	¥
166	¦	&brvbar	167	§	§	168	¨	¨
169	©	©	170	ª	ª	171	«	«
172	¬	¬	173	-	­	174	®	&reg
175	¯	¯	176	°	°	177	±	±
178	²	²	179	³	³	180	´	´
181	µ	µ	182	¶	¶	183	·	·
184	¸	¸	185	¹	¹	186	º	º
187	»	»	188	¼	¼	189	½	½
190	¾	¾	191	¿	¿	192	À	À
193	Á	Á	194	Â	Â	195	Ã	Ã
196	Ä	Ä	197	Å	Å	198	Æ	&Aelig;
199	Ç	Ç	200	È	È	201	É	É
202	Ê	Ê	203	Ë	Ë	204	Ì	Ì
205	Í	Í	206	Î	Î	207	Ï	Ï
208	Ð	Ð	209	Ñ	Ñ	210	Ò	Ò
211	Ó	Ó	212	Ô	Ô	213	Õ	Õ
214	Ö	Ö	215	×	×	216	Ø	Ø
217	Ù	Ù	218	Ú	Ú	219	Û	Û
220	Ü	Ü	221	Ý	Ý	222	Þ	Þ
223	ß	ß	224	à	à	225	á	á
226	â	â	227	ã	ã	228	ä	ä
229	å	å	230	æ	æ	231	ç	ç
232	è	è	233	é	é	234	ê	ê
235	ë	ë	236	ì	ì	237	í	í
238	î	î	239	ï	ï	240	ð	ð
241	ñ	ñ	242	ò	ò	243	ó	ó
244	ô	ô	245	õ	õ	246	ö	ö
247	÷	÷	248	ø	ø	249	ù	ù
250	ú	ú	251	û	û	252	ü	ü
253	ý	ý	254	þ	þ	255	ÿ	ÿ

```
U+0041 LATIN CAPITAL LETTER A
U+0042 LATIN CAPITAL LETTER B
U+0043 LATIN CAPITAL LETTER C

...

U+0391 GREEK CAPITAL LETTER ALPHA
U+0392 GREEK CAPITAL LETTER BETA
U+0393 GREEK CAPITAL LETTER GAMMA
```

The U+ symbol means that the number after it corresponds to a Unicode position.

Table 3.4. The Windows and Mac OS extensions to the ISO Latin 1 set represent some of the forgotten Western European characters, here Windows Latin 1 or Windows-1252.

Code	Char	Code	Char	Code	Char	Code	Char
128	€	129		130	‚	131	ƒ
132	„	133	…	134	†	135	‡
136	ˆ	137	‰	138	Š	139	‹
140	Œ	141		142	Ž	143	
144		145	'	146	'	147	"
148	"	149	•	150	–	151	—
152	˜	153	™	154	š	155	›
156	œ	157		158	ž	159	Ÿ

Unicode also allows the composition of accented characters from a base character and one or more diacritics. That is the case for the French $\hat{E}$ or the Scandinavian $\mathring{A}$, which can be defined as combinations. They are created by typing a sequence of two keys: E + ˆ and A + °, corresponding to

```
U+0045 LATIN CAPITAL LETTER E
U+0302 COMBINING CIRCUMFLEX ACCENT
U+0041 LATIN CAPITAL LETTER A
U+030A COMBINING RING ABOVE
```

Both characters also have a single code point:

```
U+00CA LATIN CAPITAL LETTER E WITH CIRCUMFLEX
U+00C5 LATIN CAPITAL LETTER A WITH RING ABOVE
```

The resulting graphical symbol is called a grapheme. A grapheme is a "natural" character or a symbol. It may correspond to a single code point as E or A, or result from a composition as $\hat{E}$ or $\mathring{A}$.

Unicode allocates contiguous blocks of code to scripts from U+0000. They start with alphabetic scripts: Latin, Greek, Cyrillic, Hebrew, Arabic, etc., then the symbols area, and Asian ideograms or alphabets. Ideograms used by the Chinese, Japanese, and Korean (CJK) languages are unified to avoid duplication. Table 3.5 shows the script allocation. The space devoted to Asian scripts occupies most of the table.

3.2.3 The Unicode Encoding Schemes

Unicode offers three major different encoding schemes: UTF-8, UTF-16, and UTF-32. The UTF schemes – Unicode transformation format – encode the same data by units of 8, 16, or 32-bits and can be converted from one to another without loss.

UTF-16 was the original encoding scheme when Unicode started with 16 bits. It uses fixed units of 16 bits – 2 bytes – to encode directly most characters. The code units correspond to the sequence of their code points using precomposed characters, such as $\hat{E}$ in *FÊTE*

Table 3.5. Unicode subrange allocation of the Universal Character Set (simplified).

Code	Name	Code	Name
U+0000	Basic Latin	U+1400	Unified Canadian Aboriginal Syllabic
U+0080	Latin-1 Supplement	U+1680	Ogham, Runic
U+0100	Latin Extended-A	U+1780	Khmer
U+0180	Latin Extended-B	U+1800	Mongolian
U+0250	IPA Extensions	U+1E00	Latin Extended Additional
U+02B0	Spacing Modifier Letters	U+1F00	Extended Greek
U+0300	Combining Diacritical Marks	U+2000	Symbols
U+0370	Greek	U+2800	Braille Patterns
U+0400	Cyrillic	U+2E80	CJK Radicals Supplement
U+0530	Armenian	U+2F80	KangXi Radicals
U+0590	Hebrew	U+3000	CJK Symbols and Punctuation
U+0600	Arabic	U+3040	Hiragana, Katakana
U+0700	Syriac	U+3100	Bopomofo
U+0780	Thaana	U+3130	Hangul Compatibility Jamo
U+0900	Devanagari, Bengali	U+3190	Kanbun
U+0A00	Gurmukhi, Gujarati	U+31A0	Bopomofo Extended
U+0B00	Oriya, Tamil	U+3200	Enclosed CJK Letters and Months
U+0C00	Telugu, Kannada	U+3300	CJK Compatibility
U+0D00	Malayalam, Sinhala	U+3400	CJK Unified Ideographs Extension A
U+0E00	Thai, Lao	U+4E00	CJK Unified Ideographs
U+0F00	Tibetan	U+A000	Yi Syllables
U+1000	Myanmar	U+A490	Yi Radicals
U+10A0	Georgian	U+AC00	Hangul Syllables
U+1100	Hangul Jamo	U+D800	Surrogates
U+1200	Ethiopic	U+E000	Private Use
U+13A0	Cherokee	U+F900	Others

```
0046 00CA 0054 0045
```

or composing it as with E+^ in FE^TE

```
0046 0045 0302 0054 0045
```

UTF-8 is a variable-length encoding. It maps the ASCII code characters U+0000 to U+007F to their byte values 00 to 7F. It then takes on the legacy of ASCII. All the other characters in the range U+007F to U+FFFF are encoded as a sequence of two or more bytes. Table 3.6 shows the mapping principles of the 32-bit character code points to 8-bit units.

Let us encode *FÊTE* in UTF-8. The letters *F*, *T*, and *E* are in the range U-00000000 – U-0000007F. Their numeric code values are exactly the same in ASCII and UTF-8. The code point of *Ê* is U+00CA and is in the range U-00000080 – U-000007FF. Its binary representation is 0000 0000 1100 1010. UTF-8 uses the 11 rightmost bits of 00CA. The first five underlined bits together with the prefix 110

Table 3.6. Mapping of 32-bit character code points to 8-bit units according to UTF-8. The xxx corresponds to the rightmost bit values used in the character code points.

Range	Encoding
U-00000000 – U-0000007F	0xxxxxxx
U-00000080 – U-000007FF	110xxxxx 10xxxxxx
U-00000800 – U-0000FFFF	1110xxxx 10xxxxxx 10xxxxxx
U-00010000 – U-001FFFFF	11110xxx 10xxxxxx 10xxxxxx 10xxxxxx
U-00200000 – U-03FFFFFF	111110xx 10xxxxxx 10xxxxxx 10xxxxxx 10xxxxxx
U-04000000 – U-7FFFFFFF	1111110x 10xxxxxx 10xxxxxx 10xxxxxx 10xxxxxx 10xxxxxx

form the octet 1100 0011 that corresponds to C3 in hexadecimal. The seven next boldface bits with the prefix 10 form the octet 1000 1010 or 8A in hexadecimal. The letter $\hat{E}$ is then encoded as 1100 0011 1000 1010 or C3 8A in UTF-8. Hence, the word FÊTE and the code points U+0046 U+00CA U+0054 U+0045 are encoded as

```
46 C3 8A 54 45
```

UTF-32 represents exactly the codes points by their code values. One question remains: How does UTF-16 represent the code points above U+FFFF? The answer is: it uses two surrogate positions consisting of a high surrogate in the range U+DC00 .. U+DFFF and a low surrogate in the range U+D800 .. U+DBFF. This is made possible because the Unicode consortium does not expect to assign characters beyond the code point U+10FFFF. Using the two surrogates, characters between U+10000 and U+10FFFF can be converted from UTF-32 to UTF-16, and vice versa.

Finally, the storage requirements of the Unicode encoding schemes are, of course, different and depend on the language. A text in English will have approximately the same size in ASCII and in UTF-8. The size of the text will be doubled in UTF-16 and four times its original size in UTF-32, because all characters take four bytes.

A text in a Western European language will be larger in UTF-8 than in ASCII because of the accented characters: a nonaccented character takes one octet, and an accented one takes two. The exact size will thus depend on the proportion of accented characters. The text size will be twice its ASCII size in UTF-16. Characters in the surrogate space take 4 bytes, but they are very rare and should not increase the storage requirements. UTF-8 is then more compact for most European languages. This is not the case with other languages. A Chinese or Indic character takes, on average, three bytes in UTF-8 and only two in UTF-16.

3.3 Locales and Word Order

3.3.1 Presenting Time, Numerical Information, and Ordered Words

In addition to using different sets of characters, languages often have specific presentations for times, dates, numbers, or telephone numbers, even when they are restricted to digits. Most European languages outside English would write $\pi = 3,14159$ instead of $\pi = 3.14159$. Inside a same language, different communities may have different presentation conventions. The US English date February 24, 2003, would be written 24 February 2003 or February 24th, 2003, in England. It would be abridged 2/24/03 in the United States, 24/02/2003 in Britain, and 2003/02/24 in Sweden. Some communities may be restricted to an administration or a company, for instance, the military in the US, which writes times and dates differently than the rest of the society.

The International Organization for Standardization (ISO) has standardized the identification of languages and communities under the name of **locales**. Each locale uses a set of rules that defines the format of dates, times, numbers, currency, and how to sort – **collate** – strings of characters. A locale is defined by three parameters: the language, the region, and the variant that corresponds to more specific conventions used by a restricted community. Table 3.7 shows some locales for English, French, and German.

Table 3.7. Examples of locales.

Locale	Language	Region	Variant
English (United States)	en	US	
English (United Kingdom)	en	GB	
French (France)	fr	FR	
French (Canada)	fr	CA	
German (Germany)	de	DE	
German (Austria)	de	AT	

One of the most significant features of a locale is the collation component that defines how to compare and order strings of characters. In effect, elementary sorting algorithms consider the ASCII or Unicode values with a predefined comparison operator such as the inequality predicate @</2 in Prolog. They determine the lexical order using the numerical ranking of the characters.

These basic sorting procedures do not arrange the words in the classical dictionary order. In ASCII as well as in Unicode, lowercase letters have a greater code value than uppercase ones. A basic algorithm would then sort *above* after *Zambia*, which would be quite misleading for most users.

Current dictionaries in English, French, and German use a different convention. The lowercase letters precede their uppercase equivalents when the strings are equal except for the case. Table 3.8 shows the collation results for some strings.

Table 3.8. Sorting with the ASCII code comparison and the dictionary order.

ASCII order	Dictionary order
ABC	abc
Abc	Abc
Def	ABC
aBf	aBf
abc	def
def	Def

A basic sorting algorithm may suffice for some applications. However, most of the time it would be unacceptable when the ordered words are presented to a user. The result would be even more confusing with accented characters, since their location is completely random in the extended ASCII tables.

In addition, the lexicographic ordering of words varies from language to language. French and English dictionaries sort accented letters as nonaccented ones, except when two strings are equal except for the accents. Swedish dictionaries treat the letters Å, Ä, and Ö as distinct symbols of the alphabet and sort them after Z. German dictionaries have two sorting standards. They process accented letters either as single characters or as couples of nonaccented letters. In the latter case, Ä, Ö, Ü, and β are considered respectively as *AE*, *OE*, *UE*, and *ss*.

3.3.2 The Unicode Collation Algorithm

The Unicode consortium has defined a collation algorithm that takes into account the different practices and cultures in lexical ordering. It can be parameterized to cover most languages and conventions. It uses three levels of difference to compare strings. We outline their features for European languages and Latin scripts:

- The primary level considers differences between base characters, for instance, between A and B.
- If there are no differences at the first level, the secondary level considers the accents on the characters.
- And finally, the third level considers the case differences between the characters.

These level features are general, but not universal. Accents are a secondary difference in many languages, but we saw that Swedish sorts accented letters as individual ones and hence sets a primary difference between A and $Å$, or o and $Ö$. Depending on the language, the levels may have other features.

To deal with the first level, the Unicode collation algorithm defines classes of letters that gather upper- and lowercase variants, accented and unaccented forms. Hence, we have the ordered sets: {a, A, á, Á, à, À, etc.} < {b, B} < {c, C, ć, Ć, ĉ, Ĉ, ç, Ç, etc.} < {e, E, é, É, è, È, ê, Ê, ë, Ë, etc.} < ....

The second level considers the accented letters if two strings are equal at the first level. Accented letters are ranked after their nonaccented counterparts. The first accent is the acute one (´), then come the grave accent (`), the circumflex (^), and the umlaut (¨). So, instances of letter E with accents, in lower- and uppercase have the order: {e, E} << {é, É} << {è, È} << {ê, Ê} << {ë, Ë}, where << denotes a difference at the second level. The comparison at the second level is done from the left to the right of a word in English and most languages. It is carried out from the right to the left in French, i.e., from the end of a word to its beginning.

Similarly, the third level considers the case of letters when there are no differences at the first and second levels. Lowercase letters are before uppercase ones, that is, {a} <<< {A}, where <<< denotes a difference at the third level.

Table 3.9 shows the lexical order of *pêcher* 'peach tree' and *Péché* 'sin', together with various conjugated forms of the verbs *pécher* 'to sin' and *pêcher* 'to fish' in French and English. The order takes the three levels into account and the reversed direction of comparison in French for the second level. German adopts the English sorting rules for these accents.

Table 3.9. Lexical order of words with accents. Note the reversed order of the second level comparison in French.

English	French
Péché	*pèche*
PÉCHÉ	*pêche*
pèche	*Pêche*
pêche	*Péché*
Pêche	*PÉCHÉ*
pêché	*pêché*
Pêché	*Pêché*
pécher	*pécher*
pêcher	*pêcher*

Some characters are expanded or contracted before the comparison. In French, the letters Œ and Æ are considered as pairs of two distinct letters: OE and AE. In traditional German used in telephone directories, Ä, Ö, Ü, and ß are expanded into AE, OE, UE, and ss and then sorted as an accent difference with the corresponding letter pairs. In traditional Spanish, *Ch* is contracted into a single letter that sorts between *Cz* and *D*.

The implementation of the collation algorithm first maps the characters onto collation elements that have three numerical fields to express the three different levels of comparison. Each character has constant numerical fields that are defined in a collation element table. The mapping may require a preliminary expansion, as for *æ* and *œ* into *ae* and *oe* or a contraction. The algorithm then forms for each string the sequence of the collation elements of its characters. It creates a sort key by rearranging the elements of the string and concatenating the fields according to the levels: the first fields of the string, then second fields, and third ones together. Finally, the algorithm compares two sort keys using a binary comparison that applies to the first level, to the second level in case of equality, and finally to the third level if levels 1 and 2 show no differences.

3.4 Markup Languages

3.4.1 A Brief Background

Corpus annotation uses sets of labels, also called markup languages. Corpus markup languages are comparable to those of standard word processors such as Microsoft Word or LaTeX. They consist of tags inserted in the text that request, for instance, to start a new paragraph, or to set a phrase in italics or in bold characters. Among the most widespread markup languages, there are the Rich Text Format (RTF) from Microsoft (2004) and the (La)TeX format designed by Donald Knuth (Knuth 1986) (Table 3.10).

Table 3.10. Some formatting tags in RTF and LaTeX.

	Text in italics	New paragraph	Accented letter *é*
RTF	{\i text in italics}	\par	\'e9
LaTeX	{\it text in italics}	\cr	\'{e}

While RTF and LaTeX are used by communities of million of persons, they are not acknowledged as standards. The Standard Generalized Markup Language (SGML) takes this place. SGML could have failed and remained a forgotten international initiative. But the Internet and the World Wide Web, which use Hypertext Markup Language (HTML), a specific implementation of SGML, have ensured its posterity. In the next sections, we introduce the Extensible Markup Language (XML), which builds on the simplicity of HTML that has secured its success, and extends it to handle any kind of data.

3.4.2 An Outline of XML

XML is a coding framework: a language to define ways of structuring documents. XML can incorporate logical and presentation markups. Logical markups describe the document structure and organization such as, for instance, the title, the sections, and inside the sections, the paragraphs. Presentation markups describe the text appearance and enable users to set a sentence in italic or bold type, or to insert a page break. Contrary to other markup languages, like HTML, XML does not have a predefined set of tags. The programmer defines them together with their meaning.

XML separates the definition of structure instructions from the content – the data. Structure instructions are described in a document type definition (DTD) that models a class of XML documents. DTDs correspond to specific tagsets that enable users to mark up texts. A DTD lists the legal tags and their relationships with other tags, for instance, to define what is a chapter and to verify that it contains a title. Among coding schemes defined by DTDs, there are:

- the Extensible Hypertext Markup Language (XHTML), a clean, XML implementation of HTML that models the Internet Web pages
- the Text Encoding Initiative (TEI), which is used by some academic projects to encode texts

A DTD is composed of three kinds of components defined in the XML jargon as elements, attributes, and entities. Comments of DTDs and XML documents are enclosed between `<!--` and `-->` tags.

Elements. Elements are the logical units of an XML document. They are delimited by surrounding tags. A start tag enclosed between angle brackets precedes the element content, and an end tag terminates it. End tags are the same as start tags with a / prefix. XML tags must be balanced, which means that an end tag must follow each start tag. Here is a simple example of an XML document:

```
<!-- My first XML document -->
<book>
  <title>Language Processing Cookbook</title>
  <author>Pierre Cagné</author>
  <!-- Image to show on the cover -->
  <img></img>
  <text>Here comes the text!</text>
</book>
```

where `<book>` and `</book>` are legal tags indicating respectively the start and the end of the book, and `<title>` and `</title>` the beginning and the end of the title. **Empty elements**, such as the image `<img></img>`, can be abridged as `<img/>`. Unlike HTML, XML tags are case sensitive: `<TITLE>` and `<title>` define different elements.

Attributes. An element can have attributes, i.e., a set of properties attached to the element. Let us complement our book example so that the `<title>` element has an alignment whose possible values are flush left, right, or center, and a character style taken from underlined, bold, or italics. Let us also indicate where `<img>` finds the image file. The DTD specifies the possible attributes of these elements and the value list among which the actual attribute value will be selected. The actual attributes of an element are supplied as name–value pairs in the element start tag.

Let us name the alignment and style attributes `align` and `style` and set them in boldface characters and centered, and let us store the image file of the `img` element in the `src` attribute. The markup in the XML document will look like:

```
<title align="center" style="bold">
  Language Processing Cookbook
</title>
```

```
<author>Pierre Cagné</author>
<img src="pierre.jpg"/>
```

Entities.   Finally, entities correspond to data stored somewhere in a computer. They can be accented characters, symbols, strings as well as text or image files. The programmer can declare or define variables referring to entities and use them subsequently. There are two different types of entities: parameter entities are used in DTDs, and general entities or simply entities are used in XML document contents. The two types of entities correspond to two different contexts. They are declared and referred to differently.

An entity is referred to within an XML document by enclosing its name between the start delimiter "&" and the end delimiter ";", such as `&EntityName;`. The XML parser will substitute the reference with the content of `EntityName` when it is encountered.

There are five predefined entities recognized by XML. They correspond to characters used by the XML standard, which cannot be used as is in a document (Table 3.11). References to parameter entities use "%" and ";" as delimiters, such as `%ParameterEntityName;`. Parameter entity references can only occur in DTDs.

Table 3.11. The predefined entities of XML.

Symbol	Entity encoding
<	`&lt;` (less than)
>	`&gt;` (greater than)
&	`&amp;`
"	`&quot;`
'	`&apos;`

3.4.3 Writing a DTD

The DTD specifies the formal structure of a document type. It enables an XML parser to determine whether a document is valid. The DTD file contains the description of all the legal elements, attributes, and entities.

Elements.   The description of the elements is enclosed between the start and end delimiters `<!ELEMENT` and `>`. It contains the element name and the content model in terms of other elements or reserved keywords (Table 3.12). The content model specifies how the elements appear, their order, and their number of occurrences (Table 3.13). For example:

```
<!ELEMENT book (title, (author | editor)?, img,
   chapter+)>
<!ELEMENT title (#PCDATA)>
```

states that a book consists of a title, a possible author or editor, an image img, and one or more chapters. The title consists of PCDATA, that is, only text with no other embedded elements.

Table 3.12. Character types.

Character type	Description
PCDATA	Parsed character data. This data will be parsed and must only be text, punctuation, and special characters; no embedded elements
ANY	PCDATA or any DTD element
EMPTY	No content – just a placeholder

Table 3.13. List separators and occurrence indicators.

List notation	Description
,	Elements must all appear and be ordered as listed
|	Only one element must appear (exclusive or)
+	Compulsory element (one or more)
?	Optional element (zero or one)
*	Optional element (zero or more)

Attributes. Attributes are the possible properties of the elements. Attribute lists are usually defined after the element they refer to. Their description is enclosed between the delimiters < !ATTLIST and >. An attribute list contains:

- the element the attribute is referring to
- the attribute name
- the kind of value the attribute may take: a predefined type (Table 3.14) or an enumerated list of values between brackets and separated by vertical bars
- the default value between quotes or a predefined keyword (Table 3.15)

For example:

```
<!ATTLIST title
   style (underlined | bold | italics) "bold"
   align (left | center | right) "left">
<!ATTLIST author
   style (underlined | bold | italics) #REQUIRED>
```

says that title has two attributes, style and align. The style attribute can have three possible values and, if not specified in the XML document, the default value will be bold. author has one style attribute that must be specified in the document.

Table 3.14. Some XML attribute types.

Attribute types	Description
CDATA	The string type: any character except <, >, &, ', and "
ID	An identifier of the element unique in the document; ID must begin with a letter, an underscore, or a colon
IDREF	A reference to an identifier
NMTOKEN	String of letters, digits, periods, underscores, hyphens, and colons. It is more restrictive than CDATA, for instance, spaces are not allowed

Table 3.15. Some default value keywords.

Predefined default values	Description
#REQUIRED	A value must be supplied
#FIXED	The attribute value is constant and must be equal to the default value
#IMPLIED	If no value is supplied, the processing system will define the value

Entities. Entities can be used to insert non-ASCII symbols or characters. Character references consist of a Unicode number delimited by "&#x" and ";", such as É for É and © for ©.

Entities also enable users to define variables. Their declaration is enclosed between the delimiters <!ENTITY and >. It contains the entity name and the entity content (possibly a sequence):

```
<!ENTITY myEntity "Introduction">
```

Parameter entities have a "%" sign before the entity name, as in

```
<!ENTITY % myEntity "<!ELEMENT textbody (para)+>">
```

A DTD Example. Let us now suppose that we want to publish cookbooks. We define a document type, and we declare the rules that will form its DTD: a book will consist of a title, a possible author or editor, an image, one or more chapters, and one or more paragraphs in these chapters. Let us then suppose that the main title and the chapter titles can be in bold, in italics, or underlined. Let us finally suppose that the chapter titles can be numbered in Roman or Arabic notation. The DTD elements and attributes are

```
<!ELEMENT book (title, (author | editor)?, img,
  chapter+)>
<!ELEMENT title (#PCDATA)>
<!ATTLIST title style (u | b | i) "b">
<!ELEMENT author (#PCDATA)>
<!ATTLIST author style (u | b | i) "i">
```

```
<!ELEMENT editor (#PCDATA)>
<!ATTLIST editor style (u | b | i) "i">
<!ELEMENT img EMPTY>
<!ATTLIST img src CDATA #REQUIRED>
<!ELEMENT chapter (subtitle, para+)>
<!ATTLIST chapter number ID #REQUIRED>
<!ATTLIST chapter numberStyle (Arabic | Roman)
   "Roman">
<!ELEMENT subtitle (#PCDATA)>
<!ELEMENT para (#PCDATA)>
```

The name of the document type corresponds to the **root element**, here book, which must be unique.

XML Schema. You probably noticed that the DTD syntax does not fit very well with that of XML. This bothered some people, who tried to make it more compliant. This gave birth to XML Schema, a document definition standard using the XML style. As of today, DTD is still "king," however, XML Schema is gaining popularity. Specifications are available from the Web consortium at www.w3.org/XML/Schema.

3.4.4 Writing an XML Document

We shall now write a document conforming to the book document type. An XML document begins with a header: a declaration describing the XML version and an optional encoding. The default encoding is UTF-8.

```
<?xml version="1.0" encoding="UTF-8"?>
```

The document can contain any Unicode character. The encoding refers to how the characters are stored in the file. This has no significance if you only use unaccented characters in the basic Latin set from position 0 to 127. If you type accented characters, the editor will have to save them as UTF-8 codes. In the document above, *Cagné* must be stored as 43 61 67 6E C3 A9, where *é* is corresponds to C3 A9.

If your text editor does not manage UTF-8, you will have to enter the accented characters as entities with their Unicode number, for instance, É for *É*, or é for *é*. Other encodings, such as Latin 1 (ISO-8859-1), Windows-1252, or MacRoman would let you simply type the characters *É* or *é* from your keyboard instead and save it with your machine's default encoding.

Then, the document declares the DTD it uses. The DTD can be inside the XML document and enclosed between the delimiters <!DOCTYPE [and] >, for instance:

```
<!DOCTYPE book [
<!ELEMENT book (title, (author | editor)?, img,
   chapter+)>
<!ELEMENT title (#PCDATA)>
...
]>
```

Or the DTD can be external to the document, for instance, in a file called book_definition.dtd. In this case, DOCTYPE indicates its location on the computer using the keyword SYSTEM:

```
<!DOCTYPE book SYSTEM
  "/home/pierre/xml/book_definition.dtd">
```

Now, we can write the document content. Let us use the XML tags to sketch a very short book. It could look like this:

```
<book>
  <title style="i">Language Processing Cookbook
  </title>
  <author style="b">Pierre Cagné</author>
  <img src="pierre.jpg"/>
  <chapter number="c1">
    <subtitle>Introduction</subtitle>
    <para>Let&apos;s start doing simple things:
      Collect texts.
    </para>
    <para>First, choose an author you like.
    </para>
  </chapter>
</book>
```

Once, we have written an XML document, we must check that is **well formed**, which means that it has no syntax errors: the brackets are balanced, the encoding is correct, etc. We must also **validate** it, i.e., check that it conforms to the DTD. This can be done with a variety of parsers available from the Internet. An easy way to do it is to use Microsoft Explorer (or any modern Web browser), which has an embedded XML parser.

3.4.5 Namespaces

In our examples, we used element names that can be part of other DTDs. The string title, for instance, is used by XHTML. The XML namespaces is a device to avoid collisions. It is a naming scheme that enables us to define groups of elements and attributes in the same document and prevent name conflicts.

We declare a namespace using the predefined xmlns attribute as <my-element xmlns:prefix="URI">. It starts a namespace inside my-element and its descendants, where prefix defines a group of names. Names members of this namespace are preceded by the prefix, as in prefix:title. URI has the syntax of a Web address. However, it is just a unique name; it is never accessed.

Declaring two namespaces in book, we can reuse title for different purposes:

```
<book
  xmlns:pierre="http://www.cs.lth.se/~pierre"
```

```
xmlns:raymond="http://www.grandecuisine.com">

<pierre:title style="i">Language Processing
  Cookbook
</pierre:title>

<raymond:title style="i">A French Cookbook
</raymond:title>

</book>
```

3.5 Codes and Information Theory

Information theory underlies the design of codes. Claude Shannon probably started the field with a seminal article (1948), in which he defined a measure of information: the **entropy**. In this section, we outline essential information theory concepts: entropy, optimal coding, cross entropy, and **perplexity**. Entropy and perplexity are used as metrics in many areas of language processing.

3.5.1 Entropy

Information theory models a text as a sequence of symbols. Let $x_1, x_2, ..., x_N$ be a discrete set of N symbols representing the characters. The **information content** of a symbol is defined as $I(x_i) = -\log_2 p(x_i) = \log_2 \frac{1}{p(x_i)}$, and it is measured in bits. When the symbols have equal probabilities, they are said to be equiprobable and $p(x_1) = p(x_2) = ... = p(x_N) = \frac{1}{N}$. The information content of x_i is then $I(x_i) = \log_2 N$.

The information content corresponds to the number of bits that is necessary to encode the set of symbols. The information content of the alphabet, assuming that it consists of 26 unaccented equiprobable characters and the space, is $\log_2(26 + 1) = 4.75$, which means that five bits are necessary to encode it. If we add 16 accented characters, the uppercase letters, 11 punctuation signs, [, . ; : ? ! " – ( ) '], and the space, we need $(26 + 16) \times 2 + 12 = 96$ symbols. Their information content is $\log_2 96 = 6.58$, and they can be encoded on seven bits.

The information content assumes that the symbols have an equal probability. This is rarely the case in reality. Therefore this measure can be improved using the concept of entropy, the average information content, which is defined as:

$$H(X) = -\sum_{x \in X} p(x) \log_2 p(x),$$

where X is a random variable over a discrete set of variables, $p(x) = P(X = x), x \in X$, with the convention $0 \log_2 0 = 0$. When the symbols are equiprobable, $H(X) = \log_2 N$. This corresponds also to the upper bound on the entropy value, and for any random variable, we have the inequality $H(X) \leq \log_2 N$.

To evaluate the entropy of printed French, we computed the frequency of the printable French characters in Gustave Flaubert's novel *Salammbô*. Table 3.16 shows the frequency of 26 unaccented letters, the 16 accented or specific letters, and the blanks (spaces).

Table 3.16. Letter frequencies in the French novel *Salammbô* by Gustave Flaubert. The text has been normalized in uppercase letters. The table does not show the frequencies of the punctuation signs or digits.

Letter	Freq	Letter	Freq	Letter	Freq	Letter	Freq
A	42471	B	5762	C	14226	D	18912
E	71178	F	4996	G	5151	H	5315
I	33669	J	1220	K	92	L	30976
M	13101	N	32919	O	22629	P	13178
Q	3965	R	33577	S	46766	T	35110
U	29276	V	6924	W	1	X	2213
Y	1232	Z	413	À	1893	Â	607
Æ	9	Ç	452	È	2002	É	7728
Ê	898	Ë	6	Î	277	Ï	66
Ô	398	Œ	121	Ù	179	Û	213
Ü	0	Ÿ	0	Blanks	101,555	**Total:**	591,676

The entropy of the text restricted to the characters in Table 3.16 is defined as:

$$H(X) = - \sum_{x \in X} p(x) \log_2 p(x).$$
$$= -p(A) \log_2 p(A) - p(B) \log_2 p(B) - ...$$
$$-p(Z) \log_2 p(Z) - p(\grave{A}) \log_2 p(\grave{A}) - ...$$
$$-p(\ddot{Y}) \log_2 p(\ddot{Y}) - p(blanks) \log_2 p(blanks).$$

If we distinguish between upper- and lowercase letters and if we include the punctuation signs, the digits, and all the other printable characters – ASCII ≥ 32 – the entropy of Gustave Flaubert's *Salammbô* in French is $H(X) = 4.39$.

3.5.2 Huffman Encoding

The information content of the French character set is less than the seven bits required by equiprobable symbols. Although it gives no cue on an encoding algorithm, it indicates that a more efficient code is theoretically possible. This is what we examine now with Huffman encoding, which is a general and simple method to build such a code.

Huffman encoding uses variable-length code units. Let us simplify the problem and use only the eight symbols A, B, C, D, E, F, G, and H with the count frequencies in Table 3.17.

Table 3.17. Frequency counts of the symbols.

	A	B	C	D	E	F	G	H
Freq	42,471	5762	14,226	18,912	71,178	4996	5151	5315
Prob	0.25	0.03	0.08	0.11	0.42	0.03	0.03	0.03

Table 3.18. A possible encoding of the symbols on 3 bits.

A	B	C	D	E	F	G	H
000	001	010	011	100	101	110	111

The information content of equiprobable symbols is $\log_2 8 = 3$ bits. Table 3.18 shows a possible code with constant-length units.

The idea of Huffman encoding is to encode frequent symbols using short code values and rare ones using longer units. This was also the idea of the Morse code, which assigns a single signal to letter E: ., and four signals to letter X: - . . -.

This first step builds a Huffman tree using the frequency counts. The symbols and their frequencies are the leaves of the tree. We grow the tree recursively from the leaves to the root. We merge the two symbols with the lowest frequencies into a new node that we annotate with the sum of their frequencies. In Fig. 3.1, this new node corresponds to the letters F and G with a combined frequency of $4996 + 5151 = 10{,}147$ (Fig. 3.2). The second iteration merges B and H (Fig. 3.3); the third one, (F, G) and (B, H) (Fig. 3.4), and so on (Figs. 3.5–3.8).

Fig. 3.1. The symbols and their frequencies.

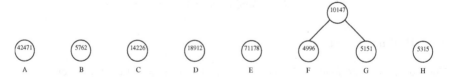

Fig. 3.2. Merging the symbols with the lowest frequencies.

The second step of the algorithm generates the Huffman code by assigning a 0 to the left branches and a 1 to the right branches (Table 3.19).

The average number of bits is the weighted length of a symbol. If we compute it for the data in Table 3.17, it corresponds to:

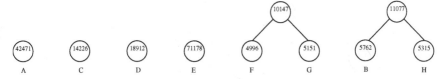

Fig. 3.3. The second iteration.

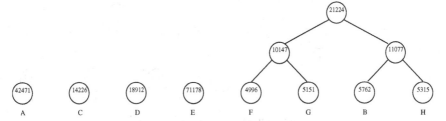

Fig. 3.4. The third iteration.

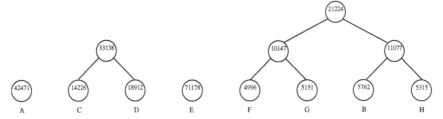

Fig. 3.5. The fourth iteration.

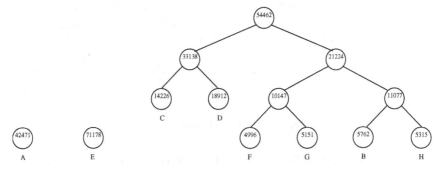

Fig. 3.6. The fifth iteration.

Table 3.19. The Huffman code.

A	B	C	D	E	F	G	H
10	11110	1100	1101	0	11100	11101	11111

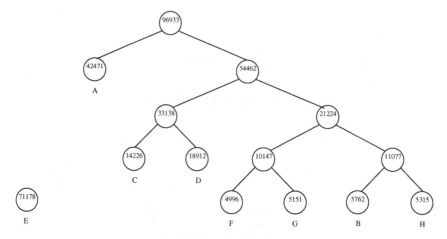

Fig. 3.7. The sixth iteration.

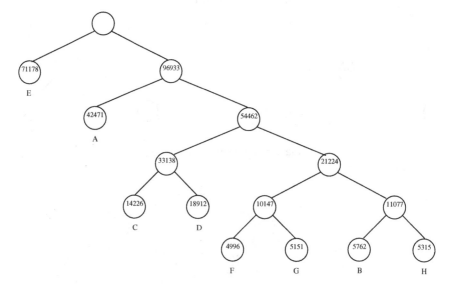

Fig. 3.8. The final Huffman tree.

$$0.25 \times 2 \text{ bit} + 0.03 \times 5 \text{ bit} + 0.08 \times 4 \text{ bit} + 0.11 \times 4 \text{ bit} + 0.42 \times 1 \text{ bit}$$
$$+0.03 \times 5 \text{ bit} + 0.03 \times 5 \text{ bit} + 0.03 \times 5 \text{ bit} = 2.35$$

Although the Huffman code reduces the average number of bits, it does not reach the entropy limit, which is, in our example, 2.27.

3.5.3 Cross Entropy

Let us now compare the letter frequencies between two parts of *Salammbô*, then between *Salammbô* and another text in French or in English. The symbol probabilities will certainly be different. Intuitively, the distributions of two parts of the same novel are likely to be close, further apart between *Salammbô* and another French text from the 21st century, and even further apart with a text in English. This is the idea of cross entropy, which compares two probability distributions.

In the cross entropy formula, one distribution is referred to as the model. It corresponds to data on which the probabilities have been trained. Let us name it m with the distribution $m(x_1), m(x_2), ..., m(x_N)$. The other distribution, p, corresponds to the test data: $p(x_1), p(x_2), ..., p(x_N)$. The cross entropy of m on p is defined as:

$$H(p, m) = - \sum_{x \in X} p(x) \log_2 m(x).$$

Cross entropy quantifies the average surprise of the distribution when exposed to the model. We have the inequality $H(p) \leq H(p, m)$ for any other distribution m with equality if and only if $m(x_i) = p(x_i)$ for all i. The difference $H(p, m) - H(p)$ is a measure of the relevance of the model: the closer the cross entropy, the better the model.

To see how the probability distribution of Flaubert's novel could fare on other texts, we trained a model on the first fourteen chapters of *Salammbô*, and we applied it to the last chapter of *Salammbô* (Chap. 15), to Victor Hugo's *Notre Dame de Paris*, both in French, and to *Nineteen Eighty-Four* by George Orwell in English. The data in Table 3.20 conform to our intuition. They show that the first chapters of *Salammbô* are a better model of the last chapter of *Salammbô* than of *Notre Dame de Paris* and even better than of *Nineteen Eighty-Four*.

Table 3.20. The entropy is measured on the file itself and the cross entropy is measured with Chapters 1–14 of Gustave Flaubert's *Salammbô* taken as the model.

	Entropy	Cross entropy	Difference
Salammbô, chapters 1-14, training set	4.39481	4.39481	0.0
Salammbô, chapter 15, test set	4.34937	4.36074	0.01137
Notre Dame de Paris, test set	4.43696	4.45507	0.01811
Nineteen Eighty-Four, test set	4.35922	4.82012	0.46090

3.5.4 Perplexity and Cross Perplexity

Perplexity is an alternate measure of information that is mainly used by the speech processing community. Perplexity is simply defined as $2^{H(X)}$. The cross perplexity is defined similarly as $2^{H(p,m)}$.

Although perplexity does not bring anything new to entropy, it presents the information differently. Perplexity reflects the averaged number of choices of a random variable. It is equivalent to the size of an imaginary set of equiprobable symbols, which is probably easier to understand.

Table 3.21 shows the perplexity and cross perplexity of the same texts measured with Chaps. 1–14 of Gustave Flaubert's *Salammbô* taken as the model.

Table 3.21. The perplexity and cross perplexity of texts measured with Chapters 1–14 of Gustave Flaubert's *Salammbô* taken as the model.

	Perplexity	Cross perplexity
Salammbô, chapters 1-14, training set	21.04	21.04
Salammbô, chapter 15, test set	20.38	20.54
Notre Dame de Paris, test set	21.66	21.93
Nineteen Eighty-Four, test set	20.52	28.25

3.6 Entropy and Decision Trees

Decision trees are useful devices to classify objects into a set of classes. They have many applications in language processing. In this section, we will describe what they are and see how entropy can help us learn – or induce – automatically decision trees from a set of data. The algorithm, which resembles a reverse Huffman encoding, is one of the simplest machine-learning techniques.

3.6.1 Decision Trees

Decision trees consider objects defined by a set of attributes – also called features – where the nodes of the trees are conditions on the features. An object is presented at the root of the tree, and its features are tested by the tree nodes from the root down to a leaf. The leaves return an output, which can be the description of an object's membership or probabilities to be the member of a class.

Quinlan (1986) gives an example of a set where objects are members of two classes N and P (Table 3.22) and a decision tree that correctly classifies these objects (Fig. 3.9).

3.6.2 Inducing Decision Trees Automatically

It is possible to design many trees that classify the objects in Table 3.22 successfully. The tree in Fig. 3.9 is interesting because it is efficient: a decision can be made with a minimal number of tests.

An efficient decision tree can be induced from a set of examples, members of mutually exclusive classes using an entropy measure. We will describe the induction using two classes of p positive and n negative examples, although this can be generalized to any number of classes. Each example is defined by a finite number of attributes. Each node in the decision tree corresponds to an attribute that has as many branches as the attribute has possible values.

Table 3.22. A set of object members of two classes: N and P. After Quinlan (1986).

Object	Attributes				Class
	Outlook	Temperature	Humidity	Windy	
1	Sunny	Hot	High	False	N
2	Sunny	Hot	High	True	N
3	Overcast	Hot	High	False	P
4	Rain	Mild	High	False	P
5	Rain	Cool	Normal	False	P
6	Rain	Cool	Normal	True	N
7	Overcast	Cool	Normal	True	P
8	Sunny	Mild	High	False	N
9	Sunny	Cool	Normal	False	P
10	Rain	Mild	Normal	False	P
11	Sunny	Mild	Normal	True	P
12	Overcast	Mild	High	True	P
13	Overcast	Hot	Normal	False	P
14	Rain	Mild	High	True	N

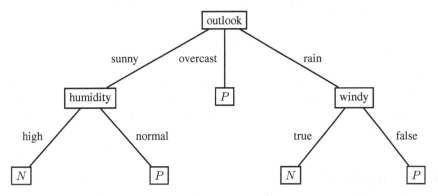

Fig. 3.9. A decision tree classifying the objects in Table 3.22. After Quinlan (1986).

At the root of the tree, the condition must be the most discriminating, that is, have branches gathering most positive examples while others gather negative examples. The ID3 (Quinlan 1986) algorithm uses the entropy to select the best attribute to be the root of the tree and recursively the next attributes of the resulting nodes. ID3 defines the information gain as the difference of entropy before and after the decision. It measures the separating power of an attribute: the more the gain, the better the attribute.

As defined previously, the entropy of a two-class set of p positive and n negative examples is:

$$I(p,n) = -\frac{p}{p+n}\log_2\frac{p}{p+n} - \frac{n}{p+n}\log_2\frac{n}{p+n}.$$

If attribute A is the root of the tree and has v possible values $\{A_1, A_2, ..., A_v\}$, there will be v resulting nodes. Each node corresponds to one value of A and contains p_i positive and n_i negative examples. Its entropy is $I(p_i, n_i)$.

The weighted average of all the nodes below A is:

$$\sum_{i=1}^{v} \frac{p_i + n_i}{p + n} I\left(\frac{p_i}{p_i + n_i}, \frac{n_i}{p_i + n_i}\right).$$

The information gain is defined as $I_{before} - I_{after}$. For the tree in Fig. 3.9, let us compute the information gain of attribute *outlook*.

$$I_{before}(p, n) = -\frac{9}{14} \log_2 \frac{9}{14} - \frac{5}{14} \log_2 \frac{5}{14} = 0.940.$$

Outlook has three values: *sunny*, *overcast*, and *rain*. Their corresponding entropies are:

$$I(p_1, n_1) = -\tfrac{2}{5} \log_2 \tfrac{2}{5} - \tfrac{3}{5} \log_2 \tfrac{3}{5} = 0.971.$$
$$I(p_2, n_2) = 0.$$
$$I(p_3, n_3) = -\tfrac{3}{5} \log_2 \tfrac{3}{5} - \tfrac{2}{5} \log_2 \tfrac{2}{5} = 0.971.$$

Thus

$$I_{after}(p, n) = \frac{5}{14} I(p_1, n_1) + \frac{4}{14} I(p_{21}, n_2) + \frac{5}{14} I(p_3, n_3) = 0.694.$$

The gain is $0.940 - 0.694 = 0.246$, which is the highest among the possible attributes.

The algorithm to build the decision tree is simple. The attribute that has the highest information gain is selected to be the root of the tree, and this process is repeated recursively for each node of the tree.

3.7 Further Reading

Many operating systems such as Windows, Mac OS, and Unix, or programming languages such as Java have adopted Unicode and take the language parameter of a computer into account. Basic lexical methods such as date and currency formatting, word ordering, and indexing are now supported at the operating system level. Operating systems or programming languages offer toolboxes and routines that you can use in applications.

The Unicode Consortium publishes books and technical reports that describe the various aspects of the standard. *The Unicode Standard, Version 4.0* (2003) is the most comprehensive document while Davis and Whistler (2002) describe in detail the Unicode collation algorithm. Both documents are available in electronic format from the Unicode Web site: http://www.unicode.org. IBM implemented a large library of Unicode components in Java and C++, which are available as open-source software (http://www.ibm.com/software/globalization/icu).

SGML started from a US DARPA initiative. Goldfarb (1990) is a difficult-to-read reference to this language by its designer. Derived markup standards such as

HTML and XML are continuously evolving. Their specifications are available from the World Wide Web consortium (http://www.w3.org). Finally, a good reference on XML is *Learning XML* (Ray 2003).

Information theory has been covered by many books, many of them requiring a good mathematical background. The text by Manning and Schütze (Chap. 2, 1999) provides a short and readable introduction oriented toward natural language processing.

We will use ID3 as a machine-learning algorithm in other chapters of this book. ID3 is one of the oldest and easiest-to-understand algorithms. There are many other machine-learning techniques that can use the same type of input data: a set of examples defined by features and members of a finite set of classes. As is the case for ID3, they automatically train classifiers from the annotated examples. Classifiers can then be reused for unannotated data. Support vector machines (Boser et al. 1992), which rely on a complex mathematic formulation, are very efficient devices. They enjoy a growing popularity in the language processing community. Their presentation is beyond the scope of this book. Fortunately, there are many free implementations of them. Schlkopf and Smola (2002) is a good reference on them.

Exercises

3.1. Implement UTF-8 that transforms a sequence of code points in a sequence of octets in Prolog.

3.2. Implement a word collation algorithm for English, French, German, or Swedish.

3.3. Modify the DTD in Sect. 3.4.4 so that the cookbook consists of meals instead of chapters, and each meal has an ingredient and a recipe section.

3.4. Modify the DTD in Sect. 3.4.4 to declare the general and parameter entities:

```
<!ENTITY myEntity "Introduction">
<!ENTITY %myEntity "<!ELEMENT textbody (para)+>">
```

Use these entities in the DTD and the document.

3.5. Write a Prolog program that removes the tags from a text encoded in HTML.

3.6. Write a Prolog program that process a text encoded in HTML: it retains headers (Hn tags) and discards the rest.

3.7. Implement the ID3 algorithm in Prolog or Perl.

4

Counting Words

4.1 Counting Words and Word Sequences

We saw in Chap. 2 that words have specific contexts of use. Pairs of words like *strong* and *tea* or *powerful* and *computer* are not random associations but the result of a preference. A native speaker will use them naturally, while a learner will have to learn them from books – dictionaries – where they are explicitly listed. Similarly, the words *rider* and *writer* sound much alike in American English, but they are likely to occur with different surrounding words. Hence, hearing an ambiguous phonetic sequence, a listener will discard the improbable *rider of books* or *writer of horses* and prefer *writer of books* or *rider of horses* (Church and Mercer 1993).

In lexicography, extracting recurrent pairs of words – collocations – is critical to finding the possible contexts of a word and citing real examples of its use. In speech recognition, the statistical estimate of a word sequence – also called a **language model** – is a key part of the recognition process. The language model component of a speech recognition system enables the system to predict the next word given a sequence of previous words: *the writer of books, novels, poetry*, etc., rather than of *the writer of hooks, nobles, poultry*.

Knowing the frequency of words and sequences of words is crucial in many fields of language processing. In addition to speech recognition and lexicography, they include parsing, semantic interpretation, and translation. In this chapter, we introduce techniques to obtain word frequencies from a corpus and to build language models. We also describe a set of related concepts that are essential to understand them.

4.2 Words and Tokens

4.2.1 What Is a Word?

The definition of what a word is, although apparently obvious, is in fact surprisingly difficult. A naïve description could be a sequence of alphabetic characters delimited by two white spaces. This is an approximation. In addition to white spaces, words can end with a comma, a question mark, a period, etc. Words can also include dashes and apostrophes that, depending on the context, have a different meaning. They may vary according to the language. Compare the French word *aujourd'hui* 'today', which forms a single word, and *l'article* 'the article', where the sequence of an article and a noun must be separated before any further processing.

In corpus processing, text elements are generally called **tokens**. Tokens include words but also punctuation, numbers, abbreviations, or any other similar type of string. Tokens may mix characters and symbols as:

- numbers: 9,812.345 (English and French from the 18th–19th century), 9 812,345 (current French and German) 9.812,345 (French from the 19th–early 20th century)
- dates: 28/02/1996 (French and British English), 2002/11/20 (Swedish)
- abbreviations and acronyms: km/h, m.p.h., S.N.C.F
- nomenclatures: A1-B45, /home/pierre/book.tex
- destinations: Paris–New York, Las Palmas–Stockholm, Rio de Janeiro–Frankfurt am Main
- telephone numbers: (0046) 46 222 96 40
- tables
- formulas: $E = mc^2$

The definition of what is a sentence is also tricky. As in the case for words, a naïve definition would be a sequence of words ended by a period. Unfortunately, periods are also ambiguous. They occur in numbers and terminate abbreviations, as in *etc.* or *Mr.*, which makes sentence isolation equally complex. In the next sections, we examine techniques to break a text into words and sentences and to count the words.

4.2.2 Breaking a Text into Words: Tokenization

Tokenization breaks a character stream, that is, a text file or a keyboard input, into tokens – separated words – and sentences. In Prolog, it results into a list of atoms. For this paragraph, such a list looks like:

```
[['Tokenization', breaks, a, character, stream, (,),
that, is, (,), a, text, file, or, a, keyboard, input,
(,), into, tokens, -, separated, words, -, and,
sentences, '.'], ['In', 'Prolog', it, results, into,
a, list, of, atoms, '.'], ['For', this, paragraph,
(,), such, a, list, looks, like, :]]
```

Tokenization is a necessary step to morphological and syntactic parsing since these analyses consider words or sentences most of the time. A tokenizer can also remove formatting instructions, such as XML tags, if any.

This section introduces tokenization techniques. For sake of simplicity, we consider that words are contiguous segments of alphanumeric characters and that other symbols mark a separation. We can then define a tokenizer by a grammar:

- A token is a sequence of alphabetic characters or digits.
- Other characters mark the token termination and consist of carriage returns, blanks, tabulations, punctuation signs, or other ASCII symbols or commands.
- A sentence is a sequence of tokens ended by a period, a colon, a semicolon, an exclamation point, or a question mark.

We provide an implementation of tokenization using Prolog and Perl. Perl is generally faster and is well suited to process large quantities of text.

4.3 Tokenizing Texts

4.3.1 Tokenizing Texts in Prolog

A Basic Program. The tokenization program `tokenize/2` takes a list of character codes as input and returns a list of tokens. The predicate `char_typ/2` determines the type of a character code: alphanumerical, blank, or other. It uses the Latin 1 character set (charset) plus some Windows extensions. The first `tokenize/2` rule corresponds to the termination condition. The second `tokenize/2` rule tests the type of the head of the list. It skips the blanks. When it reaches an alphanumerical character in the third rule, it calls `make_word/5`, which builds a word out of next letters or digits in the list. When `tokenize/2` encounters another symbol in the fourth rule, it makes a single token out of it.

You can use the `read_file/2` predicate from Appendix A, "An Introduction to Prolog," to read the character codes from a file.

```
% tokenize(+CharCodes, -Tokens)
%  breaks a list of character codes into
%  a list of tokens.
tokenize([], []).
tokenize([CharCode | RestCodes], Tokens) :-
  char_typ(CharCode, blank),
  !,
  tokenize(RestCodes, Tokens).
tokenize([CharCode | CharCodes], [Word | Tokens]) :-
  char_typ(CharCode, alnum),
  !,
  make_word(CharCode, alnum, CharCodes, WordCodes,
    RestCodes),
  name(Word, WordCodes),
  tokenize(RestCodes, Tokens).
tokenize([CharCode | CharCodes], [Char | Tokens]) :-
  !,
  name(Char, [CharCode]),
  tokenize(CharCodes, Tokens).
```

```
% make_word(+CharCode, +Type, +CharCodes, -WordCodes,
%      -RestCodes)
make_word(CharCode1, alnum, [CharCode2 | CharCodes],
     [CharCode1 | WordCodes], RestCodes) :-
  char_typ(CharCode2, alnum),
  !,
  make_word(CharCode2, alnum, CharCodes, WordCodes,
    RestCodes).
make_word(CharCode, alnum, RestCodes, [CharCode] ,
    RestCodes).


% char_typ(+CharCode, -Type)
%  Returns the type of CharCode.
%  There are several cases:
%  Blanks
char_typ(CharCode, blank) :-
  CharCode =< 32,
  !.
%  Lower-case letters without accent
char_typ(CharCode, alnum) :-
  97 =< CharCode,
  CharCode =< 122,
  !.
%  Upper-case letters without accent
char_typ(CharCode, alnum) :-
  65 =< CharCode,
  CharCode =< 90,
  !.
%  Accented characters.
%  The values 215 and 247 correspond to
%  the multiplication and division symbols:  Œ œ
char_typ(CharCode, alnum) :-
  192 =< CharCode,
  CharCode =< 255,
  CharCode =\= 215,
  CharCode =\= 247,
  !.
%  Digits
char_typ(CharCode, alnum) :-
  48 =< CharCode,
  CharCode =< 57,
  !.
%  The oe, OE, and Y" letters
char_typ(CharCode, alnum) :-
  (CharCode =:= 140 ; CharCode =:= 156 ;
```

```
CharCode =:= 159),
!.
```

Improving the Tokenizer.   The program we have written may work badly for some strings. For instance, it does not process the point of decimal numbers such as 3.14, and inserts a sentence end between 3 and 14. This can be fixed using two-pass processing. The first pass recognizes decimal numbers with an appropriate grammar and annotates them. The second one runs the tokenizer on the resulting text.

We can generalize this strategy to improve the tokenizer with specific grammars recognizing numbers, dates, and percentages that will be run as as many different processing stages. However, there will remain cases where the program fails, notably with abbreviations, which often have fixed and variable parts as in *Dr. Watson. Dr.* is a common fixed title, and *Watson* a possible name. We can bring a second improvement to the tokenizer using rules and a lexicon of common abbreviations: *Mr.*, *Sen.*, *Rep.*, *Oct.*, *Fig.*, *pp.*, etc. Rules may recognize likely abbreviations by testing whether the period is followed either by a comma, a semicolon, a question mark or a lowercase letter. The tokenizer can test words ending with a period using the rules or the lexicon to decide whether they are a sentence end or not (Grefenstette and Tapanainen 1994). Mikheev (2002) describes a more efficient method that learns tokenization rules from the set of ambiguous tokens distributed in a document.

4.3.2 Tokenizing Texts in Perl

Perl offers a simple and very fast way to tokenize files into words using the `tr` operator. We will consider that contiguous sequences of characters, including the dash and the quote, are words, and we will isolate them on a single line. We will isolate the punctuation symbols on a single line as well.

The Perl program formulates this a little differently:

* If the character is not a letter or punctuation sign, then replace it by a new line. Note that the dash character in `tr` as well as in character classes means an interval and that we have to quote it to process it in a text.
* If it is a punctuation sign, then insert it between two new lines.
* Finally, reduce contiguous sequences of new lines to a single occurrence.

```
$text = <>;
while ($line = <>) {
  $text .= $line;
}
$text =~ tr/a-zåàâäæçéèêëîïôöœùûüßA-
ZÅÀÂÄÆÇÉÈÊËÎÏÔÖŒÙÛÜ' ()\-,.?!:;/\n/cs;
$text =~ s/([,.?!:;()'\-])/\n$1\n/g;
$text =~ s/\n+/\n/g;
print $text;
```

4.4 *N*-grams

4.4.1 Some Definitions

The first step of lexical statistics consists in extracting the list of **word types** or
types, i.e., the distinct words, from a corpus, along with their frequencies. Within
the context of lexical statistics, word types are opposed to word tokens, the sequence
of running words of the corpus. The excerpt from George Orwell's *Nineteen Eighty-
Four*:

> *War is peace*
> *Freedom is slavery*
> *Ignorance is strength*

has nine tokens and seven types. The type-to-token ratio is often used as an elementary measure of a text's density.

Collocations and language models also use the frequency of pairs of adjacent
words: **bigrams**, for example how many *of the* there are in this text; of word triplets:
trigrams; and more generally of fixed sequences of *n* words: *n*-**grams**. In lexical
statistics, single words are called **unigrams**.

Jelinek (1985) exemplified corpus statistics and trigrams with the phrase

> *We need to resolve all the important issues*

selected from a 90-million-word corpus of IBM office correspondences. Table 4.1
shows each word of this phrase, its rank in the corpus, and other words ranking before
it according to a linear combination of trigram, bigram, and unigram probabilities.
In this corpus, *We* is the ninth most probable word to begin a sentence. More likely
words are *The*, *This*, etc. Following *We*, *need* is the seventh most probable word.
More likely bigrams are *We are*, *We will*, *We the*, *We would*.... Knowing that words
We need have been written, *to* is the most likely word to come after them. Similarly,
the is the most probable word to follow *all of*.

Table 4.1. Trigram generation. After Jelinek (1985).

Word	Rank	More likely alternatives
We	9	*The This One Two A Three Please In*
need	7	*are will the would also do*
to	1	
resolve	85	*have know do...*
all	9	*the this these problems...*
of	2	*the*
the	1	
important	657	*document question first...*
issues	14	*thing point to...*

4.4.2 Counting Unigrams in Prolog

Counting unigrams in a corpus consists simply in tokenizing it, sorting the words, and counting the number of times a type occurs in the corpus. We will not use the Prolog predefined `sort/2` predicate because it removes the duplicates. Instead, we can use a predicate implementing the quicksort algorithm or `msort/2` in some Prologs.

The predicate `count_duplicates/2` counts the duplicates. It takes the ordered list of words as an input and returns a list of pairs with the frequency of each word [N, Word] in the output list:

```prolog
count_duplicates(OrderedList, CountedList) :-
  count_duplicates(OrderedList, 1, [],
    CountedListRev),
  reverse(CountedListRev, CountedList).

count_duplicates([X, X | Ordered], N, Counting,
    Counted) :-
  N1 is N + 1,
  !,
  count_duplicates([X | Ordered], N1, Counting,
    Counted).
count_duplicates([X | Ordered], N, Counting,
    Counted) :-
  !,
  count_duplicates(Ordered, 1, [[N, X] | Counting],
    Counted).
count_duplicates([], _, L, L).
```

We get the unigrams with their counts with

```prolog
?- read_file(myFile, CharacterList),
   tokens(TokenList, CharacterList, []),
   quicksort(TokenList, OrderedTokens),
   count_duplicates(OrderedTokens, UnigramList).
```

4.4.3 Counting Unigrams with Perl

Counting unigrams is straightforward and very fast with Perl. We can obtain them with the following algorithm:

1. Tokenize the text file, putting one word per line with `tr`.
2. Count the words using a hash table.
3. Possibly, sort the words according to their alphabetical order and numerical ranking.

The tokenizing part is the same as in the previous section, and we use the `split` function to assign each word of the text to the elements of an array. As we saw in Chap. 2, `split` takes two arguments: a regular expression, which describes a delimiter, and a string, which is split everywhere the delimiter matches. The resulting fragments are assigned sequentially to an array. Let `$text` be a big string containing the whole text with one word per line. The instruction:

```
@words = split(/\n/, $text);
```

assigns the first line and hence the first word to `$words[0]`, the second word to `$words[1]`, and so on. A useful generalization of this instruction is

```
@words = split(/\s+/, $text);
```

which splits the text at each sequence of white space characters.

Then, we use a hash table or associative array. Instead of being indexed by consecutive numbers, as in classical arrays, hash tables are indexed by strings. The next three lines

```
$wordcount{"a"} = 21;
$wordcount{"And"} = 10;
$wordcount{"the"} = 18;
```

create a hash table `$wordcount` with three indices called the keys: a, And, the, whose values are 21, 10, and 18. Hash keys can be numbers as well as strings. We refer to the whole array using the notation `%wordcount`. The instruction `keys` return the keys of the array as in

```
keys %wordcount
```

A hash entry is created when a value is assigned to it. Its existence can be tested using the `exists` Boolean function.

The counting program scans the `@words` array and increments the frequency of the words as they occur. We finally introduce two new instructions and functions. The instruction `foreach item (list)` iterates over the items of an array, and `sort(array)` returns a sorted array.

```
$text = <>;
while ($line = <>) {
  $text .= $line;
}
$text =~ tr/a-zåàâäæçéèêëîïôöœùûüßA-
  ZÅÀÂÄÆÇÉÈÊËÎÏÔÖŒÙÛÜ' ()\-,.?!:;/\n/cs;
$text =~ s/([,.?!:;()'\-])/\n$1\n/g;
$text =~ s/\n+/\n/g;
@words = split(/\n/, $text);
for ($i = 0; $i <= $#words; $i++) {
  if (!exists($frequency{$words[$i]})) {
```

```
      $frequency{$words[$i]} = 1;
    } else {
      $frequency{$words[$i]}++;
    }
}
foreach $word (sort keys %frequency){
    print "$frequency{$word} $word\n";
}
```

4.4.4 Counting Bigrams with Perl

We count bigrams and n-grams just as we did with unigrams. The only difference is that we create an array of bigrams by concatenating the adjacent words. The following Perl program enables us to obtain them:

```
$text = <>;
while ($line = <>) {
    $text .= $line;
}
$text =~ tr/a-zåâãäæçéèêëîïôöœùûüßA-
ZÅÂÃÄÆÇÉÈÊËÎÏÔÖŒÙÛÜ'()\-,.?!:;/\n/cs;
$text =~ s/([,.?!:;()'\-])/\n$1\n/g;
$text =~ s/\n+/\n/g;
@words = split(/\n/, $text);
for ($i = 0; $i < $#words; $i++) {
    $bigrams[$i] = $words[$i] . " " . $words[$i + 1];
}
for ($i = 0; $i < $#words; $i++) {
    if (!exists($frequency_bigrams{$bigrams[$i]})) {
        $frequency_bigrams{$bigrams[$i]} = 1;
    } else {
        $frequency_bigrams{$bigrams[$i]}++;
    }
}
foreach $bigram (sort keys %frequency_bigrams){
    print "$frequency_bigrams{$bigram} $bigram \n";
}
```

4.5 Probabilistic Models of a Word Sequence

4.5.1 The Maximum Likelihood Estimation

We observed in Table 4.1 that some word sequences are more likely than others. Using a statistical model, we can quantify these observations. The model will enable us to assign a probability to a word sequence as well as to predict the next word to follow the sequence.

Let $S = w_1, w_2, ..., w_i, ..., w_n$ be a word sequence. Given a training corpus, an intuitive estimate of the probability of the sequence, $P(S)$, is the relative frequency of the string $w_1, w_2, ..., w_i, ..., w_n$ in the corpus. This estimate is called the *maximum likelihood estimate* (MLE):

$$P_{MLE}(S) = \frac{C(w_1, ..., w_n)}{N},$$

where $C(w_1, ..., w_n)$ is the frequency or count of the string $w_1, w_2, ..., w_i, ..., w_n$ in the corpus, and N is the total number of strings of length n.

Most of the time, however, it is impossible to obtain this estimate. Even when corpora reach billions of words, they have a limited size, and it is unlikely that we can always find the exact sequence we are searching. We can try to simplify the computation and decompose $P(S)$ a step further as:

$$\begin{aligned} P(S) &= P(w_1, ..., w_n), \\ &= P(w_1)P(w_2|w_1)P(w_3|w_1, w_2)P(w_n|w_1, ..., w_{n-1}), \\ &= \prod_{i=1}^{n} P(w_i|w_1, ..., w_{i-1}). \end{aligned}$$

The probability $P(It\ was\ a\ bright\ cold\ day\ in\ April)$ from *Nineteen Eighty-Four* corresponds then to the probability of having *It* to begin the sentence, then *was* knowing that we have *It* before, then *a* knowing that we have *It was* before, and so on until the end of the sentence. It yields the product of conditional probabilities:

$$\begin{aligned} P(S) = P(It) &\times P(was|It) \times P(a|It, was) \times P(bright|It, was, a) \times ... \\ &\times P(April|It, was, a, bright, ..., in). \end{aligned}$$

To estimate $P(S)$, we need to know unigram, bigram, trigram, so far, so good, but also 4-gram, 5-gram, and even 8-gram statistics. Of course, no corpus is big enough to produce them. A practical solution is then to limit the n-gram length to 2 or 3, and thus to approximate them to bigrams:

$$P(w_i|w_1, w_2, ..., w_{i-1}) \approx P(w_i|w_{i-1}),$$

or trigrams:

$$P(w_i|w_1, w_2, ..., w_{i-1}) \approx P(w_i|w_{i-2}, w_{i-1}).$$

Using a trigram language model, $P(S)$ is approximated as:

$$\begin{aligned} P(S) \approx P(It) &\times P(was|It) \times P(a|It, was) \times P(bright|was, a) \times ... \\ &\times P(April|day, in). \end{aligned}$$

Using a bigram grammar, the general case of a sentence probability is:

$$P(S) \approx P(w_1) \prod_{i=2}^{n} P(w_i|w_{i-1}),$$

with the estimate

$$P_{MLE}(w_i|w_{i-1}) = \frac{C(w_{i-1}, w_i)}{\sum\limits_{w} C(w_{i-1}, w)} = \frac{C(w_{i-1}, w_i)}{C(w_{i-1})}.$$

Similarly, the trigram maximum likelihood estimate is:

$$P_{MLE}(w_i|w_{i-2}, w_{i-1}) = \frac{C(w_{i-2}, w_{i-1}, w_i)}{C(w_{i-2}, w_{i-1})}.$$

And the general case of n-gram estimation is:

$$P_{MLE}(w_{i+n}|w_{i+1}, ..., w_{i+n-1}) = \frac{C(w_{i+1},...,w_{i+n})}{\sum\limits_{w} C(w_{i+1},...,w_{i+n-1},w)},$$
$$= \frac{C(w_{i+1},...,w_{i+n})}{C(w_{i+1},...,w_{i+n-1})}.$$

4.5.2 Using ML Estimates with *Nineteen Eighty-Four*

Training and Testing the Language Model.   Before computing the probability of a word sequence, we must train the language model. The corpus used to derive the n-gram frequencies is classically called the **training set**, and the corpus on which we apply the model, the **test set**. Both sets should be distinct. If we apply a language model to a word sequence, which is part of the training corpus, its probability will be biased to a higher value, and thus will be inaccurate. The training and test sets can be balanced or not, depending on whether we want them to be specific of a task or more general.

For some models, we need to optimize parameters in order to obtain the best results. Again, it would bias the results if at the same time, we carry out the optimization on the test set and run the evaluation on it. For this reason some models need a separate **development set** to fine-tune their parameters.

In some cases, especially with small corpora, a specific division between training and test sets may have a strong influence on the results. It is then preferable to apply the training and testing procedure several times with different sets and average the results. The method is to divide randomly the corpus into two sets. We learn the parameters from the training set, apply the model to the test set, and repeat the process with a new random division, for instance, ten times. This method is called **cross-validation**, or 10-fold cross-validation if we repeat it 10 times. Cross-validation smoothes the impact of a specific partition of the corpus.

Marking up the Corpus.   Most corpora use some sort of markup language. The most common markers of N-gram models are the sentence delimiters <s> to mark the start of a sentence and </s> at its end. For example:

<s> *It was a bright cold day in April* </s>

Depending on the application, both symbols can be counted in the n-gram frequencies just as the other tokens or can be considered as context cues. Context cues are vocabulary items that appear in the condition part of the probability but are never predicted – they never occur in the right part. In many models, <s> is a context cue and </s> is part of the vocabulary. We will adopt this convention in the next examples.

The Vocabulary. We have defined language models that use a finite and predetermined set of words. This is never the case in reality, and the models will have to handle out-of-vocabulary (OOV) words. Training corpora are typically of millions, or even billions, of words. However, whatever the size of a corpus, it will never have a complete coverage of the vocabulary. Some words that are unseen in the training corpus are likely to occur in the test set. In addition, frequencies of rare words will not be reliable.

There are two main types of methods to deal with OOV words:

- The first method assumes a **closed vocabulary**. All the words both in the training and the test sets are known in advance. Depending on the language model settings, any word outside the vocabulary will be discarded or cause an error. This method is used in some applications, like voice control of devices.
- The **open vocabulary** makes provisions for new words to occur with a specific symbol, <UKN>, called the unknown token. All the OOV words are mapped to <UNK>, both in the training and test sets.

The vocabulary itself can come from an external dictionary. It can also be extracted directly from the training set. In this case, it is common to exclude the rare words, notably those seen only once – the *hapax legomena*. The vocabulary will then consist of the most frequent types of the corpus, for example, the 20,000 most frequent types. The other words, unseen or with a frequency lower than a cutoff value, 1, 2, or up to 5, will be mapped to <UKN>.

Computing a Sentence Probability. We trained a bigram language model on a very small corpus consisting of the three chapters of *Nineteen Eighty-Four*. We kept the appendix, "The Principles of Newspeak," as the test set and we selected this sentence from it:

> <s> *A good deal of the literature of the past was, indeed, already being transformed in this way* </s>

We first normalized the text: We created a file with one sentence per line. We inserted automatically the delimiters <s> and </s>. We removed the punctuation, parentheses, quotes, stars, dashes, tabulations, and double white spaces. We set all the words in lowercase letters. We counted the words, and we produced a file with the unigram and bigram counts.

The training corpus has 115,212 words; 8,635 types, including 3,928 hapax legomena; and 49,524 bigrams, where 37,365 bigrams have a frequency of 1. Table 4.2 shows the unigram and bigram frequencies for the words of the test sentence. It excludes <s> from the unigram probabilities.

Table 4.2. Frequencies of unigrams and bigrams.

w_i	$C(w_i)$	$P_{MLE}(w_i)$	w_{i-1}, w_i	$C(w_{i-1}, w_i)$	$P_{MLE}(w_i|w_{i-1})$
\<s\>	7072	–	–	–	–
A	2482	0.023	\<s\> a	133	0.019
good	53	0.00049	a good	14	0.006
deal	5	$4.62\ 10^{-5}$	good deal	0	0.0
of	3310	0.031	deal of	1	0.2
the	6248	0.058	of the	742	0.224
literature	7	$6.47\ 10^{-5}$	the literature	1	0.0002
of	3310	0.031	literature of	3	0.429
the	6248	0.058	of the	742	0.224
past	99	0.00092	the past	70	0.011
was	2211	0.020	past was	4	0.040
indeed	17	0.00016	was indeed	0	0.0
already	64	0.00059	indeed already	0	0.0
being	80	0.00074	already being	0	0.0
transformed	1	$9.25\ 10^{-6}$	being transformed	0	0.0
in	1759	0.016	transformed in	0	0.0
this	264	0.0024	in this	14	0.008
way	122	0.0011	this way	3	0.011
\</s\>	7072	0.065	way \</s\>	18	0.148

All the words of the sentence have been seen in the training corpus, and we can compute a probability estimate of it using the unigram relative frequencies:

$$P(S) \approx P(a) \times P(good) \times \ldots \times P(way) \times P(</s>),$$
$$\approx 1.18 \times 10^{-48}.$$

The bigrams estimate is defined as

$$P(S) \approx P(a|<s>) \times P(good|a) \times \ldots \times P(way|this) \times P(</s>|way).$$

and has a zero probability, which is due to **sparse data**: the fact that the corpus is not big enough to have all the bigrams covered with a realistic estimate. We shall see in the next section how to handle them.

4.6 Smoothing N-gram Probabilities

4.6.1 Sparse Data

The approach using the maximum likelihood estimation has an obvious disadvantage because of the unavoidably limited size of the training corpora. Given a vocabulary of 20,000 types, the potential number of bigrams is $20,000^2 = 400,000,000$, and with trigrams, it amounts to the astronomic figure of $20,000^3 = 8,000,000,000,000$. No corpus yet has the size to cover the corresponding word combinations.

Among the set of potential n-grams, some are almost impossible, except as random sequences generated by machines; others are simply unseen in the corpus. This phenomenon is referred to as **sparse data**, and the maximum likelihood estimator gives no hint on how to estimate their probability.

In this section, we introduce **smoothing** techniques to estimate probabilities of unseen n-grams. As the sum of probabilities of all the n-grams of a given length is 1, smoothing techniques also have to re-arrange the probabilities of the observed n-grams. Smoothing allocates a part of the probability mass to the unseen n-grams that, as a counterpart, it shifts – or **discounts** – from the other n-grams.

4.6.2 Laplace's Rule

Laplace's rule (Laplace 1820, p. 17) is probably the oldest published method to cope with sparse data. It just consists in adding one to all the counts. For this reason, some authors also call it the add-one method. The frequency of unseen n-grams is equal to 1 and the general estimate of a bigram probability is:

$$P_{Laplace}(w_{i+1}|w_i) = \frac{C(w_i, w_{i+1}) + 1}{\sum_{w}(C(w_i, w) + 1)} = \frac{C(w_i, w_{i+1}) + 1}{C(w_i) + Card(V)},$$

where $Card(V)$ is the number of word types. The denominator correction is necessary to have the probability sum equal to 1.

Table 4.3. Frequencies of bigrams using Laplace's rule.

w_i, w_{i+1}	$C(w_i, w_{i+1})$	$C(w_i) + Card(V)$	$P_{Lap}(w_{i+1}|w_i)$
<s> a	133	7072 + 8634	0.0085
a good	14	2482 + 8634	0.0013
good deal	0	53 + 8634	0.00012
deal of	1	5 + 8634	0.00023
of the	742	3310 + 8634	0.062
the literature	1	6248 + 8634	0.00013
literature of	3	7 + 8634	0.00046
of the	742	3310 + 8634	0.062
the past	70	6248 + 8634	0.0048
past was	4	99 + 8634	0.00057
was indeed	0	2211 + 8634	0.000092
indeed already	0	17 + 8634	0.00012
already being	0	64 + 8634	0.00011
being transformed	0	80 + 8634	0.00011
transformed in	0	1 + 8634	0.00012
in this	14	1759 + 8634	0.0014
this way	3	264 + 8634	0.00045
way </s>	18	122 + 8634	0.0022

With Laplace's rule, we can use bigrams to compute the sentence probability (Table 4.3):

$$P(S) \approx P(a| <s>) \times P(good|a) \times ... \times P(</s> |way),$$
$$\approx 4.62 \times 10^{-57}.$$

Laplace's method is easy to understand and implement. It has an obvious drawback however: it shifts an enormous mass of probabilities to the unseen n-grams and gives them a considerable importance. The frequency of the unlikely bigram *the of* will be 1, a quarter of the much more common *this way*.

The **discount** value is the ratio between the smoothed frequencies and their actual counts in the corpus. The bigram *this way* has been discounted by $\frac{0.011}{0.00045} = 24.4$ to make place for the unseen bigrams. This is unrealistic and shows the major drawback of this method.

If adding 1 is too much, why not try less, for instance, 0.5. This is the idea of the Lidstone's rule. This value is denoted λ. The new formula is then:

$$P_{Lidstone}(w_{i+1}|w_i) = \frac{C(w_i, w_{i+1}) + \lambda}{C(w_i) + \lambda Card(V)},$$

which, however, is not a big improvement.

4.6.3 Good–Turing Estimation

The Good–Turing estimation (Good 1953) is one of the most efficient smoothing methods. As with Laplace's rule, it reestimates the counts of the n-grams observed in the corpus by discounting them, and it shifts the probability mass it has shaved to the unseen bigrams. The discount factor is variable, however, and depends on the number of times a n-gram has occurred in the corpus. There will be a specific discount value to n-grams seen once, another one to bigrams seen twice, a third one to those seen three times, and so on.

Let us denote N_c the number of n-grams that occurred exactly c times in the corpus. N_0 is the number of unseen n-grams, N_1 the number of n-grams seen once, N_2 the number of n-grams seen twice, and so on. If we consider bigrams, the value N_0 is $Card(V)^2$ minus all the bigrams we have seen.

The Good–Turing method reestimates the frequency of n-grams occurring c times using the formula:

$$c* = (c+1)\frac{E(N_{c+1})}{E(N_c)},$$

where $E(x)$ denotes the expectation of the random variable x. This formula is usually approximated as

$$c* = (c+1)\frac{N_{c+1}}{N_c}.$$

Hence, the Good–Turing estimation of the unseen n-grams is $c* = \frac{N_1}{N_0}$, and the n-grams that have been seen once in the training corpus are reestimated to $c* = \frac{2N_2}{N_1}$.

The three chapters in *Nineteen Eighty-Four* contain 37,365 unique bigrams and 5820 bigrams seen twice. Its vocabulary of 8634 words generates $8634^2 = 74{,}545{,}956$ bigrams, of which 74,513,701 are unseen. The Good–Turing method reestimates the frequency of each unseen bigram to $37{,}365/74{,}513{,}701 = 0.0005$ and unique bigrams to $2 \times (5820/37{,}365) = 0.31$. Table 4.4 shows the complete the reestimated frequencies for the n-grams up to 9.

In practice, only high values of N_c are reliable, which correspond to low values of c. In addition, above a certain threshold, most frequencies of frequency will be equal to zero. Therefore, the Good–Turing estimation is applied for $c < k$, where k is a constant set to $5, 6, \ldots$, or 10. Other counts are not reestimated.

The probability of a n-gram is given by the formula

$$P_{GT}(w_1, ..., w_n) = \frac{c * (w_1, ..., w_n)}{N},$$

where $c*$ is the reestimated count of $w_1...w_n$, and N the original count of n-grams in the corpus. The conditional frequency is

$$P_{GT}(w_n | w_1, ..., w_{n-1}) = \frac{c * (w_1, ..., w_n)}{C(w_1, ..., w_{n-1})}.$$

Table 4.5 shows the conditional frequencies where only frequencies less than 10 have been reestimated.

Table 4.4. The reestimated frequencies of the bigrams.

Frequency of occurrence	N_c	$c*$
0	74,513,701	0.0005
1	37,365	0.31
2	5,820	1.09
3	2,111	2.02
4	1,067	3.37
5	719	3.91
6	468	4.94
7	330	6.06
8	250	6.44
9	179	8.93

4.7 Using N-grams of Variable Length

In the previous section, we used smoothing techniques to reestimate the probability of n-grams of constant length, whether they occurred in the training corpus or not. A property of these techniques is that they assign a same probability to all the unseen n-grams.

Table 4.5. The conditional frequencies using the Good–Turing method.

w_i, w_{i+1}	$C(w_i, w_{i+1})$	$c * (w_i, w_{i+1})$	$P_{GT}(w_{i+1}|w_i)$
`<s>` *a*	133	133	0.019
a good	14	14	0.006
good deal	0	0.0005	$9.46 \ 10^{-6}$
deal of	1	0.31	0.062
of the	742	742	0.224
the literature	1	0.31	$4.99 \ 10^{-5}$
literature of	3	2.02	0.29
of the	742	742	0.224
the past	70	70	0.011
past was	4	3.37	0.034
was indeed	0	0.0005	$2.27 \ 10^{-7}$
indeed already	0	0.0005	$2.95 \ 10^{-5}$
already being	0	0.0005	$7.84 \ 10^{-6}$
being transformed	0	0.0005	$6.27 \ 10^{-6}$
transformed in	0	0.0005	0.00050
in this	14	14	0.008
this way	3	2.02	0.0077
way `</s>`	18	18	0.148

Another strategy is to rely on the frequency of observed sequences but of lesser length: $n - 1$, $n - 2$, and so on. As opposed to smoothing, the estimate of each unseen n-gram will be specific to the words it contains. In this section, we introduce two techniques: the linear interpolation and the Katz back-off model.

4.7.1 Linear Interpolation

Linear interpolation, also called deleted interpolation (Jelinek and Mercer 1980), combines linearly the maximum likelihood estimates from length 1 to n. For trigrams, it corresponds to:

$$P_{DelInterpolation}(w_n|w_{n-2}, w_{n-1}) = \lambda_1 P_{MLE}(w_n|w_{n-2}w_{n-1}) + \\ \lambda_2 P_{MLE}(w_n|w_{n-1}) + \lambda_3 P_{MLE}(w_n),$$

where $0 \leq \lambda_i \leq 1$ and $\sum_{i=1}^{3} \lambda_i = 1$.

The values can be constant and set by hand, for instance, $\lambda_1 = 0.6$, $\lambda_2 = 0.3$, and $\lambda_3 = 0.1$. They can also be trained and optimized from a corpus (Jelinek 1997).

We can now understand why bigram *we the* is ranked so high in Table 4.1 after *we are* and *we will*. Although, it can occur in English, as in the American constitution, *We, the people...*, it is not a very frequent combination. In fact, the estimation has been obtained with an interpolation where the term $\lambda_3 P_{MLE}(the)$ boosted the bigram to the top because of the high frequency of *the*.

4.7.2 Back-off

The idea of the back-off model (Katz 1987) is to use the frequency of longest available n-grams, and if no n-gram is available to back off to the $(n-1)$-gram, and then to $(n-2)$-gram, and so on. If n is 3, we first try trigrams, then bigrams, and finally unigrams. This can be expressed as:

$$P_{Backoff}(w_i|w_{i-2}, w_{i-1}) = \begin{cases} \tilde{P}(w_i|w_{i-2}, w_{i-1}), & \text{if } C(w_{i-2}, w_{i-1}, w_i) \neq 0, \\ \alpha_1 P(w_i|w_{i-1}), & \text{if } C(w_{i-2}, w_{i-1}, w_i) = 0 \\ & \text{and } C(w_{i-1}, w_i) \neq 0, \\ \alpha_2 P(w_i), & \text{otherwise.} \end{cases}$$

So far, this model does not tell us how to estimate the n-gram probabilities to the right of the formula. A first idea would be to use the maximum likelihood estimate,

$$P_{MLE}(w_i|w_{i-2}, w_{i-1}) = \frac{C(w_{i-2}, w_{i-1}, w_i)}{C(w_{i-2}, w_{i-1})},$$

but in this case, the sum of all the probabilities would be more than 1. Therefore we need the α_1 and α_2 values to ensure that the sum of probabilities is equal to 1. In addition, to make room for them, we need to discount the trigram estimates.

The back-off model is often used in conjunction with the Good–Turing discounting and the estimation is solved recursively. Let us first assume that for all the possible trigrams, we can back off to an observed bigram. We use the Good–Turing estimate,

$$\tilde{P}(w_i|w_{i-2}, w_{i-1}) = \frac{C^*(w_{i-2}, w_{i-1}, w_i)}{C(w_{i-2}, w_{i-1})},$$

to discount the observed trigrams and we assign the remaining probability mass to the unseen trigrams. That is,

$$1 - \sum_{w_i, C(w_{i-2}, w_{i-1}, w_i) > 0} \tilde{P}(w_i|w_{i-2}, w_{i-1}).$$

We compute α_1 so that the probability mass of the observed bigrams fits this value.

But we are not finished yet. In case of an unseen bigram, the model uses a unigram estimate. To compute it, the Katz model recursively applies the method it used with the trigrams. It further discounts the observed bigrams with the Good–Turing estimation to make room for the unigrams. It then adjusts the α_2 value so that the sum of probabilities of the discounted observed bigrams and the weighted unigram probabilities is equal to 1.

4.8 Quality of a Language Model

4.8.1 Intuitive Presentation

We can compute the probability of sequences of any length or of whole texts. As each word in the sequence corresponds to a conditional probability less than 1, the product will naturally decrease with the length of the sequence. To make sense, we normally average it by the number of words in the sequence and extract its nth root. This measure, which is a sort of a per-word probability of a sequence L, is easier to compute using a logarithm:

$$H(L) = -\frac{1}{n} \log_2 P(w_1, ..., w_n).$$

We have seen that trigrams are better predictors than bigrams, which are better than unigrams. This means that the probability of a very long sequence computed with a bigram model will normally be higher than with a unigram one. The log measure will then be lower.

Intuitively, this means that the $H(L)$ measure will be a quality marker for a language model where lower numbers will correspond to better models. This intuition has mathematical foundations, as we will see in the two next sections.

4.8.2 Entropy Rate

We used entropy with characters in Chap. 3. We can use it with any symbols such as words, bigrams, trigrams, or any n-grams. When we normalize it by the length of the word sequence, we define the **entropy rate**:

$$H_{rate} = -\frac{1}{n} \sum_{w_1,...,w_n \in L} p(w_1, ..., w_n) \log_2 p(w_1, ..., w_n),$$

where L is the set of all possible sequences of length n.

It has been proven that when $n \to \infty$ or n is very large and under certain conditions, we have

$$H_{rate}(L) = \lim_{n \to \infty} -\frac{1}{n} \sum_{w_1,...,w_n \in L} p(w_1, ..., w_n) \log_2 p(w_1, ..., w_n),$$
$$= \lim_{n \to \infty} -\frac{1}{n} \log_2 p(w_1, ..., w_n),$$

which means that we can compute $H_{rate}(L)$ from a very long sequence, ideally infinite, instead of summing of all the sequences of a definite length.

4.8.3 Cross Entropy

We can also use cross entropy, which is measured between a text, called the language and governed by an unknown probability p, and a language model m. Using the same definitions as in Chap. 3, the cross entropy of m on p is given by:

$$H(p, m) = -\frac{1}{n} \sum_{w_1,...,w_n \in L} p(w_1, ..., w_n) \log_2 m(w_1, ..., w_n).$$

As for the entropy rate, it has been proven that, under certain conditions

$$H(p,m) = \lim_{n \to \infty} -\frac{1}{n} \sum_{w_1,\ldots,w_n \in L} p(w_1, \ldots, w_n) \log_2 m(w_1, \ldots, w_n),$$
$$= \lim_{n \to \infty} -\frac{1}{n} \log_2 m(w_1, \ldots, w_n).$$

In applications, we generally compute cross entropy on the complete word sequence of a test set, governed by p, using a bigram or trigram model, m, derived from a training set.

In Chap. 3, we saw the inequality $H(p) \leq H(p,m)$. This means that the cross entropy will always be an upper bound of $H(p)$. As the objective of a language model is to be as close as possible to p, the best model will be the one yielding the lowest possible value. This forms the mathematical background of the intuitive presentation in Sect. 4.8.1.

4.8.4 Perplexity

The perplexity of a language model is defined as:

$$PP(p,m) = 2^{H(p,m)}.$$

Perplexity is interpreted as the average "branching factor" of a word: the statistically weighted number of words that follow a given word. Perplexity is equivalent to entropy. The only advantage of perplexity is that it results in numbers more comprehensible for human beings. It is then more popular to measure the quality of language models. As is the case for entropy, the objective is to minimize it: the better the language model, the lower the perplexity.

4.9 Collocations

Collocations are recurrent combinations of words. They are ubiquitous and arbitrary in English, French, German, and other languages (Smadja 1993). Simplest collocations are fixed n-grams such as *The White House*, and *Le Président de la République*. Other collocations involve some morphological or syntactic variation such as the one linking *make* and *decision* in American English: *to make a decision, decisions to be made, made an important decision*. Smadja (1993) calls the latter collocations predicative relations.

Collocations underlie word preferences that most of the time cannot easily be explained by a syntactic or semantic reasoning: they are merely resorting to usage. Collocations are in the mind of a native speaker. S/he can recognize them as valid. On the contrary, nonnative speakers may make mistakes when they are not aware of them or try to produce word-for-word translations. For this reason, many second language learners' dictionaries describe most frequent associations. In English, the *Oxford Advanced Learner's Dictionary*, *The Longman Dictionary of Contemporary English*, *The Cambridge International Dictionary*, and *The Collins COBUILD* carefully list verbs and prepositions or particles commonly associated such as phrasal verbs *set up*, *set off*, and *set out*.

Lexicographers used to identify collocations by introspection and by observing corpora, at the risk of forgetting some of them. Statistical tests can automatically extract associated words or "sticky" pairs from raw corpora. We introduce three of these tests in this section together with programs in Perl to compute them.

4.9.1 Word Preference Measurements

Mutual information (Church and Hanks 1990), t-score (Church and Mercer 1993), and the likelihood ratio (Dunning 1993) are statistical tests that are widely used to measure the strength of word associations:

- Mutual information is defined as

$$I(w_i, w_j) = \log_2 \frac{P(w_i, w_j)}{P(w_i)P(w_j)} \approx \log_2 \frac{NC(w_i, w_j)}{C(w_i)C(w_j)}.$$

- t-scores are defined as

$$t(w_i, w_j) = \frac{mean(P(w_i,w_j)) - mean(P(w_i))mean(P(w_j))}{\sqrt{\sigma^2(P(w_i,w_j)) + \sigma^2(P(w_i))\sigma^2(P(w_j))}},$$
$$\approx \frac{C(w_i,w_j) - \frac{1}{N}C(w_i)C(w_j)}{\sqrt{C(w_i,w_j)}}.$$

where $C(w_i)$ and $C(w_j)$ are respectively the frequencies of word w_i and word w_j in the corpus, $C(w_i, w_j)$ is the frequency of bigram w_i, w_j, and N is the total number of words in the corpus. The bigram count can be extended to the frequency of word w_i when it is followed or preceded by w_j in a window of k words. The latter definition is a generalization of the former with $k = 1$ and $j = i + 1$.

High t-scores show recurrent combinations of grammatical or very frequent words such as *of the, and the*, etc. Table 4.6 shows collocates of *set* extracted from the Bank of English using the t-score test. High mutual information shows pairs of words occurring together but generally with a lower frequency, such as technical terms. Table 4.7 gives collocates of the word *surgery*.

Table 4.6. Collocates of set extracted from Bank of English using the t-score test.

Word	Frequency	Bigram *set* + word	t-score
up	134,882	5512	67.980
a	1,228,514	7296	35.839
to	1,375,856	7688	33.592
off	52,036	888	23.780
out	12,3831	1252	23.320

Dunning (1993) criticized the t-score test and proposed an alternative based on likelihood ratios:

Table 4.7. Collocates of *surgery* extracted from the Bank of English using the mutual information test. Note the misspelled word *pioneeing*.

Word	Frequency	Bigram word + *surgery*	Mutual info
arthroscopic	3	3	11.822
pioneeing	3	3	11.822
reconstructive	14	11	11.474
refractive	6	4	11.237
rhinoplasty	5	3	11.085

$$LR(w_1, w_2) = 2 \log \frac{L(p_1, k_1, n_1) L(p_2, k_2, n_2)}{L(p, k_1, n_1) L(p, k_2, n_2)},$$

where

$p = \frac{C(w_2)}{N}$, $p_1 = \frac{C(w_1, w_2)}{C(w_1)}$, $p_2 = \frac{C(w_2) - C(w_1, w_2)}{N - C(w_1)}$, and $L(p, n, k) = p^k (1 - p)^{n-k}$.

4.9.2 Extracting Collocations with Perl

Both programs use unigram and bigram statistics. To compute them, we must first tokenize the text, and count words and bigrams using the tools we have described before:

```
$text = <>;
while ($line = <>) {
  $text .= $line;
}
$text =~ tr/a-zåàâäæçéèêëîïôöœùûüßA-
ZÅÀÂÄÆÇÉÈÊËÎÏÔÖŒÙÛÜ' ()\-,.?!:;/\n/cs;
$text =~ s/([,.?!:;()'\-])/\n$1\n/g;
$text =~ s/\n+/\n/g;
@words = split(/\n/, $text);
for ($i = 0; $i < $#words; $i++) {
  $bigrams[$i] = $words[$i] . " " . $words[$i + 1];
}
for ($i = 0; $i <= $#words; $i++) {
  $frequency{$words[$i]}++;
}
for ($i = 0; $i < $#words; $i++) {
  $frequency_bigrams{$bigrams[$i]}++;
}
```

Finally, we must know the number of words in the corpus. This corresponds to the size of the word array: $#word.

Mutual Information.   The Perl program iterates over the word array and applies the mutual information formula. The program is not optimal and computes the same value several times:

```
for ($i = 0; $i < $#words; $i++) {
  $mutual_info{$bigrams[$i]} = log(($#words + 1) *
    $frequency_bigrams{$bigrams[$i]}/
      ($frequency{$words[$i]} *
        $frequency{$words[$i + 1]}))/log(2);
}

foreach $bigram (keys %mutual_info){
  @bigram_array = split(/ /, $bigram);
  print $mutual_info{$bigram}, " ", $bigram, "\t",
  $frequency_bigrams{$bigram}, "\t",
  $frequency{$bigram_array[0]}, "\t",
  $frequency{$bigram_array[1]}, "\n";
}
```

t-**Scores.**   The program is similar to the previous one except the formula:

```
for ($i = 0; $i < $#words; $i++) {
  $t_scores{$bigrams[$i]} =
    ($frequency_bigrams{$bigrams[$i]} -
      $frequency{$words[$i]} *
        $frequency{$words[$i + 1]}/($#words + 1))
          /sqrt($frequency_bigrams{$bigrams[$i]});
}

foreach $bigram (keys %t_scores ){
  @bigram_array = split(/ /, $bigram);
  print $t_scores{$bigram}, " ", $bigram, "\t",
  $frequency_bigrams{$bigram}, "\t",
  $frequency{$bigram_array[0]}, "\t",
  $frequency{$bigram_array[1]}, "\n";
}
```

4.10 Application: Retrieval and Ranking of Documents on the Web

The advent of the Web in the mid-1990s made it possible to retrieve automatically quantities of electronic documents at a modest cost. Companies providing such a service are among the most popular sites on the Internet. The most notable ones include Google, Yahoo, and MSN Search.

Web search systems or engines are based on "spiders" or "crawlers" that visit Internet addresses, follow links they encounter, and collect all the pages they traverse. Crawlers can amass billions of pages every month. They necessitate massive network bandwidth, storage capacity, and computing power.

All the pages the crawlers download are tokenized and undergo a full text indexing. The engine lists all the words of its collection of documents and links each word with the pages where this word occurs in. This is pretty much like a book index except that it considers all the words. When a user asks for a specific word, the search system answers with the pages that contain it.

Search engines represent documents internally using statistical or popularity models. A popular representation is the vector space model (Salton 1988). The idea is to represent the documents in a vector space whose directions are the words. Then documents are vectors in a space of words. Let us first suppose that the document coordinates are the occurrence count of each word. A document would be represented as: $\mathbf{d} = (C(w_1), C(w_2), C(w_3), ..., C(w_n))$. Table 4.8 shows the matrix representing a collection of documents where each cell (D_i, w_j) contains the frequency of w_j in document D_i.

Table 4.8. The word by document matrix. Each cell (D_i, w_j) contains the frequency of w_j in document D_i.

Words\Documents	D_1	D_2	D_3	...	D_m
W_1					
W_2					
...					
W_n					

Using the vector space model, we can measure the similarity of two documents by the angle they form in the vector space. It is easier to computer the cosine of the angle:

$$\cos(\mathbf{q}, \mathbf{d}) = \frac{\sum_{i=1}^{n} q_i d_i}{\sqrt{\sum_{i=1}^{n} q_i^2} \sqrt{\sum_{i=1}^{n} d_i^2}}.$$

In fact, the rough word count is replaced by a more elaborate term: the term frequency times the inverted document frequency, better known as $tf \times idf$ (Salton 1988). To examine how it works, let us take the phrase *Internet in Somalia* as an example.

A document that contains many *Internet* words is probably more relevant than a document that has only one. The frequency $tf_{i,j}$ of a term j in a document i reflects this. It is a kind of a "mass" relevance. However, since *Internet* is a very common word, it is not specific. The number of documents that contain it must downplay its importance. This is the role of $idf_j = \log(\frac{N}{n_j})$, where N is the total number of documents in the collection – the total number of pages the crawler has collected – divided by the number of pages n_j, where a term j occurs at least once. *Somalia* probably appears in fewer documents than *Internet* and idf_j will give it a chance. The weight of a term j in document i is finally defined as $tf_{i,j} \times \log(\frac{N}{n_j})$.

The user may query a search engine with a couple of words or a phrase. Most systems will then answer with the pages that contain all the words and any of the words of the question. Some questions return hundreds or even thousands of valid documents. Ranking a document consists in projecting the space to that of the question words using the cosine. With this model, higher cosines will indicate better relevance. In addition to $tf \times idf$, search systems may employ heuristics such as giving more weight to the words in the title of a page (Mauldin and Leavitt 1994).

Google's PageRank algorithm (Brin and Page 1998) uses a different technique that takes into account the page popularity. PageRank considers the "backlinks", the links pointing to a page. The idea is that a page with many backlinks is likely to be a page of interest. Each backlink has a specific weight, which corresponds to the rank of the page it comes from. The page rank is simply defined as the sum of the ranks of all its backlinks. The importance of a page is spread through its forward links and contributes to the popularity of the pages it points to. The weight of each of these forward links is the page rank divided by the count of the outgoing links. The ranks are propagated in a document collection until they converge.

4.11 Further Reading

Statistical techniques have been applied first to speech recognition, lexicography, and later to other domains of linguistics. Their use has been a matter of debate because they opposed Chomsky's competence model. For a supporting review and a historical turning point, see the special issues of *Computational Linguistics* (1993, 1 and 2).

Interested readers will there find details on χ^2 tests and likelihood ratios to improve collocation detection in Dunning (1993). Other methods to obtain semantic clusters have been described by Brown et al. (1992). Manning and Schütze (1999) describe statistical methods in detail.

There are several language modeling toolkits available from the Internet. The SRI Language Modeling collection (Stolcke 2002) is a C++ package to create and experiment language models (http://www.speech.sri.com). The CMU-Cambridge Statistical Language Modeling Toolkit (Clarkson and Rosenfeld 1997) is another set of tools (http://svr-www.eng.cam.ac.uk/˜prc14/toolkit.html).

Exercises

4.1. Retrieve a text you like on the network. Give the five most frequent words.

4.2. Write a Prolog program that connects to a Web site, and explore hypertext Web links using a breadth-first strategy.

4.3. Implement a Prolog program to obtain bigrams and their statistics.

4.4. Implement a Prolog program to obtain trigrams and their statistics.

4.5. Retrieve a text you like on the network. Give the five most frequent bigrams and trigrams.

4.6. Retrieve a text you like on the network. Divide it into a training set and a test set. Implement the Laplace rule either in Perl or in Prolog. Learn the probabilities on the training set and compute the perplexity of the test set.

4.7. Retrieve a text you like on the network. Divide it into a training set and a test set. Implement the Good–Turing estimation either in Perl or in Prolog. Learn the probabilities on the training set and compute the perplexity of the test set.

4.8. Implement the mutual information test in Prolog.

4.9. Implement the t-score test in Prolog.

4.10. Implement the likelihood ratio in Perl.

4.11. Implement the mutual information test with a window of five words to the left and to the right of the word.

5

Words, Parts of Speech, and Morphology

5.1 Words

5.1.1 Parts of Speech

We can divide the lexicon into **parts of speech** (POS), that is, classes whose words share common grammatical properties. The concept of part of speech dates back to the classical antiquity philosophy and teaching. Plato made a distinction between the verb and the noun. After him, the word classification further evolved and parts of speech grew in number until Dionysius Thrax fixed and formulated them under a form that we still use today. Aelius Donatus popularized the list of the eight parts of speech: noun, pronoun, verb, participle, conjunction, adverb, preposition, and interjection, in his work *Ars grammatica*, a reference reading in the Middle Ages:

> "Partes orationis quot sunt? Octo. Quae? Nomen pronomen verbum adverbium participium coniunctio praepositio interiectio."

The word parsing comes from the Latin phrase *partes orationis* 'parts of speech'. It corresponds to the identification of the words' parts of speech in a sentence. In natural language processing, POS tagging is the automatic annotation of words with grammatical categories also called POS tags. Parts of speech are also sometimes called lexical categories.

Most European languages have inherited the Greek and Latin part-of-speech classification with a few adaptations. The word categories as they are taught today roughly coincide in English, French, and German in spite of some inconsistencies. This is not new. To manage the nonexistence of articles in Latin, Latin grammarians tried to get the Greek article into the Latin pronoun category.

The definition of the parts of speech is sometimes arbitrary and has been a matter of debate. From Dionysius Thrax, tradition has defined the parts of speech using morphological and grammatical properties. We shall adopt essentially this viewpoint here. However, words of a certain part of speech share semantic properties and some grammars contain statements like a noun denotes a thing and a verb an action.

Parts of speech can be clustered into two main classes: the **closed class** and the **open class**. Closed class words are relatively stable over time and have a functional role. They include words such as articles, like English *the*, French *le*, or German *der*, which change very slowly. Among the closed class, there are the determiners, the pronouns, the prepositions, the conjunctions, and the auxiliary and modal verbs (Table 5.1).

Open class words form the bulk of a vocabulary. They appear or disappear with the evolution of the language. If a new word is created, say a *hedgedog*, breed of a hedgehog and a Yorkshire terrier, it will belong to an open class category: here a noun. The main categories of the open class are the nouns, the adjectives, the verbs, and the adverbs (Table 5.2). We can add interjection to this list. Interjections are words such as *ouch*, *ha*, *oh*, and so on, that express sudden surprise, pain, or pleasure.

Table 5.1. Closed class categories.

Part of speech	English	French	German
Determiners	*the, several, my*	*le, plusieurs, mon*	*der, mehrere, mein*
Pronouns	*he, she, it*	*il, elle, lui*	*er, sie, ihm*
Prepositions	*to, of*	*vers, de*	*nach, von*
Conjunctions	*and, or*	*et, ou*	*und, oder*
Auxiliaries and modals	*be, have, will, would*	*être, avoir, pouvoir*	*sein, haben, können*

Table 5.2. Open class categories.

Part of speech	English	French	German
Nouns	*name, Frank*	*nom, François*	*Name, Franz*
Adjectives	*big, good*	*grand, bon*	*groß, gut*
Verbs	*to swim*	*nager*	*schwimmen*
Adverbs	*rather, very, only*	*plutôt, très, uniquement*	*fast, nur, sehr, endlich*

5.1.2 Features

Basic categories can be further refined, that is **subcategorized**. Nouns, for instance, can be split into singular nouns and plural nouns. In French and German, nouns can also be split according to their gender: masculine and feminine for French, and masculine, feminine, and neuter for German.

Genders do not correspond in these languages and can shape different visions of the world. Sun is a masculine entity in French – *le soleil* – and a feminine one in German – *die Sonne*. In contrast, moon is a feminine entity in French – *la lune* – and a masculine one in German – *der Mond*.

Additional properties that can further specify main categories are often called the **features**. Features vary among European languages and include notably the number, gender, person, case, and tense. Each feature has a set of possible values; for instance, the number can be singular or plural.

Word features are different according to their parts of speech. In English, a verb has a tense, a noun has a number, and an adjective has neither tense nor number. In French and German, adjectives have a number but no tense. The feature list of a word defines its part of speech together with its role in the sentence.

5.1.3 Two Significant Parts of Speech: The Noun and the Verb

The Noun. Nouns are divided into proper and common nouns. Proper nouns are names of persons, people, countries, companies, and trademarks, such as: *England, Robert, Citroën*. Common nouns are the rest of the nouns. Common nouns are often used to qualify persons, things, ideas.

A noun definition referring to semantics is a disputable approximation, however. More surely, nouns have certain syntactic features, namely the number, gender, and case (Table 5.3). A noun group is marked with these features, and other words of the group, that is, determiners, adjectives, must agree with the features they share.

Table 5.3. Features of common nouns.

Features\Values	English	French	German
Number	singular, plural *waiter/waiters, book/books*	singular, plural *serveur/serveurs, livre/livres*	singular, plural *Buch/Bücher*
Gender		masculine, feminine *serveur/table*	masculine, feminine, neuter *Ober/Gabel/Tuch*
Case			nominative, accusative, genitive, dative *Junge/Jungen/Jungen/Jungen*

While number and gender are probably obvious, case might be a bit obscure for non-German speakers. Case is a function marker that inflects words such as nouns or adjectives. In German, there are four cases: nominative, accusative, genitive, and dative. The nominative case corresponds to the subject function, the accusative case to the direct object function, and the dative case to the indirect object function. Genitive denotes a possession relation. These cases are still marked in English and French for pronouns.

In addition to these features, the English language makes a distinction between nouns that can have a plural: count nouns, and nouns that cannot: mass nouns. *Milk, water, air* are examples of mass nouns.

Verbs. Semantically, verbs often describe an action, an event, a state, etc. More positively, and as for the nouns, verbs in European languages are marked by their morphology. This morphology is quite elaborate in a language like French, notably due to the tense system. Verbs can be basically classified into three main types: auxiliaries, modals, and main verbs.

Auxiliaries are helper verbs such as *be* and *have* that enable us to build some of the main verb tenses (Table 5.4). Modal verbs are verbs immediately followed by another verb in the infinitive. They usually indicate a modality, a possibility (Table 5.5). Modal verbs are more specific to English and German. In French, semiauxiliaries correspond to a similar category.

Table 5.4. Auxiliary verbs.

English	French	German
to be: am, are, is, was, were	**être**: suis, es, est, sommes,	**sein**: bin, bist, ist, war, waren
to have: has, have, had	sont, étais, était	**haben**: habe, hast, hat,
to do: does, did, done	**avoir**: ai, as, a, avons, ont,	haben, habt
	avais, avait, avions	**werden**: werde, wirst, wird,
		wurde

Table 5.5. Modal verbs.

English	French (semiauxiliaries)	German
can, could,	**pouvoir**: peux, peut, pouvons,	**können**: kann, können, konnte
must, may, might,	pourrai, pourrais	**dürfen**: darf, dürfen, dürfte
shall, should	**devoir**: dois, doit, devons, devrai,	**mögen**: mag, mögen, möchte
	devrais	**müssen**: muß, müssen, mußte
	vouloir: veux, veut, voulons,	**sollen**: soll, sollen, sollte
	voudrai, voudrais	

Main verbs are all the other verbs. Traditionally, main verbs are categorized according to their complement's function (Table 5.6):

- Copula or link verb – verbs linking a subject to an (adjective) complement. Copulas include **verbs of being** such as *be, être, sein* when not used as auxiliaries, and other verbs such as *seem, sembler, scheinen*.
- Intransitive – verbs taking no object.
- Transitive – verbs taking an object.
- Ditransitive – verbs taking two objects.

Verbs have more features than other parts of speech. First, the verb group shares certain features of the noun (Table 5.7). These features must agree with corresponding ones of the verb's subject.

Verbs have also specific features, namely the tense, the mode, and the voice:

Table 5.6. Verb types.

	English	French	German
Copulas	*Man is mortal*	*l'homme est mortel*	*Der Mensch ist*
	She seems intelligent	*Elle paraît intelligente*	*sterblich*
			Sie scheint intelligent
Intransitive verbs	*Frank sleeps*	*François dort*	*Franz schläft*
	Charlotte runs	*Charlotte court*	*Charlotte rennt*
Transitive verbs	*You take the book*	*Tu prends le livre*	*Du nimmst das Buch*
	Susan reads the paper	*Suzanne lis l'article*	*Susan liest den Artikel*
Ditransitive verbs	*I give my neighbors the notes*	*Je donne les notes à mon voisin*	*Ich gebe die Notizen meinem Nachbarn*

Table 5.7. Features common to verbs and nouns.

Features\Values	English	French	German
Person	1, 2, and 3	1, 2, and 3	1, 2, and 3
	I am	*je suis*	*ich bin*
	you are	*tu es*	*du bist*
	she is	*elle est*	*sie ist*
Number	singular, plural	singular, plural	singular, plural
	I am/we are	*je suis/nous sommes*	*ich bin/wir sind*
	She eats/they eat	*elle mange/elles mangent*	*sie ißt/sie essen*
Gender		masculine, feminine	
	–	*il est mangé/elle est mangée*	–

- **Tense** locates the verb, and the sentence, in time. Tense systems are elaborate in English, French, and German, and do not correspond. Tenses are construed using form variations (Table 5.8) or auxiliaries (Table 5.9). Tenses are a source of significant form variation in French.
- **Mood** enables the speaker to present or to conceive the action in various ways (Table 5.10).
- **Voice** characterizes the sequence of syntactic groups. Active voice corresponds to the "subject, verb, object" sequence. The reverse sequence corresponds to the passive voice. This voice is possible only for transitive verbs. Some constructions in French and German use a reflexive pronoun. They correspond to the pronominal voice.

5.2 Lexicons

A lexicon is a list of words, and in this context, lexical entries are also called the **lexemes**. Lexicons often cover a particular domain. Some focus on a whole language, like English, French, or German, while some specialize in specific areas such

Table 5.8. Tenses constructed using inflection.

	English	French	German
Base	*I like to **sing***	*j'aime **chanter***	*Ich **singe** gern*
Present	*I **sing** everyday*	*Je **chante** tous les jours*	*Ich **singe** alltags*
Preterit (Simple past)	*I **sang** in my youth*	*Je **chantai** dans ma jeunesse*	*Ich **sang** in meiner Jugend*
Imperfect	–	*Je **chantais** dans ma jeunesse*	–
Future	–	*Je **chanterai** plus tard*	–
Present participle	*I am **singing***	*En **chantant** tous les jours*	***Singend***
Past participle	*I have **sung** before*	*J'ai **chanté***	*Ich habe **gesungen***

Table 5.9. Some tenses constructed using auxiliaries. Values do not correspond across languages.

	English	French	German
Present progressive	*I am singing*	–	–
Future	*I shall (will) sing*	–	*Ich werde singen*
Present perfect	*I have sung*	*J'ai chanté*	*Ich habe gesungen*
Pluperfect	*I had sung*	*J'avais chanté*	*Ich hatte gesungen*
Passé antérieur	–	*J'eus chanté*	–
Future perfect	*I will have sung*	*J'aurai chanté*	*Ich werde gesungen haben*
Futur antérieur	*I would have sung*	*J'aurais chanté*	*Ich würde gesungen haben*
Past progressive	*I was singing*	–	–
Future progressive	*I will be singing*	–	–
Present perfect progressive	*I have been singing*	–	–
Future perfect progressive	*I will have been singing*	–	–
Past perfect progressive	*I had been singing*	–	–

Table 5.10. Moods (Present only).

	English	French	German
Indicative	*I am singing*	*Je chante*	*Ich singe*
Imperative	*sing*	*chante*	*singe*
Conditional	*I should (would) sing*	*Je chanterais*	*Ich würde singen*
Subjunctive	Rare, it appears in expressions such as: *God save the queen*	*Il faut que je chante*	*Ich singe*

as proper names, technology, science, and finance. In some applications, lexicons try to be as exhaustive as is humanly possible. This is the case of Internet crawlers, which index all the words of all the Web pages they can find. Computerized lexicons are now embedded in many popular applications such as in spelling checkers, thesauruses, or definition dictionaries of word processors. They are also the first building block of most language processing programs.

Several options can be taken when building a computerized lexicon. They range from a collection of words – a word list – to words carefully annotated with their pronunciation, morphology, and syntactic and semantic labels. Words can also be related together using semantic relationships and definitions.

A key point in lexicon building is that many words are ambiguous both syntactically and semantically. Therefore, each word may have as many entries as it has syntactic or semantic readings. Table 5.11 shows words that have two or more parts of speech and senses. In this chapter, we only examine the syntactic part. Chap. 13 will cover semantic issues.

Table 5.11. Word ambiguity.

	English	**French**	**German**
Part of speech	*can* modal	*le* article	*der* article
	can noun	*le* pronoun	*der* pronoun
Semantic	*great* big	*grand* big	*groß* big
	great notable	*grand* notable	*groß* notable

Many computerized lexicons are now available from the industry and from sources on the Internet. English sources are the most numerous at present, but the situation is rapidly changing for other languages. Most notable ones in English include word lists derived from the *Longman Dictionary of Contemporary English* (Procter 1978) and the *Oxford Advanced Learner's Dictionary* (Hornby 1974). Table 5.12 shows the first lines of letter *A* of an electronic version of the OALD.

BDLex – standing for *Base de Données Lexicale* – is an example of a simple French lexicon (Pérennou and de Calmès 1987). BDLex features a list of words in a lemmatized form together with their part of speech and a syntactic type (Table 5.13).

5.2.1 Encoding a Dictionary

Letter trees (de la Briandais 1959) or tries (pronounce try ees) are a useful data structures to store large lexicons and to search words quickly. The idea behind a trie is to store the words as trees of characters and to share branches as far as the letters of two words are identical. Figure 5.1 shows a graphical representation of a trie encoding the words *bin*, *dark*, *dawn*, *tab*, *table*, *tables*, and *tablet*.

In Prolog, we can represent this trie as embedded lists, where each branch is a list. The first element of a branch is the root letter: the first letter of all the subwords that correspond to the branch. The leaves of the trie are the lexical entries, here the

Table 5.12. The first lines the *Oxford Advanced Learner's Dictionary*.

Word	Pronunciation	Syntactic tag	Syllable count or verb pattern (for verbs)
a	@	S-*	1
a	EI	Ki$	1
a fortiori	eI ,fOtI'OraI	Pu$	5
a posteriori	eI ,p0sterI'OraI	OA$,Pu$	6
a priori	eI ,praI'OraI	OA$, Pu$	4
a's	Eiz	Kj$	1
ab initio	&b I'nISI@U	Pu$	5
abaci	'&b@saI	Kj$	3
aback	@'b&k	Pu%	2
abacus	'&b@k@s	K7%	3
abacuses	'&b@k@sIz	Kj%	4
abaft	@'bAft	Pu$,T-$	2
abandon	@'b&nd@n	H0%,L@%	36A,14
abandoned	@'b&nd@nd	Hc%,Hd%,OA%	36A,14
abandoning	@'b&nd@nIN	Hb%	46A,14
abandonment	@'b&nd@nm@nt	L@%	4
abandons	@'b&nd@nz	Ha%	36A,14
abase	@'beIs	H2%	26B
abased	@'beIst	Hc%,Hd%	26B
abasement	@'beIsm@nt	L@%	3

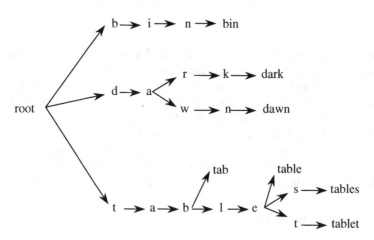

Fig. 5.1. A letter tree encoding the words *tab*, *table*, *tablet*, and *tables*.

Table 5.13. An excerpt from BDLex. Digits encode accents on letters. The syntactical tags of the verbs correspond to their conjugation type taken from the *Bescherelle* reference.

Entry	Part of speech	Lemma	Syntactic tag
a2	Prep	a2	Prep_00_00;
abaisser	Verbe	abaisser	Verbe_01_060_**;
abandon	Nom	abandon	Nom_Mn_01;
abandonner	Verbe	abandonner	Verbe_01_060_**;
abattre	Verbe	abattre	Verbe_01_550_**;
abbe1	Nom	abbe1	Nom_gn_90;
abdiquer	Verbe	abdiquer	Verbe_01_060_**;
abeille	Nom	abeille	Nom_Fn_81;
abi3mer	Verbe	abi3mer	Verbe_01_060_**;
abolition	Nom	abolition	Nom_Fn_81;
abondance	Nom	abondance	Nom_Fn_81;
abondant	Adj	abondant	Adj_gn_01;
abonnement	Nom	abonnement	Nom_Mn_01;
abord	Nom	abord	Nom_Mn_01;
aborder	Verbe	aborder	Verbe_01_060_**;
aboutir	Verbe	aboutir	Verbe_00_190_**;
aboyer	Verbe	aboyer	Verbe_01_170_**;
abre1ger	Verbe	abre1ger	Verbe_01_140_**;
abre1viation	Nom	abre1viation	Nom_Fn_81;
abri	Nom	abri	Nom_Mn_01;
abriter	Verbe	abriter	Verbe_01_060_**;

words themselves that we represent as atoms. Of course, these entries could contain more information, such as the part of speech, the pronunciation, etc.

```
[
  [b, [i, [n, bin]]]
  [d, [a, [r, [k, dark]],
          [w, [n, dawn]]]]
  [t, [a, [b, tab,
              [l, [e, table,
                      [s, tables],
                      [t, tablet]]]]]]]
]
```

5.2.2 Building a Trie in Prolog

The make_trie/2 predicate builds a trie from a lexicon represented as an ordered list of atoms.

```
% make_trie(+WordList, -Trie)
make_trie([Word | WordList], Trie) :-
```

```
    make_trielist(Word, Word, WordTrie),
    make_trie(WordList, [WordTrie], Trie).

% make_trie(+WordList, -Trie, -FinalTrie)
make_trie([], T, T) :- !.
make_trie([Word | WordList], Trie, FinalTrie) :-
    insert_word_in_trie(Word, Word, Trie, NewTrie),
    make_trie(WordList, NewTrie, FinalTrie).
```

The make_trie/2 predicate uses make_trielist/3 to transform an atom into a trie representing a single word. The make_trielist/3 predicate takes the word and the lexical entry as an input:

```
?- make_trielist(tab, noun, TL).
TL = [t, [a, [b, noun]]]

%make_trielist(+Word, +Leave, -WordTtrie)
% Creates the trie for a single word.
% Leaf contains the type of the word.
make_trielist(Word, Leaf, WordTrie) :-
    atom_chars(Word, CharList),
    make_trielist_aux(CharList, Leaf, WordTrie).

make_trielist_aux([X], Leaf, [X, Leaf]) :- !.
make_trielist_aux([X | L], Leaf, [X | [LS]]) :-
    make_trielist_aux(L, Leaf, LS).
```

Finally, make_trie/2 inserts a word trie into the lexicon trie using insert_-word_in_trie/4:

```
%Inserts a word in a trie.
%The Leaf argument contains the type of the word
%insert_word_in_trie(+Word, +Leaf, +Trie, -NewTrie)
insert_word_in_trie(Word, Leaf, Trie, NewTrie) :-
    make_trielist(Word, Leaf, WordTrie),
    insert_wordtrie_in_trie(WordTrie, Trie, NewTrie).

%Inserts a word trie in a trie
%insert_wordtrie_in_trie(+WordTrie, +Trie, -NewTrie)
insert_wordtrie_in_trie([H | [T]],
    [[H, Leaf | BT] | LT], [[H, Leaf | NB] | LT]) :-
    atom(Leaf),
    !,
    insert_wordtrie_in_trie(T, BT, NB).
% Traverses a segment shared between the trie and
% the word and encounters a leaf.
```

```
% It assumes that the leaf is an atom.

insert_wordtrie_in_trie([H | [T]], [[H | BT] | LT],
    [[H | NB] | LT]) :-
  !,
  insert_wordtrie_in_trie(T, BT, NB).
% Traverses a segment shared between the trie and
% the word.

insert_wordtrie_in_trie([H | T], [[HT | BT] | LT],
    [[HT | BT] | NB]) :-
  !,
  insert_wordtrie_in_trie([H | T], LT, NB).
% Traverses a nonshared segment

insert_wordtrie_in_trie(RW, RT, NB) :-
  append(RT, [RW], NB),
  !.
% Appends the remaining part of the word to the trie.
```

5.2.3 Finding a Word in a Trie

The rules to find a word in a trie are easier to write. A first rule compares the first letter of the word to the trie and unifies with the branch starting with this letter. It continues recursively with the remaining characters of the word. A second rule extracts the lexical entries that we assume to be atoms.

```
% Checks if a word is in a trie
% is_word_in_trie(+WordChars, +Trie, -Lex)
is_word_in_trie([H | T], Trie, Lex) :-
  member([H | Branches], Trie),
  is_word_in_trie(T, Branches, Lex).
is_word_in_trie([], Trie, LexList) :-
  findall(Lex, (member(Lex, Trie), atom(Lex)),
    LexList),
  LexList \= [].
% We assume that the word lexical entry is an atom
```

5.3 Morphology

5.3.1 Morphemes

From a morphological viewpoint, a language is a set of morphemes divided into **lexical** and **grammatical** morphemes. Lexical morphemes correspond to the word stems and form the bulk of the vocabulary. Grammatical morphemes include grammatical words and the affixes. In European languages, words are made of one or more morphemes (Table 5.14). The affixes are concatenated to the stem (bold): before it – the prefixes (underlined) – and after it – the suffixes (double underlined). When a prefix and a suffix surrounding the stem are bound together, it is called a circumfix, as in the German part participle (wavy underlines).

Table 5.14. Morpheme decomposition. We replaced the stems with the corresponding lemmas.

	Word	Morpheme decomposition
English	*disentangling*	*dis+en+**tangle**+ing*
	rewritten	*re+**write**+en*
French	*désembrouillé*	*dé+em+**brouiller**+é*
	récrite	*re+**écrire**+te*
German	*entwirrend*	*ent+**wirren**+end*
	wiedergeschrieben	*wieder+ge+**schreiben**+en*

Affixing grammatical morphemes to the stem is general property of most European languages, which is **concatenative morphology** (Fig. 5.2). Although there are numerous exceptions, it enables us to analyze the structure of most words.

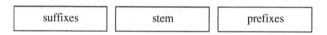

Fig. 5.2. Concatenative morphology where prefixes and suffixes are concatenated to the stem.

Concatenative morphology is not universal, however. The Semitic languages, like Arabic or Hebrew, for instance, have a **templatic morphology** that interweaves the grammatical morphemes to the stem. There are also examples of nonconcatenative patterns in European languages like in irregular verbs of German. The verb *singen* 'sing' has the forms *sangst* 'you sang' and *gesungen* 'sung' where the stem [s–ng] is embedded into the grammatical morphemes [–a–st] for the second-person preterit (Fig. 5.3) and [ge–u–en] for the past participle (Fig. 5.4).

5.3.2 Morphs

Grammatical morphemes represent syntactic or semantic functions whose realizations in words are called **morphs**. Using an object-oriented terminology, morphemes would be the classes, while morphs would be the objects. The **allomorphs** correspond to the set of all the morphs in a morpheme class.

The plural morpheme of English and French nouns is generally realized with an *s* suffix – an *s* added at the end of the noun. It can also be *es* or nothing ($\emptyset$) in English and *ux* in French. In German, the plural morpheme can take several shapes, such as suffixes *e*, *en* , *er*, *s*, or an umlaut on the first vowel of the word (Table 5.15):

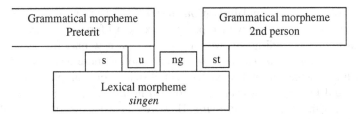

Fig. 5.3. Embedding of the stem into the grammatical morphemes in the German verb *sangst* (second-person preterit of *singen*). After Simone (1998, p. 144).

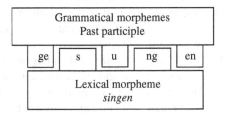

Fig. 5.4. Embedding of the stem into the grammatical morphemes in the German verb *gesungen* (past participle of *singen*). After Simone (1998, p. 144).

- In English, suffixes *-s*, *-es*, etc.
- In French, *-s*, *-ux*, etc.
- In German, an umlaut on the first vowel and the *-e* suffix, or simply the *-e* suffix.

Table 5.15. Plural morphs.

	Plural of nouns	Morpheme decomposition
English	*hedgehogs*	*hedgehog+s*
	churches	*church+es*
	sheep	*sheep+∅*
French	*hérissons*	*hérisson+s*
	chevaux	*cheval+ux*
German	*Gründe*	*Grund+(¨)e*
	Hände	*Hand+(¨)e*
	Igel	*Igel+∅*

Plurals also offer exceptions. Many of the exceptions, such as *mouse* and *mice*, are not predictable and have to be listed in the lexicon.

5.3.3 Inflection and Derivation

Some Definitions. We saw in Chap. 1 that morphology can be classified into **inflection**, the form variation of a word according to syntactic features such as gender, number, person, tense, etc., and **derivation**, the creation of a new word – a new meaning – by concatenating a word with a specific affix. A last form of construction is the **composition (compounding)** of two words to give a new one, for instance, *part of speech, can opener, pomme de terre*. Composition is more obvious in German, where such new words are not separated with a space, for example, *Führerschein*. In English and French, some words are formed in this way, such as *bedroom*, or are separated with a hyphen, *centre-ville*. However, the exact determination of other compounded words – separated with a space – can be quite tricky.

Inflection.   Inflection corresponds to the application of a grammatical feature to a word, such as putting a noun into the plural or a verb into the past participle (Table 5.16). It is also governed by its context in the sentence; for instance, the word is bound to agree in number with some of its neighbors.

Inflection is relatively predictable – regular – depending on the language. Given a lemma, its part of speech, and a set of grammatical features, it is possible to construct a word form using rules, for instance, gender, plural, or conjugation rules. The past participle of regular English, French, and German verbs can be respectively formed with an *ed* suffix, an *é* suffix, and the *ge* prefix and the *t* suffix. Morphology also includes frequent exceptions that can sometimes also be described by rules.

Table 5.16. Verb inflection with past participle.

	English	French	German
Base form	*work*	*travailler, chanter*	*arbeiten*
	sing	*paraître*	*singen*
Past participle (regular)	*worked*	*travaillé, chanté*	*gearbeitet*
Past participle (exception)	*sung*	*paru*	*gesungen*

Inflectional systems are similar in European languages but show differences according to the syntactic features. In English, French, and German, nouns are inflected with plurals and are consequently decorated with a specific suffix. However, in French and other Romance languages, verbs are inflected with future. Verb *chanterons* is made of two morphs: *chant* 'sing' and *-erons*. The first one is the stem (root) of *chanter*, and the second one is a suffix indicating the future tense, the first person, and the plural number. In English and German, this tense is rendered with an auxiliary: *we shall sing* or *wir werden singen*.

Derivation.   Derivation is linked to lexical semantics and involves another set of affixes (Table 5.17). Most affixes can only be attached to a specific lexical category (part of speech) of words: some to nouns, others to verbs, etc. Some affixes leave the derived word in the same category, while some others entail a change of category. For instance, some affixes transform adjectives into adverbs, nouns into adjectives, and verbs into nouns (Table 5.18). Derivation rules can be combined and are sometimes complex. For instance, the word *disentangling* features two prefixes: *dis-* and *en-*, and a suffix *-ing*.

Table 5.17. Derivational affixes.

	English	French	German
Prefixes	*foresee, unpleasant*	*prévoir, déplaisant*	*vorhersehen, unangenehm*
Suffixes	*manageable, rigorous*	*gérable, rigoureux*	*vorsichtich, streitbar*

Table 5.18. Derivation related to part of speech.

	Adjectives	Adverbs	Nouns	Adjectives	Verbs	Nouns
English	*recent*	*recently*	*air*	*aerial*	*compute*	*computation*
	frank	*frankly*	*base*	*basic*		
French	*récent*	*récemment*	*lune*	*lunaire*	*calculer*	*calcul*
	franc	*franchement*	*air*	*aérien*		
German	*glücklich*	*glücklicherweise*	*Luft*	*luftig*	*rechnen*	*Rechnung*
	möglich	*möglicherweise*	*Grund*	*gründlich*		

Some semantic features of words, such as the contrary or the possibility, can be roughly associated to affixes, and so word meaning can be altered using them (Table 5.19). However, derivation is very irregular. Many words cannot be generated as simply, because the word does not exist or sounds weird. In addition, some affixes cannot be mapped to clear semantic features.

Table 5.19. Word derivation.

	Word	Contrary	Possibility
English	*pleasant*	*unpleasant*	**pleasable*
	do	*undo*	*doable*
French	*plaisant*	*déplaisant*	**plaisable*
	faire	*défaire*	*faisable*
German	*angenehm*	*unangenehm*	**angenehmbar*
	tun	**untun*	*tunlichst*

Compounding is a feature of German, Dutch, and the Scandinavian languages. It resembles the English noun sequences with the difference that nouns are not separated with a white space. English open compounds (e.g., *word processor*) are.

Morphological Processing. Morphological processing includes parsing and generation (Table 5.20). Parsing consists in splitting an inflected, derived, or compounded word into morphemes; this process is also called a **lemmatization**. Lemmatization refers to transforming a word into its canonical dictionary form, for example, *retrieving* into *retrieve*, *recherchant* into *rechercher*, or *suchend* into *suchen*. Stemming consists of removing the suffix from the rest of the word. Taking the previous examples, this yields *retriev*, *recherch*, and *such*. Lemmatization and stemming are often mistaken. Conversely, generation consists of producing a word – a lexical form – from a set of morphemes.

Table 5.20. Morphological generation and parsing.

Generation →					
English		**French**		**German**	
dog+s	*dogs*	*chien+s*	*chiens*	*Hund+e*	*Hunde*
work+ing	*working*	*travailler+ant*	*travaillant*	*arbeiten+end*	*arbeitend*
un+do	*undo*	*dé+faire*	*défaire*		

← **Parsing**

In French, English, and German, derivation operates on open class words. In English and French, a word of this class consists of a stem preceded by zero or more derivational prefixes and followed by zero or more derivational suffixes. An inflectional suffix can be appended to the word. In German, a word consists of one or more stems preceded by zero or more derivational prefixes and followed zero or more derivational suffixes. An inflectional prefix and an inflectional suffix can be appended to the word (Table 5.21). As we saw earlier, these rules are general principles of concatenative morphology that have exceptions.

Table 5.21. Open class word morphology, where ⋆ denotes zero or more elements and ? denotes an optional element.

English and French	`prefix⋆ stem suffix⋆ inflection?`
German	`inflection? prefix⋆ stem⋆ suffix⋆ inflection?`

Ambiguity. Word lemmatization is often ambiguous. An isolated word can lead to several readings: several bases and morphemes, and in consequence several categories and features as exemplified in Table 5.22.

Lemmatization ambiguities are generally resolved using the word context in the sentence. Usually only one reading is syntactically or semantically possible, and others are not. The correct reading of a word's part of speech is determined considering the word's relations with the surrounding words and with the rest of the sentence. From a human perspective, this corresponds to determining the word's function in the sentence. As we saw in the introduction, this process has been done by genera-

Table 5.22. Lemmatization ambiguities.

	Words	Words in context	Lemmatization
English	*Run*		
		1. *A **run** in the forest*	1. **run**: noun singular
		2. *Sportsmen **run** everyday*	2. **run**: verb present third person plural
French	*Marche*		
		1. *Une **marche** dans la forêt*	1. **marche**: noun singular feminine
		2. *Il **marche** dans la cour*	2. **marcher**: verb present third person singular
German	*Lauf*		
		1. *Der **Lauf** der Zeit*	1. **Der Lauf**: noun, sing, masc
		2. ***Lauf** schnell!*	2. **laufen**: verb, imperative, singular

tions of pupils dating as far back as the schools of ancient Greece and the Roman Empire.

5.3.4 Language Differences

Paper lexicons do not include all the words of a language but only lemmas. Each lemma is fitted with a morphological class to relate it to a model of inflection or possible exceptions. A French verb will be given a class of conjugation or its exception pattern – one among a hundred. English or German verbs will be marked as regular or strong and in this latter case will be given their irregular forms. Then, a reader can apply morphological rules to produce all the lexical forms of the language.

Automatic morphological processing tries to mimic this human behavior. Nevertheless, it has not been so widely implemented in English as in other languages. Programmers have often preferred to pack all the English words into a single dictionary instead of implementing a parser to do the job. This strategy is possible for European languages because morphology is finite: there is a finite number of noun forms, adjective forms, or verb forms. It is clumsy, however, to extend it to languages other than English because it considerably inflates the size of dictionaries.

Statistics from Xerox (Table 5.23) show that techniques available for storing English words are very costly for many other languages. It is not a surprise that the most widespread morphological parser – KIMMO – was originally built for Finnish, one of the most inflection-rich languages. In addition, while English inflection is tractable by means of storing all the forms in a lexicon, it is often necessary to resort to a morphological parser to deal with forms such as: *computer, computerize, computerization, recomputerize* (Antworth 1994), which cannot all be foreseen by lexicographers.

Table 5.23. Some language statistics from a Xerox promotional flyer.

Language	Number of stems	Number of inflected forms	Lexicon size (kb)
English	55,000	240,000	200–300
French	50,000	5,700,000	200–300
German	50,000	350,000 or	450
		infinite (compounding)	
Japanese	130,000	200 suffixes	500
		20,000,000 word forms	500
Spanish	40,000	3,000,000	200–300

5.4 Morphological Parsing

5.4.1 Two-Level Model of Morphology

Using a memory expensive method, lemmatization can be accomplished with a lexicon containing all the words with all their possible inflections. A dictionary lookup yields then the lemma of each word in a text. Although it has often been used for English, this method is not very efficient for many other languages. We now introduce the two-level model of Kimmo Koskenniemi (1983), which is universal and has been adopted by many morphological parsers.

The two-level morphology model enables us to link the **surface form** of a word – the word as it is actually in a text – to its **lexical** or **underlying form** – its sequence of morphemes. Karttunen (1983) did the first implementation of this model, which he named KIMMO. A later implementation – PC-KIMMO 2 – was carried out by Antworth (1995) in C. PC-KIMMO 2 is available from the Summer Institute of Linguistics through the Internet.

Table 5.24 shows examples of correspondence between surface forms and lexical forms. Morpheme boundaries in lexical forms are denoted by +.

Table 5.24. Surface and lexical forms.

	Generation: Lexical to surface form →	
English	*dis+en+tangle+ed*	*disentangled*
	happy+er	*happier*
	move+ed	*moved*
French	*dés+em+brouiller+é*	*désembrouillé*
	dé+chanter+erons	*déchanterons*
German	*ent+wirren+end*	*entwirrend*
	wieder+ge+schreiben+en	*wiedergeschrieben*
	Parsing: ← Surface to lexical form	

In the two-level model, the mapping between the surface and lexical forms is synchronous. Both strings need to be aligned with a letter-for-letter correspondence.

That is, the first letter of the first form is mapped to the first letter of the second form, and so on. To maintain the alignment, possible null symbols are inserted in either form and are denoted ε or 0, if the Greek letters are not available. They reflect a letter deletion or insertion. Table 5.25 shows aligned surface and lexical forms.

Table 5.25. Correspondence between lexical and surface forms.

English	`dis+en+tangle+ed`	`happy+er`	`move+ed`
	↕ ⋯	↕ ⋯	↕ ⋯
	`dis0en0tangl00ed`	`happi0er`	`mov00ed`
French	`dé+chanter+erons`	`cheval+ux`	`cheviller+é`
	↕ ⋯	↕ ⋯	↕ ⋯
	`dé0chant000erons`	`cheva00ux`	`chevill000é`
German	`singen+st`	`Grund+¨e`	`Igel+Ø`
	↕ ⋯	↕ ⋯	↕ ⋯
	`singe00st`	`Gründ00e`	`Igel00`

5.4.2 Interpreting the Morphs

Considering inflection only, it is easier to interpret the morphological information using grammatical features rather than morphs. Most morphological parsers represent the lexical form as a concatenation of the stem and its features instead of morphs. For example, the Xerox parser output for *disentangle*, *happier*, and *Gründe* is:

```
disentangle+Verb+PastBoth+123SP
happy+Adj+Comp
Grund+Noun+Masc+Pl+NomAccGen
```

where the feature `+Verb` denotes a verb, `+PastBoth`, either past tense or past participle, and `+123SP` any person, singular or plural; `+Adj` denotes an adjective and `+Comp`, a comparative; `+Noun` denotes a noun, `+Masc` masculine, `+Pl`, plural, and `+NomAccGen` either nominative, accusative, or genitive. (All these forms are ambiguous, and the Xerox parser shows more than one interpretation per form.)

Given these new lexical forms, the parser has to align the feature symbols with letters or null symbols. The principles do not change, however (Fig. 5.5).

5.4.3 Finite-State Transducers

The two-level model is commonly implemented using finite-state transducers (FST). Transducers are automata that accept, translate, or generate pairs of strings. The arcs are labeled with two symbols: the first symbol is the input and the second is the output. The input symbol is transduced into the output symbol as a transition occurs on the arc. For instance, the transducer in Fig. 5.6 accepts or generates the string *abbbc* and translates into *zyyyx*.

Lexical	d	i	s	e	n	t	a	n	g	l	e	+Verb	+PastBoth	+123sp
Surface	d	i	s	e	n	t	a	n	g	l	0	0	e	d

Lexical	h	a	p	p	y	+Adj	+Comp
Surface	h	a	p	p	i	e	r

Lexical	G	r	u	n	d	+Noun	+Masc	+Pl	+NomAccGen
Surface	G	r	ü	n	d	0	0	0	e

Fig. 5.5. Alignments with features.

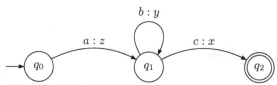

Fig. 5.6. A transducer.

Finite-state transducers have a formal definition, which is similar to that of finite-state automata. A FST consists of five components $(Q, \Sigma, q_0, F, \delta)$, where:

1. Q is a finite set of states.
2. Σ is a finite set of symbol or character pairs $i : o$, where i is a symbol of the input alphabet and o of the output alphabet. As we saw, both alphabets may include epsilon transitions.
3. q_0 is the start state, $q_0 \in Q$.
4. F is the set of final states, $F \subseteq Q$.
5. δ is the transition function $Q \times \Sigma \to Q$, where $\delta(q, i, o)$ returns the state where the automaton moves when it is in state q and consumes the input symbol pair $i : o$.

The quintuple, which defines the automaton in Fig. 5.6 is $Q = \{q_0, q_1, q_2\}$, $\Sigma = \{a : z, b : y, c : x\}$, $\delta = \{\delta(q_0, a : z) = q_1, \delta(q_1, b : y) = q_1, \delta(q_1, c : x) = q_2\}$, and $F = \{q_2\}$.

5.4.4 Conjugating a French Verb

Morphological FSTs encode the lexicon and express all the legal transitions. Arcs are labeled with pairs of symbols representing letters of the surface form – the word – and the lexical form – the set of morphs.

Table 5.26 shows the future tense of regular French verb *chanter*, where suffixes are specific to each person and number, but are shared by all the verbs of the so-called first group. The first group accounts for the large majority of French verbs. Table 5.27 shows the aligned forms and Fig. 5.7 the corresponding transducer. The arcs are annotated by the input/output pairs, where the left symbol corresponds to the lexical form and the right one to the surface form. When the lexical and surface characters are equal, as in c:c, we just use a single symbol in the arc.

Table 5.26. Future tense of French verb *chanter*.

Number\Person	First	Second	Third
singular	*chanterai*	*chanteras*	*chantera*
plural	*chanterons*	*chanterez*	*chanteront*

Table 5.27. Aligned lexical and surface forms.

Number\Pers.	First	Second	Third
singular	chanter+erai	chanter+eras	chanter+era
	chant000erai	chant000eras	chant000era
plural	chanter+erons	chanter+erez	chanter+eront
	chant000erons	chant000erez	chant000eront

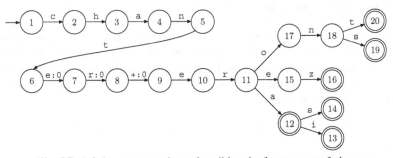

Fig. 5.7. A finite-state transducer describing the future tense of *chanter*.

This transducer can be generalized to any regular French verb of the first group by removing the stem part and inserting a self-looping transition on the first state (Fig. 5.8).

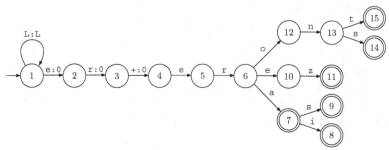

Fig. 5.8. A finite-state transducer describing the future tense of French verbs of the first group.

The transducer in Fig. 5.8 also parses and generates forms that do not exist. For instance, we can forge an imaginary French verb *palimoter* that still can be conjugated by the transducer. Conversely, the transducer will successfully parse the improbable *palimoterons*. This process is called overgeneration (both in parsing and generation).

Overgeneration is not that harmful provided that inputs are well formed. However, it can lead to some wrong parses. Consider English and German comparatives that are formed with -*er* suffix. Raw implementation of a comparative transducer would rightly parse *greater* as *great+er* but could also parse *better* or *reader*. Overgeneration is reduced by a lexical lookup, where the parse result is searched in a dictionary. This eliminates nonexistent words. It can also be limited by a set of constraints on affixes restricting the part of speech of the word to which they can be appended – here adjectives.

5.4.5 Prolog Implementation

Finite-state transducers can easily be implemented in Prolog. In this section, we implement the future tense of regular French verbs corresponding to Fig. 5.8, and we remove null symbols by inserting a mute transition in the surface form. The transducer has four parameters: the start state, normally 1, a final state, together with a lexical form and a surface one:

```
transduce(+Start, ?Final, ?Lexical, ?Surface).
```

The transducer parses surface forms:

```
?- transduce(1, Final, Lexical, [r, ê, v, e, r, a]).
  Final = 7,
  Lexical = [r, ê, v, e, r, +, e, r, a]
```

It also generates surface forms from lexical ones:

```
?- transduce(1, Final,
    [r, ê, v, e, r, +, e, r, e, z], Surface).
  Final = 11,
  Surface = [r, ê, v, e, r, e, z]
```

Finally, the transducer conjugates verbs (generates the verbal forms):

```
?- transduce(1, 11, [r, ê, v, e, r | L], Surface).
  L = [+, e, r, e, z],
  Surface = [r, ê, v, e, r, e, z]
```

Here is the Prolog code:

```
% arc(Start, End, LexicalChar, SurfaceChar)
%   describes the automaton

arc(1, 1, C, C) :- letter(C).
arc(1, 2, e, 0).    arc(2, 3, r, 0).    arc(3, 4, +, 0).
arc(4, 5, e, e).    arc(5, 6, r, r).    arc(6, 7, a, a).
arc(7, 8, i, i).    arc(7, 9, s, s).
arc(6, 10, e, e).   arc(10, 11, z, z).
arc(6, 12, o, o).   arc(12, 13, n, n).
arc(13, 14, s, s).  arc(13, 15, t, t).


% final_state(S)
%   gives the stop condition

final_state(7).    final_state(8).    final_state(9).
final_state(11).   final_state(14).   final_state(15).


% letter(+L)
%   describes the French lower-case letters

letter(L) :-
  name(L, [Code]),
  97 =< Code, Code =< 122, !.
letter(L) :-
  member(L,
    [à, â, ä, ç, é, è, ê, ë, î, ï, ô, ö, ù, û,
     ü, 'œ']),
  !.
```

```
% transduce(+Start, ?Final, ?LexicalString,
%    ?SurfaceString)
%  describes the transducer. The first and second
%  rules include mute transitions and
%  enable to remove 0s

transduce(Start, Final, [U | LexicalString],
     SurfaceString) :-
  arc(Start, Next, U, 0),
  transduce(Next, Final,LexicalString,SurfaceString).
transduce(Start, Final, LexicalString,
     [S | SurfaceString]) :-
  arc(Start, Next, 0, S),
  transduce(Next, Final,LexicalString,SurfaceString).
transduce(Start, Final, [U | LexicalString],
     [S | SurfaceString]) :-
  arc(Start, Next, U, S),
  U \== 0,
  S \== 0,
  transduce(Next, Final,LexicalString,SurfaceString).
transduce(Final, Final, [], []) :-
  final_state(Final).
```

We can associate a final state to a part of speech. For instance, state 11 corresponds to the second-person plural of the future.

5.4.6 Ambiguity

In the transducer for future tense, there is no ambiguity. That is, a surface form has only one lexical form with a unique final state. This is not the case with the present tense (Table 5.28), and

(je) chante 'I sing'
(il) chante 'he sings'

have the same surface form but correspond respectively to the first- and third-person singular.

Table 5.28. Present tense of French verb *chanter*.

Number\Person	First	Second	Third
singular	*chante*	*chantes*	*chante*
plural	*chantons*	*chantez*	*chantent*

This corresponds to the transducer in Fig. 5.9, where final states 5 and 7 are the same. The implementation in Prolog is similar to that of the future tense. Using backtracking, the transducer can yield all the final states reflecting the morphological ambiguity.

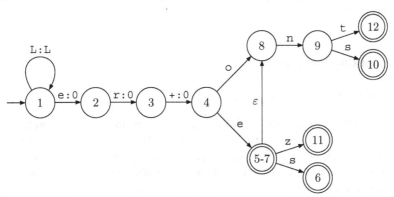

Fig. 5.9. A finite-state transducer encoding the present tense of verbs of the first group.

5.4.7 Operations on Finite-State Transducers

Finite-state transducers have mathematical properties similar to those of finite-state automata. In addition, they can be inverted and composed:

- Let T be transducer. The inversion T^{-1} reverses the input and output symbols of the transition function. The transition function of the transducer in Fig. 5.6 is then $\delta = \{\delta(q_0, z : a) = q_1, \delta(q_1, y : b) = q_1, \delta(q_1, x : c) = q_2\}$.
- Let T_1 and T_2 be two transducers. The composition $T_1 \circ T_2$ is a transducer, where the output of T_1 acts as the input of T_2.

Both the inversion and composition operations result in new transducers. This is obvious for the inversion. The proof is slightly more complex for the composition. Let $T_1 = (\Sigma, Q_1, q_1, F_1, \delta_1)$ and $T_2 = (\Sigma, Q_2, q_2, F_2, \delta_2)$ be two transducers. The composition $T_3 = T_1 \circ T_2$ is defined by $(\Sigma, Q_1 \times Q_2, \langle q_1, q_2 \rangle, F_1 \times F_2, \delta_3)$. The transition function δ_3 is built using the transition functions δ_1 and δ_2, and generating all the pairs where they interact (Kaplan and Kay 1994):

$$\delta_3(\langle s_1, s_2 \rangle, i, o) = \{\langle t_1, t_2 \rangle | \exists c \in \Sigma \cup \varepsilon, t_1 \in \delta_1(s_1, i, c) \wedge t_2 \in \delta_2(s_2, c, o)\}.$$

The inversion property enables transducers to operate in generating or parsing mode. They accept both surface and lexical strings. Each symbol of the first string is mapped to the symbol of the second string. So you can walk through the automaton and retrieve the lexical form from the surface form, or conversely, as we saw with the Prolog example.

Composition enables us to break down morphological phenomena. It is sometimes easier to formulate a solution then using intermediate forms between the surface and lexical forms. The correspondence between the word form and the sequence of morphemes is not direct but is obtained as a cascade of transductions. Composition enables us to compact the cascade and to replace the transducers involved in it by a single one (Karttunen et al. 1992). We will see an example of it with French irregular verbs in Sect. 5.5.3.

5.5 Morphological Rules

5.5.1 Two-Level Rules

Originally, Koskenniemi (1983) used declarative rules to describe morphology. These two-level rules enumerate the correspondences between lexical characters and surface ones and the context where they occur. Context corresponds to left and right characters of the current character and can often be expressed in terms of vowels (V) or consonants (C).

In the two-level formalism, a rule is made of a correspondence pair (`lexical:surface`), a rule operator, and the immediate left and right context. Operators can be $\Rightarrow$, $\Leftarrow$, $\Leftrightarrow$, or $/\Leftarrow$, and mean respectively only in that context, always in that context, always and only, and never in that context. Left and right contexts where the rule applies are separated by the symbol __ (Table 5.29).

Table 5.29. Two-level rules.

Rules	Description
`a:b` $\Rightarrow$ `lc __ rc`	a is transduced as b **only** when it has `lc` to the left and `rc` to the right
`a:b` $\Leftarrow$ `lc __ rc`	a is **always** transduced as b when it has `lc` to the left and `rc` to the right
`a:b` $\Leftrightarrow$ `lc __ rc`	a is transduced as b **always and only** when it has `lc` to the left and `rc` to the right
`a:b` $/\Leftarrow$ `lc __ rc`	a is **never** transduced as b when it has `lc` to the left and `rc` to the right

In English, the comparative *happier* is decomposed into two morphemes *happy + er*, where the lexical *y* corresponds to a surface *i* (Table 5.30). This correspondence occurs more generally when *y* is preceded by a consonant and followed by *-er*, *-ed*, or *-s*. This can be expressed by three rules, where C represents any consonant:

1. `y:i` $\Leftarrow$ `C:C __ +:0 e:e r:r`
2. `y:i` $\Leftarrow$ `C:C __ +:e s:s`
3. `y:i` $\Leftarrow$ `C:C __ +:0 e:e d:d`

Once written, all the rules are applied in parallel. This parallel application is the main distinctive feature of the two-level morphology compared with other, older models. This means that when processing a string, every rule must be successfully

Table 5.30. The y : i transduction rules.

Examples	happy+er	party+s	marry+ed
	happi0er	parties	marri0ed
Rules	Cy+er	Cy+s	Cy+ed
	Ci0er	Cies	Ci0ed

applied to the current pair of characters lexical:surface before moving to the next pair (Fig. 5.10).

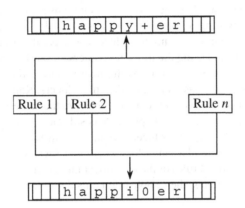

Fig. 5.10. Applying the rules in parallel.

The left and right contexts of a rule can use a wildcard, the ANY symbol @, which stands for any alphabetical character, as in

y:x ⇐ __ @:c

This rule means that a lexical y corresponds to a surface x when it is before a surface c. The corresponding lexical character in the right context is not specified in the rule, however, the unspecified character represented by the ANY symbol must be compatible with the correspondence rule that can apply to it. The ANY symbol is not, strictly speaking, any character then, but any character so that it forms a "feasible pair", here with c.

5.5.2 Rules and Finite-State Transducers

It has been demonstrated that any two-level rule can be compiled into an equivalent transducer (Johnson 1972, Kaplan and Kay 1994). Rule 1, for instance, corresponds to the automaton in Fig. 5.11, where the pair @:@ denotes any pair that cannot pass the other transitions.

In practice, morphological phenomena are easier to describe and to understand using individual rules rather than writing a complex transducer. For this reason, the

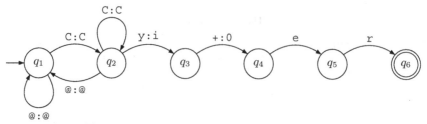

Fig. 5.11. A transducer to parse the y:i correspondence.

development of parsers based on the two-level method uses this strategy (Karttunen 1994). It consists in writing a collection of rules to model a language's morphology and compiling them into as many transducers. The parallel transducers are then combined into a single one using the transducer intersection (Fig. 5.12).

However, while the intersection of two finite automata defines a finite-state automaton, it is not always the case for finite-state transducers. Kaplan and Kay (1994) demonstrated that when surface and lexical pairs have the same length – without ε – the intersection is a transducer. This property is sufficient to intersect the rules in practical applications. In fact, transducers obtained from two-level rules are intersected by treating the ε symbol as an ordinary symbol (Beesley and Karttunen 2003, p. 55). Parallel application of rules or the transducer intersection removes one of their major harmful the side effects: their application outside of their intended context.

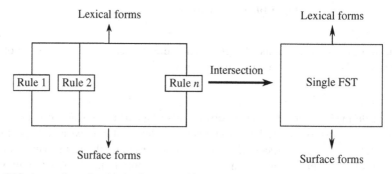

Fig. 5.12. A set of two-level rules intersected into a single FST. After Karttunen et al. (1992).

Originally, rules were compiled by hand. However, this problem can quickly become intractable, especially when it comes to managing conflicting rules or when rule contexts interfere with transduced symbols. To solve it, we can use a compiler that creates transducers automatically from two-level rules. The Xerox XFST is an example of it. It is a publicly available tool, and to date it is the only serious implementation of a morphological rule compiler.

5.5.3 Rule Composition: An Example with French Irregular Verbs

When developing a complete morphological parser, it is often convenient to introduce intermediate levels between the lexical and surface strings. This is especially true when the lexical and surface forms are distant and involve complex morphological relations. Intermediate levels enable us then to decompose the morphological system into smaller parts that are easier to treat.

Chanod (1994) gives an example of decomposition with the notoriously difficult morphology of French irregular verbs (Bescherelle 1980). The French verb system has about 100 models of inflection – paradigms. Two of them are said to be regular, the first and second group, and gather the vast majority of the verbs. The third group is made of irregular verbs and gathers the rest. The irregular group contains the most frequent verbs: *faire* 'do', *savoir* 'know', *connaître* 'know', *dormir* 'sleep', *courir* 'run', *battre* 'beat', *écrire* 'write', etc.

Table 5.31 shows the conjugation of some irregular verbs. We can see that there is a set of regular suffixes: *s*, *s*, *t*, *ons*, *ez*, and *ent*, and that most irregularities, also called alternations, occur at the junction of the stem and the suffix. The stem and suffix can be directly concatenated, as in *courir*, but not in *dormir*, *peindre*, or *battre*.

Table 5.31. Conjugation of irregular French verbs, present tense. *Courir* has regular suffixes in underlined bold characters. In the other verbs, irregular infections are shown in bold characters.

Infinitive	courir	dormir	battre	peindre	écrire
First person singular	cour**s**	**dors**	**bats**	**peins**	écris
Second person singular	cour**s**	**dors**	**bats**	**peins**	écris
Third person singular	cour**t**	**dort**	**bat**	**peint**	écrit
First person plural	cour**ons**	dormons	battons	peignons	**écrivons**
Second person plural	cour**ez**	dormez	battez	peignez	**écrivez**
Third person plural	cour**ent**	dorment	battent	peignent	**écrivent**

Although apparently complex, general rules can model these alternations using local contexts corresponding to specific substrings. In the case of *dormir*, a general principle in French makes it impossible to have an *m* followed by an *s* or *t*. It then must be deleted in the three singular persons. For *battre*, the pairs *tt* or *dt* do not occur in the end of a word or before a final *s*. Such rules are not tied to one specific verb but can be applied across a variety of inflection paradigms and persons. Figure 5.5.3 shows the rule sequence that produces the correct surface form of *dors*.

The verbs *peindre* and *écrire* are more complex cases because their conjugation uses two stems: *pein* and *peign* – *écri* and *écriv*. Chanod (1994) solves these difficulties using a transduction between the infinitive and a first intermediate form that will then be regular. Then *peindre*+IndP+SG+P1 is associated to *peign*+IndP+SG+P1, and *écrire*+IndP+SG+P1 to *écriv*+IndP+SG+P1. The second intermediate form uses two-level rules to obtain the correct surface forms: *v* or *gn* must be followed by a vowel or deleted (Fig. 5.5.3). The rule that Chanod uses is, in fact:

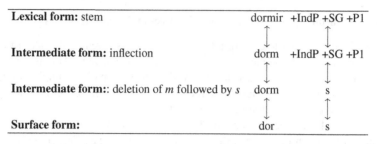

Fig. 5.13. Sequence of rules applied to *dormir*. After Chanod (1994).

$$\mathtt{n:0 \Leftrightarrow g \_\_ [s|t]}$$

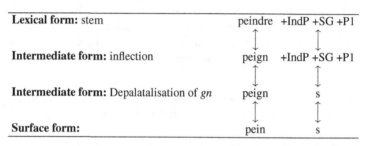

Fig. 5.14. Sequence of rules applied to *peindre*. After Chanod (1994).

The FST resulting from the surface, lexical, and intermediate levels are ultimately combined with the lexicon and composed into a single transducer (Fig. 5.15).

5.6 Application Examples

The Xerox language tools give a good example of what morphological parsers and part-of-speech taggers can do. These parsers are available for demonstration on the Internet using a Web browser. Xerox tools let you enter English, French, German, Italian, Portuguese, and Spanish words, and the server returns the context-free morphological analysis for each term (Tables 5.32–5.34). You can also type in phrases or sentences and Xerox taggers will disambiguate their part of speech. In addition to demonstrations, Xerox lists examples of industrial applications that make use of its tools.

5.7 Further Reading

Dionysius Thrax fixed the parts of speech for Greek in the 2nd century BCE. They have not changed since and his grammar is still interesting to read, see Lallot (1998).

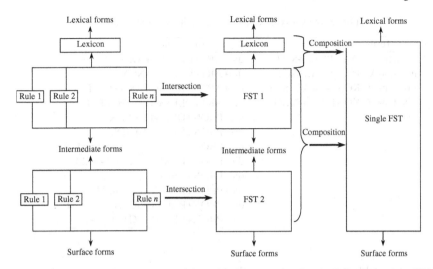

Fig. 5.15. Intersection and composition of finite-state transducers. After Karttunen (1994).

Table 5.32. Xerox morphological parsing in English.

Input Term(s): works	Input Term(s): round	Input Term(s): this
work+Vsg3	round+Vb	this+Psg
work+Npl	round+Prep	this+Dsg
	round+Adv	this+Adv
	round+Adj	
	round+Nsg	

Table 5.33. Xerox morphological parsing in French.

Input Term(s): <'>etions	Input Term(s): porte
étions 1	porte 6
être+IndI+PL+P1+Verb	porter+SubjP+SG+P1+Verb
	porter+SubjP+SG+P3+Verb
	porter+Imp+SG+P2+Verb
	porter+IndP+SG+P1+Verb
	porter+IndP+SG+P3+Verb
	porte+Fem+SG+Noun

Table 5.34. Xerox morphological parsing in German.

Input Term(s): arbeite	Input Term(s): die
arbeiten+V+IMP+PRÄS+SG2	die+ART+DEF+PL+AKK
arbeiten+V+IND+PRÄS+SG1	die+ART+DEF+PL+NOM
arbeiten+V+KONJ+PRÄS+SG1	die+ART+DEF+SG+AKK+FEM
arbeiten+V+KONJ+PRÄS+SG3	die+ART+DEF+SG+NOM+FEM
	die+PRON+DEM+PL+AKK
	die+PRON+DEM+PL+NOM
	die+PRON+DEM+SG+AKK+FEM
	die+PRON+DEM+SG+NOM+FEM
	die+PRON+RELAT+PL+AKK
	die+PRON+RELAT+PL+NOM
	die+PRON+RELAT+SG+AKK+FEM
	die+PRON+RELAT+SG+NOM+FEM

A short and readable introduction in French to the history of parts of speech is Ducrot (1995).

Accounts on finite-state morphology can be found in Sproat (1992) and Ritchie et al. (1992). Roche and Schabes (1997) is useful book that describes fundamental algorithms and applications of finite-state machines in language processing, especially for French. Kornai (1999) covers other aspects and languages. Kiraz (2001) on the morphology of Semitic languages: Syriac, Arabic, and Hebrew. Beesley and Karttunen (2003) is an extensive description of the two-level model in relation with the Xerox tools. It contains a CD-ROM with the Xerox rule compiler.

Antworth (1995) provides a free implementation of KIMMO named PC-KIMMO 2 with source and executable programs. The system is available from the Internet (http://www.sil.org). It comes with an English lexicon and English morphological rules. It is open to extensions and modifications. General-purpose finite-state transducers toolkits are also available. They include the FSA utilities (van Noord and Gerdemann 2001), the FSM library (Mohri et al. 1998), and Unitex (http://www-igm.univ-mlv.fr/~unitex/).

Exercises

5.1. Find a dictionary on the Web in English, French, German, or another language you would like to study and extract all the articles, conjunctions, prepositions, and pronouns.

5.2. Implement a morphological parser to analyze regular plurals of nouns in English or French.

5.3. Add a lexical look-up to Exercise 5.2.

5.4. Implement a morphological parser to analyze plurals of nouns in English or French, taking a list of exceptions into account.

5.5. Implement a morphological parser to analyze regular preterits of verbs in English or German.

5.6. Implement a morphological parser to conjugate French verbs of first group in the imperfect tense.

5.7. Implement a morphological parser to conjugate regular German verbs in the present tense.

5.8. Build a morphological parser implementing regular English verb inflection: *-s*, *-ed*, *-ing*.

5.9. Some verbs have their final *-e* deleted, for instance, *chase* (*chase+ed, chase+ing*). In the KIMMO formalism, the *-e* deletion rule is expressed as e:0 ⇔ C:C __ 0:+ V:V. Draw the corresponding transducer and write the Prolog rules that will parse these verbs.

5.10. Break the following words into morphemes: *computer*: *computers, computerize, computerization, recomputerize*.

5.11. Build a morphological parser that will parse words derived from *computer*: *computers, computerize, computerization, recomputerize*.

5.12. Break the following words into morphemes: *chanter*: *enchanter, rechanter, déchanter, désenchanter*.

5.13. Build a morphological parser that will parse words derived from *chanter*: *enchanter, rechanter, déchanter*, and *désenchanter*.

6

Part-of-Speech Tagging Using Rules

6.1 Resolving Part-of-Speech Ambiguity

6.1.1 A Manual Method

We saw that looking up a word in a lexicon or carrying out a morphological analysis on it can leave it with an ambiguous part of speech. The word *chair*, which can be assigned two tags, noun or verb, is an example of ambiguity. It is a noun in the phrase *a chair*, and a verb in *to chair a session*. Ambiguity resolution, that is, retaining only one part of speech (POS) and discarding the others, is generally referred to as POS tagging or POS annotation.

As children we learned to carry out a manual disambiguation by considering the grammatical context of the word. In the first phrase, *chair* is preceded by an article and therefore is part of a noun phrase. Since there is no other word here, *chair* is a noun. In the second phrase, *chair* is preceded by *to*, which would not precede a noun, and therefore is a verb.

Voutilainen and Järvinen (1995) describe a more complex example with the sentence

That round table might collapse.

While the correct part-of-speech tagging is:

That/determiner *round*/adjective *table*/noun *might*/modal verb *collapse*/verb.

a simple dictionary lookup or a morphological analysis produces many ambiguities, as shown in Table 6.1.

6.1.2 Which Method to Use to Automatically Assign Parts of Speech

Grammatical constraints are not always sufficient to resolve ambiguous tags. Church and Mercer (1993) exemplify this with the phrase *I see a bird*, which can be annotated as

Table 6.1. Ambiguities in part-of-speech annotation with the sentence: *That round table might collapse.*

Words	Possible tags	Example of use
that	Subordinating conjunction	*That he can swim is good*
	Determiner	*That white table*
	Adverb	*It is not that easy*
	Pronoun	*That is the table*
	Relative pronoun	*The table that collapsed*
round	Verb	*Round up the usual suspects*
	Preposition	*Turn round the corner*
	Noun	*A big round*
	Adjective	*A round box*
	Adverb	*He went round*
table	Noun	*That white table*
	Verb	*I table that*
might	Noun	*The might of the wind*
	Modal verb	*She might come*
collapse	Noun	*The collapse of the empire*
	Verb	*The empire can collapse*

I/noun *see*/noun *a*/noun *bird*/noun

This tagging corresponds to: *I*/letter of alphabet, *see*/noun as in *Holy See*, *a*/letter of alphabet, *bird*/noun. Although, this tag sequence makes no sense here, it cannot be ruled out as syntactically ill formed, because the parser must accept sequences of four nouns in other situations, as in *city school committee meeting*. The proper tagging is, of course, *I*/pronoun *see*/verb *a*/article *bird*/noun.

Semantic rules could implement common-sense reasoning and prevent inconsistencies. However, this method is no longer favored. It would imply writing many rules that could operate in very specific applications, and not on unrestricted texts.

Instead of using general grammar rules, we can consider word preferences. Most words taken from a dictionary have only one part of speech or have a strong preference for only one of them, although frequent words tend to be more ambiguous. From text statistics based on different corpora, in English and in French, Merialdo (1994) and Vergne (1999) report that 50% to 60% of words have a unique possible tag and 15% to 25% have only two tags. In both languages, tagging a word with its most common part of speech yields a success rate of more than 75%. Charniak (1993) reports a score of more than 90% for English. This figure is called the **base-line**. It corresponds to the accuracy obtained with a minimal algorithm, here the word annotation with its most frequent tag.

Two efficient methods applied locally have emerged to improve this figure and to solve reasonably well POS tagging. The first one uses rule-based constraints. Rules consider the left and right context of the word to disambiguate, that is, either discard or replace a wrong part of speech. Rules are symbolic and can be designed by hand or derived automatically from hand-annotated corpora.

The second method is based on statistics. Sequence statistics are automatically learned from hand-annotated corpora, and probabilistic models are applied that assign the most likely tags to words of a sentence. Both methods enable to tag successfully more than 95% of the words of a text. We will describe the first one in this chapter and the second one in the next chapter.

6.2 Tagging with Rules

Part-of-speech tagging with rules is relatively old (Klein and Simmons 1963). In the beginning, rules were hand-coded and yielded good results at the expense of thoroughly and painfully crafting the rules (Voutilainen el al. 1992). The field has been completely renewed by Brill (1995), who proposed a very simple scheme to tag a text with rules and an algorithm to learn automatically the rules from annotated corpora. A good deal of the current work on part-of-speech tagging with rules is now inspired by his foundational work.

6.2.1 Brill's Tagger

Brill's tagger uses a dictionary and assumes that it contains all the words to tag. Each word in the dictionary is labeled with its most likely (frequent) part of speech and includes the list of its other legal – possible – parts of speech. Part-of-speech distributions and statistics for each word can be derived from annotated corpora and using methods described in Chaps. 2 and 4.

The tagger first assigns each word with its most likely part of speech. It does not depend on a morphological parser, although it could use one as a preprocessor. It also features a module to tag unknown words that we will examine in Sect. 6.3. Examples of likely tags assigned to words are given in Table 6.2.

Table 6.2. Initial step of Brill's algorithm.

	Likely tags yielding a correct tagging	Likely tags yielding a wrong tagging
English	*I*/pro *can*/modal *see*/verb *a*/art *bird*/noun	*The*/art *can*/**modal** *rusted*/verb
French	*Je*/pro *donne*/verb *le*/art *cadeau*/noun	*Je*/pro *le*/**art** *fais*/verb *demain*/adv
German	*Der*/art *Mann*/noun *kommt*/verb	*Wer*/pro *ist*/verb *der*/art *Mann*/noun , *der*/**art** *kommt*/verb *?*

The tagger then applies a list of transformations to alter the initial tagging. Transformations are contextual rules that rewrite a word tag into a new one. The transformation is performed only if the new tag of the word is legal – is in the dictionary. If so, the word is assigned the new tag. Transformations are executed sequentially and each transformation is applied to the text from left to right. Examples of transformations are:

1. In English: Change the tag from modal to noun if the previous word is an article.
2. In French: Change the tag from article to pronoun if the previous word is a pronoun.
3. In German: Change the tag from article to pronoun if the previous word is a noun (or a comma.)

These rules applied to the sentences in Table 6.2 yield:

1. In English: *The*/art *can*/noun *rusted*/verb
2. In French: *Je*/pro *le*/pro *fais*/verb *demain*/adv
3. In German: *Wer*/pro *ist*/verb *der*/art *Mann*/noun , *der*/pro *kommt*/verb ?

Rules conform to a limited number of transformation types, called templates. For example, the rule

Change the tag from modal to noun if the previous word is an article.

corresponds to template:

Change the tag from X to Y if the previous tag is Z.

The tagger uses in total 11 templates shown in Table 6.3. Brill reports that less than 500 rules – instantiated templates – are needed in English to obtain an accuracy of 97%.

Table 6.3. Contextual rule templates, where A, B, C, and D denotes parts of speech, members of the POS tagset.

Rules	Explanation
alter(A, B, prevtag(C))	Change A to B if preceding tag is C
alter(A, B, nexttag(C))	Change A to B if the following tag is C
alter(A, B, prev2tag(C))	Change A to B if tag two before is C
alter(A, B, next2tag(C))	Change A to B if tag two after is C
alter(A, B, prev1or2tag(C))	Change A to B if one of the two preceding tags is C
alter(A, B, next1or2tag(C))	Change A to B if one of the two following tags is C
alter(A, B, prev1or2or3tag(C))	Change A to B if one of the three preceding tags is C
alter(A, B, next1or2or3tag(C))	Change A to B if one of the three following tags is C
alter(A, B, surroundingtag(C, D))	Change A to B if surrounding tags are C and D
alter(A, B, nextbigram(C, D))	Change A to B if next bigram tag is C D
alter(A, B, prevbigram(C, D))	Change A to B if previous bigram tag is C D

6.2.2 Implementation in Prolog

We will exemplify the tagging algorithm with an implementation of two rule templates:

```
alter(A, B, prevtag(C))
alter(A, B, prev1or2tag(C))
```

These rules being instantiated under the form of:

```
alter(verb, noun, prevtag(art)).
alter(verb, noun, prev1or2tag(art)).
```

The first rule changes the tag from `verb` to `noun` if the previous word is an `article`, and the second changes the tag from `verb` to `noun` if one of the two previous words is an `article`. The second rule is more general that the first one. We give the code of the first one because it is easier to start with it.

The `tag` predicate enables us to alter an initially tagged text:

```
?- tag([the/art, holy/adj, see/verb], L).
L = [the/art, holy/adj, see/noun]

% tag(+InitialTaggedText, -TaggedText)
% Implementation of Brill's algorithm

tag(InitialTaggedText, TaggedText) :-
  bagof(alter(FromPOS, ToPOS, Condition),
    alter(FromPOS, ToPOS, Condition), Rules),
  forall(Rules, InitialTaggedText, TaggedText).

% Collect all the rules and apply them sequentially

forall([Rule | Rules], Text, TaggedText) :-
  apply(Rule, Text, AlteredText),
  forall(Rules, AlteredText, TaggedText).
forall([], TaggedText, TaggedText).

%Apply prevtag template
apply(alter(FromPOS, ToPOS, prevtag(POS)),
  [PrevWord/POS, Word/FromPOS | RemainingText],
  [PrevWord/POS, Word/ToPOS | RemainingText1] ) :-
  !,
  apply(alter(FromPOS, ToPOS, prevtag(POS)),
    [Word/ToPOS | RemainingText],
    [Word/ToPOS | RemainingText1] ).
apply(alter(FromPOS, ToPOS, prevtag(POS)),
  [X, Y| RemainingText], [X, Y| RemainingText1] ) :-
```

```
    apply(alter(FromPOS, ToPOS, prevtag(POS)),
       [Y| RemainingText], [Y | RemainingText1] ).
apply(alter(_, _, prevtag(_)), [X], [X]).

% Apply prev1or2tag template
% The first two rules take into account that the rule
% can apply to the second word of the text
apply(alter(FromPOS, ToPOS, prev1or2tag(POS)),
    [FirstWord/POS, Word/FromPOS | RemainingText],
    [FirstWord/POS, Word/ToPOS | RemainingText1] ) :-
    apply_aux(alter(FromPOS, ToPOS, prev1or2tag(POS)),
       [FirstWord/POS, Word/ToPOS | RemainingText],
       [FirstWord/POS, Word/ToPOS | RemainingText1] ).
apply(alter(FromPOS, ToPOS, prev1or2tag(POS)),
    [X, Y| RemainingText], [X, Y| RemainingText1] ) :-
    apply_aux(alter(FromPOS, ToPOS, prev1or2tag(POS)),
       [X, Y| RemainingText], [X, Y| RemainingText1] ).

apply_aux(alter(FromPOS, ToPOS, prev1or2tag(POS)),
    [Prev2Word/POS, Prev1Word/POS1, Word/FromPOS |
     RemainingText],
    [Prev2Word/POS, Prev1Word/POS1, Word/ToPOS |
     RemainingText1] ) :-
    !,
    apply_aux(alter(FromPOS, ToPOS, prev1or2tag(POS)),
       [Prev1Word/POS1, Word/ToPOS | RemainingText],
       [Prev1Word/POS1, Word/ToPOS | RemainingText1] ).
apply_aux(alter(FromPOS, ToPOS, prev1or2tag(POS)),
    [Prev2Word/POS2, Prev1Word/POS, Word/FromPOS |
     RemainingText], [Prev2Word/POS2, Prev1Word/POS,
     Word/ToPOS | RemainingText1] ) :-
    !,
    apply_aux(alter(FromPOS, ToPOS, prev1or2tag(POS)),
       [Prev1Word/POS, Word/ToPOS | RemainingText],
       [Prev1Word/POS, Word/ToPOS | RemainingText1] ).
apply_aux(alter(FromPOS, ToPOS, prev1or2tag(POS)),
    [X, Y, Z | RemainingText],
    [X, Y, Z| RemainingText1] ) :-
    apply_aux(alter(FromPOS, ToPOS, prev1or2tag(POS)),
       [Y, Z| RemainingText], [Y, Z | RemainingText1] ).
apply_aux(alter(FromPOS, ToPOS, prev1or2tag(POS)),
    [PrevWord/POS, Word/FromPOS],
       [PrevWord/POS, Word/ToPOS]).
apply_aux(alter(_, _, prev1or2tag(_)), [X,Y], [X,Y]).
```

```
%The ordered contextual rules
alter(verb, noun, prevtag(art)).
alter(verb, noun, prev1or2tag(art)).
```

6.2.3 Deriving Rules Automatically

One of the most interesting features of Brill's rules is that they can be learned automatically from a hand-annotated corpus. This type of algorithm is called transformation-based learning (TBL). Let us denote *Corpus* this corpus and *AnnotationReference* its hand-annotation. In the context, the hand-annotation is often called the **Gold Standard**.

The TBL algorithm first assigns the most likely (frequent) tag to each word. It produces errors, and all rules templates are instantiated for each tagging error measured against *AnnotationReference*. The rule that yields the greatest error reduction is selected and applied to alter the *Corpus* tagging. This process is iterated as long as the annotation results are not close enough to *AnnotationReference*.

Table 6.4 shows the steps of the algorithm. *Corpus* annotated at iteration i of the process is denoted *AnnotatedCorpus(i)*. Each iteration enables us to derive a new rule, which is denoted *Rule(i)*.

Table 6.4. Brill's learning algorithm.

St.	Operation	Input	Output
1.	Annotate each word of the corpus with its most likely part of speech	*Corpus*	*AnnotatedCorpus(1)*
2.	Compare pairwise the part of speech of each word of the *AnnotationReference* and *AnnotatedCorpus(i)*	*AnnotationReference* *AnnotatedCorpus(i)*	List of errors
3.	For each error, instantiate the rule templates to correct the error	List of errors	List of tentative rules
4.	For each instantiated rule, compute on *AnnotatedCorpus(i)* the number of good transformations minus the number of bad transformations the rule yields	*AnnotatedCorpus(i)* Tentative rules	Scored tentative rules
5.	Select the rule that has the greatest error reduction and append it to the ordered list of transformations	Tentative rules	*Rule(i)*
6.	Apply *Rule(i)* to *AnnotatedCorpus(i)*	*AnnotatedCorpus(i)* *Rule(i)*	*AnnotatedCorpus(i+1)*
7.	If number of errors is under predefined threshold, end the algorithm else go to step 2.	–	List of rules

As hand-annotated corpus, Brill (1995) used the Penn Treebank (Marcus et al. 1993). Table 6.5 lists the five most productive rules that the algorithm learned from the *Wall Street Journal* annotated section of the corpus (Brill 1995).

Table 6.5. The five first transformations learned from the *Wall Street Journal* corpus (Brill 1995), where NN is a singular noun; VB is a verb, base form; TO is the word *to*; VBP is a verb, non-third person singular present; MD is a modal; DT is a determiner; VBD is a verb, past tense; and VBZ is a verb, third-person singular present. These tags are defined by the Penn Treebank, and Sect. 6.4.2 details the complete tagset.

	Change		
#	From	To	Condition
1	NN	VB	Previous tag is TO
2	VBP	VB	One of the previous three tags is MD
3	NN	VB	One of the previous two tags is MD
4	VB	NN	One of the previous two tags is DT
5	VBD	VBN	One of the previous three tags is VBZ

6.2.4 Confusion Matrices

At each iteration of TBL algorithm, we can derive a confusion matrix that shows for each tag how many times a word has been wrongly labeled. Table 6.6 shows an example of it (Franz 1996), which enables us to understand and track errors. Again, parts of speech use the Penn Treebank tagset described in Sect. 6.4.2. The diagonal shows the breakdown of the tags correctly assigned, for example, 99.4% for determiners (DT). The rest of the table shows the tags wrongly assigned, i.e. for determiners: 0.3% to prepositions (IN) and 0.3% to adverbs (RB). This table is only an excerpt, therefore the sum of rows and columns is not equal to 100.

6.3 Unknown Words

We have made the assumption of a finite vocabulary. This is never the case in practice. Many words will likely be absent from the dictionary: proper and common nouns, verbs, adjectives, or adverbs.

There is no standard technique to deal with the unknown words. The baseline is to tag unknown words as nouns since it is the most frequent part of speech. Another technique is to use suffixes. Brill (1995) proposes a combination of both to extend the transformation-based algorithm. The initial step tags unknown words as proper nouns for capitalized words and as common nouns for the rest. Then it applies transformations from a set of predefined templates: change the tag of an unknown word from X to Y if:

Table 6.6. A confusion matrix. The first column corresponds to the correct tags, and for each tag, the rows give the assigned tags. Excerpt from Franz (1996, p. 124). IN is a preposition, RB is an adverb, JJ is an adjective, RP is a particle, VBG is a verb, gerund (complete tagset in Sect. 6.4.2).

↓Correct	Tagger →									
	DT	IN	JJ	NN	RB	RP	VB	VBD	VBG	VBN
DT	99.4	0.3	–	–	0.3	–	–	–	–	–
IN	0.4	97.5	–	–	1.5	0.5	–	–	–	–
JJ	–	0.1	93.9	1.8	0.9	–	0.1	0.1	0.4	1.5
NN	–	–	2.2	95.5	–	–	0.2	–	0.4	–
RB	0.2	2.4	2.2	0.6	93.2	1.2	–	–	–	–
RP	–	24.7	–	1.1	12.6	61.5	–	–	–	–
VB	–	–	0.3	1.4	–	–	96.0	–	–	0.2
VBD	–	–	0.3	–	–	–	–	94.6	–	4.8
VBG	–	–	2.5	4.4	–	–	–	–	93.0	–
VBN	–	–	4.6	–	–	–	–	4.3	–	90.6

1. Deleting the prefix (suffix) x, $|x| \leq 4$, results in a word (x is any string of length 1 to 4).
2. The first (last) (1, 2, 3, 4) characters of the word are x.
3. Adding the character string x as a prefix (suffix) results in a word.
4. Word w ever appears immediately to the left (right) of the word.
5. Character z appears in the word.

These templates are specific to English, but they can easily be modified to accommodate other European languages. Table 6.7 shows the first five transformations learned from the *Wall Street Journal* corpus.

Table 6.7. The first five transformations for unknown words (Brill 1995), where NN is a noun, singular; NNS a noun, plural; CD cardinal number; JJ an adjective; VBN a verb, past participle; VBG a verb, gerund (complete tagset in Sect. 6.4.2).

#	Change From	To	Condition
1	NN	NNS	Has suffix **s**
2	NN	CD	Has character **.**
3	NN	JJ	Has character **-**
4	NN	VBN	Has suffix **ed**
5	NN	VBG	Has suffix **ing**

6.4 Standardized Part-of-Speech Tagsets

While basic parts of speech are relatively well defined: determiners, nouns, pronouns, adjectives, verbs, auxiliaries, adverbs, conjunctions, and prepositions, there is a debate on how to standardize them for a computational analysis. One issue is the level of detail. Some tagsets feature a dozen tags, some over a hundred. Another issue that is linked to the latter and is that of subcategories. How many classes for verbs? Only one or should we create auxiliaries, modal, gerund, intransitive, transitive verbs, etc.?

The debate becomes even more complicated when we consider multiple languages. In French and German, the main parts of speech can be divided into subclasses depending on their gender, case, and number. In English, these divisions are useless. Although it is sometimes possible to map tagsets from one language to another, there is no universal scheme, even within the same language.

A few years ago, many computational linguists had a personal tagset. There are now standards, but the discussion is not over. We will examine here a multilingual part-of-speech scheme (MULTEXT), a widely accepted tagset for English (the Penn Treebank), and a tagset for Swedish.

6.4.1 Multilingual Part-of-Speech Tags

Building a multilingual tagset imposes the condition of having a set of common classes, which enables a comparison between languages. These classes correspond to traditional parts of speech and gather a relatively large consensus among European languages. However, they are not sufficiently accurate for any language in particular. Dermatas and Kokkinakis (1995) retained the traditional parts of speech to tag texts in seven European languages using statistical methods. They also added features (subcategories) specific to each language (Table 6.8).

Table 6.8. Parts of speech and grammatical features.

Main parts of speech	Features (subcategories)
Adjective, noun, pronoun	Regular base comparative superlative interrogative person number case
Adverb	Regular base comparative superlative interrogative
Article, determiner, preposition	Person case number
Verb	Tense voice mood person number case

MULTEXT (Ide and Véronis 1995) is a multinational initiative that aims at providing an annotation scheme for all the Western and Eastern European languages. MULTEXT also retains the traditional parts of speech (Table 6.9) that are common to all languages and complements them by a set of features, which they call attributes. Attributes enable us to subcategorize words and reconcile specific features of different European languages. Attributes for nouns and verbs are shown in Tables 6.10 and 6.11.

MULTEXT attributes concern only the morpho-syntactic layer and represent a superset of what is needed by all the languages. Some attributes may not be relevant for a specific language. For instance, English nouns have no gender, and French ones have no case. In addition, applications may not make use of some of the attributes even if they are part of the language. Tense, for instance, may be useless for some applications.

Table 6.9. MULTEXT's main parts of speech.

Part of speech	Code
Noun	N
Verb	V
Adjective	A
Pronoun	P
Determiner	D
Adverb	R
Adposition (Preposition)	S
Conjunction	C
Numeral	M
Interjection	I
Residual	X

Table 6.10. Features (attributes) and values for nouns.

Position	Attribute	Value	Code
1	Type	Common	c
		Proper	p
2	Gender	Masculine	m
		Feminine	f
		Neuter	n
3	Number	Singular	s
		Plural	p
4	Case	Nominative	n
		Genitive	g
		Dative	d
		Accusative	a

A part-of-speech tag is a string where the first character is the main class of the word to annotate and then a sequence of attribute values. Attribute positions correspond to their rank in the table, such as those defined in Tables 6.10 and 6.11 for nouns and verbs. When an attribute is not applicable, it is replaced by a dash (-). An English noun could receive the tag:

```
N[type=common number=singular] Nc-s-
```

Table 6.11. Attributes (features) and values for verbs.

Position	Attribute	Value	Code
1	Type	Main	m
		Auxiliary	a
		Modal	o
2	Mood/form	Indicative	i
		Subjunctive	s
		Imperative	m
		Conditional	c
		Infinitive	i
		Participle	p
		Gerund	g
		Supine	s
3	Tense	Base	b
		Present	p
		Imperfect	i
		Future	f
		Past	s
4	Person	First	1
		Second	2
		Third	3
5	Number	Singular	s
		Plural	p
6	Gender	Masculine	m
		Feminine	f
		Neuter	n

a French one:

    N[type=common gender=masculine number=singular] Ncms-

and a German one:

    N[type=common gender=neuter number=singular
       case=nominative] Ncnsn

A user can extend the coding scheme and add attributes if the application requires it. A noun could be tagged with some semantic features such as country names, currencies, etc.

6.4.2 Parts of Speech for English

The Penn Treebank is a large corpus of texts annotated with part-of-speech and syntactic tags (Marcus et al. 1993). The Penn Treebank part-of-speech tagset features 48 tags (Table 6.12).

Unlike MULTEXT, the Penn Treebank tagset concerns only English and shows little possibility of being adapted to another language. However, it is now widely established in the North American language processing community and in industry. Lancaster University (UK) has defined another important tagset for English.

Table 6.12. The Penn Treebank tagset.

1.	CC	Coordinating conjunction	25.	TO	*to*
2.	CD	Cardinal number	26.	UH	Interjection
3.	DT	Determiner	27.	VB	Verb, base form
4.	EX	Existential *there*	28.	VBD	Verb, past tense
5.	FW	Foreign word	29.	VBG	Verb, gerund/present participle
6.	IN	Preposition/sub. conjunction	30.	VBN	Verb, past participle
7.	JJ	Adjective	31.	VBP	Verb, non-third pers. sing. pres.
8	JJR	Adjective, comparative	32.	VBZ	Verb, third-pers. sing. present
9.	JJS	Adjective, superlative	33.	WDT	*wh*-determiner
10.	LS	List item marker	34.	WP	*wh*-pronoun
11.	MD	Modal	35.	WP$	Possessive *wh*-pronoun
12.	NN	Noun, singular or mass	36.	WRB	*wh*-adverb
13.	NNS	Noun, plural	37.	#	Pound sign
14.	NNP	Proper noun, singular	38.	$	Dollar sign
15.	NNPS	Proper noun, plural	39.	.	Sentence final punctuation
16.	PDT	Predeterminer	40.	,	Comma
17.	POS	Possessive ending	41.	:	Colon, semicolon
18.	PRP	Personal pronoun	42.	(	Left bracket character
19.	PP$	Possessive pronoun	43.	)	Right bracket character
20.	RB	Adverb	44.	"	Straight double quote
21.	RBR	Adverb, comparative	45.	'	Left open single quote
22.	RBS	Adverb, superlative	46.	"	Left open double quote
23.	RP	Particle	47.	'	Right close single quote
24.	SYM	Symbol	48.	"	Right close double quote

Figure 6.1 shows an annotated excerpt from the Penn Treebank. The Penn Treebank team proceeded in two steps to annotate their corpus. They first tagged the texts with an automatic stochastic tagger. They then reviewed and manually corrected the annotation.

Battle-tested/JJ industrial/JJ managers/NNS here/RB always/RB buck/VBP up/RP nervous/JJ newcomers/NNS with/IN the/DT tale/ NN of/IN the/DT first/JJ of/IN their/PP$ countrymen/NNS to/TO visit/VB Mexico/NNP ,/, a/DT boatload/NN of/IN samurai/FW warriors/NNS blown/VBN ashore/RB 375/CD years/NNS ago/RB ./.
"/" From/IN the/DT beginning/NN ,/, it/PRP took/VBD a/DT man/NN with/IN extraordinary/JJ qualities/NNS to/TO succeed/VB in/IN Mexico/NNP "/" says/VBZ Kimihide/NNP Takimura/NNP ,/, president/NN of/IN the/DT Mitsui/NNP group/NN 's/POS Kensetsu/NNP Engineering/NNP Inc./NNP unit/NN ./.

Fig. 6.1. Sample of annotated text from the Penn Treebank. After Marcus et al. (1993).

6.4.3 An Annotation Scheme for Swedish

Current annotation schemes often use XML to encode data. This enables a stricter definition of codes through a DTD and makes it easier to use and share data. The annotation is often split into levels that reflect the processing stages. We describe here an example drawn from the Granska and CrossCheck projects to process Swedish (Carlberger et al. 2006) from the Kungliga Tekniska Högskolan in Stockholm. The annotation scheme uses the reference tagset for Swedish defined by the Stockholm-Umeå Corpus (Ejerhed et al. 1992).

The annotation has four levels, and we will describe two of them. The first one corresponds to tokenization. Figure 6.2 shows the token annotation of sentence:

Bilen framför justitieministern svängde fram och tillbaka över vägen så att hon blev rädd.
'The car in front of the Justice Minister swung back and forth and she was frightened.'

```
<tokens>
  <token id="1">Bilen</token>
  <token id="2">framför</token>
  <token id="3">justitieministern</token>
  <token id="4">svängde</token>
  <token id="5">fram</token>
  <token id="6">och</token>
  <token id="7">tillbaka</token>
  <token id="8">över</token>
  <token id="9">vägen</token>
  <token id="10">så</token>
  <token id="11">att</token>
  <token id="12">hon</token>
  <token id="13">blev</token>
  <token id="14">rädd</token>
  <token id="15">.</token>
</tokens>
```

Fig. 6.2. Token annotation, where the identifier id corresponds to the word position.

The second level contains the part-of-speech information, either with lemmas (Fig. 6.3) or without (Fig. 6.4). In both annotations, the tokens have been replaced by their positions. The tag attribute gives the part of speech and its features as a list separated by dots. The first item of the list the main category; for example, nn is a noun. The rest describes the features: utr is the utrum gender, sin is the singular number, def means definite, and nom is the nominative case.

```
<taglemmas>
  <taglemma id="1" tag="nn.utr.sin.def.nom" lemma="bil"/>
  <taglemma id="2" tag="pp" lemma="framför"/>
  <taglemma id="3" tag="nn.utr.sin.def.nom"
lemma="justitieminister"/>
  <taglemma id="4" tag="vb.prt.akt" lemma="svänga"/>
  <taglemma id="5" tag="ab" lemma="fram"/>
  <taglemma id="6" tag="kn" lemma="och"/>
  <taglemma id="7" tag="ab" lemma="tillbaka"/>
  <taglemma id="8" tag="pp" lemma="över"/>
  <taglemma id="9" tag="nn.utr.sin.def.nom" lemma="väg"/>
  <taglemma id="10" tag="ab" lemma="så"/>
  <taglemma id="11" tag="sn" lemma="att"/>
  <taglemma id="12" tag="pn.utr.sin.def.sub" lemma="hon"/>
  <taglemma id="13" tag="vb.prt.akt.kop" lemma="bli"/>
  <taglemma id="14" tag="jj.pos.utr.sin.ind.nom"
lemma="rädd"/>
  <taglemma id="15" tag="mad" lemma="."/>
</taglemmas>
```

Fig. 6.3. Tokens annotated with their part of speech and lemma. Tokens are indicated by their position. The tag specifies the part of speech and its features.

```
<tags>
  <tag id="1" name="nn.utr.sin.def.nom"/>
  <tag id="2" name="pp"/>
  <tag id="3" name="nn.utr.sin.def.nom"/>
  <tag id="4" name="vb.prt.akt"/>
  <tag id="5" name="ab"/>
  <tag id="6" name="kn"/>
  <tag id="7" name="ab"/>
  <tag id="8" name="pp"/>
  <tag id="9" name="nn.utr.sin.def.nom"/>
  <tag id="10" name="ab"/>
  <tag id="11" name="sn"/>
  <tag id="12" name="pn.utr.sin.def.sub"/>
  <tag id="13" name="vb.prt.akt.kop"/>
  <tag id="14" name="jj.pos.utr.sin.ind.nom"/>
  <tag id="15" name="mad"/>
</tags>
```

Fig. 6.4. Tokens annotated with their part of speech only. Tokens are indicated by their position.

6.5 Further Reading

Part-of-speech tagging has a long history in language processing, although many researchers in computational linguistics neglected it in the beginning. Early works include Harris (1962) and Klein and Simmons (1963). Harris' TDAP system was reconstructed and described by Joshi and Hopely (1999).

Brill's tagging program marked a breakthrough in tagging with symbolic techniques. It is available from the Internet for English. Roche and Schabes (1995) proposed a dramatic optimization of it that proved ten times faster than and one third the size of stochastic methods. Constant (1991) and Vergne (1998, 1999) give examples of efficient symbolic taggers that use manually crafted rules.

Exercises

6.1. Complement Brill's tagging algorithm in Prolog with rules `alter(A, B, nexttag(C))` and `alter(A, B, surroundingtag(C, D))`.

6.2. Implement Brill's learning algorithm in Prolog or Perl with all the rule templates.

7

Part-of-Speech Tagging Using Stochastic Techniques

7.1 The Noisy Channel Model

7.1.1 Presentation

Like transformation-based tagging, statistical (or stochastic) part-of-speech tagging assumes that each word is known and has a finite set of possible tags. These tags can be drawn from a dictionary or a morphological analysis. When a word has more than one possible tag, statistical methods enable us to determine the optimal sequence of part-of-speech tags $T = t_1, t_2, t_3, ..., t_n$, given a sequence of words $W = w_1, w_2, w_3, ..., w_n$.

Optimal part-of-speech sequence refers to Shannon's (1948) noisy channel model, where a sequence of symbols is transmitted over a noisy channel and received under the form of a sequence of signals. Here, we suppose that part-of-speech tags are transmitted and come out under the form of words:

$$t_1, t_2, t_3, ..., t_n \rightarrow \text{noisy channel} \rightarrow w_1, w_2, w_3, ..., w_n.$$

The optimal part-of-speech sequence knowing the word sequence corresponds to the maximization of the conditional probability:

$$\hat{T} = P(t_1, t_2, t_3, ..., t_n | w_1, w_2, w_3, ..., w_n).$$

Bayes' theorem on conditional probabilities of events A and B states that:

$$P(A|B)P(B) = P(B|A)P(A).$$

We denote $P(W) = P(w_1, w_2, w_3, ..., w_n)$ and $P(T) = P(t_1, t_2, t_3, ..., t_n)$. Using Bayes' theorem, the most probable estimate of the part-of-speech sequence is given by:

$$\hat{T} = \arg\max \frac{P(T)P(W|T)}{P(W)}.$$

For a given word sequence, $w_1, w_2, w_3, ..., w_n$, $P(W)$ is constant and we can leave it out. We can rewrite the formula as:

$$\hat{T} = \arg\max P(T)P(W|T).$$

7.1.2 The N-gram Approximation

Statistics on sequences of any length are impossible to obtain, and at this point we need to make some approximations on $P(T)$ and $P(W|T)$ to make the estimation tractable. A product of trigrams usually approximates the complete part-of-speech sequence:

$$P(T) = P(t_1, t_2, t_3, ..., t_n) \approx P(t_1)P(t_2|t_1) \prod_{i=3}^{n} P(t_i|t_{i-2}, t_{i-1}).$$

If we use a start-of-sentence delimiter <s>, the two first terms of the product, $P(t_1)P(t_2|t_1)$, are rewritten as $P(< s >)P(t_1| < s >)P(t_2| < s >, t_1)$, where $P(< s >) = 1$.

We estimate the probabilities with the maximum likelihood, P_{MLE}:

$$P_{MLE}(t_i|t_{i-2}, t_{i-1}) = \frac{C(t_{i-2}, t_{i-1}, t_i)}{C(t_{i-2}, t_{i-1})}.$$

Probabilities on trigrams $P(t_i|t_{i-2}, t_{i-1})$ require an estimate for any sequence of three parts-of-speech tags. This is obtained from hand-annotated corpora. If N_p is the number of the different parts-of-speech tags, there are $N_p \times N_p \times N_p$ values to estimate. Most of the time, annotated data is not sufficient and some sequences are missing. Few corpora are likely to contain a reliable number of the article–article–article sequence, for instance. We already encountered this problem of sparse data in Chap. 4. We can solve it using a back-off strategy or a linear interpolation.

If data are missing, we can back-off to bigrams:

$$P(T) = P(t_1, t_2, t_3, ..., t_n) \approx P(t_1) \prod_{i=2}^{n} P(t_i|t_{i-1}).$$

We can further approximate the part-of-speech sequence as the product of part-of-speech probabilities:

$$P(T) = P(t_1, t_2, t_3, ..., t_n) \approx \prod_{i=1}^{n} P(t_i).$$

And finally, we can combine linearly these approximations:

$$P_{LinearInter}(t_i|t_{i-2}t_{i-1}) = \lambda_1 P(t_i|t_{i-2}t_{i-1}) + \lambda_2 P(t_i|t_{i-1}) + \lambda_3 P(t_i),$$

with $\lambda_1 + \lambda_2 + \lambda_3 = 1$, for example, $\lambda_1 = 0.6, \lambda_2 = 0.3, \lambda_3 = 0.1$.

Using the maximum likelihood estimate, this yields:

$$P_{LinearInter}(t_i|t_{i-2}t_{i-1}) = \lambda_1 \frac{C(t_{i-2}, t_{i-1}, t_i)}{C(t_{i-2}, t_{i-1})} + \lambda_2 \frac{C(t_{i-1}, t_i)}{C(t_{i-1})} + \lambda_3 \frac{C(t_i)}{N},$$

where N is the count of words in the corpus.

We can obtain optimal λ values by using a development set: a part of the hand-annotated corpus distinct from the training set and the test set dedicated to the fine-tuning of parameters. After learning the probabilities from the training set, we will run the part-of-speech (POS) tagger on the development set. We will vary the λ values until we find the triplet that yields the best accuracy. We will finally apply the POS tagger to the test set to know its real accuracy.

The complete word sequence knowing the part-of-speech sequence is usually approximated as:

$$P(W|T) = P(w_1, w_2, w_3, ..., w_n | t_1, t_2, t_3, ..., t_n) \approx \prod_{i=1}^{n} P(w_i|t_i).$$

Like the previous probabilities, $P(w_i|t_i)$ is estimated from hand-annotated corpora using the maximum likelihood:

$$P_{MLE}(w_i|t_i) = \frac{C(w_i, t_i)}{C(t_i)}.$$

For N_w different words, there are $N_p \times N_w$ values to obtain. But in this case, many of the estimates will be 0.

7.1.3 Tagging a Sentence

We will now give an example of sentence tagging in French with *Je le donne* 'I give it'. Word *Je* is an unambiguous pronoun. Word *le* is either an article or a pronoun, and *donne* can be a noun (*deal*) or a verb (*donner*). Probabilistic tagging consists in finding the optimal path from the four possible in Fig. 7.1.

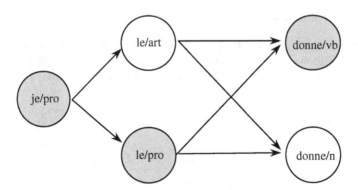

Fig. 7.1. Possible sequences of part-of-speech tags, where *pro* denotes a pronoun, *art* an article, *n* a noun, and *vb* a verb.

Using the formulas given before, we associate each transition with a probability product: $P(w_i|t_i) \times P(t_i|t_{i-2}, t_{i-1})$. We compute the estimate of part-of-speech sequences along the four paths by multiplying the probabilities. The optimal tagging corresponds to the maximum of these four values:

1. $P(pro| < s >) \times P(art| < s >, pro) \times P(verb|pro, art) \times$
   $P(je|pro) \times P(le|art) \times P(donne|verb)$
2. $P(pro| < s >) \times P(art| < s >, pro) \times P(noun|pro, art) \times$
   $P(je|pro) \times P(le|art) \times P(donne|noun)$
3. $P(pro| < s >) \times P(pro| < s >, pro) \times P(verb|pro, pro) \times$
   $P(je|pro) \times P(le|pro) \times P(donne|verb)$
4. $P(pro| < s >) \times P(pro| < s >, pro) \times P(noun|pro, pro) \times$
   $P(je|pro) \times P(le|pro) \times P(donne|noun)$

This method is very simple. However, it is very costly for long sequences. The computation with a sentence of N words and a tagset of T tags will have an upper bound complexity of N^T, which means it is exponential.

7.1.4 The Viterbi Algorithm: An Intuitive Presentation

Using the noisy channel model as we described it is not efficient in terms of speed and memory. This is because the algorithm has to maintain nonoptimal paths for all the intermediate nodes in the automaton. The Viterbi algorithm is a common way to optimize the search.

In the naïve implementation, we traversed all the paths and we computed the most probable POS sequence at the final node of the automaton, i.e., at the final word of the sentence. The Viterbi algorithm determines the optimal subpaths for each node in the automaton while it traverses the automaton and discards the others. We shall extend the example of the previous section to

> *Je le donne demain dans la matinée.*
> 'I give it tomorrow morning.'

and let us consider bigrams instead of trigrams to simplify the presentation.

Figure 7.2 shows the possible POS tags and the number of possible paths, which is $1 \times 2 \times 2 \times 1 \times 1 \times 2 \times 1 = 8$. Let us traverse the automaton from *Je* to *dans*.

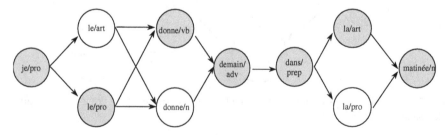

Fig. 7.2. The search space, where *adv* denotes an adverb and *prep* a preposition; the other tags are as given in Fig. 7.1.

The words *demain* and *dans* are not ambiguous, and we saw in the last section that there are four possible paths at this point. Up to *demain*, the most likely sequence will correspond to the most probable path out of the four we saw before:

1. $P(pro| < s >) \times P(art|pro) \times P(verb|art) \times P(adv|verb)$
   $P(je|pro) \times P(le|art) \times P(donne|verb) \times P(demain|adv)$
2. $P(pro| < s >) \times P(art|pro) \times P(noun|art) \times P(adv|noun)$
   $P(je|pro) \times P(le|art) \times P(donne|noun) \times P(demain|adv)$
3. $P(pro| < s >) \times P(pro|pro) \times P(verb|pro) \times P(adv|verb)$
   $P(je|pro) \times P(le|pro) \times P(donne|verb) \times P(demain|adv)$
4. $P(pro| < s >) \times P(pro|pro) \times P(noun|pro) \times P(adv|noun)$
   $P(je|pro) \times P(le|pro) \times P(donne|noun) \times P(demain|adv)$

Demain has still the memory of the ambiguity of *donne*: $P(adv|verb)$ and $P(adv|noun)$. This is no longer the case with *dans*. According to the noisy channel model and the bigram assumption, the term brought by the word *dans* is $P(dans|prep) \times P(prep|adv)$. It does not show the ambiguity of *le* and *donne*. The subsequent terms will ignore it as well.

This means that the optimal POS tag sequence of words before *dans* is already determined even if we have not yet reached the end of the sentence. It corresponds to the highest value of the four paths. It is then sufficient to keep it with the corresponding path. We can forget the others. This is the idea of the Viterbi optimization. We will describe the algorithm rigorously in the next section.

7.2 Markov Models

When we tagged words with a stochastic technique, we assumed that the current word's part of speech depended only on a couple of words before it. This limited history is a frequent property of many linguistic phenomena. It has been studied extensively since the end of the 19th century, starting with Andrei Markov. Markov processes form the theoretical background to stochastic tagging and can be applied to many problems. We introduce them now.

7.2.1 Markov Chains

A Markov chain or process is a sequence $\{X_1, X_2, ..., X_T\}$ where X_t denotes a random variable at time t. Variables have their values in a finite set of states $\{q_1, ..., q_N\}$ called the state space. Following Rabiner (1989), processes are Markovian if they have the following properties:

- A limited history. The current state depends only on a constant number of previous states: one in first-order processes, $P(X_t = q_j|X_1, ..., X_{t-1}) = P(X_t = q_j|X_{t-1})$, and two in second-order processes $P(X_t = q_j|X_1, ..., X_{t-1}) = P(X_t = q_j|X_{t-2}, X_{t-1})$.

- Independent of time t. For first-order processes, this means that they can be represented as a transition matrix with coefficients $P(X_t = q_j | X_{t-1} = q_i) = a_{ij}$, $1 \leq i, j \leq N$, with ordinary probability constraints $\sum_{j=1}^{N} a_{ij} = 1$, and $a_{ij} \geq 0$.

Markov chains define random transitions from one state to another one. We can represent them as **probabilistic** or **weighted automata**. We just need to augment transitions of automata we used in Chap. 2 with a probability. Unlike ordinary automata, the initial state can be any state in the set and will be modeled by a probability at time 1. The probability of initial states is $\pi_i = P(X_1 = q_i)$, with $\sum_{i=1}^{N} \pi_i = 1$.

In the case of natural language processing, "time sequence" is not the most relevant term to describe the chain. More appropriately, the sequence corresponds to the word flow from left to right and t to the word position in the sequence. It is easy then to see that first-order processes reflect part-of-speech bigrams, while second-order processes correspond to trigrams. Figure 7.3 shows partial bigram probabilities using a Markov chain (numbers are fictitious and transitions are not complete). For part-of-speech tagging, a_{ij} coefficients correspond to probabilities of part-of-speech bigrams computed over the tagset.

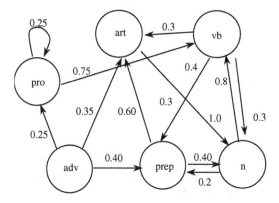

Fig. 7.3. A Markov chain representing bigram probabilities as part-of-speech transitions (numbers are fictitious, and transitions are not complete).

Instead of using an automaton, we can represent a Markov process as a trellis where states are a function of the time (the word's positions, here). In part-of-speech tagging, the vertical axis corresponds to the different part-of-speech values (the states) and the horizontal axis corresponds to the part-of-speech sequence (Fig. 7.4). All the possible bigram combinations are represented as arrows from states at time $t - 1$ to states at time t. T is the sentence length.

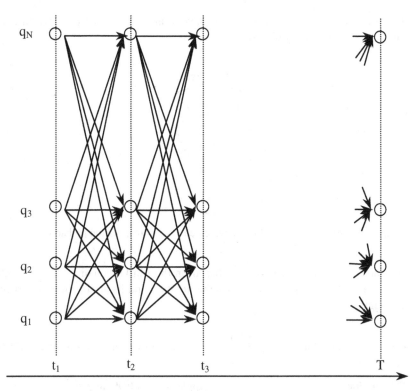

Fig. 7.4. Trellis that represents the states as the vertical axis and the time as the horizontal axis. The states correspond to part-of-speech values, and the discrete time values are the indices in the part-of-speech sequence. T is the sentence length.

7.2.2 Hidden Markov Models

Markov chains provide a model to the part-of-speech sequence. However, this sequence is not directly accessible since we usually only have the word sequence. Hidden Markov models (HMM) are an extension to the Markov chains that make it possible to include the words under the form of observed symbols. Each state of an HMM emits a symbol taken from an output set along with an emission probability. HMMs are then a stochastic representation of an observable output generated by a hidden sequence of states. They enable us to compute the probability of a state sequence (the parts of speech) given an output or observation sequence (the words).

We saw that part-of-speech tagging uses a stochastic formula that comprises two terms: $P(T)$ and $P(W|T)$. The first one, $P(T)$, corresponds to a Markov chain where transition probabilities between states represent the part-of-speech bigrams. The second term, $P(W|T)$, is an HMM superimposed on the chain. It augments each state with the capacity to emit a word using a probability function $P(w_i|t_i)$ that measures the association between the parts of speech and the words (Fig. 7.5). Although a state – a part of speech – can emit any word in the model, most probabilities will be 0 in reality. This is because words have a finite number of possible parts of speech, most of the time, as we saw, only one or two.

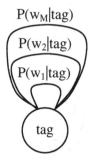

Fig. 7.5. Each state in the trellis is augmented with word emission probabilities.

The formal definition of HMMs is based on the Markov chains where we add the emission properties. Table 7.1 shows the notation and its application in part-of-speech tagging.

Table 7.1. The hidden Markov model notation and its application to part-of-speech (POS) tagging.

HMM notation	Application to POS tagging
$S = \{q_1, q_2, q_3, ..., q_N\}$ is a finite set of states.	The set of parts of speech.
$V = \{v_1, v_2, v_3, ..., v_M\}$ is an output alphabet: a finite set of symbols.	The set of words, the vocabulary.
$O = \{o_1, o_2, o_3, ..., o_T\}$ is the output or observation sequence, with $o_i \in V$ obtained from a sequence of states.	Each part of speech emits one word taken in the vocabulary. This is what we observe.
$A = \{a_{ij}\}$ is a state transition matrix.	The bigram probabilities $P(t_k = q_j \mid t_{k-1} = q_i)$.
$B = \{b_j(v_k)\}$ are the emission probabilities of symbol v_k in state j.	The conditional probability to observe a word given a part of speech $P(w \mid t)$.
$\Pi = \{\pi_i\}$ are the initial state probabilities.	The probability of the first part of speech.

7.2.3 Three Fundamental Algorithms to Solve Problems with HMMs

Hidden Markov models are able represent associations between word and parts-of-speech sequences. However, they do not tell how to solve the annotation problem. We need complementary algorithms for them to be useful. More generally, problems to solve fall into three categories that correspond to three fundamental algorithms (Rabiner 1989):

- Estimate the probability of an observed sequence. This corresponds to the sum of all the paths producing the observation. It is solved using the forward procedure. In the specific case of POS tagging, it will determine the probability of the word sequence. Although the forward procedure is not of primary importance here, it is fundamental and has many other applications.
- Determine the most likely path of an observed sequence. This is a decoding problem that is solved using the Viterbi algorithm.
- Determine (learn) the parameters given a set of observations. This algorithm is used to build models when we do not know the parameters. It is solved using the forward–backward algorithm.

We now present the algorithms where we follow Rabiner's notation (1989).

7.2.4 The Forward Procedure

The first problem to solve is to compute the probability of an observation sequence $O = \{o_1, o_2, o_3, ..., o_T\}$, given an HMM model $\lambda = (A, B, \pi)$.

If we consider only one specific sequence of states $Q = \{s_1, s_2, s_3, ..., s_T\}$, with $s_i \in S$, we compute it with the observation probability given the state sequence

$$P(O|Q, \lambda) = \prod_{t=1}^{T} P(o_t|s_t, \lambda),$$
$$= b_{s_1}(o_1)b_{s_2}(o_2)b_{s_3}(o_3)...b_{s_T}(o_T).$$

multiplied by the state sequence probability

$$P(Q|\lambda) = \pi_{s_1} \prod_{t=2}^{T} P(s_t|s_{t-1}),$$
$$= \pi_{s_1} a_{s_1 s_2} a_{s_2 s_3} ... a_{s_{T-1} s_T}.$$

In HMMs, any sequence of state can produce the observation. This means that the observation probability is the sum of observation probabilities for all the possible state combinations:

$$P(O|\lambda) = \sum_{\text{All } Q} P(O|Q, \lambda)P(Q|\lambda),$$
$$= \sum_{\text{All } s_1, s_2, ..., s_T} \pi_{s_1} b_{s_1}(o_1) a_{s_1 s_2} b_{s_2}(o_2) a_{s_2 s_3} b_{s_3}(o_3) ... a_{s_{T-1} s_T} b(o_T).$$

This method, however, is intractable for long sequences because of its complexity, N^T.

The forward procedure simplifies the brute-force method by factoring all paths incoming into a state at time t. This means that at each instant of time of the observation sequence, we maintain exactly N paths: the number of different states.

Let us denote $\alpha_t(j)$ the probability of an observation $o_1, o_2, o_3, ..., o_t$, with the condition that we are in state q_j at time t: $P(o_1, o_2, o_3, ..., o_t, s_t = q_j|\lambda)$. We compute $\alpha_{t+1}(i)$ by induction with transitions from all states at time t to state i at time $t + 1$. Figure 7.6 shows how α_t values are summed to obtain $\alpha_{t+1}(i)$.

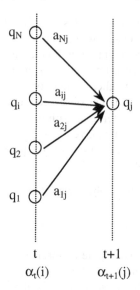

Fig. 7.6. Transitions from states $q_1, q_2, q_3, ..., q_N$ at time t to state q_j at time $t+1$.

We can compute an observation probability with a matrix reproducing the structure of the trellis in Fig. 7.4. The algorithm iteratively fills the trellis' columns from left to right. Each column is an array of length N corresponding to the number of states where we store the probabilities of the observation so far. The element of index i in the tth column contains the $\alpha(i)$ value at time t.

The first step of the algorithm fills the first column with the initial probabilities. The induction loop updates the values from t to $t+1$ by summing all the incoming transitions for each element in the $(t+1)$th column from the tth column (Table 7.2). Finally, we obtain the observation probability by summing all the elements of the last column in the matrix. The complexity of this algorithm is $O(N^2 T)$.

Table 7.2. The forward procedure.

Steps	Operations
1. Initialization	$\alpha_1(i) = \pi_i b_i(o_1), 1 \leq i \leq N$
2. Induction	$\alpha_{t+1}(j) = b_j(o_{t+1}) \times \sum_{i=1}^{N} \alpha_t(i)a_{ij}, 1 \leq j \leq N,$ and $1 \leq i \leq T-1$
3. Termination	$P(O\|\lambda) = \sum_{i=1}^{N} \alpha_T(i)$

7.2.5 Viterbi Algorithm

The Viterbi algorithm is an efficient method to find the optimal sequence of states given an observation. As with the forward procedure, it iterates from $t = 1$ to $t = T$ and searches the optimal path leading to each state in the trellis at time t.

Let us denote $\delta_t(j)$ the maximal probability of an observation $o_1, o_2, o_3, ..., o_t$ with the condition that we are in state q_j at time t:

$$\max_{s_1, s_2, ..., s_{t-1}} P(s_1, s_2, ..., s_{t-1}, o_1, o_2, o_3, ..., o_t, s_t = q_j | \lambda),$$

and $\psi_t(j)$ the corresponding optimal path.

The Viterbi algorithm resembles the forward procedure. It moves from left to right iteratively to fill the columns in the trellis. Each column element contains the most probable path, $\psi(j)$, to reach this element and its probability $\delta(j)$. In fact, $\psi(j)$ just needs to store the preceding state in the optimal path.

The first step of the algorithm fills the first column with the initial probabilities. The induction loop updates the values from t to $t + 1$ by taking the maximum of all the incoming transitions for each element in the $(t + 1)$th column and the node that led to it. Finally, we determine the most probable path from the maximum of all the elements of the last column in the matrix. We backtrack in the matrix to find the state sequence that led to it (Table 7.3).

Table 7.3. The Viterbi algorithm.

Steps	Operations
1. Initialization	$\delta_1(i) = \pi_i b_i(o_1), 1 \leq i \leq N$
	$\psi_1(i) = null$
2. Induction	$\delta_{t+1}(j) = b_j(o_{t+1}) \times \max_{1 \leq i \leq N} \delta_t(i) a_{ij}, 1 \leq j \leq N$, and $1 \leq i \leq T - 1$
	$\psi_{t+1}(j) = \arg \max_{1 \leq i \leq N} \delta_t(i) a_{ij}$
3. Termination	$P* = \max_{1 \leq i \leq N} \delta_T(i)$
	$s_T* = \arg \max_{1 \leq i \leq N} \delta_T(i)$
	The optimal path sequence is given by the backtracking: $s_T^*, s_{T-1}^* = \psi_T(s_T^*), s_{T-2}^* = \psi_{T-2}(s_{T-1}^*), ...$

The Viterbi algorithm is a dynamic programming technique comparable to the computation of the min-edit distance. Its implementation also uses a table. Table 7.4 shows how to fill the three first columns with the sentence <s> *Je le donne demain dans la matinée.*

We start the sentence with $\delta_1(< s >) = 1.0$ and $\delta_1(i) = 0$ for the rest of indices $i \neq < s >$. This means that in the first column, all the cells equal 0, except for one. The computation of the second column is easy. Each cell i is filled with the term $P(i| < s >) \times P(Je|i)$, with $i \in \{prep, adverb, pronoun, verb, noun, art, <$

$s >$}. The algorithm really starts with the third column. For each cell j, we compute $\max_i P(j|i) \times P(le|j) \times \delta_2(i)$. The *pronoun* cell, for instance, is filled with $\max_i P(pronoun|i) \times P(le|pronoun) \times \delta_2(i)$. This process is iterated for each column to the end of the matrix.

Table 7.4. The Viterbi algorithm applied to the sentence <s> *Je le donne demain dans la matinée.*

$i \backslash \delta$	δ_1	δ_2	δ_3	δ_4	δ_5	δ_6	δ_7	δ_8
prep	0							
adverb	0							
pronoun	0							
verb	0							
noun	0							
art	0							
<s>	1.0	0	0	0	0	0	0	0
	<s>	*Je*	*le*	*donne*	*demain*	*dans*	*la*	*matinée*

7.2.6 The Backward Procedure

We have computed the estimation of an observation from left to right. Although less natural, we can also compute it from right to left. We now present this backward procedure to introduce the forward–backward algorithm in the next section.

The backward variable $\beta_t(j) = P(o_{t+1}, o_{t+2}, o_{t+3}, ..., o_T, s_t = q_j|\lambda)$ is the probability of an observation $o_{t+1}, o_{t+2}, o_{t+3}, ..., o_T$ with the condition that we are in state q_j at time t. We compute $\beta_t(i)$ by induction with transitions from state i at time t to all states at time $t + 1$. Figure 7.7 shows how $\beta_{t+1}(i)$ values are summed to obtain β_t, and Table 7.5 shows the procedure.

Table 7.5. The backward procedure.

Steps	Operations
1. Initialization	$\beta_T(i) = 1, 1 \leq i \leq N$
2. Induction	$\beta_t(i) = \sum_{j=1}^{N} a_{ij} b_j(o_{t+1}) \beta_{t+1}(i), 1 \leq j \leq N$, and for $t = T - 1$ to $t = 1$.
3. Termination	$P(O|\lambda) = \sum_{i=1}^{N} \pi_i b_i(o_1) \beta_1(i)$

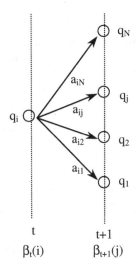

Fig. 7.7. Transitions from state q_i at time t to states $q_1, q_2, q_3, ..., q_N$ at time $t + 1$.

7.2.7 The Forward–Backward Algorithm

The forward–backward algorithm will enable us to derive the a_{ij} and $b_j(o_t)$ coefficients, here $P(w_i|t_i)$ and $P(t_i|t_{i-1})$, from raw, unannotated texts. Although this yields results inferior to those obtained from a hand-annotated corpus, it makes it possible to build a part-of-speech tagger when no annotation is available.

The forward–backward algorithm is referred to as an **unsupervised learning** method, because no additional information is available except the text. This is opposed to **supervised learning**, when the algorithm has access to some sort of reference annotation.

Informal Presentation. The idea of the forward–backward algorithm is to guess initial estimates to $P(t_i|t_{i-1})$ and $P(w_i|t_i)$ and tag the corpus. Once we have a tagged corpus, we can derive new estimates of $P(w_i|t_i)$ and $P(t_i|t_{i-1})$ that we will use to retag the corpus. We repeat the process until it converges (Table 7.6).

However, we have no guarantee that the algorithm converges, and when it converges, we can also hit a local maximum. In the latter case, the learning procedure will stop without finding correct figures. This is the drawback of this method. For this reason some quantity of hand-annotated data is always preferrable to a raw corpus (Merialdo 1994).

The Algorithm. In the presentation above, we had to tag the text before we could derive new estimates of probabilities $P(t_i|t_{i-1})$ and $P(w_i|t_i)$, or more generally a_{ij} and $b_j(o_t)$. In fact, we can avoid the tagging stage. The coefficients can be computed directly using the forward procedure. We will reestimate $\hat{a}_{ij}$ at step n of the estimation process from estimates a_{ij} at step $n - 1$.

Table 7.6. Iterative estimation of $P(t_i|t_{i-1})$ (figures are fictitious).

Steps	Estimates used to tag the corpus	Estimates derived from the tagged corpus
Initial estimates	$P(pronoun|pronoun) = 0.2$ $P(art|pronoun)\quad = 0.2$ $P(verb|pronoun)\quad = 0.6$	
We tag the corpus and we derive new estimates.		$P(pronoun|pronoun) = 0.15$ $P(art|pronoun)\quad = 0.05$ $P(verb|pronoun)\quad = 0.8$
Second estimates	$P(pronoun|pronoun) = 0.15$ $P(art|pronoun)\quad = 0.05$ $P(verb|pronoun)\quad = 0.8$	
We retag the corpus and we derive estimates.		$P(pronoun|pronoun) = 0.18$ $P(art|pronoun)\quad = 0.02$ $P(verb|pronoun)\quad = 0.9$
Third estimates	$P(pronoun|pronoun) = 0.18$ $P(art|pronoun)\quad = 0.02$ $P(verb|pronoun)\quad = 0.9$	

The algorithm idea is to consider one observation – one word – and then to average it on all the other observations – the whole sentence. For one specific observation $b_j(o_{t+1})$ at time $t + 1$, corresponding here to the word of index $t + 1$, the transition probability from state $s_t = q_i$ to state $s_{t+1} = q_j$ corresponds to

$$\xi_t(i,j) = P(s_t = q_i, s_{t+1} = q_j|O, \lambda),$$
$$= \frac{P(s_t=q_i, s_{t+1}=q_j, O|\lambda)}{P(O|\lambda)},$$
$$= \frac{P(s_t=q_i, s_{t+1}=q_j, O|\lambda)}{\sum\limits_{1 \le i \le N}\sum\limits_{1 \le j \le N} P(s_t=q_i, s_{t+1}=q_j, O|\lambda)}.$$

We can use the forward and backward probilities to determine the estimate. Figure 7.8 shows how to introduce them in the equation.

We have:

$$\xi_t(i,j) = \frac{\alpha_t(i)a_{ij}b_j(o_{t+1})\beta_{t+1}(j)}{\sum\limits_{i=1}^{N}\sum\limits_{j=1}^{N}\alpha_t(i)a_{ij}b_j(o_{t+1})\beta_{t+1}(j)}.$$

We denote $\gamma_t(i) = \sum\limits_{j=1}^{N}\xi_t(i,j)$ the probability to be in state q_i at time t.

To consider all the observations, we sum $\xi_t(i,j)$ from $t = 1$ to $t = T-1$. The expected number of transitions from state q_i to state q_j is $\sum\limits_{t=1}^{T-1}\xi_t(i,j)$, and the expected

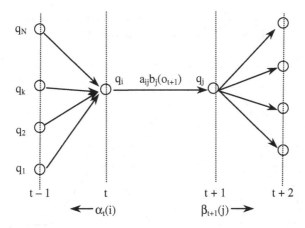

Fig. 7.8. Transition from state q_i at time t to state q_j at time $t+1$ with observation o_{t+1}. After Rabiner (1989).

number of transitions from state q_i is $\sum_{t=1}^{T-1} \gamma_t(i)$. The last sum also corresponds to the number of times we are in state q_i. We derive:

- The new estimate of a_{ij}:

$$\hat{a}_{ij} = \frac{\text{expected number of transitions from state } q_i \text{ to state } q_j}{\text{expected number of transitions from state } q_i},$$

$$= \frac{\sum_{t=1}^{T-1} \xi_t(i,j)}{\sum_{t=1}^{T-1} \gamma_t(i)}.$$

- The initial state estimates $\pi_i = \gamma_1(i)$.
- The observation estimates:

$$\hat{b}_i(v_k) = \frac{\text{expected number of times in state } q_i \text{ and observing symbol } v_k}{\text{expected number of times in state } q_i},$$

$$= \frac{\sum_{o_t = v_k, 1 \leq t \leq T}^{T} \gamma_t(i)}{\sum_{t=1}^{T} \gamma_t(i)}.$$

7.3 Tagging with Decision Trees

So far, we used the maximum likelihood to estimate part of speech and word proba-bilities. We can replace it with decision trees induced from an annotated corpus. The tagging performance could be superior when the training set is small.

TreeTagger (Schmid 1994, 1995) is a stochastic tagger that replaces the max-imum likelihood estimate with a binary decision tree to estimate $P(t_i|t_{i-2}, t_{i-1})$. Figure 7.9 shows an example of an imaginary tree where the conditional probability

$P(NN|DET, ADJ)$ is read from the tree by examining t_{-1} and t_{-2}, here ADJ and DET, respectively. The probability estimate is 0.70.

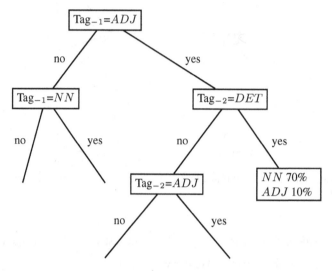

Fig. 7.9. A decision tree to estimate POS frequencies where is a noun, DET, a determiner, and ADJ, an adjective. After Schmid (1994).

The decision tree is built from a training set of POS trigrams t_{-2}, t_{-1}, t_0 extracted from an annotated corpus. The condition set is $t_{-i} = v$, with $i \in \{1, 2\}$ and $v \in T$, where T is the tagset.

The idea is to use the entropy of the POS trigams where the random variable is t_0. The entropy is then defined as:

$$- \sum_{t_0 \in T} P(t_0) \log_2 P(t_0).$$

If the total number of tokens is N, the entropy is estimated as:

$$- \sum_{t_0 \in T} \frac{C(t_0)}{N} \log_2 \frac{C(t_0)}{N}.$$

The decision tree minimizes the information it needs to identify the third tag, t_0, given the two preceding tags, t_{-2} and t_{-1}. This reflects the minimal amount of information brought by the third tag of a trigram.

To find the root node, the algorithm creates all the possible partitions of the training set according to the values of t_{-2} and t_{-1}. It computes the weighted average of the entropy of the positive and negative examples. The root condition corresponds to the values i and v with $i \in \{1, 2\}$ and $v \in T$ that minimize

$$-\frac{p}{p+n}\sum_{t_0\in T}\frac{C(t_0,t_{-i}=v)}{p}\log_2\frac{C(t_0,t_{-i}=v)}{p} - \frac{n}{p+n}\sum_{t_0\in T}\frac{C(t_0,t_{-i}\neq v)}{n}\log_2\frac{C(t_0,t_{-i}\neq v)}{n},$$

where p is the count of the trigrams that pass the test to be the root condition, and n is the count of trigrams that do not pass the test. $C(t_0, t_{-1} = v)$ is the count of trigrams t_{-2}, t_{-1}, t_0 that pass the test and where the third tag is t_0, and $C(t_0, t_{-1} \neq v)$ the count of trigrams that do not pass the test and where the third tag is t_0.

The algorithm stops expanding the tree and creates a leaf when the next node would gather a number of positive or negative trigrams below a certain threshold, 2, for example.

7.4 Unknown Words

For stochastic taggers, the main issue to tag unknown words is to estimate $P(w|t)$. Carlberger and Kann (1999) proposed to use suffixes or more precisely word endings to compute the estimate. They counted the number of word types with common word endings of length i, $C(w_{end-i}, t)$, for each tag t in the tagset, with i ranging from 0 to L. The estimate $P(w|t)$ for unknown word is then

$$P_{est}(w|t) = \sum_{i=0}^{L}\alpha_i\frac{C(w_{end-i}, t)}{\sum_{\tau\in\text{tagset}}C(w_{end-i}, \tau)}.$$

where α_i are parameters optimized on the training set. They tried their formula with increasing values of L, and they found that tagging accuracy did not improve for $L > 5$.

If $L = 0$, $P_{est}(w|t) = \frac{C(t)}{\sum_{\tau\in\text{tagset}}C(\tau)}$ corresponds to the proportion of part of speech t among the word types.

7.5 An Application of the Noisy Channel Model: Spell Checking

An interesting application of the noisy channel model is to help a spell checker rank candidate corrections (Kernighan et al. 1990). In this case, the source sequence is a correct string c that produces an incorrect one called the typo t through the noisy channel. The most likely correction is modeled as

$$\hat{c} = \arg\max P(c)P(t|c).$$

Possible typos are deletion, insertion, substitutions, and transpositions. In their original paper, Kernighan et al. allowed only one typo per word. Typo frequencies are estimated from a corpus where:

- $del(xy)$ is the number of times the characters xy in the correct word were typed x in the training set.
- $ins(xy)$ is the number of times x is typed as xy in the training set.

- $sub(xy)$ is the number of times the character x is typed y.
- $trans(xy)$ is the number of times xy is typed as yx in the training set.

$P(t|c)$ is estimated as:

$$P(t|c) = \begin{cases} \frac{del(c_{p-1},c_p)}{C(c_{p-1},c_p)} & \text{if deletion,} \\ \frac{ins(c_{p-1},t_p)}{C(c_{p-1})} & \text{if insertion,} \\ \frac{sub(t_p,c_p)}{C(c_p)} & \text{if substitution,} \\ \frac{trans(c_p,c_{p+1})}{C(c_{p-1},c_p)} & \text{if transposition.} \end{cases}$$

where c_p is the pth character of c, and t_p the pth of t.

The algorithm needs four confusion matrices, of size 26×26 for English, that contain the frequencies of deletions, insertions, substitutions, and transpositions. The *del* matrix will give the counts $del(xy)$, how many times y was deleted after x for all the letter pairs, for instance, $del(ab)$.

The matrices can be obtained through hand-annotation or automatically. Hand-annotation is expensive, and Kernighan et al. described an algorithm to train automatically the matrices. It resembles the forward–backward procedure (Sect. 7.2.7).

The training phase initializes the matrices with equal values and applies the spelling algorithm to generate a correct word for each typo in the text. The pairs typo/corrected word are used to update the matrices. The algorithm is repeated on the original text to obtain new pairs and is iterated until the matrices converge.

7.6 A Second Application: Language Models for Machine Translation

Natural language processing was born with machine translation, which was one of its first applications. Facing competition from Russia after the Second World War, the government of the United States decided to fund large-scale translation programs to have a quick access to documents written in Russian. It started the field and resulted in programs like SYSTRAN, which are still in use today.

Given the relatively long history of machine translation, a variety of methods have been experimented on and applied. In this section, we outline how language models and statistical techniques can be used to translate a text from one language into another one. IBM teams pioneered statistical models for machine translation in the early 1990s (Brown et al. 1993). Their work is still the standard reference.

7.6.1 Parallel Corpora

Parallel corpora are the main resource of statistical language translation. Administrative or parliamentary texts of multilingual countries are widely used because they are easy to obtain and are often free. The Canadian Hansard or the European Parliament

Table 7.7. Parallel texts from the Swiss federal law on milk transportation.

German	French	Italian
Art. 35 Milchtransport	**Art. 35 Transport du lait**	**Art. 35 Trasporto del latte**
1 Die Milch ist schonend und hygienisch in den Verarbeitungsbetrieb zu transportieren. Das Transportfahrzeug ist stets sauber zu halten. Zusammen mit der Milch dürfen keine Tiere und milchfremde Gegenstände transportiert werden, welche die Qualität der Milch beeinträchtigen können.	1 Le lait doit être transporté jusqu'à l'entreprise de transformation avec ménagement et conformément aux normes d'hygiène. Le véhicule de transport doit être toujours propre. Il ne doit transporter avec le lait aucun animal ou objet susceptible d'en altérer la qualité.	1 Il latte va trasportato verso l'azienda di trasformazione in modo accurato e igienico. Il veicolo adibito al trasporto va mantenuto pulito. Con il latte non possono essere trasportati animali e oggetti estranei, che potrebbero pregiudicarne la qualità.
2 Wird Milch ausserhalb des Hofes zum Abtransport bereitgestellt, so ist sie zu beaufsichtigen.	2 Si le lait destiné à être transporté est déposé hors de la ferme, il doit être placé sous surveillance.	2 Se viene collocato fuori dall'azienda in vista del trasporto, il latte deve essere sorvegliato.
3 Milchpipelines sind nach den Anweisungen des Herstellers zu reinigen und zu unterhalten.	3 Les lactoducs des exploitations d'estivage doivent être nettoyés et entretenus conformément aux instructions du fabricant.	3 I lattodotti vanno puliti e sottoposti a manutenzione secondo le indicazioni del fabbricante.

proceedings are examples of them. Table 7.7 shows an excerpt of the Swiss federal law in German, French, and Italian on the quality of milk production.

The idea of machine translation with parallel texts is simple: given a sentence, a phrase, or a word in a **source language**, find its equivalent in the **target language**. The translation procedure splits the text to translate into fragments, finds a correspondence for each source fragment in the parallel corpora, and composes the resulting target pieces to form a translated text. Using the titles in Table 7.7, we can build pairs from the phrases *transport du lait* 'milk transportation' in French, *Milchtransport* in German, and *trasporto del latte* in Italian.

The idea of translating with the help of parallel texts is not new and has been applied by many people. A notable example is the Egyptologist and linguist Jean-François Champollion, who used the famous Rosetta stone, an early parallel text, to decipher Egyptian hieroglyphs from Greek.

7.6.2 Alignment

The parallel texts must be aligned before using them in machine translation. This corresponds to a preliminary segmentation and mark-up that determines the corresponding paragraphs, sentences, phrases, and words across the texts. Inside sentences, aligned fragments are called **beads**. Alignment of texts in Table 7.7 is made easier because paragraphs are numbered and have the same number of sentences in each language. This is not always the case, however, and some texts show a significantly different sentence structure.

Gale and Church (1993) describe a simple and effective method based on the idea that

> "longer sentences in one language tend to be translated into longer sentences in the other language, and that shorter sentences tend to be translated into shorter sentences."

Their method generates pairs of sentences from the target and source texts, assigns them a score, which corresponds to the difference of lengths in characters of the aligned pairs, and uses dynamic programming to find the maximum likelihood alignment of sentences.

The sentences in the source language are denoted $s_i, 1 \leq i \leq I$, and the sentences in the target language $t_i, 1 \leq i \leq J$. $D(i, j)$ is the minimum distance between sentences $s_1, s_2, ..., s_i$ and $t_1, t_2, ..., t_j$, and $d(source_1, target_1; source_2, target_2)$ is the distance function between sentences. The algorithm identifies six possible cases of alignment through insertion, deletion, substitution, expansion, contraction, or merger. They are expressed by the formula below:

$$D(i,j) = \min \begin{pmatrix} D(i, j - 1) + d(0, t_j; 0, 0) \\ D(i - 1, j) + d(s_i, 0; 0, 0) \\ D(i - 1, j - 1) + d(s_i, t_j; 0, 0) \\ D(i - 1, j - 2) + d(s_i, t_j; 0, t_{j-1}) \\ D(i - 2, j - 1) + d(s_i, t_j; s_{i-1}, 0) \\ D(i - 2, j - 2) + d(s_i, t_j; s_{i-1}, t_{j-1}) \end{pmatrix}.$$

The distance function is defined as $-\log P(alignment|\delta)$, with $\delta = (l_2 - l_1 c)/\sqrt{l_1 s^2}$, and where l_1 and l_2 are the lengths of the sentences under consideration, c the average number of characters in the source language L_2 per character in the target language L_1, and s^2 its variance. Gale and Church (1993) found a value of c of 1.06 for the pair French–English and 1.1 for German–English. This means that French and German texts are longer than their English counterparts: 6% longer for French and 10% for German. They found $s^2 = 7.3$ for German–English and $s^2 = 5.6$ for French–English.

Using Bayes' theorem, we can derive a new distance function:

$$-\log P(\delta|alignment) - \log P(alignment).$$

Gale and Church (1993) estimated the probability $P(alignment)$ of their six possible alignments with these figures: substitution 1–1: 0.89, deletion and substitution 0–1 or 1–0: 0.0099, expansion and contraction 2–1 or 1–2: 0.089, and merger 2–2: 0.011. They rewrote $P(\delta|alignment)$ as $2(1 - P(|\delta|))$, which can be computed from statistical tables. See Gale and Church's original article.

Alignment of words and phrases uses similar techniques, however, it is more complex. Figures 7.10 and 7.11 show examples of alignment from Brown et al. (1993).

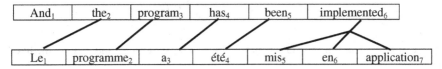

Fig. 7.10. Alignment. After Brown et al. (1993).

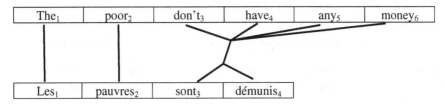

Fig. 7.11. A general alignment. After Brown et al. (1993).

7.6.3 Translation

Using a statistical formulation, given a source text, S, the most probable target text, T, corresponds to $\arg\max_T P(T|S)$, which can be rewritten as $\arg\max_T P(T)P(S|T)$. The first term, $P(T)$, is a language model, for instance, a trigram model, and the second one, $P(S|T)$, is the translation model. In their original article, Brown et al. (1993) used French as the source language and English as the target language with the notations F and E. They modeled the correspondence between a French string $f = f_1, f_2, ..., f_m$ and an English string, $e = e_1, e_2, ..., e_l$.

The first step is to rewrite the translation model as

$$P(f|e) = \sum_a P(f, a|e),$$

where a is the alignment between the source and target sentences and where each source word has one single corresponding target word. The target word can be the empty string. The alignment is represented by the string $a = a_1, a_2, ..., a_m$, where a_j is the position of the corresponding word in the English string as $a_j = i$, which denotes that word j in the French string is connected to word i in the English string. When there is no connection $a_j = 0$. In the example of Fig. 7.10, we have the alignment $a = (2, 3, 4, 5, 6, 6, 6)$.

Brown et al. (1993) proposed five models ranging from relatively simple to pretty elaborate to work out concretely the formula. In their simplest model 1, they introduce the simplification:

$$P(f, a|e) = \frac{\varepsilon}{(l+1)^m} \prod_{j=1}^{m} t(f_j|e_{a_j}),$$

where $t(f_j|e_{a_j})$ is the translation probability of f_j given e_{a_j} and ε a small, fixed number.

Using the example in Fig. 7.10, the product in

P(Le programme a été mis en application, a|And the program has been implemented)

for $a = (2, 3, 4, 5, 6, 6, 6)$ corresponds to the terms:

t(Le|the) $\times$ t(programme|program) $\times$ t(a|has) $\times$ t(été|been)$\times$
t(mis|implemented) $\times$ t(en|implemented) $\times$ t(application|implemented)

where t values are derived from aligned corpora. Summing over all the possible alignments, we obtain the probability of the translation of *Le programme a été mis en application* into *And the program has been implemented*.

7.7 Further Reading

A complete introduction to stochastic methods can be found in Charniak (1993). It notably includes a description of the Viterbi algorithm that enables users to speed the search of the optimal part-of-speech sequence. Magerman (1995) noted some errors in Charniak's book that are worth being corrected. Carlberger and Kann (1999) is a very readable and complete text to implement a stochastic tagger.

Brown et al. (1993) started the field on statistical translation models. The original article is worth reading. GIZA++ (Och and Ney 2000), a free software to train translation models, is available from: http://www.fjoch.com/GIZA++.html.

Exercises

7.1. Implement the stochastic part-of-speech tagging algorithm in Prolog or Perl using unigrams.

7.2. Implement the stochastic part-of-speech tagging algorithm in Prolog or Perl using bigrams.

7.3. Implement the Viterbi search for the bigram part-of-speech tagger.

7.4. Implement a spell checker in Prolog or Perl.

8

Phrase-Structure Grammars in Prolog

8.1 Using Prolog to Write Phrase-Structure Grammars

This chapter introduces parsing using phrase-structure rules and grammars. It uses the Definite Clause Grammar (DCG) notation (Pereira and Warren 1980), which is a feature of virtually all Prologs. The DCG notation enables us to transcribe a set of phrase-structure rules directly into a Prolog program.

Prolog was designed from the very beginning for language processing. It has built-in search and unification mechanisms that make it naturally suited to implement formal models of linguistics with elegance and concision. Parsing with DCG rules comes down to a search in Prolog. Prolog recognizes the rules at load time and translates them into clauses. Its engine automatically carries out the parse without the need for additional programming.

Many natural language processing systems, both in academia and in industry, have been written in Prolog. Other languages like Perl, Python, Java, or C++ are now widely used in language engineering applications. However, much programming is often necessary to implement an idea or a linguistic theory. Prolog gets to the heart of the problem in sometimes only a few lines of code. It thus enables us to capture fundamental concepts while setting aside coding chores.

8.2 Representing Chomsky's Syntactic Formalism in Prolog

8.2.1 Constituents

Chomsky's syntactic formalism (1957) is based on the concept of constituents. Constituents can be defined as groups of words that fit together and act as relatively independent syntactic units. We shall illustrate this idea with the sentences:

The waiter brought the meal.
The waiter brought the meal to the table.
The waiter brought the meal of the day.

Phrases such as *the waiter, the meal, of the day*, or *brought the meal of the day* are constituents because they sound natural. On the contrary, the groups of words *meal to* or *meal of the* sound odd or not complete and therefore are not constituents.

The set of constituents in a sentence includes all the phrases that meet this description. Simplest constituents are the sentence's words that combine with their neighbors to form larger constituents. Constituents combine again and extend up to the sentence itself. Constituents can be pictured by boxed groups of sentence chunks (Figs. 8.1 and 8.2).

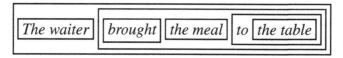

Fig. 8.1. The constituent structure of *The waiter brought the meal to the table*.

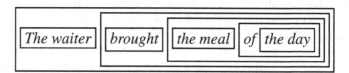

Fig. 8.2. The constituent structure of *The waiter brought the meal of the day*.

In Fig. 8.2, the phrase *the meal of the day* fits in a box, while in Fig. 8.1, *the meal* and *to the table* are separated. The reason is semantic. *The meal of the day* can be considered as a single entity, and so *of the day* is attached to *the meal*. Both can merge in a single constituent and hence fit in the same box. *To the table* is related to the sentence verb rather than to *the meal*: this phrase specifies where the waiter brought something. That is why the next enclosing box frames the phrase *brought the meal to the table* and not *the meal to the table*.

Constituents are organized around a headword that usually has the most significant semantic content. The constituent category takes its name from the headword part of speech. So, *the waiter, the meal, the day*, and *the meal of the day* are noun phrases (NPs), and *brought the meal of the day* is a verb phrase (VP). Prepositional phrases (PPs) are noun phrases beginning with prepositions such as *to the table* and *of the day*.

8.2.2 Tree Structures

Tree structures are an alternate representation to boxes where constituent names annotate the tree nodes. The symbol S denotes the whole sentence and corresponds to the top node. This node divides into two branches that lead to the NP and VP

nodes, and so on. Figure 8.3 shows the structure of *The waiter brought the meal to the table*, and Fig. 8.4 the structure of *The waiter brought the meal of the day*.

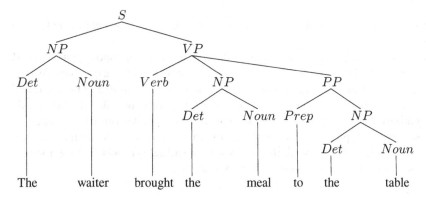

Fig. 8.3. Tree structure of *The waiter brought the meal to the table*.

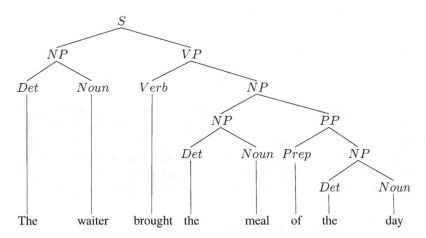

Fig. 8.4. Tree structure of *The waiter brought the meal of the day*.

8.2.3 Phrase-Structure Rules

Phrase-structure rules (PS rules) are a device to model constituent structures. PS rules rewrite the sentence or phrases into a sequence of simpler phrases that describe the composition of the tree nodes. More precisely, a PS rule has a left-hand side that is the parent symbol and a right-hand side made of one, two, or more symbols labeling the downward-connected nodes. For instance, rule

$S \rightarrow NP\ VP$

describes the root node of the tree: a sentence can consist of a noun phrase and a verb phrase.

A phrase-structure grammar is a set of PS rules that can decompose sentences and phrases down to the words and describe complete trees. The phrase categories occurring in Figs. 8.3 and 8.4 are sentence, noun phrase, verb phrase, and prepositional phrase. In the phrase-structure formalism, these categories are called the **nonterminal symbols**. Parts of speech or lexical categories here are determiners (or articles), nouns, verbs, and prepositions. PS rules link up categories to rewrite the sentence and the phrases until they reach the words – the **terminal symbols**. Table 8.1 shows a grammar to parse the sentences in Figs. 8.1 and 8.2.

Table 8.1. A phrase-structure grammar.

Phrases	Lexicon	
$S \rightarrow NP\ VP$	$Determiner \rightarrow the$	$Noun \rightarrow day$
$NP \rightarrow Determiner\ Noun$	$Noun \rightarrow waiter$	$Verb \rightarrow brought$
$NP \rightarrow NP\ PP$	$Noun \rightarrow meal$	$Preposition \rightarrow to$
$VP \rightarrow Verb\ NP$	$Noun \rightarrow table$	$Preposition \rightarrow of$
$VP \rightarrow Verb\ NP\ PP$		
$PP \rightarrow Preposition\ NP$		

The first rule in Table 8.1 means that the sentence consists of a noun phrase followed by a verb phrase. The second and third rules mean that a noun phrase can consist either of a determiner and a noun, or a noun phrase followed by a prepositional phrase, and so on. The left constituent is called the **mother** of the rule, and the right constituents are its **expansion** or its **daughters**. The sequence of grammar rules applied from the sentence node to get to the words is called a **derivation**.

8.2.4 The Definite Clause Grammar (DCG) Notation

The translation of PS rules into DCG rules is straightforward. The DCG notation uses the - - >/2 built-in operator to denote that a constituent can consist of a sequence of simpler constituents. DCG rules look like ordinary Prolog clauses except that the operator - - >/2 separates the head and body instead of : - /2. Let us use the symbols s, np, vp, and pp to represent phrases. The grammar in Table 8.1 corresponds to DCG rules:

```
s --> np, vp.
np --> det, noun.
np --> np, pp.
```

```
vp --> verb, np.
vp --> verb, np, pp.
pp --> prep, np.
```

DCG rules encode the vocabulary similarly. The left-hand side of the rule is the part of speech, and the right-hand side is the word put inside a list – enclosed between brackets:

```
det --> [the].
det --> [a].
noun --> [waiter].
noun --> [meal].
noun --> [table].
noun --> [day].
verb --> [brought].
prep --> [to].
prep --> [of].
```

The Prolog search mechanism checks whether a fact is true or generates all the solutions. Applied to parsing, the search checks whether a sentence is acceptable to the grammar or generates all the sentences accepted by this grammar.

Once the Prolog interpreter has consulted the DCG rules, we can query it using the input word list as a first parameter and the empty list as a second. Both queries:

```
?- s([the, waiter, brought, the, meal, to, the,
table], []).
Yes

?- s([the, waiter, brought, the, meal, of, the,
day], []).
Yes
```

succeed because the grammar accepts the sentences.

In addition to accepting sentences, the interpreter finds all the sentences generated by the grammar. It corresponds to the so-called syntactically correct sentences:

```
?-s(L, []).
L = [the, waiter, brought, the, waiter] ;
L = [the, waiter, brought, the, meal] ;
L = [the, waiter, brought, the, table] ;
...
```

In the grammar above, the two first lexical rules mean that a determiner can be either *the* or *a*. This rule could have been compacted in a single one using Prolog's disjunction operator ; /2 as:

```
det --> [the] ; [a].
```

However, like for Prolog programs, using the semicolon operator sometimes impairs the readability and is not advisable.

In our grammar, nonterminal symbols of lexical rules are limited to a single word. They can also be a list of two or more words as in:

```
prep --> [in, front, of].
```

which means that the word sequence *in front of* corresponds to a preposition.

DCG rules can mix terminal and nonterminal symbols in their expansion as in:

```
np --> noun, [and], noun.
```

Moreover, Prolog programs can mix Prolog clauses with DCG rules, and DCG rules can include Prolog goals in the expansion. These goals are enclosed in braces:

```
np --> noun, [and], noun, {prolog_code}.
```

as, for example:

```
np -->
  noun, [and], noun,
  {write('I found two nouns'), nl}.
```

8.3 Parsing with DCGs

8.3.1 Translating DCGs into Prolog Clauses

Prolog translates DCG rules into Prolog clauses when the file is consulted. The translation is nearly a mapping because DCG rules are merely a notational variant of Prolog rules and facts. In this section, we will first consider a naïve conversion method. We will then outline how most common interpreters adhering to the Edinburgh's Prolog (Pereira 1984) tradition carry out the translation.

A tentative translation of DCG rules in Prolog clauses would add a variable to each predicate. The rule

```
s --> np, vp.
```

would then be converted into the clause

```
s(L) :- np(L1), vp(L2) ...
```

so that each variable unifies with the word list corresponding to the predicate name. With this kind of translation and the input sentence *The waiter brought the meal*, variable

- L would match the input list [the, waiter, brought, the, meal];
- L1 would match the noun phrase list [the, waiter]; and
- L2 would match the verb phrase [brought, the, meal].

To be complete, the Prolog clause requires an `append/3` predicate at the end to link L1 and L2 to L:

```
s(L) :- np(L1), vp(L2), append(L1, L2, L).
```

Although this clause might seem easy to understand, it would not gracefully scale up. If there were three daughters, the rule would require two appends, and if there were four daughters, the rule would then need three appends, and so on.

In most Prologs, the translation predicate adds two variables to each DCG symbol to the left-hand side and the right-hand side of the rule. The DCG rule

```
s --> np, vp.
```

is actually translated into the Prolog clause

```
s(L1, L) :- np(L1, L2), vp(L2, L).
```

where L1, L2, and L are lists of words. As with the naïve translation, the clause expresses that a constituent matching the head of the rule is split into subconstituents matching the goals in the body. However, constituent values correspond to the difference of each pair of arguments.

- *The waiter brought the meal* corresponds to the s symbol and unifies with L1\L, where L1\L denotes L1 minus L.
- *The waiter* corresponds to the np symbol and unifies with L1\L2.
- *brought the meal* corresponds to the vp symbol and unifies with L2\L.

In terms of lists, L1\L corresponds to [the, waiter, brought, the, meal]; L1\L2 corresponds to the first noun phrase [the, waiter]; and L2\L corresponds to the verb phrase and [brought, the, meal].

L1 is generally set to the input sentence and L to the empty list, [], when querying the Prolog interpreter, as in:

```
?- s([the, waiter, brought, the, meal], []).
Yes
```

So the variables L1 and L2 unify respectively with [the, waiter, brought, the, meal] and [brought, the, meal].

The lexical rules are translated the same way. The rule

```
det --> [the].
```

is mapped onto the fact:

```
det([the | L], L).
```

Sometimes, terminal symbols are rewritten using the 'C'/3 (connects) built-in predicate. In this case, the previous rule could be rewritten into:

```
det(L1, L) :- 'C'(L1, the, L).
```

The 'C'/3 predicate links L1 and L so that the second parameter is the head of L1 and L, its tail. 'C'/3 is defined as:

```
'C'([X | Y], X, Y).
```

In many Prologs, the translation of DCG rules into Prolog clauses is carried out by a predicate named expand_term/2.

8.3.2 Parsing and Generation

DCG parsing corresponds to Prolog's top-down search that starts from the **start symbol**, s. Prolog's search mechanism rewrites s into subgoals, here np and vp. Then it rewrites the leftmost symbols starting with np and goes down until it matches the words of the input list with the words of the vocabulary. If Prolog finds no solution with a set of rules, it backtracks and tries other rules.

Let us illustrate a search tracing the parser with the sentence *The waiter brought the meal* in Table 8.2. The interpreter is launched with the query

```
?- s([the, waiter, brought, the, meal], []).
```

The Prolog clause

```
s(L1, L) :- np(L1, L2), vp(L2, L).
```

is called first (Table 8.2, line 1). The leftmost predicate of the body of the rule, np, is then tried. Rules are examined in the order they occur in the file, and

```
np(L1, L) :- det(L1, L2), noun(L2, L).
```

is then called (line 2). The search continues with det (line 3) that leads to the terminal rules. It succeeds with the fact

```
det([the | L], L).
```

and unifies L with [waiter, brought, the, meal] (line 4). The search skips from det/2 to noun/2 in the rule

```
np(L1, L) :- det(L1, L2), noun(L2, L).
```

noun/2 is searched the same way (lines 5 and 6). np succeeds and returns with L unified with [brought, the, meal] (line 7). The rule

```
s(L1, L) :- np(L1, L2), vp(L2, L).
```

proceeds with vp (line 8) until s succeeds (line 18).

The search is pictured in Fig. 8.5.

Table 8.2. Trace of *The waiter brought the meal.*

```
 1  Call: s([the, waiter, brought, the, meal], [])
 2  Call: np([the, waiter, brought, the, meal], _2)
 3  Call: det([the, waiter, brought, the, meal], _6)
 4  Exit: det([the, waiter, brought, the, meal], [waiter,
            brought, the, meal])
 5  Call: noun([waiter, brought, the, meal], _2)
 6  Exit: noun([waiter, brought, the, meal], [brought,
            the, meal])
 7  Exit: np([the, waiter, brought, the, meal], [brought,
            the, meal])
 8  Call: vp([brought, the, meal], [])
 9  Call: verb([brought, the, meal], _10)
10  Exit: verb([brought], [the, meal])
11  Call: np([the, meal], [])
12  Call: det([the, meal], _11)
13  Exit: det([the, meal], [meal])
14  Call: noun([meal], [])
15  Exit: noun([meal], [])
16  Exit: np([the, meal], [])
17  Exit: vp([brought, the, meal], [])
18  Exit: s([the, waiter, brought, the, meal], [])
```

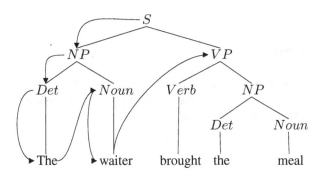

Fig. 8.5. The DCG parsing process.

8.3.3 Left-Recursive Rules

We saw that the DCG grammar in Table 8.1 accepts and generates correct sentences, but what about incorrect ones? A first guess is that the grammar should reject them. In fact, querying this grammar with *The brought the meal* (*) never returns or even crashes Prolog. This is due to the left-recursive rule

```
np --> np, pp.
```

Incorrect strings, such as:

The brought the meal (*)

trap the parser into an infinite loop. Prolog first tries to match *The brought* to

```
np --> det, noun.
```

Since *brought* is not a noun, it fails and tries the next rule

```
np --> np, pp.
```

Prolog calls np again, and the first np rule is tried anew. The parser loops hopelessly.

The classical method to get rid of the left-recursion is to use an auxiliary rule with an auxiliary symbol (ngroup), which is not left-recursive, and to rewrite the noun phrase rules as:

```
ngroup --> det, noun.
np --> ngroup.
np --> ngroup, pp.
```

When a grammar does not contain left-recursive rules, or once left-recursion has been removed, any sentence not accepted by the grammar makes Prolog fail:

```
?- s([the, brought, the, meal, to, the, table], []).
No
```

8.4 Parsing Ambiguity

The tree structure of a sentence reflects the search path that Prolog is traversing. With the rule set we used, verb phrases containing a prepositional phrase can be parsed along to two different paths. The rules

```
vp --> verb, np.
np --> np, pp.
```

give a first possible path. Another path corresponds to the rule

```
vp --> verb, np, pp.
```

This alternative corresponds to a syntactic ambiguity.

Two parse trees reflect the result of a different syntactic analysis for each sentence. Parsing

The waiter brought the meal to the table

corresponds to the trees in Figs. 8.3 and 8.6. Parsing

The waiter brought the meal of the day

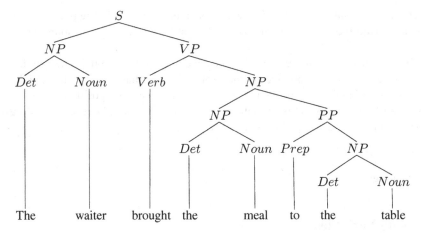

Fig. 8.6. A possible parse tree for *The waiter brought the meal to the table*.

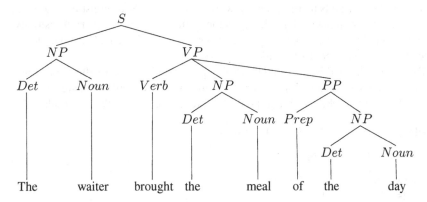

Fig. 8.7. A possible parse tree for *The waiter brought the meal of the day*.

corresponds to the trees in Figs. 8.4 and 8.7.

In fact, only Figs. 8.3 and 8.4 can be viewed as correct because the prepositional phrases attach differently in the two sentences. In

The waiter brought the meal to the table

the object is *the meal* that the waiter brings to a specific location, *the table*. These are two distinct entities. In consequence, the phrase *to the table* is a verb adjunct and must be attached to the verb phrase node.

In the sentence

The waiter brought the meal of the day

the verb object is *the meal of the day*, which is an entity in itself. The phrase *of the day* is a **postmodifier** of the noun *meal* and must be attached to the noun phrase node.

When we hear such ambiguous sentences, we unconsciously retain the one that is acceptable from a pragmatic viewpoint. Prolog does not have this faculty, and the parser must be hinted. It can be resolved by considering verb, preposition, and noun types using logical constraints or statistical methods. It naturally requires adding some more Prolog code. In addition, sentences such as

> *I saw a man with a telescope*

remain ambiguous, even for humans.

8.5 Using Variables

Like Prolog, DCG symbols can have variables. These variables can be used to implement a set of constraints that may act on words in a phrase. Such constraints govern, for instance, the number and gender agreement, the case, and the verb transitivity. Variables can also be used to get the result from a parse. They enable us to build the parse tree and the logical form while parsing a sentence.

DCG variables will be kept in their Prolog predicate counterpart after consulting. Variables of a DCG symbol appear in front of the two list variables that are added by expand_term/2 while building the Prolog predicate. That is, the DCG rule

```
np(X, Y, Z) --> det(Y), noun(Z).
```

is translated into the Prolog clause

```
np(X, Y, Z, L1, L) :-
    det(Y, L1, L2),
    noun(Z, L2, L).
```

8.5.1 Gender and Number Agreement

French and German nouns have a gender and a number that must agree with that of the determiner and the adjective. Genders in French are masculine and feminine. German also has a neuter gender. Number is singular or plural. Let us use variables Gender and Number to represent them in the noun phrase rule and to impose the agreement:

```
np(Gender, Number) -->
    det(Gender, Number), noun(Gender, Number).
```

To keep the consistency along with all the rules of the grammar, lexical rules must also describe the gender and number of words (Table 8.3).

A Prolog query on np with the French vocabulary loaded generates two noun phrases whose determiner and noun agree in gender:

Table 8.3. A vocabulary with gender and number.

French	German
det(masc, sing) --> [le].	det(masc, sing) --> [der].
det(fem, sing) --> [la].	det(fem, sing) --> [die].
det(_, plur) --> [les].	det(neut, sing) --> [das].
noun(masc, sing) --> [garçon].	det(_, plur) --> [die].
noun(fem,sing) --> [serveuse].	noun(masc, _) --> ['Ober'].
	noun(fem,sing) --> ['Speise'].

```
?- np(Gender, Number, L, []).
Gender = masc, Number = sing, L = [le, garçon];
Gender = fem, Number = sing, L = [la, serveuse];
No
```

In addition to number and gender, German nouns are marked with four cases: nominative, dative, genitive, and accusative. Determiner case must agree with that of the adjective and the noun. To implement the case agreement, let us mark the noun phrase rule with an extra variable Case.

```
np(Gender, Number, Case) -->
  det(Gender, Number, Case),
  adj(Gender, Number, Case),
  noun(Gender, Number, Case).
```

Let us also write a small vocabulary:

```
det(masc, sing, nominative) --> [der].
det(masc, sing, dative) --> [dem].
det(masc, sing, genitive) --> [des].
det(masc, sing, accusative) --> [den].

adj(masc, sing, nominative) --> [freundliche].
adj(masc, sing, dative) --> [freundlichen].
adj(masc, sing, genitive) --> [freundlichen].
adj(masc, sing, accusative) --> [freundlichen].

noun(masc, _, Case) -->
  ['Ober'],
  {Case \= genitive}.
noun(masc, _, genitive) --> ['Obers'].
```

Querying np with the German vocabulary

```
?- np(G, N, C, L, []).
```

generates four noun phrases whose determiner, adjective, and noun agree in gender and case:

```
G = masc, N = sing, C = nominative,
   L = [der, freundliche, 'Ober'];
G = masc, N = sing, C = dative,
   L = [dem, freundlichen, 'Ober'];
G = masc, N = sing, C = genitive,
   L = [des, freundlichen, 'Obers'];
G = masc, N = sing, C = accusative,
   L = [den, freundlichen, 'Ober'];
No
```

So far, we have seen agreement within the noun phrase. It can also be applied to categorize verbs. Some verbs such as *sleep*, *appear*, or *rushed* are never followed by a noun phrase. These verbs are called intransitive (iv). Transitive verbs such as *bring* require a noun phrase after them: the object (tv). We can rewrite two verb phrase rules to mark transitivity:

```
vp --> verb(iv).
vp --> verb(tv), np.


verb(tv) --> [brought].
verb(iv) --> [rushed].
```

8.5.2 Obtaining the Syntactic Structure

We used variables to implement constraints. Variables can also return the parse tree of a sentence. The idea is to unify variables with the syntactic structure of a constituent while it is being parsed. To exemplify this, let us use a simplified version of our grammar:

```
s --> np, vp.
np --> det, noun.
vp --> verb, np.
```

The parse tree of

The waiter brought the meal

is reflected by the Prolog term

```
T = s(np(det(the), noun(waiter)),
      vp(verb(brought), np(det(the), noun(meal))))
```

To get this result, the idea is to attach an argument to all the symbols of rules, where each argument represents the partial parse tree of its corresponding symbol. Each right-hand-side symbol will have a variable that corresponds to the structure it matches, and the argument of the left-hand-side symbol will unify with the structure it has parsed. Each rule carries out a part of the tree construction when it is involved in the derivation. Let us consider the rule:

```
s --> np, vp.
```

We add two variables to np and vp, respectively NP and VP, that reflect the partial structure they map. When the whole sentence has been parsed, NP and VP should be

```
NP = np(det(the), noun(waiter))
```

and

```
VP = vp(verb(brought), np(det(the), noun(meal)))
```

When NP and VP are unified, s combines them into a term to form the final structure. This term is s(NP, VP). We obtain the construction of the parse tree by changing rule

```
s --> np, vp
```

into

```
s(s(NP, VP)) --> np(NP), vp(VP).
```

The rest of the rules are modified in the same way:

```
np(np(D, N)) --> det(D), noun(N).
vp(vp(V, NP)) --> verb(V), np(NP).

det(det(the)) --> [the].
det(det(a)) --> [a].

noun(noun(waiter)) --> [waiter].
noun(noun(meal)) --> [meal].
noun(noun(table)) --> [table].
noun(noun(tray)) --> [tray].

verb(verb(bring)) --> [brought].
```

The query:

```
?- s(Structure, L, [])
```

generates all the sentences together with their syntactic structure:

```
Structure = s(np(det(the), noun(waiter)),
    vp(verb(brought), np(det(the), noun(waiter)))),
L = [the, waiter, brought, the, waiter] ;

Structure = s(np(det(the), noun(waiter)),
    vp(verb(brought), np(det(the), noun(meal)))),
L = [the, waiter, brought, the, meal] ;
```

```
Structure = s(np(det(the), noun(waiter)),
   vp(verb(brought), np(det(the), noun(table)))),
L = [the, waiter, brought, the, table]
...
```

8.6 Application: Tokenizing Texts Using DCG Rules

We can use DCG rules for many applications other than sentence parsing, which we exemplify here with a tokenization grammar.

8.6.1 Word Breaking

The first part of a tokenizer takes a character list as an input and breaks it into tokens. Let us implement this with a DCG grammar. We start with rules describing a sequence of tokens (tokens) separated by blanks. Blank characters (blank) are white spaces, carriage returns, tabulations, or control codes. A token (token) is a sequence of alphanumeric characters (alphanumerics) or another symbol (other). Finally, alphanumerics are digits, uppercase letters, lowercase letters, or accented letters:

```
tokens(Tokens) --> blank, {!}, tokens(Tokens).
tokens([FirstT | Tokens]) -->
  token(FirstT), {!}, tokens(Tokens).
tokens([]) --> [].

% A blank is a white space or a control character
blank --> [B], {B =< 32, !}.

% A token is a sequence of alphanumeric characters
% or another symbol

token(Word) -->
  alphanumerics(List), {name(Word, List), !}.
token(Symbol) -->
  other(CSymbol), {name(Symbol, [CSymbol]), !}.

% A sequence of alphanumerics is an alphanumeric
% character followed by the rest of alphanumerics
% or a single alphanumeric character.

alphanumerics([L | LS]) -->
  alphanumeric(L), alphanumerics(LS).
alphanumerics([L]) --> alphanumeric(L).
```

```
% Here comes the definition of alphanumeric
% characters: digits, uppercase letters without
% accent, lowercase letters without accent,
% and accented characters. Here we only consider
% letters common in French, German, and Swedish

% digits
alphanumeric(D) --> [D], { 48 =< D, D =< 57, !}.

% uppercase letters without accent
alphanumeric(L) --> [L], {65 =< L, L =< 90, !}.

% lowercase letters without accent
alphanumeric(L) --> [L], {97 =< L, L =< 122, !}.

% accented characters
alphanumeric(L) -->
  [L], {name(A, [L]), accented(A), !}.

accented(L) :-
  member(L,
    ['à', 'â', 'ä', 'å', 'æ, 'ç', 'é', 'è', 'ê', 'ë',
     'î', 'ï', 'ô', 'ö', 'œ', 'ù', 'û', 'ü', 'ß',
     'À', 'Â', 'Ä', 'Å', 'Æ', 'Ç', 'É', 'È', 'Ê', 'Ë',
     'Î', 'Ï', 'Ï', 'Ô', 'Ö', 'Œ', 'Ù', 'Û', 'Ü']).

% All other symbols come here
other(Symbol) --> [Symbol], {!}.
```

Before applying the `tokens` rules, we need to read the file to tokenize and to build a character list. We do it with the `read_file/2` predicate. We launch the complete word-breaking program with

```
?- read_file(myFile, CharList), tokens(TokenList,
   CharList, []).
```

8.6.2 Recognition of Sentence Boundaries

The second role of tokenization is to delimit sentences. The corresponding grammar takes the token list as an input. The sentence list (`sentences`) is a list of words making a sentence (`words_of_a_sentence`) followed by the rest of the sentences. The last sentence can be a punctuated sentence or a string of words with no final punctuation (`words_without_punctuation`). We define a sentence as tokens terminated by an end punctuation: a period, a colon, a semicolon, an exclamation point, or a question mark.

```
sentences([S | RS]) -->
  words_of_a_sentence(S),
  sentences(RS).
% The last sentence (punctuated)
sentences([S]) --> words_of_a_sentence(S).
% Last sentence (no final punctuation)
sentences([S]) --> words_without_punctuation(S).

words_of_a_sentence([P]) -->
  end_punctuation(P).
words_of_a_sentence([W | RS]) -->
  word(W),
  words_of_a_sentence(RS).

words_without_punctuation([W | RS]) -->
  word(W),
  words_without_punctuation(RS).
words_without_punctuation([W]) --> [W].

word(W) --> [W].

end_punctuation(P) --> [P], {end_punctuation(P), !}.

end_punctuation(P) :-
  member(P, ['.', ';', ':', '?', '!']).
```

We launch the whole tokenization program with

```
?- read_file(myFile, CharacterList),
   tokens(TokenList, CharacterList, []),
   sentences(SentenceList, TokenList, []).
```

8.7 Semantic Representation

8.7.1 λ-Calculus

One of the goals of semantics is to map sentences onto logical forms. In many applications, this is a convenient way to represent meaning. It is also a preliminary step to further processing such as determining whether the meaning of a sentence is true or not.

In some cases, the logical form can be obtained simultaneously while parsing. This technique is based on the principle of compositionality, which states that it is possible to compose the meaning of a sentence from the meaning of its parts. We shall explain this with the sentence

Bill is a waiter

and its corresponding logical form

```
waiter('Bill').
```

If *Pierre* replaces *Bill* as the waiter, the semantic representation of the sentence is

```
waiter('Pierre').
```

This means that the constituent *is a waiter* retains the same meaning independently of the value of the subject. It acts as a property or a function that is applied to other constituents. This is the idea of compositional analysis: combine independent constituents to build the logical form of the sentence.

The λ-calculus (Church 1941) is a mathematical device that enables us to represent intermediate constituents and to compose them gracefully. It is a widely used tool in compositional semantics. The λ-calculus maps constituents onto abstract properties or functions, called λ-expressions. Using a λ-expression, the property *is a waiter* is represented as

$$\lambda x.waiter(x)$$

where λ is a right-associative operator. The transformation of a phrase into a property is called a λ-abstraction. The reverse operation is called a β-reduction. It is carried out by applying the property to a value and is denoted

$$\lambda x.waiter(x)(Bill)$$

which yields

$$waiter(Bill)$$

Since there is no λ character on most computer keyboards, the infix operator ^ classically replaces it in Prolog programs. So $\lambda x.waiter(x)$ is denoted `X^waiter(X)`. λ-expressions are also valid for adjectives, and *is fast* is mapped onto `X^fast(X)`. A combination of nouns and adjectives, such as *is a fast waiter*, is represented as: `X^(fast(X), waiter(X))`.

While compositionality is an elegant tool, there are also many sentences where it does not apply. *Kick* is a frequently cited example. It shows compositional properties in *kick the ball* or *kick the box*. A counter example is the idiom *kick the bucket*, which means to die, and where *kick* is not analyzable alone.

8.7.2 Embedding λ-Expressions into DCG Rules

It is possible to use DCG rules to carry out a compositional analysis. The idea is to embed λ-expressions into the rules. Each rule features a λ-expression corresponding to the constituent it can parse. Parsing maps λ-expressions onto constituents rule-by-rule and builds the semantic representation of the sentence incrementally.

The sentence we have considered applies the property of being a waiter to a name: *Pierre* or *Bill*. In this sentence, the verb *is*, as other verbs of being, only links a name to the predicate `waiter(X)`. So the constituent *is a waiter* is roughly equivalent to *waiter*. Then, the semantic representation of common nouns or adjectives is that of a property: $\lambda x.waiter(x)$. Nouns incorporate their semantic representation as an argument in DCG rules, as in:

```
noun(X^waiter(X)) --> [waiter].
```

As we saw, verbs of being have no real semantic content. If we only consider these verbs, verb phrase rules only pass the semantics of the complement to the sentence. Therefore, the semantics of the verb phrase is simply that of its noun phrase:

```
vp(Semantics) --> verb, np(Semantics).
```

The `Semantics` variable is unified to `X^waiter(X)`, where `X` is to represent the sentence's subject. Let us write this in the sentence rule that carries out the β-reduction

```
s(Predicate) --> np(Subject),
vp(Subject^Predicate).
```

The semantic representation of a name is just this name:

```
np('Bill') --> ['Bill'].
np('Mark'] --> ['Mark'].
```

We complement the grammar with an approximation: we consider that determiners have no meaning. It is obviously untrue. We do it on purpose to keep the program simple. We will get back to this later:

```
np(X) --> det, noun(X).
det --> [a].
verb --> [is].
```

Once the grammar is complete, querying it with a sentence results in a logical form:

```
?- s(S, ['Mark', is, a waiter], []).
S = waiter('Mark').
```

The reverse operation generates a sentence from the logical form:

```
?- s(waiter('Bill'), L, []).
L = ['Bill, is, a, waiter].
```

8.7.3 Semantic Composition of Verbs

We saw that verbs of being played no role in the representation of a sentence. On the contrary, other types of verbs, as in

Bill rushed
Mr. Schmidt called Bill

are the core of the sentence representation. They correspond to the principal functor of the logical form:

```
rushed('Bill')
called('Mr. Schmidt', 'Bill')
```

Their representation is mapped onto a λ-expression that requires as many arguments as there are nouns involved in the logical form. *Rushed* in the sentence *Bill rushed* is intransitive. It has a subject and no object. It is represented as

```
X^rushed(X)
```

where X stands for the subject. This formula means that to be complete the sentence must supply rushed(X) with X = 'Bill' so that it reduces to rushed('Bill').

Called in the sentence *Mr. Schmidt called Bill* is transitive: it has a subject and an object. We represent it as

```
Y^X^called(X, Y)
```

where X and Y stand respectively for the subject and the object. This expression means that it is complete when X and Y are reduced.

Let us now examine how the parsing process builds the logical form. When the parser considers the verb phrase

called Bill

it supplies an object to the verb's λ-expression. The λ-expression reduces to one argument, $\lambda x.called(x, Bill)$, which is represented in Prolog by

```
X^called(X, 'Bill')
```

When the subject is supplied, the expression reduces to

```
called('Mr. Schmidt', 'Bill').
```

Figure 8.8 shows graphically the composition.

Let us now write a complete grammar accepting both sentences. We add a variable or a constant to the left-hand-side symbol of each rule to represent the constituent's or the word's semantics. The verb's semantics is a λ-expression as described previously, and np's value is a proper noun. The semantic representation is built compositionally – at each step of the constituent parsing – by unifying the argument of the left-hand-side symbol.

```
s(Semantics) --> np(Subject),
vp(Subject^Semantics).
vp(Subject^Semantics) --> verb(Subject^Semantics).
vp(Subject^Semantics) -->
  verb(Object^Subject^Semantics), np(Object).
np('Bill') --> ['Bill'].
np('Mr. Schmidt') --> ['Mr. Schmidt'].

verb(X^rushed(X)) --> [rushed].
verb(Y^X^called(X, Y)) --> [called].

?- s(Semantics, ['Mr. Schmidt', called, 'Bill'], []).
Semantics = called('Mr. Schmidt', 'Bill')
```

In this paragraph, proper nouns were the only noun phrases we considered. We have set aside common nouns and determiners to simplify the presentation. In addition, prepositions and prepositional phrases can also be mapped onto λ-expressions in the same way as verbs and verb phrases. We will examine the rest of semantics in more detail in Chap. 12.

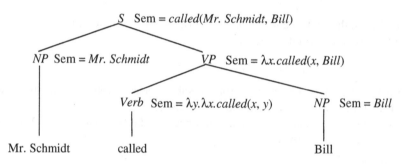

Fig. 8.8. Parse tree with a semantic composition.

8.8 An Application of Phrase-Structure Grammars and a Worked Example

As we saw in Chap. 1, the Microsoft Persona agent uses a phrase-structure grammar module to parse sentences and gets a logical form from them. Ball et al. (1997) give an example of order:

I'd like to hear something composed by Mozart.

that Persona transforms in the logical form:

```
like1 (+Modal +Past +Futr)
   Dsub: i1 (+Pers1 +Sing)
   Dobj: hear1
      Dsub: i1
      Dobj: something1 (+Indef +Exis +Pers3 +Sing)
         Prop: compose1
               Dsub: mozart1 (+Sing)
               Dobj: something1
```

Although Persona uses a different method (Jensen et al. 1993), a small set of DCG rules can parse this sentence and derive a logical form using compositional techniques. To write the grammar, let us simplify the order and proceed incrementally. The core of the sentence means that the user would like something or some Mozart. It is easy to write a grammar to parse sentences such as:

I would like something
I would like some Mozart

The sentence and the noun phrase rules are close to those we saw earlier:

```
s(Sem) --> np(Sub), vp(Sub^Sem).
```

In anticipation of a possible left-recursion, we use an auxiliary npx symbol to describe a nonrecursive noun phrase:

```
npx(SemNP) --> pro(SemNP).
npx(SemNP) --> proper_noun(SemNP).
npx(SemNP) --> det, proper_noun(SemNP).

np(SemNP) --> npx(SemNP).
```

The verb phrase is slightly different from those of the previous sections because it contains an auxiliary verb. A possible expansion would consist of the auxiliary and a recursive verb phrase:

```
vp --> aux, vp.
```

Although some constituent grammars are written this way, the treatment of auxiliary *would* is disputable. In some languages – notably in Romance languages – the conditional auxiliary is rendered by the inflection of the main verb, as in French: *j'aimerais*. A better modeling of the verb phrase uses a verb group that corresponds either to a single verb or to a sequence, including an auxiliary to the left and the main verb, here

```
verb_group(SemVG) --> aux(SemAux), verb(SemVG).
verb_group(SemVG) --> verb(SemVG).

vp(SemVP) --> verb_group(SemVP).
vp(SemVP) --> verb_group(Obj^SemVP), np(Obj).
```

The vocabulary is also similar to what we saw previously:

```
verb(Obj^Sub^like(Sub, Obj)) --> [like].
verb(Obj^Sub^hear(Sub, Obj)) --> [hear].

aux(would) --> [would].

pro('I') --> ['I'].
pro(something) --> [something].

proper_noun('Mozart') --> ['Mozart'].

det --> [some].
```

This grammar answers queries such as:

```
?- s(Sem, ['I', would, like, some, 'Mozart'], []).
Sem = like('I', 'Mozart')
```

Now let us take a step further toward the original order, and let us add the infinitive verb phrase *to hear*:

I would like to hear something
I would like to hear some Mozart

The infinitive phrase has a structure similar to that of a finite verb phrase except that it is preceded by the infinitive marker *to*:

```
vp_inf(SemVP) --> [to], vp(SemVP).
```

We must add a new verb phrase rule to the grammar to account for it. Its object is the subordinate infinitive phrase:

```
vp(SemVP) --> verb_group(Obj^SemVP), vp_inf(Obj).
```

The new grammar accepts queries such as:

```
?- s(Sem, ['I', would, like, to, hear, some,
   'Mozart'], []).
Sem = like('I', X^hear(X, 'Mozart'))
```

In the resulting logical form, the subject of *hear* is not reduced. In fact, this is because it is not explicitly indicated in the sentence. This corresponds to an anaphora within the sentence – an intrasentential anaphora – where both verbs *like* and *hear* implicitly share the same subject.

To solve the anaphora and to understand how Prolog composes the logical forms, instead of using the variable Obj, let us exhibit all the variables of the λ-expressions at the verb phrase level. The nonreduced λ-expression for *hear* is

```
ObjectHear^SubjectHear^hear(SubjectHear, ObjectHear).
```

When the infinitive verb phrase has been parsed, the `ObjectHear` is reduced and the remaining expression is

```
SubjectHear^hear(SubjectHear, 'Mozart').
```

The original λ-expression for *like* is

```
ObjectLike^SubjectLike^like(SubjectLike, ObjectLike)
```

where `ObjectLike` unifies with the λ-expression representing *hear*. Since both subjects are identical, λ-expressions can be rewritten so that they share a same variable in **Subject**^SemInf for *hear* and SemInf^**Subject**^SemVP for *like*. The verb phrase is then:

```
vp(Subject^SemVP) -->
  verb_group(SemInf^Subject^SemVP),
  vp_inf(Subject^SemInf).
```

and the new grammar now solves the anaphora:

```
?- s(Sem, ['I', would, like, to, hear, some,
  'Mozart'], []).
Sem = like('I', hear('I', 'Mozart'))
```

Let us conclude with the complete order, where the track the user requests is *something composed by Mozart*. This is a noun phrase, which has a passive verb phrase after the main noun. We model it as:

```
np(SemNP) --> npx(SemVP^SemNP), vp_passive(SemVP).
```

We also need a model of the passive verb phrase:

```
vp_passive(SemVP) -->
  verb(Sub^SemVP), [by], np(Sub).
```

and of the verb:

```
verb(Sub^Obj^compose(Sub, Obj)) --> [composed].
```

Finally, we need to modify the pronoun *something* so that it features a property:

```
pro(Modifier^something(Modifier)) --> [something].
```

Parsing the order with the grammar yields the logical form:

```
?- s(Sem, ['I', would, like, to, hear, something,
composed, by, 'Mozart'], []).
Sem = like('I', hear('I',
          X^something(compose('Mozart', X))))
```

which leaves variable X uninstantiated.[1] A postprocessor would then be necessary to associate X with *something* and reduce it.

---

[1] Prolog probably names it _Gxxx using an internal numbering scheme.

8.9 Further Reading

Colmerauer (1970, 1978) created Prolog to write language processing applications and, more specifically, parsers. Pereira and Warren (1980) designed the Definite Clause Grammar notation, although it is merely a variation on the Prolog syntax. Most Prolog environments now include a compiler that is based on the Warren Abstract Machine (WAM, Warren 1983). This WAM has made Prolog's execution very efficient.

Textbooks on Prolog and natural language processing delve mostly into syntax and semantics. Pereira and Shieber (1987) provide a good description of phrase-structure grammars, parsing, and formal semantics. Other valuable books include Gazdar and Mellish (1989), Covington (1994), and Gal et al. (1989).

SRI's Core Language Engine (Alshawi 1992) is an example of a comprehensive development environment based on Prolog. It is probably the most accomplished industrial system in the domain of syntax and formal semantics. Using it, Agnäs et al. (1994) built the Spoken Language Translator (SLT) to translate spoken English to spoken Swedish in the area of airplane reservations. The SLT has been adapted to other language pairs.

Exercises

8.1. Translate the sentences of Sect. 8.2.1 into French or German and write the DCG grammar accepting them.

8.2. Underline constituents of the sentence *The nice hedgehog ate the worm in its nest.*

8.3. Write a grammar accepting the sentence *The nice hedgehog ate the worm in its nest.* Draw the corresponding tree. Do the same in French or German.

8.4. The previous grammar contains a left-recursive rule. Transform it as indicated in this chapter.

8.5. Give a sentence generated by the previous grammar that is not semantically correct.

8.6. Verbs of being can be followed by adjective phrases or noun phrases. Imagine a new constituent category, `adjp`, describing adjective phrases. Write the corresponding rules. Write rules accepting the sentences *the waiter is tall*, *the waiter is very tall*, and *Bill is a waiter.*

8.7. How does Prolog translate the rule `lex -> [in, front].`?

8.8. How does Prolog translate the rule `lex -> [in], {prolog_code}, [front].`?

8.9. Write the `expand_term/2` predicate that converts DCG rules into Prolog clauses.

8.10. Write a grammar accepting the sentence *The nice hedgehog ate the worm in its nest* with variables building the parse tree.

8.11. Replace all nouns of the previous sentence by personal pronouns, and write the grammar.

8.12. Translate the sentence in Exercise 8.10 into French or German, and add variables to the rules to check number, gender, and case agreement.

8.13. Calculate the β-reductions of expressions $\lambda x.f(x)(y)$ and $\lambda x.f(x)(\lambda y.f(y))$.

8.14. Write a grammar that accepts the noun phrase *the nice hedgehog* and that builds a syntactic representation of it.

8.15. Persona's parser accepts orders like *Play before you accuse me*. Draw the corresponding logical form. Write grammar rules that parse the order *Play a song* and that build a logical form from it.

9

Partial Parsing

9.1 Is Syntax Necessary?

The description of language in terms of layers – sounds, words, and syntax – can suggest that a parse tree is a necessary step to obtain the semantic representation of a sentence. Yet, many industrial applications do not rely on syntax as we presented it before. The reason is that it is difficult to build a syntactic parser with large grammatical coverage, expensive in terms of resources, and sometimes it is not worth the cost.

Some applications need only to detect key words, as in some telephone speech servers. There, the speech recognition module spots meaningful words and sets the others aside. It enables the system to deal with the noisy environment or the fragmented nature of speech by telephone. Other applications rely on the detection of word groups such as noun phrases. Although sentences are not fully parsed, the result is sufficient to make use of it. Information retrieval and extraction are typical applications relying on group detection techniques.

In this chapter, we will examine a collection of techniques to extract incomplete syntactic representations. These techniques are generally referred to as partial or shallow parsing and operate on groups of words, often called **chunks**. Some of them just carry out the detection of key words or specific word patterns. Others use phrase-structure rules describing groups such as noun groups or verb groups. Finally, some techniques are an extension of part-of-speech tagging and resort to similar methods.

9.2 Word Spotting and Template Matching

9.2.1 ELIZA

A first shallow technique consists in matching predefined templates. It appeared with the popular ELIZA program that mimics a dialogue between a psychotherapist and his/her patient (Weizenbaum 1966). In fact, ELIZA understands merely nothing. She "spots" a handful of words or patterns such as *yes, no, why, I'm afraid of X, I like X,* etc., where *X* is a name or any group of words. When a template matches the user's sentence, ELIZA has a set of ready-made answers or questions mapped onto it. When no template matches, ELIZA tries to guess whether the sentence is a declaration, a negation, or an interrogation, and has repartees like *in what way, can you think of a specific example, go on*, etc. It enables the machine to follow the conversation with a semblance of realism. Table 9.1 shows some user/psychotherapist templates.

Table 9.1. Some ELIZA templates.

User	Psychotherapist
...I like X...	*Why do you like X?*
...I am X...	*How long have you been X?*
...father...	*Tell me more about your father*

ELIZA's dialogue pays a specific attention to words like *mother* and *father*. Whenever one of these words occurs, ELIZA asks for more details. We remind the reader that this program was created when Freudian theories were still very influential. Although the approach is now considered simplistic, at best, the psychoanalytical settings secured ELIZA a mainstream popularity.

9.2.2 Word Spotting in Prolog

A word spotting program can easily be written using DCG rules. Utterances are modeled as phrase-structure rules consisting of a beginning, the word or pattern to search, and an end. The translation into a DCG rule is straightforward:

```
utterance(U) --> beginning(B), [the_word], end(E).
```

Each predicate has a variable that unifies with the part of the utterance it represents. Variables B and E unify respectively with the beginning and the end of the utterance. The variable U is used to build the system answer as in the templates in Table 9.1.

Prolog translates the DCG rules into clauses when they are consulted. It adds two arguments to each predicate, and the previous rule expands into:

```
utterance(U, L1, L) :-
   beginning(B, L1, L2),
   c(L2, the_word, L3),
   end(E, L3, L).
```

We saw in Chap. 8 that each predicate in the rule covers a word sequence, and that it corresponds to the difference of the two new arguments: L1 minus L corresponds to utterance; L1 minus L2 corresponds to beginning; L3 minus L corresponds to end. Figure 9.1 shows the composition of the utterance with respect to the new lists.

Utterance

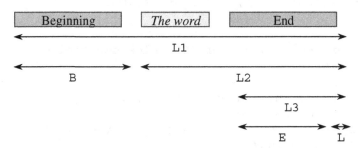

Fig. 9.1. The composition of utterance.

To match B and E, the trick is to define `beginning/3` and `end/3` as append-like predicates:

```
beginning(X, Y, Z) :- append(X, Z, Y).
end(X, Y, Z) :- append(X, Z, Y).
```

ELIZA is then a loop that reads the user input, tries to find a matching utterance, and answers with the corresponding template. It stops when the user writes the word *bye*. The next program is a simplified version of ELIZA. It matches the user/psychoanalyst pairs in Table 9.1.

```
%% A simplified version of ELIZA in Prolog
%%

% The main loop reads the input and calls process/1
% It stops when the input is the word bye.

eliza :-
    write('Hello, I am ELIZA. How can I help you?'),
    nl,
    repeat,
    write('> '),
    tokenize(In),
    process(In).

% process/1 accepts the user's utterance.
% It either terminates or tries to find a
% template matching the user's utterance

process([bye | _]) :-
    write('ELIZA: bye'), nl, !.
process(In) :-
    utterance(Out, In, []),
```

```
    !,
    write('ELIZA: '), write_answer(Out),
    fail.

% utterance is a set of DCG rules describing
% templates

utterance(['Why', aren, '''', t, you | Y]) -->
    ['I', am, not], end(Y).
utterance(['How', long, have, you, been | Y]) -->
    ['I', am], end(Y).
utterance(['Why', do, you, like | Y]) -->
    ['I', like], end(Y).
utterance(['Do', you, often, think, of | Y]) -->
    beginning(_), ['I', remember], end(Y).
utterance(['Please', tell, me, more, about, your,
       X, .]) -->
    beginning(_), [X], end(_), {important(X)}.
utterance(['Why', are, so, negative, '?']) -->
    [no].
utterance(['Tell', me, more, .]) -->
    [_].
utterance(['Please', go, on, .]) -->
    beginning(_).

% The Prolog clauses beginning/3 and end/3
% link the pieces of the utterance

beginning(X, Y, Z) :- append(X, Z, Y).
end(X, Y, Z) :- append(X, Z, Y).

% The Freudian facts
important(father).
important(mother).
important(brother).
important(sister).

% write_answer/1 prints the content of the list
% containing Eliza's answer.

write_answer([Head | Tail]) :-
    write(Head), write(' '),
    write_answer(Tail).
  write_answer([]) :- nl.
```

The next lines are a sample dialogue with ELIZA:

```
?- eliza.
Hello, I am ELIZA. How can I help you?
> yes
ELIZA: Tell me more .
> I like apples
ELIZA: Why do you like apples
>I went out with my father
ELIZA: Please tell me more about your father .
> no
ELIZA: Why are so negative ?
> I am cold
ELIZA: How long have you been cold
> bye
ELIZA: bye

Yes
?-
```

9.3 Multiword Detection

9.3.1 Multiwords

While ELIZA has no real application, the techniques we used in it can serve to detect specific patterns in texts or in speech. Finding multiple word expressions or multi-words is an example.

Multiwords – or multiword expressions (MWE) – are sequences of two or more words that act as a single lexical unit. They include proper nouns (names) of persons, companies, organizations, temporal expressions describing times and dates, and numerical expressions. Multiwords also include complex prepositions, adverbs, conjunctions, or phrasal verbs where each of the words taken separately cannot be clearly understood (Table 9.2). Multiwords corresponding to people or organization names are frequent in the press and the media, where new denominations surge and quickly disappear.

Although the identification of multiwords may seem intuitive, there are many tricky cases. In addition, people do not always agree on their exact definition.

9.3.2 A Standard Multiword Annotation

In the 1990s, The US Department of Defense organized series of competitions to measure the performance of commercial and academic systems on multiword detection. It called them the Message Understanding Conferences (MUC). To help benchmarking the various systems, MUC-6 and MUC-7 defined an annotation scheme that

Table 9.2. Multiwords in English and French.

Type	English	French
Prepositions	*to the left hand side*	*À gauche de*
Adverbs	*because of*	*à cause de*
Conjunctions		
Names	*British gas plc.*	*Compagnie générale d'électricité SA*
Titles	*Mr. Smith*	*M. Dupont*
	The President of the United States	*Le président de la République*
Verbs	*give up*	*faire part*
	go off	*rendre visite*

was shared by all the participants. This annotation has subsequently been adopted by commercial applications.

The MUC annotation restricts the annotation to information useful for its main funding source: the US military. It considers named entities (persons, organizations, locations), time expressions, and quantities. The annotation scheme defines a corresponding XML element for each of these three classes: <ENAMEX>, <TIMEX>, and <NUMEX> (Chinchor 1997), with which it brackets the relevant phrases in a text. The phrases can be real multiwords, consisting of two or more words, or they can be restricted to a single word.

The <ENAMEX> element identifies proper nouns and uses a TYPE attribute with three values to categorize them: ORGANIZATION, PERSON, and LOCATION, as in

```
the <ENAMEX TYPE="PERSON">Clinton</ENAMEX> government
<ENAMEX TYPE="ORGANIZATION">Bridgestone Sports Co.</ENAMEX>
<ENAMEX TYPE="ORGANIZATION">European Community</ENAMEX>
<ENAMEX TYPE="ORGANIZATION">University of California</ENAMEX>
in <ENAMEX TYPE="LOCATION">Los Angeles</ENAMEX>
```

The <TIMEX> element identifies time expressions and uses a TYPE attribute to distinguish between DATE and TIME, as in

```
<TIMEX TYPE="TIME">twelve o'clock noon</TIMEX>
<TIMEX TYPE="TIME">5 p.m. EST</TIMEX>
<TIMEX TYPE="DATE">January 1990</TIMEX>
```

The <NUMEX> element is used to bracket quantities. It has also a TYPE attribute to categorize MONEY and PERCENT, as in

```
<NUMEX TYPE="MONEY">20 million New Pesos</NUMEX>
<NUMEX TYPE="MONEY">$42.1 million</NUMEX>
<NUMEX TYPE="MONEY">million-dollar</NUMEX> conferences
<NUMEX TYPE="PERCENT">15 pct</NUMEX>
```

9.3.3 Detecting Multiwords with Rules

The detection of multiwords with rules is an extension of word spotting. Just as for word spotting, we represent multiwords using DCG rules. We use variables and Prolog code to extract them from the word stream and annotate them.

Compounded prepositions, conjunctions, and phrasal verbs are often listed in dictionaries and can be encoded as Prolog constants. Other multiwords raise more problems. Their identification generally requires specialized dictionaries of surnames, companies, countries, and trademarks. Some of these dictionaries, called **gazetteers**, are available on the Internet. They are built from the compilation of lexical sources such as economic and legal newspapers, directories, or Internet Web sites.

The extraction of multiwords also relies on hints that vary according to the type of entity to detect. Locations may include words such as *Ocean, Range, River*, etc. Legal denominations will be followed by acronyms such as *Ltd, Corp., SA*, and *GMBH*. Persons might be preceded by titles such as *Mr., Mme, Herr, Dr.*, by a surname, or have a capitalized initial. Currency phrases will include a sign such as €, $, £, etc., and a number. Such techniques can be applied to any measuring expression: length, time, etc.

Let us write rules to detect the phrasal verb *give up*, the French title *M. XXXX*, such as *M. Dupont*, and the European money worth *XXXX euros*, such as *200 euros*. As a result, the detector appends the multiword parts using an underscore character: give_up, or builds a list with surrounding XML tags [<ENAMEX>, 'M.', 'Dupont', </ENAMEX>], and [<NUMEX>, 200, euros, </NUMEX>]. The corresponding rules are:

```
multiword(give_up) --> [give, up].
multiword(['<ENAMEX>', 'M.', Name, '</ENAMEX>']) -->
   ['M.'], [Name],
   {
     name(Name, [Initial | _]),
     Initial >= 65, % must be an upper-case letter
     Initial =< 90
   }.
multiword(['<NUMEX>', Value, euros, '</NUMEX>']) -->
   [Value], [euros],
   {
     number(Value)
   }.
```

9.3.4 The Longest Match

Among the set of multiwords we want to detect, some may have a common suffix, as for the phrases *in front* and *in front of*. This corresponds to the rules:

```
multiword(in_front) --> [in, front].
multiword(in_front_of) --> [in, front, of].
```

With the sentence

The car in front of the house

rules as they are ordered above yield two solutions. The first multiword to be matched is *in front*, and if Prolog backtracks, it will find *in front of*. A backtracking strategy is not acceptable in most cases. What we generally want is the longest possible match (Table 9.3).

Table 9.3. Longer matches are preferred.

	English	**French**
Competing multiwords	*in front of*	*en face de*
	in front	*en face*
Examples	*The car in front*	*La voiture en face*
	In front of me	*En face de moi*

Prolog interpreters consider rules sequentially and downwards (from the beginning to the end). We implement the longest match by ordering the DCG rules properly. When several multiwords compete, i.e., have the same beginning, the longest one must be searched first, as in the sequence:

```
multiword(in_front_of) --> [in, front, of].
multiword(in_front) --> [in, front].
```

9.3.5 Running the Program

Now we will write a rule to embed the multiword description. If the word stream contains a multiword, it should be modeled as a beginning, the multiword, and an end, as in ELIZA. Its transcription into a DCG rule is straightforward:

```
word_stream_multiword(Beginning, Multiword, End) -->
  beginning(Beginning),
  multiword(Multiword),
  end(End).
```

Extracting the list of multiwords means that the whole word stream must be matched against the rule set. The multiword detector scans the word stream from the beginning, and once a multiword has been found, it starts again with the remaining words.

`multiword_detector/2` is a Prolog predicate. It takes the word stream `In` as the input and the multiword list `Out` as the output. It searches a multiword within the word stream using the `word_stream_multiword` DCG rule.

Each `word_stream_multiword` rule is translated into a Prolog predicate when consulted and two new variables are added. Thus, `word_stream_multi- word` is of arity 5 in the `multiword_detector` rule. The two last variables are unified respectively to the input list and to the empty list.

When `word_stream_multiword` reaches a multiword, `Beginning` is unified with the beginning of the word stream and `End` with the rest. The program is called recursively with `End` as the new input value.

```
multiword_detector(In, [Multiword | Out]) :-
  word_stream_multiword(Beginning, Multiword, End,
    In, []),
  multiword_detector(End, Out).
multiword_detector(_, []).
```

Using the detector with the sentence *M. Dupont was given 500 euros in front of the casino* results into `['<ENAMEX>', 'M. ', 'Dupont', '</ENAMEX>']`, `['<NUMEX>', 500, euros, '</NUMEX>']`, and `in_front_of`:

```
?- multiword_detector(['M.', 'Dupont', was, given,
500, euros, in, front, of, the, casino], Out).
Out = [[<ENAMEX>, M., Dupont, </ENAMEX>],
[<NUMEX>, 500, euros, </NUMEX>], in_front_of]
```

The result is a list containing sublists. The `flatten/2` predicate can replace recursively all the sublists by their elements and transform them into a flat list.

```
?- flatten([['<ENAMEX>', 'M. ', Dupont,
'</ENAMEX>'], ['<NUMEX>', 500, 'DM', '</NUMEX>'],
in_front_of], Out).
Out = [<ENAMEX>, M., Dupont, </ENAMEX>, <NUMEX>,
500, DM, </NUMEX>, in_front_of]
```

The multiword detector can be modified to output the whole stream. That is, the multiwords are tagged and other words remain unchanged. In this program, `Beginning` is appended to the multiword `Multiword` that has been detected to form the `Head` of the word stream. The `Head` and the result of the recursive call `Rest` form the `Output`. We must not forget the `End` in the termination fact.

```
multiword_detector(In, Out) :-
  word_stream_multiword(Beginning, Multiword, End,
    In, []),
  !,
  multiword_detector(End, Rest),
  append(Beginning, [Multiword], Head),
  append(Head, Rest, Out).
multiword_detector(End, End).
```

Let us now execute a query with this new detector with `flatten/2`:

```
?- multiword_detector(['M.', 'Dupont', was, given,
500, euros, in, front, of, the, casino], Res),
flatten(Res, Out).
Out = [<ENAMEX>, M., Dupont, </ENAMEX>, was,
given, <NUMEX>, 500, euros, </NUMEX>, in_front_of,
the, casino]
```

9.4 Noun Groups and Verb Groups

The word detection techniques enabled us to search certain word segments, with no consideration of their category or part of speech. The detection can extend to syntactic patterns.

The two most interesting word groups are derived from the two major parts of speech: the noun and the verb. They are often called **noun groups** and **verb groups**, although **noun chunks** and **verb chunks** are also widely used. In a sentence, noun groups (Table 9.4) and verb groups (Table 9.5) correspond to verbs and nouns and their immediate depending words. This is often understood, although not always, as words extending from the beginning of the constituent to the head noun or the head verb. That is, the groups include the headword and its dependents to the left. They exclude the postmodifiers. For the noun groups, this means that modifying prepositional phrases or, in French, adjectives to the right of the nouns are not part of the groups.

The principles we exposed above are very general, and exact definitions of groups may vary in the literature. They reflect different linguistic viewpoints that may coexist or compete. However, when designing a parser, precise definitions are of primary importance. Like for part-of-speech tagging, hand-annotated corpora will solve the problem. Most corpora come with annotation guidelines. They are usually written before the hand-annotation process. As definitions are often difficult to formulate the first time, they are frequently modified or complemented during the annotation process. Guidelines normally contain definitions of groups and examples of them. They should be precise enough to enable the annotators to bracket consistently the groups. The guidelines will provide the grammar writer with accurate definitions, or when using machine learning techniques, the annotated texts will encapsulate the linguistic knowledge about groups and make it accessible to the automatic analysis.

Table 9.4. Noun groups.

English	French	German
The waiter is bringing *the very big dish* on the table	*Le serveur* apporte *le très grand plat* sur la table	*Der Ober* bringt *die sehr große Speise* an dem Tisch
Charlotte has eaten *the meal* of the day	*Charlotte* a mangé *le plat* du jour	*Charlotte* hat *die Tagesspeise* gegessen

Table 9.5. Verb groups.

English	French	German
*The waiter **is bringing** the very big dish on the table*	*Le serveur **apporte** le très grand plat sur la table*	*Der Ober **bringt** die sehr große Speise an den Tisch*
*Charlotte **has eaten** the meal of the day*	*Charlotte **a mangé** le plat du jour*	*Charlotte **hat** die Tagesspeise **gegessen***

9.4.1 Groups Versus Recursive Phrases

The rationale behind word group detection is that a group structure is simpler and more tractable than that of a sentence. Group detection uses a local strategy that can accept errors without making subsequent analyses of the rest of the sentence fail. It also leaves less room for ambiguity because it sets aside the attachment of prepositional phrases. As a result, partial parsers are more precise. They can capture roughly 90% of the groups successfully (Abney 1996).

Like for complete sentences, phrase-structure rules can describe group patterns. They are easier to write, however, because verb groups and noun groups have a relatively rigid and well-defined structure. In addition, local rules usually do not describe complex recursive linguistic structures. That is, there is no subgroup inside a group and, for instance, the noun group is limited to a unique head noun. This makes the parser very fast. Moreover, in addition to phrase-structure rules, finite-state automata or regular expressions can also describe group structures.

9.4.2 DCG Rules to Detect Noun Groups

A noun group consists of an optional determiner *the*, *a*, or determiner phrase such as *all of the*, one or more optional adjectives, and one or more nouns. It can also consist of a pronoun or a proper noun – a name. This definition is valid in English. In German, sequences of nouns usually form a single word through compounding. In French, noun groups also include adjectives to the right of the head noun that we set aside.

The core of the noun group is a sequence of nouns also called a nominal expression. A first possibility would be to write as many rules as we expect nouns. However, this would not be very elegant. A recursive definition is more concise: a nominal is then either a noun or a noun and a nominal. Symbols noun and nominal have variables that unify with the corresponding word. This corresponds to the rules:

```
nominal([NOUN | NOM]) --> noun(NOUN), nominal(NOM).
nominal([N]) --> noun(N).
```

The simplest noun groups consist of a determiner and a nominal. The determiners are the articles, the possessive pronouns, etc. They are sometimes more complex phrases that we set aside here. Determiners are optional and the group definition must also represent its absence. A noun group can also be a proper noun or a pronoun:

```
% noun_group(-NounGroup)
% detects a list of words making a noun group and
% unifies NounGroup with it

noun_group([D | N]) --> det(D), nominal(N).
noun_group(N) --> nominal(N).
noun_group([PN]) --> proper_noun(PN).
noun_group([PRO]) --> pronoun(PRO).
```

The adjective group serves as an auxiliary in the description of noun group. It can feature one or more adjectives and be preceded by an adverb. If we set aside the commas, this corresponds to:

```
% adj_group(-AdjGroup)
% detects a list of words making an adjective
% group and unifies AdjGroup with it

adj_group_x([RB, A]) --> adv(RB), adj(A).
adj_group_x([A]) --> adj(A).

adj_group(AG) --> adj_group_x(AG).
adj_group(AG) -->
  adj_group_x(AGX),
  adj_group(AGR),
  {append(AGX, AGR, AG)}.
```

Past participles and gerunds can replace adjectives as in *A flying object* or *The endangered species*:

```
adj(A) --> past_participle(A).
adj(A) --> gerund(A).
```

We must be aware that these rules may conflict with a subsequent detection of verb groups. Compare the ambiguous phrase *detected words* in *the detected words* and *The partial parser detected words*.

Adjectives can precede the noun. Using the adjective group, we add two rules to the noun group:

```
noun_group(NG) -->
  adj_group(AG), nominal(NOM),
  {append(AG, NOM, NG)}.
noun_group(NG) -->
  det(D), adj_group(AG), nominal(NOM),
  {append([D | AG], NOM, NG)}.
```

9.4.3 DCG Rules to Detect Verb Groups

Verb groups can be written in a similar way. In English, the simplest group consists of a single tensed verb:

```
verb_group([V]) --> tensed_verb(V).
```

Verb groups also include adverbs that may come before the verb:

```
verb_group([RB, V]) --> adv(RB), tensed_verb(V).
```

Verb groups can combine auxiliary and past participles, or auxiliary and gerund, or modal and infinitive, or *to* and infinitive, or be simply an auxiliary:

```
verb_group([AUX, V]) --> aux(AUX),past_participle(V).
verb_group([AUX, G]) --> aux(AUX), gerund(G).
verb_group([MOD, I]) --> modal(MOD), infinitive(I).
verb_group([to, I]) --> [to], infinitive(I).
verb_group([AUX]) --> aux(AUX).
```

Verb groups can include adverbs and have more auxiliaries:

```
verb_group([AUX, RB, V]) -->
  aux(AUX), adv(RB), past_participle(V).
verb_group([AUX1, AUX2, V]) -->
  aux(AUX1), aux(AUX2), past_participle(V).
verb_group([MOD, AUX, V]) -->
  modal(MOD), aux(AUX), past_participle(V).
```

Now let us write a rule that describes a group inside a word stream: word_-
stream_group. As for with the multiwords, such a stream consists of a beginning, the group, and an end. Its transcription into a DCG rule is:

```
word_stream_group(Beginning, Group, End) -->
  beginning(Beginning),
  group(Group),
  end(End).
```

Finally, a group can either be a noun group or a verb group. As for multiwords, noun groups and verb groups are annotated using the XML tags <NG> and <VG>:

```
group(NG) -->
  noun_group(Group),
  {append(['<NG>' | Group], ['</NG>'], NG)}.
group(VG) -->
  verb_group(Group),
  {append(['<VG>' | Group], ['</VG>'], VG)}.
```

9.4.4 Running the Rules

Let us write a Prolog program using an approximation of the longest match algorithm to run the rules. The program is similar to the multiword detector:

```
group_detector(In, Out) :-
  word_stream_group(Beginning, Group, End, In, []),
  group_detector(End, Rest),
  append(Beginning, [Group], Head),
  append(Head, Rest, Out).
group_detector(End, End).
```

Since these rules match the longest segments first, they must be written from the longest to the shortest.

Although the grammar is certainly not comprehensive, it can fare reasonably well for a first step. We shall apply it to a text from the *Los Angeles Times* "Flying Blind With the Titans", December 17, 1996):

> *Critics question the ability of a relatively small group of big integrated prime contractors to maintain the intellectual diversity that formerly provided the Pentagon with innovative weapons. With fewer design staffs working on military problems, the solutions are likely to be less varied.*

The lexical rules for this text are:
The query results in:

```
?- group_detector([critics, question, the,
ability, of, a, relatively, small, group, of, big,
integrated, prime, contractors, to, maintain, the,
intellectual, diversity, that, formerly, provided,
the, pentagon, with, innovative, weapons, with,
fewer, design, staffs, working, on, military,
problems, the, solutions, are, likely, to, be,
less, varied], L), flatten(L, Out).
```

```
Out = [<NG>, critics, </NG>, <VG>, question,
</VG>, <NG>, the, ability, </NG>, of, <NG>, a,
relatively, small, group, </NG>, of, <NG>, big,
integrated, prime, contractors, </NG>, <VG>, to,
maintain, </VG>, <NG>, the, intellectual,
diversity, </NG>, that, <VG>, formerly, provided,
</VG>, <NG>, the, pentagon, </NG>, with, <NG>,
innovative, weapons, </NG>, with, <NG>, fewer,
design, staffs, </NG>, working, on, <NG>,
military, problems, </NG>, <NG>, the, solutions,
</NG>, <VG>, are, </VG>, likely, <VG>, to, be,
</VG>, less, varied]
```

```
det(the) --> [the].              adj(small) --> [small].
det(a) --> [a].                  adj(big) --> [big].
det(null_det) --> [].            adj(prime) --> [prime].
noun(critics) --> [critics].     adj(intellectual) -->
noun(ability) --> [ability].         [intellectual].
noun(group) --> [group].         adj(innovative) -->
noun(contractors) -->                [innovative].
    [contractors].               adj(military) --> [military].
noun(diversity) -->              adj(fewer) --> [fewer].
    [diversity].                 infinitive(be) --> [be].
noun(pentagon) -->               infinitive(maintain) -->
    [pentagon].                      [maintain].
noun(weapons) --> [weapons].     tensed_verb(question) -->
noun(design) --> [design].           [question].
noun(staffs) --> [staffs].       tensed_verb(provided) -->
noun(problems) -->                   [provided].
    [problems].                  past_participle(integrated) -->
noun(solutions) -->                  [integrated].
    [solutions].                 past_participle(varied) -->
adv(relatively) -->                  [varied].
    [relatively].                aux(are) --> [are].
adv(formerly) --> [formerly].
adv(likely) --> [likely].
adv(less) --> [less].
```

Though our detector misses groups, we realize that a limited effort has rapidly produced results.

9.5 Group Detection as a Tagging Problem

Group detection results in bracketing a word sequence with opening and closing annotations. This can be recast as a tagging problem. However, the detector inserts brackets between words instead of assigning tags to words. The most intuitive annotation is then probably to tag intervals. We can use algorithms very similar to part-of-speech tagging. They give us an alternate method to DCG rules describing verb groups and noun groups.

For the sake of simplicity, we will only present the noun group detection. Verb group detection uses exactly the same method. We first describe which tags to use to annotate the intervals. We will then see that we can equivalently tag the words instead of the gaps.

9.5.1 Tagging Gaps

Below are examples of noun group bracketing from Ramshaw and Marcus (1995). They insert brackets between the words where appropriate.

[$_{NG}$ The government $_{NG}$] has [$_{NG}$ other agencies and instruments $_{NG}$] for pursuing [$_{NG}$ these other objectives $_{NG}$] .

Even [$_{NG}$ Mao Tse-tung $_{NG}$] [$_{NG}$'s China $_{NG}$] began in [$_{NG}$ 1949 $_{NG}$] with [$_{NG}$ a partnership $_{NG}$] between [$_{NG}$ the communists $_{NG}$] and [$_{NG}$ a number $_{NG}$] of [$_{NG}$ smaller, non-communists parties $_{NG}$] .

If we only consider noun groups, the tagset must include opening and ending brackets. There must also be a tag to indicate a separation between two contiguous noun groups. The rest of the gaps are to be labeled with a "no bracket" tag.

As noun group detection usually considers nonrecursive sequences, we avoid nested brackets, as in this sequence: [. . . [or in this one:] . . .] . To check nesting while processing the stream, we must make a distinction between a "no bracket" inside a group and "no bracket" outside a group. The tagger can then prevent an inside "no bracket" to be followed by a closing bracket. We complement the tagset with no bracket tags denoting either we are within a group or outside (Table 9.6)

Table 9.6. Tagset to annotate noun groups.

Beginning	End	Between	No bracket (outside)	No bracket (inside)
[$_{NG}$	$_{NG}$]	$_{NG}$] [$_{NG}$	Outside	Inside

In addition to nested groups, other inconsistencies can occur, such as the sequences:

- [Outside
-] Inside or
- Outside]

The tagger must keep track of the preceding bracket to refuse illegal tags.

9.5.2 Tagging Words

Instead of tagging the gaps, we can equivalently tag the words. Ramshaw and Marcus (1995) defined a tagset of three elements {I, O, B}, where I means that the word is inside a noun group, O means that the word is outside, and B means that the word is at the beginning of a noun group that immediately follows another noun group. Using this tagging scheme, an equivalent annotation of the sentences in Sect. 9.5.1 is:

The/I government/I has/O other/I agencies/I and/I instruments/I for/O pursuing/O these/I other/I objectives/I ./O

Even/O Mao/I Tse-tung/I 's/B China/I began/O in/O 1949/I with/O a/I partnership/I between/O the/I communists/I and/O a/I number/I of/O smaller/I ,/I non-communists/I parties/I ./O

As in the case for gap tagging, some inconsistencies can occur, such as the sequence: O B. The tagger can refuse such sequences, mapping them to a plausible annotation. That is, in the example above, to change the B tag into an I tag.

As with part-of-speech tagging, group detection uses statistical and symbolic rules methods. Both statistics and rules are learned from hand-annotated corpora. Church (1988) first addressed group detection as a tagging problem and used statistical methods. Church tagged the gaps with brackets. Ramshaw and Marcus (1995) used a symbolic strategy. They adapted Brill's (1995) algorithm to learn rules to detect groups from annotated corpora. They used the {I, O, B} tagset.

9.5.3 Using Symbolic Rules

The symbolic rules algorithm is very similar to that of Brill's part-of-speech tagging method. The initial tagging considers the part of speech of the word and assigns the group annotation tag that is most frequently associated with it, that is, I, O, or B. Then, rules applied sequentially modify annotation tags.

Rules consider the immediate context of the tag to be modified, spanning a few words to the left and a few words to the right of the current word. More precisely, they take into account group annotation tags, parts-of-speech tags, and words around the current word. When the context of the current word matches that of the rule being applied, the current tag is altered.

Ramshaw and Marcus (1995) applied a set of 100 templates using a combination of 10 word contexts and 10 part-of-speech contexts, 20 templates in total, and 5 group annotation tag contexts spanning up to three words to the left and to the right:

- W_0, W_{-1}, W_1 being respectively the current word, the first word to the left, and the first word to the right.
- P_0, P_{-1}, P_1 being respectively the part of speech of the current word, of the first word to the left, and of the first word to the right.
- T_0, T_{-1}, T_1 being respectively the group annotation tag of the current word, of the first word to the left, and of the first word to the right.

Table 9.7 shows the complete set of templates. Word and part-of-speech templates are the same.

After training the rules on the Penn Treebank using its part-of-speech tagset, they could retrieve more than 90% of the noun groups. The five most productive rules are given in Table 9.8. The first rule means that an I tag is changed into an O tag when the current part of speech is an adjective (JJ) and the following word is tagged O. The second rule sets the tag to B if the two previous tags are I and the current word's part of speech is a determiner (DT).

9.5.4 Using Statistical Tagging

The maximum likelihood estimator determines the optimal sequence of gap tags $G = g_2, g_3, ..., g_n$, given a sequence of part-of-speech tags $T = t_1, t_2, t_3, ..., t_n$ and of

Table 9.7. Patterns used in the templates.

Word patterns		Noun group patterns	
Pattern	**Meaning**	**Pattern**	**Meaning**
W_0	Current word	T_0	Current noun group tag
W_{-1}	First word to left	T_{-1}, T_0	Tag bigram to left of current word
W_1	First word to right	T_0, T_1	Tag bigram to right of cur. word
W_{-1}, W_0	Bigram to left of current word	T_{-2}, T_{-1}	Tag bigram to left of current word
W_0, W_1	Bigram to right of current word	T_1, T_2	Tag bigram to right
W_{-1}, W_1	Surrounding words		
W_{-2}, W_{-1}	Bigram to left		
W_1, W_2	Bigram to right		
$W_{-1,-2,-3}$	Words 1 or 2 or 3 to left		
$W_{1,2,3}$	Words 1 or 2 or 3 to right		

Table 9.8. The five first rules from Ramshaw and Marcus (1995).

Pass	Old tag	Context	New tag
1	I	T_1 = O, P_0 = JJ	O
2	-	T_{-2} = I, T_{-1} = I, P_0 = DT	B
3	-	T_{-2} = O, T_{-1} = I, P_{-1} = DT	I
4	I	T_{-1} = I, P_0 = WDT	B
5	I	T_{-1} = I, P_0 = PRP	B

words $W = w_1, w_2, w_3, ..., w_n$. It maximizes Eq. (9.1), where w_{i-1} and w_i are the words before and after each gap together with the surrounding parts of speech: t_{i-1} and t_i. Church (1988) used a simpler equation in considering parts of speech only, see Eq. (9.2).

$$P(G) = \prod_{i=2}^{n} P(g_i|w_{i-1}, t_{i-1}, w_i, t_i). \tag{9.1}$$

$$P(G) = \prod_{i=2}^{n} P(g_i|t_{i-1}, t_i). \tag{9.2}$$

Finally, the equation can take the preceding tag into account to prevent illegal transitions. That is, to assign:

$$P(g_i|t_{i-1}, t_i, g_{i-1})$$

to 0 when $g_i = [$ and $g_{i-1} = Outside$, for instance.

9.6 Cascading Partial Parsers

We saw that partial phrase-structure rules could detect multiwords and groups. We can combine both detectors into a multilevel parser and add more layers. A tokenizer is necessary to read the text before it can be passed to the parsers. The applications generally use a part-of-speech tagger before the group detector (or **chunker**) and sometimes a morphological parser. The parser's structure is then a pipeline of analyzers, where each parsing level has a definite task to achieve. This technique is referred to as cascaded parsing.

With this approach, the exact number and nature of levels of cascaded parsers depends on the application and the expected result. In addition, some layers are relatively generic, while others are more specific and depend on the application goal. However, the principle is that one level uses the output of the lower level and passes on the result to the next layer (Fig. 9.2).

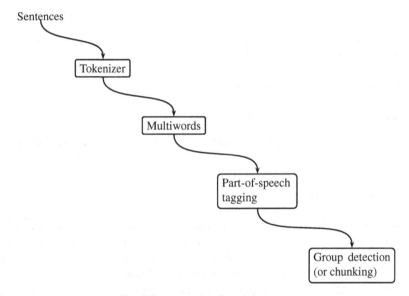

Fig. 9.2. A cascade of partial parsers.

9.7 Elementary Analysis of Grammatical Functions

9.7.1 Main Functions

In a previous section, we named groups according to the part of speech of their main word, that is, noun groups and verb groups. We can also consider their grammatical function in the sentence. We already saw that main functions (or relations) are subject, direct object, and indirect object. An accurate detection of function is difficult, but we can write a simplified one using cascaded parsing and phrase-structure rules.

We can recognize grammatical functions using a layer above those we have already described and thus complement the cascade structure. In English, the subject is generally the first noun group of a sentence in the active voice. It is marked with the nominative case in German, while case inflection is limited to pronouns in English and French. The direct object is the noun group just after the verb if there is no preposition in-between. It is marked with the accusative case in German.

We will now write a small set of DCG rules to encode this simplified description. The structure of a simple sentence consists of a subject noun group, a verb group in the active voice, and an object noun group. It corresponds to the rules:

```
sentence(S, V, O) -->
    subject(S),
    verb(V, active),
    object(O),
    ['.'].

subject(S) --> noun_group(S).

object(O) --> noun_group(O).

verb(V, active) --> verb_group(V, active).
```

We must modify the description of verbs in the terminal symbols to add an active/passive feature.

9.7.2 Extracting Other Groups

The Subject–Verb–Object relation is the core of most sentences. However, before extracting them, it is useful to skip some groups between them. Among the groups, there are prepositional phrases and embedded clauses, as in the two sequences: subject, prepositional groups, verb and subject, relative clause, verb.

A prepositional group can be defined as a preposition followed by a noun group. Using a DCG rule, this translates into:

```
prep_group([P | [NG]]) --> prep(P), ng(NG).
```

The detection of prepositional groups is a new layer in the cascade structure. A new rule describing ng as a terminal symbol is then necessary to be consistent with the noun groups detected before:

```
ng(['<NG>' | NG]) --> [['<NG>' | NG]].
```

Embedded clauses can be relative, infinitive, or subordinate. Here we will only consider relative and infinitive clauses that may modify a noun.

A relative clause is an embedded sentence whose subject or object has been replaced with a relative pronoun. The relative pronoun comes in front of the clause. For simple clauses, this translates into two rules:

```
%Relative clause: The relative pronoun is the subject
relative_clause(RC) -->
  relative_pronoun(R),
  vg(VG),
  ng(NG),
  {append([R | [VG]], [NG], RC)}.

% Relative clause: The relative pronoun is the object
relative_clause(RC) -->
  relative_pronoun(R),
  ng(NG),
  vg(VG),
  {append([R | [NG]], [VG], RC)}.
```

An infinitive clause is simply a verb phrase set in the infinitive. For simple examples, it translates into a verb group possibly followed by a noun group, where the verb group begins with *to*:

```
infinitive_clause([['<VG>', to | VG], NG]) -->
  vg(['<VG>', to | VG]),
  ng(NG).
infinitive_clause([['<VG>', to | VG]]) -->
  vg(['<VG>', to | VG]).
```

Like for noun groups, we must describe verb groups as a terminal symbol:

```
vg(['<VG>' | VG]) --> [['<VG>' | VG]].
```

Now let us write the rules to describe the modifiers and annotate them:

```
modifier(MOD) -->
  prep_group(PG),
  {append(['<PG>' | PG], ['</PG>'], MOD)}.
modifier(MOD) -->
  relative_clause(RC),
  {append(['<RC>' | RC], ['</RC>'], MOD)}.
modifier(MOD) -->
  infinitive_clause(IC),
  {append(['<IC>' | IC], ['</IC>'], MOD)}.
```

Finally, we write the detector to run the program:

```
modifier_detector(In, Out) :-
  word_stream_modifier(Beginning, Group, End, In, []),
  modifier_detector(End, Rest),
  append(Beginning, [Group], Head),
  append(Head, Rest, Out).
modifier_detector(End, End).
```

```
word_stream_modifier(Beginning, Group, End) -->
  beginning(Beginning),
  modifier(Group),
  end(End).
```

Let us apply these rules on the first sentence of the *Los Angeles Times* excerpt. We must add prepositions and a relative pronoun to the vocabulary:

```
prep(of) --> [of].
prep(with) --> [with].

relative_pronoun(that) --> [that].
```

And the query yields:

```
?- modifier_detector([[<NG>, critics, </NG>],
[<VG>, question, </VG>], [<NG>, the, ability,
</NG>], of, [<NG>, a, relatively, small, group,
</NG>], of, [<NG>, big, integrated, prime,
contractors, </NG>], [<VG>, to, maintain, </VG>],
[<NG>, the, intellectual, diversity, </NG>], that,
[<VG>, formerly, provided, </VG>], [<NG>, the,
pentagon, </NG>], with, [<NG>, innovative,
weapons, </NG>], with, [<NG>, fewer, design,
staffs, </NG>], working, on, [<NG>, military,
problems, </NG>], [<NG>, the, solutions, </NG>],
[<VG>, are, </VG>], likely, [<VG>, to, be, </VG>],
less, varied], O).

O = [[<NG>, critics, </NG>], [<VG>, question,
</VG>], [<NG>, the, ability, </NG>], [<PG>, of,
[<NG>, a, relatively, small, group, </NG>],
</PG>], [<PG>, of, [<NG>, big, integrated, prime,
contractors, </NG>], </PG>], [<IC>, [<VG>, to,
maintain, </VG>], [<NG>, the, intellectual,
diversity, </NG>], </IC>], [<RC>, that, [<VG>,
formerly, provided, </VG>], [<NG>, the, pentagon,
</NG>], </RC>], [<PG>, with, [<NG>, innovative,
weapons, </NG>], </PG>], [<PG>, with, [<NG>,
fewer, design, staffs, </NG>], </PG>], working,
on, [<NG>, military, problems, </NG>], [<NG>, the,
solutions, </NG>], [<VG>, are, </VG>], likely,
[<IC>, [<VG>, to, be, </VG>], </IC>], less, varied]
```

Prepositional phrases and relative clauses are labeled with <PG>, <IC>, and <RC> tags. Remaining groups are [<NG>, critics, </NG>], [<VG>, question, `</VG>`], and [`<NG>`, the, ability, `</NG>`], which correspond to heads of the subject, main verb, and the object of the sentence.

9.8 An Annotation Scheme for Groups in French

The PEAS initiative (Protocole d'évaluation des analyseurs syntaxiques, Gendner et al. 2003) defines an XML annotation scheme for syntactic groups (chunks) and functional relations for French. It was created to reconcile different annotation practices and enable the evaluation of parsers. We present here the chunk annotation that applies to continuous, nonrecursive constituents.

The PEAS annotation identifies six types of chunks:

1. verb groups (noyau verbal): `<NV></NV>`
2. noun groups (groupe nominal): `<GN></GN>`
3. prepositional groups: `<GP></GP>`
4. adjective groups: `<GA></GA>`
5. adverb groups: `<GR></GR>`
6. verb groups starting with a preposition: `<PV></PV>`

The sentence *En quelle année a-t-on vraiment construit la première automobile?* 'Which year the first automobile was really built?' is bracketed as

<GP> En quelle année </GP> <NV> a –t-on </NV> <GR> vraiment </GR> <NV> construit </NV> <GN> la première automobile</GN> ?

The annotation first identifies the sentence in the corpus:

```
<E id="2"> En quelle année a -t-on vraiment
construit la première automobile ? </E>
```

The second step tokenizes the words:

```
<DOCUMENT fichier="Guide.1">
  <E id="E2">
    <F id="E2F1">En</F>
    <F id="E2F2">quelle</F>
    <F id="E2F3">année</F>
    <F id="E2F4">a</F>
    <F id="E2F5">-t-on</F>
    <F id="E2F6">vraiment</F>
    <F id="E2F7">construit</F>
    <F id="E2F8">la</F>
    <F id="E2F9">première</F>
    <F id="E2F10">automobile</F>
    <F id="E2F11">?</F>
  </E>
</DOCUMENT>
```

using the DTD

```
<!ELEMENT DOCUMENT ( E+ ) >
<!ATTLIST DOCUMENT fichier NMTOKEN #REQUIRED >
<!ELEMENT E ( F)+>
<!ATTLIST E id NMTOKEN #REQUIRED >
<!ELEMENT F ( #PCDATA ) >
<!ATTLIST F id ID #REQUIRED >
```

The third step brackets the groups:

```
<DOCUMENT fichier="Guide.1.ph1.IR.xml">
  <E id="E2">
    <Groupe type="GP" id="E2G1">
     <F id="E2F1">En</F>
     <F id="E2F2">quelle</F>
     <F id="E2F3">année</F>
    </Groupe>
    <Groupe type="NV" id="E2G2">
     <F id="E2F4">a</F>
     <F id="E2F5">-t-on</F>
    </Groupe>
    <Groupe type="GR" id="E2G3">
     <F id="E2F6">vraiment</F>
    </Groupe>
    <Groupe type="NV" id="E2G4">
     <F id="E2F7">construit</F>
    </Groupe>
    <Groupe type="GN" id="E2G5">
     <F id="E2F8">la</F>
     <F id="E2F9">première</F>
     <F id="E2F10">automobile</F>
    </Groupe>
     <F id="E2F11">?</F>
  </E>
</DOCUMENT>
```

using the DTD

```
<!ELEMENT DOCUMENT ( E+ ) >
<!ATTLIST DOCUMENT fichier NMTOKEN #REQUIRED >
<!ELEMENT E ( F | Groupe )+>
<!ATTLIST E id NMTOKEN #REQUIRED >
<!ELEMENT Groupe ( F+ ) >
<!ATTLIST Groupe id ID #REQUIRED >
<!ATTLIST Groupe type ( GA | GN | GP | GR | NV |
```

```
PV ) #REQUIRED >
<!ELEMENT F ( #PCDATA ) >
<!ATTLIST F id ID #REQUIRED >
```

9.9 Application: The FASTUS System

9.9.1 The Message Understanding Conferences

The FASTUS system was designed at the Stanford Research Institute to extract information from free-running text (Hobbs et al. 1997, Appelt et al. 1993). It was implemented within the course of the Message Understanding Conferences (MUCs) that we introduced in Sect. 9.3.2. MUCs were organized to measure the performance of information extraction systems. They were held regularly until MUC-7 in 1997, under the auspices of DARPA, an agency of the US Department of Defense. The performances improved dramatically in the beginning and then stabilized. DARPA discontinued the competitions when it realized that the systems were no longer improving.

MUCs are divided into a set of tasks that have changed over time. The most basic task is to extract people and company names. The most challenging one is referred to as information extraction. It consists of the analysis of pieces of text ranging from one to two pages, the identification of entities or events of a specified type, and filling a predefined template with relevant information from the text. Information extraction then transforms free texts into tabulated information. Here is an example news wire cited by Hobbs et al. (1997) and its corresponding filled template drawn from MUC-3 (Table 9.9):

San Salvador, 19 Apr 89 (ACAN-EFE) – [TEXT] Salvadoran President-elect Alfredo Cristiani condemned the terrorist killing of Attorney General Roberto Garcia Alvarado and accused the Farabundo Marti National Liberation Front (FMLN) of the crime.

...

Garcia Alvarado, 56, was killed when a bomb placed by urban guerrillas on his vehicle exploded as it came to a halt at an intersection in downtown San Salvador.

...

Vice President-elect Francisco Merino said that when the attorney general's car stopped at a light on a street in downtown San Salvador, an individual placed a bomb on the roof of the armored vehicle.

...

According to the police and Garcia Alvarado's driver, who escaped unscathed, the attorney general was traveling with two bodyguards. One of them was injured.

Table 9.9. A template derived from the previous text. After Hobbs et al. (1997).

Template slots	Information extracted from the text
Incident: Date	19 Apr 89
Incident: Location	El Salvador: San Salvador (city)
Incident: Type	Bombing
Perpetrator: Individual ID	*urban guerrillas*
Perpetrator: Organization ID	*FMLN*
Perpetrator: Organization confidence	Suspected or accused by authorities: *FMLN*
Physical target: Description	*vehicle*
Physical target: Effect	Some damage: *vehicle*
Human target: Name	*Roberto Garcia Alvarado*
Human target: Description	*Attorney general*: *Roberto Garcia Alvarado*
	driver
	bodyguards
Human target: Effect	Death: *Roberto Garcia Alvarado*
	No injury: *driver*
	Injury: *bodyguards*

9.9.2 The Syntactic Layers of the FASTUS System

FASTUS uses partial parsers that are organized as a cascade of finite-state automata. It includes a tokenizer, a multiword detector, and a group detector as first layers. The detector uses a kind of longest match algorithm. Verb groups are tagged with active, passive, gerund, and infinitive features. Then FASTUS combines some groups into more complex phrases. Complex groups include notably the combination of adjacent nouns groups (appositives):

The joint venture, <u>Bridgestone Sports Taiwan Co.</u>
First noun group   Second noun group

of noun groups separated by prepositions *of* or *for* (noun postmodifiers):

The board of <u>directors</u>

and of noun group conjunctions:

<u>*a local concern*</u> and <u>*a Japanese trading house*</u>

Complex groups also include verb expressions such as:

plan to set up
announced a plan to form

Such complex groups can be found in French and German, where they have often a one-word counterpart in another language:

mettre une lettre à la poste 'mail a letter'
jemanden kennen lernen 'know somebody'

They merely reduce to a single semantic entity that is formed differently from one language to another.

FASTUS' upper layers then deal with grammatical functions and semantics. FASTUS attempts to reduce sentences to a basic pattern consisting of a subject, a verb, and an object. Finally, FASTUS assigns a sense to some groups by annotating them with a semantic category such as company, product, joint venture, location, and so on.

SRI first used a full parser called TACITUS, and FASTUS as a front-end to off-load it of some tasks. Seeing the excellent results and speed of FASTUS, SRI completely replaced TACITUS with FASTUS. It had a considerable influence on the present evolution of parsing techniques. FASTUS proved that the local and cascade approach was more efficient and much faster than other global analyses for information extraction. It had a considerable number of followers.

9.9.3 Evaluation of Information Extraction Systems

The MUCs introduced a metric to evaluate the performance of information extraction systems using three figures: recall, precision, and the F-measure. This latter metric, originally borrowed from library science, proved very generic to summarize the overall effectiveness of a system. It has been used in many other fields of language processing since then.

To explain these figures, let us stay in our library and imagine we want to retrieve all the documents on a specific topic, say *morphological parsing*. An automatic system to query the library catalog will, we hope, return some of them, but possibly not all. On the other hand, everyone who has searched a catalog knows that we will get irrelevant documents: *morphological pathology, cell morphology*, and so on. Table 9.10 summarizes the possible cases into which documents fall.

Table 9.10. Documents in a library returned from a catalog query and split into relevant and irrelevant books.

	Relevant documents	Irrelevant documents
Retrieved	A	B
Not retrieved	C	D

Recall measures how much relevant information the system has retrieved. It is defined as the number of relevant documents retrieved by the system divided by number of relevant documents in the library:

$$\text{Recall} = \frac{A}{A \cup C}.$$

Precision is the accuracy of what has been returned. It measures how much of the information is actually correct. It is defined as the number of correct documents returned divided by the total number of documents returned.

$$\text{Precision} = \frac{A}{A \cup B}.$$

Recall and precision are combined into the F-**measure**, which is defined as the harmonic mean of both numbers:

$$F = \frac{2PR}{P + R}.$$

The F-measure is a composite metric that reflects the general performance of a system. It does not privilege precision at the expense of recall, or vice versa. An arithmetic mean would have made it very easy to reach 50% using, for example, very selective rules with a recall of 100 and a precision of 0.

Using a β-coefficient, it is possible to give an extra weight to either precision, $\beta > 1$, or recall, $\beta < 1$, however:

$$F = \frac{(\beta^2 + 1)PR}{\beta^2 P + R}.$$

Finally, a **fallout** figure is also sometimes used that measures the proportion of irrelevant documents that have been selected.

$$\text{Fallout} = \frac{B}{B \cup D}.$$

9.10 Further Reading

Partial or shallow parsing has attracted a considerable interest in the 1990s and has renewed the field. This is largely due to the simplicity of the methods it involves. It is also due to its recent successes in information extraction competitions such as the MUCs (see, for instance, MUC-5 (1993)). The definition of the Named Entity annotation can be read from the MUC-7 web page: www.itl.nist.gov/iaui/894.02/-related_projects/muc/proceedings/muc_7_toc.html.

One of the first partial parsing systems is due to Ejerhed (1988). Appelt et al. (1993) describe with eloquence the history and structure of the FASTUS system. Abney (1994) has surveyed partial parsing with much detail and provides a comprehensive bibliography of 200 papers! Roche and Schabes (1997) and Kornai (1999) are other sources for partial parsing techniques.

Partial parsing was the topic of a series of conferences on Computational Natural Language Learning (CoNLL). Each year, the CoNLL conference organizes a "shared task" where it provides an annotated training set. Participants can train their system on this set, evaluate it on a common test set, and report a description of their algorithms and results in the proceedings. In 1999, the shared task was dedicated to noun group chunking (http://www.cnts.ua.ac.be/conll99/npb/); in 2000, it was extended to other chunks (http://www.cnts.ua.ac.be/conll2000/chunking/), and in 2001, the topic was the identification of clauses (http://www.cnts.ua.ac.be/conll2001/clauses/). The

CoNLL sites and proceedings are extremely valuable as they provide data sets, annotation schemes, a good background literature, and an excellent idea of the state of the art.

The development of partial parsing has been driven by applications without concern for a specific linguistic framework. This is a notable difference from many other areas of language processing, where theories abound. Functional and dependency grammars (Tesnière 1966, Mel'cuk 1988) may offer background and provide readers with a sound theory perspective.

Exercises

9.1. Complement the ELIZA program and add possible templates and answers.

9.2. Implement a multiword detector to detect dates in formats such as in English: 04/04/1997 or April 4, 1997, and in French: 20/04/1997 or 20 avril 1997.

9.3. Complement the noun group grammar and write down the vocabulary to recognize the noun groups of the text:
The big tobacco firms are fighting back in the way that served them well for 40 victorious years, pouring their wealth into potent, relentless legal teams. But they are also starting to talk of striking deals – anathema for those 40 years, and a sure sign that, this time, victory is less certain.
(*The Economist*, no. 8004, 1997).

9.4. See Exercise 9.3; do the same for verb groups.

9.5. Write a noun group grammar to parse the French text:
Les limites de la régulation de l'audiovisuel sont clairement définies aujourd'hui par la loi. C'est le principal handicap du CSA : son champ d'action est extrêmement limité. Alors que la télévision numérique prend son essor, le CSA, dont les compétences s'arrêtent au câble et à l'hertzien, n'a aucun pouvoir pour contrôler ou sanctionner la télévision de demain formée par les chaînes satellitaires.
(*Le Monde*, mercredi 3 septembre 1997).

9.6. See Exercise 9.5; do the same for verb groups.

9.7. Write a noun group grammar to parse the German text:
Die Freude über das neue große Europa wird also nur von kurzer Dauer sein. Die Probleme, die sich aus einer Union der 25 ergeben, dürften dagegen Regierungen und Völker über Jahre hinweg in Atem halten. Zunächst einmal wird es alles andere als leicht sein, die 10 neuen Mitgliedsstaaten zu integrieren. Die Migrationswellen, die von ihnen ausgehen, werden der „alten" EU reichlich Kopfschmerzen bereiten. Vor allem stellt sich der Entscheidungsprozess innerhalb der Union künftig noch weitaus schwieriger dar.
(*Die Zeit*, 30 April 2004).

9.8. See Exercise 9.7; do the same for verb groups.

9.9. Adapt the Prolog code of Brill's tagger from Chap. 6 so that it can detect noun groups.

9.10. Write rules that detects some complex noun groups:
- Adjacent nouns groups linked by the prepositions *of* or *for*
- Noun group conjunctions

9.11. Find press wires on football matches on the Web and implement a program to retrieve teams' names and final scores. Use a base of football team names, and adopt a cascaded architecture.

10

Syntactic Formalisms

10.1 Introduction

Studies on syntax have been the core of linguistics for most of the 20th century. While the goals of traditional grammars had been mostly to prescribe what the correct usage of a language is, the then-emerging syntactic theories aimed at an impartial description of language structures. These ideas revolutionized the field. Research activity was particularly intense in the years 1940–1970, and the focus on syntax was so great that, for a time, it nearly eclipsed phonetics, morphology, semantics, and other disciplines of linguistics.

Among all modern syntax researchers, Noam Chomsky has had a considerable and indisputable influence. Chomsky's seminal work, *Syntactic Structures* (1957), is still considered by many as a key reading in linguistics. In his book (in Sect. 6.1), Chomsky defined grammars as *essentially a theory of* [a language] that should be (1) adequate: whose correctness should be measurable using corpora; (2) general: extendible to a variety of languages, and, as far as possible, (3) simple. As goals, he assigned grammatical rules to describe syntactic structures:

> "These rules express structural relations among the sentences of the corpus and the indefinite number of sentences generated by the grammar beyond the corpus (predictions)."

More specifically (in Sect. 5.5), Chomsky outlined a formal model of syntax under the form of grammars that was precise enough to be programmable and verifiable.

Chomsky's ideas appealed to the linguistics community because they featured an underlying analogy between human languages and computer – or formal – languages together with a mathematical formalism that was already used for compilers. Chomsky came at a convergence point where advances in computer technology, mathematical logic, and programming languages made his theory possible and acceptable. Chomsky's theories on syntactic structures have originated much research in the domain and an astounding number of followers, notably in the United States.

In addition, his theories spurred a debate that went well beyond linguistic circles reaching psychology and philosophy.

In the meantime, linguists in Europe developed other structural approaches and also tried to derive generic linguistic structures. But instead of using the computer operation as a model or to posit cognition universals, as Chomsky did, some of them tried to study and expose examples from a variety of languages to prove their theories. The most prominent figure of the European school is Lucien Tesnière. Although Tesnière's work (1959, 2nd edn., 1966, both posthumous) is less known it is gaining recognition and it is used with success in implementations of grammars and parsers for English, French, German, and many other languages.

Many computational models of syntactic structures are presently based on the notion of constituent. They are inherited from the American school and are a part of Chomskyan grammars – although Chomsky does not limit grammars to a constituent decomposition. The European school has its origin in an older tradition. It is based on the notion of connections between words where each word of a sentence is linked to another one under a relation of subordination or dependence. For this reason, these syntactic models are also called dependency grammars. This chapter introduces both structural approaches – **constituency** and **dependency** – and associated formalisms.

10.2 Chomsky's Grammar in Syntactic Structures

Chomsky fractionates a grammar into three components. The first level consists of phrase-structure (PS) rules expressing constituency. The second one is made of transformation rules that complement PS rules. **Transformations** enable us to derive automatically new constructions from a given structure: a declarative form into an interrogative or a negative one; an active sentence into a passive one. Transformation rules apply to constituent structures or trees and describe systematic mappings onto new structures.

Initially, PS and transformation rules used a vocabulary made of morphemes, roots, and affixes, as well as complete words. The inflection of a verb with the past participle tense was denoted [*en + verb*] where *en* represented the past participle affix, for example, [*en + arrive*]. A third **morphophonemic** component handled the final word generation, mapping forms such as [*en + arrive*] onto *arrived*.

10.2.1 Constituency: A Formal Definition

Constituency is usually associated with context-free grammars. Formally, such grammars are defined by:

1. A set of designated start symbols, Σ, covering the sentences to parse. This set can be reduced to a single symbol, such as `sentence`, or divided into more symbols: `declarative_sentence`, `interrogative_sentence`.
2. A set of nonterminal symbols enabling the representation of the syntactic categories. This set includes the sentence and phrase categories.

3. A set of terminal symbols representing the vocabulary: words of the lexicon, possibly morphemes.
4. A set of rules, F, where the left-hand-side symbol of the rule is rewritten in the sequence of symbols of the right-hand side.

Chomsky (1957) portrayed PS rules with an example generating *the man hit the ball*. It has a straightforward equivalent in DCG:

```
sentence --> np, vp.
np --> t, n.
vp -- verb, np.
t --> [the].
n --> [man] ; [ball] ; etc.
verb --> [hit] ; [took] ; etc.
```

A set of such PS rules can generate sentences. Chomsky illustrated it using a mechanism that resembles the top-down algorithm of Prolog (Fig. 10.1).

Sentence	0
NP + VP	1
T + N + VP	2
T + N + Verb + NP	3
the + N + Verb + NP	4
the + man + Verb + NP	5
the + man + hit + NP	6
the + man + hit + T + N	7
the + man + hit + the + N	8
the + man + hit + the + ball	9

Fig. 10.1. Generation of sentences.

Generation was the main goal of Chomsky's grammars: to produce all potential sentences – word and morpheme sequences – considered to be syntactically correct or acceptable by native speakers. Chomsky introduced recursion in grammars to give a finite set of rules an infinite capacity of generation.

From the initial goal of generation, computational linguists wrote and used grammars to carry out recognition – or parsing – of syntactically correct sentences. A sentence has then to be matched against the rules to check whether it falls within the generative scope of the grammar. Parsing results in a parse tree – the sequence of grammar rules that were applied. The parsing process can be carried out using:

- a top-down mechanism, which starts from the initial symbol – the sentence – down to the words of the sentence to be parsed
- a bottom-up mechanism, which starts from the words of the sentence to be parsed up to the sentence symbol

Some parsing algorithms run more efficiently with a restricted version of context-free grammars called the **Chomsky normal form** (CNF). Rules in the CNF have either two nonterminal symbols to their right-hand side or one nonempty terminal symbol:

```
lhs --> rhs1, rhs2.
lhs --> [a].
```

Any grammar can be converted into an equivalent CNF grammar using auxiliary symbols and rules as for

```
lhs --> rhs1, rhs2, rhs3.
```

which is equivalent to

```
lhs --> rhs1, lhs_aux.
lhs_aux --> rhs2, rhs3.
```

The equivalence is said to be weak because the resulting grammar generates the same sentences but does not yield exactly the same parse trees.

10.2.2 Transformations

The transformational level consists of the mechanical rearrangement of sentences according to some syntactic relations: active/passive, declarative/interrogative, etc. A transformation operates on a sentence with a given phrase structure and converts it into a new sentence with a new derived phrase structure. Transformations use rules – transformational rules or T-rules – to describe the conversion mechanism as:

```
T1: np1, aux, v, np2 →
    np2, aux, [be], [en], v, [by], np1
```

which associates an active sentence to its passive counterpart. The active part of the rule matches sentences such as

the man will hit the ball

and its passive part enables us to generate the equivalent passive sentence:

the ball will be (en hit) by the boy

where *(en hit)* corresponds to the past participle of verb *to hit*. An additional transformational rule permutes these two elements:

```
T2: affix, v →
    v, affix, #
```

where # marks a word boundary. Once applied, it yields

the ball will be hit en # by the boy

Hit en # is then rewritten into *hit* by morphophonemic rules. Finally, the transformational process yields:

the ball will be hit by the boy

A tree-to-tree mapping as shown in Fig. 10.2 can also reflect transformation rules.

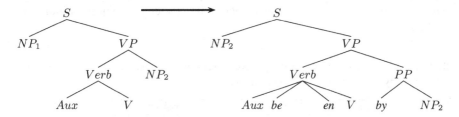

Fig. 10.2. A tree-to-tree mapping representing the active/passive transformational rule.

Other common transformations include (Chomsky 1957):

- Negations. *John comes → John doesn't come.*
- Yes/no questions. *they arrive → do they arrive; they have arrived → have they arrived; they can arrive → can they arrive; they arrived → did they arrive*
- Interrogatives. *John ate an apple → did John eat an apple; John ate an apple → what did John eat; John ate an apple → who ate an apple*
- Conjunction. *(the scene of the movie was in Chicago; the scene of the play was in Chicago) → the scene of the movie and of the play was in Chicago.*
- Topicalization. that is, moving a constituent in front of a sentence to emphasize it. *the waiter brought the meal to the table → to the table, the waiter brought the meal; I don't like this meal → this meal, I don't like.*

In Chomsky's formalism, PS rules are written so that certain generated sentences require a transformation to be correct. Such transformations are said to be obligatory. An example is given by the affix permutation rule (T_2). Other rules are optional, such as the passive/active transformation (T_1). PS rules and obligatory transformations account for the "kernel of a language" and generate "kernel sentences". All other sentences can be unfolded and mapped onto this kernel using one or more transformations.

According to Chomsky, transformations simplify the description of a grammar, and make it more compact. Writing a grammar only requires the phrase structure of kernel sentences, and all others are derived from transformations. Later Chomsky related kernel sentences to a deep structure, while transformed sentences correspond to a surface structure. Transformations would then map the surface structure of a sentence onto its deep structure. The deep structure would consist of a set of obligatory transformations and a core phrase structure on which no transformation could be carried out.

10.2.3 Transformations and Movements

Transformation theory evolved into the concept of movement (Chomsky 1981). A movement is a sentence rearrangement where a constituent is moved to another location. The moved constituent leaves a **trace**: an empty symbol representing its initial location. Passives correspond to a composition of two movements: one that moves the subject noun phrase into the position of a prepositional phrase headed by *by*; and another that moves the object noun phrase into the empty subject position (Table 10.1).

Table 10.1. Movements to obtain the passive of sentence *The man hit the ball*. Traces are represented by —. Original positions of traces are in bold.

Movements	Traces	Passives
First movement	***The man** hit ...*	*... — is hit by the man*
Second movement	*... hit **the ball***	*The ball is hit —*

Paradigms of movement are questions beginning with an interrogative pronoun or determiner: the *wh*-movements. A *wh*-word – *who, which, what, where* – is moved to the beginning of the sentence to form a question. Consider the sentence *John ate an apple in the dining room*. According to questions and to the *wh*-word type in front of the question, a trace is left at a specific location in the original sentence (Table 10.2). Traces correspond to noun phrases.

Table 10.2. Questions beginning with a *wh*-word and their traces (—).

Questions	Traces
Who ate an apple in the dining room?	*— ate an apple in the dining room*
What did John eat in the dining room?	*John ate — in the dining room*
Which apple did John eat in the dining room?	*John ate — in the dining room*
Where did John eat an apple?	*John ate an apple —*

Transformations or movements use a syntactic model of both the original phrase – or sentence – and its transformed counterpart. These models form the left and right members of a *T*-rule. Applying a transformation to a phrase or conversely unfolding a transformation from it, requires knowing its tree structure. In consequence, transformational rules or movements need a prior PS analysis before being applied.

10.2.4 Gap Threading

Gap threading is a technique to parse *wh*-movements (Pereira 1981, Pereira and Shieber 1987). Gap threading uses PS rules that consider the sentence after the movement has occurred. This requires new rules to account for interrogative pronouns or interrogative determiners moved in front of sentence, as for:

John ate an apple
What did John eat?

with a rule to parse the declaration

```
s --> np, vp.
```

and a new one for the question

```
s --> [what, did], np, vp.
```

One aim of gap threading is to keep changes in rules minimal. Thus the trace – or **gap** – should be handled by rules similar to those of a sentence before the movement. The rule describing a verb phrase with a transitive verb should remain unchanged:

```
vp --> v, np.
```

with the noun phrase symbol being possibly empty in case of a gap.

```
np --> [].
```

However, such a rule is not completely adequate because it would not differentiate a gap: the absence of a noun phrase resulting from a movement, from the pure absence of a constituent. Rules could insert empty lists wrongly in sentences such as

John ate

To handle traces properly, gap threading keeps a list of the moved constituents – or **fillers** – as the parsing mechanism reads them. In our example, fillers are *wh*-terms. When a constituent contains a moved term, it is stored in the filler list. When a constituent contains a gap – a missing noun phrase – a term is reclaimed from the head of the filler list.

Gap threading uses two lists as arguments that are added to each constituent of the DCG rules. These lists act as input and output of gaps in the current constituent, as in:

```
s(In, Out) --> np(In, Out1), vp(Out1, Out).
```

At a given point of the analysis, the first list holds fillers that have been stored before, and the second one returns the remaining fillers once gaps have been filled in the constituent.

In the sentence

What did John eat —?

the verb phrase *eat* — contains a gap. Before processing this phrase, the filler list must have accumulated *what*, which is removed when the verb phrase is completely parsed. Hence, input and output arguments of the vp constituent must be:

```
% vp(In, Out)
vp([what], [])
```

or, to be more general,

```
vp([what | T], T)
```

The noun phrase rule handling the gap accepts no word as an input (because it is a gap). Its right-hand side is then an empty list. The real input is received from the filler list. The rule collects the filler from the first argument of np and returns the resulting list in the second one:

```
np([what | T], T) --> [].
```

The whole set of rules is finally:

```
s(In, Out) -->
  [what, did],
   np([ what | In], Out1),
   vp(Out1, Out).
s(In, Out) --> np(In, Out1), vp(Out1, Out).

np(X, X) --> ['John'].        % no gap here
np(X, X) --> det, n.          % no gap here
np([what | T], T) --> [].     % the gap

vp(In, Out) --> v, np(In, Out).

v --> [eat]; [ate].

det --> [an].

n --> [apple].
```

When parsing a sentence with a movement, initial and final filler lists are set to empty lists:

```
?- s([], [], [what, did, 'John', eat], []).
Yes
```

as in the initial declaration:

```
?- s([], [], ['John', ate, an, apple], []).
Yes
```

10.2.5 Gap Threading to Parse Relative Clauses

Gap threading can also be used to parse relative clauses. Relative clauses are sentences complementing a noun phrase whose subject or object has been replaced by a relative pronoun. Consider the noun phrase

The meal that the waiter brought

The rule describing such a phrase is

```
np --> ngroup, relative
```

where `ngroup` maps *the meal* and `relative` maps *that the waiter brought*.
The modified sentence corresponding to the relative clause here is

The waiter brought the meal

where the noun phrase *the meal* has been moved from its object position to the front
of the relative and has been replaced by the object pronoun *that* (Fig. 10.3). The
phrase

The waiter who brought the meal

is similar, but the movement occurs on the subject noun phrase, which is replaced by
subject pronoun *who*.

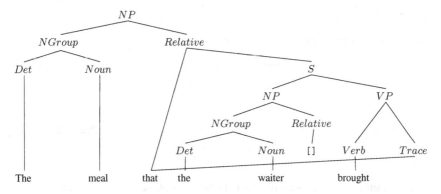

Fig. 10.3. The parse tree of *The meal that the waiter brought* with gap threading.

Let us write a grammar using gap threading to parse such noun phrases. The top
rule has two new variables to hold fillers:

```
np(In, Out) -->
    ngroup(In, Out1),
    relative(Out1, Out).
```

The relative clause is a sentence that starts with a pronoun, and this pronoun is
stored in the filler input list of the sentence symbol:

```
relative(In, Out) --> [that], s([that | In], Out).
relative(In, Out) --> [who], s([who | In], Out).
```

There might also be no relative clause

```
relative(X, X) --> [].
```

When we encounter a trace, a noun phrase is missing. The head pronoun is then removed from the filler list

```
np([PRO | T], T) --> [].
```

The rest of the grammar is straightforward

```
s(In, Out) --> np(In, Out1), vp(Out1, Out).

vp(In, Out) --> v, np(In, Out).

ngroup(X, X) --> det, n.

det --> [the].
n --> [waiter].
n --> [meal].
v --> [brought].
```

When launching the parse, both filler lists are empty

```
?- np([], [],[the, meal, that, the, waiter, brought],
   []).
Yes

?- np([], [], [the, waiter, who, brought, the, meal],
   []).
Yes
```

In the examples above, we have made no distinction between object and subject pronouns. The program could have been refined to take this difference into account.

10.3 Standardized Phrase Categories for English

The aim of a standard for phrase categories is to define an annotation set that would be common to people working on syntax. Such a standard would facilitate corpus and program sharing, assessment, and communication between computational linguists. Currently, there is no universally accepted standard. Defining an annotation set requires finding a common ground on the structure or the denomination of a specific group of words. It proves to be more difficult than expected. There is a consensus on main categories but details are sometimes controversial.

Most annotation schemes include phrase categories mapping the four main parts of speech, namely nouns, verbs, adverbs, and adjectives. Category names correspond to those of constituent heads:

• **Noun phrases** (NP), phrases headed by a noun.

- **Verb phrases** (VP), phrases headed by a verb together with its objects.
- **Adjective phrase** (AdjP), a phrase headed by an adjective, possibly with modifiers.
- **Adverbial phrase** (AdvP), a phrase headed by an adverb.
- Most annotation sets also feature **prepositional phrases** (PP): noun phrases beginning with a preposition.

The Penn Treebank (Marcus et al. 1993) is a corpus annotated with part-of-speech labels. Parts of it are also fully bracketed with syntactic phrase categories, and it was one of the first corpora widely available with such an annotation. Table 10.3 shows its set of phrase labels.

Table 10.3. The Penn Treebank phrase labels. After Marcus et al. (1993).

	Categories	Description
1.	ADJP	Adjective phrase
2.	ADVP	Adverb phrase
3.	NP	Noun phrase
4.	PP	Prepositional phrase
5.	S	Simple declarative clause
6.	SBAR	Clause introduced by subordinating conjunction or 0 (see below)
7.	SBARQ	Direct question introduced by *wh*-word of *wh*-phrase
8.	SINV	Declarative sentence with subject-aux inversion
9.	SQ	Subconstituent of SBARQ excluding *wh*-word of *wh*-phrase
10.	VP	Verb phrase
11.	WHADVP	*wh*-adverb phrase
12.	WHNP	*wh*-noun phras
13.	WHPP	*wh*-prepositional phrase
14.	X	Constituent of unknown or uncertain category
	Null elements	
1.	*	"Understood" subject of infinitive or imperative
2.	0	Zero variant of *that* in subordinate clauses
3.	T	Trace – marks position where moved *wh*-constituent is interpreted
4.	NIL	Marks position where preposition is interpreted in pied-piping context

As an example, Fig. 10.4 shows the bracketing of the sentence

Battle-tested industrial managers here always buck up nervous newcomers with the tale of the first of their countrymen to visit Mexico, a boatload of samurai warriors blown ashore 375 years ago.

in the Penn Treebank, where `pseudo-attach` denotes an attachment ambiguity for `VP-1`. In effect, *blown ashore* can modify either *boatload* or *samurai warriors*. Both attachments mean roughly the same thing, and there is no way to remove the ambiguity. In this bracketing, *blown ashore* has been attached arbitrarily to *warriors*, and a pseudo-attach has been left to indicate a possible attachment to *boatload*.

```
(  (S
    (NP Battle-tested industrial managers
        here)
      always
    (VP buck
        up
        (NP nervous newcomers)
        (PP with
            (NP the tale
            (PP of
                (NP (NP the
                        (ADJP first
                                (PP of
                                    (NP their countrymen)))
                        (S (NP *)
                            to
                            (VP visit
                                (NP Mexico))))
                    '
                    (NP (NP a boatload
                            (PP of
                                (NP (NP samurai warriors)
                                    (VP-1 blown
                                        ashore
                                        (ADVP (NP 375 years)
                                                ago)))))
                    (VP-1 *pseudo-attach*)))))))))
  .)
```

Fig. 10.4. Bracketed text in the Penn Treebank. After Marcus et al. (1993, p. 325).

Bracketing of phrases is done semiautomatically. A first pass uses an automatic parser. The output is then complemented or corrected by hand by human annotators.

10.4 Unification-Based Grammars

10.4.1 Features

In the examples above, there is no distinction between types of noun phrases. They appeared under a unique category: np. However, noun phrases are often marked with additional grammatical information, that is, depending on the language, a person, a number, a gender, a case, etc. In German, cases correspond to a specific inflection visible on the surface form of the words (Table 10.4). In English and French, noun phrases are inflected with plural, and in French with gender. We saw in Chap. 5 that such grammatical characteristics are called **features**. Case, gender, or number are

Table 10.4. Inflection imposed to noun group *der kleine Ober* 'the small waiter' by the case feature in German.

Cases	Noun groups
Nominative	*der kleine Ober*
Genitive	*des kleinen Obers*
Dative	*dem kleinen Ober*
Accusative	*den kleinen Ober*

features of the noun that are also shared by the components of the noun phrase to which it belongs.

If we adopt the generative framework, it is necessary to take features into account to have correct phrases. We can get a picture of it with the German cases and a very simple noun phrase rule:

```
np --> det, adj, n.
```

Since we do not distinguish between np symbols, the rule will output ungrammatical phrases as:

```
?-np(L, []).
[der, kleinen, Ober];     %wrong
[der, kleinen, Obers];    %wrong
[dem, kleine, Obers]      %wrong
...
```

To avoid such a wrong generation, we need to consider cases and other features and hence to refine our model. In addition, beyond generation features are necessary in many applications such as spelling or grammar checking, style critique, and so on.

A solution could be to define new noun phrase symbols corresponding to cases such as np_nominative, np_genitive, np_dative, np_accusative. We need others to consider number, np_nominative_singular, np_nominative_plural, ..., and it is not over, because of gender: np_nominative_-singular_masc, np_nominative_singular_fem, ... This process leads to a division of main categories, such as noun phrases, nouns, and adjectives, into subcategories to account for grammatical features.

10.4.2 Representing Features in Prolog

Creating a new category for each grammatical feature is clumsy and is sometimes useless in applications. Instead of it, features are better represented as arguments of main grammatical categories. This is straightforward in Prolog using the DCG notation. To account for cases in noun phrases, let us rewrite np into:

```
np(case:C)
```

where the C value is a member of list [nom, gen, dat, acc] denoting nominative, genitive, dative, and accusative cases.

We can extend the number of arguments to cover the rest of grammatical information. Prolog functors then represent main categories such as noun phrases, and arguments represent the grammatical details. Arguments are mapped onto feature structures consisting of pairs feature/values as for gender, number, case, person, and type of determiner:

```
np(gend:G, num:N, case:C, pers:P, det:D)
```

Using Prolog's unification, features are easily shared among constituents making up a noun phrase as in the rule:

```
np(gend:G, num:N, case:C, pers:P, det:D) -->
   det(gend:G, num:N, case:C, pers:P, det:D),
   adj(gend:G, num:N, case:C, pers:P, det:D),
   n(gend:G, num:N, case:C, pers:P).
```

Let us exemplify it with a small fragment of the German lexicon:

```
det(gend:masc, num:sg, case:nom, pers:3, det:def) -->
   [der].
det(gend:masc, num:sg, case:gen, pers:3, det:def) -->
   [des].
det(gend:masc, num:sg, case:dat, pers:3, det:def) -->
   [dem].
det(gend:masc, num:sg, case:acc, pers:3, det:def) -->
   [den].

adj(gend:masc, num:sg, case:nom, pers:3, det:def) -->
   [kleine].
adj(gend:masc, num:sg, case:gen, pers:3, det:def) -->
   [kleinen].
adj(gend:masc, num:sg, case:dat, pers:3, det:def) -->
   [kleinen].
adj(gend:masc, num:sg, case:acc, pers:3, det:def) -->
   [kleinen].

n(gend:masc, num:sg, case:nom, pers:3) --> ['Ober'].
n(gend:masc, num:sg, case:gen, pers:3) --> ['Obers'].
n(gend:masc, num:sg, case:dat, pers:3) --> ['Ober'].
n(gend:masc, num:sg, case:acc, pers:3) --> ['Ober'].
```

To consult this lexicon, Prolog needs a new infix operator ":" that we define using the op/3 built-in predicate:

```
:- op(600, xfy, ':').
```

And our grammar generates correct noun phrases only:

```
?- np(_, _, _, _, _, L, []).
   L = [der, kleine, 'Ober'] ;
   L = [des, kleinen, 'Obers'] ;
   L = [dem, kleinen, 'Ober'] ;
   L = [den, kleinen, 'Ober'] ;
No
```

10.4.3 A Formalism for Features and Rules

In the previous section, we directly wrote features as arguments of Prolog predicates. More frequently, linguists use a notation independent of programming languages, which is referred to as unification-based grammars. This notation is close to Prolog and DCGs, however, and is therefore easy to understand. The noun phrase rule

```
np(gend:G, num:N, case:C, pers:P, det:D) -->
   det(gend:G, num:N, case:C, pers:P, det:D),
   adj(gend:G, num:N, case:C, pers:P, det:D),
   n(gend:G, num:N, case:C, pers:P).
```

is represented as:

$$
\begin{array}{ccccc}
NP & \rightarrow & DET & ADJ & N \\
\begin{bmatrix} gend:G \\ num:N \\ case:C \\ pers:P \\ det:D \end{bmatrix} & &
\begin{bmatrix} gend:G \\ num:N \\ case:C \\ pers:P \\ det:D \end{bmatrix} &
\begin{bmatrix} gend:G \\ num:N \\ case:C \\ pers:P \\ det:D \end{bmatrix} &
\begin{bmatrix} gend:G \\ num:N \\ case:C \\ pers:P \end{bmatrix}
\end{array}
$$

Rules of a grammar describing complete sentences are similar to those of DCGs. They consist, for example, of:

$$
\begin{array}{ccc}
S & \rightarrow & NP \qquad VP \\
 & & \begin{bmatrix} num:N \\ case:nom \\ pers:P \end{bmatrix} \begin{bmatrix} num:N \\ pers:P \end{bmatrix}
\end{array}
$$

$$
\begin{array}{ccc}
VP & \rightarrow & V \\
\begin{bmatrix} num:N \\ pers:P \end{bmatrix} & & \begin{bmatrix} trans:i \\ num:N \\ pers:P \end{bmatrix}
\end{array}
$$

$$
\begin{array}{ccc}
VP & \rightarrow & V \qquad NP \\
\begin{bmatrix} num:N \\ pers:P \end{bmatrix} & & \begin{bmatrix} trans:t \\ num:N \\ pers:P \end{bmatrix} \begin{bmatrix} case:acc \end{bmatrix}
\end{array}
$$

$$NP \rightarrow Pronoun$$

$$\begin{bmatrix} gen : G \\ num : N \\ pers : P \\ case : C \end{bmatrix} \quad \begin{bmatrix} gen : G \\ num : N \\ pers : P \\ case : C \end{bmatrix}$$

with lexicon entries such as:

$$DET \rightarrow der$$

$$\begin{bmatrix} gend : masc \\ num : sg \\ case : nom \\ det : def \end{bmatrix}$$

10.4.4 Features Organization

A feature structure is a set of pairs consisting of a feature name – or attribute – and its value.

$$\begin{bmatrix} feature_1 : value_1 \\ feature_2 : value_2 \\ \vdots \\ feature_n : value_n \end{bmatrix}$$

Unlike arguments in Prolog or DCGs, the feature notation is based solely on the name and not on the position of the argument. Hence, both

$$\begin{bmatrix} gen : fem \\ num : pl \\ case : acc \end{bmatrix} \text{ and } \begin{bmatrix} num : pl \\ case : acc \\ gen : fem \end{bmatrix}$$

denote the same feature structure. Feature structures can be pictured by a graph as shown in Fig. 10.5.

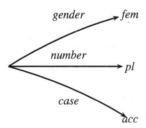

Fig. 10.5. Graph representing a feature structure.

The value of a feature can be an atomic symbol, a variable, or another feature structure to yield a hierarchical organization as in:

$$\begin{bmatrix} f_1 : v_1 \\ f_2 : \begin{bmatrix} f_3 : v_3 \\ f_4 : \begin{bmatrix} f_5 : v_5 \\ f_6 : v_6 \end{bmatrix} \end{bmatrix} \end{bmatrix}$$

whose corresponding graph is shown in Fig. 10.6.

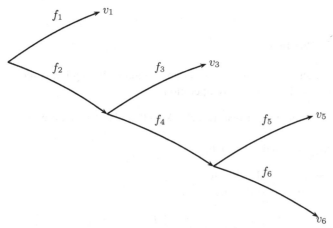

Fig. 10.6. Graph corresponding to embedded feature structures.

Grouping a set of features into a substructure enables the simplification of notations or rules. A feature denoted `agreement` can group gender, number, and person, and can be encoded as a single structure. German nominative and accusative pronouns *er* 'he' and *ihn* 'him' can then be represented as:

$$\begin{bmatrix} Pronoun \\ agreement : \begin{bmatrix} gender : masc \\ number : sg \\ pers : 3 \end{bmatrix} \\ case : nom \end{bmatrix} \rightarrow er$$

$$\begin{bmatrix} Pronoun \\ agreement : \begin{bmatrix} gender : masc \\ number : sg \\ pers : 3 \end{bmatrix} \\ case : acc \end{bmatrix} \rightarrow ihn$$

which enables us to simplify the noun phrase rule in:

$$\begin{bmatrix} NP \\ agreement : X \\ case : C \end{bmatrix} \rightarrow \begin{bmatrix} Pronoun \\ agreement : X \\ case : C \end{bmatrix}$$

We can even push categories into structures and rewrite the previous rule as

$$\begin{bmatrix} cat : np \\ agreement : X \\ case : C \end{bmatrix} \rightarrow \begin{bmatrix} cat : pronoun \\ agreement : X \\ case : C \end{bmatrix}$$

Unlike the case for DCGs, unspecified or nonshared features are simply omitted in unification-based grammars. There is no need for an equivalent of the anonymous variable then.

10.4.5 Features and Unification

Unification of feature structures is similar to term unification of Prolog but is more general. It is a combination of two recursive operations:

- Structures merge the set of all their features, checking that identical features have compatible values.
- Variables unify with values and substructures.

Feature structure unification is usually denoted $\cup$.
  Unification results in a merger of features as in

$$\begin{bmatrix} feature_1 : v_1 \\ feature_2 : v_2 \end{bmatrix} \cup \begin{bmatrix} feature_2 : v_2 \\ feature_3 : v_3 \end{bmatrix} = \begin{bmatrix} feature_1 : v_1 \\ feature_2 : v_2 \\ feature_3 : v_3 \end{bmatrix}.$$

Variable unification considers features of same name and applies to values, other variables, or recursive feature structures, just as in Prolog but regardless of their position. Here are a couple of examples:

- $[feature_1 : v_1]$ and $[feature_1 : v_2]$ fail to unify if $v_1 \neq v_2$.

- $$\begin{bmatrix} f_1 : v_1 \\ f_2 : X \end{bmatrix} \cup \begin{bmatrix} f_5 : v_5 \\ f_2 : \begin{bmatrix} f_3 : v_3 \\ f_4 : v_4 \end{bmatrix} \end{bmatrix} = \begin{bmatrix} f_1 : v_1 \\ f_2 : \begin{bmatrix} f_3 : v_3 \\ f_4 : v_4 \end{bmatrix} \\ f_5 : v_5 \end{bmatrix}$$

- $$\begin{bmatrix} f_1 : v_1 \\ f_2 : X \end{bmatrix} \cup \begin{bmatrix} f_5 : X \\ f_2 : \begin{bmatrix} f_3 : v_3 \\ f_4 : v_4 \end{bmatrix} \end{bmatrix} = \begin{bmatrix} f_1 : v_1 \\ f_2 : \begin{bmatrix} f_3 : v_3 \\ f_4 : v_4 \end{bmatrix} \\ f_5 : \begin{bmatrix} f_3 : v_3 \\ f_4 : v_4 \end{bmatrix} \end{bmatrix}$$

In the last example, both features f_2 and f_5 result of the unification of X and are therefore identical. They are said to be re-entrant. However, the structure presentation does not make it clear because it duplicates the X value as many times as it occurs in the structure: twice here. Different structures could yield the same result, as with the unification of

$$\begin{bmatrix} f_1 : v_1 \\ f_2 : \begin{bmatrix} f_3 : v_3 \\ f_4 : v_4 \end{bmatrix} \end{bmatrix} \text{ and } \begin{bmatrix} f_5 : \begin{bmatrix} f_3 : v_3 \\ f_4 : v_4 \end{bmatrix} \\ f_2 : X \end{bmatrix}$$

where feature f_2 and f_5 have (accidentally) the same value.

To improve the structure presentation, identical features are denoted with a label. Here [1] indicates that f_2 and f_5 are the same:

$$\begin{bmatrix} f_1 : v_1 \\ f_2 : [1] \begin{bmatrix} f_3 : v_3 \\ f_4 : v_4 \end{bmatrix} \\ f_5 : [1] \end{bmatrix}$$

and Fig. 10.7 shows the corresponding graph.

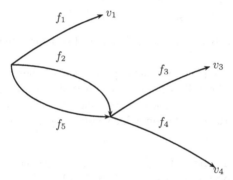

Fig. 10.7. Graph with re-entrant feature structures.

10.4.6 A Unification Algorithm for Feature Structures

Unification of feature structures is close to that of terms in Prolog. However, feature structures provide partial specifications of the entities they represent, while Prolog terms are complete. Feature structure unification is merely a union of compatible characteristics, as in the example

$$[case : nom] \cup [gender : masc] = \begin{bmatrix} case : nom \\ gender : masc \end{bmatrix}$$

where both structures merge into a more specific set. As is, corresponding Prolog terms `struct(case: nom)` and `struct(gender: masc)` would fail to unify.

There are possible workarounds. Given a syntactic category, we could itemize all its possible attributes and map them onto a Prolog term. We would have to assign each feature to a specific argument rank, for instance, `case` to the first argument, `gender` to the second one, and so on. We would then fill the specified arguments and leave the others empty using the anonymous variable '_'. For the example above, this would yield terms

```
struct(case: nom, gender:_)
```

and

```
struct(case: _, gender: masc)
```

that unify properly:

```
?- X = struct(case: nom, gender:_), Y =
struct(case: _, gender: masc), X = Y.

X = struct(case: nom, gender: masc)
Y = struct(case: nom, gender: masc)
```

However, when there are many features and hierarchical structures such a method could be tedious or difficult.

A better idea is to use incomplete lists. Incomplete lists have their tails uninstantiated as [a, b, c | X]. Such lists can represent partial structures as [case: nom | X] or [gender: masc | Y] and be expanded through a Prolog unification. Merging both feature structures is simple. It consists in the unification of X with [gender: masc | Y]:

```
?- STRUCT = [case: nom | X], X = [gender: masc | Y].
STRUCT = [case: nom, gender: masc | Y]
```

To be more general, we will use the anonymous variable as a tail. Converting a feature structure then consists in representing features as members of a list where closing brackets are replaced by | _]. Hence, structures $[case : nom]$ and $[gender : masc]$ are mapped onto [case: nom | _] and [gender: masc | _], and their unification yields [case: nom, gender: masc | _]. Hierarchical features as:

$$\begin{bmatrix} cat : np \\ agreement : \begin{bmatrix} gender : masc \\ number : sg \\ pers : 3 \end{bmatrix} \\ case : acc \end{bmatrix}$$

are represented by embedded incomplete lists:

```
[cat: np,
agreement: [gender: masc, number: sg, pers: 3 | _],
case: acc | _]
```

Let us now implement the unification algorithm for feature structures due to Boyer (1988). The unif/2 predicate consists of a fact expressing the end of unification – both structures are the same – and two main rules:

- The first rule considers the case where the heads of both lists represent features of the same name. The rule unifies the feature values and unifies the rest.
- When feature names are different, the second rule uses a double recursion. The first recursion unifies the tail of the first list with the head of the second list. It yields a new list, Rest3, which is the unification result minus the head features F1 and F2. The second recursion unifies the rest of the second list with the list made up of the head of the first list and Rest3:

```
:- op(600, xfx, ':').

unif(FStr, FStr) :-
  !.
unif([F1:V1 | Rest1], [F1:V2 | Rest2]) :-
  !,
  unif(V1, V2),
  unif(Rest1, Rest2).
unif([F1:V1 | Rest1], [F2:V2 | Rest2]) :-
  F1 \= F2,
  unif(Rest1, [F2:V2 | Rest3]),
  unif(Rest2, [F1:V1 | Rest3]).
```

Consulting unif/2 and querying Prolog with:

```
?- X = [case: nom | _], Y =[gender: masc | _],
   unif(X, Y).
```

results in:

```
X = [case: nom, gender: masc | _]
Y = [gender: masc, case: nom | _]
```

10.5 Dependency Grammars

10.5.1 Presentation

Dependency grammars form an alternative to constituent-based theories. These grammars describe a sentence's structure in terms of syntactic links – or connections or dependencies – between its words (Tesnière, 1966). Each link reflects a dominance relation (conversely a dependence) between a headword and a dependent word. Examples of simple dependencies tie a determiner to its noun, or a subject noun to its main verb. Dependency links are pictured by arrows flowing from headwords to their dependents (or the reverse).

In noun groups, determiners and adjectives depend on their noun; adverbs depend on their adjective (Fig. 10.8), as in

The very big cat

where the noun *cat* is the head of *the* and *big* and the adjective *big* is the head of *very*. In addition, *cat* is the head – or the root – of the whole phrase.

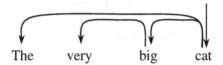

The   very   big   cat

Fig. 10.8. Dependency graph of the noun group *The very big cat*.

Figure 10.9 shows an alternate equivalent representation of the dependencies.

Fig. 10.9. Tree representing dependencies in the noun group *The very big cat*.

According to the classical dependency model, each word is the dependent of exactly one head with the exception of the head of the sentence. Conversely, a head may have several dependents (or modifiers). This means a dependency graph is equivalent to a tree. Figure 10.10 shows a graph representing the structure of a simple sentence where determiners depend on their noun; nouns depend on the main verb, which is the root of the sentence. Tesnière used the word **stemma** – garland or stem in Greek – to name the graphic representation of these links.

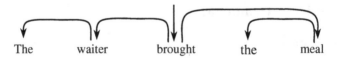

The   waiter   brought   the   meal

Fig. 10.10. Dependency graph or stemma of the sentence *The waiter brought the meal*.

Although dependency and constituency are often opposed, stemmas embed sorts of constituents that Tesnière called *nœuds*. Deriving a *nœud* from a dependency graph simply consists in taking a word, all its dependents, and dependents of dependents recursively. It then corresponds to the subtree below a certain word.[1] And in many cases stemmas and phrase-structure trees yield equivalent structures hinting that dependency and constituency are in fact comparable formalisms.

There are a couple of differences, however. One is the importance given to words in dependency grammars. There are no intermediate representation symbols such as phrases of constituent grammars. Syntactic relations involve words only, and nodes in stemmas are purely lexical.

Another difference is that dependency grammars do not need a fixed word order or word contiguity in the *nœuds* to establish links. In that sense dependency theory is probably more suited than constituent grammars to model languages where the word order is flexible. This is the case for Latin, Russian, and German to a lesser extent. Figure 10.11 gives an example with the sentence (Bröker 1998):

Den Mann hat der Junge gesehen
The man$_{/obj}$ has the boy$_{/subj}$ seen 'The boy has seen the man.'

where positions of noun groups *den Mann* and *der Junge* can be inverted and yield another acceptable sentence: *Der Junge hat den Mann gesehen*. Meaning is preserved because functions of noun groups are marked by cases, nominative and accusative here.

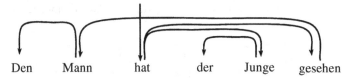

Den   Mann   hat   der   Junge   gesehen

Fig. 10.11. Dependency graph of *Den Mann hat der Junge gesehen*, modified from Bröker (1998).

In the example above, stemmas of both sentences are the same, whereas a phrase-structure formalism requires more rules to take the word order variability into account. Modeling the verb phrase needs two separate rules to describe the position of the accusative noun group

hat <u>den Mann</u> gesehen

and the nominative one

hat <u>der Junge</u> gesehen

$$VP \rightarrow AUX \quad NP \quad V$$
$$\begin{bmatrix} num : N \\ pers : P \end{bmatrix} \quad \begin{bmatrix} num : N \\ pers : P \end{bmatrix} \quad [case : acc] \quad \begin{bmatrix} tense : pastpart \\ num : N \\ pers : P \end{bmatrix}$$

---

[1] *Nœud* is the French word for node. It shouldn't be mistaken with a node in a graph, which is a single element. Here a nœud is a whole subtree.

and

$$
\begin{array}{cccc}
VP & \rightarrow & AUX & NP & V \\
\begin{bmatrix} num : N \\ pers : P \end{bmatrix} & & \begin{bmatrix} num : N \\ pers : P \end{bmatrix} & [case : nom] & \begin{bmatrix} tense : pastpart \\ num : N \\ pers : P \end{bmatrix}
\end{array}
$$

When word order shows a high degree of freedom, the constituent structure tends to become combinatorial making grammars resorting on it impracticable. For this reason, many linguists, especially in Europe, believe dependency grammar to be a more powerful formalism than constituency. On the contrary, constituency is a property of English that possibly makes dependency less useful in this language.

10.5.2 Properties of a Dependency Graph

After Tesnière, followers extended or modified the definition of dependency grammars. This has led to variations from the original theory. However, some common principles have emerged from the variety of definitions. We expose here features that are the most widely accepted. They result in constraints on dependency graphs. As for constituent grammars, dependency grammars also received formal mathematical definitions.

The first principle is that dependency graphs are acyclic. This means that there is no loop in the graph. Figure 10.12 shows two structures that are not acceptable.

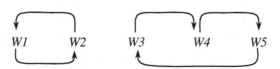

Fig. 10.12. Cyclic dependencies in a graph.

The second principle is that dependency graphs should be connected. This corresponds to the assumption that a sentence has one single head, the root, to which all the other words are transitively connected. Figure 10.13 shows a sentence $w_1 w_2 w_3 w_4 w_5$ with two nonconnected subgraphs.

Fig. 10.13. A nonconnected graph spanning sentence $w_1 w_2 w_3 w_4 w_5$.

The third principle is called **projectivity** or **adjacency**. It assumes that all the dependents of a word, direct and indirect, form a contiguous sequence. This means that each pair of words $(Dep, Head)$ in the graph, which is directly or transitively connected, is only separated by direct or indirect dependents of $Head$ or Dep. All the words in-between are hence dependents of *Head*. In a dependency graph, projectivity results in the absence of crossing arcs.

The projectivity principle is much more controversial that the two first ones. Although less frequent than projective examples, there are many cases of nonprojective sentences. Figures 10.14 and 10.15 show two examples in English and Latin. The sentence *What would you like me to do?* shows a dependency link between *what* and *do*. The projectivity principle would require that *would*, *you*, and *like* are dependent of *do*, which is untrue. The sentence is thus nonprojective.

The Latin verse *Ultima Cumaei venit iam carminis aetas* 'The last era of the Cumean song has now arrived' shows a dependency link between *carminis* and *Cumaei*, but neither *venit* nor *iam* are dependent of *carminis*. We can then better reformulate projectivity as a general principle that suffers exceptions.

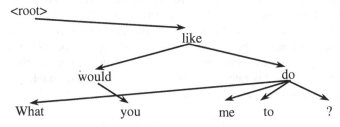

Fig. 10.14. Dependency graph of *What would you like me to do?* After Järvinen and Tapanainen (1997).

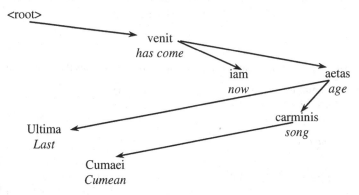

Fig. 10.15. Dependency graph of *Ultima Cumaei venit iam carminis aetas*. 'The last era of the Cumean song has now arrived' (Vergil, *Eclogues* IV.4). After Covington (1990).

10.5.3 Valence

Tesnière and others stressed the importance of verbs in European languages: main verbs have the highest position in the node hierarchy and are the structural centers of sentences. All other types of phrases are organized around them. Hence verbs tend to impose a certain structure to sentences. Connected to this observation, a major claim of dependency grammars is that verbs have specific complement patterns. Verb complements in a broad sense include groups that accompany it: subject, objects, and adjuncts.

Different verbs combine differently with their complements. Certain complements are essential to a verb, like its subject, most of the time. Essential complements cannot be removed from the sentence without making it incorrect or incomplete. Other complements are optional – or circumstantial – like adjuncts that give information on space, time, or manner. Removing them would modify the meaning of the sentence but would still result into something acceptable.

The valence is the number of essential complements of a verb. Using an analogy with chemistry, valence is the attraction power of a verb for potential complements and a specific property of each verb. Just as for chemical elements, the valence is not a strict requirement but rather reflects a sort of most current, stable construction. Common valence values are (Table 10.5):

- 0, for verbs describing weather, *it's raining, snowing*
- 1, corresponding to the subject of intransitive verbs, *he's sleeping, vanishing*
- 2, the subject and object of transitive verbs, *she read this book.*
- 3, the subject and two objects – direct and indirect objects – of ditransitive verbs, *Elke gave a book to Wolfgang, I said it to my sister.*
- 4, the subject, object, source, and destination of certain verbs like *move* or *shift: I moved the car from here to the street* (Heringer 1993).

Table 10.5. Valence values and examples, where *iobject* denotes the indirect object.

Valences	Examples	Frames
0	*it's raining*	$raining\ []$
1	*he's sleeping*	$sleeping\ [subject:he]$
2	*she read this book*	$read\ \begin{bmatrix} subject:she \\ object:book \end{bmatrix}$
3	*Elke gave a book to Wolfgang*	$gave\ \begin{bmatrix} subject:Elke \\ object:book \\ iobject:Wolfgang \end{bmatrix}$
4	*I moved the car from here to the street*	$moved\ \begin{bmatrix} subject:I \\ object:car \\ source:here \\ destination:street \end{bmatrix}$

From a quantitative definition: the number of slots or arguments attached to a verb and filled with its essential complements, valence is also frequently extended to cover qualitative aspects. It includes the grammatical form and the meaning of these slots. Grammatical properties include possible prepositions and syntactic patterns allowed to each complement of a verb: noun group, gerund, or infinitive. Many dictionaries, especially learners' dictionaries, itemize these patterns, also referred to as **subcategorization frames**. Tables 10.6–10.8 summarize some verb–complement structures.

Table 10.6. Verb–complement structures in English.

Verb	Complement structure	Example
slept	None (Intransitive)	*I slept*
bring	NP	*The waiter brought the meal*
bring	NP + to + NP	*The waiter brought the meal to the patron*
depend	on + NP	*It depends on the waiter*
wait	for + NP + to + VP	*I am waiting for the waiter to bring the meal*
keep	VP(ing)	*He kept working*
know	that + S	*The waiter knows that the patron loves fish*

Table 10.7. Verb–complement structures in French.

Verb	Complement structure	Example
dormir	None (Intransitive)	*J'ai dormi*
apporter	NP (Transitive)	*Le serveur a apporté un plat*
apporter	NP + à + NP	*Le serveur a apporté un plat au client*
dépendre	de + NP	*Ça dépend du serveur*
attendre	que + S(Subjunctive)	*Il a attendu que le serveur apporte le plat*
continuer	de + VP(INF)	*Il a continué de travailler*
savoir	que + S	*Le serveur sait que le client aime le poisson*

In addition, typical complements of a verb often belong to broad semantic categories. The verb *read* generally involves a person as a subject and a written thing as an object. This extension of valence to the semantic domain is called the selectional restrictions of a verb and is exemplified by the frame structure of *gave*:

$$gave \begin{bmatrix} subject : PERSON \\ object : THING \\ iobject : PERSON \end{bmatrix}$$

Chap. 13 gives more details on this aspect.

Table 10.8. Verb–complement structure in German.

Verb	Complement structure	Example
schlafen	None (Intransitive)	*Ich habe geschlafen*
bringen	NP(Accusative)	*Der Ober hat eine Speise gebracht*
bringen	NP(Dative) + NP(Accusative)	*Der Ober hat dem Kunde eine Speise gebracht*
abhängen	von + NP(Dative)	*Es hängt vom Ober ab*
warten	auf + S	*Er wartete auf dem Ober, die Speise zu bringen*
fortsetzen	NP	*Er hat die Arbeit fortgesetzt*
wissen	NP(Final verb)	*Der Ober weiß, das der Kunde Fisch liebt*

10.5.4 Dependencies and Functions

The dependency structure of a sentence – the stemma – generally reflects its traditional syntactic representation and therefore its links can be annotated with function
labels. In a simple sentence, the two main functions correspond to subject and object
relations that link noun groups to the sentence's main verb (Fig. 10.16).

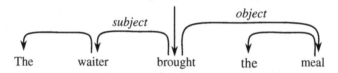

Fig. 10.16. Dependency graph of the sentence *The waiter brought the meal*.

Adjuncts form another class of functions that modify the verb they are related to.
They include prepositional phrases whose head is set arbitrarily to the front prepo-
sition (Fig. 10.17). In the same way, adjuncts include adverbs that modify a verb
(Fig. 10.18).

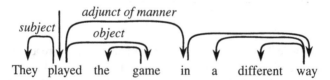

Fig. 10.17. Dependency graph of the sentence *They played the game in a different way*. After
Järvinen and Tapanainen (1997).

As for phrase categories in constituent grammars, a fixed set of function labels
is necessary to annotate stemmas. Tables 10.9 and 10.10 reproduce the set of dependency functions proposed by Järvinen and Tapanainen (1997). Figures 10.19 and
10.20 show examples of annotations.

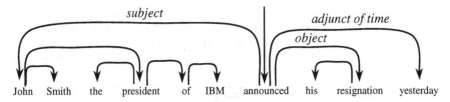

Fig. 10.18. Dependency graph of the sentence *John Smith, the president of IBM, announced his resignation yesterday.* After Collins (1996).

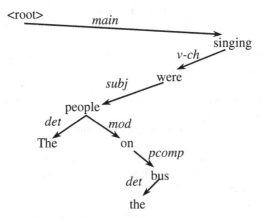

Fig. 10.19. Stemma representing *The people on the bus were singing.* After Järvinen and Tapanainen (1997).

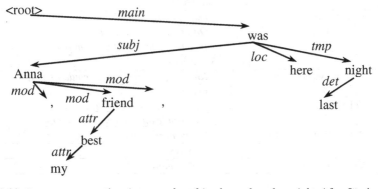

Fig. 10.20. Stemma representing *Anna, my best friend, was here last night.* After Järvinen and Tapanainen (1997).

Table 10.9. Main functions used by Järvinen and Tapanainen (1997) in their functional dependency parser for English. Intranuclear links combine words inside a *nœud* (a consituent). Verb complementation links a verb to its core complements. Determinative functions generally connect determiners to nouns. Modifiers are pre- or postmodifiers of a noun, i.e., dependents of a noun before or after it.

Name	Description	Example
	Main functions	
main	Main element, usually the verb	*He doesn't **know** whether to send a gift*
qtag	Question tag	*Let's play another game, **shall** we?*
	Intranuclear links	
v-ch	Verb chain, connects elements in a complex verb group	*It **may have been being** examined*
pcomp	Prepositional complement, connects a preposition to the noun group after it.	*They played the game **in** a different way*
phr	Verb particle, connects a verb to a particle or preposition.	*He asked me who would look **after** the baby*
	Verb complementation	
subj	Subject	
obj	Object	*I gave him my **address***
comp	Subject complement, the second argument of a copula.	*It has become **marginal***
dat	Indirect object	*Pauline gave it **to Tom***
oc	Object complement	*His friends call him **Ted***
copred	Copredicative	*We took a swim **naked***
voc	Vocative	*Play it again, **Sam***
	Determinative functions	
qn	Quantifier	*I want **more** money*
det	Determiner	***Other** members will join...*
neg	Negator	*It is **not** coffee that I like, but tea*
	Modifiers	
attr	Attributive nominal	***Knowing** no French, I couldn't express my thanks*
mod	Other postmodifiers	*The baby, **Frances Bean**, was...* *The people **on the bus** were singing*
ad	Attributive adverbial	*She is **more** popular*
	Junctives	
cc	Coordination	*Two **or** more cars...*

Table 10.10. Adverbial functions used by Järvinen and Tapanainen (1997). Adverbial functions connect adjuncts to their verb.

Name	Description	Example
		Adverbial functions
tmp	Time	*It gives me very great pleasure this **evening***
dur	Duration	*They stay in Italy all **summer** through*
frq	Frequency	*I **often** catch her playing*
qua	Quantity	*It weighed almost a **ton***
man	Manner	*They will support him, however **grudgingly**...*
loc	Location	*I don't know **where** to meet him*
sou	Source	*They travelled slowly **from** Hong Kong*
goa	Goal	*They moved **into** the kitchen every stick of furniture they possessed*
cnd	Condition	*If I were **leaving**, you should know about it*
meta	Clause adverbial	*Will somebody **please** open the door?*
cla	Clause initial element	***In** the view of the authorities, Jones was...*

10.6 Further Reading

Literature on Chomsky's works and generative transformational grammar is uncountable. Most linguistics textbooks in the English-speaking world retain this approach. Recent accounts include Radford (1988), Ruwet (1970), Haegeman and Gueron (1999), Lasnik et al. (2000).

Principles of dependency grammars stem from an old tradition dating back to the ancient Greek and Latin grammar schools. Tesnière (1966) proposes a modern formulation. Heringer (1993) provides a short and excellent summary of his work. Other accounts include Hays (1964), Gaifman (1965), and Mel'cuk (1988). Implementations of dependency theories include the Functional Dependency Grammar (Järvinen and Tapanainen 1997) and Link Grammar (Sleator and Temperley 1993).

Within the work of Tesnière, valence has been a very productive concept although it has not always been explicitly acknowledged. It provides theoretical grounds for verb subcategorization, cases, and selectional restrictions that we find in other parts of this book (Chapter 13). In addition to verbs, valence can apply to adjectives and nouns.

Unification-based grammars were born when Alain Colmerauer designed the *systèmes-Q* (1970) and later the Prolog language with his colleagues. *Systèmes-Q* have been applied in the MÉTÉO system to translate weather reports from English to French (TAUM 1971). MÉTÉO is still in use today. Prolog is derived from them and was also implemented for a project aimed at dialogue and language analysis (Colmerauer et al. 1972). For a review of its history, see Colmerauer and Roussel (1996).

Unification-based grammars have been used in many syntactic theories. The oldest and probably the simplest example is that of Definite Clause Grammars (Colmerauer 1978; Pereira and Warren 1980). Since then there have been many followers.

The most notable include head-driven phrase structure grammars (HPSG, Pollard and Sag 1994) and lexical function grammars (LFG, Kaplan and Bresnan 1982). Unification-based grammars do not depend on a specific syntactic formalism. They are merely a tool that we used with PS rules in this chapter. Dependency grammars can also make use of them. Dependency unification grammar (DUG, Hellwig 1980, 1986) and unification dependency grammar (UDG, Maxwell 1995) are examples. Accounts of unification formalisms in French include Abeillé (1993) and in German, Müller (1999).

Exercises

10.1. Describe step-by-step how the Prolog search mechanism would generate the sentence *the boy hit the ball*, and compare this trace with that of Fig. 10.1.

10.2. Write a Prolog program that converts a DCG grammar into its Chomsky normal form equivalent.

10.3. Write a grammar using the DCG notation to analyze simple sentences: a noun phrase and a verb phrase, where the verb phrase is either a verb or a verb and an object. Write transformation rules that map declarative sentences into their negation.

10.4. Complement PS rules of Exercise 10.3 to parse a possible prepositional phrase within the verb phrase. Write transformation rules that carry out a topicalization of the prepositional phrase.

10.5. Write DCG rules using the gap threading technique to handle sentences and questions of Table 10.2.

10.6. Find a text of 10 to 20 lines in a language you know and bracket the constituents with the phrase labels of Table 10.3.

10.7. Unify $\begin{bmatrix} gen : fem \\ case : acc \end{bmatrix}$ and $\begin{bmatrix} gen : fem \\ num : pl \end{bmatrix}$, $\begin{bmatrix} gen : fem \\ num : pl \\ case : acc \end{bmatrix}$ and $\begin{bmatrix} gen : fem \\ num : sg \end{bmatrix}$,
$\begin{bmatrix} gen : masc \\ num : X \\ case : nom \end{bmatrix}$ and $\begin{bmatrix} gen : masc \\ num : pl \\ case : Y \end{bmatrix}$ when possible.

10.8. Unify $\begin{bmatrix} f_1 : v_1 \\ f_2 : X \end{bmatrix}$ and $\begin{bmatrix} f_1 : v_5 \\ f_2 : \begin{bmatrix} f_3 : v_3 \\ f_4 : v_4 \end{bmatrix} \end{bmatrix}$, $\begin{bmatrix} f_1 : v_1 \\ f_2 : X \end{bmatrix}$ and $\begin{bmatrix} f_1 : Y \\ f_2 : \begin{bmatrix} f_3 : v_3 \\ f_4 : Y \end{bmatrix} \end{bmatrix}$,
$\begin{bmatrix} f_1 : v_1 \\ f_2 : X \end{bmatrix}$ and $\begin{bmatrix} f_5 : X \\ f_2 : Y \\ f_1 : Y \end{bmatrix}$.

10.9. Using the unification grammar formalism write rules describing the noun group in a language you know.

10.10. Write a `norm/2` predicate that transforms complete lists into incomplete ones as, for example, `[a, b, [c, d], e]` into `[a, b, [c, d | _], e, | _]`.

10.11. Find a text of approximately ten lines in a language you know and draw the stemmas (dependency links).

10.12. Draw stemmas of sentences in Table 10.9.

10.13. Annotate stemmas of sentences in Table 10.9 with their corresponding functions.

11

Parsing Techniques

11.1 Introduction

In the previous chapters, we used Prolog's built-in search mechanism and the DCG notation to parse sentences and constituents. This search mechanism has drawbacks however. To name some of them: its depth-first strategy does not handle left-recursive rules well and backtracking is sometimes inefficient. In addition, if DCGs are appropriate to describe constituents, we haven't seen means to parse dependencies until now.

This chapter describes algorithms and data structures to improve the efficiency of constituents parsing and to parse dependencies. It begins with a basic bottom-up algorithm and then introduces techniques using well-formed substring tables or charts. Charts are arrays to store parsing results and hypotheses. They are popular parsing devices because of some superior features: charts accept left-recursive rules, avoid backtracking, and can work with a top-down or bottom-up control.

Frequently, sentences show an ambiguous structure – exhibit more than one possible parse. Search strategies, either bottom-up or top-down, produce solutions blindly; the ordering of the resulting parse trees being tied to that of the rules. For most cases however sentences are not ambiguous to human readers who retain one single sensible analysis. To come to a similar result, parsers require a disambiguation mechanism.

Early disambiguation methods implemented common sense rules to assess parse trees and to discard implausible ones. Current solutions, inspired from speech recognition and part-of-speech tagging, use statistical techniques. They enable us to parse properly most ambiguous sentences. Recent approaches based on dependencies yield a very high rate of performance for unrestricted texts. This chapter outlines symbolic techniques as well as probabilistic methods applicable to constituency and dependency grammars.

11.2 Bottom-up Parsing

11.2.1 The Shift–Reduce Algorithm

We saw in Chap. 8 that left-recursive rules may cause top-down parsing to loop infinitely. Left-recursion is used to express structures such as noun phrases modified by a prepositional phrase, or conjunctions of noun phrases as, for example,

```
np --> np, pp.
np --> np, conj, np.
```

It is possible to eliminate left-recursive rules using auxiliary symbols and rules. However, this results in larger grammars that are less regular. In addition, parsing with these new rules yields slightly different syntactic trees, which are often less natural.

A common remedy to handle left-recursive rules is to run them with a bottom-up search strategy. Instead of expanding constituents from the top node, a bottom-up parser starts from the words. It looks up their parts of speech, builds partial structures out of them, and goes on from partial structure to partial structure until it reaches the top node. Figure 11.1 shows the construction order of partial structures that goes from the annotation of *the* as a determiner up to the root s.

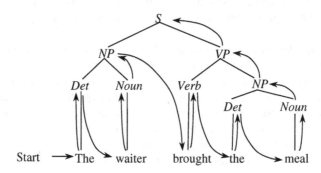

Fig. 11.1. Bottom-up parsing. The parser starts with the words and builds the syntactic structure up to the top node.

The shift and reduce algorithm is probably the simplest way to implement bottom-up parsing. As input, it uses two arguments: the list of words to parse and a symbol, s, np, for example, representing the parsing goal. The algorithm gradually reduces words, parts of speech, and phrase categories until it reaches the top node symbol – the parsing goal. The algorithm consists of a two-step loop:

1. **Shift** a word from the phrase or sentence to parse onto a stack.
2. Apply a sequence of grammar rules to **reduce** elements of the stack.

This loop is repeated until there are no more words in the list and the stack is reduced to the parsing goal. Table 11.1 shows an example of shift and reduce operations applied to the sentence *The waiter brought the meal.*

Table 11.1. Steps of the shift–reduce algorithm to parse *the waiter brought the meal*. At iteration 7, a further reduction of the stack yields [s], which is the parsing goal. However, since there are remaining words in the input list, the algorithm fails and backtracks to produce the next states of the stack. The table does not show the exploration of paths leading to a failure.

It.	Stack	S/R	Word list
0			[the, waiter, brought, the, meal]
1	[the]	Shift	[waiter, brought, the, meal]
2	[det]	Reduce	[waiter, brought, the, meal]
3	[det, waiter]	Shift	[brought, the, meal]
4	[det, noun]	Reduce	[brought, the, meal]
5	[np]	Reduce	[brought, the, meal]
6	[np, brought]	Shift	[the, meal]
7	[np, v]	Reduce	[the, meal]
8	[np, v, the]	Shift	[meal]
9	[np, v, det]	Reduce	[meal]
10	[np, v, det, meal]	Shift	[]
11	[np, v, det, n]	Reduce	[]
12	[np, v, np]	Reduce	[]
13	[np, vp]	Reduce	[]
14	[s]	Reduce	[]

11.2.2 Implementing Shift–Reduce Parsing in Prolog

We implement both arguments of the shift_reduce/2 predicate as lists: the words to parse and the symbol – or symbols – corresponding to the parsing goal. We represent grammar rules and the vocabulary as facts, as shown in Table 11.2.

Table 11.2. Rules and vocabulary of a shift–reduce parser.

Rules	Vocabulary	
rule(s, [np, vp]).	word(d, [the]).	word(v, [brought]).
rule(np, [d, n]).	word(n, [waiter]).	word(v, [slept]).
rule(vp, [v]).	word(n, [meal]).	
rule(vp, [v, np]).		

Using this grammar, shift_reduce should accept the following queries:

```
?- shift_reduce([the, waiter, brought, the, meal],
   [s]).
Yes
```

```
?- shift_reduce([the, waiter, brought, the, meal],
   [np, vp]).
Yes
```

```
?- shift_reduce([the, waiter, slept], X).
X = [s];
X = [np, vp];
X = [np, v];
...
```

To implement this predicate, we need an auxiliary stack to hold words and categories where we carry out the reduction step. This initial value of the stack is an empty list

```
% shift_reduce(+Sentence, ?Category)
shift_reduce(Sentence, Category) :-
  shift_reduce(Sentence, [], Category).
```

Then shift_reduce/3 uses two predicates, shift/4 and reduce/2. It repeats the reduction recursively until it no longer finds a reduction. It then applies shift. The parsing process succeeds when the sentence is an empty list and Stack is reduced to the parsing goal:

```
% shift_reduce(+Sentence, +Stack, ?Category)
shift_reduce([], Category, Category).
shift_reduce(Sentence, Stack, Category) :-
  reduce(Stack, ReducedStack),
  write('Reduce: '), write(ReducedStack), nl,
  shift_reduce(Sentence, ReducedStack, Category).
shift_reduce(Sentence, Stack, Category) :-
  shift(Sentence, Stack, NewSentence, NewStack),
  write('Shift: '), write(NewStack), nl,
  shift_reduce(NewSentence, NewStack, Category).
```

shift/4 removes the first word from the word list currently being parsed and puts it on the top the stack – here appends it to the end of the Stack list – to produce a NewStack.

```
% shift(+Sentence, +Stack, -NewSentence, -NewStack)
shift([First | Rest], Stack, Rest, NewStack) :-
  append(Stack, [First], NewStack).
```

reduce/2 simplifies the Stack. It searches the rules that match a sequence of symbols in the stack using match_rule/2 and match_word/2.

```
%reduce(+Stack, -NewStack)
reduce(Stack, NewStack) :-
  match_rule(Stack, NewStack).
reduce(Stack, NewStack) :-
  match_word(Stack, NewStack).
```

`match_rule/2` attempts to find the `Expansion` of a rule on the top of `Stack`, and replaces it with `Head` to produce `ReducedStack`:

```
match_rule(Stack, ReducedStack) :-
  rule(Head, Expansion),
  append(StackBottom, Expansion, Stack),
  append(StackBottom, [Head], ReducedStack).
```

`match_word/2` is similar:

```
match_word(Stack, NewStack) :-
  append(StackBottom, Word, Stack),
  word(POS, Word),
  append(StackBottom, [POS], NewStack).
```

The stack management of this program is not efficient because `shift/4`, `match_word/2`, and `match_rule/2` have to traverse it using `append/3`. It is possible to avoid the traversal using a reversed stack. For an optimization, see Exercise 11.1.

11.2.3 Differences Between Bottom-up and Top-down Parsing

Top-down and bottom-up strategies are fundamental approaches to parsing. The top-down exploration is probably more intuitive from the viewpoint of a Prolog programmer, at least for a neophyte. Once a grammar is written, Prolog relies on its built-in search mechanism to parse a sentence. On the contrary, bottom-up parsing requires additional code and may not be as natural.

Whatever the parsing strategy, phrase-structure rule grammars are written roughly in the same way. There are a couple of slight differences, however. As we saw, bottom-up parsing can handle left-recursive rules such as those describing conjunctions. In contrast, top-down parsers can handle null constituents like

```
det --> [].
```

Bottom-up parsers could not use such a rule with an empty symbol because they are able to process actual words only.

Both parsing methods may fail to find a solution, but in a different way. Top-down parsing explores all the grammar rules starting from the initial symbol, whatever the actual tokens. It leads to the expansion of trees that have no chance to yield any solution since they will not match the input words. On the contrary, bottom-up parsing starts with the words and hence builds trees that conform to the input. However, a bottom-up analysis annotates the input words with every possible part of speech, and generates the corresponding partial trees, even if they have no chance to result into a sentence.

For both strategies, Prolog produces a solution – whenever it exists – using backtracking. When Prolog has found a dead-end path, whether in the bottom-up or the top-down mode, it selects another path and explores this path until it completes the parse or fails. Backtracking may repeat a same operation since Prolog does not store intermediate or partial solutions. We will see in the next section a parsing technique that stores incomplete solutions using a table or a **chart** and thus avoids parsing repetitions.

11.3 Chart Parsing

11.3.1 Backtracking and Efficiency

Backtracking is an elegant and simple mechanism, but it frequently leads to reparsing a same substructure to produce the final result. Consider the noun phrase *The meal of the day* and DCG rules in Fig. 11.2 to parse it.

```
np --> npx.        npx --> det, noun.
np --> npx, pp.

pp --> prep, np.
```

Fig. 11.2. A small set of DCG rules where left-recursion has been eliminated.

The DCG search algorithm first tries rule np --> npx, uses npx to parse *The meal*, and fails because of the remaining words *of the day*. It then backtracks with the second np rule, reuses npx to reparse *The meal*, and finally completes the analysis with pp. Backtracking is clearly inefficient here. The parser twice applies the same rule to the same group of words because it has forgotten a previous result: *The meal* is an npx.

Chart – or tabular – parsing is a technique to avoid a parser repeating a same analysis. A chart is a memory where the parser stores all the possible partial results at a given position in the sentence. When it needs to process a subsequent word, the parser fetches partial parse structures obtained so far in the chart instead of reparsing them. At the end of the analysis, the chart contains all possible parse trees and subtrees that it represents tidily and efficiently.

11.3.2 Structure of a Chart

A chart represents intervals between words as nodes of a graph. Considering a sentence of N words, nodes are numbered from left to right, from 0 to N. The chart – which can also be viewed as a table – then has $N + 1$ entries or positions. Figure 11.3 shows word numbering of the sentence *Bring the meal* and the noun phrase *The meal of the day*. A chart node is also called a vertex.

Directed arcs (or edges) connect nodes and define constituents. Each arc has a label that corresponds to the syntactic category of the group it spans (Fig. 11.4). Charts

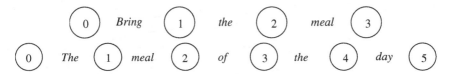

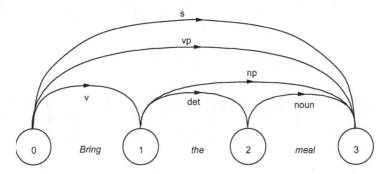

Fig. 11.3. Nodes of a chart.

Fig. 11.4. Nodes and arcs of a chart associated with the sentence *Bring the meal*.

consist then of sets of nodes and directed labeled arcs. This algorithmic structure is also called a directed acyclic graph (DAG).

A chart can store alternative syntactic representations. As we saw in Chap. 8, the grammar in Fig. 11.5 yields two parse trees for the sentence

Bring the meal of the day.

```
s  --> vp.             np --> det, noun.
vp --> v, np, pp.      np --> det, adj, noun.
vp --> v, np.          np --> np, pp.
                       pp --> prep, np.
```

Fig. 11.5. A small grammar for restaurant orders in English.

The chart of Fig. 11.6 shows the possible parses of this sentence. Rules vp --> v, np and vp --> v, np, pp create two paths that connect node 0 to node 6. Starting from node 0, the first one traverses nodes 1 and 6: arc v from 0 to 1, then np from 1 to 6. The second sequence of arcs traverses nodes 1, 3, 6: arc v from 0 to 1, then np from 1 to 3, and finally pp from 3 to 6.

11.3.3 The Active Chart

So far, we used charts as devices to represent partial or complete parse trees. Charts can also store representations of constituents currently being parsed. In this case, a chart is said to be active.

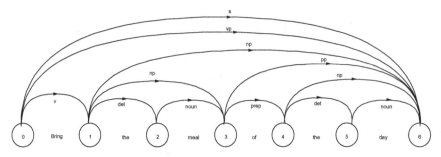

Fig. 11.6. A chart representing alternative parse trees.

In the classical chart notation, the parsing progress of a constituent is indicated using a dot (•) inserted in the right-hand side of the rules. A **dotted rule** represents what has been parsed so far, with the dot marking the position of the parser relative to the input. Thus

```
np --> det noun •
```

is a completely parsed noun phrase composed of a determiner and a noun. Since the constituent is complete, the arc is said to be inactive. Rules

```
np --> det • noun
np --> • det noun
```

describe noun phrases being parsed. Both correspond to constituent hypotheses that the parser tries to find. In the first rule, the parser has found a determiner and looks for a noun to complete the parse. The second rule represents the constituent being sought originally. Both arcs are said to be active since the parser needs more words from the input to confirm them.

Consider the sentence *Bring the meal*. Table 11.3 shows dotted-rules and arcs during the parsing process, and Fig. 11.7 shows a graphic representation of them.

Table 11.3. Some dotted-rules and arcs in the chart while parsing *Bring the meal of the day*.

Positions	Rules	Arcs	Constituents
0	s --> • vp	[0, 0]	• *Bring the meal*
1	vp --> v • np	[0, 1]	*Bring* • *the meal*
1	np --> • det noun	[1, 1]	• *the meal*
1	np --> • np pp	[1, 1]	• *the meal*
2	np --> det • noun	[1, 2]	*the* • *meal*
3	np --> det noun •	[1, 3]	*the meal* •
3	np --> np • pp	[1, 3]	*the meal* •
3	vp --> v np •	[0, 3]	*Bring the meal* •
3	s --> vp •	[0, 3]	*Bring the meal* •

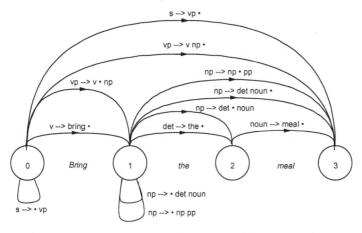

Fig. 11.7. Some arcs of a chart labeled with dotted-rules while parsing *Bring the meal of the day*.

Charts can be used with top-down, bottom-up, or more sophisticated strategies. We introduce now a top-down version due to Earley (1970). Its popularity comes from its complexity, which has been demonstrated as $0(N^3)$.

11.3.4 Modules of an Earley Parser

An Earley parser consists of three modules, the predictor, the scanner, and the completer, which are chained by the parsing process. The initial goal of the algorithm is to parse the start symbol, which is generally a sentence s. Here, we illustrate the algorithm with the noun phrase *The meal of the day* and the rules in Fig. 11.5. The start symbol is then np and is represented by the dotted-rule

```
start --> • np
```

The Predictor. At a given position of the parsing process, the predictor determines all possible further parses. To carry this out, the predictor selects all the rules that can process active arcs. Considering the dotted rule, lhs --> c_1 c_2 ... • c... c_n, the predictor searches all the rules where c is the left-hand-side symbol: c --> x_1 ... x_k. The predictor introduces them into the chart as new parsing goals under the form c --> • x_1 ... x_k. The predictor proceeds recursively with nonterminal symbols until it reaches the parts of speech. Considering *The meal of the day* with np as the starting parsing goal and applying the predictor results in new goals shown in Fig. 11.8 and graphically in Fig. 11.9.

The Scanner. Once all possible predictions are done, the scanner accepts a new word from the input, here *the*. The parts of speech to the right of a dot are matched against the word, here in our example, rules np --> • det noun and np --> • det adj noun. The scanner inserts the word into the chart with all its matching

```
start --> • np            [0, 0]
np --> • det noun         [0, 0]
np --> • det adj noun     [0, 0]
np --> • np pp            [0, 0]
```

Fig. 11.8. Dotted-rules resulting from the recursive run of the predictor with starting goal np.

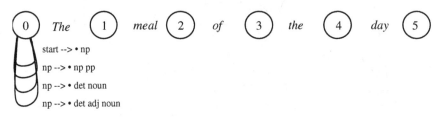

Fig. 11.9. Graphic representation of the predictor results.

part-of-speech readings under the form `pos --> word •` and advances the parse position to the next node, here

```
det --> the •     [0, 1]
```

as shown in Fig. 11.10.

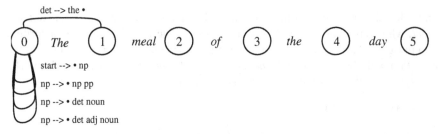

Fig. 11.10. The scanner accepts word *The* from the input.

The Completer. The scanner introduces new constituents under the form of parts of speech in the chart. The completer uses them to advance the dot of active arcs expecting them, and possibly complete the corresponding constituents. Once a constituent has been completed, it can in turn modify others expecting it in active arcs. The completer thus is applied to propagate modifications and to complete all possible arcs. It first determines which constituents are complete by looking for dots that have reached the end of a rule: $c --> x_1 \ldots x_k$ •. The completer then searches all the active arcs expecting c, that is, the rules with a dot to the right of it: $lhs --> c_1 c_2 \ldots • c \ldots c_n$, moves the dot over c: $lhs --> c_1 c_2 \ldots c$ •

... c_n, and inserts the new arc into the chart. It proceeds recursively from the parts of speech to all the possible higher-level constituents.

In our example, the only completed constituent is the part of speech det. The completer advances the dot over it in two active arcs and inserts them into the chart. It does not produce new completed constituents (Fig. 11.11).

```
np --> det • noun        [0, 1]
np --> det • adj noun    [0, 1]
```

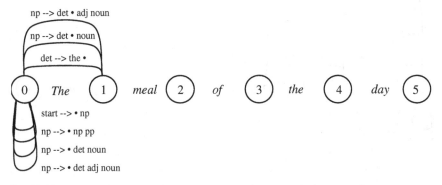

Fig. 11.11. The completer looks for completed constituents and advances the dot over them.

From node 1, the predictor is run again, but it does not yield new arcs. The scanner accepts word *meal*, advances the position to 2, and inserts

```
noun --> meal •    [1, 2]
```

as shown in Fig. 11.12.

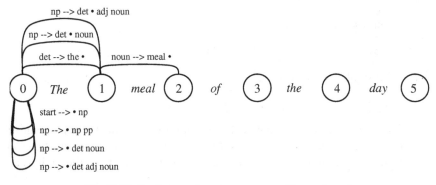

Fig. 11.12. Predictor and scanner are run with word *meal*.

At node 2, the completer can advance active arc

```
np --> det noun •        [0, 2]
```

and complete a higher-level constituent (Fig. 11.13).

```
np --> np • pp        [0, 2]
```

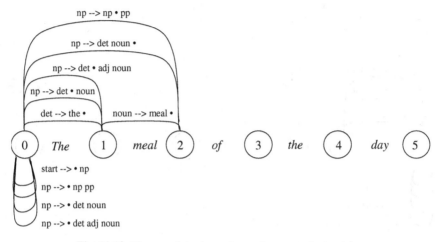

Fig. 11.13. The completer is run to produce new chart entries.

11.3.5 The Earley Algorithm in Prolog

To implement the algorithm in Prolog, we must first represent the chart. It consists of arcs such as

```
np --> np • pp        [0, 2]
```

which we represent as facts

```
arc(np, [np, '.', pp], 0, 2).
```

The start symbol is encoded as:

```
arc(start, ['.', np], 0, 0).
```

Although this data representation is straightforward from the description of dotted-rules, it is not efficient from the speed viewpoint. The arc representation can be improved easily, but an optimization may compromise clarity. We leave it as an exercise.

New arcs are stored in the chart, a list called Chart, using the expand_-chart/1 predicate, which checks first that the new entry is not already in the chart:

```
expand_chart([], Chart, Chart).
expand_chart([Entry | Entries], Chart, NewChart) :-
   \+ member(Entry, Chart),
   !,
   expand_chart(Entries, [Entry | Chart], NewChart).
expand_chart([_ | Entries], Chart, NewChart) :-
   expand_chart(Entries, Chart, NewChart).
```

The Earley algorithm is implemented by the predicate `earley_parser/2`. It uses five arguments: the input word sequence, the current position in the sequence `CurPos`, the final position `FinalPos`, the current chart, and the final chart. The `earley_parser` main rule consists of calling the `predictor`, `scanner`, and `completer` predicates through the $N + 1$ nodes of the chart:

```
earley_parser([], FinalPos, FinalPos, Chart, Chart) :-
   !.
earley_parser(Words, CurPos, FinalPos, Chart,
      FinalChart) :-
   predictor(CurPos, Chart, PredChart),
   NextPos is CurPos + 1,
   scanner(Words, RestWords, CurPos, NextPos,
      PredChart, ScanChart),
   completer(NextPos, ScanChart, NewChart),
   !,
   earley_parser(RestWords, NextPos, FinalPos,
      NewChart, FinalChart).
```

The Earley algorithm is called by `parse/2`, which takes the word sequence `Words` and the start `Category` as arguments. The `parse/2` predicate initializes the chart with the start symbol and launches the parse. The parsing success corresponds to the presence of a completed start symbol, which is, in our example, the `arc(start, [np, '.'], 0, FinalNode)` fact in the Prolog database:

```
parse(Words, Category, FinalChart) :-
   expand_chart([arc(start, ['.', Category], 0, 0)],
      [], Chart),
   earley_parser(Words, 0, FinalPos, Chart,
      FinalChart),
   member(arc(start, [Category, '.'], 0, FinalPos),
      FinalChart).
```

Table 11.4 shows the transcription of np rules in Fig. 11.5 encoded as Prolog facts. It contains a small vocabulary to parse the phrase *The meal of the day*.

The Predictor. The predictor looks for rules to expand arcs from a current position (`CurPos`). To carry this out, `predictor/3` searches all the arcs containing the pattern: `[..., X, '.', CAT, ...]`, where `CAT` matches the left-hand side of a rule: `rule(CAT, RHS)`. This is compactly expressed using the

Table 11.4. Rules and vocabulary for the chart parser.

Rules	Words	
rule(np, [d, n]).	word(d, [the]).	word(prep, [of]).
rule(np, [d, a, n]).	word(n, [waiter]).	word(v, [brought]).
rule(np, [np, pp]).	word(n, [meal]).	word(v, [slept]).
rule(pp, [prep, np]).	word(n, [day]).	

findall/3 built-in predicate. predictor/3 then adds arc(CAT, ['.' |
RHS], CurPos, CurPos) to the chart NewChart. predictor/3 is run re-
cursively until no new arc can be produced, that is, NewChartEntries == [].
It then returns the predictor's chart PredChart.

```
predictor(CurPos, Chart, PredChart) :-
  findall(
    arc(CAT, ['.' | RHS], CurPos, CurPos),
    (
      member(arc(LHS, ACTIVE_RHS, InitPos, CurPos),
        Chart),
      append(B, ['.', CAT | E], ACTIVE_RHS),
      rule(CAT, RHS),
      \+ member(arc(CAT, ['.' | RHS], CurPos,CurPos),
        Chart)
    ),
    NewChartEntries),
  NewChartEntries \== [],
  expand_chart(NewChartEntries, Chart, NewChart),
  predictor(CurPos, NewChart, PredChart),
  !.
predictor(_, PredChart, PredChart).
```

Using chart entry arc(np, [np, '.', pp], 0, 2) and rules in Table 11.4:

```
?- predictor(2,[arc(np, [np, '.', pp], 0, 2)],Chart).
```

adds

```
arc(pp, ['.', prep, np], 2, 2)
```

to the Chart list.

The Scanner. The scanner gets a new word from the input and looks for active
arcs that match its possible parts of speech to the right of the dot. The scanner stores
the word with its compatible parts of speech as new chart entries. Again, we use
findall/3 to implement this search.

```
scanner([Word | Rest], Rest, CurPos, NextPos, Chart,
      NewChart) :-
   findall(
      arc(CAT, [Word, '.'], CurPos, NextPos),
      (
         word(CAT, [Word]),
         once((
            member(arc(LHS, ACTIVE_RHS, InitPos, CurPos),
               Chart),
            append(B, ['.', CAT | E], ACTIVE_RHS)))
      ),
      NewChartEntries),
   NewChartEntries \== [],
   expand_chart(NewChartEntries, Chart, NewChart).
```

The Completer. The completer looks for completed constituents, that is, for arcs with a dot at the end of the right-hand-side part of the rule. They correspond to arc(LHS, COMPLETE_RHS, InitPos, CurPos), where COMPLETE_-RHS matches [..., X, '.']. We use the goal append(_, ['.'], COM-PLETE_RHS) to find them. The completer then searches arcs with a dot to the right of the LHS category of completed constituents: [..., '.', LHS, ...], advances the dot over LHS: [..., LHS, '.', ...], and stores the new arc with updated node positions. We use findall/3 to implement the search, and completer/3 is run recursively until there is no arc to complete.

```
completer(CurPos, Chart, CompChart) :-
   findall(
      arc(LHS2, RHS3, PrevPos, CurPos),
      (
         member(arc(LHS, COMPLETE_RHS, InitPos, CurPos),
            Chart),
         append(_, ['.'], COMPLETE_RHS),
         member(arc(LHS2, RHS2, PrevPos, InitPos), Chart),
         append(B, ['.', LHS | E], RHS2),
         append(B, [LHS, '.' | E], RHS3),
         \+ member(arc(LHS2, RHS3, PrevPos, CurPos),
            Chart)
      ),
      CompletedChartEntries),
   CompletedChartEntries \== [],
   expand_chart(CompletedChartEntries, Chart, NewChart),
   completer(CurPos, NewChart, CompChart),
   !.
completer(_, CompChart, CompChart).
```

An Execution Example. Table 11.5 shows the arcs added to the chart while parsing the phrase *The meal of the day*. The parser is queried by:

```
?- parse([the, meal, of, the, day], np, Chart).
```

Note that the `completer` calls at position 2 that completes np, and at position 5 that completes np, pp, and the starting goal np.

Table 11.5. Additions to the Prolog database.

Module	New Chart Entries in the Database
	Position 0
start	arc(start, ['.', np], 0, 0)
predictor	arc(np, [., d, n], 0, 0), arc(np, [., d, a, n], 0, 0), arc(np, [., np, pp], 0, 0)
	Position 1
scanner	arc(d, [the, .], 0, 1)
completer	arc(np, [d, ., a, n], 0, 1), arc(np, [d, ., n], 0, 1)
predictor	[]
	Position 2
scanner	arc(n, [meal, .], 1, 2)
completer	arc(np, [d, n, .], 0, 2)
completer	arc(np, [np, ., pp], 0, 2), arc(start, [np, .], 0, 2)
predictor	arc(pp, [., prep, np], 2, 2)
	Position 3
scanner	arc(prep, [of, .], 2, 3)
completer	arc(pp, [prep, ., np], 2, 3)
predictor	arc(np, [., d, n], 3, 3), arc(np, [., d, a, n], 3, 3), arc(np, [., np, pp], 3, 3)
	Position 4
scanner	arc(d, [the, .], 3, 4)
completer	arc(np, [d, ., a, n], 3, 4), arc(np, [d, ., n], 3, 4)
predictor	[]
	Position 5
scanner	arc(n, [day, .], 4, 5)
completer	arc(np, [d, n, .], 3, 5)
completer	arc(np, [np, ., pp], 3, 5), arc(pp, [prep, np, .], 2, 5)
completer	arc(np, [np, pp, .], 0, 5)
completer	arc(np, [np, ., pp], 0, 5), arc(start, [np, .], 0, 5)

11.3.6 The Earley Parser to Handle Left-Recursive Rules and Empty Symbols

The Earley parser handles left-recursive rules without looping infinitely. In effect, the predictor is the only place where the parser could be trapped into an infinite execution. This is avoided because before creating a new arc, the `predictor` predicate checks that it is not already present in the chart using the goal

```
\+ member(arc(CAT, ['.' | RHS], CrPos, CrPos), Chart)
```

So

```
start --> • np          [0, 0]
```

predicts

```
np --> • np pp          [0, 0]
np --> • det noun       [0, 0]
np --> • det adj noun   [0, 0]
```

but `np --> • np pp` predicts nothing more since all the possible arcs are already in the chart.

The Earley algorithm can also parse null constituents. It corresponds to examples such as *meals of the day*, where the determiner is encoded as `word(d, [])`. As we wrote it, the scanner would fail on empty symbols. We need to add a second rule to it to handle empty lists:

```
% The first scanner rule
scanner([Word | Rest], Rest, CurPos, NextPos, Chart,
      NewChart) :-
  findall(
    arc(CAT, [Word, '.'], CurPos, NextPos),
    (
      word(CAT, [Word]),
      once((
        member(arc(LHS, ACTIVE_RHS, InitPos, CurPos),
          Chart),
        append(B, ['.', CAT | E], ACTIVE_RHS)))
    ),
    NewChartEntries),
  NewChartEntries \== [],
  expand_chart(NewChartEntries, Chart, NewChart),
  !.

% The second rule to handle empty symbols
scanner(Words, Words, CurPos, NextPos, Chart,
      NewChart) :-
  findall(
    arc(CAT, [[], '.'], CurPos, NextPos),
```

```
(
  word(CAT, []),
  once((
    member(arc(LHS, ACTIVE_RHS, InitPos, CurPos),
      Chart),
    append(B, ['.', CAT | E], ACTIVE_RHS)))
  ),
  NewChartEntries),
NewChartEntries \== [],
expand_chart(NewChartEntries, Chart, NewChart),
!.
```

Let us add

```
word(d, []).
word(n, [meals]).
```

to the database to be able to parse *meals of the day*:

```
?- parse([meals, of , the, day], np, Chart).
```

11.4 Probabilistic Parsing of Context-Free Grammars

So far, parsing methods made no distinction between possible parse trees of an ambiguous sentence. They produced trees either through a systematic backtracking or simultaneously in a chart with the Earley algorithm. The reason is that the parsers considered all rules to be equal and tried them sequentially.

We know this is not the case in reality. Some rules describe very frequent structures, while others are rare. As a solution, a parser could try more frequent rules first, prefer certain rules when certain words occur, and rank trees in an order of likelihood. To do that, the parser can integrate statistics derived from bracketed corpora. Because annotation is done by hand, frequencies captured by statistics reflect preferences of human beings.

There are many possible **probabilistic parsing** techniques. They all aim at finding an optimal analysis considering a set of statistical parameters. A major difference between them corresponds to the introduction of lexical statistics or not – statistics on words as opposed to statistics on rules. We begin here with a description of nonlexicalized probabilistic context-free grammars, or PCFG.

11.5 A Description of PCFGs

A PCFG is a constituent context-free grammar where each rule describing the structure of a left-hand-side symbol is augmented with its probability $P(lhs \rightarrow rhs)$

Table 11.6. A small set of phrase-structure rules augmented with probabilities, P.

Rules		P	Rules		P
s	--> np vp	0.8	det	--> the	1.0
s	--> vp	0.2	noun	--> waiter	0.4
np	--> det noun	0.3	noun	--> meal	0.3
np	--> det adj noun	0.2	noun	--> day	0.3
np	--> pronoun	0.3	verb	--> bring	0.4
np	--> np pp	0.2	verb	--> slept	0.2
vp	--> v np	0.6	verb	--> brought	0.4
vp	--> v np pp	0.1	pronoun	--> he	1.0
vp	--> v pp	0.2	prep	--> of	0.6
vp	--> v	0.1	prep	--> to	0.4
pp	--> prep np	1.0	pronoun	--> he	1.0
			adj	--> big	1.0

(Charniak 1993). Table 11.6 shows a small set of grammar rules with imaginary probabilities.

According to figures in the table, the structure of a sentence consists 4 times out of 5 in a noun phrase and a verb phrase – $P(s \rightarrow np, vp) = 0.8$ – and 1 time out of 5 in a verb phrase – $P(s \rightarrow vp) = 0.2$. Such figures correspond in fact to conditional probabilities: knowing the left-hand-side symbol they describe proportions among the right-hand-side expansions. The probability could be rewritten then as

$$P(lhs \rightarrow rhs|lhs).$$

The sum of probabilities of all possible expansions of a left-hand-side symbol must be equal to 1.0.

Probabilities in Table 11.6 are fictitious and incomplete. A sentence has, of course, many more possible structures than those shown here. Real probabilities are obtained from syntactically bracketed corpora – treebanks. The probability of a given rule $lhs \rightarrow rhs_i$ is obtained by counting the number of times it occurs in the corpus and by dividing it by the count of all the expansions of symbol lhs.

$$P(lhs \rightarrow rhs_i|lhs) = \frac{Count(lhs \rightarrow rhs_i)}{\sum_j Count(lhs \rightarrow rhs_j)}.$$

Parsing with a PCFG is just the same as with a context-free grammar except that each tree is assigned with a probability. The probability for sentence S to have the parse tree T is defined as the product of probabilities attached to rules used to produce the tree:

$$P(T, S) = \prod_{rule(i) producing T} P(rule(i)).$$

Let us exemplify probabilistic parsing for an ambiguous sentence using the grammar in Table 11.6. *Bring the meal of the day* has two possible parse trees, as shown in Table 11.7. We consider trees up to the verb phrase symbol only.

Table 11.7. Possible parse trees for *Bring the meal of the day.*

Parse trees
T1: `vp(verb(bring),`
`        np(np(det(the), noun(meal)),`
`                    pp(prep(of), np(det(the), noun(day))))))`
T2: `vp(verb(bring),`
`        np(np(det(the), noun(meal))),`
`        pp(prep(of), np(det(the), noun(day)))))`

The probability of T_1 is defined as (Fig. 11.14):

$P(T_1, \text{Bring the meal of the day}) =$
$P(vp \rightarrow v, np) \times P(v \rightarrow Bring) \times P(np \rightarrow np, pp) \times$
$P(np \rightarrow det, noun) \times P(det \rightarrow the) \times P(noun \rightarrow meal) \times$
$P(pp \rightarrow prep, np) \times P(prep \rightarrow of) \times P(np \rightarrow det, noun) \times$
$P(det \rightarrow the) \times P(noun \rightarrow day) =$
$0.6 \times 0.4 \times 0.2 \times 0.3 \times 1.0 \times 0.3 \times 1.0 \times 0.6 \times 0.3 \times 1.0 \times 0.3 = 0.00023328,$

and that of T_2 as (Fig. 11.15) as:

$P(T_2, \text{Bring the meal of the day}) =$
$P(vp \rightarrow v, np, pp) \times P(v \rightarrow Bring) \times P(np \rightarrow det, noun) \times$
$P(det \rightarrow the) \times P(noun \rightarrow meal) \times P(pp \rightarrow prep, np) \times P(prep \rightarrow of) \times$
$P(np \rightarrow det, noun) \times P(det \rightarrow the) \times P(noun \rightarrow day) =$
$0.1 \times 0.4 \times 0.3 \times 1.0 \times 0.3 \times 1.0 \times 0.6 \times 0.3 \times 1.0 \times 0.3 = 0.0001944.$

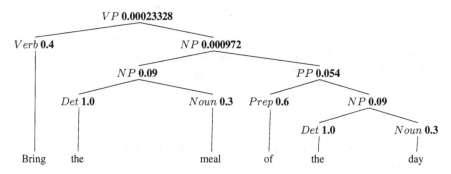

Fig. 11.14. Parse tree T_1 with nodes annotated with probabilities.

T_1 has a probability higher than that of T_2 and then corresponds to the most likely parse tree. Thus PCFG would properly disambiguate among alternative structures for this sentence. However, we can notice that PCFGs are certainly not flawless because they would not properly rank trees of *Bring the meal to the table.*

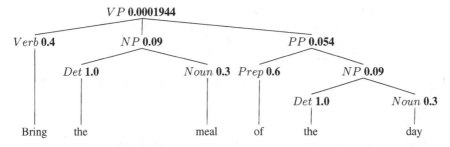

Fig. 11.15. Parse tree T_2 with nodes annotated with probabilities.

11.5.1 The Bottom-up Chart

Figures 11.14 and 11.15 show a calculation of parse tree probabilities using a bottom-up approach. Although it is possible to use other types of parsers, this strategy seems the most natural because it computes probabilities as it assembles partial parses. In addition, a chart would save us many recalculations. We will combine these techniques to build a probabilistic context-free parser. We introduce them in two steps. First, we present a symbolic bottom-up chart parser also known as the Cocke–Younger–Kasami (CYK) algorithm (Kasami 1965). We then extend it to probabilistic parsing in a next section.

The CYK algorithm uses grammars in Chomsky normal form (CNF, Chap. 10) where rules are restricted to two forms:

```
lhs --> rhs1, rhs2.
lhs --> [terminal_symbol].
```

However, the CYK algorithm can be generalized to any type of grammar (Graham et al. 1980).

Let N be the length of the sentence. The idea of the CYK parser is to consider constituents of increasing length from the words – length 1 – up to the sentence – length N. In contrast to the Earley parser, the CYK algorithm stores completely parsed constituents in the chart. It proceeds in two steps. The first step annotates the words with all their possible parts of speech. Figure 11.16 shows the result of this step with the sentence *Bring the meal of the day*. It results in chart entries such as `arc(v, [bring, '.'], 0, 1)`, `arc(det, [the, '.'], 1, 2)`, etc. This first step is also called the base case.

The second step considers contiguous pairs of chart entries that it tries to reduce in a constituent of length l, l ranging from 2 to N. Considering rule `lhs --> rhs1, rhs2`, the parser searches couples of arcs corresponding to `arc(rhs1, [..., '.'], i, k)` and `arc(rhs2, [..., '.'], k, j)` such that $i < k < j$ and $j - i = l$. It adds then a new arc: `arc(lhs, [rhs1, rhs2, '.'], i, j)` to the chart. Since constituents of length 2, 3, 4, ... N are built in that order, it ensures that all constituents of length less than l have already been built. This second step is called the recursive case.

length

verb	det	noun	prep	det	noun

1

Bring   the   meal   of   the   day

0   1   2   3   4   5   6

Fig. 11.16. Annotation of the words with their possible part of speech. Here words are not ambiguous.

Let us consider constituents of length 2 of our example. We can add two noun phrases that we insert in the second row, as shown in Fig. 11.17. They span nodes 1–3 and 4–6. Since their length is 2, no constituent can start in cell 5–6, otherwise it would overflow the array. We insert the symbol "—" in the corresponding cell. This property is general for any constituent of length l and yields a triangular array.

length

2

	np			np	—
verb	det	noun	prep	det	noun

1

Bring   the   meal   of   the   day

0   1   2   3   4   5   6

Fig. 11.17. Constituents of length 1 and 2.

The parse is complete and successful when length N, here 6, has been reached with the start symbol. Figure 11.18 shows constituents of length 3, and Fig. 11.19 shows the completed parse, where constituents are indexed vertically according to their length.

length

3

s			pp	—	—
	np			np	—
verb	det	noun	prep	det	noun

2

1

Bring   the   meal   of   the   day

0   1   2   3   4   5   6

Fig. 11.18. Constituent of lengths 1, 2, and 3.

11.5.2 The Cocke–Younger–Kasami Algorithm in Prolog

From the algorithm description, the Prolog implementation is relatively straight-forward. We use two predicates to carry out the base case and the recursive case: tag_words/5 and cyk_loop/4.

Since we use a CNF, we need to rewrite some rules in Table 11.6:

length						
6	s	—	—	—	—	—
5		np	—	—	—	—
4			—	—	—	—
3	s			pp	—	—
2		np			np	—
1	verb	det	noun	prep	det	noun
	Bring	the	meal	of	the	day

0   1   2   3   4   5   6

Fig. 11.19. The completed parse.

- `rule(np, [d, a, n])` is rewritten into `rule(np, [det, np])` and `rule(np, [a, n])`.
- `rule(vp, [v, np, pp])` is rewritten into `rule(vp, [vp, pp])` and `rule(vp, [v, np])`.
- `rule(s, [vp])` is rewritten into `rule(s, [vp, pp])` and `rule(s, [v, np])`.
- `rule(vp, [v])` is rewritten into `word(vp, [brought])`, `word(vp, [bring])`, and `word(vp, [slept])`.
- `rule(np, [pronoun])` is rewritten into `word(np, [he])`.

The parsing predicate `parse/2` consists of tagging the words (the base case) and calling the reduction loop (the recursive case).

```
parse(Sentence, Chart) :-
    tag_words(Sentence, 0, FinalPosition,[],WordChart),
    cyk_loop(2, FinalPosition, WordChart, Chart).
```

`tag_words/3` tags the words with their possible parts of speech and adds the corresponding arcs using the `expand_chart/1` predicate.

```
tag_words([], FinalPos, FinalPos, Chart, Chart).
tag_words([Word | Rest], Pos, FinalPos, Chart,
        WordChart) :-
    NextPos is Pos + 1,
    findall(
        arc(LHS, [Word, '.'], Pos, NextPos),
        word(LHS, [Word]),
        ChartEntries),
    expand_chart(ChartEntries, Chart, NewChart),
    tag_words(Rest, NextPos, FinalPos, NewChart,
        WordChart).
```

`cyk_loop/4` implements the recursive case. It proceeds from length 2 to the sentence length and attempts to reduce constituents using `inner_loop/5`. The new constituents are added to the chart using `expand_chart/3`.

```
cyk_loop(FinalPos, FinalPos, Chart, FinalChart) :-
   inner_loop(0, FinalPos, FinalPos,Chart,FinalChart).
cyk_loop(Length, FinalPos, Chart, FinalChart) :-
   inner_loop(0, Length, FinalPos, Chart, ILChart),
   NextLength is Length + 1,
   cyk_loop(NextLength, FinalPos, ILChart,FinalChart).


inner_loop(StartPos, Length, FinalPos, Chart,Chart):-
   FinalPos < StartPos + Length.
inner_loop(StartPos, Length, FinalPos, Chart,
       ILChart) :-
   EndPos is StartPos + Length,
   findall(
     arc(LHS3, [LHS1, LHS2, '.'], StartPos, EndPos),
     (
       member(arc(LHS1, RHS1,StartPos,MidPos), Chart),
       member(arc(LHS2, RHS2, MidPos, EndPos), Chart),
       StartPos < MidPos,
       MidPos < EndPos,
       rule(LHS3, [LHS1, LHS2])
     ),
     ChartEntries),
   expand_chart(ChartEntries, Chart, NewChart),
   NextStartPos is StartPos + 1,
   inner_loop(NextStartPos, Length, FinalPos,
       NewChart, ILChart).
```

11.5.3 Adding Probabilities to the CYK Parser

Considering sentence S, the parser has to find the most likely tree T defined as the maximum probability

$$T(S) = \arg\max P(T).$$

Let us suppose that sentence S consists of constituents A and B: $S \rightarrow A, B$. The most likely parse tree corresponds to that yielding the maximum probability of both A and B. This is valid recursively for substructures of A and B down to the words.

To obtain most likely constituents for any given length, we need to maintain an array that stores the maximum probability for all the possible constituents spanning all the word intervals $i...j$ in the chart. In other words, that means that if there are two or more competing constituents with the same left-hand-side label spanning $i...j$, the parser retains the maximum and discards the others. Let lhs be the constituent label and $\pi(i, j, lhs)$ this probability.

The base case initializes the algorithm with part of speech probabilities:

$$\pi(i, i+1, part\_of\_speech \rightarrow word).$$

The recursive case maintains the probability of the most likely structure of lhs. It corresponds to

$$\pi(i, j, lhs) = \max(\pi(i, k, rhs_1) \times \pi(k, j, rhs_2) \times P(lhs \rightarrow rhs_1, rhs_2),$$

where the maximum is taken over all the possible values of k with $i < k < j$ and all possible values of rhs_1, rhs_2 with $lhs \rightarrow rhs_1, rhs_2$ in the grammar.

11.6 Parser Evaluation

11.6.1 Constituency-Based Evaluation

We have a variety of techniques to evaluate parsers. The PARSEVAL measures (Black et al. 1991) are the most frequently cited for constituent parsing. They take a manually bracketed treebank as the reference – the gold standard – and compare it to the results of a parser.

PARSEVAL uses a metric similar to that of information extraction, that is, recall and precision. Recall is defined as the number of correct constituents generated by the parser, i.e., exactly similar to that of the manually bracketed tree, divided by the number of constituents of the treebank. The precision is the number of correct constituents generated by the parser divided by the total number of constituents – wrong and correct ones – generated by the parser.

$$\text{Recall} = \frac{\text{Number of correct constituents generated by the parser}}{\text{Number of constituents in the manually bracketed corpus}}.$$

$$\text{Precision} = \frac{\text{Number of correct constituents generated by the parser}}{\text{Total number of constituents generated by the parser}}.$$

A third metric is the number of crossing brackets. It corresponds to the number of constituents produced by the parser that overlap constituents in the treebank. Table 11.8 shows two possible analyses of *Bring the meal of the day* with crossing brackets between both structures. The number of crossing brackets gives an idea of the compatibility between structures and whether they can be combined into a single structure.

Table 11.8. Bracketing of order *Bring the meal of the day* and crossing brackets.

Bracketing	Crossing brackets
(((bring) (the meal)) (of the day))	( ) ( )
((bring) ((the meal) (of the day)))	( ) ( )

11.6.2 Dependency-Based Evaluation

Lin (1995) proposed another evaluation metric based on dependency trees. It also considers a treebank that it compares to the output of a parser. The error count is the number of words that are assigned a wrong head (governor). Figure 11.20 shows a reference dependency tree and a possible parse of *Bring the meal to the table*. The error count is 1 out of 6 links and corresponds to the wrong attachment of *to*. Lin (1995) also described a method to adapt this error count to constituent structures. This error count is probably simpler and more intuitive than the PARSEVAL metrics.

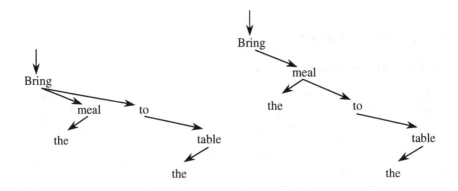

Fig. 11.20. Evaluation of dependency trees: The reference dependency tree (left) and a possible parse output (right).

11.6.3 Performance of PCFG Parsing

PCFGs rank the possible analyses. This enables us to select the most probable parse tree and to evaluate it. Charniak (1997) reports approximately 70% recall and 75% precision for this parsing method.

In terms of accuracy, PCFG parsing does not show the best performances. This is mainly due to its poor use of lexical properties. An example is given with prepositional-phrase attachment. While prepositional phrases attach to the preceding noun phrase 6 to 7 times out of 10 on average, there are specific lexical preferences. Some prepositions attach more often to verbs in general, while others attach to nouns. There are also verb/preposition or noun/preposition couples, showing strong affinities.

Let us exhibit them with orders

Bring the meal to the table

and

Bring the meal of the day

for which a parser has to decide where to attach prepositional phrases *to the table* and *of the day*. Alternatives are the verb *Bring* and the noun phrase *the meal*. Prepositional phrases headed by *of* attach systematically to the preceding noun phrase, here *the meal*, while *to* attaches here to the verb. Provided that part-of-speech annotation of both sentences is the same, the ratio

$$\frac{P(T1|\text{Bring the meal of the day})}{P(T2|\text{Bring the meal of the day})} = \frac{P(T1|\text{Bring the meal to the table})}{P(T2|\text{Bring the meal to the table})},$$

$$= \frac{P(vp \rightarrow v,np) \times P(np \rightarrow np,pp)}{P(vp \rightarrow v,np,pp)}$$

depends only on rule probabilities and not on the lexicon. In our example, the PCFG does not take the preposition value into account: any prepositional phrase would always attach to the preceding noun, thus accepting an average error rate of 30 to 40%

11.7 Parsing Dependencies

Parsing dependencies consists of finding links between governors – or heads – and dependents – one word being the root of the sentence (Fig. 11.21). In addition, each link can be annotated with a grammatical function as shown in Table 11.9.

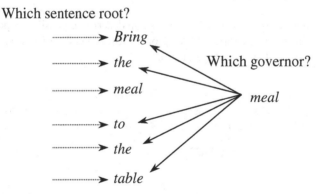

Fig. 11.21. Possible sentence roots and governors for word meal. There are N possible roots and each remaining word has theoretically $N - 1$ possible governors.

The dependency graph of a sentence is compactly expressed by the sequence

$$D = \{< \text{Head}(1), \text{Rel}(1) >, < \text{Head}(2), \text{Rel}(2) >, ..., < \text{Head}(n), \text{Rel}(n) >\},$$

which maps each word of index i to its head, Head(i), with relation Rel(i). The head is defined by its position index in the sentence. The sentence *Bring the meal to the table* would yield

Table 11.9. A representation of dependencies due to Lin (1995). Direction gives the direction of the governor. Symbol '>' means that it is the first occurrence of the word to the right, '>>' the second one, etc. '*' denotes the root of the sentence.

Word position	Word	Direction	Governor	Governor position	Function
1	*Bring*	*		Root	Main verb
2	*the*	>	*meal*	3	Determiner
3	*meal*	<	*Bring*	1	Object
4	*to*	<	*Bring*	1	Location
5	*the*	>	*table*	6	Determiner
6	*table*	<	*to*	4	Prepositional complement

$$D = \{< nil, \text{root} >, < 3, \text{det} >, < 1, \text{object} >, < 1, \text{loc} >, < 6, \text{det} >, < 4, \text{pcomp} >\},$$

where $< nil, \text{root} >$ denotes the root of the dependency graph.

There is a large range of techniques to parse dependencies. We introduce some of them in an order of increasing complexity, where more elaborate methods produce, in general, better results. We will begin with dependency rules, then shift–reduce for dependencies, constraint satisfaction, and finally statistical lexical dependencies.

11.7.1 Dependency Rules

Writing dependency rules or D-rules consists in describing possible dependency relations between word categories (Covington 1990): typically a head part of speech to a dependent part of speech (Fig. 11.22).

```
1. determiner ← noun.   4. noun ← verb.
2. adjective ← noun.    5. preposition ← verb.
3. preposition ← noun.  6. verb ← root.
```

Fig. 11.22. Examples of D-rules.

These rules mean that a determiner can depend on a noun (1) (or that a noun can be the head of a determiner), an adjective can depend on a noun (2) and a noun can depend on a verb (4). The rules express ambiguity. A preposition can depend either on a verb (5) as in *Bring the meal to the table* or on a noun (3) as in *Bring the meal of the day*. Finally, rule 6 means that a verb can be the root of the sentence.

D-rules are related to one or more functions. The first rule expresses the determinative function, the second one is an attributive function, and the third rule can be a subject, an object, or an indirect object function. Using a unification-based formalism, rules can encapsulate functions, as in:

$$\begin{bmatrix} category : noun \\ number : N \\ person : P \\ case : nominative \end{bmatrix} \leftarrow \begin{bmatrix} category : verb \\ number : N \\ person : P \end{bmatrix}$$

which indicates that a noun marked with the nominative case can depend on a verb. In addition, the noun and verb share the person and number features. Unification-based D-rules are valuable because they can easily pack properties into a compact formula: valence, direction of dependency relation (left or right), lexical values, etc. (Covington 1989; Koch 1993).

11.7.2 Extending the Shift–Reduce Algorithm to Parse Dependencies

Once we have written the rules, we need an algorithm to run a grammar on sentences. Nivre (2003) proposed a dependency parser that creates a graph that he proved to be both projective and acyclic. The parser is an extension to the shift–reduce algorithm. It uses oriented D-rules to represent left, $LEX(n') \leftarrow LEX(n)$, and right, $LEX(n) \rightarrow LEX(n')$, dependencies.

As with the regular shift–reduce, Nivre's parser uses a stack S and a list of input words W. However, instead of finding constituents, it builds a set of arcs A representing the graph of dependencies. The triplet $\langle S, W, A \rangle$ represents the parser state.

Nivre's parser uses two operations in addition to shift and reduce: left-arc and right-arc:

- Left-arc adds an arc $n' \rightarrow n$ from the next input word n' to the top of the stack n and reduces n from the top of the stack. The grammar must contain the rule $LEX(n') \leftarrow LEX(n)$ and there must not be an arc $n'' \rightarrow n$ already in the graph.
- Right-arc adds an arc $n \rightarrow n'$ from the top of the stack n to the next input word n' and pushes n' on the top of the stack. The grammar must contain the rule $LEX(n) \rightarrow LEX(n')$ and there must not be an arc $n'' \rightarrow n'$ already in the graph.

Table 11.10 shows the operations and their conditions.

The parsing algorithm is simple. The first step uses a POS tagger to annotate each word of the input list with its part of speech. Then, the parser applies a sequence of operations: left-arc, right-arc, reduce, and shift. Nivre (2003) experimented with three parsing strategies that depended on the operation priorities. The two first ones are:

- The parser uses constant priorities for the operations: left-arc > right-arc > reduce > shift.
- The second parser uses the constant priorities left-arc > right-arc and a rule to resolve shift/reduce conflicts. If the top of the stack can be a transitive head of the next input word, then shift; otherwise reduce.

Table 11.10. The parser transitions where W is the initial word list; I, the current input word list; A, the graph of dependencies; and S, the stack.

Actions	Parser actions	Conditions
Initialization	$\langle nil, W, \emptyset \rangle$	
Termination	$\langle S, nil, A \rangle$	
Left-arc	$\langle n|S, n'|I, A \rangle \rightarrow \langle S, n'|I, A \cup \{(n', n)\} \rangle$	$LEX(n) \leftarrow LEX(n') \in R$
		$\neg \exists n''(n'', n) \in A$
Right-arc	$\langle n|S, n'|I, A \rangle \rightarrow \langle n'|n|S, I, A \cup \{(n, n')\} \rangle$	$LEX(n) \rightarrow LEX(n') \in R$
		$\neg \exists n''(n'', n') \in A$
Reduce	$\langle n|S, I, A \rangle \rightarrow \langle S, I, A \rangle$	$\exists n'(n', n) \in A$
Shift	$\langle S, n|I, A \rangle \rightarrow \langle n|S, I, A \rangle$	

Nivre's parser can be extended to predict the parser's sequence of actions and to handle nonprojectivity. It then uses probabilities derived from a hand-annotated corpus and a machine-learning algorithm (memory-based learning or support vector machines). The extensions are described in Nivre and Scholz (2004) and Nivre and Nilsson (2005).

11.7.3 Nivre's Parser in Prolog

Before we start to write the parser, we need to represent the dependency rules, the arcs, and the input sentence.

- We encode the D-rules with a d/4 predicate that describes the function and the dependency direction:
```
%drule(+HeadPOS, +DependentPOS, +Function,+Direction)
drule(noun, determiner, determinative, left).
drule(noun, adjective, attribute, left).
drule(verb, noun, subject, left).
drule(verb, pronoun, subject, left).
drule(verb, noun, object, right).
drule(verb, pronoun, object, right).
drule(verb, prep, adv, _).
drule(noun, prep, pmod, right).
drule(prep, noun, pcomp, right).
```
- We store the words and their position using the predicate w(word, position), and we represent the sentence *The waiter brought the meal* as the list [w(the, 1), w(waiter, 2), w(brought, 3), w(the, 4), w(meal, 5)].
- Finally, we store the dependency arcs as d(Head, Dependent, Function).

The parser code is an extension of the regular shift–reduce. The shift_reduce/2 predicate takes the sentence as input and returns the graph of dependencies.

To implement it, we need an auxiliary `shift_reduce/4` predicate with two additional variables: a stack and graph where we will store the current arcs. This initial value of the stack as well as the graph is the empty list.

```
% shift_reduce(+Sentence, -Graph)

shift_reduce(Sentence, Graph) :-
   shift_reduce(Sentence, [], [], Graph).
```

Then `shift_reduce/4` consists of four predicates: `left_arc/6`, `right_-arc/6`, `shift/4`, and `reduce/3`. They are applied in the order just listed until the sentence is an empty list:

```
% shift_reduce(+Words, +Stack, +CurrentGraph,
%    -FinalGraph)

shift_reduce([], _, Graph, Graph).
shift_reduce(Words, Stack, Graph, FinalGraph) :-
   left_arc(Words, Stack, NewStack, Graph, NewGraph),
   write('left arc'), nl,
   shift_reduce(Words, NewStack, NewGraph,FinalGraph).
shift_reduce(Words, Stack, Graph, FinalGraph) :-
   right_arc(Words, NewWords, Stack, NewStack, Graph,
      NewGraph),
   write('right arc'), nl,
   shift_reduce(NewWords, NewStack, NewGraph,
      FinalGraph).
shift_reduce(Words, Stack, Graph, FinalGraph) :-
   reduce(Stack, NewStack, Graph),
   write(reduce), nl,
   shift_reduce(Words, NewStack, Graph, FinalGraph).
shift_reduce(Words, Stack, Graph, FinalGraph) :-
   shift(Words, NewWords, Stack, NewStack),
   write(shift),nl,
   shift_reduce(NewWords, NewStack, Graph,FinalGraph).
```

The `shift/4` predicate removes the first word from the word list currently being parsed and puts it on the top the stack. Here appends it to the end of the `Stack` list – to produce a `NewStack`

```
% shift(+WordList, -NewWordList, +Stack, -NewStack)

shift([First | Words], Words, Stack, [First| Stack]).
```

The `reduce/3` predicate reduces the `Stack` provided that the word has a head already in the graph.

```
% reduce(+Stack, -NewStack, +Graph)

reduce([w(Top, PosT) | Stack], Stack, Graph) :-
  member(d(_, w(Top, PosT), _), Graph).
```

The `right_arc/6` predicate adds an arc to the graph linking the top of the stack to the first word of the list with the conditions described in Table 11.9.

```
% right_arc(+WordList, -NewWordList, +Stack,
%   -NewStack, +Graph, -NewGraph)

right_arc([w(First, PosF) | Words], Words,
    [w(Top, PosT) |
    Stack], [w(First, PosF), w(Top, PosT) | Stack],
    Graph, [d(w(Top, PosT), w(First, PosF),
    Function) | Graph]) :-
  word(First, FirstPOS),
  word(Top, TopPOS),
  drule(TopPOS, FirstPOS, Function, right),
  \+ member(d(_, w(First, PosF), _), Graph).
```

The `left_arc/6` predicate adds an arc to the graph linking the first word of the list to the top of the stack with the conditions described in Table 11.9.

```
% left_arc(+WordList, +Stack, -NewStack, +Graph,
%   -NewGraph)

left_arc([w(First, PosF) |_], [w(Top, PosT) | Stack],
    Stack, Graph, [d(w(First, PosF), w(Top, PosT),
    Function) | Graph]) :-
  word(First, FirstPOS),
  word(Top, TopPOS),
  drule(FirstPOS, TopPOS, Function, left),
  \+ member(d(_, w(Top, PosT), _), Graph).
```

Let us use the words:

```
%word(+Word, +PartOfSpeech)

word(waiter, noun).
word(meal, noun).
word(the, determiner).
word(a, determiner).
word(brought, verb).
word(ran, verb).
```

Applying the parser to *The waiter brought the meal* yields:

```
?- shift_reduce([w(the, 1), w(waiter, 2),
w(brought, 3), w(the, 4), w(meal, 5)], G).

shift
left arc
shift
left arc
shift
shift
left arc
right arc

G = [d(w(brought, 3), w(meal, 5), object),
d(w(meal, 5), w(the, 4), determinative),
d(w(brought, 3), w(waiter, 2), subject),
d(w(waiter, 2), w(the, 1), determinative)]
```

11.7.4 Finding Dependencies Using Constraints

Another strategy to parse dependencies is to use constraints in addition to D-rules. The parsing algorithm is then framed as a constraint satisfaction problem.

Constraint dependency parsing annotates words with dependencies and functions tags. It then applies a set of constraints to find a tag sequence consistent with all the constraints. Some methods generate all possible dependencies and then discard inconsistent ones (Maruyama 1990, Harper et al. 1999). Others assign one single dependency per word and modify it (Tapanainen and Järvinen 1997).

Let us exemplify a method inspired by Harper et al. (1999) with the sentence *Bring the meal to the table.* Table 11.11 shows simplified governor and function assignments compatible with a word's part of speech.

Table 11.11. Possible functions according to a word's part of speech.

Parts of speech	Possible governors	Possible functions
Determiner	Noun	det
Noun	Verb	object, iobject
Noun	Prep	pcomp
Verb	Root	root
Prep	Verb, noun	mod, loc

The first step generates all possible governor and function tags. Using Table 11.11, tagging yields:

Words	*Bring*	*the*	*meal*	*to*	*the*	*table*
Position	1	2	3	4	5	6
Part of speech	verb	det	noun	prep	det	noun
Possible tags	<nil, root>	<3, det>	<4, pcomp>	<3, mod>	<3, det>	<4, pcomp>
		<6, det>	<1, object>	<1, loc>	<6, det>	<1, object>
			<1, iobject>			<1, iobject>

Then, a second step applies and propagates the constraint rules. It checks that the constraints do not conflict and enforces the consistency of tag sequences. Rules for English describe for instance, adjacency (links must not cross), function uniqueness (there is only one subject, one object, one indirect object), and topology:

- A determiner has its governor to its right-hand side.
- A subject has its governor to its right-hand side when the verb is at the active form.
- An object and an indirect object have their governor to their left-hand side (active form).
- A prepositional complement has its governor to its left-hand side.

Applying this small set of rules discards some wrong tags but leave some ambiguity.

Words	*Bring*	*the*	*meal*	*to*	*the*	*table*
Position	1	2	3	4	5	6
Part of speech	verb	det	noun	prep	det	noun
Possible tags	<nil, root>	<3, det>	<1, object>	<3, mod>	<6, det>	<4, pcomp>
			<1, iobject>	<1, loc>		

11.7.5 Parsing Dependencies Using Statistical Techniques

Using constraints and statistics, it is possible to build a dependency parser that reaches very high rates of accuracy. Here, we introduce an algorithm derived from that of Collins (1996, 1999, 2003) where parsing corresponds to finding the most likely dependency tree DT given a sentence S. This can be formulated as

$$DT_{best} = \arg\max P(DT\,|S) \ .$$

Collins' statistical dependency parser uses a cascade of three statistical modules: a part-of-speech tagger, a noun group detector, and a dependency model. Inside a noun group, dependency links are not ambiguous and can be determined in a fairly straightforward fashion. Therefore the algorithm represents noun groups by their main nouns and thus decreases its complexity. It takes the reduced tagged sentence as an input.

Collins' algorithm uses a statistical model composed of two terms: one corresponding to noun groups, NG, and the other to dependencies, D. It can be rewritten as:

$$P(DT\,|S) = P(NG, D\,|S) = P(NG\,|S) \times P(\,D\,|S, NG) \ .$$

We will focus here on dependencies only and for sake of simplicity, we will suppose that noun groups are perfectly detected. The input of the parser is then a reduced sentence whose words are tagged for part of speech:

$$S =< (w_1, t_1), (w_2, t_2), ..., (w_n, t_n) > .$$

For *Bring the meal to the table*, this yields

Position	1	2	3	4
Word	*Bring*	*meal*	*to*	*table*
POS	verb	noun	prep	noun

A dependency link for word i is represented as $AF(i) = (h_i, R_i)$, where h_i is the position of the governor and R_i is the relation linking both words. In our example, $AF(2) = (1, object)$ means that the governor of *meal* is word 1, i.e., *bring*, with the object relation. According to the model, the most likely parse is the maximum of

$$P(D|NG, S) = \prod_{j=1}^{m} P(AF(j)|NG, S).$$

Probability estimates are obtained using a dependency treebank. Let $C(R, \langle a, b \rangle, \langle c, d \rangle)$ be the number of times dependency relation R links words a and c with respective part-of-speech tags b and d in a same sentence in the training corpus and $C(\langle a, b \rangle, \langle c, d \rangle)$, the number of times words a and c with part-of-speech tags b and d are seen in a same sentence in the training corpus. $F(R| \langle a, b \rangle, \langle c, d \rangle)$ is the probability that $\langle a, b \rangle$ is a dependent of $\langle c, d \rangle$ with relation R given that $\langle a, b \rangle$ and $\langle c, d \rangle$ appear in the same sentence. Its estimate is defined by:

$$F(R| \langle a, b \rangle, \langle c, d \rangle) = \frac{C(R, \langle a, b \rangle, \langle c, d \rangle)}{C(\langle a, b \rangle, \langle c, d \rangle)}.$$

Dependencies are computed in a stochastic way. Link determination between words corresponds to the maximum of

$$\prod_{j=1}^{m} F(R_j| \langle w_j, t_j \rangle, \langle w_{h_j}, t_{h_j} \rangle),$$

where m is the total number of words in the sentence, F represents the probability of a dependency link R_j between word w_j of index j with part-of-speech tag t_j and word w_{h_j} with index h_j and part of speech t_{h_j}.

Since there is a great likelihood of sparse data – the figure of counts $C(\langle w_i, t_i \rangle, \langle w_j, t_j \rangle)$ are too low or equal to 0 – a combination of estimates has to be devised. Collins (1999) proposed considering, ranging from more to less accurate:

1. both words and both tags
2. w_j and the two POS tags
3. w_{h_j} and the two POS tags

4. the two POS tags alone

Estimate 1) is used first when it is available, else a combination of 2) and 3) else 4).

Estimate 4) is given by

$$\frac{C(R, \langle t_j \rangle, \langle t_{h_j} \rangle)}{C(\langle t_j \rangle, \langle t_{h_j} \rangle)}.$$

These probabilities do not take into account the distance between words and the directions between governor and dependents. This is introduced by a Δ variable whose approximation could be $\Delta_{j,h_j} = h_j - j$. In fact, Collins (1999) uses a more sophisticated measure that takes into account:

- The word order between the dependents, because, according to categories, some words tend to have their governor to their left-hand side or to their right-hand side. English is said to be right-branching: complements often occur to the right of the head. An example is given by prepositions, whose governor is almost systematically to the left.
- The distance, because most dependencies tend to be between adjacent or very close words.
- The verb crossings, because dependencies rarely jump over a verb.
- Punctuation.

As a simple example, we will give possible combinations for the reduced sentence *Bring meal to table*. Table 11.12 shows the dependencies with lexical statistics, and Table 11.13 gives dependencies with part of speech only. The probability figure is the product of four terms, one per word index. The maximum value corresponds to the most likely dependency tree.

Table 11.12. Probability of dependencies between words with a model including distances. The probability figure corresponds to the product of four probabilities. One is chosen per word index.

Word 1	Word 2
$P(root \rightarrow bring/vb, \Delta_{root})$	$P(root \rightarrow meal/noun, \Delta_{root})$
$P(meal/noun \rightarrow bring/vb, \Delta_{1,2})$	$P(bring/vb \rightarrow meal/noun, \Delta_{2,1})$
$P(to/prep \rightarrow bring/vb, \Delta_{1,3})$	$P(to/prep \rightarrow meal/noun, \Delta_{2,3})$
$P(table/noun \rightarrow bring/vb, \Delta_{1,4})$	$P(table/noun \rightarrow meal/noun, \Delta_{2,4})$

Word 3	Word 4
$P(root \rightarrow to/prep, \Delta_{root})$	$P(root \rightarrow table/noun, \Delta_{root})$
$P(bring/vb \rightarrow to/prep, \Delta_{3,1})$	$P(bring/vb \rightarrow table/noun, \Delta_{4,1})$
$P(meal/noun \rightarrow to/prep, \Delta_{3,2})$	$P(to/prep \rightarrow table/noun, \Delta_{4,2})$
$P(table/noun \rightarrow to/prep, \Delta_{3,4})$	$P(meal/noun \rightarrow table/noun, \Delta_{4,3})$

Table 11.13. Probability of dependencies between part of speech with a model including distances. The probability figure corresponds to the product of four probabilities, one per word index.

Word 1	Word 2
$P(root \rightarrow vb, \Delta_{root})$	$P(root \rightarrow noun, \Delta_{root})$
$P(noun \rightarrow vb, \Delta_{1,2})$	$P(vb \rightarrow noun, \Delta_{2,1})$
$P(prep \rightarrow vb, \Delta_{1,3})$	$P(prep \rightarrow noun, \Delta_{2,3})$
$P(noun \rightarrow vb, \Delta_{1,4})$	$P(noun \rightarrow noun, \Delta_{2,4})$

Word 3	Word 4
$P(root \rightarrow prep, \Delta_{root})$	$P(root \rightarrow noun, \Delta_{root})$
$P(vb \rightarrow prep, \Delta_{3,1})$	$P(vb \rightarrow noun, \Delta_{4,1})$
$P(noun \rightarrow prep, \Delta_{3,2})$	$P(prep \rightarrow noun, \Delta_{4,2})$
$P(noun \rightarrow prep, \Delta_{3,4})$	$P(noun \rightarrow noun, \Delta_{4,3})$

Collins used dependencies to parse constituents. To do this, he mapped function relations R described in this section onto phrase-structure rules and represented dependencies between their respective words using a lexical head in each rule. He singled out one symbol in the right-hand side of each phrase-structure rule to be the governor of the remaining symbols. For example, the rules

```
s --> np, vp.
vp --> verb, np.
np --> det, noun.
```

select a noun as the head of a noun phrase, a verb as the head of the verb phrase, and vp as the head of the sentence. Proceeding from the bottom up, the Collins parser annotates dependencies with phrase-structure rules. In our example, the sentence rule is obtained, while the verb percolates to the root of the sentence through the verb phrase.

11.8 Further Reading

Parsing techniques have been applied to compiler construction as well as to human languages. There are numerous references reviewing formal parsing algorithms, both in books and articles. Aho et al. (1986) is a starting point.

Most textbooks in computational linguistics describe parsing techniques for natural languages. Pereira and Shieber (1987), Covington (1994), Gazdar and Mellish (1989), and Gal et al. (1989) introduce symbolic techniques and include implementations in Prolog. Allen (1994), Jurafsky and Martin (2000), and Manning and Schütze (1999) are other references that include surveys of statistical parsing. All these books mostly describe, if not exclusively, constituent parsing.

Prepositional phrase attachment is a topic that puzzled many of those adopting the constituency formalism. It often receives special treatment – a special section in books. For an introduction, see Hindle and Rooth (1993). Techniques to solve it involved the investigation of lexical preferences that probably started a shift of interest toward dependency grammars.

While most research in English has been done using the constituency formalism – and many computational linguists still use it – dependency inspires much of the present work. Covington (1990) is an early example that can parse discontinuous constituents. Tapanainen and Järvinen (1997) describe a parsing algorithm using constraint rules and producing a dependency structure where links are annotated with functions. Constant (1991), El Guedj (1996), and Vergne (1998) provide accounts in French; Hellwig (1980, 1986) was among the pioneers in German. Some authors reformulated parsing a constraint satisfaction problem (CSP) sometimes combining it with a chart. Constraint handling rules (CHR) is a simple, yet powerful language to define constraints (Frühwirth 1998). Constraint handling rules are available in some Prologs, notably SWI Prolog. In 2006, the Tenth Conference on Computational Natural Language Learning (CoNLL-X) organized its shared task on multilingual dependency parsing. The conference site provides background literature, data sets, and an evaluation scheme (http://www.cnts.ua.ac.be/conll/). It is an extremely valuable source of information on dependency parsing.

Statistical parsing is more recent than symbolic approaches. Charniak (1993) is a good account to probabilistic context-free grammars, PCFG. Manning and Schütze (1999) is a comprehensive survey of statistical techniques used in natural language processing. See also the two special issues of *Computational Linguistics* (1993, vol. 19, nos. 1 and 2). Collins' dissertation (1999) is an excellent and accessible description of statistical dependency parsing. Bikel (2004) is a complement to it. Charniak (2000) describes another efficient parser.

Quality of statistics and rules is essential to get good parsing performance. Probabilities are drawn from manually bracketed corpora, and their quality depends on the annotation and the size of the corpus. A key problem is sparse data. For a good review on how to handle sparse data, see Collins (1999) again. Symbolic rules can be tuned manually by expert linguists or obtained automatically using inductive logic techniques, either for constituents or dependencies. Zelle and Mooney (1997) propose an inductive logic programming method in Prolog to obtain rules from annotated corpora.

Exercises

11.1. The shift–reduce program we have seen stores words at the end of the list representing the stack. Subsequently, we use append/3 to traverse the stack and match it to grammar rules. Modify this program so that words are added to the beginning of the list.

Hint: you will have to reverse the stack and the rules so that rule s --> np, vp is encoded rule([vp, np | X], [s | X]).

11.2. Trace the shift–reduce parser with a null symbol word(d, []) and describe what happens.

11.3. Modify the shift–reduce parser so that it can handle lists of terminal symbols such as `word(d, [all, the])`.

11.4. Complete arcs of Fig. 11.13 with the Earley algorithm.

11.5. Trace the Earley algorithm in Prolog with the sentence *Bring the meal of the day*.

11.6. In the implementation of the Earley's algorithm, we represented dotted rules as
`np --> np • pp            [0, 2]`
by Prolog facts as
`arc(np, [np, '.', pp], 0, 2).`
This representation involves searching a dot in a list, which is inefficient. Modify the program so that it can use an arc representation, where the sequence of categories to the left and to the right of the dot are split into two lists, as with `arc(np, [np], [pp], 0, 2).`

11.7. The Earley chart algorithm accepts correct sentences and rejects ill-formed ones, but it does not provide us with the sentence structure. Write a `retrieve` predicate that retrieves parse trees from the chart.

11.8. Modify the Cocke, Younger, and Kasami Prolog program to include parsing probabilities to constituents in the chart.

11.9. Modify the Cocke, Younger, and Kasami Prolog program to produce the best parse tree as a result of the analysis. Hint: to retrieve the tree more easily, use an array of back pointers: an array storing for each best constituent over the interval i ...j, the rule that produced it, and the value of k.

11.10. Implement the Collins dependency parser in Prolog.

12

Semantics and Predicate Logic

12.1 Introduction

Semantics deals with the meaning of words, phrases, and sentences. It is a wide and open subject intricately interwoven with the structure of the mind. The potential domain of semantics is immense and covers many of the human cognitive activities. It has naturally spurred a great number of theories. From the philosophers of ancient and medieval times, to logicians of the 19th century, psychologists and linguists of the 20th century, and now computer scientists, a huge effort has been made on this subject.

Semantics is quite subtle to handle or even to define comprehensively. It would be a reckless challenge to claim to introduce an exhaustive view of the topic. It would be even more difficult to build a unified point of view of all the concepts that are attached to it. In this chapter, we will cover formal semantics. This approach to semantics is based on logic and is the brainchild of both linguists and mathematicians. It addresses the representation of phrases and sentences, the definition of truth, the determination of reference (linking words to the world's entities), and some reasoning. In the next chapter, we will review lexical semantics.

12.2 Language Meaning and Logic: An Illustrative Example

Roughly defined, formal semantics techniques attempt to map sentences onto logical formulas. They cover areas of sentence representation, reference, and reasoning. Let us take an example to outline and illustrate layers involved in such a semantic processing. Let us suppose that we want to build a robot to serve us a dinner. To be really handy, we want to address and control our beast using natural language. So far, we need to implement a linguistic interface that will understand and process our orders and a mechanical device that will carry out the actions in the real world. Given the limits of this book, we set aside the mechanical topics and we concentrate on the linguistic part.

To avoid a complex description, we confine the scope of the robot's understanding to a couple of orders and questions. The robot will be able to bring meals to the table, to answer a few questions from the patrons, and to clear the table once the meals have been eaten. Now, let us imagine a quick dialogue between the two diners, Socrates and Pierre, and the robot (Table 12.1).

Table 12.1. A dialogue between diners and the robot.

Dialogue turns	Sentences
Socrates orders the dinner from the robot	*Bring the meal to the table*
The robot, after it has brought the meal, warns the diners	*The meal is on the table. It is hot*
Pierre, who was not listening	*Is this meal cold?*
...	*Miam miam*
Socrates, after the dinner is finished	*Clear the table*

Processing the sentences' meaning from a logical viewpoint requires a set of steps that we can organize in operating modules making parts of a semantic interpretation system. The final organization of the modules may vary, depending on the final application.

- The first part has to **represent** the state of the world. There is a table, diners around the table, a meal somewhere, and a robot. A condition to any further processing is to have them all in a knowledge base. We represent real entities, persons, and things using symbols that we store in a Prolog database. The database should reflect at any moment the current state of the world and the properties of the entities. That is, any change in the world should update the Prolog database correspondingly. When the robot mechanically modifies the world or when it asserts new properties on objects, a corresponding event has to appear in the database.
- The second part has to **translate** phrases or sentences such as *The robot brought the meal* or *the meal on the table* into formulas a computer can process. This also involves a representation. Let us consider the phrase *the meal on the table*. There are two objects, x and y, with x being a meal and y being a table. In addition, both objects are linked together by the relation that x is on y. A semantic module based on formal logic will translate such a phrase into a **logical form** compatible with the representation of objects into the database. This module has also to assert it into the database.
- A third part has to **reference** the logical forms to real objects represented in the database. Let us suppose that the robot asserts: *The meal is on the table. It is hot.* Referencing a word consists of associating it to an object from the real world (more accurately, to its corresponding symbol in the database). Referencing is sometimes ambiguous. There might be two meals: one being served and another one in the refrigerator. The referencing module must associate the word *meal* to the right object. In addition, referencing has also to keep track of entities men-

tioned in the discourse and to relate them. *It* in the second sentence refers to the same object as *the meal on the table* in the first sentence, and not to another meal in the refrigerator.

- A fourth part has to **reason** about the world and the sentences. Consider the utterance *The meal is on the table. Is it cold?* Is the latter assertion true? Is it false? To answer this question, the semantic interpreter must determine whether there is really a meal on the table and whether it is cold. To check it, the interpreter needs either to look up whether this fact is in the database or to have external devices such as a temperature sensor and a definition of cold. In addition, if a fact describes the meal as hot, a reasoning process must be able to tell us that if something is hot, it is not cold. We can implement such reasoning in Prolog using rules and an inference mechanism.

12.3 Formal Semantics

Of the many branches of semantics, formal semantics is one of the best-established in the linguistic community. The main assumption behind it is that logic can model language and, by extension, human thought. This has many practical consequences because, at hand, there is an impressive set of mathematical models and tools to exploit. The most numerous ones resort to the first-order predicate calculus. Such tools were built and refined throughout the 20th century by logicians such as Jacques Herbrand, Bertrand Russell, and Alfred Tarski.

The formal semantics approach is also based on assumptions linking a sentence to its semantic representation and most notably the principle of compositionality. This principle assumes that a sentence's meaning depends on the meaning of the phrases that compose it: "the meaning of the whole is a function of the meaning of its parts." A complementary – and maybe more disputable – assumption is that the phrases carrying meaning can be mapped onto syntactic units: the constituents. As a result, the principle of compositionality ties syntax and semantics together. Though there are many utterances in English, French, or German that are not compositional, these techniques have proved of interest in some applications.

12.4 First-Order Predicate Calculus to Represent the State of Affairs

The first concrete step of semantics is to represent the **state of affairs**: objects, animals, people, and observable facts together with properties of things and relations between them. A common way to do this is to use **predicate-argument structures**. The role of a semantic module will then be to map words, phrases, and sentences onto symbols and structures characterizing things or properties in a given context: the **universe of discourse**.

First-order predicate calculus (FOPC) is a convenient tool to represent things and relations. FOPC has been created by logicians and is a proven tool to express and handle knowledge. It features constants, variables, and terms that correspond exactly to predicate-argument structures. We examine here these properties with Prolog, which is based on FOPC.

12.4.1 Variables and Constants

We can map things, either real or abstract, onto constants – or atoms – and subsequently identify the symbols to the things. Let us imagine a world consisting of a table and two chairs with two persons in it. This could be represented by five constants stored in a Prolog database. Then, the state of affairs is restrained to the database:

```
% The people:
  'Socrates'.
  'Pierre'.

% The chairs:
  chair1.     % chair #1
  chair2.     % chair #2

% The unique table:
  table1.     % table #1
```

A second kind of device, Prolog's variables such as X, Y, or Z, can unify with any entity of the universe and hold its value. And variable X can stand for any of the five constants.

12.4.2 Predicates

Predicates to Encode Properties. Predicates are symbols representing properties or relations. Predicates indicate, for instance, that 'Pierre' has the property of being a person and that other things have the property of being objects. We state this simply using the person and object symbols as functors (predicate names) and 'Pierre' and table1 as their respective arguments. We add these facts to the Prolog database to reflect the state of the world:

```
person('Pierre').
person('Socrates').

object(table1).
object(chair1).
object(chair2).
```

We can be more specific and use other predicates describing that table1 is a table, and that chair1 and chair2 are chairs. We assert this using the table/1 and chair/1 predicates:

```
table(table1).

chair(chair1).
chair(chair2).
```

Predicates to Encode Relations. Predicates can also describe relations between objects. Let us imagine that chair `chair1` is in front of table `table1`, and that `Pierre` is on `table1`. We can assert these relative positions using functors, such as `in_front_of/2` or `on/2`, linking respectively arguments `chair1` and `table1`, and `'Pierre'` and `table1`:

```
in_front_of(chair1, table1).
```

```
on('Pierre', table1).
```

So far, we have only used constants (atoms) as arguments in the properties and in the predicates representing them. If we want to describe more accurately three-dimensional scenes such as that in Fig. 12.1, we need more elaborate structures.

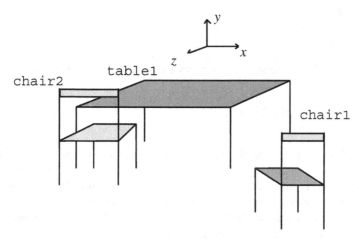

Fig. 12.1. A three-dimensional scene.

In such a scene, a coordinate system is necessary to locate precisely entities of the world. Since we are in a 3D space, 3D vectors give the position of objects that we can represent using the `v/3` predicate. `v(?x, ?y, ?z)` indicates the coordinate values of a point on x, y, and z axes. To locate objects, we will make use of `v/3`.

For sake of simplicity here, we approximate an object's position to its gravity center. We locate it with the `position/2` predicate. Position facts are compound terms that take the name of an object and the vector reflecting its gravity center as arguments:

```
position(table1, v(0, 0, 0)).
```

```
position(chair1, v(1, 1, 0)).
position(chair2, v(10, -10, 0)).
```

12.5 Querying the Universe of Discourse

Now, we have a database containing facts, i.e., properties and relations uncondition-ally true that describe the state of affairs. Using queries, the Prolog interpreter can check whether a fact is true or false:

```
?- table(chair1).
No

?- chair(chair2).
Yes
```

In addition, unification enables Prolog to determine subsets covering certain properties:

```
?- chair(X).
X = chair1;
X = chair2
```

We can get the whole subset in one shot using `bagof/3`. The alternate query yields:

```
?- bagof(X, chair(X), L).
L = [chair1, chair2]
```

The built-in `bagof/3` predicate has a cousin: `setof/3`. The difference is that `setof/3` sorts the elements of the answer and removes possible duplicates.

We may want to intersect properties and determine the set of the corresponding matching objects. Prolog can easily do this using conjunctions and shared variables. For instance, we may want to select from the set of chairs those that have the property of being in front of a table. The corresponding query is:

```
?- chair(X), in_front_of(X, Y), table(Y).
X = chair1, Y = table1
```

12.6 Mapping Phrases onto Logical Formulas

Using predicate-argument structures, we can map words, phrases, and sentences onto logical formulas. Simplifying a bit, nouns, adjectives, or verbs describe properties and relations that we can associate to predicates. Having said this, we have solved one part of the problem. We need also to determine the arguments that we will represent as logical variables.

Arguments refer to real-world entities, and the state of affair should define their value. We then need a second process to have a complete representation that will replace – unify – each variable with a logical constant. We will first concentrate on the representation of words or phrases and leave the arguments uninstantiated for now.

As a notation, we use λ-expressions that provide an abstraction of properties or relations. The λ symbol denotes variables that we can substitute with an entity of the real world, such as:

$$\lambda x.property(x)$$

or

$$\lambda y.\lambda x.property(x, y)$$

where λx indicates that we may supply an expression or a value for x.

Supplying such a value is called a β-reduction. It replaces all the occurrences of x in the expression and eliminates λx:

$$(\lambda x.property(x))entity\#1$$

yields

$$property(entity\#1)$$

λ is a right-associative operator that we cannot get with Western keyboards. We use the symbol ^ to denote it in Prolog. And X^property (X) is equivalent to $\lambda x.property(x)$.

12.6.1 Representing Nouns and Adjectives

Nouns or adjectives such as *waiter, patron, yellow,* or *hot* are properties that we map onto predicates of arity 1. For example, we represent the noun *chair* by:

$$\lambda x.chair(x)$$

whose equivalent notation in Prolog is X^chair (X). Let us suppose that *chair1* is an entity in the state of affairs. We can supply it to this λ-expression:

$$(\lambda x.chair(x))chair1$$

and carry out a β-reduction that yields:

$$chair(chair1).$$

Table 12.2 shows some examples of representation of nouns and adjectives.

We can consider proper nouns as well as common nouns. In this case, we will have predicates such as X^pierre (X) and X^socrates (X). This means that there are several Pierres and Socrates that can be unified with variable X. We can also make a nice distinction between them and treat proper nouns as constants like we have done before. In this case, there would be one single Pierre and one single Socrates in the world. Such a choice depends on the application.

Table 12.2. Representation of nouns and adjectives.

Lexical representations	Sentences	Semantic representations
Nouns		
X^chair(X)	*chair1 is a chair*	chair(chair1)
X^patron(X)	*Socrates is a patron*	patron('Socrates')
Adjectives		
X^yellow(X)	*table1 is yellow*	yellow(table1)
X^hot(X)	*meal2 is hot*	hot(meal2)

12.6.2 Representing Noun Groups

Noun groups may consist of a sequence of adjectives and a head noun. We form their semantic representation by combining each representation in a conjunction of properties (Table 12.3).

Table 12.3. Noun groups.

Noun groups	Semantic representation
hot meal	X^(hot(X), meal(X))
fast server	X^(fast(X), server(X))
yellow big table	X^(yellow(X), big(X), table(X))

The case is trickier when we have compounded nouns such as:

computer room
city restaurant
night flight

Noun compounds are notoriously ambiguous and require an additional interpretation. Some compounds should be considered as unique lexical entities such a *computer room*. Others can be rephrased with prepositions. *A city restaurant* is similar to *a restaurant in the city*. Others can be transformed using an adjective. A *night flight* could have the same interpretation as a *late flight*.

12.6.3 Representing Verbs and Prepositions

Verbs such as *run*, *bring*, or *serve* are relations. We map them onto predicates of arity 1 or 2, depending on whether they are intransitive or transitive, respectively (Table 12.4).

Prepositions usually link two noun groups, and like transitive verbs, we map them onto predicates of arity 2 (Table 12.5).

Table 12.4. Representation of verbs.

Lexical representations	Sentences	Sentence representations
Intransitive verbs		
X^ran(X)	*Pierre ran*	ran('Pierre')
X^sleeping(X)	*Socrates is sleeping*	sleeping('Socrates')
Transitive verbs		
Y^X^brought(X,Y)	*Roby served a meal*	served('Roby', Z^meal(Z))
Y^X^served(X, Y)	*Roby brought a plate*	brought('Roby',Z^plate(Z))

Table 12.5. Preposition representation.

Lexical representations	Phrases	Phrase representations
Y^X^in(X, Y)	*The fish in the plate*	in(Z^fish(Z), T^plate(T))
Y^X^from(X,Y)	*Pierre from Normandy*	from('Pierre', 'Normandy')
Y^X^with(X,Y)	*The table with a napkin*	with(Z^table(Z), T^napkin(T))

12.7 The Case of Determiners

12.7.1 Determiners and Logic Quantifiers

So far, we have dealt with adjectives, nouns, verbs, and prepositions, but we have not taken determiners into account. Yet, they are critical in certain sentences. Compare:

1. *A waiter ran*
2. *Every waiter ran*
3. *The waiter ran*

These three sentences have a completely different meaning, although they differ only by their determiners. The first sentence states that there is a waiter and that s/he ran. We can rephrase it as there is an x that has a conjunction of properties: $waiter(x)$ and $ran(x)$. The second sentence asserts that all x having the property $waiter(x)$ also have the property $ran(x)$.

Predicate logic uses two quantifiers to transcribe these statements into formulas:

- The existential quantifier, denoted ∃, and read *there exists*, and
- The universal quantifier, denoted ∀, and read *for all*

that we roughly associate to determiners *a* and *every*, respectively.

The definite determiner *the* refers to an object supposedly unique over the whole universe of discourse. We can connect it to the restricted existential quantifier denoted ∃! and read *there exists exactly one*. *The waiter ran* should then be related to a unique waiter.

We can also use the definite article to designate a specific waiter even if there are two or more in the restaurant. Strictly speaking, *the* is ambiguous in this case because it matches several waiters. *The* refers then to an object unique in the mind of the speaker as s/he mentions it, for instance, the waiter s/he can see at the very moment s/he is saying it or the waiter taking care of her/his table. The universe of discourse is then restricted to some pragmatic conditions. We should be aware that these conditions may bring ambiguity in the mind of the hearer – and maybe in that of the speaker.

12.7.2 Translating Sentences Using Quantifiers

Let us now consider determiners when translating sentences and let us introduce quantifiers. For that, we associate determiner *a* with quantifier $\exists$ and *every* with $\forall$. Then, we make the quantifier the head of a logical formula that consists either of a conjunction of predicates for determiner *a* or of an implication with *every*. The arguments are different depending on whether the verb is transitive or intransitive.

With intransitive verbs, the logical conjunctions or implications link the subject to the verb. Table 12.6 shows a summary of this with an alternate notation using Prolog terms. Predicates – principal functors – are then the quantifiers' names: `all/3`, `exists/3`, and `the/3`.

Table 12.6. Representation of sentences with intransitive verbs using determiners.

Sentences	Logical representations
A waiter ran	$\exists x(waiter(x) \wedge ran(x))$
	`exists(X, waiter(X), ran(X))`
Every waiter ran	$\forall x(waiter(x) \Rightarrow ran(x))$
	`all(X, waiter(X), ran(X))`
The waiter ran	$\exists! x(waiter(x) \wedge ran(x))$
	`the(X, waiter(X), ran(X))`

When sentences contain a transitive verb like:

A waiter brought a meal
Every waiter brought a meal
The waiter brought a meal

we must take the object into account. In the previous paragraph, we have represented subject noun phrases with a quantified logical statement. Processing the object is similar. In our examples, we map the object *a meal* onto the formula:

$$\exists y(meal(y))$$

Then, we link the object's variable y to the subject's variable x using the main verb as a relation predicate:

$$brought(x, y)$$

Finally, sentence *A waiter brought a meal* is represented by:

$$\exists x(waiter(x) \wedge \exists y(meal(y) \wedge brought(x, y)))$$

Table 12.7 recapitulates the representation of the examples.

Table 12.7. Logical representation of sentences with transitive verbs using determiners.

Sentences	Logical representation

A waiter brought a meal	$\exists x(waiter(x) \wedge \exists y(meal(y) \wedge brought(x, y)))$
	 `exists(X, waiter(X),`
	 `              exists(Y, meal(Y), brought(X, Y))`

Every waiter brought a meal	$\forall x(waiter(x) \Rightarrow \exists y(meal(y) \wedge brought(x, y)))$
	 `all(X, waiter(X),`
	 `              exists(Y, meal(Y), brought(X, Y))`

The waiter brought a meal	$\exists! x(waiter(x) \wedge \exists y(meal(y) \wedge brought(x, y)))$
	 `the(X, waiter(X),`
	 `              exists(Y, meal(Y), brought(X, Y))`

12.7.3 A General Representation of Sentences

The quantifiers we have used so far are the classical ones of logic. Yet, in addition to *a*, *every*, and *the*, there are other determiners such as numbers: *two*, *three*, *four*; indefinite adjectives: *several*, *many*, *few*; possessive pronouns: *my*, *your*; demonstratives: *this*, *that*; etc. These determiners have no exact counterpart in the world of logic quantifiers.

A more general representation uses determiners themselves as functors of Prolog terms instead of logic quantifier names. The subject noun phrase's determiner will be the principal functor of term mapping the whole sentence. Subsequent determiners will be the functors of inner terms. For example,

Two waiters brought our meals

is translated into

`two(X, waiter(X), our(Y, meal(Y), brought(X, Y)))`

Figure 12.2 depicts this term graphically.

Such a formalism can be extended to other types of sentences that involve more complex combinations of phrases (Colmerauer 1982). The basic idea remains the same: we map sentences and phrases onto trees – Prolog terms – whose functor names are phrases' determiners and whose arity is 3. Such terms are also called ternary trees. The top node of the tree corresponds to the sentence's first determiner (Fig. 12.3). The three arguments are:

• a variable that the determiner introduces into the semantic representation, say X

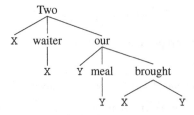

Fig. 12.2. Semantic representation of *Two waiters brought our meals*.

- the representation of the first noun phrase bound to the latter variable, that is X here
- the representation of the rest of the sentence, which we give the same recursive structure

As a result, a sentence is transformed into the Prolog predicate: `determiner(X, SemNP, SemRest)` (Fig. 12.3).

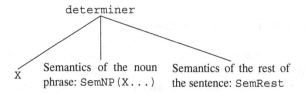

Fig. 12.3. Semantic representation using ternary trees.

This representation also enables us to process relative clauses and adjuncts. We represent them as a conjunction of properties. For example,

The waiter who has a cap

is translated into

`the(X, (waiter(X), a(Y, cap(X), has(X, Y))), P)`

where the second argument corresponds to the relative clause, the comma (,) between `waiter(X)` and `a(Y, cap(X), has(X, Y))` stands for a conjunction of these properties, and where P is linked with a possible rest of the sentence. If we complement this phrase with a verb phrase:

The waiter who has a cap brought a meal

we can give a value to P and the complete sentence representation will be (Fig. 12.4):

```
the(X,
    (waiter(X), a(Y, cap(X), has(X, Y))),
    a(Z, meal(Z), brought(X, Z))).
```

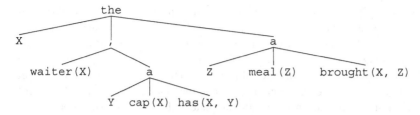

Fig. 12.4. Representation of *The waiter who has a cap brought a meal.*

12.8 Compositionality to Translate Phrases to Logical Forms

In Chap. 8, we used λ-calculus and compositionality to build a logical form out of a sentence. We will resort to these techniques again to incorporate the representation of determiners. Just like the case for nouns and verbs, we will process determiners using arguments in the DCG rules that will carry their partial semantic representation. The construction of the logical form will proceed incrementally using Prolog's unification while parsing the phrases and the sentence. The semantic composition of a sentence involves:

1. the translation of the first noun phrase – the subject
2. the translation of the verb phrase – the predicate – that contains a possible second noun phrase – the object

From the representation we provided in Chap. 8, the main change lies in the noun phrase translation. We approximated its semantics to the noun itself. Now we refine it into:

```
determiner(X, SemNP, SemRest).
```

12.8.1 Translating the Noun Phrase

To obtain `SemNP`, we have to compose the semantics of the determiner and of the noun, knowing that the noun's representation is:

```
noun(X^waiter(X)) --> [waiter].
```

Since the determiner must form the top node of the semantic tree, it has to embed an incomplete representation of the whole phrase. If we go back to the principles of λ-calculus, we know that the λ-variable indicated roughly that we request a missing value. In this case, the determiner needs the noun representation to reduce it. In consequence, variables in the noun phrase rule must be:

```
np(Sem) --> det((X^SemNP)^Sem), noun(X^SemNP).
```

We need to specify a variable X in the λ-expression of this rule, because it unifies with the Sem term, that is, with its first argument, as well as with SemNP and SemRest.

To write the determiner's lexical rule, we have now to proceed down into the structure details of Sem. The term Sem reflects a logical form of arity 3. It obtained its second argument SemNP from the subject – it did this in the np rule. It has to get its third argument, SemRest, from the verb and the object. SemRest will be built by the verb phrase vp, and since it is not complete at the moment, we denote it with a λ-expression. So, variables in the determiner rules are:

```
det((X^SemNP)^(Y^SemRest)^a(X, SemNP, SemRest)) -->
   [a].
```

Again, we must specify the Y variable that is to be bound in SemRest.
Using these rules, let us process *a waiter*. They yield the logical form:

```
(Y^SemRest)^a(X, waiter(X), SemRest)
```

whose λ-variable (Y^SemRest) ^ requests the semantic value of the verb phrase. The sentence rule s provides it and builds the complete representation, where vp brings SemRest:

```
s(Sem) --> np((Y^SemRest)^Sem), vp(SemRest).
```

12.8.2 Translating the Verb Phrase

Now, let the verb phrase rules compose the semantics of the rest (SemRest). The representation of the verbs remains unchanged. The verbs feature a single variable when intransitive, as in:

```
verb(X^rushed(X)) --> [rushed].
```

and two variables when transitive:

```
verb(Y^X^ordered(X, Y)) --> [ordered].
```

Verb phrase semantics is simple with an intransitive verb:

```
vp(X^SemRest) --> verb(X^SemRest).
```

It is a slightly more complicated when there is an object. As for the subject, the object's determiner embeds a ternary tree as a representation (Fig. 12.2). It introduces a new variable Y and contains a λ-expression that requests the representation of the verb. This λ-expression surfaces at the verb phrase level to bind the verb semantics to the third argument in the ternary tree. Let us name it (Y^SemVerb) ^. It enables us to write the vp rule:

```
vp(X^SemRest) -->
   verb(Y^X^SemVerb),
   np((Y^SemVerb)^SemRest).
```

Finally, the whole program consists of these rules put together:

```
s(Sem) --> np((X^SemRest)^Sem), vp(X^SemRest).

np((X^SemRest)^Sem) -->
  determiner((X^SemNP)^(X^SemRest)^Sem),
  noun(X^SemNP).

vp(X^SemRest) --> verb(X^SemRest).
vp(X^SemRest) -->
  verb(Y^X^SemVerb),
  np((Y^SemVerb)^SemRest).
```

Let us also write a couple of vocabulary rules:

```
noun(X^waiter(X)) --> [waiter].
noun(X^patron(X)) --> [patron].
noun(X^meal(X)) --> [meal].

verb(X^rushed(X)) --> [rushed].
verb(Y^X^ordered(X, Y)) --> [ordered].
verb(Y^X^brought(X, Y)) --> [brought].

determiner((X^SemNP)^(X^SemRest)^a(X, SemNP,
SemRest)) --> [a].
determiner((X^SemNP)^(X^SemRest)^the(X, SemNP,
SemRest)) --> [the].
```

These rules applied to the sentence *The patron ordered a meal* yield:

```
?- s(Sem, [the, patron, ordered, a, meal], []).

Sem =
  the(_4,patron(_4),a(_32,meal(_32),ordered(_4,_32)))
```

where _4 and _32 are Prolog internal variables. Let us rename them X and Y to provide an easier and equivalent reading:

```
Sem = the(X, patron(X), a(Y, meal(Y), ordered(X, Y)))
```

Similarly, *the waiter rushed* produces

```
Sem = the(X, waiter(X), rushed(X))
```

12.9 Augmenting the Database and Answering Questions

Now that we have built a semantic representation of a sentence, what do we do with it? This has two answers, depending on whether it is a declaration or a question.

We must keep in mind that the state of affairs – here the Prolog database – reflects the total knowledge available to the interpretation system. If it is a declaration – a statement from the user – we must add something because it corresponds to new information. Conversely, if the user asks a question, we must query the database to find a response. In this section, we will review some straightforward techniques to implement it.

12.9.1 Declarations

When the user utters a declaration, the system must add its semantic representation to the description of the state of affairs. With a Prolog interpreter, the resulting semantic fact – corresponding, for example, to `determiner(X, NP, Rest)` – will have to be asserted to the database.

We can carry this out using one of the `asserta` or `assertz` predicates. The system builds the semantic representation while parsing and asserts the new fact when it has finished, that is, after the `sentence` rule. Since `asserta` is a Prolog predicate and we are using DCG rules, we enclose it within curly brackets (braces). The rule

```
sentence(Sem) -->
    np(...), vp(...), {asserta(Sem), ...}.
```

will result into a new `Sem` predicate asserted in the database once the sentence has been parsed.

12.9.2 Questions with Existential and Universal Quantifiers

In the case of a question, the parser must also build a representation. But the resulting semantic formula should be interpreted using inference rules that query the system to find an answer. Questions may receive *yes* or *no* as an answer. They may also provide the value of a fact from the database.

Yes/no questions generally correspond to sentences beginning with an auxiliary verb such as *do, is, have* in English, with *Est-ce que* in spoken French, and with a verb in German. Other types of questions begin with *wh*-words such as *what, who, which* in English, with *qu*-words in French such as *quel, qui*, with *w*-words in German such as *wer, wen*.

We must bring some modifications to the parser's rules to accept questions, although basically the sentence structure remains the same. Let us suppose that we deal with very simple *yes/no* questions beginning with auxiliary *do*. The rule structure after the auxiliary is that of a declaration. Once the question has been parsed, the system must "call" the semantic fact resulting from the parsing to answer it. We do this using the `call` predicate at the end of rules describing the `sentence` structure. The system will thus succeed and report a yes, or fail and report a no:

```
sentence(Sem) -->
    [do], np(...), vp(...), {call(Sem), ...}.
```

If the sentence contains determiners, the Sem fact will include them. Notably, the subject noun phrase's determiner will be the predicate functor: determiner(X, Y, Z). For example,

Did a waiter rush

will produce Sem = a(X, waiter(X), rushed(X))

To call such predicates, we must write inference rules corresponding to the determiner values. The most general cases correspond to the logical quantifiers exists, which roughly maps *a*, *some*, *certain*, ..., and to the universal quantifier all.

Intuitively, a formula such as:

exists(X, waiter(X), rushed(X)),

corresponding to the sentence:

A waiter rushed

should be mapped onto to the query:

?- waiter(X), rushed(X).

and

a(X, waiter(X), a(Y, meal(Y), brought(X, Y))).

should lead to the recursive call:

?- waiter(X), a(Y, meal(Y), brought(X, Y)).

In consequence, exists can be written in Prolog as simply as:

```
exists(X, Property1, Property2) :-
  Property1,
  Property2,
  !.
```

We could have replaced exists/3 with a/3 or some/3 as well.

The universal quantifier corresponds to logical forms such as:

all(X, waiter(X), rushed(X))

and

all(X, waiter(X), a(Y, meal(Y), brought(X, Y))).

We map these forms onto Prolog queries using a double negation, which produces equivalent statements. The first negation creates an existential quantifier corresponding to

There is a waiter who didn't rush
and
There is a waiter who didn't brought a meal

And the second one is interpreted as:

There is no waiter who didn't rush
and
There is no waiter who didn't brought a meal

Using the same process, we translate the double negation in Prolog by the rule:

```
all(X, Property1, Property2) :-
  \+ (Property1, \+ Property2),
  !.
```

We may use an extra call to `Property1` before the negation to ensure that there are *waiters*.

12.9.3 Prolog and Unknown Predicates

To handle questions, we want Prolog to retrieve the properties that are in the database and instantiate the corresponding variables. If no facts matching these properties have been asserted before, we want the predicate call to fail. With compiled Prologs, supporting ISO exception handling, a call will raise an exception if the predicate is not in the database. Fortunately, there are workarounds. If you want that the unknown predicates fail silently, just add:

```
:- unknown(_, fail).
```

in the beginning of your code.

If you know the predicate representing the property in advance, you may define it as `dynamic`:

```
:- dynamic(predicate/arity).
```

Finally, instead of calling the predicate using

```
Property
```

or

```
call(Property)
```

you can also use

```
catch(Property,
  error(existence_error(procedure, _Proc), _),
  fail)
```

which behaves like `call(Property)` except that if the predicate is undefined it will fail.

12.9.4 Other Determiners and Questions

Other rules corresponding to determiners such as *many*, *most*, and *more* are not so easy to write as the previous ones. They involve different translations depending on the context and application. The reader can examine some of them in the exercise list.

Questions beginning with *wh*-words are also more difficult to process. Sometimes, they can be treated in a way similar to yes/no questions. This is the case for *which* or *who*, which request the list of the possible solutions to predicate `exists`. Other *wh*-words, such as *where* or *when*, involve a deeper understanding of the context, possibly spatial or time reasoning. These cases are out of the scope of this book.

From this chapter, the reader should also be aware that the presentation has been simplified. In "real" natural language, many sentences are very difficult to translate. Notably, ambiguity is ubiquitous, even in benign sentences such as

Every caterpillar is eating a hedgehog

where two interpretations are possible.

Mapping an object must also take the context into account. If a patron says *This meal*, pointing to it with his/her finger, no ambiguity is possible. But, we then need a camera or tracking means to spot what is the user's gesture.

12.10 Application: The Spoken Language Translator

12.10.1 Translating Spoken Sentences

The Core Language Engine (CLE, Alshawi 1992) is a workbench aimed at processing natural languages such as English, Swedish, French, and Spanish. The CLE has a comprehensive set of modules to deal with morphology, syntax, and semantics. It provides a framework for mapping any kind of sentence onto logical forms. The CLE, which was designed at the Stanford Research Institute in Cambridge, England, is implemented in Prolog.

CLE has been used in applications, the most dramatic of which is definitely the Spoken Language Translator (SLT, Agnäs et al. 1994). This system translates spoken sentences from one language into another for language pairs such as English/Swedish, English/French, and Swedish/Danish.

Translation operates nearly in real time and has reached promising quality levels. Although SLT never went beyond the demonstration stage, it was reported that it could translate more than 70% of the sentences correctly for certain language pairs. Table 12.8 shows examples from English into French (Rayner and Carter 1995). SLT is limited to air travel information, but it is based on principles general enough to envision an extension to any other domain.

Table 12.8. Examples of French–English translations provided by the SLT. After Rayner and Carter (1995).

English	*What is the earliest flight from Boston to Atlanta?*
French	*Quel est le premier vol Boston–Atlanta?*
English	*Show me the round trip tickets from Baltimore to Atlanta*
French	*Indiquez-moi les billets aller-retour Baltimore–Atlanta*
English	*I would like to go about 9 am*
French	*Je voudrais aller aux environs de 9 heures*
English	*Show me the fares for Eastern Airlines flight one forty seven*
French	*Indiquez-moi les tarifs pour le vol Eastern Airlines cent quarante sept*

12.10.2 Compositional Semantics

The CLE's semantic component maps sentences onto logical forms. It uses unification and compositionality as a fundamental computation mechanism. This technique makes it easy to produce a representation while parsing and to generate the corresponding sentence in the target language.

Agnäs et al. (1994, pp. 42–43) give an example of the linguistic analysis of the sentence

I would like to book a late flight to Boston

whose semantic structure corresponds to the Prolog term:

```
would(like_to(i,
              book(i,
                   np_pp(a(late(flight)),
                         X^to(X, boston)))))
```

The parse rule notation is close to that of DCGs, but instead of the rule

```
Head --> Body_1, Body_2, ..., Body_n.
```

CLE uses the equivalent Prolog term

```
rule(<RuleId>,
  Head,
  [Body_1,
   Body_2,
   ...
   Body_n])
```

Table 12.9 shows the rules involved to parse this sentence. For example, rule 1 describes the sentence structure and is equivalent to

```
s --> np, vp.
```

Table 12.9. Rules in the CLE formalism. After Agnäs et al. (1994, p. 42).

#	Rules

1	```rule(s_np_vp,```
	``` s([sem=VP]),```
	``` [np([sem=NP,agr=Ag]),```
	``` vp([sem=VP,subjsem=NP,aspect=fin,agr=Ag])]).```

2	```rule(vp_v_np,```
	``` vp([sem=V,subjsem=Subj,aspect=Asp,agr=Ag]),```
	``` [v([sem=V,subjsem=Subj,aspect=Asp,agr=Ag,```
	``` subcat=[np([sem=NP])]]),```
	``` np([sem=NP,agr=_])]).```

3	```rule(vp_v_vp,```
	``` vp([sem=V,subjsem=Subj,aspect=Asp,agr=Ag]),```
	``` [v([sem=V,subjsem=Subj,aspect=Asp,agr=Ag,```
	``` subcat=[vp([sem=VP,subjsem=Subj])]]),```
	``` vp([sem=VP,subjsem=Subj,aspect=ini,agr=])]).```

4	```rule(vp_v_to_vp,```
	``` vp([sem=V,subjsem=Subj,aspect=Asp,agr=Ag]),```
	``` [v([sem=V,subjsem=Subj,aspect=Asp,agr=Ag,```
	``` subcat=[inf([]),vp([sem=VP,subjsem=Subj])]]),```
	``` inf([]),```
	``` vp([sem=VP,subjsem=Subj,aspect=inf,agr=])]).```

5	```rule(np_det_nbar,```
	``` np([sem=DET,agr=(3-Num)]),```
	``` [(det([sem=DET,nbarsem=NBAR,num=Num]),```
	``` nbar([sem=NBAR,num=Num])]).```

6	```rule(nbar_adj_nbar,```
	``` nbar([sem=ADJ,num=Num])```
	``` [adj([sem=ADJ,nbarsem=NBAR]),```
	``` nbar([sem=NBAR,num=Num])]).```

7	```rule(np_np_pp,```
	``` np([sem=np_pp(NP,PP),agr=Ag]),```
	``` [np([sem=NP,agr=Ag]),```
	``` pp([sem=PP])]).```

8	```rule(pp_prep_np,```
	``` pp([sem=PREP]),```
	``` [prep([sem=PREP,npsem=NP]),```
	``` np([sem=NP,agr=_])]).```

Rules embed variables with values under the form of pairs `Feature = Value` to implement syntactic constraints and semantic composition.

The lexicon entries follow a similar principle and map words onto Prolog terms:

```
lex(<Wordform>, <Category> (Features>))
```

Table 12.10 shows lexical entries of the sentence *I would like to book a late flight to Boston*, and Fig. 12.5. shows its parse tree

Table 12.10. Lexicon entries in the CLE formalism. After Agnäs et al. (1994, p. 42).

#	Lexicon entries
1	`lex(boston,np([sem=boston,agr=(3-s)])).`
2	`lex(i,np([sem,agr=(1-s)])).`
3	`lex(flight,n([sem=flight,num=s])).`
4	`lex(late,adj([sem=late(NBAR),nbarsem=NBAR])).`
5	`lex(a,det([sem=a(NBAR),nbarsem=NBAR,num=s])).`
6	`lex(to,prep([sem=X^to(X,NP),npsem=NP])).`
7	`lex(to,inf([])).`
8	`lex(book,v([sem=have(Subj,Obj),subjsem=Subj,aspect=ini,` `agr=_,subcat=[np([sem=Obj])]])).`
9	`lex(would,v([sem=would(VP),subjsem=Subj,aspect=fin,` `agr=_,subcat=[vp([sem=VP,aubjsem=Subj])]])).`
10	`lex(like,v([sem=like_to(Subj,VP),subjsem=Subj,aspect=ini,` `agr=_,subcat=[inf([]),vp([sem=VP,subjsem=Subj])]])).`

The semantic value of words or phrases is denoted with the `sem` constant in the rules. For instance, *flight* has the semantic value `flight` (Table 12.10, line 3) and *a* has the value `a(NBAR)` (Table 12.10, line 5), where `NBAR` is the semantic value of the adjective/noun sequence following the determiner.

The parser composes the semantic value of the noun phrase *a flight* applying the `np_det_nbar` rule (Table 12.9, line 5) equivalent to

```
np --> det, nbar.
```

in the DCG notation. It results in `sem = a(flight)`.

All the semantic values are unified compositionally and concurrently with the parse in an upward movement, yielding the sentence's logical form.

12.10.3 Semantic Representation Transfer

The complete CLE's semantic layer relies on two stages. The first one maps a sentence onto a so-called quasi-logical form. Quasi-logical forms are basic predicate-argument structures, as we saw in this chapter, where variables representing real objects remain uninstantiated. The second layer links these variables to values, taking the context into account and so constructing fully resolved logical forms.

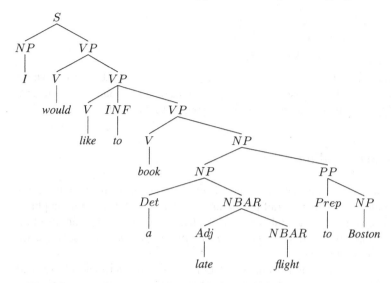

Fig. 12.5. Parse tree for *I would like to book a late flight to Boston*. After Agnäs et al. (1994, p. 43).

Translation from one language to another need not resolve variables. So the SLT builds a quasi-logical form from the source sentence and transfers it into the target language at the same representation level. SLT uses then a set of recursive transfer rules to match patterns in the source sentence and to replace them with their equivalent in the target language. Rules have the following format (Rayner et al. 1996):

```
trule(<Comment>
   <QLF pattern 1>
   <Operator>
   <QLF pattern 2>).
```

where `Operator` describes whether the rule is applicable from source to target (`>=`), the reverse (`=<`), or bidirectional (`==`).

Some rules are lexical, such as

```
trule([eng, fre],
      flight1 >= vol1).
```

which states that *flight* is translated as *vol*, but not the reverse. Others involve syntactic information such as:

```
trule([eng, fre],
      form(tr(relation,nn),
           tr(noun1),
           tr(noun2))
      >=
```

```
[and, tr(noun2),
       form(prep(tr(relation)),
            tr(noun1))]).
```

which transfers English compound nouns like *arrival time* – noun1 noun2. These nouns are rendered in French as: *heure d'arrivée* with a reversed noun order – noun2 noun1 and with a preposition in-between *d'* – prep(tr(relation)).

12.11 Further Reading

Relations between logic and language have been a core concern for logicians, linguists, and philosophers. For a brief presentation and a critical discussion on philosophical issues, you may read Habermas (1988, Chap. 5). The reader can also find good and readable introductions in *Encyclopédie philosophique universelle* (Jacob 1989) and in Morton (2003).

Modern logic settings stem from foundational works of Herbrand (1930) and Tarski (1944). Later, Robinson (1965) proposed algorithms to implement logic programs. Robinson's work eventually gave birth to Prolog (Colmerauer 1970, 1978). Burke and Foxley (1996) provide a good introductory textbook on logic and notably on Herbrand bases. Sterling and Shapiro (1994) also give some insights on relations between Prolog and logic.

Some books attribute the compositionality principle to Frege (1892). In fact, Frege said exactly the opposite. The investigation of rational ways to map sentences onto logical formulas dates back to the ancient Greeks and the Middle Ages. Later, Montague (1974) extended this work and developed it systematically to English. Montague has had a considerable influence on modern developments of research in this area. For a short history of compositionality, see Godart-Wendling et al. (1998). The *Handbook of Logic and Language* (van Benthem and Ter Meulen (eds) 1997) provides a comprehensive treatment on current theories in the field. A shorter and very readable introduction on the philosophy of language is that of Taylor (1998).

Exercises

12.1. Write facts to represent
Tony is a hedgehog
A hedgehog likes caterpillars
Tony likes caterpillars
All hedgehogs likes caterpillars

12.2. Write DCG rules to get the semantic structure out of sentences of Exercise 12.1.

12.3. Write DCG rules to obtain the semantic representation of noun phrases made of one noun and one and more adjectives such as *The nice hedgehog, the nice little hedgehog.*

12.4. Write rules accepting sentences with embedded relative clauses, such as *The waiter that ran brought a meal* and producing a logical form out of them:
`the(X, (waiter(X), ran(X)), a(Y, meal(Y), brought(X, Y))`

12.5. Write rules to carry out the semantic interpretation of determiner *two*, as in the sentence *Two waiters rushed.*

12.6. Write rules to carry out the semantic interpretation of determiner *No*, as in *No waiter rushed.*

12.7. Write rules to carry out the semantic interpretation of *how many*, as in *how many waiters rushed.*

12.8. Write rules to parse questions beginning with relative pronouns *who* and *what* in sentences, such as *Who brought the meal?* and *What did the waiter bring?* and build logical forms out of them.

12.9. Write a small dialogue system accepting assertions and questions and answering them. A transcript of a session could be:
User: *the patron ordered the meal*
System: *OK*
User: *who brought the meal*
System: *I don't know*
User: *who ordered the meal*
System: *the patron*
User: *the waiter brought the meal*
System: *OK*
User: *who brought the meal*
System: *the waiter*

12.10. Some sentences such as *all the patrons ordered a meal* may have several readings. Cite two possible interpretations of this sentence and elaborate on them.

13

Lexical Semantics

13.1 Beyond Formal Semantics

13.1.1 *La langue et la parole*

Formal semantics provides clean grounds and well-mastered devices for bridging language and logic. Although debated, the assumption of such a link is common sense. There is obviously a connection – at least partial – between sentences and logical representations. However, there are more controversial issues. For instance, can the whole language be handled in terms of logical forms? Language practice, psychology, or pragmatics are not taken into account. These areas pertain to cognition: processes of symbolization, conceptualization, or understanding.

Bibliography on nonformal semantics is uncountable. Let us have a glimpse at it with Ferdinand de Saussure (1916), the founder of modern linguistics. Much of Saussure's work, but not exclusively, was devoted to the area of what we would call now real-world semantics. He first made the distinction between the cultural background of a community of people of a same language embodied in words and grammatical structures and physical messages of individuals expressed by the means of a tongue. He called these two layers language and speech – *la langue et la parole*, in his words.

13.1.2 Language and the Structure of the World

Starting from the crucial distinction between *langue* and *parole*, Saussure went on to consider linguistic values of words, taking examples from various languages (1916, Chap. 4). Comparing words to economic units, Saussure described them as structural units tied together into a net of relationships. These units would have no sense isolated, but taken together are the mediators between thought and the way individuals express themselves. Accepting Saussure's theory, languages are not only devices to communicate with others but also to seize and understand reality. This entails that the structure of knowledge and thought is deeply intermingled within a linguistic structure. And of course, to fit communication, this device has to be shared by a community of people.

In this chapter, we will limit ourselves to some aspects on how a language and, more specifically, words relate to the structure of the world. Words of a specific tongue also embed a specific view of the universe. We believe that most concepts are common to all languages and can be structured in the same way. However, certain words cover concepts somewhat differently according to languages. In addition, the ambiguity they introduce is puzzling since it rarely corresponds from one language to another. We will present techniques to structure a lexicon and to resolve ambiguity. Within this framework, we will examine verb structures and case grammars that will provide us with a way to loop back to sentence representation and to formal semantics.

13.2 Lexical Structures

13.2.1 Some Basic Terms and Concepts

To organize words, we must first have a clear idea of what they express. In dictionaries, this is given by definitions. **Definitions** are statements that explain the meaning of words or phrases. Some words have nearly the same definition and hence nearly the same meaning. They are said to be **synonyms**. In fact, perfect synonyms are rare if they ever exist. We can relax the synonymy definition and restate it as: synonyms are words that have the same meaning in a specific context. Synonymy is then rather considered as a graded similarity of meaning. **Antonyms** are words with opposite meanings.

Contrary to synonymy, a same word – or string of characters – may have several meanings. It is then said to be ambiguous. Word ambiguity is commonly divided between **homonymy** (or **homography**) and **polysemy**:

- When words of a same spelling have completely unrelated meanings, such as for the strings *lot* in *a lot of* and *a parking lot*, they are said to be **homonyms** or **homographs**.
- When a word extends its meaning from concrete to abstract and to concepts tied by analogy, it is said to be **polysemous**. Consider the example of *tools* used in *computer tools* and in *carpenter tools*, where the latter is a concrete object and the former a computer program.

13.2.2 Ontological Organization

There are several ways to organize words within a lexicon. Most dictionaries for European languages sort words alphabetically. An obvious advantage of this method is to provide an easy access to words. However, alphabetical organization is of little help when we want to process semantic properties. A more intuitive way is to organize words according to their meaning. The lexicon structure then corresponds to broad categories where we arrange and group the words. Such a classification certainly better reflects the structure of our knowledge of the world and is more adequate for semantic processing.

A first classification dates back to ancient Greek philosophy when Aristotle established his famous division of words into ten main categories (Fig. 13.1). Such a lexicon structure, and beyond it, the representation of the world it entails, is often called an **ontology** in computational linguistics.

> Expressions, which are in no way composite, signify substance, quantity, quality, relation, place, time, position, state, action, or affection. To sketch my meaning roughly, examples of substance are "man" or "the horse", of quantity, such terms as "two cubits long" or "three cubits long", of quality, such attributes as "white", "grammatical". "Double", "half", "greater", fall under the category of relation; "in the market place", "in the Lyceum", under that of place; "yesterday", "last year", under that of time. "Lying", "sitting", are terms indicating position, "shod", "armed", state; "to lance", "to cauterize", action; "to be lanced", "to be cauterized", affection.
>
> Aristotle, *Categories*, IV. (trans. E.M. Edghill)

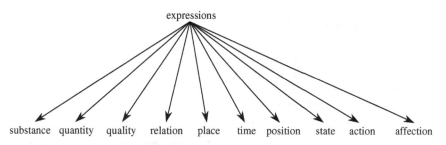

Fig. 13.1. Aristotle's ontology.

We can deepen the classification hierarchy. Aristotle's substance is what we could call now an entity. It includes *man* and *horse* as well as *meal* and *table*. It is easy to introduce further divisions between these words. To refine them, we insert new nodes under the *substance* class. Figure 13.2 shows a symbolic tree distinguishing between *animates, human beings, animals, food*, and *furniture*. This tree representation – now ubiquitous – is traditionally attributed to Porphyry.

13.2.3 Lexical Classes and Relations

An ontological structure defines classes and relationships relative to each word of the lexicon. The most obvious way to group words within an ontological tree is to cut a branch under a word. The branch contains then the **hyponyms** of that word: more specific and specialized terms. For instance, hyponyms of *animals* are *mammals*,

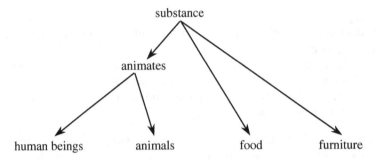

Fig. 13.2. Extending Aristotle's ontology.

carnivores, *felines*, or *cats*. We can go the reverse direction, from specific to more general, and abstract heading to the root of the tree. Thus we get the **hypernyms** of a word. Hypernyms of *hedgehogs* are *insectivores*, *mammals*, *animals*, and *substance*.

It is easy to express hypernymy and hyponymy using Prolog facts. Let us define the is_a/2 predicate to connect two concepts. We can represent the hierarchy of the previous paragraph as:

```
%% is_a(?Word, ?Hypernym)

is_a(hedgehog, insectivore).
is_a(cat, feline).
is_a(feline, carnivore).
is_a(insectivore, mammal).
is_a(carnivore, mammal).
is_a(mammal, animal).
is_a(animal, animate_being).
```

Hypernymy and hyponymy are reversed relationships and are both transitive. This can trivially be expressed in Prolog:

```
hypernym(X, Y) :- is_a(X, Y).
hypernym(X, Y) :- is_a(X, Z), hypernym(Z, Y).

hyponym(X, Y) :- hypernym(X, Y).
```

Beyond the tree structure, we can enrich relationships and link parts to the whole. *Feet*, *legs*, *hands*, *arms*, *chest*, and *head* are parts of *human beings*. This relation is called **meronymy**. Meronymy is also transitive. That is, if *nose*, *mouth*, *brain* are meronyms of *head*, they are also meronyms of *human beings*. Again it is easy to encode this relation using Prolog facts. Let us use the has_a/2 predicate:

```
%% has_a(?Word, ?Meronym).

has_a(human_being, foot).
```

```
has_a(human_being, leg).
has_a(human_being, hand).
has_a(human_being, arm).
has_a(human_being, chest).
has_a(human_being, head).
has_a(head, nose).
has_a(head, mouth).
has_a(head, brain).
```

The opposite of meronymy is called **holonymy**.

13.2.4 Semantic Networks

We can generalize the organization of words and knowledge and extend it to any kind of relationships that may link two concepts. Words are figured as a set of nodes, and relationships are labeled arcs that connect them. This representation is called a semantic network (Quillian 1967).

Figure 13.3 shows an extension of Fig. 13.2 where we have added the relations *eat* and *possess*. As we see, the graph contains two *eat* links: the first one between *carnivores* and *meat*, and the second one between *animates* and *food*. Once a semantic net has been designed, we search relations between two concepts, climbing up from specific to general. Inheritance enables then to assign relations eat(X, meat) to nodes X under *carnivores*, and eat(Y, food) to other nodes Y under *animates*.

Inheritance makes the design of a semantic network easier, therefore the core structure of the graph remains centered on hypernymy, that is "is a" links. Other properties come as a supplement to it. There are then many ways to augment a net. Design decisions depend on the application. The verbs linking words representing the agent of an action and its object are among common and useful arcs.

13.3 Building a Lexicon

Dictionaries – or lexicons – are repositories of a language's words. They are organized as a set of entries – the words – containing one or more senses. Current dictionaries attempt to itemize all the senses of words and typically contain more than 50,000 entries. Others are focused on specific domains. Dictionaries associate words or senses with grammatical models and definitions. Grammatical models such as the part of speech or a verb's conjugation class indicate morphological and syntactic properties of words; this enables their lemmatization and parsing. Models can also extend to semantic and pragmatic classifications. Many dictionaries cross-reference words using synonyms and give usage examples to show how a word is used in context.

As we could have guessed, wide-coverage lexical databases are central to most natural language processing applications. Instead of creating a new base from scratch,

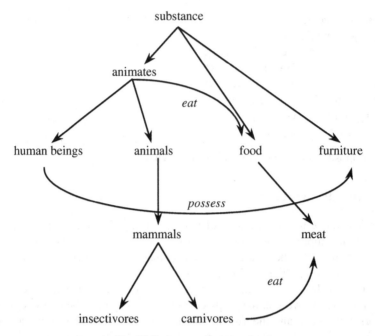

Fig. 13.3. A semantic network.

many computerized dictionaries have been derived from existing paper lexicons and transcribed in a computer readable format, which are called machine-readable dictionaries (MRDs). Computerized dictionaries often take the structure of their paper counterparts and are organized as a set of entries corresponding to word senses with their syntactical model, semantic annotations, and definition.

Learner or nonnative speaker dictionaries are often preferred as primary resources to derive lexical databases. They describe precisely pronunciation and syntactical features, such as a verb's subcategory or an inflection paradigm, while other dictionaries sometimes take it for granted by native speakers. Some dictionaries also tie words to specialized domains with labels such as: anatomy, computer science, linguistics, etc. or to general semantic codes: life, body, people, food, etc. Finally, most learner's dictionaries define each entry with a controlled vocabulary limited to two to three thousand words. This ensures a consistency in definitions, ease of understanding, and avoids circular – looping – definitions.

General lexicographic sources for English include the *Longman Dictionary of Contemporary English* (LDOCE, Procter 1978), the *Oxford Advanced Learner's Dictionary* (OALD, Hornby 1995), the *Collins Cobuild English Language Dictionary* (COBUILD, Sinclair 1987) or the *Cambridge International Dictionary of English* (CIDE, Procter 1995). Among them, the computerized version of the LDOCE gained the largest popularity within the academic computational linguistics community.

13.3.1 The Lexicon and Word Senses

As we saw in Chap. 1, many words are ambiguous, that is, a same string of letters has more than one meaning. Most dictionaries arrange homonyms that have clearly different meanings under different entries. The OALD, (1995 edition) lists three entries for *bank*: two nouns, *organization* and *raised ground*, and a verb *turn*. Polysemy, which refers to meaning variations within a same entry, is subtler. Dictionaries divide entries into submeanings with more or less precision according to the dictionary. These are the senses of a word. Let us take the example of the sentence

The patron ordered a meal

to realize concretely what word senses are. We will annotate each word of the sentence with its correct sense, and we will use definitions of the OALD to carry out this operation.

In the sentence, there are three content words: *patron, order*, and *meal*. For each of these words, the OALD lists more than one sense. *Patron* has one main entry for which the dictionary makes out two meanings:

1. a person who gives money or support to a person, an organization, a cause or an activity
2. a customer of a shop, restaurant, theater

Order has two entries. The first one is a noun and the other is a verb for which the OLAD details four sub-meanings:

1. to give an order to somebody
2. to request somebody to supply or make goods, etc.
3. to request somebody to bring food, drink, etc. in a hotel, restaurant, etc.
4. to put something in order

And finally, *meal* has two entries – two homographs – one as in *oatmeal*, and the other being divided into two submeanings:

1. an occasion where food is eaten
2. the food eaten on such occasion

That is, with such a simple sentence, we already have 16 choices ($2 \times 4 \times 2$; Table 13.1).

Classically, senses of a word are numbered relatively to a specific dictionary using the entry number and then the sense number within the entry. So *requesting somebody to bring food, drink, etc. in a hotel, restaurant, etc.*, which is the 3rd sense of the 2nd entry of *order* in the OALD is denoted **order (2.3)**. The proper sense sequence of *The patron ordered a meal* is then *patron* (1.2) *order* (2.3) *meal* (1.2).

Table 13.1. Sense ambiguity in the sentence *The patron ordered a meal.*

Words	Definitions	OALD sense numbers
The patron	**Correct sense:**	
	A customer of a shop, restaurant, theater	**1.2**
	Alternate sense:	
	A person who gives money or support to a person, an organization, a cause or an activity	**1.1**
ordered	**Correct sense:**	
	To request somebody to bring food, drink, etc in a hotel, restaurant etc.	**2.3**
	Alternate senses:	
	To give an order to somebody	**2.1**
	To request somebody to supply or make goods, etc.	**2.2**
	To put something in order	**2.4**
a meal	**Correct sense:**	
	The food eaten on such occasion	**1.2**
	Alternate sense:	
	An occasion where food is eaten	**1.1**

13.3.2 Verb Models

Dictionaries contain information on words' pronunciations, parts of speech, declension, and conjugation models. Some enrich their annotations with more precise syntactic structures such as the verb construction. In effect, most verbs constrain their subject, object, or adjuncts into a relatively rigid construction (Table 13.2).

Table 13.2. Some verb constructions.

English	*depend* + *on* + object noun group
	I like + verb-*ing* (gerund)
	require + verb-*ing* (gerund)
French	*dépendre* + *de* + object noun group
	Ça me plaît de + infinitive
	demander + *de* + infinitive
German	*hängen* + *von* + dative noun group + *ab*
	es gefällt mir + *zu* + infinitive
	verlangen + accusative noun group

Some dictionaries such as the OALD or the LDOCE provide the reader with this argument structure information. They include the traditional transitive and intransitive verb distinction, but descriptions go further. The OALD itemized 28 different types of verb patterns. Intransitive verbs, for example, are subdivided into four categories:

- **V** are verbs used alone.
- **Vpr** are verbs followed by a prepositional phrase.
- **Vadv** are verbs followed by an adverb.
- **Vp** are verbs followed by a particle.

A verb entry contains one or more of these models to indicate possible constructions.

Some dictionaries refine verb patterns with semantic classes. They indicate precisely the ontological type of the subject, direct object, indirect object, and sometimes adjuncts. Verbs with different argument types will be mapped onto as many lexical senses. For instance, Rich and Knight (1991) quote three kinds of *wanting*:

1. wanting something to happen
2. wanting an object
3. wanting a person

We can map the 2nd construction onto a DCG rule specifying it in its arguments:

```
%% word(+POS, +Construction, +Subject, +Object)

word(verb, transitive, persons, phys_objects) -->
   [want].
```

Argument types enforce constraints, making sure that the subject is a person and that the object is a physical object. These are called **selectional restrictions**. They may help parsing by reducing syntactic ambiguity.

The LDOCE lists selectional restrictions of frequent verbs that give the expected semantic type of their subject and objects. It uses semantic classes such as inanimate, human, plant, vehicle, etc. The Collins Robert French–English dictionary (Atkins 1996) is another example of a dictionary that includes such ontological information with a large coverage.

13.3.3 Definitions

The main function of dictionaries is to provide the user with definitions, that is, short texts describing a word. The typical definition of a noun first classifies it in a *genus* or superclass using a hypernym. Then, it describes in which way the noun is specific using attributes to differentiate it from other members of the superclass. This part of the definition is called the *differentia specifica*. Examples from the OALD include (general in bold and specific underlined):

bank (1.1): *a land* sloping up along each side of a canal or a river.
hedgehog: *a small animal* with stiff spines covering its back.
waiter: *a person* employed to serve customers at their table in a restaurant, etc.

from *Le Robert Micro* (Rey 1988)

bord (1.1): ***contour, limite, extrémité*** *d'une surface.*
hérisson (1.1): ***petit mammifère*** *au corps recouvert de piquants, qui se nourrit essentiellement d'insectes.*
serveur (1.1): ***personne*** *qui sert les clients dans un café, un restaurant.*

and from *Der kleine Wahrig* (Wahrig 1978)

Ufer (1.1): ***Rand*** *eines Gewässers, Gestade.*
Igel (1.1): ***ein kleines insektfressendes Säugetier*** *mit kurzgedrungenem Körper und auf dem Rücken aufrichtbaren Stacheln.*
Ober (1.2) –> Kellner: ***Angestellter*** *in einer Gaststätte zum Bedienen der Gäste.*

13.4 An Example of Exhaustive Lexical Organization: WordNet

WordNet (Miller 1995, Fellbaum 1998) is a lexical database of English. It is probably the most successful attempt to organize word information with a computer. It has served as a research model for other languages such as Dutch, German, Italian, or Spanish. A key to this success is WordNet's coverage – it contains more than 120,000 words – and its liberal availability online: users can download it under the form of Prolog facts from its home at Princeton University.

WordNet arranges words or word forms along with word meanings into a lexical matrix (Fig. 13.4). The lexical matrix addresses both synonymy and polysemy. A horizontal line defines a set of synonymous words – a *synset* in WordNet's parlance. A column shows the different meanings of a word form. In Fig. 13.4, F_1 and F_2 are synonyms (both have meaning M_1) and F_2 is polysemous (it has meanings M_1 and M_2). Synsets are the core of WordNet. They represent concepts and knowledge that they map onto words.

Word meanings	Word forms				
	F_1	F_2	...	...	F_n
M_1	$E_{1,1}$	$E_{1,2}$			
M_2		$E_{2,2}$			
M_m					$E_{m,n}$

Fig. 13.4. The lexical matrix (Miller et al. 1993).

From synonymy and synsets, WordNet sets other semantic relations between words, taking their part of speech into account. WordNet creators found this property relevant, citing cognitive investigations: when people have to associate words spontaneously, they prefer consistently to group words with the same part of speech rather than words that have a different one.

WordNet considers open class words: nouns, verbs, adjectives, and adverbs. It has set aside function words. According to classes, the organization and relationships between words are somewhat different. However, semantic relations remain based on synsets and thus are valid for any word of a synset.

13.4.1 Nouns

WordNet singles out twenty-five primitive concepts or **semantic primes** (Fig. 13.5), and it partitions the noun set accordingly. Within each of the corresponding topics, WordNet uses a hypernymic organization and arranges nouns under the form of a hierarchical lexical tree. WordNet contains 95,000 nouns.

{*act, action, activity*}	{*food*}	{*possession*}
{*animal, fauna*}	{*group, collection*}	{*process*}
{*artifact*}	{*location, place*}	{*quantity, amount*}
{*attribute*}	{*motive*}	{*relation*}
{*body, corpus*}	{*natural object*}	{*shape*}
{*cognition, knowledge*}	{*natural phenomenon*}	{*state, condition*}
{*communication*}	{*person, human being*}	{*substance*}
{*event, happening*}	{*plant, flora*}	{*time*}
{*feeling, emotion*}		

Fig. 13.5. WordNet's 25 semantic primes.

In addition to the 25 base domains, WordNet adds top divisions (Fig. 13.6). This enables it to gather some classes and to link them to a single node. Figure 13.7 shows the hierarchy leading to {*thing, entity*}.

{*entity, something*}	{*state*}	{*group, grouping*}
{*psychological feature*}	{*event*}	{*possession*}
{*abstraction*}	{*act, human action, human activity*}	{*phenomenon*}

Fig. 13.6. Nouns' top nodes.

To picture the word hierarchy and synsets with an example, let us take *meal*. It has two senses in WordNet:

1. *meal, repast* – (the food served and eaten at one time)
2. *meal* – (coarsely ground foodstuff; especially seeds of various cereal grasses or pulse)

For sense 1, synonyms are *nutriment, nourishment, sustenance, aliment, alimentation*, and *victuals*; and hypernyms are (from the word up to the root):

- *nutriment, nourishment, sustenance, aliment, alimentation, victuals* – (a source of nourishment)

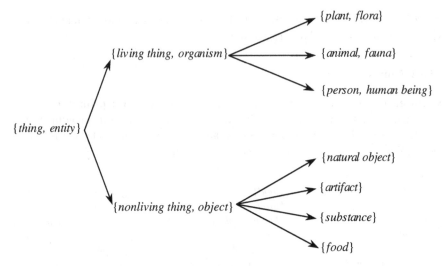

Fig. 13.7. {*thing, entity*} node of WordNet's hierarchy.

- *food, nutrient* – (any substance that can be metabolized by an organism to give energy and build tissue)
- *substance, matter* – (that which has mass and occupies space; "an atom is the smallest indivisible unit of matter")
- *object, physical object* – (a physical (tangible and visible) entity; "it was full of rackets, balls, and other objects")
- *entity, something* – (anything having existence (living or nonliving))

13.4.2 Adjectives

WordNet divides adjectives into two general classes: descriptive and relational, and into a more specific one: color adjectives. WordNet contains 20,000 adjectives.

Descriptive adjectives modify a noun and qualify one of its attributes. Examples include *hot* and *cold*, as in *hot meal* and *cold meal*, where *hot* and *cold* both describe the temperature attribute of *meal*. Another example is *heavy* and *light*, which give a value to the weight attribute of a noun (more precisely to the object it represents). As for other words, adjectives are grouped into synsets, and for each adjective synset, there is a link to the attribute it describes.

In addition to synonymy, WordNet uses antonymy as a core concept to organize descriptive adjectives. It clusters all of them around bipolar couples: word–antonym together with their respective synsets. *Hot* and *cold* or *wet* and *dry* are typical couples of antonyms, and WordNet enumerates 2,500 of them.

Antonymy relation, however, is not valid for all the members of a synset. *Torrid* is a synonym of *hot* but it cannot be considered as an antonym of *cold*. To cope with this, WordNet makes a distinction between bipolar antonymy and opposite concepts

– or indirect antonyms. There is no direct antonym for *torrid*, but using its synset, WordNet can link it indirectly to *cold* via *hot*.

Relational adjectives (**pertainyms**) such as *fraternal*, *contextual*, or *dental* are modified nouns and behave much like them on the semantic side, although they have the syntactic properties of adjectives. WordNet encodes them with a reference to their related noun: *fraternal* with *fraternity* or *brother*, *contextual* with *context*, and *dental* with *teeth* or *dentistry*. As opposed to descriptive adjectives, WordNet does not associate them to an attribute.

13.4.3 Verbs

WordNet partitions verbs into 15 categories. Fourteen of these categories are semantic domains: bodily functions and care, change, cognition, communication, competition, consumption, contact, creation, emotion, motion, perception, possession, social interaction, and weather. A last part contains verbs referring to states: verbs of being, having, and spatial relations (Table 13.3). WordNet has a total of 10,300 verbs.

Table 13.3. Name and description of verb files provided with the WordNet 1.6 distribution.

File	Description
Body	Verbs of grooming, dressing, and bodily care
Change	Verbs of size, temperature change, intensifying, etc.
Cognition	Verbs of thinking, judging, analyzing, doubting
Communication	Verbs of telling, asking, ordering, singing
Competition	Verbs of fighting and athletic activities
Consumption	Verbs of eating and drinking
Contact	Verbs of touching, hitting, tying, digging
Creation	Verbs of sewing, baking, painting, performing
Emotion	Verbs of feeling
Motion	Verbs of walking, flying, swimming
Perception	Verbs of seeing, hearing, feeling
Possession	Verbs of buying, selling, owning
Social	Verbs of political and social activities and events
Stative	Verbs of being, having, spatial relations
Weather	Verbs of raining, snowing, thawing, thundering

The first relation WordNet sets between verbs is synonymy, as for other words. However, synonymy is more delicate to delimit because verb meanings are quite sensitive to the context. That is, two verbs with apparently the same meaning, such as *rise* and *ascend*, do not occur with the same type of subject. This is a general case, and most verbs are selective with the type of their nominal arguments: subject, object, or adjunct. Moreover, as a verb often has no lexical synonym, WordNet encodes synsets with a small explanation – a gloss. For example, the verb *order* has nine senses whose sense 2 is represented by the synset {*order, make a request for something*}. *Bring* has 11 senses, and sense 1 is the synset {*bring, convey, take, take something or somebody with oneself somewhere*}.

Then, WordNet organizes verbs according principles similar to hyponymy and meronymy for nouns. However, it cannot apply these principles directly because they do not match exactly that of nominals. WordNet replaces them respectively with troponymy and entailment.

WordNet designers found the `is_a` relationship not relevant or clumsy for verbs (Fellbaum 1998, p. 79):

> *to amble* is a kind of *to walk* is not a felicitous sentence.

To name specializations of more generic verbs, they coined the word **troponyms**. *Amble* is then a troponym of *walk*. This is roughly a kind of verbal hyponymy related to a manner, a cause, or an intensity that makes the description of an action more precise. Since *tropos* is a Greek word for manner or fashion, it enables us to rephrase the hierarchical relation between *amble* and *walk* as *to amble is to walk in a particular manner*.

The second principle of verb organization is **entailment** – or implication – as *he is snoring* implies *he is sleeping*, or *she is limping* implies *she is walking*. Relations between verbs in these examples are not of the same kind. The latter is related to troponymy: *limping* is a specialization or an extension of *walking*. The former is an inclusion: the action of *snoring* is always included in an action of *sleeping*. In total, WordNet makes out four kinds of entailments. In addition to extension and inclusion, the two other entailments are backward presupposition – an action must have been preceded by another one, as with the pair *succeed/try* – and cause – an action leads to another one, as with *give/have*.

13.5 Automatic Word Sense Disambiguation

Although ambiguity is ubiquitous in texts, native speakers recognize the proper sense of a word intuitively. In the beginning of computational linguistics, some people declared it a human faculty impossible to reproduce automatically. This is no longer the case. There have been considerable improvements recently, and researchers have good reason to believe that a computer will be able to discriminate among word senses. Here we will present an overview of techniques to carry out word sense disambiguation, that, alone or combined, show promising results.

13.5.1 Senses as Tags

Let us again consider the sentence *The patron ordered a meal*. Solving ambiguity has an obvious definition. It consists in linking a word with its correct sense entry in a dictionary. We can recast this as a tagging problem. We regard a dictionary as a sense inventory and senses as a finite set of labels that we call semantic tags. The number of tags per word ranges from one to more than a dozen. Ambiguous words can receive several tags, and disambiguation consists in retaining one single tag – a unique sense – per word. Semantic tagging applies most frequently to open class words: nouns, verbs, adjectives, and adverbs.

Compared to part-of-speech tagging, a major contrast comes from the tagset. Dictionaries have somewhat different classifications of word senses and there is no complete consensus on them. According to authors, sense division is also finer or coarser. Applications can even use sets of word senses specifically designed for them. If broad categories of senses are common across most dictionaries and can be transcoded, there always will be some cases with a lack of agreement. The dissimilarity in classification and how we perceive senses can be measured by asking two or more different people to annotated a same text. The agreement between manual annotators – or **interannotator agreement** – is usually significantly lower for semantic tagging than, say, for part-of-speech annotation. There is no definitive solution to it, however. We must be aware of it and live with it.

We can carry out semantic tagging using techniques similar to those that we have used with parts of speech. Namely, we can resort to numerical or symbolic techniques. Numerical techniques attempt to optimize a sequence of semantic tags using statistics from a hand-annotated corpus. Symbolic techniques apply constraints to discard wrong semantic readings and retain the good ones.

SemCor (Landes et al. 1998) is a frequently used resource to train systems for English. It comes as a freely available corpus in which all the words are annotated with the WordNet nomenclature.

13.5.2 Associating a Word with a Context

The basic idea of most disambiguation techniques is to use the context of a word (Wilks et al. 1996, Chap. 11). The noun *bank*, for example, has two major senses[1] that will probably appear in clear-cut contexts. Sense one (**bank1**) resorts to finance and money; sense 2 (**bank2**) pertains to riversides and sloping ground. Context may be given by the words of the sentence or of the paragraph where the word occurs. This means that, depending on the words surrounding *bank* or what the text is about, a reader can select one of its two senses.

Some finer and more local relations such as the order of two words or the grammatical relations may also give the context. Disambiguating *meal* in *The patron ordered a meal* requires such considerations, because the two senses of this word belong to the same topic:

1. an occasion where food is eaten
2. the food eaten on such occasion

13.5.3 Guessing the Topic

The idea of this technique is first to define a limited number of topics, that is, a list of general areas, to attach a topic to each sense of words, and then to guess the

---

[1] OALD lists a third sense of *bank* as being a row of similar objects.

topic (or topics) of a paragraph or of a sentence. This technique implies that correct word senses will make the paragraph topic converge and enable us to discard senses attached to other topics. To make disambiguation possible, topics must, of course, be different along with each sense of a word.

According to applications, topics may come from dictionaries that flag some words with broad classifications – subject tags. For instance, the LDCOE categorizes words with 300 subject codes or domains that we can use as topics: agriculture, business, economics, engineering, etc. These tags usually annotate more specialized words.[2] Topics could also be a small set of hypernyms drawn from a comprehensive lexical database. For instance, using WordNet, **bank1** could be attached to financial institution (finance or institution) and **bank2** to slope:

```
%% topic(?Word, ?OALD_Sense, ?Topic).

topic(bank, bank1, [finance, institution]).
topic(bank, bank2, [slope]).
```

The disambiguation algorithm operates on a context that corresponds to a sequence of words such as a paragraph, a fixed number of sentences, or a fixed number of words, from 10 to 100, where the topic is supposed to be stable. A procedure annotates the words in the window with the possible subject tags when they are available. It yields possible sense sequences. The algorithm then retains the sense sequence that has the maximum of subject tags in common. A variation of this algorithm annotates nouns only. This method is referred to as a **bag-of-words** approach because it does not take the word order into account.

13.5.4 Naïve Bayes

The naïve Bayes classifier is an alternate statistical strategy that uses the bag-of-word approach. It also computes the sense of a word given its context. For a polysemous word w with n senses $s_1, s_2, \ldots, s_n$, the context C is defined as the sequence of words surrounding it: $w_{-m}, w_{-m+1}, \ldots, w_{-1}, w, w_1, \ldots, w_{m-1}, w_m$. The optimal sense $\hat{s}$ corresponds to $\arg\max_{s_i, 1 \le i \le n} P(s_i|C)$.

Using the Bayes rules, we have:

$$\hat{s} = \arg\max_{s_i, 1 \le i \le n} P(s_i)P(C|s_i),$$
$$= \arg\max_{s_i, 1 \le i \le n} P(s_i)P(w_{-m}, w_{-m+1}, \ldots, w_{-1}, w_1, \ldots, w_{m-1}, w_m|s_j).$$

And using the bag-of-word assumption, we replace

$$P(w_{-m}, w_{-m+1}, \ldots, w_{-1}, w_1, \ldots, w_{m-1}, w_m|s_j)$$

with the product of probabilities:

---

[2] LDOCE annotates the rest of nonspecialized words with another set of semantic codes: the key concepts.

$$\hat{s} = \underset{s_i, 1 \le i \le n}{\arg\max} P(s_j) \prod_{i=-m, i \ne 0}^{m} P(w_i | s_j).$$

$P(s_j)$ and $P(w_i | s_j)$ are both estimated from hand-annotated corpora.

13.5.5 Using Constraints on Verbs

As we saw, most verb arguments have a structure and a semantic type that is relatively rigid. Another set of disambiguation techniques exploits these properties and takes verb constructions and local relations into account. We start here from clauses, and for each one we detect the verb group and noun groups. The idea is to apply the selectional restrictions imposed by the verb group to its depending noun groups and thus reject wrong senses.

This technique needs a group detector and a shallow parser to identify the verbs' subject and object. The sense tagger operates on headwords, that is, here on the main noun and the main verb of each group. The tagger goes through the verbs that it annotates with their possible semantic constructions. It also annotates nouns with their possible senses. Finally, for each verb sense, the tagger retains subject and object senses that agree with the selectional restrictions.

Although this technique sets aside some parts of sentences, such as adjuncts, it reduces ambiguity and can be used with a combination of other techniques. In contrast to the previous technique, it has a more local viewpoint.

In addition, we can operate a disambiguation within groups using other selectional restrictions on adjectives and adverbs. We need to extend the description of adjectives with features giving the semantic type of the noun they expect to modify. Adverbs also have to include their modifier type. As an example, the word *mean* can have the properties of being an adjective and of qualifying only persons:

```
%% word(+Category, +Qualify)

word(adjective, persons) --> [mean].
```

13.5.6 Using Dictionary Definitions

We saw that using the naïve Bayes approach to tag senses in unrestricted texts requires an immense hand-annotation effort. It is possible to avoid it using unsupervised methods. Unsupervised methods have no training step or are trained on raw texts. These techniques are very appealing, especially in word sense disambiguation, because they avoid the need of human labor to annotate the words.

Wilks and Stevenson (1997) described an algorithm that only uses word definitions from general dictionaries as semantic resource. Their method was inspired by a paper by Lesk (1986).

The algorithm tags each word with all its possible senses listed in the dictionary and links each sense with its definition in a dictionary. It first applies constraints on parts of speech and then identifies the context using the definitions: it selects senses whose definitions overlap best within the range of a window of N words, a sentence, or a paragraph. This is made easier with dictionaries, such as the LDOCE, whose definitions are written using a controlled defining vocabulary. Simplified main steps of the program are:

1. A name recognition module identifies the proper nouns of the text.
2. A lemmatization module transforms each word into its canonical form. It associates each content word with its set of possible senses listed in the dictionary and with the corresponding textual definitions. Words occurring in definitions are also lemmatized.
3. A part-of-speech tagger annotates each word with its part of speech. At this step, the program can discard some senses because they have grammatical categories different from that of the words in the sentence.
4. The algorithm then computes the definition overlap for each sequence of possible senses. The overlap function considers a sequence of senses and their textual definition – one definition per word. The algorithm concatenates definitions of this sequence and counts the occurrences of each definition word: n. Each definition word brings a score of $n - 1$. So, if a definition word appears once, it will contribute nothing to the function; if it appears twice, it will contribute 1, and so on. Then, the algorithm adds up the counts and associates this score to the sense sequence.
5. The algorithm retains the sequence that has the maximum overlap, which is the largest number of definition words in common.

Wilks and Stevenson (1997) improved this algorithm using topics as defined in Sect. 13.5.3. Basically, they compute an overlap function for topics within the range of a paragraph:

6. The algorithm annotates nouns of a paragraph with possible subject tags when available. It retains the sequence that has the maximum of subject tags in common. This computation is similar to that of step 4.
7. The results of steps 4 and 6 are combined in a simplistic way. When both tags do not correspond, the first one in the dictionary entry list is retained. This is based on the assumption that entries are ordered by frequency of occurrence.

Step 4 of this algorithm can lead to very intensive computations. If a sentence has 15 words with 6 senses each, it leads to $6^{15} \sim 4.7 \, 10^{11}$ intersections. Wilks and Stevenson used simulated annealing to approximate the function. See also Wilks et al. (1996, Chap. 11).

13.5.7 An Unsupervised Algorithm to Tag Senses

Yarowsky (1995) proposed a slightly supervised and effective algorithm based on two assumptions on sense distribution:

• Nearby words provide strong clues to the sense of a word. This means that a word has **one sense per collocation**.

- The sense of a word is consistent within any given document. This means that a word has **one sense per discourse**.

The algorithm is basically a classifier. Given a polysemous word w with n senses $s_1, s_2, \ldots, s_n$ and a set of examples of the word surrounded by the neighboring words, the algorithm assigns each example a class corresponding to one of the senses. Each word in the examples is defined by a set of features, which are, as for naïve Bayes, the surrounding words. The algorithm starts from a few manually annotated examples that serve as a seed set to derive incrementally a sequence of classifiers for the remaining unlabeled examples. It uses an objective function that measures the performance of the classification. The algorithm is repeated until it has classified all the examples.

The algorithm has an initialization step and two loops. It extracts the set of all the examples of word w with the surrounding words from the training corpus. It results in N contexts $c_1, \ldots, c_N$ of, say, ten words, centered around w. These examples will be the input. In its original article, Yarowsky used the word *plant* and its two main senses $s_1 = living$ and $s_2 = factory$. The algorithm gradually annotates all the examples of the corpus with one of the two senses. It produces a sequence of annotated corpora $Corpus(0), Corpus(1), \ldots, Corpus(n)$ and builds classifiers that correspond to the sets of collocations of the first sense, $Coll_1^k$, and of the second one, $Coll_2^k$. $Corpus(0)$ is the original, unannotated set of examples.

1. **Initialization**. This step manually identifies initial collocations, and the first sense classifier tags the examples whose context contains one of the collocations with the corresponding sense label. Yarowsky used the words *life* for the first sense, $Coll_1^1 = \{life\}$, and *manufacturing* for the second one, $Coll_2^1 = \{manufacturing\}$. Both words enabled the disambiguation 2% of the examples in $Corpus(1)$.

2. **Outer Loop**. This loop uses the "one sense per collocation" principle. It identifies the examples where the intersection of the context and one of the collocation sets is nonempty: $c_k \cap Coll_i^j \neq \emptyset$ with $1 \leq k \leq N$, $i = 1, 2$, and j is the iteration index of the loop. It annotates the corresponding examples with the sense s_i. It results in $Corpus(j)$. In Yarowksy's paper, contexts of *plant* that contained one word of the first set were tagged with the first sense, and others that contained one word of the second set were tagged with the second sense. The algorithm applies optionally the "one sense per discourse" constraint.

   - **Inner Loop**. The objective function determines for each sense other collocations that partition the training data $Corpus(j)$ and ranks them by the purity of the distribution. It builds new sets of classifiers $Coll_i^{j+1}$ with collocations where the objective function is above a certain threshold. This step identifies *cell, microscopic, animal,* and *species* as collocates of the first sense $Coll_1^{j+1} = \{life, cell, microscopic, animal, species\}$ and *equipment, employee,* and *automate* as collocates of the second sense: $Coll_2^{j+1} = \{manufacturing, equipment, employee, automate\}$.

3. Repeat the outer loop until it converges (the partition is stable).

The algorithm identifies collocations with an objective function that determines the "strongest feature." It uses the log-likelihood ratio that is defined for a word w with two senses as $\log \frac{P(Sense_1|w_k)}{P(Sense_2|w_k)}$. It ranks the resulting values depending on w_k for all w_k members of the contexts $w_{-m}, w_{-m+1}, ..., w_{-1}, w, w_1, ..., w_{m-1}, w_m$, where the collocations the most strongly tied to a specific sense will show the largest values, either positive or negative.

The "one sense per collocation" principle implies that counts of 0 are frequent. In another paper, Yarowsky (1996) describes techniques to smooth data. Once the collocation sets have been built, the resulting classifiers can be applied to other corpora.

13.5.8 Senses and Languages

Word senses do not correspond in a straightforward way across languages. In a famous comparison, Hjelmslev (1943) exemplified it with the values of French words *arbre* 'tree', *bois* 'wood', and *forêt* 'forest' and their mapping onto German and Danish scales (Table 13.4). He went on and remarked that the word covering the material sense in French (*bois*) and in Danish (*træ*) could also have the plant sense but in different ways: a group of trees in French, a single tree in Danish. In a more striking example, Hjelmslev cited color naming that is roughly common to European languages with the exception of Celtic languages such as Welsh or Breton, which does not makes the same distinction between blue and green (Table 13.5).

Table 13.4. Values of *arbre*, *bois*, and *forêt* in German and Danish.

French	German	Danish
arbre	Baum	
	Holz	Træ
bois		
forêt	Wald	Skov

Table 13.5. Color values in French and Welsh.

French	Welsh
	gwyrdd
vert	
bleu	glas
gris	
	llwyd
brun	

There are many other examples where one word in English can be rendered by more words in French or German, or the reverse. Finding the equivalent word from one language to another often requires identifying its correct sense in both languages. It is no great surprise that word sense disambiguation was attempted first within the context of automatic machine translation projects.

This raises some questions about the proper granularity of sense division for a translation application. In some cases, sense division that is available in monolingual dictionaries is not sufficient and must be split within as many senses as there are in both languages combined. In other cases, all senses of one word correspond from one language to another. Therefore their distinction is not necessary and the senses can be merged. This problem is still wide open and is beyond the scope of this book.

13.6 Case Grammars

13.6.1 Cases in Latin

Some languages, like Latin, Russian, and to a lesser extent German, indicate grammatical functions in a sentence by a set of inflections: the cases. Basically, Latin cases are relative to the verb, and a case is assigned to each noun group: the noun and its depending adjectives. Latin has six cases that we can roughly associate to a semantic property:

- **Nominative** marks the subject of the sentence.
- **Accusative** indicates the object of the verb.
- **Dative** describes the beneficiary of a gift or of an action. It corresponds to the indirect object of the verb.
- **Genitive** describes the possession. As opposed to other cases, it is relative to a noun that the word in the genitive modifies or qualifies.
- **Ablative** describes the manner, the instrument, or the cause of an action. It corresponds to the adjunct function.
- **Vocative** is used to name and to address a god or a person.
- **Locative** is a seventh and an archaic case. It indicates the location of the speaker in some particular expressions.

Latin, like Russian, has quite a flexible word order. That is, we can arrange words of a sentence in different manners without modifying its meaning. The subject can appear at the beginning as well as at the end of a sentence. It has no specific location as in English or in French.

A flexible word order makes cases necessary for a sentence to be understandable. They indicate functions of groups: *who did what to whom, when, and where* and hence the arguments of a verb. Searching the subject, for example, corresponds to searching the noun phrase at the nominative case. Let us apply these principles to parse the following example:

Servus	*senatoris*	*domino*	*januam*	*clave*	*aperit*
Slave	senator	master	door	key	opens

Aperit is the verb in the third-person singular of present and means open (*aperire*). It is the predicate relative to which nouns will be the arguments. Each Latin noun has a model of inflection, also called a declension, five in total. *Servus* follows the second declension and means the slave. It is in the nominative case and hence the subject of the sentence. *Senatoris*, third declension, is the genitive case of *senator* and is the noun complement of *servus*. *Domino*, second declension, means master and is the dative of *dominus*. It corresponds to the indirect object of the verb. *Januam*, first declension, is the accusative of *janua* – door – and is the object. Finally, *clave*, third declension, is the ablative of *clavis* – the key – and the instrument of the action. Once we have identified cases, we can safely translate the sentence as:

The slave of the senator opens the door to the master with a key.

Cases are also useful to discover what goes with what such as an adjective and its head noun. Both will have the same case even if the noun group is fragmented within the sentence.

13.6.2 Cases and Thematic Roles

Case grammars stem from the idea that each verb – or each verb sense – has a finite number of possible cases. Case grammars rest on syntactic and semantic observations of languages like Latin and offer a framework to represent sentences. Hjelmslev (1935), and more recently, Fillmore (1968) are known to have posited that cases were universal and limited to a handful. Because of declensions, cases are obvious to those who learned Latin. However, it is somewhat hidden to speakers of English or French only. That is probably why, compared to compositionality, the acceptance of the case theory and its transposition to English or French has been slower.

Surveying a set of languages ranging from Estonian to Walapai, Fillmore percolated a dozen core cases, or **thematic roles**. A first classification led him to define (Fillmore 1968, p. 24):

- **Agentive** (A) – the case of the instigator of the action, which is typically animate
- **Instrumental** (I) – the case of the force or object typically inanimate causing the event
- **Dative** (D) – the case of the entity typically animate affected by the action
- **Factitive** (F) – the case of the object or being resulting from the event
- **Locative** (L) – the case of the identifying the place of the event or the orientation of the action
- **Objective** (O) – the most general case indicating the entity that is acted upon or that changes

As an example, Fillmore (1968, p. 27) attached to the verb *open* a frame containing an objective case that always occurs in the sentence, and optional instrumental and agentive cases denoted in parentheses: [O, (I), (A)]. This frame enables us to represent sentences in Table 13.6. One must note that the objective case, here filled with *the door*, sometimes corresponds to the grammatical subject and sometimes to the grammatical object.

Table 13.6. Examples of case frames (Fillmore 1968, p. 27).

Sentences	Case frames
The door opened	[O = door, (I), (A)]
John opened the door	[O = door, (I), (A) = John]
The wind opened the door	[O = door, (I), (A) = wind]
John opened the door with a chisel	[O = door, (I) = chisel, (A) = John]

To be complete and represent our Latin sentence, we add a dative case:

The slave of the senator opens the door to the master with a key.
[O = the door, (I) = a key, (A) = the slave of the senator, (D) = the master]

Later a multitude of authors proposed extensions to these cases. Most general and useful are:

* **Source** – the place from which something moves
* **Goal** – the place to which something moves
* **Beneficiary** – the being, typically animate, on whose behalf the event occurred
* **Time** – the time at which the event occurred

Over the time, Fillmore himself slightly changed the structure and name of his cases. Here is a more abstract classification of cases together with their description.

* **Agent** – primary animate energy source
* **Experiencer** – psychological locus of an experience
* **Theme** – primary moving object
* **Patient** – object which undergoes a change
* **Source** – starting point of a motion or change
* **Goal** – destination, target of a motion
* **Location** – location of an object or event
* **Path** – trajectory of a motion, between source and goal
* **Content** – content of an event of feeling, thinking, speaking, etc.

Some verbs do not fit into this case scheme, in spite of its generality. Fillmore again cited some of them such as the verb set *buy, sell, pay, spend, charge*, etc., whose cases are the quadruplet **buyer, seller, goods, money**, and the set *replace, substitute, swap*, etc., whose cases are **old, new, position, causer**. In addition, some applications may require other more specific cases.

13.6.3 Parsing with Cases

Parsing with the case grammar formalism transforms a sentence – or a part of it – into a kind of logical form: the frame. The predicate is the main verb, and its arguments represent the cases (or the roles). The parsing process merely maps noun groups or other features such as the tense or adverbs onto the cases. According to the verbs, some cases will be obligatory, such as the agent for most verbs. They will be assigned with exactly one argument. Others cases will be optional. They will be assigned with at most one value. In addition, cases are constrained by an ontological type. Table 13.7. shows a representation of the sentence

The waiter brought the meal to the patron

which links noun groups and the verb tense to cases.

Table 13.7. *Bring* cases with constraints.

Case	Type		Value
Agentive	Animate	(Obligatory)	*The waiter*
Objective (or theme)		(Obligatory)	*the meal*
Dative	Animate	(Optional)	*the patron*
Time		(Obligatory)	past

We can relate verbs cases to Tesnière's *actants* and *circonstants* (1966), which are idiosyncratic patterns of verbs encapsulated into a predicate argument structure. Tesnière first made a distinction between the typical cases of a verb – *actants* – and its optional modifiers – *circonstants*. A verb attracts a definite number of actants corresponding to its **valence**. Drawing on the semantic side, cases fit well an ontology of nouns and lead to subcategories of verb patterns. The agent, or the subject, of verb *eat* is generally animate. The instrument of *open* should comply with the instrument ontological subtree. These semantic properties related to verb cases are another viewpoint on sectional restrictions.

13.6.4 Semantic Grammars

Originally, parsing with a case grammar was carried out using a combination of techniques: shallow parsing and "expectations" on verb arguments. First, the parser detects the verb group and its depending noun groups or noun phrases. Then, the parser fills the cases according to "markers": topological relations, ontological compatibility (selectional restrictions), prepositions, tense, and for German, syntactic cases.

In many circumstances, we can assimilate the Agent to the subject of a sentence and the Theme to the object. Languages like English and French have a rather rigid word order in a sentence, and functions correspond to a specific location relative to a the verb. The subject is generally the first noun phrase; the object comes after the verb. In German, they are inflected respectively with the nominative and accusative cases.

Adjuncts are more mobile, and a combination of constraints on prepositions and selectional restrictions can be productive to fill modifier cases such as Source, Goal, and Instrument. Prepositions such as *from*, *to*, or *into* often indicate a Source and a Goal. We can add a double-check and match them to location classes such as places, cities, countries, etc. Other prepositions are more ambiguous, such as *by* in English, *pour* in French, and *auf* in German. Ontological categories come first as conditions to carry out the parse. They enable us to attach noun groups to classes and to choose a case complying with the selectional restrictions of the verb.

Phrase-structure rules can help us implement a limited system to process cases. It suffices to replace parts of speech and phrase categories with ontological classes in rules. This leads to **semantic grammars** dedicated to specific applications, such as this one describing a piece of the real and gory life of animals:

```
sentence --> npInsectivores, ingest,
npCrawlingInsects.
npInsectivores --> det, insectivores.
npCrawlingInsects --> det, crawlingInsects.

insectivores --> [mole].
insectivores --> [hedgehog].
ingest --> [devoured].
ingest --> [ate].
crawlingInsects --> [worms].
crawlingInsects --> [caterpillars].
det --> [the].
```

Rules describe prototypic situations, and parsing checks the compatibility of the types in the sentence. They produce a semantic parse tree.

Semantic grammars were once popular because they were easy to implement. However, they are limited to one application. Changing context or simply modifying it often requires a complete redesign of the rules.

13.7 Extending Case Grammars

13.7.1 FrameNet

The FrameNet research project started from Fillmore's theory on case grammars (1968). Reflecting on it, Fillmore noticed how difficult (impossible?) it was to work out a small set of generic cases applicable to all the verbs. He then altered his original ideas to form a new theory on **frame semantics** (Fillmore 1976). With frame semantics, Fillmore no longer considers universal cases but a set of frames resembling predicate-argument structures, where each frame is specific to a class of verbs. Frames are supposed to represent prototypical conceptual structures shared by a language community, i.e., here English.

FrameNet is a concrete outcome of the frame semantics theory. It aims at describing the frame properties of all the English verbs as well as some nouns and adjectives, and at annotating them in a large corpus. Like WordNet, FrameNet takes the shape of an extensive lexical database, which associates a word sense to a frame with a set frame elements (FEs). FrameNet also links the frames to annotations in the 100-million word British National Corpus.

Ruppenhofer et al. (2005) list Revenge as an example of frame, which features five frame elements: Avenger, Punishment, Offender, Injury, and Injured_party. The Revenge frame serves as a semantic model to 15 lexical units, i.e., verb, noun, or adjective senses:

> *avenge.v, avenger.n, get back (at).v, get_even.v, retaliate.v, retaliation.n, retribution.n, retributive.a, retributory.a, revenge.n, revenge.v, revengeful.a, revenger.n, vengeance.n, vengeful.a,* and *vindictive.a*

where the *.v* suffix denotes a verb, *.n* a noun, and *.a* an adjective.

Once the frame was defined, the FrameNet team annotated the corresponding lexical units in sentences extracted from its corpus. The annotation identifies one lexical unit per sentence, which is the **target**, and brackets its frame elements as in these examples from Ruppenhofer et al. (2005):

1. [$_{<Avenger>}$ His brothers] **avenged** [$_{<Injured\_party>}$ him].
2. With this, [$_{<Agent>}$ El Cid] at once **avenged** [$_{<Injury>}$ the death of his son].
3. [$_{<Avenger>}$ Hook] tries to **avenge** [$_{<Injured\_party>}$ himself] [$_{<Offender>}$ on Peter Pan] [$_{<Punishment>}$ by becoming a second and better father].

Each frame element contains semantic and grammatical information split into three levels of annotation. The first level is the name of the semantic role. The second and third ones describe how a frame element is realized in the sentence: the phrase syntactic category and its grammatical function. The phrase syntactic category, i.e., noun phrases, prepositional phrases, and so on, is called the phrase type (PT). FrameNet uses a small set of grammatical functions (GFs), which are specific to the target's part of speech (i.e., verbs, adjectives, prepositions, and nouns). For the verbs, FrameNet defines four GFs: Subject, Object (Obj), Complement (Comp), and Modifier (Mod), i.e., modifying adverbs ended by *-ly* or indicating manner. FrameNet renames the subjects as external arguments (Ext).

Table 13.8 shows the three-level annotation of the sentences above. Altogether, these levels form a **valence group**. Each sentence shows a **valence pattern**, a specific set of valence groups.

13.7.2 A Statistical Method to Identify Semantic Roles

We saw that it was possible to develop a case parser using manually written rules. However, such parsers require much labor, testing, and debugging, and have an unavoidably limited coverage. We introduce now a statistical technique that uses FrameNet to identify semantic roles for unrestricted text.

Gildea and Jurafsky's (2002) algorithm takes a sequence of sentences as input and consists conceptually of two steps. The first step segments the sentences to identify a target word and the constituents that will serve as frame elements. The second step labels the frame elements with their semantic roles.

Table 13.8. The valence patterns of avenge in the sentences above and their three levels of annotations: frame element (FE), phrase type (PT), and grammatical function (GF).

Sent. 1 *avenge*	FE	Avenger	Injured_party		
	PT	NP	NP		
	GF	Ext	Object		
Sent. 2 *avenge*	FE	Agent	Injury		
	PT	NP	NP		
	GF	Ext	Obj		
Sent. 3 *avenge*	FE	Avenger	Injured_party	Offender	Punishment
	PT	NP	NP	PP	PPing
	GF	Ext	Obj	Comp	Comp

We present here a simplified version of the algorithm where we first describe the two-step procedure starting from the second step: the role identification of presegmented constituents. We then outline the constituent segmentation that uses a similar probability model. Finally, we merge the two steps into a single model that yields the best results.

Two-Step Labeling. The algorithm is based on the observation that a semantic role depends both on the phrase type and on its grammatical function, for instance, noun phrase and agent, agent and subject. The idea is then to find a set of features that expresses both dependencies. While the phrase type is accessible using a parser, this is not the case for the grammatical function. Gildea and Jurafsky use a set of three parameters to capture this function:

- The simplest one is the constituent position relative to the target, before or after. This feature correlates the fact that in English, the subject is often before the verb, while the object is after.
- The second feature is the constituent governor in the parse tree. The governor is the highest node in the tree to go from the target to the constituent. It concerns only noun phrases and has two possible values: sentence (S) or verb phrase (VP). A subject will have S as typical governor and an object VP, as shown in Fig. 13.8.
- The third feature is the path from the target to the constituent. A typical object path for a subject is $VB \uparrow VP \uparrow S \downarrow NP$ and $VB \uparrow VP \downarrow NP$ for an object. This feature is used in the boundary detection of the frame elements and not in the role-labeling step.

We add three more features: the target, constituent headwords, and sentence voice. We have seen with selectional restrictions that semantic roles in a sentence depend on an interaction between the target and the frame elements. We express these restrictions through the constituent headword. The voice value active/passive also plays a role, because it inverts the subject/agent roles. Given the features we have described, the resulting statistical model of role identification is then:

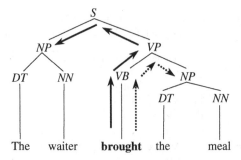

Fig. 13.8. Paths from the target to the subject (*solid lines*) and object (*dashed lines*).

$$P(r|h, pt, gov, position, voice, t),$$

where r denotes the role; h, the headword; pt, the phrase type; gov, the governor; *position*, the position of the constituent relative to the target; *voice*, the sentence voice; and t, the target.

Using the maximum likelihood, we can estimate this value from an annotated corpus:

$$P_{MLE}(r|h, pt, gov, position, voice, t) = \frac{C(r, h, pt, gov, position, voice, t)}{C(h, pt, gov, position, voice, t)}.$$

In fact, due to sparse data, it is generally not possible to compute it. Gildea and Jurafsky proposed workarounds that include linear interpolation and backoff. Both show similar performance, and here is the formula they used for linear interpolation:

$$\begin{aligned} P(r|constituent) = \ & \lambda_1 P(r|t) + \lambda_2 P(r|pt, t) \\ & + \lambda_3 P(r|pt, gov, t) + \lambda_4 P(r|pt, position, voice) \\ & + \lambda_5 P(r|pt, position, voice, t) + \lambda_6 P(r|h) \\ & + \lambda_7 P(r|h, t) + \lambda_8 P(r|h, pt, t), \end{aligned}$$

where $\sum_i \lambda_i = 1$.

The probability above does not identify the frame element boundaries. Gildea and Jurafsky proposed a model to determine if a constituent is a frame element from the path, the headword of the constituent, and the target word. The three last features appear in the condition part of the probability. To handle sparse data, they used linear interpolation:

$$P(fe|path, h, t) = \lambda_1 P(fe|path) + \lambda_2 P(fe|path, t) + \lambda_3 P(fe|h, t),$$

and set the threshold at 0.5.

Using the two-step procedure, boundary detection of frame elements and labeling of semantic roles, Gildea and Jurafsky report a precision of 67 and a recall of 48.7.

Combining Models. The valence patterns of a lexical unit, such as those shown in Table 13.7 for *avenge*: {Avenger, Injured_party}, {Agent, Injury}, and {Avenger, Injured_party, Offender, Punishment}, are not equally probable. Gildea and Jurafsky used this observation to improve the role-labeling step of their system. The most likely role assignment over a sentence of n constituents is modeled as

$$r^* = \arg \max_{r_{1...n}} P(r_{1...n}|t, f_{1...n}),$$

where r^* is the optimal role assignment over the n constituents of a sentence; t, the target word; and f_i, the constituent features. These features are the same as in the first version of the role labeler.

Using Bayes' theorem, we rewrite the equation as

$$r^* = \arg \max_{r_{1...n}} P(\{r_{1...n}\}|t) \prod_i \frac{P(r_i|f_i, t)}{P(r_i|t)},$$

where $P(\{r_{1...n}\}|t)$ is the probability of a valence pattern given a target word t.

Finally, Gildea and Jurafsky combined the two probability models from the frame element segmenter and the improved role labeler into a single equation:

$$r^* = \arg \max_{r_{1...n}} P(\{r_{1...n}\}|t) \prod_i \frac{P(r_i|f_i, fe_i, t)P(fe_i|f_i)}{P(r_i|t)},$$

where fe_i is a Boolean variable indicating whether sentence constituent i is a frame element or not. $P(fe_i|f_i)$ is computed as in the first step of the previous method. The combined equation yielded better results, with a precision of 64.6 and a recall of 61.2.

13.8 An Example of Case Grammar Application: EVAR

The EVAR application (Mast et al. 1994) is a spoken dialogue system that answers inquiries about train connections in Germany. EVAR uses a dedicated ontology to represent the domain and a case grammar to process the utterances. It is able to process exchanges like the one in Table 13.9.

13.8.1 EVAR's Ontology and Syntactic Classes

EVAR organizes nouns as a classical ontological tree restricted to the railway domain in Germany (Fig. 13.9). For instance, *train* is linked to "transport," *Hamburg* to "location," etc.

Table 13.9. A dialogue with the EVAR system.

Turn	Utterance
EVAR	*Guten Tag. Hier ist die automatische Intercityauskunft.* 'Hello, this is the automatic Intercity information system.'
User	*Ich will nach Hamburg* 'I want to go to Hamburg'
EVAR	*Sie wollen nach Hamburg fahren?* 'You want to go to Hamburg' *Wo wollen sie abfahren?* 'Where do you want to start?'
User	*In Erlangen*
EVAR	*Sie wollen von Erlangen abfahren?* 'You want to start from Erlangen' *An welchem Tag?* 'Which day?'
User	*Morgen früh* 'Tomorrow morning'
EVAR	*Sie wollen am Donnerstag den 26. Juni zwischen 6 und 12 Uhr fahren?* 'You want to travel on Thursday 26th of June between 6 and 12 AM'
User	*genau* 'Yes'
EVAR	*Ich habe mehrere Verbindungen gefunden.* 'I found connections' *Nach Hamburg HBF fahren sie ab Erlangen um 11 Uhr 1, Ankunft in Hamburg HBF...* 'To Hamburg, you can start from Erlangen at 11.01, arrival in Hamburg...' *Soll ich die Verbindungen wiederholen?* 'Shall I repeat?'
User	*Nein Danke*
EVAR	*Möchten Sie weitere Auskünfte?* 'Would you like more information?'
User	*Nein*
EVAR	*Auf wiederhören* 'Good bye'

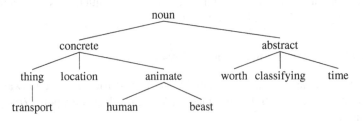

Fig. 13.9. Semantic classes in the EVAR application. After Mast et al. (1994).

13.8.2 Cases in EVAR

EVAR uses a partial parser to detect syntactic groups, notably noun groups, prepositional groups, infinitive groups, verb groups, and time and date expressions. It represents utterances with a case grammar tied to the train domain and uses the ontology in Fig. 13.9. The case system is relatively detailed – it is said to be fine grained – and consists of about 30 cases associated to verbs and also to nouns and adjectives. Table 13.10 shows some examples of case frames together with their constraints.

Table 13.10. Some verbs and nouns with their cases in the EVAR system. After Mast et al. (1994).

Word senses	Examples and cases
Fahren1.1	*Der Zug fährt von Hamburg nach München*
	'The train is going from Hamburg to Munich'
	Instrument: noun group (nominative), Transport, obligatory
	Source: prepositional group (Origin), Location, optional
	Goal: prepositional group (Direction), Location, optional
Fahren1.2	*Ich fahre mit dem Zug von Hamburg nach München*
	'I am going by train from Hamburg to Munich'
	Agent: noun group (nominative), Animate, obligatory
	Instrument: prepositional group (prep=mit), Transport, optional
	Source: prepositional group (Origin), Location, optional
	Goal: prepositional group (Direction), Location, optional
Abfahrt1.1	*Die Abfahrt des Zuges von Hamburg nach München*
	'The departure of the train at Hamburg for Munich'
	Object: noun group (genitive), Transport, optional
	Location: prepositional group (Place), Location, optional
	Time: prepositional group (Moment), Time, optional
Verbindung1.5	*Eine Verbindung von Hamburg nach München*
	'A connection from Hamburg to Munich'
	Source: prepositional group (Origin), Location, optional
	Goal: prepositional group (Direction), Location, optional

Sagerer (1990) gives the full description of the semantic cases related to EVAR.

13.9 Further Reading

Although it may not serve for immediate applications, Saussure's *Cours de linguistique générale* (1916) offers a fundamental background introduction on links between language and though. Also of interest, is Hjelmslev's *Prolegomena to a Theory of Language* (1943), which provides a complement to Saussure's views. A good introduction to the classical texts is the historical presentation on linguistics by Harris and Taylor (1997).

Electric Words by Wilks et al. (1996) provides an account on semantics that focuses on computerized dictionaries. It contains many mistakes however. Boguraev and Pustejovsky (1996) have similar concerns but address more specific points of lexical acquisition. Mel'cuk et al. (1995) propose a detailed dictionary model for French. Fellbaum (1998) gives an in-depth description of WordNet and its design. The WordNet lexical database is regularly updated and its content is available for download from http://wordnet.princeton.edu. Pustejovsky (1995) presents an alternate viewpoint on lexical structure. Dutoit (1992) describes another model that governed the implementation of Dicologique, a lexical database in French of size comparable to WordNet.

Literature on word sense disambiguation is countless. The reader can find a starting point in a dedicated special issue of *Computational Linguistics*, especially in its Introduction (Ide and Véronis 1998), which lists more than 300 references! Word sense disambiguation has made considerable progress recently. The SENSEVAL workshops benchmark competing systems for a variety of languages. Proceedings are available from the ACL Anthology (http://www.aclweb.org/anthology).

In a classical text, Fillmore (1968) gives the rationale behind case grammars. Jackendoff (1990) gives another detailed description of cases for English. Later, Fillmore started the FrameNet project that itemizes the frame elements of all the verbs. Although it is an ongoing project, the FrameNet database is well underway. Its description and content is available for download from http://framenet.icsi.berkeley.edu. Propbank or Proposition bank is a similar project aimed at annotating the Penn Treebank with semantic data (Kingsbury et al. 2002).

Automatic role labeling using statistical techniques has received considerable interest recently and was the theme of two conferences on Computational Natural Language Learning (CoNLL-2004 and CoNLL-2005). Annotated data, descriptions, and performance of the competing systems are available from the conference Web pages (http://www.cnts.ua.ac.be/conll2004/ and http://www.cnts.ua.ac.be/conll2005/).

Exercises

13.1. Implement the complete semantic net of Fig. 13.3.

13.2. Implement a graph search that finds entities linked by properties using inheritance, and test it using the `eat/2` relation.

13.3. Annotate each word of the following sentences with their possible senses:
The waiter brought the starter to the customers.
Le serveur a apporté l'entrée aux clients
Der Ober hat die Vorspeise zum Kunden gebracht.
You may use any dictionary.

13.4. Write verb syntactical models corresponding to senses of *order* in Table 13.1.

13.5. Write selectional restrictions corresponding to senses of *order* in Table 13.1.

13.6. Take a dozen or so words and, using their definition, build the corresponding ontological tree.

13.7. According to WordNet, *bring* entails *come, come up* (move toward, travel toward something or somebody or approach something or somebody). Classify this type of entailment as coextensiveness, proper inclusion, backward presupposition, or cause.

13.8. In this exercise, you will implement the word sense disambiguation algorithm outlined in Sect. 13.5.3.

- Write a Prolog program that produces all sense sequences of a given sentence. Implement the lexical database representing possible senses of *patron, ordered,* and *meal,* and test the program with *The patron ordered the meal.*
- Find topics associated with senses of words *patron, order,* and *meal.* Set these topics under the form of Prolog facts.
- Write a Prolog program that collects all the topics associated with a sense sequence.
- What is the main condition for the algorithm to produce good results?

13.9. Disambiguate by hand the senses of words in the sentence: *the patron ordered the meal* using word definitions and the algorithm of Sect. 13.5.6. You may use any dictionary.

13.10. Program the algorithm of the Exercise 13.9.

14

Discourse

14.1 Introduction

The grammatical concepts we have seen so far apply mostly to isolated words, phrases, or sentences. Texts and conversations, either full or partial, are out of their scope. Yet to us, human readers, writers, and speakers, language goes beyond the simple sentence. It is now time to describe models and processing techniques to deal with a succession of sentences. Although analyzing texts or conversations often requires syntactic and semantic treatments, it goes further. In this chapter, we shall make an excursion to the discourse side, that is, paragraphs, texts, and documents. In the next chapter, we shall consider dialogue, that is, a spoken or written interaction between a user and a machine.

Most basically, a discourse is made of **referring expressions**, i.e., words or phrases that refer to real – or possibly imaginary – things: the **discourse entities** or **discourse referents**. A first objective of discourse processing techniques is then to identify and track sets of referring expressions – phrases or words – along with sentences and to relate them to entities – real-world objects.

A discourse normally links the entities together to address topics, issues throughout the sentences, paragraphs, chapters such as, for instance, the quality of food in restaurants, the life of hedgehogs and toads, and so on. At a local level, i.e., within a single sentence, grammatical functions such as the subject, the verb, and the object provide a model of relations between entities. A model of discourse should extend and elaborate relations that apply not to an isolated sentence but to a sequence and hence to the entities that this sequence of sentences covers.

Models of discourse structures are still a subject of controversy. As for semantics, discourse has spurred many theories, and it seems relatively far off to produce a synthesis of them. In consequence, we will merely adopt a bottom-up and pragmatic approach. We will start from what can be a shallow-level processing of discourse and application examples; we will then introduce theories, namely centering, rhetoric, and temporal organization, which provide hints for a discourse structure.

14.2 Discourse: A Minimalist Definition

14.2.1 A Description of Discourse

Intuitively what defines a discourse, and what differentiates it from unstructured pieces of text, is its coherence. A discourse is a set of more or less explicit topics addressed in a sequence of sentences: what the discourse is about at a given time. Of course, there can be digressions, parentheses, interruptions, etc., but these are understood as exceptions in the flow of a normal discourse. Distinctive qualities of a discourse are clarity, expressiveness, or articulation, which all relate to the ease of identification of discourse topics and their logical treatment. Discourse coherence ideally takes the shape of a succession of stable subjects (or contexts) that are chained rationally along with the flow of sentences.

More formally, we describe a discourse as a sequence of utterances or segments, $S_1, S_2, S_3, ..., S_n$, so that each of these segments is mapped onto a stationary context. Segments are related to sentences, but they are not equivalent. A segment can span one or more sentences, and conversely a sentence can also contain several segments. Segments can be produced by a unique source, which is the case in most texts, or by more interacting participants, in the case of a dialogue.

14.2.2 Discourse Entities

Discourse entities – or discourse referents – are the real, abstract, or imaginary objects introduced by the discourse. Usually they are not directly accessible to a language processing system because it would require sensors to "see" or "feel" them. In a language like Prolog, discourse entities are represented as a set of facts stored in a database. Referring expressions are mentions of the discourse entities along with the text. Table 14.1 shows entities and references of sentences adapted from Suri and McCoy (1994):

1. *Susan drives a Ferrari*
2. *She drives too fast*
3. *Lyn races her on weekends*
4. *She often beats her*
5. *She wins a lot of trophies*

Table 14.1. Discourse entities and referring expressions.

Referring expressions	Discourse entities (or referents)	Logic properties
Susan, she, her	'Susan'	'Susan'
Lyn, she	'Lyn'	'Lyn'
A Ferrari	X	ferrari(X)
A lot of trophies	E	E ⊂ {X, trophy(X)}

Discourse entities are normally stable – constant – over a segment, and we can use them to delimit a segment's boundaries. That is, once we have identified the entities, we can delimit the segment boundaries. Let us come back to our example. There are two sets of relatively stable entities that we can relate to two segments. The first one is about Susan and her car. It consists of sentences 1 and 2. The second one is about Susan and Lyn, and it extends from 3 to 6 (Table 14.2).

Table 14.2. Context segmentation.

Contexts	Sentences	Entities
C1	1. *Susan drives a Ferrari*	Susan, Ferrari
	2. *She drives too fast*	
C2	3. *Lyn races her on weekends*	Lyn, Susan, trophies
	4. *She often beats her*	
	5. *She wins a lot of trophies*	

14.3 References: An Application-Oriented View

As a starting point of discourse processing, we will focus on referring expressions, i.e., words or phrases that correspond to the discourse entities. This treatment can be done fairly independently without any comprehensive treatment of the text. In addition, the identification of discourse entities is interesting in itself and has an industrial significance in applications such as information extraction.

In this section, we will take examples from the Message Understanding Conferences (MUCs) that we already saw in Chap. 9. We will learn how to track the entities along with sentences and detect sets of phrases or words that refer to the same thing in a sentence, a paragraph, or a text.

14.3.1 References and Noun Phrases

In MUC, information extraction consists in converting a text under the form of a file card. Cards are predefined templates whose entries are formatted tabular slots that represent the information to be extracted: persons, events, or things. For each text, information extraction systems have to generate a corresponding card whose slots are filled with the appropriate entities.

Detecting – generating – the entities is a fundamental step of information extraction; a system could not fill the templates properly otherwise. To carry it out, the basic idea is that references to real-world objects are equivalent to noun groups or noun phrases of the text. So detecting the entities comes down to recognizing the nominal expressions.

To realize in concrete terms what it means, let us take an example from Hobbs et al. (1997) and identify the entities. We just have to bracket the noun groups and to assign them with a number that we increment with each new group:

[$_{entity1}$ Garcia Alvarado], 56, was killed when [$_{entity2}$ a bomb] placed by [$_{entity3}$ urban guerrillas] on [$_{entity4}$ his vehicle] exploded as [$_{entity5}$ it] came to [$_{entity6}$ a halt] at [$_{entity7}$ an intersection] in [$_{entity8}$ downtown] [$_{entity9}$ San Salvador].

We have detected nine nominal expressions and hence nine candidates to be references that we represent in Table 14.3.

Table 14.3. References in the sentence: *Garcia Alvarado, 56, was killed when a bomb placed by urban guerrillas on his vehicle exploded as it came to a halt at an intersection in downtown San Salvador.*

Entities	Noun groups
Entity 1	*Garcia Alvarado*
Entity 2	*a bomb*
Entity 3	*urban guerrillas*
Entity 4	*his vehicle*
Entity 5	*it*
Entity 6	*a halt*
Entity 7	*an intersection*
Entity 8	*downtown*
Entity 9	*San Salvador*

Typical discourse analyzers integrate modules into an architecture that they apply on each sentence. Depending on applications, they use a full-fledged parser or a combination of part-of-speech tagger, group detector, semantic role identifier, or ontological classifier. Here, we could have easily created these entities automatically with the help of a noun group detector. A few lines more of Prolog to our noun group detector (Chap. 9) would have numbered and added each noun group to an entity database.

14.3.2 Finding Names – Proper Nouns

In unrestricted texts, in addition to common nouns, many references correspond to names (or proper nouns). Their detection is then central to a proper reference processing. Names include:

- Persons: Mrs. Smith, François Arouet, Dottore Graziani, Wolfgang A. Mozart, H.C. Andersen, Sammy Davis, Jr.
- Companies or organizations: IBM Corp., Fiat SpA, BT Limited, Banque National de Paris, Siemens GMBH, United Nations, Nations unies
- Countries, nations, or provinces: England, France, Deutchland, Romagna, Vlanderen
- Cities or geographical places: Paris, The Hague, Berlin, le Mont Blanc, la Città del Vaticano, the English Channel, la Manche, der Rhein

Name recognition frequently uses a dedicated database and the help of some heuristics. Such name databases can sometimes be downloaded from the Internet. However, for many applications, they have to be compiled manually or bought from specialized companies. A name recognition system can then be implemented with local DCG rules and a word spotting program (see Chap. 9).

However, name databases are rarely complete or up-to-date. Peoples' names particularly are tricky and may sometimes be confused with common names. The same can be said of names of companies, which are created every day, and those of countries, which appear and disappear with revolutions and wars. If we admit that there will be names missing in the database, we have to design the word spotter to cope with it and to implement some rules to guess them.

Guessing a person's name is often done through titles and capitalization. A few rules of thumb attempt to match:

- A first name, a possible initial, and a surname that is two strings of characters with a capitalized first letter followed by lower case letters:
  Robert Merryhill, Brigitte Joyard, Max Hübnisch
  A possible enhancement is to try to match the first string to common first names.
- A title, possible first names or initials and a surname where common titles have to be itemized:
  Sir Robert Merryhill, Dr. B. K. Joyard, Herr Hübnisch
- A person's name and a suffix:
  R. Merryhill Sr., Louis XXII, Herr Hübnisch d. med.

These heuristics can be implemented with a word spotter and DCG rules to match titles and first names. A short piece of Prolog code will also have to test the case of certain characters. We can also use regular expressions or a stochastic classifer.

14.4 Coreference

14.4.1 Anaphora

In the example of the previous section, we have numbered eight objects corresponding to noun groups and one corresponding to the pronoun *it*. Such a pronoun is generally related to a previous expression in the text and depends on this expression to be interpreted. Here, the reader can easily guess that *it* and the noun group *his vehicle* designate the same entity. This means that entities 5 and 4 in Table 14.3 are equal and that nominal expressions *his vehicle* and *it* **corefer** to a same thing (Fig. 14.1).

The pair of expressions *his vehicle* and *it* form an **anaphora** where the first reference to the object – *his vehicle* – is the **antecedent** and subsequent references – here *it* – are **anaphors**. Antecedent and anaphors are then a set of references to a same entity in a text. The antecedent acts as the semantic source of the set and enables the understanding of the anaphors (Tesnière 1966).

Third-person and relative pronouns (*he/she/it/who*) are typical examples of anaphors. In addition to them, anaphora uses demonstrative pronouns such as *this/that*

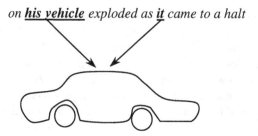

*on **his vehicle** exploded as **it** came to a halt*

Fig. 14.1. Coreferencing an entity with a noun group and a pronoun.

in *He did that*, or location adverbs such as *here/there* in *He was there*. Demonstrative pronouns (or adjectives) can be used as determiners as in *this vehicle*. The possessive pronouns (or adjectives) are similar and also denote an anaphora as *his* in *his vehicle* that is tied to the vehicle's possessor.

While normally anaphors have their antecedent before they occur, there are sometimes examples of forward references or **cataphora**. For example, in the sentence:

*I just wanted to touch **it**, this stupid animal.*

It refers to the *stupid animal*. It has been shown that in most structured discourses, cataphoras occur in the same sentence. However, this is not always the case, and sometimes the referent is never mentioned, either because it is obvious given the context, because it is unknown, or for some other reasons:

They have stolen my bicycle.

14.4.2 Solving Coreferences in an Example

Although we had no difficulty recognizing the identity of the two expressions, *his vehicle* and *it* in the example above, coreference resolution is not as straightforward as it may appear at a first sight. Let us come back to our example in Table 14.3 to show this, and let us make our method explicit to outline an algorithm. We will first admit that coreferences of a pronoun are always located before the pronoun occurs in the text. Then, in the example, in addition to *his vehicle* (entity 4), pronoun *it* (entity 5) has four possible candidates: *it* could be *Garcia Alvarado* (entity 1), *a bomb* (entity 2), or *urban guerrillas* (entity 3).

We can rule out entities 1 and 3 from the coreference set because they do not match the pronoun's number or gender. If entity 5 had been *Garcia Alvarado* – a man – the pronoun would have been *he*, and if it had been *urban guerrillas* – a plural – the pronoun would have been *they*. The noun group *A bomb* is more difficult to discard. We do not retain it because of a semantic incompatibility. Selectional restrictions of the verb *came* likely require that its subject is a vehicle or a person.

We saw examples of anaphora where a same entity is specified by a noun and a pronoun. Pairs of references can also consist of nouns or noun groups. They can simply be a repetition of identical expressions, (*the vehicle, the vehicle*). Sometimes there might be a different determiner, a different denomination, synonyms, or aliases to refer to a same thing. For instance, in an economic wire, we can first have *Bayerische Motoren Werke*, then *BMW*, and finally *the German automaker*.

Coreference is a far-reaching concept that can prove very complex. The definition of anaphora may also vary: most authors restrain anaphors to be pronouns and certain types of adverbs. Others extend it to noun phrases, either definite or not. In the rest of the text, we will make no distinction, and we will define coreference resolution or coreference recognition as the retrieval of sets of references to identical entities in a text – what we have just come to do. We will also keep the terms antecedent and anaphor to refer to the first and second term of a coreferring pair, even if the anaphor is not a pronoun.

14.4.3 A Standard Coreference Annotation

Before we explain general methods to solve coreferences, let us first examine an annotation scheme proposed in the sixth and seventh Message Understanding Conferences (MUC-6 and MUC-7) to tag them. While there are various mark-up models, this one, based on XML tags, is widely public and can be considered as a standard. In addition, as the MUC's final objective is to extract information, these tags have an application interest.

The annotation of references and coreferences in a text consists first of identifying of the referring expressions and then assigning a unique label to expressions referring to a same entity. Hirschman and Chinchor (1997) proposed to annotate nominal expressions, that is nouns, noun phrases, and pronouns, here considered as referring expressions, and their antecedents, with the XML-defined COREF element. COREF has five possible attributes: ID, REF, TYPE, MIN, and STAT.

ID is an arbitrary integer that assigns a unique number to each nominal expression of the text. REF is an optional integer that links a nominal expression to a coreferring antecedent. REF value is then the ID of its antecedent. From Hirschman and Chinchor's annotated examples, the text

```
<COREF ID="100">Lawson Mardon Group Ltd.</COREF> said <COREF
ID="101" TYPE="IDENT" REF="100">it</COREF>
```

indicates that *Lawson Mardon Group Ltd.* and *it* are assigned respectively with ID 100 and 101, and that *it* refers to the same entity as *Lawson Mardon Group Ltd* through REF="100".

In the MUC competitions, coreference is defined as symmetric and transitive, that is, if A is coreferential with B, the reverse is also true. And if A is coreferential with B, and B is coreferential with C, then A is coreferential with C. Such a coreference set then forms an equivalence class called a **coreference chain**. This is stated with the TYPE attribute that specifies the link between the anaphor and its antecedent: "IDENT" is the only possible value of the attribute, and it indicates that coreferences are identical. One may imagine other types of coreference such as part, subset, etc.

Other attributes are MIN and STAT. Some denominations may have a variable length and yet refer to the same entity, such as *Queen Elisabeth of England* and

Queen Elisabeth. In a text where the denomination appears in full, a coreference analyzer could bracket both. The COREF tag MIN indicates the minimum valid string. From Hirschman and Chinchor's guidelines,

```
<COREF ID="100" MIN="Haden MacLellan PLC">Haden MacLel-
lan PLC of Surrey, England</COREF> ... <COREF ID="101" TYPE=
"IDENT" REF="100">Haden MacLellan</COREF>
```

indicates that *Haden MacLellan PLC of Surrey, England* and *Haden MacLellan PLC* are both valid bracketing.

Finally, STAT ("status") means that the annotation is optional. It is used when coreference is tricky or doubtful. The only value for this attribute is OPT ("optional"). From Hirschman and Chinchor's guidelines,

```
<COREF ID="102" MIN="Board of Education">Our Board of
Education</COREF> budget is just too high, the Mayor said. <COREF
ID="103" STAT="OPT" TYPE="IDENT" REF="102">Livingston
Street </COREF> has lost control.
```

indicates that *Board of Education* and *Livingston Street* refers to the same entity, but that it can bewilder the reader and the annotation is left optional.

14.5 References: A More Formal View

14.5.1 Generating Discourse Entities: The Existential Quantifier

In Chap. 12, we introduced a logical notation to represent nominal expressions that differs from that of the previous section. If we take the formal semantics viewpoint, a sentence such as:

A patron ordered a meal.

exposes two new terms: *a patron* and *a meal*. These entities are tied to indefinite noun phrases and hence to logical forms headed by the existential quantifier $\exists$:

$$\exists x, patron(x)$$
$$\exists y, meal(y)$$

A discourse interpretation program should reflect them in a Prolog database and augment the database with the corresponding semantic facts:

```
patron(patron#3).
meal(meal#15).
```

We generate the entities by creating new constants – new atoms – making sure that they have a unique name, here patron#3 or meal#15. Then, we can add them in the database under the form of facts using the asserta/1 built-in predicate.

New entities are only a part of the whole logical set because the complete semantic representation of the sentence is:

```
a(X, patron(X), a(Y, meal(Y), ordered(X, Y)))
```

To be consistent with this representation, we must also add the predicate `ordered(Subject, Object)` to link the two new entities. We carry this out by asserting a last fact:

```
ordered(patron#3, meal#15).
```

14.5.2 Retrieving Discourse Entities: Definite Descriptions

While indefinite noun phrases introduce new entities, definite ones usually refer to entities created previously. A possible subsequent sentence in the discourse could be:

The patron ate the meal,

which should not create new entities. This simply declares that the patron already mentioned ate the meal he ordered. Such definite noun phrases are then anaphors.

The logic interpretation of definite descriptions usually translates as:

$$\exists!x, patron(x)$$
$$\exists!y, meal(y)$$

where properties are quantified with $\exists!$ meaning that x and y are unique. To reflect this in the Prolog database, we could identify x and y among the entities previously created and then assert the new fact:

```
ate(patron#3, meal#15).
```

An alternate processing of the `ate/2` relation – and probably a more alert one – is to first create new atoms, that is, new names:

```
patron(patron#5).
meal(meal#17).
```

to link them with `ate/2`:

```
ate(patron#5, meal#17).
```

and to assert later that some names are identical:

```
equals(patron#3, patron#5).
equals(meal#15, meal#17).
```

This method is precisely the coreference recognition that we described previously. Besides, proceeding in two steps enables a division of work. While a first task generates all potential entities, a second one resolves coreferences using techniques that we will review in Sect. 14.7.

14.5.3 Generating Discourse Entities: The Universal Quantifier

We saw that determiners can also correspond to the universal quantifier $\forall$. An example of such a sentence is:

Every patron ordered a meal.

Its corresponding logic representation is:

$$\forall x, patron(x) \Rightarrow \exists y, meal(y), ordered(x, y)$$

or in a predicate form:

```
all(X, patron(X), a(Y, meal(Y), ordered(X, Y)))
```

In such a logical form, each value of X should be mapped onto a specific value of Y: each patron has eaten his/her own and unique meal. A definition in extension of this sentence – that is, the list of all the facts it encompasses – could be:

Pierre ordered a cassoulet,
Charlotte ordered a pytt i panna, and
Dave ordered a Yorkshire pudding.

Doing so, we have defined a function linking each value of X with a unique value of Y, that is, *Pierre* with a specific *cassoulet*, *Charlotte* with a *pytt i panna*, and *Dave* with a *Yorkshire pudding*. In logic, this is called a Skolem function (Table 14.4).

Table 14.4. A Skolem function.

X	Y	Skolem function values
pierre	cassoulet#2	f(pierre) = cassoulet#2
charlotte	pytt_i_panna#4	f(charlotte) = pytt_i_panna#4
dave	yorkshire_pudding#4	f(dave) = yorkshire_pudding#4

Our Skolem function has eliminated variable y and the existential quantifier. It has replaced them by $f(x)$ in the logical form:

$$\forall x, patron(x) \Rightarrow ordered(x, f(x))$$

or

```
all(X, patron(X), a(f(X), meal(f(X)),
        ordered(X, f(X))))
```

More generally, Skolemization handles logical formulas with universally quantified variables, $x_1, x_2, ..., x_n$, and a variable existentially quantified y on its left-hand side:

$$\forall x_1, \forall x_2, ..., \forall x_n, \exists y, pred(x_1, x_2, ..., x_n, y)$$

It substitutes y by a function of the universally quantified variables:

$$y = f(x_1, x_2, ..., x_n)$$

yielding unique values for each n-tuplet $(x_1, x_2, ..., x_n)$.

Skolemization results in a new formula, where variable y has disappeared:

$$\forall x_1, \forall x_2, ..., \forall x_n, pred(x_1, x_2, ..., x_n, f(x_1, x_2, ..., x_n))$$

and where $f(x_1, x_2, ..., x_n)$ is called a Skolem function.

14.6 Centering: A Theory on Discourse Structure

Of the many theories on discourse structure, Grosz and Sidner's (1986) has been very influential in the computational linguistics community. Grosz and Sidner modeled a discourse as being a composite of three components:

- the linguistic structure of the actual sequence of utterances in the discourse
- a structure of intentions
- an attentional state

Grosz and Sidner's first assumption is that the linguistic structure of a discourse is made of segments. They substantiated this claim using psychological studies showing a relative agreement among individuals over the segmentation a text: given a text, individuals tend to fractionate it in a same way. Segments have a nonstrict embedded (hierarchical) organization (Fig. 14.2). It is roughly comparable to that of the phrase structure decomposition of a sentence. Segment boundaries are often delimited by clues and **cue phrases**, also called markers, that indicate transitions.

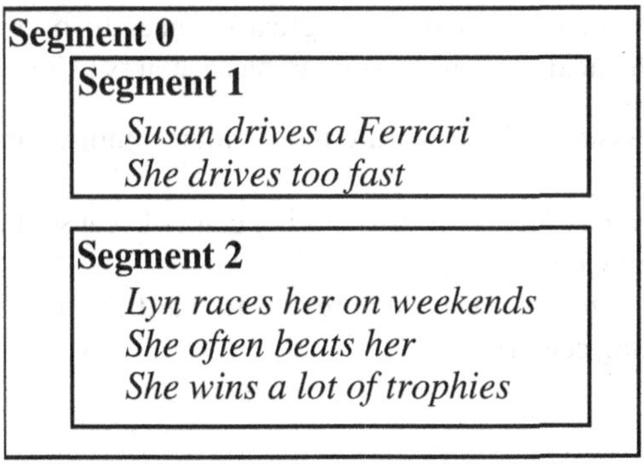

> **Segment 0**
>> **Segment 1**
>>> *Susan drives a Ferrari*
>>> *She drives too fast*
>>
>> **Segment 2**
>>> *Lyn races her on weekends*
>>> *She often beats her*
>>> *She wins a lot of trophies*

Fig. 14.2. The embedded structure of discourse. Segment 0 covers the five sentences and spans segment 1 (1 and 2) and segment 2 (3–5).

The intentional structure is what underlies a discourse. It is the key to how segments are arranged and their internal coherence. It has global and local components.

From a global viewpoint, intention relates to the **discourse purpose**, which is the main objective of the discourse and why it takes place. Within each segment there is a **discourse segment purpose** that is local and that contributes to the main purpose. Discourse segment purposes are often easier to determine than the overall discourse intention.

The attentional state is the dynamic set of objects, relations, and properties along with the discourse. The attentional state is closely related to segments. For each of them there is a focus space made of salient entities, properties of entities, and relations between entities, that is, predicates describing or linking the entities. The attentional state also contains the discourse segment purpose.

While Grosz and Sidner's general model may prove difficult to implement, Grosz et al. (1995) derived a simpler concept of **centering** from it. Centering retains the idea of segment, defined as a set of utterances, along which a limited number of dynamic centers turn up. Centers are the "useful" entities of an utterance that link it to other utterances of a segment. Since centers are a subset of entities, they are easier to detect than the intention or the whole attentional state. They provide a tentative model to explain discourse coherence and coreference organization.

Centers of an utterance are split into a set of **forward-looking centers** and a unique **backward-looking center**, except for the first utterance of the segment, which has no backward-looking center:

- The backward-looking center, or simply the center, is the entity that connects the current utterance with the previous one and hence with one of the previous forward-looking centers. It is often a pronoun.
- Forward-looking centers are roughly the other discourse entities of a segment. More precisely, they are limited to entities serving to link the utterance to other utterances.

Forward-looking centers can be ordered according to syntactic, semantic, and pragmatic factors, and the first one has great chances to become the backward-looking center of the next utterance. As examples, centers in Table 14.1 are:

- In sentence 1, *Susan* and *Ferrari* are the discourse entities and forward-looking centers.
- In sentence 2, *she* is the backward-looking center because it connects the utterance with the previous one.
- In sentence 3, *Lyn* and *weekends* are the forward-looking centers; *her* is the backward-looking center.

14.7 Solving Coreferences

Although coreferences to a same object are frequently ambiguous, they generally raise no understanding problem to a human reader, with the exception of poorly written texts. However, they represent a tricky issue for a machine. The field has long been dominated by complex linguistic theories that are difficult to implement and to process. Fortunately, as with partial parsing, the MUCs have focused research on concrete problems and robust algorithms that revolutionized coreference resolution.

In the next sections, we will describe algorithms to automatically resolve coreferences. We will first introduce systems based on manually written rules and then describe an efficient machine-learning approach. Even if coreference algorithms do not reach the performance of POS taggers or noun group detectors, they have greatly improved recently and can now be applied to unrestricted texts.

14.7.1 A Simplistic Method: Using Syntactic and Semantic Compatibility

A basic rule that links an anaphor and its antecedent is that their number and gender are identical. This yields the idea of a simplistic method to resolve anaphoric pronouns. The algorithm first collects a list of all the discourse's referents. When an anaphor occurs, the antecedent is searched backward in this list. We set aside cataphoras here. The resolution retains the first antecedent it finds in the list – the most recent one – that agrees in gender and number.

This method may seem naïve, but in fact, most of the time the first antecedent occurring in the sentence or in the previous one with matching gender and number is the good one. This **recency** principle has been observed in many experimental studies. The methods ranks properly potential antecedents of *it* in the sentence:

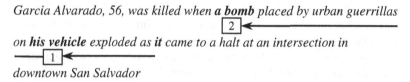

Garcia Alvarado, 56, was killed when **a bomb** *placed by urban guerrillas*

*on **his vehicle** exploded as **it** came to a halt at an intersection in*

downtown San Salvador

We can extend this resolution method to find antecedents of definite noun phrases. The recency principle remains the same, but in addition to syntactic features such as gender and number, we add semantic constraints. We search the antecedent of a definite noun phrase, considered as an anaphor, among the entities semantically compatible. Compatibility takes the form of:

- the identity – identical noun groups indicate a same reference
- a direct ontological link between groups – generalization or specialization as in *a car* and *the vehicle*, or
- compatible modifiers – adjectives and complements as in *car*, *white car* or *police car*, but not in *police car* and *ambulance*

Huls et al. (1995) report that such a method identifies pronoun anaphor coreferences with an accuracy of 95%. Although this figure would probably degrade in some cases, it proves the power and effectiveness of this very simple model. The existence of gender for nouns in French and in German makes the search probably more accurate in these languages.

14.7.2 Solving Coreferences with Shallow Grammatical Information

Kameyama (1997) proposed an algorithm using manually written rules that produced good results in the MUC contest for the coreference resolution task. Here is a slightly modified version of his algorithm. It operates on pronouns and definite noun groups only. It sets aside others such as indefinite and possessive noun groups.

The algorithm first extracts all nominal expressions of the text. Then, it scans these expressions in left-to-right order, and for each pronoun or definite noun group, it collects preceding nominal expressions – the potential antecedents – within a definite span of a couple of sentences. The exact window size depends on the type of referring expression:

- The entire MUC text preceding the current expression for proper names.
- Narrower for definite noun phrases. Kameyama suggests 10 sentences.
- Even narrower for pronouns. Again, Kameyama suggests 3 sentences.
- The current sentence for reflexive pronouns.

The algorithm applies constraints on the collected nominal expressions to check the compatibility between the current entity E and possible antecedents:

- Number and gender consistency: both must coincide. In some cases, such as with organizations, plural pronouns may denote a singular antecedent.
- Ontological consistency: type of E must be equal to the type of the antecedent or subsume it. For instance, *the automaker* is a valid antecedent of *the company*, but not the reverse.
- Modifier consistency: modifiers such as adjectives must not contradict such as in *the British company* and *the French company*.

Then, among possible candidates, the algorithm retains the one whose **salience** is the highest. This salience is based on the prominence of certain elements in a sentence, such as subjects over objects, and on obliteration with time (or recency). It has its origin in a rough model of human memory. Memory tends to privilege recent facts or some rhetoric or syntactic forms. A linear ordering of candidates approximates salience in English because subjects have a relatively rigid location in front of the sentence. Kameyama's salience ranks candidates from:

1. the preceding part of the same sentence in left–right order (subject salience)
2. the immediately preceding sentence in left–right order (subject salience)
3. other preceding sentences within the window in right–left order (recency)

In addition, the algorithm improves the name recognition with aliases. Companies are often designated by full names, partial names, and acronyms to avoid repetitions. For example, consider *Digital Equipment Corporation, Digital, DEC*. An improvement to coreference recognition is to identify full names with substrings of them and their acronyms.

14.7.3 Salience in a Multimodal Context

EDWARD (Huls et al. 1995) is a model that extends salience to a gesture designation of entities. EDWARD is part of a system that is intended to control a graphical user interface made of windows containing icons that represent files. The interface accepts natural language and mouse commands to designate objects, that is, to name them and to point at them. This combination of modes of interaction is called **multimodality**.

The multimodal salience model keeps the idea of recency in language. The subject of the sentence is also supposed to be retained better than its object, and an object better than an adjunct. In addition, the model integrates a graphical salience and a possible interaction. It takes into account the visibility of entities and pointing gestures. Syntactic properties of an entity are called linguistic context factors, and visual ones are called perceptual context factors. All factors: subject, object, visibility, interaction, and so on, are given a numerical value. A pointed object has the highest possible mark.

The model uses a time sliding window that spans a sentence. It creates the discourse entities of the current window and assigns them a weight corresponding to their contextual importance. Computation of an entity's weight simply sums up all the factors attached to it. An entity salience is then mapped onto a number: its weight. Then the window is moved to the next sentence, and each factor weight attached to each entity is decremented by one. An entity mentioned for the first time and in the position of an object has a context factor weight – a salience – of 3. The next sentence, its worth will be 2, then 1, and finally 0 (Table 14.5).

The model sequentially processes the noun phrases of a sentence. To determine coreferring expressions of the current noun phrase, the model selects all entities semantically compatible with it that have been mentioned before. The one that has the highest salience value among them is retained as a coreference. Both salience values are then added: the factor brought by the current phrase and the accumulated salience of its coreference. All entities are assigned a value that is used to interpret the next sentence. Then, the decay algorithm is applied and the window is moved to the next sentence.

Table 14.6 shows a processing example. It indicates the salience values of *Lyn*, *Susan*, and *Ferrari*. In case of ambiguous reference, the system would ask the user to indicate which candidate is the right one.

14.7.4 Using a Machine-Learning Technique to Resolve Coreferences

Algorithms we have seen so far are based on manually engineered rules. This strategy requires a good deal of expertise and considerable clerical work to test and debug the rules. In this section, we introduce a machine learning approach where the coreference solver uses rules obtained automatically from a hand-annotated corpus (Soon et al. 2001).

The coreference solver is a decision tree. It considers pairs of noun phrases (NP_i, NP_j), where each pair is represented by a feature vector of 12 parameters.

Table 14.5. Context factors (simplified) according to Huls et al. (1995). Note that a subject appears twice in the context factor list, as a subject and as a major constituent.

Context factors (CF)	Objects in Scope	Successive weights
Linguistic CFs		
Major-constituent referents CF	Referents of subject, (in)direct object, and modifier	$[3, 2, 1, 0]$
Subject referent CF	Referent of the subject phrase	$[2, 1, 0]$
Nested-term referent CF	Referents of the noun phrase modifiers (e.g., prepositional phrase, relative clause)	$[1, 0]$
Perceptual CFs		
Visible referent CF	Referents visible in the current viewpoint. Typically icons visible in a window	$[1, \ldots, 1, 0]$
Selected referent CF	Referents selected in the model world. Typically icons selected – highlighted – with the mouse or by a natural language command	$[2, \ldots, 2, 0]$
Indicated referent CF	Referents indicated by a pointing gesture. Typically an icon currently being pointed at with a mouse	$[30, 1, 0]$

Table 14.6. Computation of the salience value (SV) of *Lyn*, *Susan*, and *Ferrari*.

	SV of Susan	SV of Lyn	SV of Ferrari
Initial values	0	0	0
Susan drives a Ferrari	$3 + 2 = 5$ major + subject	0 major	3
Decay after completion	$3 - 1 + 2 - 1 = 3$		$3 - 1 = 2$
She drives too fast	$3 + 3 + 2 = 8$ existing + major + subject	0	2
Decay after completion	$3 - 1 - 1 + 2 - 1 - 1 + 3 - 1 + 2 - 1 = 4$		$3 - 1 - 1 = 1$
Lyn races her on weekends	$4 + 3 = 7$ existing + major	$3 + 2 = 5$ major + subject	1
Decay after completion	$3 - 1 - 1 - 1 + 3 - 1 - 1 + 2 - 1 - 1 + 3 - 1 = 3$	$3 - 1 + 2 - 1 = 3$	$3 - 1 - 1 - 1 = 0$
She often beats her	$3 + 3 + 2 = 8$ existing + major + subject	$3 + 3 = 6$ existing + major	0

The solver first extracts pairs of noun phrases and computes feature vectors for each pair. It then takes the set of NP pairs as input and decides for each pair whether it corefers or not. Using the transitivity property, it identifies all the coreference chains in the text.

The ID3 learning algorithm (Quinlan 1986) automatically induces the decision tree from annotated texts using the MUC annotation standard (Sect. 14.4.3).

Noun Phrase Extraction. The engine first identifies all the noun phrases – the coreference candidates – from a text using a pipeline of language processing modules. The pipeline is similar to what we have seen in information extraction: tokenization, morphological processing, POS tagging, noun phrase identification, named entity recognition, nested noun phrase extraction, and semantic class determination (Fig. 14.3).

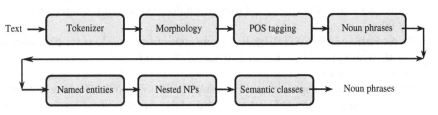

Fig. 14.3. A cascade of NL modules.

The four first modules are generic to many language processing applications. The named entities module follows the MUC style and extracts organization, person, location, date, time, money, and percent entities. When a noun phrase and a named entity overlap, they are merged to form a single noun phrase. The Nested NPs module splits some noun phrases and is more specific to coreference resolution:

1. It brackets possessive noun phrases and possessive pronouns, as in *his long-term strategy*, to form two phrases, *his* and *his long-term strategy*.
2. It also brackets modifier nouns in nominal compounds, as in *wage reductions*, to generate two noun phrases, *wage* and *wage reduction*.

Features. As input, the coreference engine takes a pair of extracted noun phrases (NP_i, NP_j), where NP_i is before NP_j in the text. The engine considers NP_i as a potential antecedent and NP_j as an anaphor and classifies the pair as positive if both NPs corefer, or negative if they do not. Each pair is described by a feature vector of 12 parameters that correspond to positional, grammatical, semantic, and lexical properties:

- Positional feature:
  1. Distance (DIST): This feature is the distance between the two noun phrases measured in sentences: 0, 1, 2, 3, ... The distance is 0 when the noun phrases are in the same sentence.

- Grammatical features:
  2. i-Pronoun (I_PRONOUN): Is NP_i a pronoun i.e. personal, reflexive, or possessive pronoun? Possible values are true or false.
  3. j-Pronoun (J_PRONOUN): Is NP_j a pronoun? Possible values are true or false.
  4. Definite noun phrase (DEF_NP): Is NP_j a definite noun phrase, i.e., that starts with *the*? Possible values are true or false.
  5. Demonstrative noun phrase (DEM_NP): Is NP_j a demonstrative noun phrase, i.e., that starts with *this, that, these, those*? Possible values are true or false.
  6. Number agreement (NUMBER): Do NP_i and NP_j agree in number? Possible values are true or false.
  7. Gender agreement (GENDER): Do NP_i and NP_j agree in gender? Possible values are true, false, or unknown.
  8. Both proper nouns (PROPER_NOUN): Are NP_i and NP_j both proper nouns? Proper nouns are determined using capitalization. Possible values are true or false.
  9. Appositive (APPOSITIVE): Is NP_j an apposition to NP_i, as *the chairman of Microsoft* in *Bill Gates, the chairman of Microsoft*, ...
- Semantic features:
  10. Semantic class agreement (SEMCLASS): Do NP_i and NP_j have the same semantic class? Possible values are true, false, or unknown. Classes are organized as a small ontology with two main parts, person and object, themselves divided respectively into male and female, and organization, location, date, time, money, and percent. The head nouns of the NPs are linked to this ontology using the WordNet hierarchy.
  11. Alias (ALIAS): Are NP_i and NP_j aliases, for instance, *IBM* and *International Business Machines*? Possible values are true or false.
- Lexical feature:
  12. String match (STR_MATCH): Are NP_i and NP_j equal after removing articles and demonstratives from both noun phrases? Possible values are true or false.

Figure 14.3 shows an example of feature vector for the pair *Frank Newman* and *vice chairman* excerpted from the next sentence (Soon et al. 2001):

> Separately, Clinton transition official said that *Frank Newman*, 50, *vice chairman* and chief financial officer of BankAmerica Corp., is expected to be nominated as assistant Treasury secretary for domestic finance.

Training Examples. The classifier is a decision tree. It is trained from positive and negative examples extracted from the annotated corpus using the ID3 algorithm:

- The training procedure generates the positive examples using pairs of adjacent coreferring noun phrases. If $NP_{a1} - NP_{a2} - NP_{a3} - NP_{a4}$ is a coreference chain in a text, the positive examples correspond to pairs: (NP_{a1}, NP_{a2}),

Table 14.7. Feature vector of the noun phrase pair: NP_i = *Frank Newman* and NP_j = *vice chairman*. After Soon et al. (2001).

Feature type	Feature	Value	Comments
Positional	DIST	0	NP_i and NP_j are the same sentence
Grammatical	I_PRONOUN	–	NP_i is not a pronoun
	J_PRONOUN	–	NP_j is not a pronoun
	DEF_NP	–	NP_j is not a definite NP
	DEM_NP	–	NP_j is not a demonstrative NP
	NUMBER	+	NP_i and NP_j are both singular
	GENDER	1	NP_i and NP_j are both males (false = 0, true = 1, unknown = 2)
	PROPER_NOUN	–	Only NP_i is a proper noun
	APPOSITIVE	+	NP_j is not an apposition to NP_i
Semantic	SEMCLASS	1	NP_i and NP_j are both persons (false = 0, true = 1, unknown = 2)
	ALIAS	–	NP_j is not an alias of NP_i
Lexical	STR_MATCH	–	NP_i and NP_j do not match

(NP_{a2}, NP_{a3}), (NP_{a3}, NP_{a4}), where the first noun phrase is always considered to be the antecedent and the second one the anaphor.

- To create the negative examples, the training procedure considers the same adjacent pairs antecedent, anaphor (NP_i, NP_j), and the noun phrases intervening between them $NP_{i+1}, NP_{i+2}, ..., NP_{j-1}$. For each positive pair (NP_i, NP_j), the training procedure generates negative pairs, which consist of one intervening NP and the anaphor NP_j: (NP_{i+1}, NP_j), (NP_{i+2}, NP_j), ..., and (NP_{j-1}, NP_j). The intervening noun phrases can either be part of another coreference chain or not.

Extracting the Coreference Chains. Once the classifier has been trained, it is applied to the noun phrases in a text to identify the coreference chains. The engine first extracts all the noun phrases in the text. It traverses the text from left to right from the second noun phrase. For each current NP_j, the algorithm considers every NP_i before it as a possible antecedent. It then proceeds from right to left and submits the pairs (NP_i, NP_j) to the classifier until it reaches an antecedent or the start of the text.

The algorithm is as follows:

1. Let $NP_1, NP_2, ..., NP_N$ be the noun phrases.
2. For $j = 2$ to N.
   a) For each NP_j, generate all the pairs (NP_i, NP_j), where $i < j$.
   b) Compute the feature vector of each pair (NP_i, NP_j).
   c) For $i = j - 1$ to 1, submit the pair (NP_i, NP_j) to the classifier until a positive pair is found or the beginning of the text is reached.
   d) If a noun phrase returns positive, NP_j has an antecedent and is part of the corresponding coreference chain.

14.7.5 More Complex Phenomena: Ellipses

An **ellipsis** is the absence of certain words or phrases normally necessary to build a sentence. Ellipses occur frequently in the discourse to avoid tedious repetitions. For instance, the sequence:

I want to have information on caterpillars. And also on hedgehogs.

features a second sentence whose subject and verb are missing. The complete sentence would be:

I want to have information on hedgehogs.

Here the speaker avoids saying twice the same thing. Ellipses also occur with clauses linked by conjunctions where a phrase or a word is omitted as in the sentence:

I saw a hedgehog walking on the grass and another sleeping,

Everyone, however, can understand that it substitutes the complete sentence:

I saw a hedgehog walking on the grass and I saw another hedgehog sleeping.

Ellipses are rather difficult to handle. In many cases, however, maintaining a history of all the discourse's referents can help retrieve an omitted referent or verb. A referent missing in a sentence can be searched backward in the history and replaced with an adequate previous one.

14.8 Discourse and Rhetoric

Rhetoric also offers means to explain discourse coherence. Although rhetoric has a very long tradition dating from ancient times, modern linguists have tended to neglect it, favoring other models or methods. Recently however, interest has again increased. Modern rhetorical studies offer new grounds to describe and explain argumentation. Modeling argumentation complements parts of human discourse that cannot only be explained in terms of formal logic or arbitrary beliefs. The *Traité de l'argumentation* by Perelman and Olbrechts-Tyteca (1976) is a prominent example of this trend.

On a parallel road, computational linguistics also rediscovered rhetoric. Most of the renaissance in this community is due to influential papers on rhetorical structure theory (RST) by Mann and Thompson (1987, 1988). This section provides a short introduction to ancient rhetoric and then describes RST.

14.8.1 Ancient Rhetoric: An Outline

Rhetoric was studied in most schools of ancient Greece and Rome, and in universities in the Middle Ages. Rhetoric was then viewed as a way to define how best to compose ideas in a discourse, to make it attractive, to convince and persuade an audience. It was considered as a kind of discourse strategy defining the optimal arrangement or planning of arguments according to the type of audience, of speech case, etc.

According to the ancient rhetoric school, the production of discourse had to be organized around five canons – invention, arrangement, style, memory, and delivery.

- Invention (*inventio*) is related to the ideas or facts contained in a discourse: what to say or to write are the first things to identify to make a discourse exist. According to ancient Greeks, a key to invention was to answer the right questions in the right order.
- Arrangement (*dispositio*) is the discourse construction for which general patterns have been proposed. According to Cicero, a discourse should feature an introduction (*exordium*), a narrative (*narratio*) where the orator sets forth the issues of the problem, a proposition (*propositio*) where s/he states her/his arguments for the case, a refutation (*refutatio*), where s/he gives counterarguments, a confirmation (*confirmatio*) where s/he reinforces her/his arguments, and finally a conclusion (*peroratio*).
- Style (*elocutio*) concerns the transcription and the edition of ideas into words and sentences. Rules of style suggested to privilege clarity – use plain words and conform to a correct grammar. This was a guarantee to be understood by everybody. Style was also a literary art where efficiency mattered most. It was divided into three categories whose goals were to emote (*movere*), to explain (*docere*), or to please (*delectare*) according to the desired effect on the audience.
- Memory (*memoria*) was essential that the orator should retain what s/he had to say. The Ancients advised orators to sleep well, to be in good shape, to exercise memory by learning by heart, and to use images.
- Delivery (*actio*) concerned the uttering of the discourse: voice, tone, speed, and gestures.

Although current discourse strategies may not be the same as those designed and contrived in Athens or Sicily 2500 years ago, if elucidated they give keys to a discourse structure. Later, the historical definition of rhetoric has been sometimes superseded by a pejorative sense meaning empty political speeches or ranting.

14.8.2 Rhetorical Structure Theory

Rhetorical structure theory (RST) is a theory of text organization in terms of relations that occur in a text. As for Grosz and Sidner, RST identifies a hierarchical tree structure in texts. A text consists of nonoverlapping segments that define the tree nodes.

These segments are termed by Mann and Thompson as "text spans." They correspond typically to one or more clauses. Text spans may be terminal or nonterminal nodes that are linked in the tree by relations.

Rhetorical relations are sorts of dependencies between two text spans termed the **nucleus** and the **satellite**, where the satellite brings some sort of support or explanation to the nucleus, which is the prominent issue. To illustrate this concept, let us take the example of the *Justify* relation from Mann and Thompson (1987, pp. 9–11): "A justify satellite is intended to increase the reader's readiness to accept the writer's right to present the nuclear material." In the short text:

1. *The next music day is scheduled for July 21 (Saturday), noon–midnight*
2. *I'll post more details later,*
3. *but this is good time to reserve the place on your calendar.*

segments 2 and 3 justify segment 1, and they can be represented graphically by Fig. 14.4.

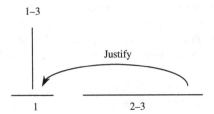

Fig. 14.4. The Justify relation.

Segments can then be further subdivided using other relations, in the example a *Concession* (Fig. 14.5).

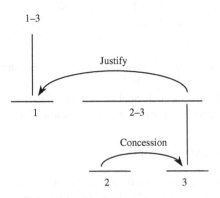

Fig. 14.5. More relations: Concession.

Relations are easy to represent in Prolog with facts
`rhetorical_relation(relation_type, satellite, nucleus)`:

```
rhetorical_relation(justify, 3, 1).
rhetorical_relation(concession, 2, 3).
```

Another example is given by this funny text about dioxin (Mann and Thompson, 1987, pp. 13–15):

1. *Concern that this material is harmful to health or the environment may be misplaced.*
2. *Although it is toxic to certain animals,*
3. *evidence is lacking that it has any serious long-term effect on human beings.*

which can be analyzed with relations *Elaboration* and *Concession* in Fig. 14.6.

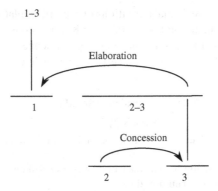

Fig. 14.6. Elaboration and Concession.

These relations are equivalent to the Prolog facts:

```
rhetorical_relation(elaboration, 3, 1).
rhetorical_relation(concession, 2, 3).
```

14.8.3 Types of Relations

The total number and the type of rhetorical relation vary much among authors and even among papers written by their creators. Their number ranges from a dozen to several hundreds. As we saw in the previous section, most relations link a nucleus and a satellite. Figure 14.7 shows a slightly simplified list of them from Mann and Thompson (1987). In some instances, relations also link two nuclei. They are shown in Fig. 14.8.

Circumstance Evidence   Otherwise
Solutionhood Justify   Interpretation
Elaboration Cause   Evaluation
Background   Antithesis Restatement
Enablement   Concession Summary
Motivation   Condition

Fig. 14.7. RST rhetorical relations linking a nucleus and a satellite.

Sequence Joint Contrast

Fig. 14.8. Relations linking two nuclei.

14.8.4 Implementing Rhetorical Structure Theory

Mann and Thompson gave formal definitions of rhetorical relations using constraints on the satellite, the nucleus, and both. Table 14.8 shows constraints holding for *evidence*. In addition, a rhetorical relation entails consequences that are described by an effect: here, with *evidence*, the reader's belief of the nucleus is increased.

Table 14.8. The EVIDENCE relation. After Mann and Thompson (1987).

Relation name	EVIDENCE
Constraints on the nucleus N	The reader R might not believe to a degree satisfactory to the writer W
Constraints on the satellite S	The reader believes S or will find it credible
Constraints on the $N + S$ **combination**	
	R's comprehending S increases R's belief of N
The effect	R's belief of N is increased
Locus of the effect	N

Such constraints are difficult – if not impossible – to implement in a computer as is because they involve knowing the thoughts of the reader and the writer. However, rhetorical relations are often indicated by a handful of specific cue words or phrases. Mann and Thompson observe that a concession is often introduced by *although*, as in the dioxin text from the previous section, or *but*. A common workaround to detect a relation is then to analyze the surface structure made of these cue phrases. They may indicate the discourse transitions, segment boundaries, and the type of relations. Many cue phrases are conjunctions, adverbial forms, or syntactic patterns (Table 14.9).

Mann and Thompson also observed that the nucleus and the satellite had typical topological orders (Table 14.10).

Recently, comprehensive works have itemized cue phrases and other constraints enabling the rhetorical parsing of a text. Marcu (1997) and Corston-Oliver (1998)

Table 14.9. Examples of cue phrases and forms.

Cues	English	French	German
Conjunctions	Because, in fact, but, and	Car, en effet, puisque, et, mais	denn, und, aber,
Adverbial forms	In addition, for example	De plus, en particulier, particulièrement, par exemple	dazu, besonders, zum Beispiel
Syntactic forms	Past participles: given	Present participles: étant donné	

Table 14.10. Typical orders for some relations.

Satellite before nucleus	
Antithesis	Condition
Background	Justify
Concession	Solutionhood

Nucleus before satellite	
Elaboration	Evidence
Enablement	Statement

are notable examples of this trend. As an example, Corston-Oliver (1998) recognizes the *Elaboration* relation with a set of necessary criteria that must hold between two clauses, clause 1 being the nucleus and clause 2 the satellite:

1. Clause 1 precedes clause 2.
2. Clause 1 is not subordinate to clause 2.
3. Clause 2 is not subordinate to clause 1.

and cues that are ranked according to an heuristic score (Table 14.11).

Corston-Oliver (1998) applied these cues to analyze the Microsoft *Encarta* encyclopedia. With the excerpt:

1. *A stem is a portion of a plant.*
2. *Subterranean stems include the rhizomes of the iris and the runners of the strawberry;*
3. *The potato is a portion of an underground stem.*

using cue H41, he could obtain the rhetoric structure shown in Fig. 14.9.

14.9 Events and Time

In most discourses, actions, events, or situations have a **temporal** context. This context is crucial to the correct representation of actions. It involves time, which is reflected by time expressions, such as adverbs or adjuncts, *now, tomorrow, in 5 minutes,* and verb **tenses**, such as present, past, or future.

Table 14.11. Cues to recognize the *Elaboration* relation. After Corston-Oliver (1998, p. 129).

Cue	Score	Cue Name
Clause 1 is the main clause of a sentence (sentence i), and clause 2 is the main clause of a sentence (sentence j), and sentence i immediately precedes sentence j, and (a) clause 2 contains an elaboration conjunction (*also, for example*), or (b) clause 2 is in a coordinate structure whose parent contains an elaboration conjunction.	35	H24
Cue H24 applies, and clause 1 is the main clause of the first sentence in the excerpt.	15	H26
Clause 2 contains a predicate nominal whose head is in the set {*portion, component, member, type, kind, example, instance*}, or clause 2 contains a predicate whose head verb is in the set {*include, consist*}	35	H41
Clauses 1 and 2 are not coordinated, and (a) clauses 1 and 2 exhibit subject continuity, or (b) clause 1 is passive and the head of the direct object of clause 1 and the head of the direct object of clause 2 have the same base form, or (c) clause 2 contains an elaboration conjunction.	10	H25
Cue H25 applies, and clause 2 contains a habitual adverb (*sometimes, usually, . . .*).	17	H25a
Cue H25 applies, and the syntactic subject of clause 2 is the pronoun *some* or contains the modifier *some*.	10	H38

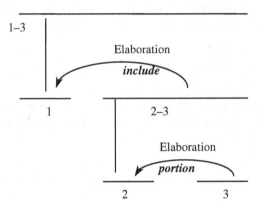

Fig. 14.9. Rhetorical structures.

Understanding temporal relations between events is difficult and may depend on the language. For instance, there is no exact correspondence for past and present tenses between French and English. In the next section, we will provide hints on theories about temporal modeling.

14.9.1 Events

Research on the representation of time, events, and temporal relations dates back to the beginning of logic. It resulted in an impressive number of formulations and models. A possible approach is to **reify** events, that is to turn them into objects, to quantify them existentially, and to connect them to other objects using predicates based on action verbs and their modifiers (Davidson 1966). The sentence *John saw Mary in London on Tuesday* is then translated into the logical form:

$$\exists \varepsilon [saw(\varepsilon, John, Mary) \wedge place(\varepsilon, London) \wedge time(\varepsilon, Tuesday),$$

where ε represents the event.

To represent the temporal context of an action sequence we can use a set of predicates. Consider:

Spring is back. Hedgehogs are waking up. Toads are still sleeping.

There are obviously three actions or events described here. These events are located in time around a reference point defined by the return of spring. From this point, the hedgehogs' waking up process extends onwards while the toads' sleeping process overlaps it (Fig. 14.10). Events have a different duration: the first sentence merely describes a single time point whereas the two last processes are defined inside intervals.

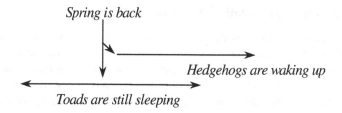

Fig. 14.10. Events.

Let us denote e1, e2, and e3 the events in Fig. 14.10, and let us portray them in Prolog. In addition, let us use the agent semantic role that we borrow from the case grammars. We have a first representation:

```
event(e1).
is_back(e1).
agent(e1, spring).
```

```
. . .
event(e2).
waking_up(e2).
agent(e2, hedgehogs).
. . .

event(e3)
sleeping(e3).
agent(e3, toads).
```

14.9.2 Event Types

Events are closely related to sentence's main verbs, and different classifications have been proposed to associate a verb with a type of event. Vendler (1967) for English, Gosselin (1996) for French, and others came to a consensus to divide verbs into four categories, denoting:

- A state – a permanent property or a usual situation (e.g., *be, have, know, think*).
- An achievement – a state change, a transition, occurring at single moment (e.g., *find, realize, learn*).
- An activity – a continuous process taking place over a period of time (e.g., *work, read, sleep*). In English, activities often use the present perfect, *-ing*.
- An accomplishment – an activity with a definite endpoint completed by a result (e.g., *write a book, eat an apple*).

Some authors have associated events to verbs only. It is safer, however, to take verb phrases – predicates – and even subjects into account to link events to Vendler's categories (Table 14.12). Compare *The water ran*, which is an activity in the past, and *The hurdlers ran* (in a competition), which depicts an achievement.

14.9.3 Temporal Representation of Events

Let us now try to represent processes in a temporal chronology. In the example in Fig. 14.10, the only process that has a definite location is e1. It is associated to a calendar period: *spring*. Other processes are then relative to it. As for these sentences, in most discourses it is impossible to map all processes onto an absolute time. Instead, we will represent them using relative, and sometimes partial, temporal relations.

Simplifying things, we will suppose that time has a linear ordering and that each event is located in time: it has a certain beginning and a certain end. This would not be true if we had considered conditional statements. Temporal relations associate processes to time intervals and set links, constraints between them. We will adopt here a model proposed by Allen (1983, 1984), whose 13 relations are listed in Table 14.13.

Using Allen's representation, relations before(e1, e2), after(e2, e1), and contains(e3, e1) depict temporal constraints on events e1, e2, and e3 in Sect. 14.9.1. Temporal relations result in constraints between all processes that enable a total or partial ordering of them.

Table 14.12. Vendler's verb categories.

	English	French	German
State	*The cat is sick*	*Le chat est malade*	*Die Katze ist krank*
	I like chocolate	*J'aime le chocolat*	*Ich esse Schokolade gern*
Activity	*She works for a company*	*Elle travaille pour une entreprise*	*Sie arbeitet für eine Firma*
	He is writing a book	*Il écrit un livre*	*Er schreibt ein Buch*
Accomplishment	*He wrote a book*	*il a écrit un livre*	*Er hat ein Buch geschrieben*
	The dormouse ate the pears	*Le loir a mangé les poires*	*Die Haselmaus hat die Birnen gegessen*
Achievement	*The sun set*	*Le soleil s'est couché*	*Die Sonne ist untergegangen*
	I realized I was wrong	*Je me suis rendu compte que j'avais tort*	*Ich habe eingesehen, ich nicht recht hatte*

Table 14.13. Allen's temporal relations.

#	Relations	Graphical representations
1. 2.	before(a, b) after(b, a)	
3. 4.	meets(a, b) met_by(b, a)	
5. 6.	overlaps(a, b) overlapped_by(b, a)	
7. 8.	starts(a, b) started_by(b, a)	
9. 10.	during(b, a) contains(a, b)	
11. 12.	finishes(b, a) finished_by(a, b)	
13.	equals(a, b)	

14.9.4 Events and Tenses

As we saw, event modeling results in time intervals and in relations between them. From event examples in Fig. 14.10, we can define two new temporal facts:

- instantaneous events, which are punctual and marking a transition
- situations, which have a duration – true over an interval

Relations as well as events or situations are not accessible directly. As for rhetorical relations or segment boundaries, we need cues or markers to track them. In the example above, we have mapped events onto verbs. This hints at detection and description methods. Although there is no definitive solution on how to detect events, many techniques rely on verbs and verb phrases to act as markers.

A first cue to create and locate an event is the verb tense. A sentence sequence defines a linear sequence of enunciation events. A basic distinction is between the moment of the enunciation and the time of the event (or situation). Figure 14.11 represents a kind of ideal time.

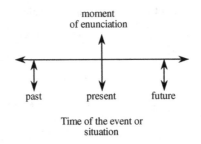

Fig. 14.11. Ideal time: past, present, and future.

The sentence

Ernest the hedgehog ate a caterpillar

creates two events; one corresponds to the processes described the sentence, e1, and the other, e2, to the time of speech. Both events are linked by the relation before(e1, e2). We could have refined the model with a beginning e1b and an end e1e of *Ernest*'s dinner. New relations would be:

```
before(e1b, e1e).
before(e1b, e2).
before(e1e, e2).
```

Using a verb classification and tenses helps determine the events location or situation boundaries. We may also rely on time adverbs and time adjuncts such as *for five minutes*, *tomorrow*, etc.

The 'ideal' representation, however, is not sufficient to describe many narrative phenomena where the writer/reader viewpoint is moved relatively to temporal events.

Reichenbach (1947) elaborated a more complex representation to take this viewpoint into account. Basically, verb tenses are mapped onto a triplet representing on a linear scale the point of the event or situation denoted E, the point of speech denoted S, and a point of reference denoted R. The reference corresponds to a sort of writer/reader viewpoint.

Let us first consider the time of speech and the event. It is clear to the reader that an event described by basic tenses, past, present, and future, is respectively before, coinciding, and after the point of speech (Fig. 14.12).

Fig. 14.12. Ideal tenses.

Reichenbach's tense model introduces the third point to position events relatively in the past or in the future. Consider the past sentence

Hedgehogs had already woken up when the sun set.

Two events are described, the hedgehogs' waking up, ewu, and the sunset, ess. Among the two events, the speaker viewpoint is focused by the clause *Hedgehogs had already woken up*: then, the action takes place. This point where the speaker moves to relate the story is the point of reference of the narrative, and the event is before it (Fig. 14.13). The point of reference of the first process enables us to locate the second one relatively to it and to order them in a sequence.

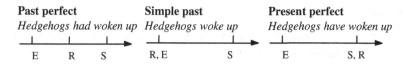

Fig. 14.13. Event, reference, and speech for some English tenses.

Some tenses describe a time stretch of the event, as for the French *imparfait* compared to the *passé composé* (Fig. 14.14), or continuous tenses of English (Fig. 14.15).

14.10 TimeML, an Annotation Scheme for Time and Events

Several schemes have been proposed to annotate temporal information in texts. Many of them were incompatible or incomplete, and in an effort to reconcile and unify the field, Ingria and Pustejovsky (2004) introduced the XML-based Time Markup Language (TimeML). TimeML is a specification language whose goal is to capture most

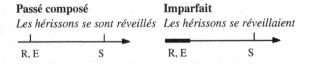

Fig. 14.14. French imparfait and passé composé.

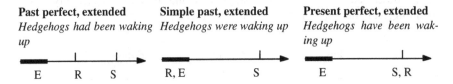

Fig. 14.15. Some English tenses involving a stretch of time.

aspects of temporal relations between events in discourses. It is based on Allen's (1984) relations and inspired by Vendler's (1967) classification of verbs.

TimeML defines the XML elements TIMEX3 to annotate time expressions (*at four o'clock*), EVENT to annotate the events (*he slept*), and "signals". The SIGNAL tag marks words or phrases indicating a temporal relation. It includes function words such as *later* and *not* (*he did not sleep*). TimeML also features elements to connect entities using different types of links, most notably temporal links, TLINKs, that describe the temporal relation holding between events or between an event and a time.

TimeML elements have attributes. For instance, events have a tense, an aspect, and a class. The seven possible classes denote the type of event, whether it is a STATE, an instantaneous event (OCCURRENCE), etc.

The sentence

All 75 people on board the Aeroflot Airbus died when it ploughed into a Siberian mountain in March 1994

is marked up as follows (Ingria and Pustejovsky 2004):

```
All 75 people
<EVENT eid="e7" class="STATE">on board</EVENT>
<MAKEINSTANCE eiid="ei7" eventID="e7" tense="NONE"
aspect="NONE"/>
<TLINK eventInstanceID="ei7" relatedToEvent="ei5"
relType="INCLUDES"/>
the Aeroflot Airbus
<EVENT eid="e5" class="OCCURRENCE" >died</EVENT>
<MAKEINSTANCE eiid="ei5" eventID="e5" tense="PAST"
aspect="NONE"/>
<TLINK eventInstanceID="ei5" signalID="s2"
```

```
relatedToEvent="ei6" relType="IAFTER"/>
<SIGNAL sid="s2">when</SIGNAL>
it
<EVENT eid="e6"
class="OCCURRENCE">ploughed</EVENT>
<MAKEINSTANCE eiid="ei6" eventID="e6" tense="PAST"
aspect="NONE"/>
<TLINK eventInstanceID="ei6" signalID="s3"
relatedToTime="t2" relType="IS_INCLUDED"/>
<TLINK eventInstanceID="ei6" relatedToEvent="ei4"
relType="IDENTITY"/>
into a Siberian mountain
<SIGNAL sid="s3">in</SIGNAL>
<TIMEX3 tid="t2" type="DATE" value="1994-04">March
1994</TIMEX3>.
```

In the example, three events e5, *died*, e6, *ploughed*, and e7, *on board*, are annotated and instantiated using the MAKEINSTANCE tag. The text contains one time expression, *March 1994*, which is annotated using TIMEX3. The events and the time expressions are connected by two temporal links, TLINK. The first link specifies that the passengers died after the plane ploughed, using the relatedToEvent attribute. The second link specifies that event ploughed is included in March 1994. A third and last TLINK refers to an event, e4, mentioned in a previous, noncited sentence. The temporal signals *when* and *in* can also be relevant, and they are tagged with a SIGNAL tag.

14.11 Further Reading

Schiffrin (1994) and Coulthard (1985) give general introductions to discourse. Ducrot and Schaeffer (1995) and Simone (1998) provide shorter and very readable accounts. Tesnière (1966) is an outstanding description of anaphora (Chap. 42) and anaphors (Chap. 43). Kamp and Reyle (1993) provide a thorough logical model of discourse that they called the discourse representation theory – DRT. Although complex and difficult to implement, it is frequently cited.

The MUCs spurred very pragmatic research on discourse, notably on coreference resolution. They produced a coreference annotation scheme that enabled researchers to evaluate competing algorithms and that became a standard. Research culminated with the design of machine learning strategies. Soon et al. (2001) were first to develop a system offering a performance matching systems with manually written rules. Ng and Cardie (2002) further improved this strategy by extending the parameters from 12 to 38 and produced results better than all other systems.

Corpus Processing for Lexical Acquisition by Boguraev and Pustejovsky (1996) covers many technical aspects of discourse processing. It includes extraction of proper nouns, which has recently developed into an active subject of research.

Introductions to rhetoric include books by Corbett and Connors (1999), Reboul (1994), and Perelman and Olbrechts-Tyteca (1976).

Time processing in texts is still a developing subject. Reichenbach (1947) described a model for all the English tenses. Starting from this foundational work, Gosselin (1996) provided an account for French that he complemented with a process duration. He described rules and an implementation valid for French verbs. Ter Meulen (1995) describes another viewpoint on time modeling in English, while Gagnon and Lapalme (1996) produce an implementation of time processing for French based on the DRT. Johansson et al. (2005) describe how semantic role labeling and time processing can be used to generate animated 3D scenes from written texts.

Exercises

14.1. Choose a newspaper text of about ten lines. Underline the references and link coreferences.

14.2. Write DCG rules to detect noun groups and pronouns of Exercise 14.1 and collect the discourse entities in a Prolog list.

14.3. Write a grammar recognizing names (proper nouns) in English, French, or German. You will consider that a name consists of a title followed by a surname whose first letter is capitalized.

14.4. Choose a newspaper text of about ten lines. Collect noun groups and pronouns in a list with a noun group detector. Write a coreference solver in Prolog to associate each pronoun to all preceding noun groups.

14.5. Using the program written for Exercise 14.4, write a first predicate that retains the first preceding noun group – first potential antecedent – and a second predicate that retains the two first noun groups.

14.6. Implement the Kameyama algorithm of Sect. 14.7.2 in Prolog.

14.7. Select a newspaper article and underline elliptical sentences or phrases.

14.8. Using the result of Exercise 14.7, describe rules that would enable you to resolve ellipses.

14.9. Select one page from a technical text and annotate clauses with rhetorical relations listed in Table 14.7.

14.10. Write rules using the model of Table 14.10 to recognize the EVIDENCE rhetorical relation.

14.11. Describe verb tenses in languages you know in terms of point of the event, of speech, and of reference, as in Sect. 14.9.4.

15

Dialogue

15.1 Introduction

While discourse materialized in texts delivers static information, dialogue is dynamic and consists of two interacting discourses. Once written, a discourse content is unalterable and will remain as it is for its future readers. On the contrary, a dialogue enables exchange information flows, to complement and to merge them in a composition, which is not known in advance. Both dialoguing parties provide feedback, influence, or modify the final content along with the course of the conversation.

In this chapter, we will envision dialogue within the framework of an interface between a system and a user. Parties have information to transmit or to request using natural language. The dialogue purpose will be to make sure that the request is complete or the information has been well captured or delivered. Naturally, as for other discourse applications, a dialogue module is only a part of the whole system using language processing techniques we have described before.

15.2 Why a Dialogue?

The first role of a dialogue module as an interface is to manage the communication and to coordinate the turn-taking between the user and the system. It is also a kind of integration shell that calls other language processing components to analyze user utterances or to generate system answers. In addition, interaction and dialogue techniques can help linguistic analysis be more flexible and recover from failures.

We saw that coreferences are sometimes difficult to resolve. They provide an example of interaction usefulness. Instead of having an interactive system conjecture about an ambiguous pronoun, it is often safer for it to ask the user himself/herself to resolve the ambiguity. Two strategies are then possible: the system can infer a missing reference and ask the user for a confirmation. Or, in case of a more difficult ambiguity, it can ask the user to reformulate completely his/her sentence.

To summarize, dialogue systems can help manage a user's discourse to:

- complement information when pieces are missing to understand a sentence or to carry out a command
- clarify some ambiguous words or constructions
- confirm information or intention to manage errors when a certain failure rate is unavoidable, e.g., with speech recognition operating on naturally flowing speech

15.3 Simple Dialogue Systems

Many simple dialogue systems in commercial operation aim to provide information through telephones. Such **speech servers** receive calls from users requesting information in a specific domain and answer interactively to questions. Although many servers still interact with a user using touch-tone telephones, more and more they feature speech recognition and speech synthesis modules.

Speech recognition conditions are difficult with telephone servers since they have usually to handle a poor acoustic environment. It naturally comes at a price: recognition is prone to errors and the number of active words – words that the system can recognize at a given time – cannot be much more than a hundred on many systems. Speech recognition is then a bottleneck that limits the whole system performance.

For reasons of robustness and cost, operating components of real-world dialogue applications rarely correspond to the integration of classical linguistic layers: morphology, syntax, and semantics. The recognition itself does not attempt to produce the full stream of words but generally uses word spotting techniques. Word spotting enables a word to be recognized within a short fragment of surrounding speech or noise. So a word will be correctly identified, even if you say *hmm* before or after it.

Because of word spotting, spoken systems do not stack a complete parsing after speech recognition. They focus on interesting words, meaningful according to context, and link them into information frames. These frames miss some words, but the important issue here is not to miss the overall meaning and to keep dialoguing with the user in real time and at a reasonable computational cost. Typical examples of such dialogue systems, elementary from a linguistic viewpoint, are based on automata.

15.3.1 Dialogue Systems Based on Automata

Dialogue systems based on finite-state automata have transitions triggered by a limited number of isolated words (Fig. 15.1). At each state, the automaton synthesizes a closed question: it proposes a finite choice of options. If the word recognition device has not understood a word, it loops onto the same state, asking for the user to repeat his/her command. If it corresponds to a legal transition, the automaton moves the user to another state.

As we said, speech recognition is not foolproof. The system avoids possible errors through a confirmation message while proceeding to a next state. On the leftmost edge of Fig. 15.1

We are happy to give you information on loans?

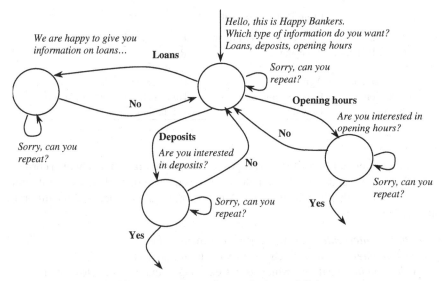

We are happy to give you
information on loans...   **Loans**

Hello, this is Happy Bankers.
Which type of information do you want?
Loans, deposits, opening hours

Sorry, can you
repeat?

No

Opening hours

Sorry, can you
repeat?

Deposits

Are you interested
in deposits?   **No**

Are you interested in
opening hours?

No

Sorry, can you
repeat?

Sorry, can you
repeat?   **Yes**

Yes

Fig. 15.1. An automaton for word-triggered dialogues.

the system uses an implicit confirmation. The user can accept the ongoing transition either explicitly by saying *yes*, or implicitly by saying nothing. It can also contradict – only if necessary – and reject the transition by saying, for instance, *no* or

No, I wanted to know about my account balance.

In this case, the user will regress to the previous state. Other edges as in the middle and rightmost transitions:

Are you interested in deposits?

correspond to explicit confirmations. They require a mandatory answer – *yes* or *no* – from the user.

As a general design rule, confirmations should not be too numerous to be acceptable by users because they tend to be tedious if overused. The first strategy is certainly preferable.

15.3.2 Dialogue Modeling

The basic structure of dialogue automata is far from providing a natural interaction. However, it implements some fundamental characteristics shared by all dialogue systems. Interactions between the user and the system correspond to pairs: the system's turns and the user's turns. These pairs, which may be nested, have been extensively studied. Levinson (1983) proposed a classification of them according to the nature of their first member. Table 15.1 shows an excerpt of Levinson's classification.

Levinson's model, however, is not sufficient to take possible errors and confirmation into account. Moeschler and others at the University of Geneva (Moeschler

Table 15.1. Classification of dialogue pairs.

First member	Preferred second member	Dispreferred second member
Offer, Invitation	Acceptance	Refusal
Request	Compliance	Refusal
Assessment	Agreement	Disagreement
Question	Expected answer	Unexpected answer, no answer
Blame	Denial	Admission

1989; Moeschler and Reboul 1994) proposed a more elaborate model, which corrects some flaws. The model divides a dialogue as a sequence of exchanges, but it complements pairs with a final assessment. An exchange is a sequence of three different interventions:

- *initiative interventions*, which open an exchange (I)
- *reaction interventions*, which are answers to initiatives (R)
- *evaluation interventions*, which assess exchanges and possibly close them (E)

In addition, exchanges may be nested and hence have a recursive structure.

Table 15.2 shows a first exchange pictured by the leftmost edge of the automaton in Fig. 15.1. It is annotated with intervention tags: I, R, and E. The two first turns are an initiative and a reaction. The last turn is an implicit acknowledgment showing that the system has understood the user command.

Table 15.2. An exchange.

Utt. no.	Turns	Utterances	Tags
1	S:	*Which type of information do you want: loans, deposits, opening hours?*	I_1
2	U:	*Loans*	R_1
3	S:	*We are happy to give you information on loans*	E_1

Along with the deposit question (middle edge), Fig. 15.1 shows a nested interaction in the evaluation. There are first an initiative and a reaction. The third turn is an evaluation, which is a recursive exchange, consisting of an initiative and a reaction (Table 15.3).

15.4 Speech Acts: A Theory of Language Interaction

Turns triggered by isolated words and phrases are a rudimentary dialogue model. Ideally, systems should handle more complicated phrases or sentences. In addition, they should take a more elaborate interaction structure into account.

Table 15.3. An exchange with a nested evaluation exchange.

Utt. no.	Turns	Utterances	Tags
1	S:	*Which type of information do you want: loans, deposits, opening hours?*	I_1
2	U:	*Deposits*	R_1
3	S:	*Are you interested in deposits?*	$\left.\begin{array}{c}I_1^2 \\ R_1^2\end{array}\right] E_1$
4	U:	*Yes*	

Language is basically a means for people to act one upon the other. However, linguistic theories as we have considered them until now do not cover this interaction aspect. Some authors have tried to remedy it and to investigate other approaches. In contrast to formal or lexical semantics, which are based on logic, they have attempted to give language a more "performative" foundation. Such a framework has interested modern linguists such as Bühler (1934, 1982) and later language philosophers such as Austin (1962) and Searle (1969).

Bühler postulated that language had three semantic functions according to his organon model:

- a representation (*Darstellung*) of objects and the state of affairs that is being described
- an expression (*Ausdruck*) materializing the psychological state of mind of the speaker – the sender of the message
- an appeal (*Appell*) corresponding to an effect on the hearer – the receiver of the message

Although Bühler admitted the dominance of the representation function of language acknowledged before him, he stressed the psychological aspects of spoken communication describing participants as "psychophysical" systems. He was the first modern linguist to introduce that speech involved a sequence of acts that he named *Sprechakt* enabling the hearer to recognize the speaker's state of mind or internal planning.

Austin came to a similar conclusion and considered also speech as a sequence of acts. For each of these acts, he distinguished what pertained to the classical side of linguistics and resorted to morphology, syntax, and semantics from pragmatics and the theory of action. He referred to the former as locutions and the latter as illocutions. From these considerations on, Austin modeled the act of saying something, with three components representing three different aspects of communication:

- *locutionary* – i.e., an act of saying something, corresponding to a phonetic utterance, a syntactic structure, and a formal semantics content
- *illocutionary* – i.e., a conversational act, which can be, for instance, to inform, to suggest, to answer, to ask
- *perlocutionary* – i.e., the effects of these acts, which can be to frighten, to worry, to convince, to persuade

Classical grammar recognizes certain links between locutionary and illocutionary content. Some types of syntactical forms are frequently associated with speech acts (Table 15.4).

Table 15.4. Syntactical forms and speech acts.

Classical speech acts	Syntactic forms
Assertions, statements	Affirmatives or declaratives
Orders, commands	Imperatives
Questions	Interrogatives

However, the association is not systematic. Speech acts are not always related to a logical – or propositional – content that could have been derived from the formal structure of sentences. Rhetorical questions such as *Can you open the door?* are in fact orders, and imperatives such as *Have a good day!* are greetings or wishes. In addition, a syntactical classification is too coarse to reflect the many needs of interaction analysis.

To cope with different aspects of communication, many authors have proposed a classification of illocutionary acts. We retain Searle's initial classes, which are best known because they probably capture essential interaction paradigms:

- **assertives**, such as stating, asserting, denying, informing.
- **directives**, such as requesting, asking, urging, commanding, ordering.
- **commissives**, such as promising, committing, threatening, consenting, refusing, offering.
- **declaratives**, such as declaring war, resigning, appointing, confirming, excommunicating. Declarative speech acts change states of affairs.
- **expressives**, which are related to emotions or feelings such as apologizing, thanking, protesting, boasting, complimenting.

Searle (1969) refines the speech act model by proposing conditions to complete an act successfully. Conditions are a set of conversational postulates that should be shared by speakers and hearers. These conditions are divided into a propositional content, a preparatory condition, a sincerity, and an essential condition. Tables 15.5 and 15.6 reproduce two success conditions to speech acts (Searle 1969, pp. 66–67).

The work of Austin and Searle has been very popular in the computational linguistics community and, far beyond it, in language in certain fields of philosophy and psychology. Although some people consider them as inventors, their findings are not completely new. Gorgias, a Greek rhetorician who lived 2500 years before them, wrote:

The effect of speech upon the condition of the soul is comparable to the power of drugs over the nature of bodies. For just as different drugs dispel different secretions from the body, and some bring an end to disease and others to life, so also in the case of speeches, some distress, others delight,

Table 15.5. Conditions to *request, order, command.* After Searle (1969).

Conditions	Values
Propositional content	Future act A of Hearer
Preparatory	
	1. Hearer is able to do A. Speaker believes Hearer is able to do A
	2. It is not obvious to both Speaker and Hearer that Hearer will do A in the normal course of events of his own accord
	3. (For *order* and *command*) Speaker must be in a position of authority over Hearer
Sincerity	Speaker wants Hearer to do A
Essential	Counts as an attempt to get Hearer to do A

Table 15.6. Conditions to *greeting.* After Searle (1969).

Conditions	Values
Propositional content	None
Preparatory	Speaker has just encountered (or has been introduced to, etc.) Hearer
Sincerity	None
Essential	Counts as courteous recognition of Hearer by Speaker

some cause fear, others make the hearers bold, and some drug and bewitch the soul with a kind of evil persuasion.

Encomium of Helen (Trans. RK Sprague)

15.5 Speech Acts and Human–Machine Dialogue

15.5.1 Speech Acts as a Tagging Model

Many language processing applications use the speech act theory as a kind of syntax to parse a discourse or a dialogue. Constituents are the discourse segments, and categories are illocution classes, termed broadly as speech acts or dialogue acts. As a result, a discourse is a sequence of segments annotated with conversation acts.

Authors may not follow the Searle's classification. Gazdar and Mellish (1989) provide a small set of "illocutionary acts," among which they quote: request, statement, suggestion, question. Using these acts, Gazdar and Mellish (1989) can label the dialogue in Table 15.7.

Acts such as challenge or concession may be more suited to analyzing a human conversation rather than a spoken human–machine interaction. In addition, applications may need different sorts of acts. Therefore, most sets of speech acts are designed for a specific dialogue system and are closely tied to it. Acts then serve as tags

Table 15.7. Illocutionary acts in a dialogue. After Gazdar and Mellish (1989, p. 385).

Turns	Utterances	Illocutionary acts
A	I really think the automobile needs servicing	Statement
B	But we had done it recently	Challenge
A	No, not for two years…	Challenge
		Interruption
A	Incidentally did you hear that gas prices are about to double?	Concession

to annotate discourse segments. Although disputable from a theoretical viewpoint, this interpretation of speech acts as tags is used as a model for scores of human–machine dialogue systems. We examine one of them in the next section.

15.5.2 Speech Acts Tags Used in the SUNDIAL Project

Bilange (1992) and Cozannet (1992) list a collection of speech acts that they used in the SUNDIAL project (Table 15.8). The acts are divided into initiatives, reactions, and evaluations following Moeschler's (1989) dialogue modeling. They are intended to enable a user to make a train ticket reservation by telephone.

Table 15.8. Speech acts used in SUNDIAL (slightly modified).

Acts	System/ User act	Descriptions
Initiatives		
request(P)	S	Open question or request for the value of P
yn_question(P, Val)	S	Is value of P Val? Answer should be *yes* or *no*
altern_question(P)	S	Alternative question: *Vanilla or strawberry?*
repeat(P)	S/U	Repetition request
inform(P)	S/U	Inform of P
recap(P)	S	Recapitulation of solved problems
Reactions		
answer(P, Val)	U	Gives a value Val on the request of P
select(P, Val)	U	Gives a value Val on an alternative question on P
accept(P, Val)	U	Accept or confirm the value Val of P
reject(P, Val)	U	Reject the value Val of P
Evaluations		
impl_valid(P, Val)	S	Implicit validation of confirmation of the value Val of P
correct(P, Val)	U	Gives a new value Val to P

Other projects such as VERBMOBIL use speech acts that are even more tied to the application (Jekat et al. 1995). VERBMOBIL provides a language support to an appointment system and its acts include INTRODUCE_NAME, ACCEPT_DATE, REJECT_DATE, SUGGEST_SUPPORT_DATE.

15.5.3 Dialogue Parsing

Dialogue applications, for example, speech servers, are aimed at answering relatively simple inquiries such as providing information on train timetables, airfares, or credit card authorizations. Their possibilities are generally well understood by users who call them and who do not expect to have a philosophical conversation with the system.

For this reason, in many applications it is possible to restrict a human–machine transaction to a dialogue opening, a negotiation where a user formulates a problem and solves it with the system, and a closing. Using Moeschler's model, we can describe each of these parts as a sequence of exchanges where utterances are divided into initiatives (I_i), reactions (I_r), and evaluations (I_e).

Table 15.9 shows a dialogue example from Andry (1992), and Table 15.10 shows the derived structure of the negotiation part. Utterances come either from the user (u) or the system (s) and consist of one or more speech acts. Utterance S2

London Paris which date?

is split into two acts. The first one (S1a)

London Paris

corresponds to an implicit confirmation that the system has understood the departure and arrival cities `Ie(s, [impl_valid])`. The second one (S2b)

which date

is an explicit question to the user `Ii(s, [request])`.

We can parse the exchange in Table 15.10 and get its structure using DCG rules. We first write a grammar to model the nonrecursive exchanges. We use variables to unify the speaker – user or system – and the type of act.

```
exchange(ex(i(X, SA1), r(Y, SA2), e(E))) -->
  initiative([X, SA1]),
  reaction([Y, SA2]),
  evaluation(E),
  {X \= Y}.
exchange(ex(i(X, SA1), r(Y, SA2))) -->
  initiative([X, SA1]),
  reaction([Y, SA2]),
  {X \= Y}.
exchange(ex(e(X, SA1), r(Y, SA2))) -->
  evaluation([X, SA1]),
  reaction([Y, SA2]),
  {X \= Y}.
```

We model initiatives, reactions, and evaluations as a sequence of speech acts:

Table 15.9. An example of dialogue with SUNDIAL.

Turns	Utterances
S1	*Bonjour puis-je vous aider?* 'Hello, can I help you?'
U1	*Je veux une réservation de Londres à Paris* 'I want a reservation from London to Paris'
S2	*Londres Paris à quelle date voulez-vous voyager?* 'London Paris which date?'
U2	*Je veux voyager le 20 juin* 'I want to travel June 20'
S3	*Le 20 juin à quelle heure?* 'June 20 which time?'
U3	*À 17 heures 15* '5.15 pm'
S4	*17 heures 15?* '5.15 pm?'
U4	*Oui* 'Yes'
S5	*Le vol BA-123 part à 17 heures 15 et arrive à Charles-de-Gaulle à 18 heures 39, est-ce que cela vous convient?* 'Flight BA-123 departure 5.15 pm and arrival 6.39 pm at Charles-de-Gaulle airport. Is that OK for you?'
U5	*Oui* 'Yes'
S6	*Quel est votre nom?* 'What is your name?'
U6	*Luc Martin*
S7	*Luc Martin une réservation pour Luc Martin sur le vol BA-123 arrivant à Charles-de-Gaulle à 18 heures 39* 'Luc Martin a reservation for Luc Martin on flight BA-123 arriving at Charles-de-Gaulle at 6.39 pm'
U7	*Oui* 'Yes'
S8	*Votre réservation a été confirmée au revoir* 'You reservation has been confirmed goodbye'
U8	*Au revoir* 'Goodbye'

```
initiative([Speaker, SpeechActs]) -->
  acts([Speaker, SpeechActs]).

reaction([Speaker, SpeechActs]) -->
  acts([Speaker, SpeechActs]).

evaluation([Speaker, SpeechActs]) -->
  acts([Speaker, SpeechActs]).
```

Table 15.10. Intervention structure.

Exch.	Interventions	Recursive interventions	Turns
	Ii(s, [request])		S1
E1	Ir(u, [answer])		U1
	Ie(S, [impl_valid])		S2a
	Ii(s, [request])		S2b
E2	Ir(u, [answer])		U2
	Ie(s, [impl_valid])		S3a
	Ii(s, [request])		S3b
E3	Ir(u, [answer])		U3
E3e		Ie(s, [impl_valid])	S4
		Ir(u, [accept])	U4
E4	Ii(s, [recap, yn_question])		S5a S5b
	Ir(u, [accept])		U5
	Ii(s, [request])		S6
E5	Ir(u, [answer])		U6
	Ie(s, [impl_valid])		S7a
	Ii(s, [recap])		S7b
E6	Ir(u, [accept])		U7
	Ie(s, [impl_valid])		S8

To take the recursive exchange into account, we have to add:

```
evaluation(S) --> exchange(S).
```

Finally, we define the dialogue as a sequence of exchanges:

```
dialogue([SE | RS]) -->
  exchange(SE), dialogue(RS).
dialogue([]) --> [].
```

Although these rules do not completely implement Moeschler's model, they give an insight to it.

15.5.4 Interpreting Speech Acts

To complete our dialogue survey, we outline ways to map utterances to speech acts, that is, in our example above, to annotate *What is you name?* as an open question. Some words, phrases, or syntactic features have a correspondence in terms of speech acts, as shown in Table 15.11. A first method is then to spot these specific patterns or cues. Cues enable us to delimit segments, to generate candidate speech acts, and to annotate the corresponding segment content. Once segments are identified, we can proceed to parse them and obtain their logical form.

However, identification is not straightforward because of ambiguity. Some words or syntactic features have more than one speech act candidate. The interrogative mode usually corresponds to questions, but not always as in *Can you do that for*

Table 15.11. Syntactic forms or templates linking utterances to speech acts.

Syntactic features	Candidate speech acts
Interrogative sentence	`yn_question, altern_question, request`
yes, right, all right, OK	`accept, impl_valid`
no, not at all	`reject`
Declarative sentence	`inform, impl_valid`
sorry, pardon, can you repeat	`repeat`
not X but Y, that's not X it's Y in fact.	`correct`

me?, which is likely to be a polite order in a human conversation. The system then produces several possible acts for each utterance or sequence of utterances: *Yes* in the dialogue in Table 15.9 is either an acceptation (U5) or an implicit validation (S4).

The identification of speech acts for unrestricted dialogues has not received a definitive solution yet. However, it has attracted much attention and reasonably good solutions for applications like speech servers. In a spoken dialogue, what matters are the user's acts that an automatic system identifies using a tagging procedure. Tagsets can be relatively generic, as in the SUNDIAL project, or application-oriented, as in VERBMOBIL. DAMSL (Allen and Core 1997) is another oft-cited tagset.

Speech act tagging uses statistical approaches or reasoning rules, or possibly a combination of both. While many systems used by speech servers are based on rules, Alexandersson (1996) describes a statistical technique similar to those used in part-of-speech tagging. He uses a dialogue corpus where the turns are annotated with illocutionary acts instead of parts of speech. The tagger is a hidden Markov model, and the training procedure derives dialogue act n-grams. As for part-of-speech tagging, the stochastic dialogue act tagging consists in finding the most likely sequence of tags given a sequence of words and features.

As general principles, the features that rules or statistical modeling take into account are:

- Cue words or phrases, which may be linked to specific speech acts.
- The syntactic and semantic forms of the utterance.
- Expectations to apply constraints on possible speech acts. These are based on transitions from a previous state to the current state of the dialogue: when the system asks a question, it expects an answer, a rejection or a failure, and it can discard other acts.
- Task modeling and goal satisfaction. This point extends the previous one. It restrains possible user acts and parameter values according to the progress point where the user is in the dialogue.

15.5.5 EVAR: A Dialogue Application Using Speech Acts

EVAR – *Erkennen, Verstehen, Antworten, Rückfragen* – is a dialogue system intended to provide information on train schedules in Germany (Mast 1993, Mast et al.

1994). It gives an example of a thorough task modeling that enables the system to restrain the number of possible dialogue acts at a given point of the inquiry process. It avoids random initiatives from the user thanks to a constant guidance process. EVAR structures the dialogue process in a sequence of phases:

- a greeting by the system
- a request from the user
- a clarification consisting of a confirmation of data requested by the user and possible requests for details and specifications
- an answer from the system
- a closing

EVAR enables transactions such as those in Table 15.12.

The finite state automaton in Fig. 15.2 models the dialogue progress. The S_ prefix denotes a system's turn, and U_ denotes a user's turn.

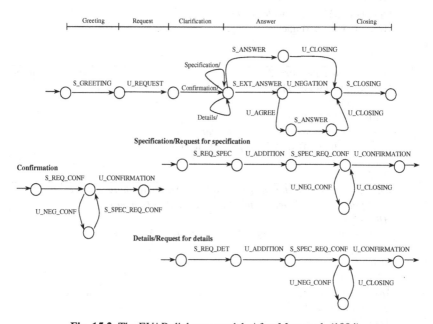

Fig. 15.2. The EVAR dialogue model. After Mast et al. (1994).

15.6 Taking Beliefs and Intentions into Account

The models of dialogue we have examined so far have an external viewpoint in the sense that they are based on observations of the user's behavior by the system. Parallel to them, some authors tried to take into account the user's beliefs, desires, and

Table 15.12. A dialogue in the EVAR prototype. After Mast et al. (1994).

Turns	Dialogue	Phases
S:	*Guten Tag. Hier ist die automatische Intercity-Auskunft.* *Welche Information benötigen Sie?* 'Hello. This is the Automatic Travel Information System. What information do you need?'	Greeting
U:	*Ich möchte morgen nach Hamburg fahren.* 'Tomorrow I want to go to Hamburg.'	Request
S:	*Sie möchten morgen nach Hamburg fahren?* 'Tomorrow you want to go to Hamburg?'	Confirmation
U:	*Ja morgen.* 'Yes tomorrow.'	
S:	*Von wo möchten Sie abfahren?* 'Where do you want to start?'	Request for details
U:	*München* 'Munich'	
S:	*Morgen von München nach Hamburg* 'Tomorrow from Munich to Hamburg'	
U:	*Ja* 'Yes'	
S:	*Wann möchten Sie fahren?* 'When do you want to leave?'	Request for speci-fication
U:	*Morgen früh* 'Early in the morning'	
S:	*Morgen früh von München nach Hamburg* 'Tomorrow morning from Munich to Hamburg'	
U:	*Ja* 'Yes'	
S:	*Ich habe mehere Verbindungen gefunden. Nach Hamburg* *HBF, fahren Sie ab München um 7 Uhr. Ankunft in Hamburg* *HBF um 15 Uhr, . . .* 'I found connections. From Munich departure 7, Arrival Hamburg 15, . . . '	Answer
U:	*Vielen Dank* 'Thank you'	
S:	*Möchten Sie weitere Auskünfte?* 'Do you want further information?'	Closing
U:	*Nein danke* 'No thank you'	
S:	*Auf wiederhören.* 'Have a nice trip.'	

intentions. They hoped to build an internal model of the user and thus to gain a deeper insight into dialogue processes.

The ambition to model beliefs and intentions is appealing because it addresses concerns and questions that often puzzle people: *What does he want from me? What does she mean?* Knowing or extracting a user's intentions would certainly help a computer serve the user better. In addition, intention modeling recasts dialogue and interaction into a framework more general than other formalisms.

However, such a model may prove difficult to implement. It is first a philosophical challenge to figure out and describe what the beliefs of individuals are. Second, if beliefs or intentions could be completely described, it would be a second challenge to box them into a program and run them with a computer. Fortunately, most dialogue applications have a goal that is plainly prosaic, and simplifications can be made. We describe now a classical representation of user modeling introduced by Allen and Perrault (1980).

15.6.1 Representing Mental States

The idea of conversational systems based on belief, desire, and intention is to model the participants as processes – agents. The agents are human users as well as artificial ones, and each agent has a specific knowledge and the desire to complete an action. The agent's core is a representation of their mental states, which uses predicates aimed at describing their beliefs or knowledge spaces, and what they can do. Agents are modeled using operators such as:

- `want(A, X)`, which means that agent A wants to do X
- `can_do(A, X)`, which means that agent A can do X
- `believe(A, X)`, which means that agent A believes X
- `know(A, X)`, which means that agent A knows X

Since beliefs are personal, that is, individual, the definition of truth is no longer universal. For this reason, predicates have two arguments, the agent who is the believer and the proposition that is believed or known. This nonuniversal logic is called modal, and refers to the various modes of truth.

From these operators, some axioms can be derived such as:

```
(know(A, X), (X ⇒ Y)) ⇒ know(A, Y)
(believe(A, X), (X ⇒ Y)) ⇒ believe(A, Y)
(believe(A, X), X) ⇒ know(A, X)
```

Mental states can be different according to dialogue participants, whether they involve human beings together or humans and machines. Let us suppose that a patron goes to a restaurant, looks at the menu, and sees as main courses *cassoulet, pytt i panna,* and *Yorkshire pudding.* Let us also suppose that the restaurant is running out of *cassoulet.* When entering the restaurant, belief spaces of the patron and the waiter are different (Table 15.13).

A short dialogue between the waiter and the patron when ordering the meal will enable them to synchronize their belief spaces (Table 15.14).

Table 15.13. Belief spaces.

Patron's belief space	Waiter's belief space
$\exists x, cassoulet(x)$	
$\exists x, pytt\_i\_panna(x)$	$\exists x, pytt\_i\_panna(x)$
$\exists x, yorkshire\_pudding(x)$	$\exists x, yorkshire\_pudding(x)$

Patron: *I feel like a cassoulet*
Waiter: *Sorry sir, we have no more of it.*

Such an exchange is also called a grounding – that is, setting a common ground. Grounding is central to dialogue system design. The user must be sure that beliefs and knowledge are shared between her/him and the system. If not, misunderstanding would creep into many exchanges.

Mutual beliefs can be expressed as believe(A, P) ∧ believe(B, P) ∧ believe(A, believe(B, P)) ∧ believe(B, believe(A, P)) ∧ believe(A, believe(B, believe(A, P))), etc. Such a infinite conjunction is denoted mutually_believe(A, B, P).

Mutual beliefs should not be explicitly listed all the time at the risk of being tedious. Most of the time, the user knows that there is an artificial system behind the box and expects something very specific from it. However, the system has to make sure the user is aware of its knowledge and beliefs, for instance, using implicit confirmation each time the user provides information.

Table 15.14. Belief spaces after dialogue.

Patron's belief space	Waiter's belief space
$\exists x, pytt\_i\_panna(x)$	$\exists x, pytt\_i\_panna(x)$
$\exists x, yorkshire\_pudding(x)$	$\exists x, yorkshire\_pudding(x)$

Representing the corresponding beliefs and intentions using Prolog is straightforward (Tables 15.15 and 15.16)

Table 15.15. Beliefs in Prolog.

Patron's belief space	Waiter's belief space
believe(patron('Pierre'), cassoulet(X))	
believe(patron('Pierre'), pytt_i_panna(X))	believe(waiter('Bill'), pytt_i_panna(X))
believe(patron('Pierre'), yorkshire_pudding(X))	believe(waiter('Bill'), yorkshire_pudding(X))

Table 15.16. Intentions in Prolog.

Patron's intentions	Waiter's intentions
`intend(patron('Pierre'),`	`intend(waiter('Bill'),`
`(cassoulet(X), order(X)))`	`take_order(X))`

Finally, modal operators can be used to transcribe speech acts. For instance, the act of informing can be associated to the operator `inform(A, B, P)` (A informs B of P), which will be applied with the following preconditions and effects:

- preconditions: `know(A, P)`, `want(A, inform(A, B, P))`
- effects: `know(B, P)`

The operator `request(A, B, P)` can be modeled as:

- preconditions: `want(A, request(A, B, P))`, `believe(A, can_-do(B, P))`
- effects: `believe(A, want(B, P))`

15.6.2 The STRIPS Planning Algorithm

Mental state consistency is usually controlled using a planning algorithm. Planning has been extensively studied, and we introduce here the STRIPS algorithm (Fikes and Nilsson 1971, Nilsson 1998). STRIPS considers planning as a search problem given an initial and a final state. It uses rules describing an action – corresponding here to the operators – with preconditions and postconditions. Postconditions are divided into an add and a delete list reflecting facts new to the world and facts to be removed.

```
%strips_rule(+operator, +preconditions, +add_list,
%    +delete_list).

strips_rule(inform(A, B, P), [know(A, P), want(A,
    inform(A, B, P))], [believe(B, P)], []).
```

Mental states or world state are described by lists of facts. The `apply/3` predicate applies an operator to a `State` that results in a `NewState`, subtracting facts to be deleted and adding facts to be added:

```
% apply(+Action, +State, -NewState)

apply(Action, State, NewState):-
    strips_rule(Action, _, _, DeleteList),
    subtract(State, DeleteList, TempState),
    strips_rule(Action, _, AddList, _),
    union(AddList, TempState, NewState).
```

where `subtract/3` and `union/3` are predicates built-in in most Prologs. They define set subtraction and union. `subtract(+Set, +Delete, -Result)` deletes all elements of list `Delete` from list `Set`, resulting in `Result`.
`union(+Set1, +Set2, -Result)` makes the union of `Set1` and `Set2`, removing duplicates and resulting in `Result`.

STRIPS represents possible states as nodes of a graph (Fig. 15.3). Each node consists of a list of facts. The actions enable movement from one node to another, adding or deleting facts when the preconditions are met. Knowing an initial and a final list of facts representing the initial state and the goal, the problem is stated as finding the action plan that modifies the world, adding or deleting facts so that the initial state is transformed into the final one. This is a search problem, where STRIPS traverses a graph to find the plan actions as follows (Nilsson 1998, pp. 376–379).

- Repeat while `Goals` are not a subset of the current `State`,
    1. Select a `Goal` from the `Goals` that is not already in the current `State`.
    2. Find a STRIP rule whose `Action` adds `Goal` to the current `State` and make sure that `Action` has not already been done.
    3. `Action` may not be possible if the `Preconditions` are not met. Therefore, use STRIPS to solve recursively `Preconditions`. This results in the intermediary state 1 (`InterState1`).
    4. Apply `Action` to add and delete facts from the intermediary state 1. This results in the intermediary state 2 (`InterState2`).
    5. Recursively solve the rest of `Goals`.

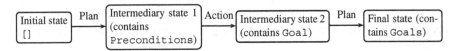

Fig. 15.3. The STRIPS schemata.

STRIPS in Prolog uses the initial state and the goals as inputs and produces the final state and the plan, where the goals must be a subset of the final state. We need some auxiliary variables to carry out the computation. The Prolog recursive rule builds the `Plan` in a reverse order, adding the current `Action` to the head of the list, and unifies it to the `FinalPlan` variable when the goal is satisfied. Prolog also builds `State`, and unifies it to `FinalState` in a same way. To avoid possible infinite loops when finding preconditions to an action, the rule keeps a copy of the corresponding plan and prohibits the repetition of actions.

```
strips(Goals, InitState, FinState, Plan) :-
    strips(Goals, InitState, [], [], FinState, RevPlan),
    reverse(RevPlan, Plan).

% strips(+Goals, +State, +Plan, +PrecondPlan,
```

```
%   -FinalState, -FinalPlan)

strips(Goals, State, Plan, _, State, Plan) :-
  subset(Goals, State).
strips(Goals, State, Plan, PrecondPlan, FinalState,
    FinalPlan) :-
  member(Goal, Goals),    %Select a goal
  \+ member(Goal, State),
  strips_rule(Action, _, AddList, _), %Find an action
  member(Goal, AddList),
  \+ member(Action, PrecondPlan),
     % Find preconditions
  strips_rule(Action, Preconditions, _, _),
  % Get the FirstPlan and InterState1
  % to achieve preconditions
  strips(Preconditions, State, Plan,
    [Action | PrecondPlan], InterState1, FirstPlan),
  % Apply Action to the world
  apply(Action, InterState1, InterState2),
  % From FirstPlan move forward
  strips(Goals, InterState2, [Action | FirstPlan],
    PrecondPlan, FinalState, FinalPlan).
```

15.6.3 Causality

Planning provides a good operation model for dialogue and for other discourse phenomena such as **causality**. Causality occurs when some sentences are logically chained and are part of a same demonstration. Consider, for instance, these sentences:

Hedgehogs are back. Caterpillars shiver.

The second sentence is a consequence of the first. Causality can be related to a logical demonstration but also depends on time-ordered events. Causal rules represent specific events, which will result in certain facts or effects. Usually, they also require preconditions. They can be expressed in Prolog using predicates whose structure is similar to:

```
causes(preconditions, event, effects).
```

As we can see, this is also closely related to planning. The causes predicate means that if the preconditions are met, and if an event occurs, then we will have effects.

Many sentences involve sequences of actions – plans – that are temporally chained. For instance:

Phileas the hedgehog was thirsty. He went out to have a pint.

These two sentences correspond to an action, which is followed by another, the second one being a consequence of the first one. For both examples, discourse understanding can be restated as a plan recognition problem.

15.7 Further Reading

Speech acts theory in dialogue is mostly known from the works of Austin (1962) and Searle (1969, 1979), although Bühler (1934) pioneered it. Searle and Vanderveken (1985) describe a logical model of illocutionary acts as well as a list of English verbs classified according to Searle's ontology. Vanderveken (1988) expands this work to French verbs. Foundations of belief and intention modeling in dialogue are due to Hintikka (1962). Carberry (1990) provides accounts to plan recognition in dialogue.

EVAR and the SUNDIAL projects have been a source of valuable research and publications about spoken dialogue processing. Bilange (1992) gives an excellent overview of dialogue processing techniques and application examples. Other works include those of Andry (1992), Mast (1993), Eckert (1996), and Sagerer (1990). The TRAINS project (Allen et al. 1995) is another example of elaborate dialogue processing. Many applications, such as train reservation systems, are now available commercially.

Planning includes a large number of applications and has spurred many algorithms. In computational linguistics, it occurs within the frameworks of temporal reasoning, intention modeling, and other forms of constraint-based reasoning. Bratko (2001) gives a short introduction to planning and a collection of Prolog programs. Russell and Norvig (2003) provides another introduction to planning.

Exercises

15.1. Write a dialogue program using Prolog clauses – no DCG rules – asking a couple of questions and accepting yes or no answers only. Collect all the answers and print them out at the end of the session.

15.2. Write a dialogue program using Prolog clauses – no DCG rules – reproducing the dialogue of Fig. 15.1. Collect all the answers and print them out at the end of the session.

15.3. Write verbs in a language you know corresponding to Searle's ontology of illocutionary classes: assertives, directives, commissives, declaratives, and expressives.

15.4. Rewrite Exercice 15.1 using SUNDIAL's speech act predicates in Table 15.8.

15.5. Rewrite Exercice 15.2 using SUNDIAL's speech act predicates in Table 15.8.

15.6. The DCG dialogue rules described in Sect. 15.5.3 are not robust. Make a parallel with sentence parsing and give examples where they would fail and why.

15.7. Modify the rules of Sect. 15.5.3 so that they would never fail but recover and start again.

15.8. Write an automaton in Prolog to model EVAR's main phases accepting a legal sequence of speech acts, such as [S_GREETING, U_REQ_INFO, ...].

15.9. Modify the EVAR automaton of Exercice 15.8 to be interactive. Design questions and messages from the system and possible answers from the user. Replace the user and system turns with them.

15.10. Modify the EVAR automaton of Exercices 15.8 and 15.9 and use the SUN-DIAL speech acts. Make the system work so that you have a more or less realistic dialogue.

A

An Introduction to Prolog

A.1 A Short Background

Prolog was designed in the 1970s by Alain Colmerauer and a team of researchers with the idea – new at that time – that it was possible to use logic to represent knowledge and to write programs. More precisely, Prolog uses a subset of predicate logic and draws its structure from theoretical works of earlier logicians such as Herbrand (1930) and Robinson (1965) on the automation of theorem proving.

Prolog was originally intended for the writing of natural language processing applications. Because of its conciseness and simplicity, it became popular well beyond this domain and now has adepts in areas such as:

- Formal logic and associated forms of programming
- Reasoning modeling
- Database programming
- Planning, and so on.

This chapter is a short review of Prolog. In-depth tutorials include: in English, Bratko (2001), Clocksin and Mellish (2003), Covington et al. (1997), Sterling and Shapiro (1994); in French, Giannesini et al. (1985); and in German, Bauman (1991). Boizumault (1988, 1993) contain a didactical implementation of Prolog in Lisp. Prolog foundations rest on first-order logic. Apt (1997), Burke and Foxley (1996), Delahaye (1986), and Lloyd (1987) examine theoretical links between this part of logic and Prolog.

Colmerauer started his work at the University of Montréal, and a first version of the language was implemented at the University of Marseilles in 1972. Colmerauer and Roussel (1996) tell the story of the birth of Prolog, including their try-and-fail experimentation to select tractable algorithms from the mass of results provided by research in logic.

In 1995, the International Organization for Standardization (ISO) published a standard on the Prolog programming language. Standard Prolog (Deransart et al. 1996) is becoming prevalent in the Prolog community and most of the available implementations now adopt it, either partly or fully. Unless specifically indicated, descriptions in this chapter conform to the ISO standard, and examples should run under any Standard Prolog implementation.

A.2 Basic Features of Prolog

A.2.1 Facts

Facts are statements that describe object properties or relations between objects. Let us imagine we want to encode that Ulysses, Penelope, Telemachus, Achilles, and others are characters of Homer's *Iliad* and *Odyssey*. This translates into Prolog facts ended with a period:

```
character(priam, iliad).
character(hecuba, iliad).
character(achilles, iliad).
character(agamemnon, iliad).
character(patroclus, iliad).
character(hector, iliad).
character(andromache, iliad).
character(rhesus, iliad).
character(ulysses, iliad).
character(menelaus, iliad).
character(helen, iliad).

character(ulysses, odyssey).
character(penelope, odyssey).
character(telemachus, odyssey).
character(laertes, odyssey).
character(nestor, odyssey).
character(menelaus, odyssey).
character(helen, odyssey).
character(hermione, odyssey).
```

Such a collection of facts, and later, of rules, makes up a **database**. It transcribes the knowledge of a particular situation into a logical format. Adding more facts to the database, we express other properties, such as the gender of characters:

```
% Male characters           % Female characters

male(priam).                female(hecuba).
male(achilles).             female(andromache).
male(agamemnon).            female(helen).
male(patroclus).            female(penelope).
male(hector).
```

```
male(rhesus).
male(ulysses).
male(menelaus).
male(telemachus).
male(laertes).
male(nestor).
```

or relationships between characters such as parentage:

```
% Fathers                % Mothers
father(priam, hector).   mother(hecuba, hector).
father(laertes,ulysses). mother(penelope,telemachus).
father(atreus,menelaus). mother(helen, hermione).
father(menelaus, hermione).
father(ulysses, telemachus).
```

Finally, would we wish to describe kings of some cities and their parties, this would be done as:

```
king(ulysses, ithaca, achaean).
king(menelaus, sparta, achaean).
king(nestor, pylos, achaean).
king(agamemnon, argos, achaean).
king(priam, troy, trojan).
king(rhesus, thrace, trojan).
```

From these examples, we understand that the general form of a Prolog fact is: `relation(object1, object2, ..., objectn)`. Symbols or names representing objects, such as `ulysses` or `penelope`, are called **atoms**. Atoms are normally strings of letters, digits, or underscores "`_`", and begin with a lowercase letter. An atom can also be a string beginning with an uppercase letter or including white spaces, but it must be enclosed between quotes. Thus `'Ulysses'` or `'Pallas Athena'` are legal atoms.

In logic, the name of the symbolic `relation` is the **predicate**, the objects `object1, object2, ..., objectn` involved in the relation are the **arguments**, and the number n of the arguments is the **arity**. Traditionally, a Prolog predicate is indicated by its name and arity: `predicate/arity`, for example, `character/2`, `king/3`.

A.2.2 Terms

In Prolog, all forms of data are called **terms**. The constants, i.e., atoms or numbers, are terms. The fact `king(menelaus, sparta, achaean)` is a **compound term** or a **structure**, that is, a term composed of other terms – **subterms**. The arguments of this compound term are constants. They can also be other compound terms, as in

```
character(priam, iliad, king(troy, trojan)).
character(ulysses, iliad, king(ithaca, achaean)).
character(menelaus, iliad, king(sparta, achaean)).
```

where the arguments of the predicate `character/3` are two atoms and a compound term.

It is common to use trees to represent compound terms. The nodes of a tree are then equivalent to the functors of a term. Figure A.1 shows examples of this.

Terms	Graphical representations

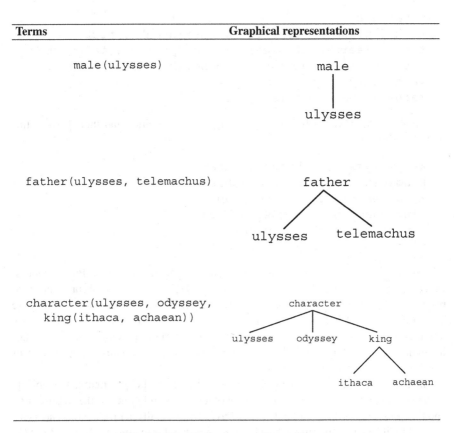

Fig. A.1. Graphical representations of terms.

Syntactically, a compound term consists of a **functor** – the name of the relation – and arguments. The leftmost functor of a term is the **principal functor**. A same principal functor with a different arity corresponds to different predicates: `character/3` is thus different from `character/2`. A constant is a special case of a compound term with no arguments and an arity of 0. The constant abc can thus be referred to as `abc/0`.

A.2.3 Queries

A query is a request to prove or retrieve information from the database, for example, if a fact is true. Prolog answers yes if it can prove it, that is, here if the fact is in the database, or no if it cannot: if the fact is absent. The question *Is Ulysses a male?* corresponds to the query:

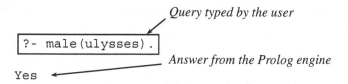

Query typed by the user

```
?- male(ulysses).
```

Answer from the Prolog engine

Yes

which has a positive answer. A same question with Penelope would give:

```
?- male(penelope).
No
```

because this fact is not in the database.

The expressions `male(ulysses)` or `male(penelope)` are **goals** to prove. The previous queries consisted of single goals. Some questions require more goals, such as *Is Menelaus a male and is he the king of Sparta and an Achaean?*, which translates into:

```
?- male(menelaus), king(menelaus, sparta, achaean).
Yes
```

where "`,`" is the conjunction operator. It indicates that Prolog has to prove both goals. The simple queries have one goal to prove, while the **compound queries** are a conjunction of two or more goals:

```
?- G1, G2, G3, ..., Gn.
```

Prolog proves the whole query by proving that all the goals G1 ... Gn are true.

A.2.4 Logical Variables

The logical variables are the last kind of Prolog terms. Syntactically, variables begin with an uppercase letter, for example, X, Xyz, or an underscore "_". Logical variables stand for any term: constants, compound terms, and other variables. A term containing variables such as `character(X, Y)` can unify with a compatible fact, such as `character(penelope, odyssey)`, with the **substitutions** X = penelope and Y = odyssey.

When a query term contains variables, the Prolog resolution algorithm searches terms in the database that unify with it. It then substitutes the variables to the matching arguments. Variables enable users to ask questions such as *What are the characters of the Odyssey?*

The variable   *The query*

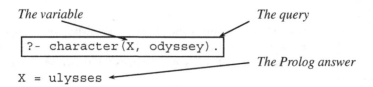

```
?- character(X, odyssey).
```
                                                    The Prolog answer
```
X = ulysses
```

Or *What is the city and the party of king Menelaus?* etc.

```
?- king(menelaus, X, Y).
X = sparta, Y = achaean
```

```
?- character(menelaus, X, king(Y, Z)).
X = iliad, Y = sparta, Z = achaean
```

```
?- character(menelaus, X, Y).
X = iliad, Y = king(sparta, achaean)
```

When there are multiple solutions, Prolog considers the first fact to match the query in the database. The user can type "`;`" to get the next answers until there is no more solution. For example:

The variable   *The query*

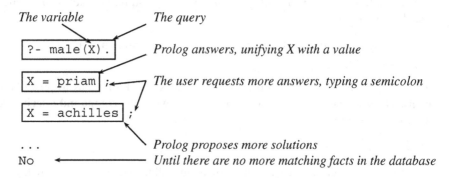

```
?- male(X).
```
                            Prolog answers, unifying X with a value
```
X = priam ;
```
                            The user requests more answers, typing a semicolon
```
X = achilles ;
```

```
...
```
                            Prolog proposes more solutions
```
No
```
                            Until there are no more matching facts in the database

A.2.5 Shared Variables

Goals in a conjunctive query can share variables. This is useful to constrain arguments of different goals to have a same value. To express the question *Is the king of Ithaca also a father?* in Prolog, we use the conjunction of two goals king(X, ithaca, Y) and father(X, Z), where the variable X is shared between goals:

```
?- king(X, ithaca, Y), father(X, Z).
X = ulysses, Y = achaean, Z = telemachus
```

In this query, we are not interested by the name of the child although Prolog responds with Z = telemachus. We can indicate to Prolog that we do not need

to know the values of Y and Z using **anonymous variables**. We then replace Y
and Z with the symbol "_", which does not return any value:

```
?- king(X, ithaca, _), father(X, _).
X = ulysses
```

A.2.6 Data Types in Prolog

To sum up, every data object in Prolog is a term. Terms divide into atomic terms,
variables, and compound terms (Fig. A.2).

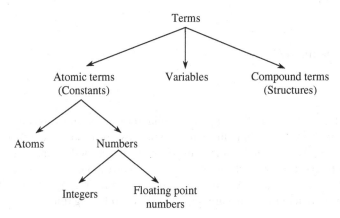

Fig. A.2. Kinds of terms in Prolog.

Syntax of terms may vary according to Prolog implementations. You should consult reference manuals for their specific details. Here is a list of simplified conventions from Standard Prolog (Deransart et al. 1996):

- Atoms are sequences of letters, numbers, and/or underscores beginning with a
  lowercase letter, as ulysses, iSLanD3, king_of_Ithaca.
- Some single symbols, called solo characters, are atoms: ! ;
- Sequences consisting entirely of some specific symbols or graphic characters are
  atoms: + - * / ^ < = > ~ : . ? @ # $ & \ '
- Any sequence of characters enclosed between single quotes is also an atom, as
  'king of Ithaca'. A quote within a quoted atom must be double quoted:
  'I"m'
- Numbers are either decimal integers, as -19, 1960, octal integers when preceded by 0o, as 0o56, hexadecimal integers when preceded by 0x, as 0xF4, or
  binary integers when preceded by 0b, as 0b101.
- Floating-point numbers are digits with a decimal point, as 3.14, -1.5. They
  may contain an exponent, as 23E-5 ($23 \; 10^{-5}$) or -2.3e5 ($2.3 \; 10^{-5}$).
- The ASCII numeric value of a character x is denoted 0'x, as 0'a (97), 0'b
  (98), etc.

- Variables are sequences of letters, numbers, and/or underscores beginning with an uppercase letter or the underscore character.
- Compound terms consist of a functor, which must be an atom, followed immediately by an opening parenthesis, a sequence of terms separated by commas, and a closing parenthesis.

Finally, Prolog uses two types of comments:

- Line comments go from the "`%`" symbol to the end of the line:
  ```
  % This is a comment
  ```
- Multiline comments begin with a "`/*`" and end with a "`*/`":
  ```
  /*
  this
  is
  a comment */
  ```

A.2.7 Rules

Rules enable to derive a new property or relation from a set of existing ones. For instance, the property of being the son of somebody corresponds to either the property of having a father and being a male, or having a mother and being a male. Accordingly, the Prolog predicate `son(X, Y)` corresponds either to conjunction `male(X)`, `father(Y, X)`, or to `male(X)`, `mother(Y, X)`. Being a son admits thus two definitions that are transcribed as two Prolog rules:

```
son(X, Y) :- father(Y, X), male(X).
son(X, Y) :- mother(Y, X), male(X).
```

More formally, rules consist of a term called the **head**, followed by symbol "`:-`", read if, and a conjunction of goals. They have the form:

```
HEAD :- G1, G2, G3, ... Gn.
```

where the conjunction of goals is the **body** of the rule. The head is true if the body is true. Variables of a rule are shared between the body and the head. Rules can be queried just like facts:

```
?- son(telemachus, Y).
Y = ulysses;
Y = penelope;
No
```

Rules are a flexible way to deduce new information from a set of facts. The `parent/2` predicate is another example of a family relationship that is easy to define using rules. Somebody is a parent if s/he is either a mother or a father:

```
parent(X, Y) :- mother(X, Y).
parent(X, Y) :- father(X, Y).
```

Rules can call other rules as with `grandparent/2`. A grandparent is the parent of a parent and is defined in Prolog as

```
grandparent(X, Y) :- parent(X, Z), parent(Z, Y).
```

where `Z` is an intermediate variable shared between goals. It enables us to find the link between the grandparent and the grandchild: a mother or a father.

We can generalize the `grandparent/2` predicate and write `ancestor/2`. We use two rules, one of them being recursive:

```
ancestor(X, Y) :- parent(X, Y).
ancestor(X, Y) :- parent(X, Z), ancestor(Z, Y).
```

This latter pattern is quite common of Prolog rules. One or more rules express a general case using recursion. Another set of rules or facts describes simpler conditions without recursion. They correspond to boundary cases and enable the recursion to terminate.

A query about the ancestors of Hermione yields:

```
?- ancestor(X, hermione).
X= menelaus;
X = helen;
X = atreus;
No
```

Facts and rules are also called **clauses**. A predicate is defined by a set of clauses with the same principal functor and arity. Facts are indeed special cases of rules: rules that are always true and `relation(X, Y)` is equivalent to `relation(X, Y) :- true`, where `true/0` is a built-in predicate that always succeeds. Most Prolog implementations require clauses of the same name and arity to be grouped together.

In the body of a rule, the comma "`,`" represents a conjunction of goals. It is also possible to use a disjunction with the operator "`;`". Thus:

```
A :-
    B
    ;
    C.
```

is equivalent to

```
A :- B.
A :- C.
```

However, "`;`" should be used scarcely because it impairs somewhat the legibility of clauses and programs. The latter form is generally better.

A.3 Running a Program

The set of facts and rules of a file makes up a **Prolog text** or program. To run it and use the information it contains, a Prolog system has to load the text and add it to the current database in memory. Once Prolog is launched, it displays a prompt symbol "?-" and accepts commands from the user.

Ways to load a program are specific to each Prolog implementation. A user should look them up in the reference manual because the current standard does not define them. There are, however, two commands drawn from the Edinburgh Prolog tradition (Pereira 1984) implemented in most systems: `consult/1` and `reconsult/1`.

The predicate `consult/1` loads a file given as an argument and adds all the clauses of the file to the current database in memory:

```
?- consult(file_name).
```

`file_name` must be an atom as, for example,

```
?- consult('odyssey.pl').
```

It is also possible to use the shortcut:

```
?- [file_name].
```

to load one file, for example,

```
?- ['odyssey.pl'].
```

or more files:

```
?- [file1, file2].
```

The predicate `reconsult/1` is a variation of `consult`. Usually, a programmer writes a program, loads it using `consult`, runs it, debugs it, modifies the program, and reloads the modified program until it is correct. While `consult` adds the modified clauses to the old ones in the database, `reconsult` updates the database instead. It loads the modified file and replaces clauses of existing predicates in the database by new clauses contained in the file. If a predicate is in the file and not in the database, `reconsult` simply adds its clauses. In some Prolog systems, `reconsult` does not exist, and `consult` discards existing clauses to replace them by the new definition from the loaded file. Once a file is loaded, the user can run queries.

The `listing/0` built-in predicate displays all the clauses in the database, and `listing/1`, the definition of a specific predicate. The `listing/1` argument format is either `Predicate` or `Predicate/Arity`:

```
?- listing(character/2).
character(priam, iliad).
character(hecuba, iliad).
character(achilles, iliad).
   ...
```

A program can also include directives, i.e., predicates to run at load time. A directive is a rule without a head: a term or a conjunction of terms with a ":-" symbol to its left-hand side:

```
:- predicates_to_execute.
```

Directives are run immediately as they are encountered. If a directive is to be executed once the program is completely loaded, it must occur at the end of the file.

Finally, `halt/0` quits Prolog.

A.4 Unification

A.4.1 Substitution and Instances

When Prolog answers a query made of a term T containing variables, it applies a **substitution**. This means that Prolog replaces variables in T by values so that it proves T to be true. The substitution $\{X = ulysses, Y = odyssey\}$ is a solution to the query `character(X, Y)` because the fact `character(ulysses, odyssey)` is in the database. In the same vein, the substitution $\{X = sparta, Y = achaean\}$ is a solution to the query `king(menelaus, X, Y)`.

More formally, a substitution is a set $\{X1 = t1, X2 = t2, ..., Xn = tn\}$, where `Xi` is a variable and `ti` is a term. Applying a substitution σ to a term T is denoted $T\sigma$ and corresponds to the replacement of all the occurrences of variable `Xi` with term `ti` in T for i ranging from 1 to n. Applying the (meaningless) substitution $\sigma_1 = \{X = ulysses\}$ to the term T1 = `king(menelaus, X, Y)` yields T1' = `king(menelaus, ulysses, Y)`. Applying the substitution $\sigma_2 = \{X = iliad, Y = king(sparta, achaean)\}$ to the term T2 = `character(menelaus, X, Y)` yields T2' = `character(menelaus, iliad, king(sparta, achaean))`.

A term T' resulting from a substitution $T\sigma$ is an **instance** of T. More generally, T' is an instance of T if there is a substitution so that $T' = T\sigma$. If T' is an instance of T, then T is **more general** than T'. Terms can be ordered according to possible compositions of instantiations. For example, `character(X, Y)` is more general than `character(ulysses, odyssey)`; `king(X, Y, Z)` is more general than `king(menelaus, Y, Z)`, which is more general than `king(menelaus, Y, achaean)`, which is itself more general than `king(menelaus, sparta, achaean)`.

A substitution mapping a set of variables onto another set of variables such as $\sigma = \{X = A, Y = B\}$ onto term `character(X, Y)` is a **renaming substitution**. Initial and resulting terms `character(X, Y)` and `character(A, B)` are said to be **alphabetical variants**. Finally, a **ground** term is a term that contains no variable such as `king(menelaus, sparta, achaean)`.

A.4.2 Terms and Unification

To equate two terms, `T1` and `T2`, Prolog uses unification, which substitutes variables in the terms so that they are identical. Unification is a logical mechanism that carries out a two-way matching, from `T1` to `T2` and the reverse, and merges them into a common term. Prolog unifies terms to solve equations such as `T1 = T2`. It also uses unification in queries to match a goal or a subgoal to the head of the rule. Figure A.3 shows the intuitive unification of terms

```
T1 = character(ulysses, Z, king(ithaca, achaean))
```

and

```
T2 = character(ulysses, X, Y)
```

through a graphical superposition.

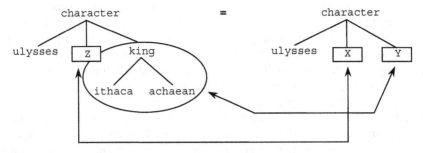

Fig. A.3. Unification of terms: a graphical interpretation.

The superposition of the two terms requires finding an instance common to both terms T_1 and T_2. This can be restated as there exist two substitutions σ_1 and σ_2 such that $T_1\sigma_1 = T_2\sigma_2$. A **unifier** is a substitution making T_1 and T_2 identical: $T_1\sigma = T_2\sigma$. In our example, there is an infinite number of possible unifiers. Candidates include the substitution $\sigma = \{$`Z = c(a)`, `X = c(a)`, `Y = king(ithaca, achaean)`$\}$, which yields the common instance: `character(ulysses,c(a), king(ithaca, achaean))`. They also include $\sigma = \{$`Z = female`, `Z = female`, `Y = king(ithaca, achaean)`$\}$, which yields another common instance: `character(ulysses, female, king(ithaca, achaean))`, etc.

Intuitively, these two previous unifiers are special cases of the unification of `T1` and `T2`. In fact, all the unifiers are instances of the substitution $\sigma = \{$`X = Z`, `Y = king(ithaca, achaean)`$\}$, which is the **most general unifier** or **MGU**.

Real Prolog systems display the unification of `T1` and `T2` in a slightly different way:

```
?- character(ulysses, Z, king(ithaca, achaean)) =
character(ulysses, X, Y).
X = _G123, Y = king(ithaca, achaean), Z = _G123
```

where _Gxyz are variable names internal to the Prolog system.

A.4.3 The Herbrand Unification Algorithm

The reference algorithm to unify terms is due to Herbrand (Herbrand 1930, Martelli and Montanari 1982). It takes the two terms to unify as input. The output is either a failure if terms do not unify or the MGU – σ.

The algorithm initializes the substitution to the empty set and pushes terms on a stack. The main loop consists in popping terms, comparing their functors, and pushing their arguments on the stack. When a variable is found, the corresponding substitution is added to σ (Sterling and Shapiro 1994, Deransart et al. 1996).

* **Initialization step**
  Initialize σ to $\{\}$
  Initialize failure to false
  Push the equation $T_1 = T_2$ on the stack
* **Loop**
  repeat {
      pop $x = y$ from the stack
      if x is a constant and $x == y$. Continue.
      else if x is a variable and x does not appear in y.
          Replace x with y in the stack and in σ. Add the substitution $\{x = y\}$ to
          σ.
      else if x is a variable and $x == y$. Continue.
      else if y is a variable and x is not a variable.
          Push $y = x$ on the stack.
      else if x and y are compounds with $x = f(x_1, ..., x_n)$ and $y = f(y_1, ..., y_n)$.
          Push on the stack $x_i = y_i$ for i ranging from 1 to n.
      else Set failure to true, and σ to $\{\}$. Break.
  } until (stack $\neq \emptyset$)

A.4.4 Example

Let us exemplify the Herbrand algorithm with terms: f(g(X, h(X, b)), Z) and f(g(a, Z), Y). We will use a two-way stack: one for the left term and one for the right term, and let us scan and push term arguments from right to left.

For the first iteration of the loop, x and y are compounds. After this iteration, the stack looks like:

Left term of the stack (x)		Right term of the stack (y)
g(X, h(X, b))	=	g(a, Z)
Z	=	Y

with the substitution $\sigma = \{\}$.

The second iteration pops the top terms of the left and right parts of the stack. The loop condition corresponds to compound terms again. The algorithm pushes the arguments of left and right terms on the stack:

Left term of the stack (x)		Right term of the stack (y)
X	=	a
h(X, b)	=	Z
Z	=	Y

with the substitution $\sigma = \{\}$.

The third iteration pops the equation X = a. The algorithm adds this substitution to σ and carries out the substitution in the stack:

Left term of the stack (x)		Right term of the stack (y)
h(X, b) ~ h(a, b)	=	Z
Z	=	Y

with the substitution $\sigma = \{X = a\}$.

The next iteration pops h(a, b) = Z, swaps the left and right terms, and yields:

Left term of the stack (x)		Right term of the stack (y)
Z	=	h(a, b)
Z	=	Y

The fifth iteration pops Z = h(a, b) and yields:

Left term of the stack (x)		Right term of the stack (y)
Z ~ h(a, b)	=	Y

with the substitution $\sigma = \{X = a, \ Z = h(a, b)\}$.

Finally, we get the MGU $\sigma = \{X = a, \ Z = h(a, b), \ Y = h(a, b)\}$ that yields the unified term f(g(a, h(a, b)), h(a, b)).

A.4.5 The Occurs-Check

The Herbrand algorithm specifies that variables X or Y must not appear – occur – in the right or left member of the equation to be a successful substitution. The unification of X and f(X) should then fail because f(X) contains X.

However, most Prolog implementations do not check the occurrence of variables to keep the unification time linear on the size of the smallest of the terms being unified (Pereira 1984). Thus, the unification X = f(X) unfortunately succeeds resulting in a stack overflow. The term f(X) infinitely replaces X in σ, yielding X = f(f(X)), f(f(f(X))), f(f(f(f(X)))), etc., until the memory is exhausted. It results into a system crash with many Prologs.

Although theoretically better, a unification algorithm that would implement an occurs-check is not necessary most of the time. An experienced programmer will not write unification equations with a potential occurs-check problem. That is why Prolog systems compromised the algorithm purity for speed. Should the occurs-check be necessary, Standard Prolog provides the unify_with_occurs_check/2 built-in predicate:

```
?- unify_with_occurs_check(X, f(X)).
No

?- unify_with_occurs_check(X, f(a)).
X = f(a)
```

A.5 Resolution

A.5.1 Modus Ponens

The Prolog resolution algorithm is based on the *modus ponens* form of inference that stems from traditional logic. The idea is to use a general rule – the major premise – and a specific fact – the minor premise – like the famous:

All men are mortal
Socrates is a man

to conclude, in this case, that

Socrates is mortal

Table A.1 shows the modus ponens in the classical notation of predicate logic and in Prolog.

Table A.1. The modus ponens notation in formal logic and its Prolog equivalent.

	Formal notation	**Prolog notation**
Facts	α	`man('Socrates').`
Rules	$\alpha \Rightarrow \beta$	`mortal(X) :- man(X).`
Conclusion	β	`mortal('Socrates').`

Prolog runs a reversed modus ponens. Using symbols in Table A.1, Prolog tries to prove that a query (β) is a consequence of the database content (α, $\alpha \Rightarrow \beta$). Using the major premise, it goes from β to α, and using the minor premise, from α to true. Such a sequence of goals is called a **derivation**. A derivation can be finite or infinite.

A.5.2 A Resolution Algorithm

Prolog uses a resolution algorithm to chain clauses mechanically and prove a query. This algorithm is generally derived from Robinson's resolution principle (1965), known as the SLD resolution. SLD stands for "linear resolution" with a "selection function" for "definite clauses" (Kowalski and Kuehner 1971). Here "definite clauses" are just another name for Prolog clauses.

The resolution takes a program – a set of clauses, rules, and facts – and a query Q as an input (Sterling and Shapiro 1994, Deransart et al. 1996). It considers a conjunction of current goals to prove, called the **resolvent**, that it initializes with Q. The resolution algorithm selects a goal from the resolvent and searches a clause in the database so that the head of the clause unifies with the goal. It replaces the goal with the body of that clause. The resolution loop replaces successively goals of the resolvent until they all reduce to true and the resolvent becomes empty. The output is then a success with a possible instantiation of the query goal Q', or a failure if no rule unifies with the goal. In case of success, the final substitution, σ, is the composition of all the MGUs involved in the resolution restricted to the variables of Q. This type of derivation, which terminates when the resolvent is empty, is called a **refutation**.

- **Initialization**
  Initialize Resolvent to Q, the initial goal of the resolution algorithm.
  Initialize σ to {}
  Initialize failure to false
- **Loop with Resolvent = G_1, G_2, ..., G_i, ..., G_m**
  while (Resolvent $\neq \emptyset$) {
  1. Select the goal $G_i \in$ Resolvent;
  2. If G_i == true, delete it and continue;
  3. Select the rule H :- B_1, ..., B_n in the database such that G_i and H unify with the MGU θ. If there is no such a rule then set failure to true; break;
  4. Replace G_i with B_1, ..., B_n in Resolvent
     % Resolvent = G_1, ..., G_{i-1}, B_1, ..., B_n, G_{i+1}, ..., G_m
  5. Apply θ to Resolvent and to Q;
  6. Compose σ with θ to obtain the new current σ;

  }

Each goal in the resolvent – i.e., in the body of a rule – must be different from a variable. Otherwise, this goal must be instantiated to a nonvariable term before it is called. The call/1 built-in predicate then executes it as in the rule:

```
daughter(X, Y) :-
  mother(Y, X), G = female(X), call(G).
```

where call(G) solves the goal G just as if it were female(X). In fact, Prolog automatically inserts call/1 predicates when it finds that a goal is a variable. G is thus exactly equivalent to call(G), and the rule can be rewritten more concisely in:

```
daughter(X, Y) :-
  mother(Y, X), G = female(X), G.
```

A.5.3 Derivation Trees and Backtracking

The resolution algorithm does not tell us how to select a goal from the resolvent. It also does not tell how to select a clause in the program. In most cases, there is more than one choice. The selection order of goals is of no consequence because Prolog has to prove all of them anyway. In practice, Prolog considers the leftmost goal of the resolvent. The selection of the clause is more significant because some derivations lead to a failure although a query can be proved by other derivations. Let us show this with the program:

```
p(X)  :- q(X), r(X).
q(a).
q(b).
r(b).
r(c).
```

and the query ?- p(X).

Let us compute the possible states of the resolvent along with the resolution's iteration count. The first resolvent (R1) is the query itself. The second resolvent (R2) is the body of p(X): q(X), r(X); there is no other choice. The third resolvent (R3) has two possible values because the leftmost subgoal q(X) can unify either with the facts q(a) or q(b). Subsequently, according to the fact selected and the corresponding substitution, the derivation succeeds or fails (Fig. A.4).

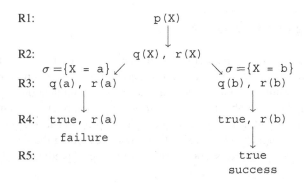

Fig. A.4. The search tree and successive values of the resolvent.

The Prolog resolution can then be restated as a search, and the picture of successive states of the resolvent as a search tree. Now how does Prolog select a clause? When more than one is possible, Prolog could expand the resolvent as many times as there are clauses. This strategy would correspond to a breadth-first search. Although it gives all the solutions, this is not the one Prolog employs because would be unbearable in terms of memory.

Prolog uses a depth-first search strategy. It scans clauses from top to bottom and selects the first one to match the leftmost goal in the resolvent. This sometimes leads to a subsequent failure, as in our example, where the sequence of resolvents is first p(X), then the conjunction q(X), r(X), after that q(a), r(a), and finally the goal r(a), which is not in the database. Prolog uses a backtracking mechanism then.

During a derivation, Prolog keeps a record of backtrack points when there is a possible choice, that is, where more than one clause unifies with the current goal. When a derivation fails, Prolog backs up to the last point where it could select another clause, undoes the corresponding unification, and proceeds with the next possible clause. In our example, it corresponds to resolvent R2 with the second possible unification: q(b). The resolvent R3 is then q(b), r(b), which leads to a success. Backtracking explores all possible alternatives until a solution is found or it reaches a complete failure.

However, although the depth-first strategy enables us to explore most search trees, it is only an approximation of a complete resolution algorithm. In some cases, the search path is infinite, even when a solution exists. Consider the program:

```
p(X) :- p(X), q(X).
p(a).
q(a).
```

where the query p(a) does not succeed because of Prolog's order of rule selection. Fortunately, most of the time there is a workaround. Here it suffices to invert the order of the subgoals in the body of the rule.

A.6 Tracing and Debugging

Bugs are programming errors, that is, when a program does not do what we expect from it. To isolate and remove them, the programmer uses a **debugger**. A debugger enables programmers to trace the goal execution and unification step by step. It would certainly be preferable to write bug-free programs, but to err is human. And debugging remains, unfortunately, a frequent part of program development.

The Prolog debugger uses an execution model describing the control flow of a goal (Fig. A.5). It is pictured as a box representing the goal predicate with four ports, where:

- The Call port corresponds to the invocation of the goal.
- If the goal is satisfied, the execution comes out through the Exit port with a possible unification.
- If the goal fails, the execution exits through the Fail port.
- Finally, if a subsequent goal fails and Prolog backtracks to try another clause of the predicate, the execution re-enters the box through the Redo port.

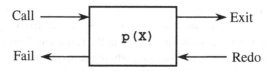

Fig. A.5. The execution model of Prolog.

The built-in predicate `trace/0` launches the debugger and `notrace/0` stops it. The debugger may have different commands according to the Prolog system you are using. Major ones are:

- `creep` to proceed through the execution ports. Simply type return to creep.
- `skip` to skip a goal giving the result without examining its subgoals. (type `s` to skip).
- `retry` starts the current goal again from an exit or redo port (type `r`).
- `fail` makes a current goal to fail (type `f`).
- `abort` to quit the debugger (type `a`).

Figure A.6 represents the rule `p(X)  :- q(X), r(X)`, where the box corresponding to the head encloses a chain of subboxes picturing the conjunction of goals in the body. The debugger enters goal boxes using the `creep` command.

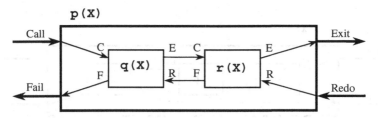

Fig. A.6. The execution box representing the rule `p(X)  :- q(X), r(X)`.

As an example, let us trace the program:

```
p(X)  :- q(X), r(X).
q(a).
q(b).
r(b).
r(c).
```

with the query `p(X)`.

```
?- trace.
Yes
?- p(X).
   Call:  (  7) p(_G106) ? creep
   Call:  (  8) q(_G106) ? creep
   Exit:  (  8) q(a) ? creep
   Call:  (  8) r(a) ? creep
   Fail:  (  8) r(a) ? creep
   Redo:  (  8) q(_G106) ? creep
   Exit:  (  8) q(b) ? creep
   Call:  (  8) r(b) ? creep
```

```
    Exit:    (  8) r(b) ? creep
    Exit:    (  7) p(b) ? creep
X = b
```

A.7 Cuts, Negation, and Related Predicates

A.7.1 Cuts

The cut predicate, written "!", is a device to prune some backtracking alternatives. It modifies the way Prolog explores goals and enables a programmer to control the execution of programs. When executed in the body of a clause, the cut always succeeds and removes backtracking points set before it in the current clause. Figure A.7 shows the execution model of the rule p(X) :- q(X), !, r(X) that contains a cut.

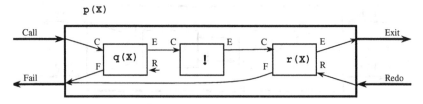

Fig. A.7. The execution box representing the rule p(X) :- q(X), !, r(X).

Let us suppose that a predicate P consists of three clauses:

```
P :- A₁, ..., Aᵢ, !, Aᵢ₊₁, ..., Aₙ.
P :- B₁, ..., Bₘ.
P :- C₁, ..., Cₚ.
```

Executing the cut in the first clause has the following consequences:

1. All other clauses of the predicate below the clause containing the cut are pruned. That is, here the two remaining clauses of P will not be tried.
2. All the goals to the left of the cut are also pruned. That is, $A_1, \ldots, A_i$ will no longer be tried.
3. However, it will be possible to backtrack on goals to the right of the cut.

$$P :- \cancel{A_1, \ldots, A_i} \ !, A_{i+1}, \ldots, A_n.$$
$$\cancel{P :- B_1, \ldots, B_m.}$$
$$\cancel{P :- C_1, \ldots, C_p.}$$

Cuts are intended to improve the speed and memory consumption of a program. However, wrongly placed cuts may discard some useful backtracking paths and solutions. Then, they may introduce vicious bugs that are often difficult to track. Therefore, cuts should be used carefully.

An acceptable use of cuts is to express determinism. Deterministic predicates always produce a definite solution; it is not necessary then to maintain backtracking possibilities. A simple example of it is given by the minimum of two numbers:

```
minimum(X, Y, X) :- X < Y.
minimum(X, Y, Y) :- X >= Y.
```

Once the comparison is done, there is no means to backtrack because both clauses are mutually exclusive. This can be expressed by adding two cuts:

```
minimum(X, Y, X) :- X < Y, !.
minimum(X, Y, Y) :- X >= Y, !.
```

Some programmers would rewrite `minimum/3` using a single cut:

```
minimum(X, Y, X) :- X < Y, !.
minimum(X, Y, Y).
```

The idea behind this is that once Prolog has compared X and Y in the first clause, it is not necessary to compare them again in the second one. Although the latter program may be more efficient in terms of speed, it is obscure. In the first version of `minimum/3`, cuts respect the logical meaning of the program and do not impair its legibility. Such cuts are called **green cuts**. The cut in the second `minimum/3` predicate is to avoid writing a condition explicitly. Such cuts are error-prone and are called **red cuts**. Sometimes red cuts are crucial to a program but when overused, they are a bad programming practice.

A.7.2 Negation

A logic program contains no negative information, only queries that can be proven or not. The Prolog built-in negation corresponds to a query failure: the program cannot prove the query. The negation symbol is written "\+" or `not` in older Prolog systems:

- If G succeeds then \+ G fails.
- If G fails then \+ G succeeds.

The Prolog negation is defined using a cut:

```
\+(P) :- P, !, fail.
\+(P) :- true.
```

where `fail/0` is a built-in predicate that always fails.

Most of the time, it is preferable to ensure that a negated goal is ground: all its variables are instantiated. Let us illustrate it with the somewhat odd rule:

```
mother(X, Y) :- \+ male(X), child(Y, X).
```

and facts:

```
child(telemachus, penelope).
male(ulysses).
male(telemachus).
```

The query

```
?- mother(X, Y).
```

fails because the subgoal male(X) is not ground and unifies with the fact male(ulysses). If the subgoals are inverted:

```
mother(X, Y) :- child(Y, X), \+ male(X).
```

the term child(Y, X) unifies with the substitution X = penelope and Y = telemachus, and since male(penelope) is not in the database, the goal mother(X, Y) succeeds.

Predicates similar to "\+" include if-then and if-then-else constructs. If-then is expressed by the built-in '->'/2 operator. Its syntax is

```
Condition -> Action
```

as in

```
print_if_parent(X, Y) :-
    (parent(X, Y) -> write(X), nl, write(Y), nl).

?- print_if_parent(X, Y).
penelope
telemachus

X = penelope, Y = telemachus
```

Just like negation, '->'/2 is defined using a cut:

```
'->'(P, Q):- P, !, Q.
```

The if-then-else predicate is an extension of '->'/2 with a second member to the right. Its syntax is

```
Condition -> Then ; Else
```

If Condition succeeds, Then is executed, otherwise Else is executed.

A.7.3 The once/1 Predicate

The built-in predicate once/1 also controls Prolog execution. once(P) executes P once and removes backtrack points from it. If P is a conjunction of goals as in the rule:

```
A :- B1, B2, once((B3, ..., Bi)), Bi+1, ..., Bn.
```

the backtracking path goes directly from B_{i+1} to B_2, skipping B_3, ..., B_i. It is necessary to bracket the conjunction inside once twice because its arity is equal to one. A single level of brackets, as in once $(B_3, ..., B_i)$, would tell Prolog that once/1 has an arity of i-3.

once (Goal) is defined as:

```
once(Goal) :- Goal, !.
```

A.8 Lists

Lists are data structures essential to many programs. A Prolog list is a sequence of an arbitrary number of terms separated by commas and enclosed within square brackets. For example:

- [a] is a list made of an atom.
- [a, b] is a list made of two atoms.
- [a, X, father(X, telemachus)] is a list made of an atom, a variable, and a compound term.
- [[a, b], [[[father(X, telemachus)]]]] is a list made of two sublists.
- [] is the atom representing the empty list.

Although it is not obvious from these examples, Prolog lists are compound terms and the square bracketed notation is only a shortcut. The list functor is a dot: ". /2", and [a, b] is equivalent to the term . (a, . (b, [])).

Computationally, lists are recursive structures. They consist of two parts: a head, the first element of a list, and a tail, the remaining list without its first element. The head and the tail correspond to the first and second argument of the Prolog list functor. Figure A.8 shows the term structure of the list [a, b, c]. The tail of a list is possibly empty as in . (c, [])).

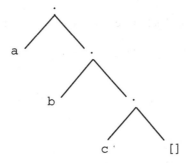

Fig. A.8. The term structure of the list [a, b, c].

The notation "|" splits a list into its head and tail, and [H | T] is equivalent to
. (H, T). Splitting a list enables us to access any element of it and therefore it is a
very frequent operation. Here are some examples of its use:

```
?- [a, b] = [H | T].
H = a, T = [b]

?- [a] = [H | T].
H = a, T = []

?- [a, [b]] = [H | T].
H = a, T = [[b]]

?- [a, b, c, d] = [X, Y | T].
X = a, Y = b, T = [c, d]

?- [[a, b, c], d, e] = [H | T].
H = [a, b, c], T = [d, e]
```

The empty list cannot be split:

```
?- [] = [H | T].
No
```

A.9 Some List-Handling Predicates

Many applications require extensive list processing. This section describes some useful predicates. Generally, Prolog systems provide a set of built-in list predicates.
Consult your manual to see which ones; there is no use in reinventing the wheel.

A.9.1 The member/2 Predicate

The member/2 predicate checks whether an element is a member of a list:

```
?- member(a, [b, c, a]).
Yes

?- member(a, [c, d]).
No
```

member/2 is defined as

```
member(X, [X | Y]).        % Termination case
member(X, [Y | YS]) :-     % Recursive case
  member(X, YS).
```

We could also use anonymous variables to improve legibility and rewrite member/2 as

```
member(X, [X | _]).
member(X, [_ | YS]) :- member(X, YS).
```

member/2 can be queried with variables to generate elements member of a list, as in:

```
?- member(X, [a, b, c]).
X = a ;
X = b ;
X = c ;
No
```

Or lists containing an element:

```
?- member(a, Z).
Z = [a | Y] ;
Z = [Y, a | X] ;
etc.
```

Finally, the query:

```
?- \+ member(X, L).
```

where X and L are ground variables, returns Yes if member(X, L) fails and No if it succeeds.

A.9.2 The append/3 Predicate

The append/3 predicate appends two lists and unifies the result to a third argument:

```
?- append([a, b, c], [d, e, f], [a, b, c, d, e, f]).
Yes

?- append([a, b], [c, d], [e, f]).
No

?- append([a, b], [c, d], L).
L = [a, b, c, d]

?- append(L, [c, d], [a, b, c, d]).
L = [a, b]

?- append(L1, L2, [a, b, c]).
L1 = [], L2 = [a, b, c] ;
L1 = [a], L2 = [b, c] ;
```

etc., with all the combinations.

append/3 is defined as

```
append([], L, L).
append([X | XS], YS, [X | ZS]) :-
  append(XS, YS, ZS).
```

A.9.3 The delete/3 Predicate

The delete/3 predicate deletes a given element from a list. Its synopsis is:
delete(List, Element, ListWithoutElement). It is defined as:

```
delete([], _, []).
delete([E | List], E, ListWithoutE):-
  !,
  delete(List, E, ListWithoutE).
delete([H | List], E, [H | ListWithoutE]):-
  H \= E,
  !,
  delete(List, E, ListWithoutE).
```

The three clauses are mutually exclusive, and the cuts make it possible to omit
the condition H \= E in the second rule. This improves the program efficiency but
makes it less legible.

A.9.4 The intersection/3 Predicate

The intersection/3 predicate computes the intersection of two sets represented
as lists: intersection(InputSet1, InputSet2, Intersection).

```
?- intersection([a, b, c], [d, b, e, a], L).
L = [a, b]
```

InputSet1 and InputSet2 should be without duplicates; otherwise
intersection/3 approximates the intersection set relatively to the first argument:

```
?- intersection([a, b, c, a], [d, b, e, a], L).
L = [a, b, a]
```

The predicate is defined as:

```
% Termination case
intersection([], _, []).
% Head of L1 is in L2
intersection([X | L1], L2, [X | L3]) :-
  member(X, L2),
```

```
  !,
  intersection(L1, L2, L3).
% Head of L1 is not in L2
intersection([X | L1], L2, L3) :-
  \+ member(X, L2),
  !,
  intersection(L1, L2, L3).
```

As for delete/3, clauses of intersection/3 are mutually exclusive, and the programmer can omit the condition \+ member(X, L₂) in the third clause.

A.9.5 The reverse/2 Predicate

The reverse/2 predicate reverses the elements of a list. There are two classic ways to define it. The first definition is straightforward but consumes much memory. It is often called the naïve reverse:

```
reverse([], []).
reverse([X | XS], YS] :-
  reverse(XS,, RXS),
  append(RX, [X], Y).
```

A second solution improves the memory consumption. It uses a third argument as an accumulator.

```
reverse(X, Y) :-
  reverse(X, [], Y).

reverse([], YS, YS).
reverse([X | XS], Accu, YS):-
  reverse(XS, [X | Accu], YS).
```

A.9.6 The Mode of an Argument

The **mode** of an argument defines if it is typically an input (+) or an output (-). Inputs must be instantiated, while outputs are normally uninstantiated. Some predicates have multiple modes of use. We saw three modes for append/3:

- append(+List1, +List2, +List3),
- append(+List1, +List2, -List3), and
- append(-List1, -List2, +List3).

A question mark "?" denotes that an argument can either be instantiated or not. Thus, the two first modes of append/3 can be compacted into append(+List1, +List2, ?List3). The actual mode of append/3, which describes all possibilities is, in fact, append(?List1, ?List2, ?List3). Finally, "@" indicates that the argument is normally a compound term that shall remain unaltered.

It is a good programming practice to annotate predicates with their common modes of use.

A.10 Operators and Arithmetic

A.10.1 Operators

Prolog defines a set of prefix, infix, and postfix operators that includes the classical arithmetic symbols: "+", "-", "*", and "/". The Prolog interpreter considers operators as functors and transforms expressions into terms. Thus, 2 * 3 + 4 * 2 is equivalent to + (* (2, 3), * (4, 2)).

The mapping of operators onto terms is governed by rules of priority and classes of associativity:

- The priority of an operator is an integer ranging from 1 to 1200. It enables us to determine recursively the principal functor of a term. Higher-priority operators will be higher in the tree representing a term.
- The associativity determines the bracketing of term A op B op C:
  1. If op is left-associative, the term is read (A op B) op C;
  2. If op is right-associative, the term is read A op (B op C).

Prolog defines an operator by its name, its **specifier**, and its priority. The specifier is a mnemonic to denote the operator class of associativity and whether it is infixed, prefixed, or postfixed (Table A.2).

Table A.2. Operator specifiers.

Operator	Nonassociative	Right-associative	Left-associative
Infix	*xfx*	*xfy*	*yfx*
Prefix	*fx*	*fy*	–
Postfix	*xf*	–	*yf*

Table A.3 shows the priority and specifier of predefined operators in Standard Prolog.

It is possible to declare new operators using the directive:

```
:- op(+Priority, +Specifier, +Name).
```

A.10.2 Arithmetic Operations

The evaluation of an arithmetic expression uses the is/2 built-in operator. is/2 computes the value of the Expression to the right of it and unifies it with Value:

```
?- Value is Expression.
```

where Expression must be computable. Let us exemplify it. Recall first that "=" does not evaluate the arithmetic expression:

Table A.3. Priority and specifier of operators in Standard Prolog.

Priority	Specifier	Operators
1200	xfx	:- -->
1200	fx	:- ?-
1100	xfy	;
1050	xfy	->
1000	xfy	','
900	fy	\+
700	xfx	= \=
700	xfx	== \== @< @=< @> @>=
700	xfx	=..
700	xfx	is =:= =\= < =< > >=
550	xfy	:
500	yfx	+ - # /\ \/
400	yfx	* / // rem mod << >>
200	xfx	**
200	xfy	^
200	fy	+ - \

```
?- X = 1 + 1 + 1.
X = 1 + 1 + 1 (or X = +(+(1, 1), 1)).
```

To get a value, it is necessary to use is

```
?- X = 1 + 1 + 1, Y is X.
X = 1 + 1 + 1, Y = 3.
```

If the arithmetic expression is not valid, is/2 returns an error, as in

```
?- X is 1 + 1 + a.
Error
```

because a is not a number, or as in

```
?- X is 1 + 1 + Z.
Error
```

because Z is not instantiated to a number. But

```
?- Z = 2, X is 1 + 1 + Z.
Z = 2, X = 4
```

is correct because Z has a numerical value when X is evaluated.

A.10.3 Comparison Operators

Comparison operators process arithmetic and literal expressions. They evaluate arithmetic expressions to the left and to the right of the operator before comparing them, for example:

```
?- 1 + 2 < 3 + 4.
Yes
```

Comparison operators for literal expressions rank terms according to their lexical order, for example:

```
?- a @< b.
Yes
```

Standard Prolog defines a lexical ordering of terms that is based on the ASCII value of characters and other considerations. Table A.4 shows a list of comparison operators for arithmetic and literal expressions.

Table A.4. Comparison operators.

	Arithmetic comparison	Literal term comparison
Equality operator	= : =	==
Inequality operator	=\=	\==
Inferior	<	@<
Inferior or equal	=<	@=<
Superior	>	@>
Superior or equal	>=	@>=

It is a common mistake of beginners to confuse the arithmetic comparison (= : =), literal comparison (==), and even sometimes unification (=). Unification is a logical operation that finds two substitutions to render two terms identical; an arithmetic comparison computes the numerical values of the left and right expressions and compares their resulting value; a term comparison compares literal values of terms but does not perform any operation on them. Here are some examples:

```
?- 1 + 2 =:= 2 + 1.        ?- 1 + 2 == 1 + 2.
Yes                        Yes
?- 1 + 2 = 2 + 1.          ?- 1 + 2 == 2 + 1.
No                         No
?- 1 + 2 = 1 + 2.          ?- 1 + X == 1 + 2.
Yes                        No
?- 1 + X = 1 + 2.          ?- 1 + a == 1 + a.
X = 2                      Yes
?- 1 + X =:= 1 + 2.
Error
```

A.10.4 Lists and Arithmetic: The `length/2` Predicate

The `length/2` predicate determines the length of a list

```
?- length([a, b, c], 3).
Yes

?- length([a, [a, b], c], N).
N = 3
```

`length(+List, ?N)` traverses the list `List` and increments a counter `N`. Its definition in Prolog is:

```
length([],0).
length([X | XS], N) :-
   length(XS, N1),
   N is N1 + 1.
```

The order of subgoals in the rule is significant because `N1` has no value until Prolog has traversed the whole list. This value is computed as Prolog pops the recursive calls from the stack. Should subgoals be inverted, the computation of the length would generate an error telling that `N1` is not a number.

A.10.5 Lists and Comparison: The `quicksort/2` Predicate

The `quicksort/2` predicate sorts the elements of a list `[H | T]`. It first selects an arbitrary element from the list to sort, here the head, `H`. It splits the list into two sublists containing the elements smaller than this arbitrary element and the elements greater. `Quicksort` then sorts both sublists recursively and appends them once they are sorted. In this program, the `before/2` predicate compares the list elements using the `@</2` literal operator.

```
% quicksort(+InputList, -SortedList)

quicksort([], []) :- !.
quicksort([H | T], LSorted) :-
   split(H, T, LSmall, LBig),
   quicksort(LSmall, LSmallSorted),
   quicksort(LBig, LBigSorted),
   append(LSmallSorted, [H | LBigSorted], LSorted).

split(X, [Y | L], [Y | LSmall], LBig) :-
   before(Y, X),
   !,
   split(X, L, LSmall, LBig).
split(X, [Y | L], LSmall, [Y | LBig]) :-
   !,
```

```
    split(X, L, LSmall, LBig).
split(_, [], [], []) :- !.

before(X, Y) :- X @< Y.
```

A.11 Some Other Built-in Predicates

The set of built-in predicates may vary according to Prolog implementations. Here is a list common to many Prologs. Consult your reference manual to have the complete list.

A.11.1 Type Predicates

The type predicates check the type of a term. Their mode of use is `type_predicate(?Term)`.

- `integer/1`: Is the argument an integer?

  ```
  ?- integer(3).
  Yes
  ```

  ```
  ?- integer(X).
  No
  ```

- `number/1`: Is the argument a number?

  ```
  ?- number(3.14).
  Yes
  ```

- `float/1`: Is the argument a floating-point number?
- `atom/1`: Is the argument an atom?

  ```
  ?- atom(abc).
  Yes
  ```

  ```
  ?- atom(3).
  No
  ```

- `atomic/1`: Is the argument an atomic value, i.e., a number or an atom?
- `var/1`: Is the argument a variable?

  ```
  ?- var(X).
  Yes
  ```

  ```
  ?- X = f(Z), var(X).
  No
  ```

- `nonvar/1`: The opposite of `var/1`.

```
?- nonvar(X).
No
```

- compound/1: Is the argument a compound term?

```
?- compound(X).
No

?- compound(f(X, Y)).
Yes
```

- ground/1: Is the argument a ground term?

```
?- ground(f(a, b)).
Yes

?- ground(f(a, Y)).
No
```

A.11.2 Term Manipulation Predicates

The term manipulation predicates enable us to access and modify elements of compound terms.

- The built-in predicate functor(+Term, ?Functor, ?Arity) gets the principal functor of a term and its arity.

```
?- functor(father(ulysses, telemachus), F, A).
F = father, A = 2
```

functor also returns the most general term given a functor name and an arity. Functor and Arity must then be instantiated: functor(-Term, +Functor, +Arity)

```
?- functor(T, father, 2).
T = father(X, Y)
```

- The predicate arg(+N, +Term, ?X) unifies X to the argument of rank N in Term.

```
?- arg(1, father(ulysses, telemachus), X).
X = ulysses
```

- The operator Term =.. List, also known as the *univ* predicate, transforms a term into a list.

```
?- father(ulysses, telemachus) =.. L.
L = [father, ulysses, telemachus]

?- T =.. [a, b, c].
T = a(b, c)
```

Univ has two modes of use: +Term =.. ?List, or -Term =.. +List.

- The predicate name (?Atom, ?List) transforms an atom into a list of ASCII codes.

```
?- name(abc, L).
L = [97, 98, 99]

?- name(A, [97, 98, 99]).
A = abc
```

Standard Prolog provides means to encode strings more naturally using double quotes. Thus

```
?- "abc" = L.
L = [97, 98, 99]
```

A.12 Handling Run-Time Errors and Exceptions

Standard Prolog features a mechanism to handle run-time errors. An error or exception occurs when the execution cannot be completed normally either successfully or by a failure. Examples of exceptions include division by zero, the attempt to evaluate arithmetically nonnumerical values with is/2, and calling a noninstantiated variable in the body of a rule:

```
?- X is 1/0.
ERROR: //2: Arithmetic evaluation error: zero_divisor

?- X is 1 + Y.
ERROR: Arguments are not sufficiently instantiated

?- X.
ERROR: Arguments are not sufficiently instantiated
```

In the normal course of a program, such faulty clauses generate run-time errors and stop the execution. The programmer can also trap these errors and recover from them using the catch/3 built-in predicate.

catch(+Goal, ?Catcher, ?Recover) executes Goal and behaves like call/1 if no error occurs. If an error is raised and unifies with Catcher, catch/3 proceeds with Recover and continues the execution.

Standard Prolog defines catchers of built-in predicates under the form of the term error(ErrorTerm, Information), where ErrorTerm is a standard description of the error and Information depends on the implementation. The query:

```
?- catch((X is 1 + Y), Error, (write(Error),nl,fail)).
error(instantiation_error,
```

```
context(system: (is)/2, _GXyz))
```

No

attempts to execute X is Y + 1, raises an error, and executes the recover goal, which prints the error and fails. The constant instantiation_error is part of the set of error cases defined by Standard Prolog.

Built-in predicates execute a throw/1 to raise exceptions when they detect an error. The throw predicate immediately goes back to a calling catch/3. If there is no such catch, by default, the execution is stopped and the control is transferred to the user.

User-defined predicates can also make use of throw(+Exception) to throw an error, as in:

```
throw_error :- throw(error(error_condition,context)).
```

The corresponding error can be caught as in the query:

```
?- catch(throw_error, Error, (write(Error),nl,fail)).
error(error_condition, context)
```

No

A.13 Dynamically Accessing and Updating the Database

A.13.1 Accessing a Clause: The clause/2 Predicate

The built-in predicate clause(+Head, ?Body) returns the body of a clause whose head unifies with Head. Let us illustrate this with the program:

```
hero(ulysses).
heroin(penelope).

daughter(X, Y) :-
  mother(Y, X),
  female(X).
daughter(X, Y) :-
  father(Y, X),
  female(X).
```

and the query:

```
?- clause(daughter(X, Y), B).
B = (mother(Y, X), female(X));
B = (father(Y, X), female(X));
No

?- clause(heroin(X), B).
X = penelope, B = true.
```

A.13.2 Dynamic and Static Predicates

The built-in predicates `asserta/1`, `assertz/1`, `retract/1`, and `abolish/1` add or remove clauses – rules and facts – during the execution of a program. They allow to update the database – and hence to modify the program – dynamically.

A major difference between Prolog implementations is whether the system interprets the program or compiles it. Roughly, an interpreter does not change the format of rules and facts to run them. A compiler translates clauses into a machine-dependent code or into more efficient instructions (Maier and Warren 1988). A compiled program runs much faster then.

Compiling occurs once at load time, and the resulting code is no longer modifiable during execution. To run properly, the Prolog engine must be told which predicates are alterable at run-time – the **dynamic** predicates – and which ones will remain unchanged – the **static** predicates. Prolog compiles static predicates and runs dynamic predicates using an interpreter.

A predicate is static by default. Dynamic predicates must either be declared using the `dynamic/1` directive or be entirely created by assertions at run time. In the latter case, the first assertion of a clause declares automatically the new predicate to be dynamic. The directive specifying that a predicate is dynamic precedes all its clauses, if any. For example, the program:

```
:- dynamic parent/2, male/1.
...
parent(X, Y) :-
...
male(xy).
...
```

declares that `parent/2` and `male/1` clauses may be added or removed at run time.

The predicates `asserta/1`, `assertz/1`, `retract/1`, and `abolish/1` can modify clauses of dynamic predicates only. Adding or removing a clause for a static predicate raises an error condition.

A.13.3 Adding a Clause: The `asserta/1` and `assertz/1` Predicates

The predicate `asserta(+P)` adds the clause P to the database. P is inserted just before the other clauses of the same predicate. As we have seen before, the predicate corresponding to the clause P must be dynamic: declared using the `dynamic/1` directive or entirely asserted at run time.

```
                                    % State of the database
                                    % Before assertion
                                    % hero(ulysses).
                                    % hero(hector).
?- asserta(hero(achilles)).
                                    % State of the database
                                    % After assertion
                                    % hero(achilles).
                                    % hero(ulysses).
                                    % hero(hector).
```

The predicate `assertz/1` also adds a new clause, but as the last one of the procedure this time.

Adding rules is similar. It requires double parentheses, as in

```
asserta((P :- B, C, D)).
```

However, it is never advised to assert rules. Modifying rules while running a program is rarely useful and may introduce nasty bugs.

Novice Prolog programmers may try to communicate the results of a procedure by asserting facts to the database. This is not a good practice because it hides what is the real output of a predicate. Results, especially intermediate results, should be passed along from one procedure to another using arguments. Assertions should only reflect a permanent change in the program state.

A.13.4 Removing Clauses: The `retract/1` and `abolish/2` Predicates

The built-in predicates `retract/1` and `abolish/1` remove clauses of a dynamic predicate. `retract(+P)` retracts clause P from the database.

```
                                    % State of the database
                                    % Before removal
                                    % hero(ulysses).
                                    % hero(achilles).
                                    % hero(hector).
?- retract(hero(hector)).
                                    % State of the database
                                    % After
                                    % hero(ulysses).
                                    % hero(achilles).
?- retract(hero(X)).
X = ulysses ;
X = achilles ;
No
?- hero(X).
No
```

The predicate `abolish(+Predicate/Arity)` removes all clauses of `Predicate` with arity `Arity` from the database.

A.13.5 Handling Unknown Predicates

When a static predicate is called and is not in the database, it is often a bug. A frequent cause is due to wrong typing as, for example, `parnet(X, Y)` instead of `parent(X, Y)`, where n and e are twiddled. For this reason, by default, Prolog raises an error in the case of such a call.

An effect of `dynamic/1` is to declare a predicate to the Prolog engine. Such a predicate 'exists' then, even if it has no clauses. A call to a dynamic predicate that has no clauses in the database is not considered as an error. It fails, simply and silently.

The Prolog engine behavior to calls to unknown predicates can be modified using the `unknown/2` directive:

```
:- unknown(-OldValue, +NewValue).
```

where `OldValue` and `NewValue` can be:

- `warning` – A call to an unknown predicate issues a warning and fails.
- `error` – A call to an unknown predicate raises an error. As we saw, this is the default value.
- `fail` – A call to an unknown predicate fails silently.

  A Prolog flag also defines this behavior. It can be set by `set_prolog_flag/2`:

```
?- set_prolog_flag(+FlagName, +NewValue).
```

where `FlagName` is set to `unknown` and possible values are `error`, `warning`, or `fail`. The current flag status is obtained by `current_prolog_flag/2`:

```
?- current_prolog_flag(+FlagName, ?Value).
```

A.14 All-Solutions Predicates

The second-order predicates `findall/3`, `bagof/3`, and `setof/3` return all the solutions to a given query. The predicate `findall` is the basic form of all-solutions predicates, while `bagof` and `setof` are more elaborate. We exemplify them with the database:

```
character(ulysses, iliad).
character(hector, iliad).
character(achilles, iliad).
character(ulysses, odyssey).
character(penelope, odyssey).
character(telemachus, odyssey).
```

`findall(+Variable, +Goal, ?Solution)` unifies `Solution` with the list of all the possible values of `Variable` when querying `Goal`.

```
?- findall(X, character(X, iliad), B).
B = [ulysses, hector, achilles]
```

```
?- findall(X, character(X, Y), B).
B = [ulysses, hector, achilles, ulysses, penelope,
telemachus]
```

The predicate `bagof(+Variable, +Goal, ?Solution)` is similar to `findall/3`, except that it backtracks on the free variables of `Goal`:

```
?- bagof(X, character(X, iliad), Bag).
Bag = [ulysses, hector, achilles]
```

```
?- bagof(X, character(X, Y), Bag).
Bag =[ ulysses, hector, achilles], Y = iliad ;
Bag = [ulysses, penelope, telemachus], Y = odyssey ;
No.
```

Variables in `Goal` are not considered free if they are existentially quantified. The existential quantifier uses the infix operator "`^`". Let X be a variable in `Goal`. `X^Goal` means that there exists X such that `Goal` is true. `bagof/3` does not backtrack on it. For example:

```
?- bagof(X, Y^character(X, Y), Bag).
Bag = [ulysses, hector, achilles, ulysses,
penelope, telemachus]
```

```
?- bagof(X, Y^(character(X, Y), female(X)), Bag).
Bag = [penelope]
```

The predicate `setof(+Variable, +Goal, ?Solution)` does the same thing as `bagof/3`, except that the `Solution` list is sorted and duplicates are removed from it:

```
?- setof(X, Y^character(X, Y), Bag).
Bag = [achilles, hector, penelope, telemachus,
ulysses]
```

A.15 Fundamental Search Algorithms

Many problems in logic can be represented using a graph or a tree, where finding a solution corresponds to searching a path going from an initial state to a goal state. The search procedure starts from an initial node, checks whether the current node meets a goal condition, and if not, goes to a next node. The transition from one node to a next one is carried out using a successor predicate, and the solution is the sequence of nodes traversed to reach the goal. In the context of search, the graph is also called the **state space**.

In this section, we will review some fundamental search strategies and as an application example, we will try to find our way through the labyrinth shown in Fig. A.9. As we saw, Prolog has an embedded search mechanism that can be used with little adaptation to implement other algorithms. It will provide us with the Ariadne's thread to remember our way in the maze with minimal coding efforts.

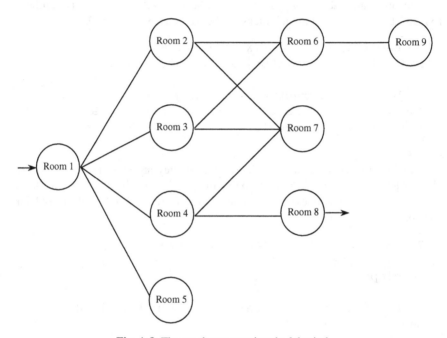

Fig. A.9. The graph representing the labyrinth.

A.15.1 Representing the Graph

We use a successor predicate s(X, Y) to represent the graph, where Y is the successor of X. For the labyrinth, the s/2 predicate describes the immediate links from one room to another. The links between rooms are:

```
link(r1, r2). link(r1, r3). link(r1, r4). link(r1,
r5). link(r2, r6). link(r2, r7). link(r3, r6).
link(r3, r7). link(r4, r7). link(r4, r8). link(r6,
r9).
```

Since links can be traversed both ways, the s/2 predicate is:

```
s(X, Y) :- link(X, Y).
s(X, Y) :- link(Y, X).
```

The goal is expressed as:

```
goal(X) :- minotaur(X).
```

where

```
minotaur(r8).
```

Finally, we could associate a cost to the link, for instance, to take into account its length. The predicate would then be:

```
s(X, Y, Cost).
```

A.15.2 Depth-First Search

A depth-first search is just the application of the Prolog resolution strategy. It explores the state space by traversing a sequence of successors to the initial node until it finds a goal. The search goes down the graph until it reaches a node without successor. It then backtracks from the bottom to the last node that has successors.

Searching a path in a labyrinth is then very similar to other programs we have written before. It consists of a first rule to describe the goal condition and second recursive one to find a successor node when the condition is not met. The depth_first_search(+Node, -Path) predicate uses the initial node as input and returns the path to reach the goal:

```
%% depth_first_search(+Node, -Path)
depth_first_search(Node, [Node]) :-
  goal(Node).
depth_first_search(Node, [Node | Path]) :-
  s(Node, Node1),
  depth_first_search(Node1, Path).
```

This short program does not work, however, because the path could include infinite cycles: Room 2 to Room 6 to Room 2 to Room 6... To prevent them, we need to remember the current path in an accumulator variable and to avoid the successors of the current node that are already members of the path. We use a depth_first_search/3 auxiliary predicate, and the new program is:

```
%% depth_first_search(+Node, -Path)
depth_first_search(Node, Path) :-
  depth_first_search(Node, [], Path).

%% depth_first_search(+Node, +CurrentPath,-FinalPath)
depth_first_search(Node, Path, [Node | Path]) :-
  goal(Node).
```

```
depth_first_search(Node, Path, FinalPath) :-
  s(Node, Node1),
  \+ member(Node1, Path),
  depth_first_search(Node1, [Node | Path],FinalPath).
```

The result of the search is:

```
?- depth_first_search(r1, L).
L = [r8, r4, r7, r3, r6, r2, r1] ;
L = [r8, r4, r7, r2, r1] ;
L = [r8, r4, r7, r2, r6, r3, r1] ;
L = [r8, r4, r7, r3, r1] ;
L = [r8, r4, r1] ;
No
?-
```

A.15.3 Breadth-First Search

The breadth-first search explores the paths in parallel. It starts with the first node, all the successors of the first node, all the successors of the successors, and so on, until it finds a solution.

If the list [Node | Path] describes a path to a node, the search needs to expand all the successors of Node. It generates the corresponding paths as lists. There are as many lists as there are successors to Node. The search then sets the successors as the heads of these lists. This is done compactly using the bagof/3 predicate:

```
expand([Node | Path], ExpandedPaths) :-
  bagof(
    [Node1, Node | Path],
    (s(Node, Node1), \+ member(Node1, Path)),
    ExpandedPaths).
```

As with the depth-first search, the breadth-first search consists of two rules. The first rule describes the goal condition. It extracts the first path from the list and checks whether the head node is a goal. The second rule implements the recursion. It expands the first path – the head of the list – into a list of paths that go one level deeper in the graph and appends them to the end of the other paths. The breadth_first_search(+Node, -Path) predicate uses the initial node as input and returns the path to reach the goal. The program needs to start with a list of lists, and it uses the auxiliary predicate bf_search_aux/2.

```
%% breadth_first_search(+Node, -Path)
breadth_first_search(Node, Path) :-
  bf_search_aux([[Node]], Path).

bf_search_aux([[Node | Path] | _], [Node | Path]) :-
  goal(Node).
```

```
bf_search_aux([CurrentPath | NextPaths],
    FinalPath) :-
  expand(CurrentPath, ExpandedPaths),
  append(NextPaths, ExpandedPaths, NewPaths),
  bf_search_aux(NewPaths, FinalPath).
```

The program is not completely correct, however, because expand/2 can fail and make the whole search fail. A failure of expand/2 means that the search cannot go further in this path and it has found no goal node in it. We can remove the path from the list then. To reflect this, we must add a second rule to expand/2 that sets the path to the empty list and prevents the first rule from backtracking:

```
expand([Node | Path], ExpandedPaths) :-
  bagof(
    [Node1, Node | Path],
    (s(Node, Node1), \+ member(Node1, Path)),
    ExpandedPaths),
  !.
expand(Path, []).
```

The result of the search is:

```
?- breadth_first_search(r1, L).
L = [r8, r4, r1] ;
L = [r8, r4, r7, r2, r1] ;
L = [r8, r4, r7, r3, r1] ;
L = [r8, r4, r7, r3, r6, r2, r1] ;
L = [r8, r4, r7, r2, r6, r3, r1] ;
No
?-
```

The breadth-first search strategy guarantees that it will find the shortest path to the solution. A disadvantage is that it must store and maintain all exploration paths in parallel. This requires a huge memory, even for a limited search depth.

A.15.4 A* Search

The A* search is a variation and an optimization of the breadth-first search. Instead of expanding the first path of the list, it uses heuristics to select a better candidate. While searching the graph, A* associates a value to paths it traverses. This value is a function f of the node being traversed. $f(n)$ at node n is the sum of two terms $f(n) = g(n) + h(n)$, where $g(n)$ is the length of the path used to reach node n and $h(n)$ is the estimate of the remaining length to reach the goal node. From a given node, A* ranks the possible subsequent nodes minimizing $f(n)$. It then explores "best nodes" first and thus avoids a blind searching.

The main difficulty of the A* search is to find a suitable h function. Its presentation is outside the scope of this appendix. Russell and Norvig (2003) examine search strategies in detail. Bratko (2001) describes an implementation of A* in Prolog.

A.16 Input/Output

The first Prolog systems had only primitive input/output facilities. Standard Prolog defines a complete new set of predicates. They represent a major change in the Prolog language, and although they are more flexible they are not universally accepted yet. This section introduces both sets of predicates. It outlines Standard Prolog input/output predicates and predicates conforming to the older tradition of Edinburgh Prolog. Most input/output predicates are deterministic, that is, they give no alternative solutions upon backtracking.

A.16.1 Reading and Writing Characters with Edinburgh Prolog

In Edinburgh Prolog, reading characters from the keyboard and writing to the screen is carried out using get0/1 and put/1. Both predicates process characters using their ASCII codes. get0/1 unifies with −1 when it reaches the end of a file. Here are some examples of use:

```
?- get0(X).
a ?

X = 97

?- put(65).
a

?- get0(X).
^D

X = -1
```

A.16.2 Reading and Writing Terms with Edinburgh Prolog

The built-in predicates read/1 and write/1 read and write terms from the current input and output streams. read(?Term) reads one term:

```
?- read(X).
character(ulysses, odyssey).

X = character(ulysses, odyssey)
```

where the input term must be terminated by a period. When reaching the end of a file, X unifies with the build-in atom end_of_file:

```
?- read(X).
^D
X = end_of_file
```

Writing terms is similar. `write(+Term)` writes one term to the current output stream and `nl/0` prints a new line:

```
?- T = character(ulysses, odyssey), write(T), nl.
character(ulysses, odyssey)

T = character(ulysses, odyssey)
?-
```

A.16.3 Opening and Closing Files with Edinburgh Prolog

Prolog input and output predicates normally write on the screen – the standard output – and read from the keyboard – the standard input. The predicates `see/1` and `tell/1` redirect the input and output so that a program can read or write any file.

    `see/1` and `tell/1` open a file for reading and for writing. Then input/output predicates such as `get0/1`, `read/1` or `put/1`, `write/1` are redirected to the current open file. Several files may be open at the same time. The program switches between open files using `see/1` or `tell/1` until they are closed. `seen/0` and `told/0` close the open input and the open output, respectively, and return to the standard input/output, that is, to the keyboard and the screen. Let us show this with an example.

`see(in_file),`	Opens `in_file` as the current input stream.
`see(user),`	The current stream becomes the user – the keyboard.
`see(in_file),`	`in_file` becomes the current input stream again with the reading the position it had before.
`seen,`	Closes the current input stream. The current stream becomes the keyboard.
`seeing(IN_STREAM),`	`IN_STREAM` unifies with the current input stream.
`tell(out_file),`	Opens `out_file` as the current output stream (creates a new file or empties a previously existing file).
`telling(OUT_STREAM),`	`OUT_STREAM` unifies with the current output stream.
`tell(user),`	The current output stream becomes the user – the screen.
`told.`	Closes the current output stream. The current output stream becomes the user.

Here is a short program to read a file:

```
read_file(FileName, CodeList) :-
  see(FileName),
  read_list(CodeList),
```

```
   seen.

 read_list([C | L]) :-
    get0(C),
    C =\= -1, % end of file
    !,
    read_list(L).
 read_list([]).
```

A.16.4 Reading and Writing Characters with Standard Prolog

Standard Prolog uses streams to read and write characters. A stream roughly corresponds to an open file. Streams are divided into output streams or sinks, and input streams or sources. By default, there are two current open streams: the standard input stream, which is usually the keyboard, and the standard output stream, the screen. Other streams are opened and closed using open/4, open/3, close/1, and close/2.

The predicates to read and write a character are get_char/1, get_char/2, put_char/1, and put_char/2:

- get_char(?Char) unifies Char with the next character of the current input stream.
- get_char(+Stream, ?Char) unifies Char with the next character of the open input stream Stream. get_char/1 and get_char/2 predicates unify with end_of_file when they reach the end of a file.
- put_char(+Char) writes Char to the current output stream.
- put_char(+Stream, ?Char) writes Char to the open output Stream.
- nl/0 and nl(+Stream) write a new line to the current output stream or to Stream.

Here is a short example:

```
?- get_char(X).
a ?

X = a

?- put_char(a).
a

?- get_char(X).
^D

X = end_of_file
```

Instead of reading and writing characters, we may want to read or write their numeric code, ASCII or Unicode, as with Edinburgh's `get0/1`. The corresponding Standard Prolog predicates are `get_code/1`, `get_code/2`, `put_code/1`, and `put_code/2`.

The predicates `get_char` and `get_code` read a character or a code, remove it from the input stream, and move to the next character. Sometimes it is useful to read a character without removing it. The predicates `peek_char` and `peek_code` do just that. They unify with the current character but stay at the same position and leave the character in the stream.

A.16.5 Reading and Writing Terms with Standard Prolog

The Standard Prolog predicates `read/1` and `write/1` are identical to those of Edinburgh Prolog:

* `read(?Term)` reads one term from the current input stream.
* `write(+Term)` writes a term to the current output stream.

  `read/2` and `write/2` read and write terms from and to a file:

* `read(+Stream, ?Term)` reads a term from `Stream`.
* `write(+Stream, ?Term)` writes a term to `Stream`.

The predicates `read_term` and `write_term` read and write terms with a list of options, either to the current input/output, `read_term/2` and `write_term/2`, or to a file, `read_term/3` and `write_term/3`. The options make it possible to adjust the printing format, for instance. They may depend on the implementation and the operating system. Consult your manual to have the complete list. The predicates `read` and `write` are equivalent to `read_term` and `write_term` with an empty list of options.

A.16.6 Opening and Closing Files with Standard Prolog

The predicates to open and close a stream are `open/4`, `open/3`, `close/1`, and `close/2`:

* `open(+SourceSink, +Mode, -Stream)` opens the file `SourceSink` in an input or output `Mode`. The `Mode` value is one of `read`, `write`, `append`, or `update`. `Stream` unifies with the opened stream and is used for the subsequent input or output operations.
* `open(+SourceSink, +Mode, -Stream, +Options)` opens the file with a list of options. `open/3` is equivalent to `open/4` with an empty list of options. Consult your manual to have the complete list.
* `close(+Stream)` closes the stream `Stream`.
* `close(+Stream, +Options)` closes the stream `Stream` with a list of options. `close/1` is equivalent to `close/2` with an empty list of options.

Here is a short program to read a file with Standard Prolog predicates:

```
read_file(FileName, CharList) :-
  open(FileName, read, Stream),
  read_list(Stream, CharList),
  close(Stream).

read_list(Stream, [C | L]) :-
  get_char(Stream, C),
  C \== end_of_file, % end of file
  !,
  read_list(Stream, L).
read_list(_, []).
```

Other useful predicates include current_input/1, current_output/1, set_input/1, and set_output/1:

- current_input(?Stream) unifies Stream with the current input stream.
- current_output(?Stream) unifies Stream with the current output.
- set_input(+Stream) sets Stream to be the current input stream.
- set_output(+Stream) sets Stream to be the current output stream.

A.16.7 Writing Loops

Programmers sometimes wonder how to write iterative loops in Prolog, especially with input/output to read or to write a sequence of terms. This is normally done with a recursive rule, as to read a file. Counting numbers down to 0 takes the form:

```
countdown(X) :-
  number(X),
  X < 0.
countdown(X) :-
  number(X),
  X >= 0,
  write(X), nl,
  NX is X - 1,
  countdown(NX).
```

For example,

```
?- countdown(4).
4
3
2
1
0
?-
```

In some other cases, backtracking using the `repeat/0` built-in predicate can substitute a loop. The `repeat/0` definition is:

```
repeat.
repeat :- repeat.
```

`repeat` never fails and when inserted as a subgoal, any subsequent backtracking goes back to it and the sequence of subgoals to its right gets executed again. So, a sequence of subgoals can be executed any number of times until a condition is satisfied. The `read_write/1` predicate below reads and writes a sequence of atoms until the atom `end` is encountered. It takes the form of a repetition (`repeat`) of reading a term X using `read/1`, writing it (`write/1`), and a final condition (X `== end`). It corresponds to the rule:

```
read_write :-
  repeat,
  read(X),
  write(X), nl,
  X == end,
  !.
```

A.17 Developing Prolog Programs

A.17.1 Presentation Style

Programs are normally written once and then are possibly read and modified several times. A major concern of the programmer should be to write clear and legible code. It helps enormously with the maintenance and debugging of programs.

Before programming, it is essential first to have a good formulation and decomposition of the problem. The program construction should then reflect the logical structure of the solution. Although this statement may seem obvious, its implementation is difficult in practice. Clarity in a program structure is rarely attained from the first time. First attempts are rarely optimal but Prolog enables an incremental development where parts of the solution can be improved gradually.

A key to the good construction of a program is to name things properly. Cryptic predicates or variable names, such as `syntproc`, `def_code`, X, Ynn, and so on, should be banned. It is not rare that one starts with a predicate name and changes it in the course of the development to reflect a better description of the solution.

Since Prolog code is compact, the code of a clause should be short to remain easy to understand, especially with recursive programs. If necessary, the programmer should decompose a clause into smaller subclauses. Cuts and asserts should be kept to a minimum because they impair the declarativeness of a program. However, these are general rules that sometimes are difficult to respect when speed matters most.

Before its code definition, a predicate should be described in comments together with argument types and modes:

```
% predicate(+Arg1, +Arg2, -Arg3).
% Does this and that
% Arg1: list, Arg2: atom, Arg3: integer.
```

Clauses of a same predicate must be grouped together, even if some Prologs permit clauses to be disjoined. The layout of clauses should also be clear and adopt common rules of typography. Insert a space after commas or dots, for instance. The rule

```
pred1 :- pred2(c,d),e,f.
```

must be rejected because of sticking commas and obfuscated predicate names. Goals must be indented with tabulations, and there should be one single goal per line. Then

```
A :-
   B,
   C,
   D.
```

should be preferred to

```
A :- B, C, D.
```

except when the body consists of a single goal. The rule

```
A :- B.
```

is also acceptable.

A.17.2 Improving Programs

Once a program is written, it is generally possible to enhance it. This section introduces three techniques to improve program speed: goal ordering, memo functions, and tail recursion.

Order of Goals.   Ordering goals is meaningful for the efficiency of a program because Prolog tries them from left to right. The idea is to reduce the search space as much as possible from the first goals. If predicate p_1 has 1000 solutions in 1 s and p_2 has 1 solution taking 1000 hours to compute, avoid conjunction:

```
p1(X), p2(X).
```

A better ordering is:

```
p2(X), p1(X).
```

Lemmas or Memo Functions. Lemmas are used to improve the program speed. They are often exemplified with Fibonacci series. Fibonacci imagined around year 1200 how to estimate a population of rabbits, knowing that:

- A rabbit couple gives birth to another rabbit couple, one male and one female, each month (one month of gestation).
- A rabbit couple reproduces from the second month.
- Rabbits are immortal.

We can predict the number of rabbit couples at month n as a function of the number of rabbit couples at month $n - 1$ and $n - 2$:

$$rabbit(n) = rabbit(n - 1) + rabbit(n - 2)$$

A first implementation is straightforward from the formula:

```
fibonacci(1, 1).
fibonacci(2, 1).
fibonacci(M, N) :-
  M > 2,
  M1 is M - 1, fibonacci(M1, N1),
  M2 is M - 2, fibonacci(M2, N2),
  N is N1 + N2.
```

However, this program has an expensive double recursion and the same value can be recomputed several times. A better solution is to store Fibonacci values in the database using `asserta/1`. So an improved version is

```
fibonacci(1, 1).
fibonacci(2, 1).
fibonacci(M, N) :-
  M > 2,
  M1 is M - 1, fibonacci(M1, N1),
  M2 is M - 2, fibonacci(M2, N2),
  N is N1 + N2,
  asserta(fibonacci(M, N)).
```

The rule is then tried only if the value is not in the database.
The generic form of the lemma is:

```
lemma(P) :-
  P,
  asserta((P :- !)).
```

with "`!`" to avoid backtracking.

484   A An Introduction to Prolog

Tail Recursion. A tail recursion is a recursion where the recursive call is the last subgoal of the last rule, as in

```
f(X)  :- fact(X).
f(X)  :- g(X, Y), f(Y).
```

Recursion is generally very demanding in terms of memory, which grows with the number of recursive calls. A tail recursion is a special case that the interpreter can transform into an iteration. Most Prolog systems recognize and optimize it. They execute a tail-recursive predicate with a constant memory size.

It is therefore significant not to invert clauses of the previous program, as in

```
f(X)  :- g(X, Y), f(Y).
f(X)  :- fact(X).
```

which is not tail recursive.

It is sometimes possible to transform recursive predicates into a tail recursion equivalent, adding a variable as for length/2:

```
length(List, Length)  :-
    length(List, 0, Length).

length([], N, N).
length([X | L], N1, N)  :-
    N2 is N1 + 1,
    length(L, N2, N).
```

It is also sometimes possible to force a tail recursion using a cut, for example,

```
f(X)  :- g(X, Y), !, f(Y).
f(X)  :- fact(X).
```

Exercises

A.1. Describe a fragment of your family using Prolog facts.

A.2. Using the model of parent/2 and ancestor/2, write rules describing family relationships.

A.3. Write a program to describe routes between cities. Use a connect/2 predicate to describe direct links between cities as facts, for example, connect(paris, london), connect(london, edinburgh), etc., and write the route/2 recursive predicate that finds a path between cities.

A.4. Unify the following pairs:

```
f(g(A, B), a)  = f(C, A).
f(X, g(a, b))  = f(g(Z), g(Z, X)).
f(X, g(a, b))  = f(g(Z), g(Z, Y)).
```

A.5. Trace the son/2 program.

A.6. What is the effect of the query

```
?- f(X, X).
```

given the database:

```
f(X, Y) :- !, g(X), h(Y).
g(a).
g(b).
h(b).
```

A.7. What is the effect of the query

```
?- f(X, X).
```

given the database:

```
f(X, Y) :- g(X), !, h(Y).
g(a).
g(b).
h(b).
```

A.8. What is the effect of the query

```
?- f(X, X).
```

given the database:

```
f(X, Y) :- g(X), h(Y), !.
g(a).
g(b).
h(b).
```

A.9. What is the effect of the query

```
?- \+ f(X, X).
```

given the databases of the three previous exercises (Exercises A.6–A.8)? Provide three answers.

A.10. Write the last(?List, ?Element) predicate that succeeds if Element is the last element of the list.

A.11. Write the nth(?Nth, ?List, ?Element) predicate that succeeds if Element is the Nth element of the list.

A.12. Write the maximum(+List, ?Element) predicate that succeeds if Element is the greatest of the list.

A.13. Write the `flatten/2` predicate that flattens a list, i.e., removes nested lists:

```
?- flatten([a, [a, b, c], [[[d]]]], L).
L = [a, a, b, c, d]
```

A.14. Write the `subset(+Set1, +Set2)` predicate that succeeds if `Set1` is a subset of `Set2`.

A.15. Write the `subtract(+Set1, +Set2, ?Set3)` predicate that unifies `Set3` with the subtraction of `Set2` from `Set1`.

A.16. Write the `union(+Set1, +Set2, ?Set3)` predicate that unifies `Set3` with the union of `Set2` and `Set1`. `Set1` and `Set2` are lists without duplicates.

A.17. Write a program that transforms the lowercase characters of a file into their uppercase equivalent. The program should process accented characters, for example, *é* will be mapped to *É*.

A.18. Implement A* in Prolog.

Index

References

(2004). *Microsoft Office Word 2003 Rich Text Format (RTF) Specification*. Microsoft. RTF Version 1.8.

Abeillé, A. (1993). *Les nouvelles syntaxes: grammaires d'unification et analyse du français*. Armand Colin, Paris.

Abney, S. (1994). Partial parsing. Tutorial given at ANLP-94, Stuttgart. http://www.vinartus.net/spa/publications.html. Cited 28 October 2005.

Abney, S. (1996). Partial parsing via finite-state cascades. In *Proceedings of the ESSLLI'96 Robust Parsing Workshop*.

Agnäs, M.-S., Alshawi, H., Bretan, I., Carter, D., Ceder, K., Collins, M., Crouch, R., Digalakis, V., Ekholm, B., Gambäck, B., Kaja, J., Karlgren, J., Lyberg, B., Price, P., Pulman, S., Rayner, M., Samuelsson, C., and Svensson, T. (1994). Spoken language translator, first-year report. Research Report R94:03, SICS, Kista, Sweden.

Aho, A. V., Sethi, R., and Ullman, J. D. (1986). *Compilers: Principles, Techniques, and Tools*. Addison-Wesley, Reading, Massachusetts.

Alexandersson, J. (1996). Some ideas for the automatic acquisition of dialogue structure. In LuperFoy, S., Nijholt, A., and van Zanten, G. V., editors, *Proceedings of the Eleventh Twente Workshop on Language Technology*, pages 149–158, Universiteit Twente, Enschede.

Allen, J. F. (1983). Maintaining knowledge about temporal intervals. *Communications of the ACM*, 26(11):832–843.

Allen, J. F. (1984). Towards a general theory of action and time. *Artificial Intelligence*, 23(2):123–154.

Allen, J. F. (1994). *Natural Language Understanding*. Benjamin/Cummings, Redwood City, California, second edition.

Allen, J. F. and Core, M. (1997). Draft of DAMSL: Dialog annotation markup in several layers. http://www.cs.rochester.edu/research/cisd/resources/damsl/. Cited 28 October 2005.

Allen, J. F. and Perrault, C. R. (1980). Analyzing intentions in utterances. *Artificial Intelligence*, 15(3):143–178.

Allen, J. F., Schubert, L. K., Ferguson, G., Heeman, P., Hwang, C. H., Kato, T., Light, M., Martin, N. G., Miller, B. W., Poesio, M., and Traum, D. R. (1995).

The TRAINS project: A case study in building a conversational planning agent. *Journal of Experimental and Theoretical AI*, 7:7–48.

Alshawi, H., editor (1992). *The Core Language Engine*. MIT Press, Cambridge, Massachusetts.

Andry, F. (1992). *Mise en œuvre de prédictions linguistiques dans un système de dialogue oral homme-machine coopératif*. PhD thesis, Université Paris Nord.

Antworth, E. L. (1994). Morphological parsing with a unification-based word grammar. In *North Texas Natural Language Processing Workshop*, University of Texas at Arlington.

Antworth, E. L. (1995). *User's Guide to PC-KIMMO, Version 2*. Summer Institute of Linguistics, Dallas. http://www.sil.org/pckimmo/. Cited 28 October 2005.

Appelt, D., Hobbs, J., Bear, J., Israel, D., Kameyama, M., and Tyson, M. (1993). SRI: Description of the JV-FASTUS system used for MUC-5. In *Fifth Message Understanding Conference (MUC-5): Proceedings of a Conference Held in Baltimore, Maryland*, pages 221–235, San Francisco. Morgan Kaufmann.

Apt, K. (1997). *From Logic Programming to Prolog*. Prentice Hall, London.

Atkins, B. T., editor (1996). *Collins-Robert French-English, English-French dictionary*. HarperCollins and Dictionnaires Le Robert, New York–Paris.

Austin, J. L. (1962). *How to Do Things With Words*. Harvard University Press, Cambridge, Massachusetts.

Ball, G., Ling, D., Kurlander, D., Miller, J., Pugh, D., Skelly, T., Stankosky, A., Thiel, D., Dantzich, M. V., and Wax, T. (1997). Lifelike computer characters: the Persona project at Microsoft Research. In Bradshaw, J. M., editor, *Software Agents*, pages 191–222. AAAI Press/MIT Press, Cambridge, Massachusetts.

Baumann, R. (1991). *PROLOG. Einführungskurs*. Klett Schulbuch, Stuttgart.

Beesley, K. R. and Karttunen, L. (2003). *Finite State Morphology*. CSLI Publications, Stanford.

Bescherelle (1980). *L'art de conjuguer*. Hatier, Paris.

Bikel, D. M. (2004). Intricacies of Collins' parsing model. *Computational Linguistics*, 30(4):479–511.

Bilange, E. (1992). *Dialogue personne-machine*. Hermès, Paris.

Black, E., Abney, S., Flickenger, D., Gdaniec, C., Grishman, R., Harrison, P., Hindle, D., Ingria, R., Jelinek, F., Klavans, J., Liberman, M., Marcus, M., Roukos, S., Santorini, B., and Strzalkowski, T. (1991). A procedure for quantitatively comparing the syntactic coverage of English grammars. In *Speech and Natural Language: Proceedings of a Workshop Held at Pacific Grove, California*, pages 306–311, San Mateo. DARPA, Morgan Kaufmann.

Boguraev, B. and Pustejovsky, J., editors (1996). *Corpus Processing for Lexical Acquisition*. MIT Press, Cambridge, Massachusetts.

Boizumault, P. (1988). *Prolog, l'implantation*. Masson, Paris.

Boizumault, P. (1993). *The Implementation of Prolog*. Princeton University Press, Princeton.

Boser, B., Guyon, I., and Vapnik, V. (1992). A training algorithm for optimal margin classifiers. In *Proceedings of the Fifth Annual Workshop on Computational Learning Theory*, pages 144–152, Pittsburgh. ACM.

Boyer, M. (1988). Towards functional logic grammars. In Dahl, V. and Saint-Dizier, P., editors, *Natural Language Understanding and Logic Programming, II*, pages 45–61. North-Holland, Amsterdam.

Bratko, I. (2001). *PROLOG Programming for Artificial Intelligence*. Addison-Wesley, Harlow, 3rd edition.

Brill, E. (1995). Transformation-based error-driven learning and natural language processing: A case study in part-of-speech tagging. *Computational Linguistics*, 21(4):543–565.

Brin, S. and Page, L. (1998). The anatomy of a large-scale hypertextual web search engine. *Computer Networks*, 30(1–7):107–117. Proceedings of WWW7.

Bröker, N. (1998). How to define a context-free backbone for DGs: Implementing a DG in the LFG formalism. In Kahane, S. and Polguère, A., editors, *Processing of Dependency-Based Grammars. Proceedings of the Workshop*, pages 29–38. COLING-ACL.

Brown, P. E., Della Pietra, V. J., Della Pietra, S. A., and Mercer, R. L. (1993). The mathematics of statistical machine translation: Parameter estimation. *Computational Linguistics*, 19(2):263–311.

Bühler, K. (1982). *Sprachtheorie. Die Darstellungsfunktion der Sprache*. UTB, Stuttgart. First edition 1934.

Burke, E. and Foxley, E. (1996). *Logic and its Applications*. Prentice Hall, London.

Carberry, S. (1990). *Plan Recognition in Natural Language Dialogue*. MIT Press, Cambridge, Massachusetts.

Carlberger, J., Domeij, R., Kann, V., and Knutsson, O. (2006). The development and performance of a grammar checker for Swedish: A language engineering perspective. *submitted*.

Carlberger, J. and Kann, V. (1999). Implementing an efficient part-of-speech tagger. *Software – Practice and Experience*, 29(2):815–832.

Chanod, J.-P. (1994). Finite-state composition of French verb morphology. Technical Report MLTT-005, Rank Xerox Research Centre, Grenoble.

Charniak, E. (1993). *Statistical Language Learning*. MIT Press, Cambridge, Massachusetts.

Charniak, E. (1997). Statistical techniques for natural language parsing. *AI Magazine*.

Charniak, E. (2000). A maximum-entropy-inspired parser. In *Proceedings of the First Meeting of the North American Chapter of the ACL*, pages 132–139, Seattle.

Chinchor, N. (1997). MUC-7 named entity task definition. Technical report. www.itl.nist.gov/iaui/894.02/related_projects/muc/proceedings/ne_task.html. Cited 2 November 2005.

Chomsky, N. (1957). *Syntactic structures*. Mouton, The Hague.

Chomsky, N. (1981). *Lectures on Government and Binding*. Foris, Dordrecht.

Church, A. (1941). *The calculi of lambda-conversion*. Princeton University Press, Princeton.

Church, K. W. (1988). A stochastic parts program and noun phrase parser for unrestricted text. In *Proceedings of the Second Conference on Applied Natural Language Processing*, pages 136–143. ACL.

Church, K. W. and Hanks, P. (1990). Word association norms, mutual information, and lexicography. *Computational Linguistics*, 16(1):22–29.

Church, K. W. and Mercer, R. L. (1993). Introduction to the special issue on computational linguistics using large corpora. *Computational Linguistics*, 19(1):1–24.

Clarkson, P. R. and Rosenfeld, R. (1997). Statistical language modeling using the CMU-Cambridge toolkit. In *Proceedings ESCA Eurospeech*.

Clocksin, W. F. and Mellish, C. S. (2003). *Programming in Prolog: Using the ISO Standard*. Springer Verlag, Berlin Heidelberg New York, 5th edition.

Collins, M. J. (1996). A new statistical parser based on bigram lexical dependencies. In *Proceedings of the 34th Annual Meeting of the Association for Computational Linguistics*, pages 184–191, Santa Cruz, California.

Collins, M. J. (1999). *Head-Driven Statistical Models for Natural Language Parsing*. PhD thesis, University of Pennsylvania.

Collins, M. J. (2003). Head-driven statistical models for natural language parsing. *Computational Linguistics*, 29(4):589–637.

Colmerauer, A. (1970). Les systèmes-Q ou un formalisme pour analyser et synthétiser des phrases sur ordinateur. Publication interne 43, Département d'informatique, Université de Montréal.

Colmerauer, A. (1978). Metamorphosis grammars. In Bolc, L., editor, *Natural language communication with computers*, volume 63 of *Lecture Notes in Computer science*, pages 133–189. Springer Verlag, Berlin Heidelberg New York.

Colmerauer, A. (1982). An interesting subset of natural language. In Clark, K. L. and Tärnlund, S., editors, *Logic Programming*, pages 45–66. Academic Press, London.

Colmerauer, A., Kanoui, H., Pasero, R., and Roussel, P. (1972). Un système de communication en français. Rapport préliminaire de fin de contrat IRIA, Groupe Intelligence Artificielle, Faculté des Sciences de Luminy, Université d'Aix-Marseille II.

Colmerauer, A. and Roussel, P. (1996). The birth of Prolog. In Bergin, T. J. and Gibson, R. G., editors, *History of Programming Languages II*. ACM Press/Addison-Wesley.

Constant, P. (1991). *Analyse syntaxique par couches*. Thèse de doctorat, École Nationale Supérieure des Télécommunications, Paris.

Cooper, D. (1999). Corpora: kwic concordances with Perl. CORPORA Mailing List Archive, Concordancing thread.

Corbett, E. P. J. and Connors, R. J. (1999). *Classical Rhetoric for the Modern Student*. Oxford University Press, New York, 4th edition.

Corston-Oliver, S. (1998). *Computing Representations of the Structure of Written Discourse*. PhD thesis, Linguistics Department, the University of California, Santa Barbara.

Coulthard, M. (1985). *An Introduction to Discourse Analysis*. Longman, Harlow, 2nd edition.

Covington, M. (1989). GULP 2.0, an extension of Prolog for unification-based grammar. Research report AI-1989-01, Artificial Intelligence Programs, University of Georgia.

Covington, M. (1990). Parsing discontinuous constituents in dependency grammar. *Computational Linguistics*, 16(4):234–236.

Covington, M. (1994). *Natural Language Processing for Prolog Programmers*. Prentice Hall, Upper Saddle River.

Covington, M., Nute, D., and Vellino, A. (1997). *Prolog Programming in Depth*. Prentice Hall, Upper Saddle River.

Cozannet, A. (1992). A model for task driven oral dialogue. In *Proceedings of the Second International Conference on Spoken Language Processing (ICSLP)*, pages 1451–1454.

Crystal, D. (1997). *The Cambridge Encyclopedia of Language*. Cambridge University Press, Cambridge, 2nd edition.

d'Arc, S. J., editor (1970). *Concordance de la Bible, Nouveau Testament*. Éditions du Cerf – Desclées De Brouwer, Paris.

Davidson, D. (1966). The logical form of action sentences. In Rescher, N., editor, *The Logic of Decision and Action*. University of Pittsburgh Press, Pittsburgh.

Davis, M. and Whistler, K. (2002). Unicode collation algorithm. Unicode Technical Standard 10, The Unicode Consortium.

de la Briandais, R. (1959). File searching using variable length keys. In *Proceedings of the Western Joint Computer Conference*, pages 295–298, San Francisco. AFIPS.

Delahaye, J.-P. (1986). *Outils logiques pour l'intelligence artificielle*. Eyrolles, Paris.

Deransart, P., Ed-Dbali, A. A., and Cervoni, L. (1996). *Prolog: The Standard, Reference Manual*. Springer Verlag, Berlin Heidelberg New York.

Dermatas, E. and Kokkinakis, G. K. (1995). Automatic stochastic tagging of natural language texts. *Computational Linguistics*, 21(2):137–163.

Ducrot, O. and Schaeffer, J.-M., editors (1995). *Nouveau dictionnaire encyclopédique des sciences du langage*. Éditions du Seuil, Paris.

Dunning, T. (1993). Accurate methods for the statistics of surprise and coincidence. *Computational Linguistics*, 19(1):61–74.

Dutoit, D. (1992). A set-theoretic approach to lexical semantics. In *Proceedings of the 15th International Conference on Computational Linguistics, COLING-92*, volume III, pages 982–987, Nantes.

Earley, J. C. (1970). An efficient context-free parsing algorithm. *Communications of the ACM*, 13(2):94–102.

Eckert, W. (1996). *Gesprochener Mensch-Machine-Dialog*. Shaker Verlag, Aachen.

Ejerhed, E. (1988). Finding clauses in unrestricted text by finitary and stochastic methods. In *Second Conference on Applied Natural Language Processing*, pages 219–227. ACL.

Ejerhed, E., Källgren, G., Wennstedt, O., and Åström, M. (1992). The linguistic annotation system of the Stockholm-Umeå corpus project. Technical Report 33, Department of General Linguistics, University of Umeå.

El Guedj, P.-O. (1996). *Analyse syntaxique par charts combinant règles de dépendance et règles syntagmatiques*. PhD thesis, Université de Caen.

Fellbaum, C., editor (1998). *WordNet: An Electronic Lexical Database (Language, Speech and Communication)*. MIT Press, Cambridge, Massachusetts.

Fikes, R. and Nilsson, N. (1971). STRIPS: A new approach to the application of theorem proving to problem solving. *Artificial Intelligence*, 2(3/4):189–208.

Fillmore, C. J. (1968). The case for case. In Bach, E. and Harms, R. T., editors, *Universals in Linguistic Theory*, pages 1–88. Holt, Rinehart and Winston, New York.

Fillmore, C. J. (1976). Frame semantics and the nature of language. *Annals of the New York Academy of Sciences: Conference on the Origin and Development of Language and Speech*, 280:20–32.

Franz, A. (1996). *Automatic Ambiguity Resolution in Natural Language Processing: An Empirical Approach*, volume 1171 of *Lecture Notes in Artificial Intelligence*. Springer Verlag, Berlin Heidelberg New York.

Frege, G. (1892). Über Sinn und Bedeutung. *Zeitschrift für Philosophie und philosophische Kritik*, pages C:25–50. English transl. in Philosophical writings of Gottlob Frege, Blackwell, 1966.

Friedl, J. E. F. (2002). *Mastering Regular Expressions*. O'Reilly, Sebastopol, California, second edition.

Fromkin, V., editor (2000). *Linguistics: An Introduction to Linguistic Theory*. Blackwell, Oxford.

Fromkin, V., Rodman, R., and Hyams, N. (2003). *An Introduction to Language*. Thomson/Heinle, Boston, 7th edition.

Frühwirth, T. (1998). Theory and practice of constraint handling rules. *Journal of Logic Programming*, 37(1–3):95–138.

Gagnon, M. and Lapalme, G. (1996). From conceptual time to linguistic time. *Computational Linguistics*, 22(1):91–127.

Gaifman, H. (1965). Dependency systems and phrase-structure systems. *Information and Control*, 8:304–337.

Gal, A., Lapalme, G., and Saint-Dizier, P. (1989). *Prolog pour l'analyse automatique du langage naturel*. Eyrolles, Paris.

Gal, A., Lapalme, G., Saint-Dizier, P., and Somers, H. (1991). *Prolog for Natural Language Processing*. Wiley, Chichester.

Gale, W. A. and Church, K. W. (1993). A program for aligning sentences in bilingual corpora. *Computational Linguistics*, 19(1):75–102.

Gazdar, G. and Mellish, C. (1989). *Natural Language Processing in Prolog: An Introduction to Computational Linguistics*. Addison-Wesley, Wokingham.

Gendner, V., Illouz, G., Jardino, M., Monceaux, L., Paroubek, P., Robba, I., and Vilnat, A. (2003). PEAS, the first instantiation of a comparative framework for evaluating parsers of French. In *Proceedings of the Research Note Sessions of the 10th Conference of the European Chapter of the Association for Computational Linguistics (EACL'03)*, volume 2, pages 95–98, Budapest.

Giannesini, F., Kanoui, H., Pasero, R., and van Caneghem, M. (1985). *Prolog*. Interéditions, Paris.

Gildea, D. and Jurafsky, D. (2002). Automatic labeling of semantic roles. *Computational Linguistics*, 28(3):245–288.

Godart-Wendling, B., Ildefonse, F., Pariente, J.-C., and Rosier, I. (1998). Penser le principe de compositionnalité : éléments de réflexion historiques et épisté-mologiques. *Traitement automatique des langues*, 39(1):9–34.

Godéreaux, C., Diebel, K., El Guedj, P.-O., Revolta, F., and Nugues, P. (1996). An interactive spoken dialog interface to virtual worlds. In Connolly, J. H. and Pemberton, L., editors, *Linguistic Concepts and Methods in CSCW*, Computer supported cooperative work, chapter 13, pages 177–200. Springer Verlag, Berlin Heidelberg New York.

Godéreaux, C., El Guedj, P.-O., Revolta, F., and Nugues, P. (1998). Ulysse: An interactive, spoken dialogue interface to navigate in virtual worlds. Lexical, syntactic, and semantic issues. In Vince, J. and Earnshaw, R., editors, *Virtual Worlds on the Internet*, chapter 4, pages 53–70, 308–312. IEEE Computer Society Press, Los Alamitos, California.

Goldfarb, C. F. (1990). *The SGML Handbook*. Oxford University Press, Oxford.

Good, I. J. (1953). The population frequencies of species and the estimation of population parameters. *Biometrika*, 40(16):237–264.

Gosselin, L. (1996). *Sémantique de la temporalité en français : un modèle calcula-toire et cognitif du temps et de l'aspect*. Duculot, Louvain-la-Neuve.

Graham, S. L., Harrison, M. A., and Ruzzo, W. L. (1980). An improved context-free recognizer. *ACM Transactions on Programming Languages and Systems*, 2(3):415–462.

Grefenstette, G. and Tapanainen, P. (1994). What is a word, what is a sentence? Problems in tokenization. MLTT Technical Report 4, Xerox.

Grosz, B. J., Joshi, A. K., and Weinstein, S. (1995). Centering: A framework for modeling the local coherence of discourse. *Computational Linguistics*, 21(2):203–225.

Grosz, B. J. and Sidner, C. L. (1986). Attention, intention, and the structure of discourse. *Computational Linguistics*, 12(3):175–204.

Habermas, J. (1988). *Nachmetaphysisches Denken*. Suhrkamp, Frankfurt am Main.

Haegeman, L. and Gueron, J. (1999). *English Grammar: A Generative Perspective*. Number 14 in Blackwell Textbooks in Linguistics. Blackwell, Malden.

Harper, M. H., Hockema, S. A., and White, C. M. (1999). Enhanced constraint dependency grammar parsers. In *Proceedings of the IASTED International Conference on Artificial Intelligence and Soft Computing*, Honolulu.

Harris, R. and Taylor, T. J. (1997). *Landmarks in Linguistic Thought, The Western Tradition from Socrates to Saussure*. Routledge, London, 2nd edition.

Harris, Z. (1962). *String Analysis of Sentence Structure*. Mouton, The Hague.

Hausser, R. (2000). *Grundlagen der Computerlinguistik. Mensch-Maschine-Kommunikation in natürlicher Sprache*. Springer Verlag, Berlin Heidelberg New York.

Hausser, R. (2001). *Foundations of Computational Linguistics. Human-Computer Communication in Natural Language*. Springer Verlag, Berlin Heidelberg New York, 2nd edition.

Hays, D. G. (1964). Dependency theory: A formalism and some observations. *Language*, 40(4):511–525.

Hellwig, P. (1980). PLAIN – a program system for dependency analysis and for simulating natural language inference. In Bolc, L., editor, *Representation and Processing of Natural Language*, pages 271–376. Hanser, München.

Hellwig, P. (1986). Dependency unification grammar (DUG). In *Proceedings of the 11th International Conference on Computational Linguistics (COLING 86)*, pages 195–198.

Herbrand, J. (1930). Recherches sur la théorie de la démonstration. *Travaux de la Société des Sciences et des Lettres de Varsovie, Classe III Sciences mathématiques et physiques*, 33.

Heringer, H.-J. (1993). Dependency syntax – basic ideas and the classical model. In Jacobs, J., von Stechow, A., Sternefeld, W., and Venneman, T., editors, *Syntax – An International Handbook of Contemporary Research*, volume 1, chapter 12, pages 298–316. Walter de Gruyter, Berlin – New York.

Hindle, D. and Rooth, M. (1993). Structural ambiguity and lexical relations. *Computational Linguistics*, 19(1):103–120.

Hintikka, J. (1962). *Knowledge and Belief, An Introduction to the Logic of the Two Notions*. Cornell University Press, Ithaca.

Hirschman, L. and Chinchor, N. (1997). MUC-7 coreference task definition. Technical report. http://www.itl.nist.gov/iaui/894.02/related_projects/muc/-proceedings/co_task.html. Cited 2 November 2005.

Hjelmslev, L. (1935-37). La catégorie des cas. *Étude de grammaire générale*, volume VII(1), IX(2) of *Acta Jutlandica*. Aarhus.

Hjelmslev, L. (1943). *Omkring sprogteoriens grundlæggelse*. Festskrift udgivet af Københavns Universiteit, Copenhagen. English translation Prolegomena to a Theory of Language.

Hobbs, J. R., Appelt, D. E., Bear, J., Israel, D., Kameyama, M., Stickel, M., and Tyson, M. (1997). FASTUS: a cascaded finite-state transducer for extracting information from natural-language text. In Roche, E. and Schabes, Y., editors, *Finite-State Language Processing*, chapter 13, pages 383–406. MIT Press, Cambridge, Massachusetts.

Hopcroft, J. E., Motwani, R., and Ullman, J. D. (2001). *Introduction to Automata Theory, Languages, and Computation*. Addison-Wesley, Boston, 2nd edition.

Hornby, A. S., editor (1974). *Oxford Advanced Learner's Dictionary of Current English*. Oxford University Press, Oxford, 3rd edition.

Hornby, A. S., editor (1995). *Oxford Advanced Learner's Dictionary of Current English*. Oxford University Press, Oxford, 5th edition.

Huang, X., Acero, A., Alleva, F., Hwang, M.-Y., Jiang, L., and Mahaja, M. (1995). Microsoft highly intelligent speech recognizer: Whisper. In *Proceedings of the International Conference on Acoustic, Speech, and Signal Processing*, Detroit.

Huls, C., Claassen, W., and Bos, E. (1995). Automatic referent resolution of deictic and anaphoric expressions. *Computational Linguistics*, 21(1):59–79.

Ide, N. and Véronis, J. (1998). Introduction to the special issue on word sense disambiguation: The state of the art. *Computational Linguistics*, 24(1):1–40.

Imbs, P. and Quemada, B., editors (1971-1994). *Trésor de la langue française. Dictionnaire de la langue française du XIXe et du XXe siècle (1789-1960).* Éditions du CNRS puis Gallimard, Paris. 16 volumes.

Ingria, B. and Pustejovsky, J. (2004). TimeML: A formal specification language for events and temporal expressions. http://www.cs.brandeis.edu/~jamesp/arda/time/-timeMLdocs/TimeML12.htm. Cited 28 October 2005.

Jackendoff, R. (1990). *Semantic Structures.* MIT Press, Cambridge, Massachusetts.

Jacob, A., editor (1989). *Encyclopédie philosophique universelle.* Presses Universitaires de France, Paris.

Järvinen, T. and Tapanainen, P. (1997). A dependency parser for English. Technical Report TR-1, Department of General Linguistics, University of Helsinki.

Jekat, S., Klein, A., Maier, E., Maleck, I., Mast, M., and Quantz, J. (1995). Dialogue acts in Verbmobil. Verbmobil-Report 65, Universität Hamburg, DFKI, Universität Erlangen, TU Berlin.

Jelinek, F. (1990). Self-organized language modeling for speech recognition. In Waibel, A. and Lee, K.-F., editors, *Readings in Speech Recognition.* Morgan Kaufmann, San Mateo. Reprinted from an IBM Report, 1985.

Jelinek, F. (1997). *Statistical Methods for Speech Recognition.* MIT Press, Cambridge, Massachusetts.

Jelinek, F. and Mercer, R. L. (1980). Interpolated estimation of Markov source parameters from sparse data. In Gelsema, E. S. and Kanal, L. N., editors, *Pattern Recognition in Practice*, pages 38–397. North-Holland, Amsterdam.

Jensen, K., Heidorn, G., and Richardson, S., editors (1993). *Natural Language Processing: The PLNLP Approach.* Kluwer Academic Publishers, Boston.

Johansson, R., Berglund, A., Danielsson, M., and Nugues, P. (2005). Automatic text-to-scene conversion in the traffic accident domain. In *IJCAI-05, Proceedings of the Nineteenth International Joint Conference on Artificial Intelligence*, pages 1073–1078, Edinburgh.

Johnson, C. D. (1972). *Formal Aspects of Phonological Description.* Mouton, The Hague.

Joshi, A. K. and Hopely, P. (1999). A parser from antiquity: an early application of finite state transducers to natural language processing. In Kornai, A., editor, *Extended Finite State Models of Language*, Studies in Natural Language Processing, pages 6–15. Cambridge University Press, Cambridge.

Jurafsky, D. and Martin, J. H. (2000). *Speech and Language Processing, An Introduction to Natural Language Processing, Computational Linguistics, and Speech Recognition.* Prentice Hall, Upper Saddle River.

Kameyama, M. (1997). Recognizing referential links: An information extraction perspective. In Mitkov, R. and Boguraev, B., editors, *Proceedings of ACL Workshop on Operational Factors in Practical, Robust Anaphora Resolution for Unrestricted Texts*, pages 46–53, Madrid.

Kamp, H. and Reyle, U. (1993). *From Discourse to Logic: Introduction to Modeltheoretic Semantics of Natural Language, Formal Logic and Discourse Representation Theory.* Kluwer Academic Press, Dordrecht.

Kaplan, R. M. and Bresnan, J. (1982). Lexical-functional grammar: A formal system for grammatical representation. In Bresnan, J., editor, *The Mental Representation of Grammatical Relations*, pages 173–281. MIT Press, Cambridge, Massachusetts.

Kaplan, R. M. and Kay, M. (1994). Regular models of phonological rule systems. *Computational Linguistics*, 20(3):331–378.

Karttunen, L. (1983). KIMMO: A general morphological processor. *Texas Linguistic Forum*, 22:163–186.

Karttunen, L. (1994). Constructing lexical transducers. In *Proceedings of the 15th Conference on Computational Linguistics, COLING-94*, volume 1, pages 406–411.

Karttunen, L., Kaplan, R. M., and Zaenen, A. (1992). Two-level morphology with composition. In *Proceedings of the 15th Conference on Computational Linguistics, COLING-92*, volume 1, pages 141–148.

Kasami, T. (1965). An efficient recognition and syntax analysis algorithm for context-free languages. Technical Report AFCRL-65-758, Air Force Cambridge Research Laboratory, Bedford, Massachusetts. Cited from Wikipedia.

Katz, S. M. (1987). Estimation of probabilities from sparse data for the language model component of a speech recognizer. *IEEE Transactions on Acoustics, Speech, and Signal Processing*, 35(3):400–401.

Kernighan, M. D., Church, K. W., and Gale, W. A. (1990). A spelling correction program based on a noisy channel model. In *Papers presented to the 13th International Conference on Computational Linguistics (COLING-90)*, volume II, pages 205–210, Helsinki.

Kingsbury, P., Palmer, M., and Marcus, M. (2002). Adding semantic annotation to the Penn Treebank. In *Proceedings of the Human Language Technology Conference*, San Diego.

Kiraz, G. A. (2001). *Computational Nonlinear Morphology: With Emphasis on Semitic Languages*. Studies in Natural Language Processing. Cambridge University Press, Cambridge.

Kleene, S. C. (1956). Representation of events in nerve nets and finite automata. In Shannon, C. E. and Carthy, J. M., editors, *Automata Studies*, pages 3–42. Princeton University Press, Princeton.

Klein, S. and Simmons, R. (1963). A computational approach to grammatical coding of English words. *Journal of the ACM*, 10(3):334–347.

Knuth, D. E. (1986). *The Texbook*. Addison-Wesley, Reading, Massachusetts.

Koch, U. (1993). The enhancement of a dependency parser for Latin. Technical Report AI-1993-03, Artificial Intelligence Programs, University of Georgia.

Kornai, A., editor (1999). *Extended Finite State Models of Language*. Studies in Natural Language Processing. Cambridge University Press, Cambridge.

Koskenniemi, K. (1983). Two-level morphology: a general computation model for word-form recognition and production. Technical Report 11, University of Helsinki, Department of General Linguistics.

Kowalski, R. A. and Kuehner, D. (1971). Linear resolution with selection function. *Artificial Intelligence*, 2:227–260.

Lallot, J., editor (1998). *La grammaire de Denys le Thrace*. CNRS Éditions, Collection Science du langage, Paris, 2e edition. Text in Greek, translated in French by Jean Lallot.

Landes, S., Leacock, C., and Tengi, R. (1998). Building semantic concordances. In Fellbaum, C., editor, *WordNet: An Electronic Lexical Database*. MIT Press, Cambridge, Massachusetts.

Laplace, P. (1820). *Théorie analytique des probabilités*. Coursier, Paris, 3e edition.

Lasnik, H., Depiante, M. A., and Stepanov, A. (2000). *Syntactic Structures Revisited: Contemporary Lectures on Classic Transformational Theory*, volume 33 of *Current Studies in Linguistics*. MIT Press, Cambridge, Massachusetts.

Lesk, M. (1986). Automatic sense disambiguation using machine readable dictionaries: how to tell a pine cone from an ice cream cone. In *Proceedings of the 5th annual international conference on systems documentation*, pages 24–26, Toronto, Ontario.

Levinson, S. (1983). *Pragmatics*. Cambridge University Press, Cambridge.

Lin, D. (1995). A dependency-based method for evaluating broad-coverage parsers. In *Proceedings of IJCAI-95*, pages 1420–1427.

Linke, A., Nussbaumer, M., and Portmann, P. R. (2004). *Studienbuch Linguistik*. Niemeyer, Tübingen, 5. edition.

Lloyd, J. W. (1987). *Foundations of Logic Programming*. Springer Verlag, Berlin Heidelberg New York, 2nd edition.

Magerman, D. (1995). Book reviews: Statistical language learning by Eugene Charniak. *Computational Linguistics*, 21(1):103–111.

Maier, D. and Warren, D. S. (1988). *Computing with Logic, Logic Programming with Prolog*. Benjamin/Cummings, Menlo Park.

Malmberg, B. (1983). *Analyse du langage au XXe siècle. Théorie et méthodes*. Presses universitaires de France, Paris.

Malmberg, B. (1991). *Histoire de la linguistique. De Sumer à Saussure*. Presses universitaires de France, Paris.

Mann, W. C. and Thompson, S. A. (1987). Rhetorical structure theory: A theory of text organization. Technical Report RS-87-190, Information Sciences Institute of the University of Southern California.

Mann, W. C. and Thompson, S. A. (1988). Rhetorical structure theory: Toward a functional theory of text organization. *Text*, 8:243–281.

Manning, C. D. and Schütze, H. (1999). *Foundations of Statistical Natural Language Processing*. MIT Press, Cambridge, Massachusetts.

Marcu, D. (1997). *The Rhetorical Parsing, Summarization, and Generation of Natural Language Texts*. PhD thesis, Department of Computer Science, University of Toronto.

Marcus, M., Marcinkiewicz, M. A., and Santorini, B. (1993). Building a large annotated corpus of English: The Penn Treebank. *Computational Linguistics*, 19(2):313–330.

Martelli, A. and Montanari, U. (1982). An efficient unification algorithm. *ACM Transactions on Programming Languages and Systems*, 4(2):258–282.

Maruyama, H. (1990). Constraint dependency grammar and its weak generative capacity. *Computer Software*.

Mast, M. (1993). *Ein Dialogmodul für ein Spracherkennungs- und Dialogsystem*, volume 50 of *Dissertationen zur Künstlichen Intelligenz*. Infix, Sankt Augustin.

Mast, M., Kummert, F., Ehrlich, U., Fink, G. A., Kuhn, T., Niemann, H., and Sagerer, G. (1994). A speech understanding and dialog system with a homogeneous linguistic knowledge base. *IEEE Transactions on Pattern Analysis and Machine Intelligence*, 16(2):179–194.

Mauldin, M. L. and Leavitt, J. R. R. (1994). Web-agent related research at the Center for Machine Translation. In *Proceedings of the ACM SIG on Networked Information Discovery and Retrieval*, McLean, Virginia.

Maxwell, D. (1995). Unification dependency grammar. ftp://ftp.ling.ohio-state.edu/pub/HPSG/Papers/UDG/. Draft. Cited 28 October 2005.

McMahon, J. G. and Smith, F. J. (1996). Improving statistical language models performance with automatically generated word hierarchies. *Computational Linguistics*, 22(2):217–247.

Mel'cuk, I. A. (1988). *Dependency Syntax: Theory and Practice*. State University Press of New York, Albany.

Mel'cuk, I. A., Clas, A., and Polguère, A. (1995). *Introduction à la lexicologie explicative et combinatoire*. Éditions Duculot, Louvain-la-Neuve.

Merialdo, B. (1994). Tagging English text with a probabilistic model. *Computational Linguistics*, 20(2):155–171.

Mikheev, A. (2002). Periods, capitalized words, etc. *Computational Linguistics*, 28(3):289–318.

Miller, G. A. (1995). WordNet: A lexical database for English. *Communications of the ACM*, 38(11):39–41.

Miller, G. A., Beckwith, R., Fellbaum, C., Gross, D., Miller, K. J., and Tangi, R. (1993). Five papers on WordNet. Technical report, Princeton University. ftp://ftp.cogsci.princeton.edu/pub/wordnet/5papers.ps. Cited 28 October 2005.

Moeschler, J. (1989). *Modélisation du dialogue : Représentation de l'inférence argumentative*. Hermès, Paris.

Moeschler, J. and Reboul, A. (1994). *Dictionnaire encyclopédique de pragmatique*. Éditions du Seuil, Paris.

Mohri, M., Pereira, F. C. N., and Riley, M. (1998). A rational design for a weighted finite-state transducer library. In Wood, D. and Yu, S., editors, *Automata implementation. Second International Workshop on Implementing Automata, WIA '97, London, Ontario, September 1997. Revised Papers*, volume 1436 of *Lecture Notes in Computer Science*, pages 144–158, Berlin Heidelberg New York. Springer Verlag.

Montague, R. (1974). *Formal Philosophy: Selected Papers*. Yale University Press, New Haven.

Morton, A. (2003). *A Guide through the Theory of Knowledge*. Blackwell, Malden, 3rd edition.

MUC-5, editor (1993). *Proceedings of the Fifth Message Understanding Conference (MUC-5)*, San Francisco. Morgan Kaufmann.

Müller, S. (1999). *Deutsche Syntax deklarativ. Head-Driven Phrase Structure Grammar für das Deutsche*, volume 394 of *Linguistische Arbeiten*. Max Niemeyer Verlag, Tübingen.

Newmeyer, F. J., editor (1988). *Linguistics: The Cambridge Survey*. Cambridge University Press, Cambridge.

Ng, V. and Cardie, C. (2002). Improving machine learning approaches to coreference resolution. In *Proceedings of the 40th Annual Meeting of the Association for Computational Linguistics*, pages 104–111.

Nguyen, L., Abdou, S., Afify, M., Makhoul, J., Matsoukas, S., Schwartz, R., Xiang, B., Lamel, L., Gauvain, J.-L., Adda, G., Schwenk, H., and Lefevre, F. (2004). The 2004 BBN/LIMSI 10xRT English broadcast news transcription system. In *Proceedings DARPA RT04*, Palisades, New York.

Nilsson, N. (1998). *Artificial Intelligence: A New Synthesis*. Morgan Kaufmann, San Francisco.

Nivre, J. (2003). An efficient algorithm for projective dependency parsing. In *Proceedings of the 8th International Workshop on Parsing Technologies (IWPT 03)*, pages 149–160, Nancy.

Nivre, J. and Nilsson, J. (2005). Pseudo-projective dependency parsing. In *Proceedings of the 43rd Annual Meeting of the Association for Computational Linguistics (ACL'05)*, pages 99–106, Ann Arbor.

Nivre, J. and Scholz, M. (2004). Deterministic dependency parsing of English text. In *Proceedings of Coling 2004*, pages 64–70, Geneva.

Och, F. J. and Ney, H. (2000). Improved statistical alignment models. In *Proceedings of the 38th Annual Meeting of the Association for Computational Linguistics*, pages 440–447, Hongkong.

Pereira, F. (1981). Extraposition grammars. *Computational Linguistics*, 7(4):243–256.

Pereira, F. (1984). *C-Prolog User's Manual, Version 1.5*. University of Edinburgh.

Pereira, F. and Warren, D. (1980). Definite clause grammar for language analysis–a survey of the formalism and a comparison with augmented transition networks. *Artificial Intelligence*, 13(3):231–278.

Pereira, F. C. N. and Shieber, S. M. (1987). *Prolog and Natural-Language Analysis*, volume 10 of *CSLI Lecture Notes*. Center for the Study of Language and Information, Stanford.

Perelman, C. and Olbrechts-Tyteca, L. (1976). *Traité de l'argumentation : la nouvelle rhétorique*. Éditions de l'Université de Bruxelles, Brussels.

Pérennou, G. and de Calmès, M. (1987). BDLex lexical data and knowledge base of spoken and written French. In *European conference on Speech Technology*, pages 393–396, Edinburgh.

Pollard, C. and Sag, I. A. (1994). *Head-Driven Phrase Structure Grammar*. University of Chicago Press, Chicago.

Procter, P., editor (1978). *Longman Dictionary of Contemporary English*. Longman, Harlow.

Procter, P., editor (1995). *Cambridge International Dictionary of English*. Cambridge University Press, Cambridge.

Pustejovsky, J. (1995). *The Generative Lexicon*. MIT Press, Cambridge, Massachusetts.

Quillian, M. R. (1967). Word concepts: a theory and simulation of some basic semantic capabilities. *Behavioral Science*, 12(5):410–430.

Quinlan, J. R. (1986). Induction of decision trees. *Machine Learning*, 1(1):81–106.

Rabiner, L. R. (1989). A tutorial on hidden Markov models and selected applications in speech recognition. *Proceedings of the IEEE*, 77(2):257–286.

Radford, A. (1988). *Transformational Grammar: A First Course*. Cambridge Textbooks in Linguistics. Cambridge University Press, Cambridge.

Ramshaw, L. and Marcus, M. P. (1995). Text chunking using transformation-based learning. In Yarowsky, D. and Church, K., editors, *Proceedings of the Third Workshop on Very Large Corpora*, pages 82–94, Cambridge, Massachusetts.

Ray, E. T. (2003). *Learning XML*. O'Reilly, Sebastopol, California, 2nd edition.

Rayner, M., Bretan, I., Wirén, M., Rydin, S., and Beshai, E. (1996). Composition of transfer rules in a multi-lingual MT system. In *Proceedings of the workshop on Future Issues for Multilingual Text Processing*, Cairns, Australia.

Rayner, M. and Carter, D. (1995). The spoken language translator project. In *Proceedings of the Language Engineering Convention*, London.

Rayner, M., Carter, D., Bouillon, P., Digalakis, V., and Wirén, M., editors (2000). *The Spoken Language Translator*. Cambridge University Press, Cambridge.

Reboul, O. (1994). *Introduction à la rhétorique : théorie et pratique*. Presses universitaires de France, Paris, 2e edition.

Reichenbach, H. (1947). *Elements of Symbolic Logic*. Macmillan, New York.

Rey, A., editor (1988). *Le Robert Micro*. Dictionnaires Le Robert, Paris.

Rich, E. and Knight, K. (1991). *Artificial Intelligence*. McGraw-Hill, New York, 2nd edition.

Ritchie, G. D., Russell, G. J., Black, A. W., and Pulman, S. G. (1992). *Computational Morphology. Practical Mechanisms for the English Lexicon*. MIT Press, Cambridge, Massachusetts.

Robins, R. H. (1997). *A Short History of Linguistics*. Longman, London, 4th edition.

Robinson, J. A. (1965). A machine-oriented logic based on the resolution principle. *Journal of the ACM*, 12(1):23–41.

Roche, E. and Schabes, Y. (1995). Deterministic part-of-speech tagging with finite-state transducers. *Computational Linguistics*, 21(2):227–253.

Roche, E. and Schabes, Y., editors (1997). *Finite-State Language Processing*. MIT Press, Cambridge, Massachusetts.

Ruppenhofer, J., Ellsworth, M., Petruck, M. R. L., and Johnson, C. R. (2005). Framenet: Theory and practice. http://framenet.icsi.berkeley.edu/book/book.html. Cited 28 October 2005.

Russell, S. J. and Norvig, P. (2003). *Artificial Intelligence, A Modern Approach*. Prentice Hall, Upper Saddle River, 2nd edition.

Ruwet, N. (1970). *Introduction à la grammaire générative*. Plon, Paris, 2e edition.

Sabah, G. (1990). *L'intelligence artificielle et le langage*. Hermès, Paris, 2e edition.

Sagerer, G. (1990). *Automatisches Verstehen gesprochener Sprache*, volume Band 74 of *Reihe Informatik*. B.I. Wissenschaftsverlag, Mannheim.

Salton, G. (1988). *Automatic Text Processing: The Transformation, Analysis, and Retrieval of Information by Computer*. Addison-Wesley, Reading, Massachusetts.

Saussure, F. (1916). *Cours de linguistique générale*. Reprinted Payot, 1995, Paris.

Schiffrin, D. (1994). *Approaches to Discourse*. Number 8 in Blackwell Textbooks in Linguistics. Blackwell, Oxford.

Schlkopf, B. and Smola, A. J. (2002). *Learning with Kernels: Support Vector Machines, Regularization, Optimization, and Beyond (Adaptive Computation and Machine Learning)*. MIT Press, Cambridge, Massachusetts.

Schmid, H. (1994). Probabilistic part-of-speech tagging using decision trees. In *Proceedings of International Conference on New Methods in Language Processing*, Manchester.

Schmid, H. (1995). Improvements in part-of-speech tagging with an application to German. In *Proceedings of the ACL SIGDAT Workshop*.

Schwartz, R. L. and Phoenix, T. (2001). *Learning Perl*. O'Reilly, Sebastopol, California, 3rd edition.

Searle, J. R. (1969). *Speech Acts. An Essay in the Philosophy of Language*. Cambridge University Press, Cambridge.

Searle, J. R. (1979). *Expression and Meaning, Studies in the Theory of Speech Acts*. Cambridge University Press, Cambridge.

Searle, J. R. and Vanderveken, D. (1985). *Foundations of Illocutionary Logic*. Cambridge University Press, Cambridge.

Shannon, C. (1948). A mathematical theory of communication. *Bell System Technical Journal*, 27:398–403 and 623–656.

Simone, R. (1998). *Fundamenti di linguistica*. Laterza, Bari, 9e edition.

Sinclair, J., editor (1987). *Collins COBUILD English Language Dictionary*. Collins, London.

Sleator, D. and Temperley, D. (1993). Parsing English with a link grammar. In *Proceedings of the Third International Workshop on Parsing Technologies*, pages 277–291.

Smadja, F. (1993). Retrieving collocations from text: Xtract. *Computational Linguistics*, 19(1):143–177.

Soon, W. M., Ng, H. T., and Lim, D. C. Y. (2001). A machine learning approach to coreference resolution of noun phrases. *Computational Linguistics*, 27(4):521–544.

Sorin, C., Jouvet, D., Gagnoulet, C., Dubois, D., Sadek, D., and Toularhoat, M. (1995). Operational and experimental French telecommunication services using CNET speech recognition and text-to-speech synthesis. *Speech Communication*, 17(3-4):273–286.

Sproat, R. (1992). *Morphology and computation*. MIT Press, Cambridge, Massachusetts.

Sterling, L. and Shapiro, E. (1994). *The Art of Prolog. Advanced Programming Techniques*. MIT Press, Cambridge, Massachusetts, 2nd edition.

Suri, L. Z. and McCoy, K. F. (1994). RAFT/RAPR and centering: A comparison and discussion of problems related to processing complex sentences. *Computational Linguistics*, 20(2):301–317.

Tapanainen, P. and Järvinen, T. (1997). A non-projective dependency parser. In *Proceedings of the Fifth Conference on Applied Natural Language Processing (ANLP'97)*, pages 64–71, Washington, D.C. ACL.

TAUM (1971). Taum 71. Rapport annuel du projet de traduction automatique de l'université de Montréal, Université de Montréal.

Taylor, K. (1998). *Truth and Meaning. An Introduction to the Philosophy of Language*. Blackwell, Oxford.

Ter Meulen, A. (1995). *Representing Time in Natural Language. The Dynamic Interpretation of Tense and Aspect*. MIT Press, Cambridge, Massachusetts.

Tesnière, L. (1966). *Éléments de syntaxe structurale*. Klincksieck, Paris, 2e edition.

The Unicode Consortium (2003). *The Unicode Standard, Version 4.0*. Addison-Wesley, Boston.

Thompson, K. (1968). Regular expression search algorithm. *Communications of the ACM*, 11(6):419–422.

van Benthem, J. and Ter Meulen, A., editors (1997). *Handbook of Logic and Language*. North Holland, Amsterdam.

van Noord, G. and Gerdemann, D. (2001). An extendible regular expression compiler for finite-state approaches in natural language processing. In Boldt, O. and Jürgensen, H., editors, *Automata Implementation. 4th International Workshop on Implementing Automata, WIA'99, Potsdam, Germany, July 1999, Revised Papers*, volume 2214 of *Lecture Notes in Computer Science*, pages 122–139, Berlin Heidelberg New York. Springer Verlag.

Vanderveken, D. (1988). *Les actes de discours : essai de philosophie du langage et de l'esprit sur la signification des énonciations*. Mardaga, Bruxelles.

Vendler, Z. (1967). *Linguistics in Philosophy*. Cornell University Press, Ithaca, New York.

Vergne, J. (1998). Entre arbre de dépendance et ordre linéaire, les deux processus de transformation: linéarisation, puis reconstruction de l'arbre. *Cahiers de grammaire*, 23.

Vergne, J. (1999). *Étude et modélisation de la syntaxe des langues à l'aide de l'ordinateur. Analyse syntaxique automatique non combinatoire. Synthèse et résultats*. Habilitation à diriger des recherches, Université de Caen.

Viterbi, A. J. (1967). Error bounds for convolutional codes and an asymptotically optimum decoding algorithm. *IEEE Transactions on Information Theory*, 13(2):260–267.

Voutilainen, A., Heikkilä, J., and Anttila, A. (1992). Constraint grammar of English: A performance-oriented introduction. Technical Report 21, Department of General Linguistics, University of Helsinki.

Voutilainen, A. and Järvinen, T. (1995). Specifying a shallow grammatical representation for parsing purposes. In *Proceedings of the Seventh Conference of the European Chapter of the ACL*, pages 210–214, Dublin.

Wahrig, G., editor (1978). *dtv-Wörterbuch der deutschen Sprache*. Deutscher Taschenbuch Verlag, Munich.

Wall, L., Christiansen, T., and Orwant, J. (2000). *Programming Perl*. O'Reilly, Sebastopol, California, 3rd edition.

Warren, D. (1983). An abstract Prolog instruction set. Technical Note 309, SRI International, Menlo Park.

Weizenbaum, J. (1966). ELIZA – a computer program for the study of natural language communication between man and machine. *Communications of the ACM*, 9(1):36–45.

Wilks, Y. and Stevenson, M. (1997). Sense tagging: Semantic tagging with a lexicon. In *Tagging Text with Lexical Semantics: Why, What, and How? Proceedings of the Workshop*, pages 74–78, Washington, DC. ACL SIGLEX.

Wilks, Y. A., Slator, B. M., and Guthrie, L. M. (1996). *Electric Words. Dictionaries, Computers, and Meanings*. MIT Press, Cambridge, Massachusetts.

Yarowsky, D. (1995). Unsupervised word sense disambiguation rivaling supervised methods. In *Proceedings of the 33rd Annual Meeting of the Association for Computational Linguistics*, pages 189–196, Cambridge, Massachusetts.

Yarowsky, D. (1996). Homograph disambiguation in speech synthesis. In van Santen, J., Sproat, R., Olive, J. P., and Hirschberg, J., editors, *Progress in Speech Synthesis*, pages 159–175, Berlin Heidelberg New York. Springer Verlag.

Zampolli, A. (2003). Past and on-going trends in computational linguistics. *The ELRA Newsletter*, 8(3-4):6–16.

Zelle, J. M. and Mooney, R. J. (1997). An inductive logic programming method for corpus-based parser construction. Technical note, University of Texas at Austin. http://www.cs.utexas.edu/users/ml/publication/ilp.html. Cited 28 October 2005.

Cognitive Technologies